ECONOMICS
Institutions and Analysis

THIRD EDITION

Gerson Antell
Walter Harris

AMSCO SCHOOL PUBLICATIONS, INC.
315 Hudson Street   New York, N.Y. 10013

Gerson Antell, Curriculum Consultant, Junior Achievement, and Former Assistant Principal for Social Studies, Hillcrest High School, New York City, is coauthor of *Economics for Everybody, Current Issues in American Democracy,* and *Western Civilization.*

Walter Harris, Former Principal at Sheepshead Bay High School, New York City, and Former Director of Education, The Kolburne School, New Marlboro, MA, is coauthor of *Economics for Everybody, Current Issues in American Democracy,* and *Western Civilization.*

When ordering this book, please specify:
R 639 P *or* ECONOMICS: I & A, THIRD EDITION, PAPERBACK
   or
R 639 H *or* ECONOMICS: I & A, THIRD EDITION, HARDBOUND

ISBN 0-87720-899-9 (Paperback edition)

ISBN 1-56765-603-X (Hardbound edition)
NYC Item 56765-603-9

Printed in the United States of America

   4 5 6 7 8 9 10   01 00 99 98

Preface

Economics: Institutions and Analysis, Third Edition, provides an introduction to one of the miracles of the modern age—the U.S. economic system. This system enables society to produce the things that people need and want. How our economic system "does its thing," some of the controversies generated by the system, and its role in the global economy is the subject matter of economics, and of this book.

Some of you may be thinking that a course in economics sounds like a journey to the far side of the moon. Unlike history, English, mathematics, and other subjects with which you are well acquainted, a course in economics may be a first-time experience. But as you read and learn more about the subject, you will find that economics is concerned with many things with which you are already familiar. For example, from the time you were born, you have been a user of goods and services. You also know something about from where those goods and services come. You have visited shops, ridden buses, gone to the movies, and in ever so many other ways seen people and places in the workaday world. You know, too, that in exchange for working at their jobs, people acquire the money they need to purchase the goods and services they want and need. And you also know from your experiences (and from the sales taxes and other taxes you have paid) that government is a major player in our economy, and that the cost of government is shared by us all. Goods and services, banks, jobs, money, taxes, government policies, and business operations are all part and parcel of the study of economics.

You probably know that economic activities extend well beyond the community or region in which you live. While the goods that you and others consume may have had their origins in the town, state, or region of the country in which you live, most have been made in other sections of the United States, or in a foreign land. More than ever before, economic activities are global in their scope. Economic topics and issues are discussed again and again on television and radio and in books, magazines, and newspapers. As the complexity of the economy increases, what you need to know in order to cope with problems of earning a living increases as well. And as government's role in the economy is enlarged, you need a better understanding of economics to be a responsible citizen. Thus, if you are to exercise your responsibilities as a consumer, citizen, and voter, you will want to learn the principles needed to understand and make reasoned decisions about economic issues.

The textbook is divided into seven units of three to four chapters each. The first unit serves as an introduction to the fundamental economic questions societies must answer and the forces affecting their decisions. The next three units focus on the principal players in the U.S. economy: business, labor, consumers, and government. The fifth unit discusses the role of money and banks. The sixth unit serves an important function: showing how the government helps manage the economy and how it meets certain economic challenges. The final unit of the text focuses on the global economy and how the United States fits into that framework.

The book contains a number of features designed to make it easier to understand. Words and phrases unique to the vocabulary of economics are italicized and defined as they are introduced, and stored in the Glossary, which may be found after the last chapter of the book. More than 200 illustrations in the form of photos, cartoons, graphs, and charts have been strategically placed throughout the text as a means of helping you to understand its contents. Many of the illustrations have captions that provide further information. Some captions have questions to challenge your understanding of the content of the illustrations.

Economics: Institutions and Analysis, Third Edition, is a thoroughgoing revision of a well-proven economics text. We carefully scrutinized all aspects of our earlier editions—organization, content, illustrations, and exercises—to determine whether they are still appropriate for today's students. As a result of this review, some topics were dropped, while others were either lengthened, shortened, or added. Throughout this new edition, we have personalized the material with references to everyday experiences.

The authors invite your criticisms, questions, and comments. We hope that your study of this book will enrich your understanding of your own life, and of your role in the nation's economy and the global economy. Finally, we hope that we will help you to become a more intelligent participant in our democratic society.

GERSON ANTELL
WALTER HARRIS

Contents

Features

UNIT I

Introduction to
Economics

Chapter 1

ECONOMICS: THE BASIC QUESTIONS

Overview

An ancient tale relates the story of Aladdin, who bought a lamp with magical qualities. Simply by rubbing the lamp, Aladdin could conjure up a genie that would grant him any wish. Food, clothing, jewels, castles, and trips to anywhere were his for the asking. No need for a job, or money, in Aladdin's world—not as long as he had that lamp and its wonderful genie.

Alas, the story of Aladdin is a myth. No one in real life, not even the world's wealthiest people, can be in more than one place at a time, or afford to buy everything they want. If they could, there would be no need for the study of economics, and this book would not have been written.

Instead of Aladdin's world, we live in a world of economics. Every day we engage in economic activities. We have to make economic decisions as buyers and sellers and as workers and business owners. After reading this book, you will have a better understanding as to why people make one economic decision rather than another. Furthermore, you will have the knowledge you will need to make sound decisions as you evaluate your own daily economic choices.

In this chapter, you will learn the answers to the following questions:

- ☐ What is economics?
- ☐ What are the four factors of production?
- ☐ What fundamental questions must all societies answer?
- ☐ How do economic systems answer the WHAT? HOW? and WHO questions?
- ☐ What do economists do?

ECONOMICS: THE STUDY OF SCARCITY AND CHOICE

Have you ever gone shopping for clothes with $75 in your wallet only to find that the things you wanted to buy added up to something around $150? Did you go home empty-handed? Perhaps you did not. Like most people, you most likely tried to get something out of your

$75 by buying those items that you needed or wanted the most, and forgoing the others.

Business firms and governments face the same kinds of decisions: none can afford everything at the same time. Instead, they try to satisfy as many of their wants with the resources available. For example, a manufacturer unable to afford both might have to choose between an advertising campaign and a factory modernization program. In a similar manner, a town might have to choose between modernizing its high school and building a parking garage

Economists refer to the things that individuals and institutions want as either goods or services. *Goods* are tangible items of value, things that we can see or touch. We can classify scissors, medicines, and textbooks as goods because they are tangible. *Services* are intangible things that have value. Intangibles can neither be seen nor touched. Haircuts, medical care, and education are examples of services.

As we use goods and services to satisfy our wants, we consume them. For that reason, those who buy goods and services for personal use are called *consumers*. The act of buying final goods and services is called *consumption*.

The ingredients that go into the production of goods and services are the *factors of production*. Whereas human wants are virtually unlimited, the factors of production needed to satisfy those wants are relatively scarce. Thus, scarcity is a fact of life, one with which every individual and institution must deal by choosing among available resources.

Economics Defined

We can define *economics* as the study of how people and societies use limited resources to satisfy their unlimited wants. To put it more simply, economics is the study of scarcity and choice.

THE FACTORS OF PRODUCTION

As we just learned, the ingredients that go into the production of goods and services are factors of production. This section discusses these four factors—human resources, natural resources, capital resources, and entrepreneurship—and shows how they are related to human wants and needs.

Human Resources

Economists use the terms *human resources, labor*, and the *workforce* to describe the people whose efforts and skills go into the production of goods and services. Without human resources, goods and services could not be produced.

Human resources influence the production of goods and services in two ways. First, the size of the workforce affects the amount of goods and services produced. If a country has too few workers, it will be unable to make full use of its other resources. It may then encourage its citizens to have larger families or it may promote immigration. It may also encourage the importation of goods produced abroad.

Numbers of workers alone, however, do not determine how much a society can produce. Even more important is *labor productivity*, which is the amount each worker produces in a specified time. Productivity, in turn, is affected by (1) the skill of the labor force, (2) the quality and quantity of machinery and tools available per worker, and (3) technology. India's population, for example, is nearly three times as large as that of the United States. Yet India produces barely one-twentieth the amount of goods and services that the United States does. United States productivity is so much higher than India's because the United States is more advanced in *technology* (a culture's methods and tools for making things). Compared to India, the United States has more advanced equipment and its workers are better educated in the use of this technology.

Natural Resources

Natural resources are materials obtained from the land, sea, and air. They include soil, minerals, fish, wildlife, water, and timber. (Economists sometimes use the word "land" to mean natural resources of all kinds.) In order to benefit from their natural resources, people must have uses for them and the means of obtaining them.

Some regions of the world have low standards of living because they have few natural resources. In economic terms, *standard of living* refers to the quantity and quality of goods and services that are available to an individual or a society. The only way to improve the living standards of these regions is to strengthen the regions' other productive factors—labor, capital, and management. Switzerland, Denmark, and Japan each has limited natural resources, but each also has a high living standard because its other resources are highly developed.

For centuries, the Native American Shoshones of present-day Utah had what we would now consider an inadequate standard of living. They ate seeds, roots, and an occasional rabbit or other animal. They created only the simplest shelters and clothing. Today, the same land produces abundant quantities of vegetables, beef, and dairy products and supports a much larger population at a much higher standard of living.

Scarcity of natural resources forces all societies to make economic choices. What choices have been made on uses for this land?

How is it possible that today's inhabitants get so much more out of the land than did the ancient Shoshones? The answer is that the present-day inhabitants apply modern technology to the land, such as drought-resistant crops and labor-saving machinery.

Although all natural resources are limited, some can be replaced or renewed while others cannot. We can replant forests after trees have been cut down. We can restock streams and lakes with fish and restock woodlands with animals. Plants and animals are examples of *renewable resources*. Mineral ores and fuels, however, cannot be replaced. They are *nonrenewable resources*, since once they are consumed they are gone forever.

Shortages of some natural resources have prompted governments to enact laws that would: (1) limit the consumption of nonrenewable resources (such as certain minerals), and (2) require the restocking of renewable resources (such as forests).

Capital Resources

The machines, tools, and buildings that we use to produce goods and services are called *capital*, or *capital goods* or *capital resources*. A factory that manufactures shirts is a form of capital because it produces those goods. Schools are capital because they house a service industry—education. The term "capital" as it is used here should not be confused with money, which in other contexts is also called "capital."

Capital is eventually used up or worn out in much the same way that an automobile or washing machine wears out from use. This process of using up or wearing out machines is a form of deterioration.

The accounting term we use to measure the decline in the value of capital goods is called *depreciation*. If new capital is not produced to replace capital that has been used up (that is, depreciated), fewer goods can be produced. In order to increase production, a nation must produce more or better capital goods than are needed merely to make up for goods that have been worn out, used up, or are just no longer useful.

Let us suppose that Country X has $100 billion in capital goods. Let us also assume that the goods have a usable life of 20 years. At the end of one year, one-twentieth, or $5 billion worth of the capital goods, will have been consumed. We can see, therefore, that unless Country X adds $5 billion worth of capital goods to its stock, it will have less capital at the end of the year than there was at the beginning. It also follows that if Country X wants to increase its supply of capital goods, it will have to invest more than $5 billion on them each year.

The production of capital goods is called *capital formation*. Because capital goods are so vital to the production of goods and services, capital formation is an essential economic process in all societies.

How Capital Formation Takes Place. Unlike consumer goods (such as food, clothing, and shelter), capital goods do not immediately satisfy human wants. Instead, they are used to produce other goods or services—either consumer goods or services or other capital goods. It is

By 1964, when this photograph was taken, Japanese industry had recovered from the destruction caused by World War II and was emphasizing heavy industry.

important to keep in mind that capital produced in the present will satisfy human wants at a future time.

There is a limit to the amount of consumer goods and services and capital goods that a nation can produce at any one time. Therefore, capital formation requires a decision to do without some consumer goods now in order to have more later. After World War II (1941–1945), for example, Japan had little capital formation and few consumer goods. Its industries had been destroyed in the bombing. For a number of years, the Japanese invested heavily in capital goods and produced very few consumer goods. They made the decision to do without consumer goods then in order to have more goods later. Today, of course, Japan is able to produce large quantities of consumer goods for its population, and for export.

Capital formation takes place when individuals and businesses set aside a portion of their income as savings. Savings enable the banks that receive the deposits to make loans to those wishing to buy capital goods. In this way, a business in need of a new machine can call upon a bank for a loan to finance the purchase.

Entrepreneurship

The process of bringing together the three factors of production (natural resources, labor, and capital) is *entrepreneurship*. The people who do this with the goal of creating and operating business enterprises are *entrepreneurs*. An entrepreneur introduces new products and techniques and improves management techniques in existing businesses. She or he invests time and money in a business in the hope of earning a profit. As risk takers, though, entrepreneurs also risk losing much money.

THE FUNDAMENTAL QUESTIONS OF ECONOMICS

As we learned earlier, the study of economics comes down to this simple fact: there is not enough of everything to go around. Unable to have everything we want, we need to pick and choose from among the alternatives so as to get the most out of our resources. What is true for individuals is also true for society as a whole. Society must try to *allocate* (distribute) its resources in such a way as to get the most for its money. Along the way, society needs to answer some fundamental economic questions. These are:

- WHAT goods and services should be produced?
- HOW should they be produced?
- WHO will receive the goods and services that are produced?

WHAT Goods and Services Should Be Produced?

When a society's resources are fully employed, production in one area can be increased only by decreasing production in another. It also follows that what is true for a society also applies to businesses. If a shopping center is built on what was once farmland, that land can no longer be used to grow food. Workers building a sports arena cannot be employed at the same time building a hospital. Machines needed to produce 100 four-door sedans and 100 convertibles can produce more sedans only by taking some of the machines away from the production of convertibles. The final result would be more sedans built but fewer convertibles. Unable to have everything, individuals and institutions need to choose between those goods and services they will buy or produce and those they will forgo.

In analyzing how people make their choices, economists generally speak of trade-offs, opportunity costs, and marginalism.

Trade-Offs and Opportunity Costs. Economic decisions (such as decisions to buy, produce, and invest) involve trade-offs. A *trade-off* takes place when one thing is given up in order to obtain something else. The answer to each of the following questions involves trade-offs:

- "Should I buy an apple pie or a cheesecake?"
- "Should the town convert this land into a parking lot or a playground?"
- "Should we apply these funds to newspaper and magazine advertising or use them for a television campaign?"

Economists refer to the trade-off of one good or service for another as the *opportunity cost* of the choice. If you choose to play basketball on a summer afternoon instead of going swimming, it could be said that the opportunity cost of your basketball game is the afternoon's swim. Similarly, the opportunity cost of building the shopping center is that many acres of farmland are lost.

Marginalism. Another explanation for economic choices involves *marginalism*. As used in economics, the term marginalism refers to the usefulness of adding one more item to the production of a product or service. For example, a fast-food restaurant with five employees hires an additional, sixth. The businessperson in this example would be applying marginalism by weighing the additional benefits resulting from the decision to hire that sixth worker against the additional costs of an added worker.

HOW Should Goods and Services Be Produced?

There is more than one way to make an automobile, build a school, or extract minerals from the ground. In producing something, management can combine factors of production in many ways. In manufacturing automobiles, for example, management decides whether to employ 100 workers using existing machinery or introduce labor-saving machinery that requires only 40 workers. In this example, management estimates how much the new equipment would reduce costs and improve output.

In considering building a new school, city planners determine whether they want a sprawling, one-story school that requires three acres of land or a multistoried building that requires less than one acre of land but will increase construction costs for the school.

In extracting ores from the ground, mining companies decide which mining technique yields the least waste and smallest cost of operation for a given output.

In each of these examples, management decides how to combine the factors of production most efficiently. In the first example, management considers a mix of labor and capital. In the second example, it considers land as well as labor and capital. The third example involves consideration of various methods of combining land and capital.

HOW goods are produced often affects an entire society. In parts of our country, the destruction of forests, the overgrazing of grasslands, and poor planting methods have resulted in soil erosion and floods. Smoke from our factories, industrial wastes emptied into our streams, and agricultural pesticides seeping into our groundwater have led to the pollution of lakes, streams, and air. The increased use of machines in factory production has changed the entire character of our labor force and has made it harder for unskilled workers to find jobs.

WHO Should Receive the Goods and Services Produced?

Since it is not possible to produce enough of everything to satisfy everyone, we might ask, "WHO shall receive the goods and services produced?"

Should everyone have an equal share? Or should some people be allowed to have more than others? Should goods and services be awarded according to people's contributions to society? Or should we divide goods and services according to need? If people are to be paid in accordance with their contributions or needs, how are these factors to be measured? Who will do the measuring?

In the United States, a neurosurgeon's income may be ten times that of a schoolteacher. In Great Britain, a neurosurgeon may earn only four times as much as a schoolteacher. In China, the difference may be less than two times.

Among the wealthiest individuals in the United States are the most successful professional athletes. In many other countries, however, professional athletes can hardly earn a living. The United States answers the question "WHO shall receive the goods and services produced by the economy?" in one way; Britain answers it in another; and China, in still another. We will learn more about the "WHO" question in our next chapter, "The United States Economic System." For a full discussion as to how wages are determined in the United States, see Chapter 8, "The Labor Force in Our Economy."

ECONOMIC SYSTEMS: SOCIETY'S ANSWER TO WHAT, HOW, AND WHO

So far we have learned that:

- Scarcity is an economic fact of life. Human wants are greater than the resources needed to satisfy them.
- In making their choices, societies have to answer three questions: WHAT goods and services should be produced? HOW should they be produced? WHO should receive the goods and services that are produced?

The way in which a society answers the WHAT, HOW, and WHO questions defines its *economic system*. Economic systems are often classified as traditional, command, or market economies.

Traditional Economy

Many of the world's people live and work in what is called a *traditional economic system,* mostly in rural areas of South America, Asia, and Africa. There are certain features common to all traditional economies. Economic life is characterized by a self-contained community. Usually the chief occupation is farming, but it might be fishing or herding. The family is the main organizational unit of economic life. Production is carried on using the same kinds of tools and techniques that were used for many generations past. People produce only enough goods to meet the needs of their family, and sometimes a little more for sale to others. WHAT is produced and HOW it is produced is not the result of conscious planning but, rather, a matter of custom and tradition.

One's career in a traditional economic system is largely determined at birth. Men learn the trades of their fathers, while women tend the home and care for the children. Men and women alike work the land or care for their herds in accordance with time-honored traditions. Inventions and innovation are less common in traditional societies than in other groups.

WHO receives the goods and services produced in a traditional society today is largely based upon the size of the family's holdings. Usually the family with the largest holding of land or livestock (such as sheep, cattle, and camels) will have more than a family with a smaller holding of land or livestock. But ownership of such property is handed down in the family from generation to generation. So, once again, it is tradition that determines the WHO answer in a traditional economic system.

Command Economy

In a *command economy*, the fundamental questions of WHAT, HOW, and WHO are pretty much decided by a central authority, usually the government. During the years of the cold war (1948–1991), the Communist nations of Eastern Europe and the Soviet Union had command economies. Although the degree of power exercised by the central authority varied from one country to another, the principal means of production in these places were in government hands.

Since government owns most of the industry in command economies, central planning agencies determine WHAT is to be produced and HOW it will be produced. In the Soviet Union, for example, Communist party leaders wanted powerful armies and increased military might. Therefore, central planning agencies allocated funds, workers,

Workers on this Soviet collective farm were bringing in the harvest in 1930. Who determined what was to be planted and who would do the work?

and other resources to build up the military power of the nation. As a result of central planners' decisions to emphasize military production, fewer resources were available for the production of consumer goods and services.

In a command economy, the central authority also decides WHO will receive the goods and services produced. Government agencies set wage scales and determine the living standards that people in different walks of life will enjoy. Since insufficient resources in the former Soviet Union were allocated to producing consumer goods, these goods were in short supply. Few Soviet workers could afford automobiles, air conditioners, or comfortable housing. Moreover, those who could have afforded to pay the price of, say, an air conditioner often found that the stores had none available for sale. Those in positions favored by the Soviet government (such as scientists, athletes, and government officials) did not have these problems. These people lived in comfortable housing. They shopped in stores especially set aside for them where they could purchase things unavailable to others.

Market Economy

Quite the opposite of the centrally directed command economy is the decentralized *market economy*. In a market system (such as we have in the United States), the major decisions as to WHAT, HOW, and WHO are made by individuals and businesses. As compared to a command system, government in a market economy plays a much less important role.

Buyers and sellers in a market system make their wishes known in a marketplace, or market. It can be any place where goods are bought and sold. A marketplace is something like a polling booth: buyers "vote" for the goods and services they want by buying them. Sellers who best satisfy the wants of buyers are "elected" to stay in business through the profits they earn from their sales. Sellers who fail to satisfy buyers' wants are, in effect, voted "out of office."

During the 1980s, the people of the Soviet Union and Eastern Europe suffered through shortages of most consumer goods. Indeed, shoppers in the Communist countries lined up outside food stores in the hope of reaching the counter before the supplies ran out. In the next decade, however, the governments of nearly all the Communist countries began dismantling their command economies. They allowed free markets to help provide the answers to the basic economic questions. By way of preparing themselves for the introduction of the market system, many of the Eastern European countries sent economists and other scholars to the United States to study the economic system there firsthand.

Adam Smith

The year 1776 was a landmark in the history of the West for at least two reasons. First, a new vision of political freedom was proclaimed in the American Declaration of Independence. Second, a new vision of economic freedom was heralded when Scottish author **Adam Smith** published *An Inquiry Into the Nature and Causes of the Wealth of Nations.* So great was Smith's impact upon Western thinking that he came to be known as the "father of modern economics."

Born in Scotland in 1723 and educated at Oxford University in England, Smith returned to his native land to teach for a time at the University of Glasgow. In 1763, he began a three-year tour of Europe, during which he met with a number of prominent thinkers. Returning to London in 1766, Smith spent the next ten years writing *The Wealth of Nations.* In 1778, Smith was placed in charge of the customs house in Glasgow, and he held that post until his death in 1790.

In Adam Smith's time, most European nations followed the doctrine of *mercantilism.* The mercantilists believed that money, gold, and silver was the source of wealth. Governments, therefore, ought to do everything they could to build up their nations' supply of these precious metals. Since most governments followed the mercantilists' doctrine, they enacted laws whose purpose was to enlarge their nations' supplies of sil-

ver and gold. These laws limited the economic activities of their colonies, thereby restricting the export of precious metals.

Smith strongly disagreed with the mercantilists. Wealth, he said, sprang from the production of goods and services, not from the accumulation of gold and silver. People cannot eat precious metals, nor can they be sheltered by them in storms, or warmed by them in winter. Those who would measure the true wealth of a nation,

Smith said, should look to the amount of goods and services available for each of its citizens, not the size of its treasury.

How then can a government encourage the production of the greatest quantity of goods and services? Here is where Smith's break with mercantilism is most clearly seen. Government, he wrote, could serve the economy best by keeping its hands off business. To the French (who had first proposed such a policy), the idea was described as *laissez-faire* (literally, "let them do"). **François Quesnay**, a French economist, had advocated *laissez-faire* in connection with the French government's farm policies. Smith expanded Quesnay's concept to apply to a nation's entire economy. *Laissez-faire* achieved enormous popularity in England as a result of *The Wealth of Nations*.

Why should government allow businesses to conduct their affairs without interference? Left to their own devices, Smith said, businesspeople would seek to make the greatest profits by turning out the greatest quantity of goods and services at the lowest possible prices. These low-cost goods and services would have to benefit society as a whole. Smith put it this way: "The businessman intends only his own gain; however, he is in this led by an invisible hand to promote an end which was not part of his intention. By pursuing his own interest, he frequently promotes that of society more effectually than when he really intends to promote it."

The "invisible hand" that Smith saw guiding business along a path of public good was, in reality, the pursuit of profits. The "chase" took place in a *market* subject to the laws of supply and demand, which we will discuss in Chapter 3. To allow these laws of the marketplace to function, Smith espoused the philosophy of *laissez-faire*. But Smith was also a realist. He recognized that government would have to intervene in the economy to preserve competition and to protect the general welfare.

The Wealth of Nations deals with many other subjects besides *laissez-faire,* among them labor, production, income distribution, rent, and taxation. Later economists would look to Smith's ideas as the springboard for the development of their own theories in each of these fields.

Smith's influence was dramatized in 1983 when the Nobel Prize in Economics was awarded to **Gerard Debreu** of the University of California at Berkeley. (See Chapter 9 for a discussion of the Nobel Prize in Economics.) Debreu's prize was awarded in recognition of his work on one of economics' fundamental questions: How do prices operate to balance what producers offer for sale with what buyers want? Debreu developed a mathematical foundation that could be used to demonstrate the laws of supply and demand in action in a modern economy. In this way, the invisible hand of the 18th century became a mathematical reality in the 20th century.

WHAT DO ECONOMISTS DO?

Economists are the professionals who study the ways in which society allocates its resources to satisfy its wants. Economists spend much of their time gathering and analyzing data. These activities enable them to identify problems and suggest solutions.

Microeconomics vs. Macroeconomics

The kinds of problems economists study can be classified as either microeconomic or macroeconomic. *Microeconomics* is the study of the effects of economic forces upon individual parts of the economy, such as business firms, households, and workers. When executives of a firm think about what would happen to sales if the firm were to increase its prices, they are wrestling with a microeconomic problem.

Macroeconomics is the study of the impact of changes on the economy as a whole. *Macroeconomists* try to answer questions like: "What will be the effect of a tax increase on consumer spending?" and "How will a decrease in the defense budget affect the nation's businesses?"

What Is vs. What Ought to Be

Economists deal with two worlds: "the world that is" and "the world that ought to be." The study of what *is* focuses on the causes and effects of specific events. For example, federal minimum wage laws set the lowest wage that most workers can be paid. If members of Congress were thinking of increasing the minimum wage, they might ask economists to find the answers to questions like: "How would a 10 percent increase in the minimum wage affect business profits?" and "What effect would such an increase have on the unemployment rate?" Both questions deal with the world that is.

Like everybody else, though, economists have sets of values that often influence how they view economic problems. For example, some economists will argue that minimum wage laws are unwise and ought not to be enacted. Others support such laws. Similarly, economists will disagree about whether government should enact programs to help special groups, such as the homeless, small business owners, farm workers, and savers.

Using Economic Models

An *economic model* is a simplified way of looking at an economic problem. It may be expressed in the form of a statement, graph, or mathematical formula. For example, an economist might say that there is an *inverse* (reverse) relationship between the price of steak and the sales of steak. The economist's verbal model could also be expressed graphically as in Figure 1.1.

Figure 1.1 Economic Model of Steak Sales

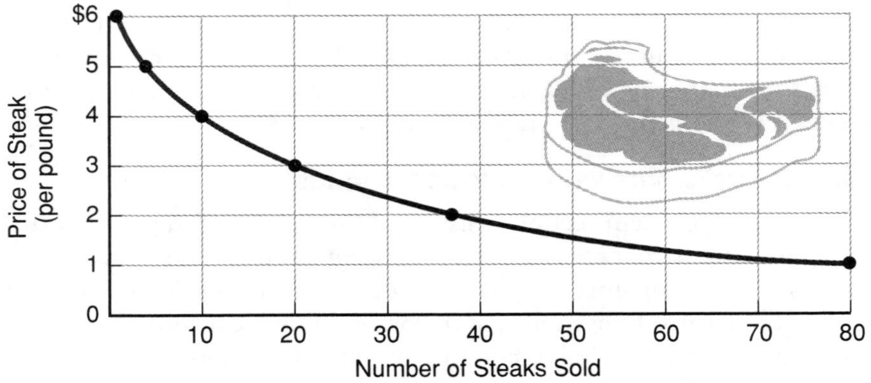

It could also be expressed mathematically as:

Sales of steak	*is*	*a function of*	*the price of steak*
(Ss)	=	f of	(Ps)

or: (Ss) = f(Ps)

Economists create models to make predictions about how a change in one variable will affect others. Suppose, for example, an economist was asked to report on the advisability of replacing existing factory equipment with new machinery. After gathering the facts, she would prepare a model (graphic, mathematical, or verbal) on which a prediction could be based.

Similarly, government economists might be asked to predict the effect of a tax cut on employment. The economists would prepare a model based on the available information. They would use the model to make their predictions.

A good model helps economists understand the consequences of economic activity and to predict changes. But even a good economic model is fallible; it cannot predict with 100 percent accuracy. In most instances, however, economic predictions are more accurately made with models than without them. For that reason, economists will continue to use models as tools of economics.

Ceteris Paribus: Other Things Being Equal

Working in laboratories, natural scientists (such as physicists and chemists) can test their theories in a controlled environment. Economists and other social scientists, however, deal with human behavior, which is often unpredictable. Such behavior can rarely be observed under laboratory conditions.

By way of bringing order into their studies, economists rely on an assumption known in Latin as *ceteris paribus* (other things being equal). Economists know, for example, that there is a relationship between the price of a good and the quantity of the good that people will buy. As prices increase, consumers buy less; as prices decrease, consumers buy more. But there can be any number of exceptions to these rules. Examples include:

- Perfume selling for $20 an ounce may outsell an identical product peddled for $.10 an ounce.
- For special occasions, some people shop in the most expensive stores in town.

By relying on *ceteris paribus*, however, economists can ignore these and other exceptions by simply saying that people will buy more of an item at a lower price than at a higher one, all other things being equal.

Ceteris paribus enables observers to focus on one or two variables while, at the same time, recognizing that other variables exist.

Summary

Economics is the study of how people and societies use scarce resources to satisfy unlimited wants. In making choices, societies have to answer three basic questions: WHAT goods and services should be produced? HOW should they be produced? WHO should receive the goods and services that are produced? The way in which a society answers these three questions depends upon whether the economic system is a traditional, command, or market economy.

Economists study the way an economy allocates its resources. Microeconomics is concerned with the effects of decisions by individuals, firms, and government on various parts of the economy. Macroeconomics is the study of changes on the economy as a whole. Economists focus on the world that is but may also be concerned with the world as they think it ought to be. Economists use models, or theories, to simplify the way they look at economic problems. A model may be expressed in the form of statements, graphs, or mathematical formulas. Economists rely on *ceteris paribus* (other things being equal) so as to focus on one or two variables while recognizing that other variables exist.

REVIEWING THE CHAPTER

Building Vocabulary

Match each term in Column A with its definition in Column B.

COLUMN A	COLUMN B
1. standard of living	*a.* the evaluation of the usefulness of adding one more item in the production of a product or service
2. good	
3. factor of production	*b.* the study of the forces affecting the economy as a whole
4. economics	*c.* the way a society answers the WHAT, HOW, and WHO questions
5. capital formation	
6. entrepreneurship	*d.* an ingredient that goes into the production of a good or service
7. trade-off	*e.* the study of how society uses limited resources to satisfy unlimited wants
8. marginalism	*f.* the production of capital goods
9. economic system	*g.* a tangible item of value
10. macroeconomics	*h.* the quantity and quality of goods and services available to an individual or society
	i. the giving up of one thing to obtain something else
	j. the bringing together of the factors of production

Understanding What You Have Read

1. "All societies must *economize* because human wants are unlimited, but resources needed to satisfy these wants are limited." This statement means that society must   (*a*) use its resources in such a way as to get the most out of them   (*b*) save as much money as possible   (*c*) keep its budgets balanced   (*d*) prohibit the use of its resources.

2. Economists differentiate between *goods* and *services*. Which of the following best illustrates a payment for a service?   (*a*) $1.95 for a hamburger   (*b*) $18.95 for a textbook   (*c*) $15,000 for a new automobile   (*d*) $10 for a haircut?

3. When a nation's resources are fully employed with maximum efficiency, additional machinery   (*a*) cannot be produced under any circumstance   (*b*) can be produced, but only under government supervision   (*c*) can be produced, but only if the production of

something else is reduced   (*d*) can be produced, but only by giant, privately owned industries.

4. Some regions of the world have low standards of living because they have few natural resources. The main way to improve the living standards of these lands is to   (*a*) place more power in the hands of government   (*b*) continue doing things as always, but work harder   (*c*) strengthen their other productive factors   (*d*) increase the population of these lands.

5. All economic systems must provide answers to three out of the four following questions. Which of the questions is not necessarily a concern of every economic system?   (*a*) What goods and services should be produced?   (*b*) How should goods and services be produced?   (*c*) Who will receive the goods and services that are produced?   (*d*) Why do not all the people in the nation share equally in the distribution of what is produced?

6. The *opportunity cost* of an increase in the local police force is   (*a*) the government goods or services that people will give up in order for the government to hire additional police   (*b*) the cost of the additional police   (*c*) the cost of training new recruits   (*d*) the amount by which taxes may be increased to pay for the additional police.

7. Which of the following is essential in order for capital formation to occur in any society?   (*a*) increased consumption   (*b*) increased savings   (*c*) decreased savings   (*d*) decreased production.

8. Which of the following is *least likely* to affect productivity?   (*a*) the skill of the labor force   (*b*) the quality and quantity of machinery and tools available per worker   (*c*) technology   (*d*) the number of workers available.

9. Which of the following is *not* a characteristic of an entrepreneur? He or she   (*a*) accepts the risk of financial loss   (*b*) introduces new products and techniques   (*c*) is satisfied to keep things as they are   (*d*) improves management techniques in existing businesses.

10. A firm sets aside funds for *depreciation* to   (*a*) prepare for a decline in business   (*b*) provide for the replacement of worn-out capital   (*c*) cover increasing labor costs   (*d*) insure against falling prices.

11. "An individual's role in the economy is most likely determined at birth, and goods and services are produced according to time-honored methods." Which economic system would fit this description?   (*a*) traditional   (*b*) command   (*c*) market   (*d*) highly specialized.

12. Skyscrapers are found in large cities but not in small towns. Economists would explain this in terms of   (a) differences in architectural tastes between residents of cities and those of small towns   (b) the lower costs of labor in cities   (c) the scarcity and high costs of land in the cities   (d) the relatively low construction costs of tall buildings compared to those of one- or two-story buildings.

13. In which type of economic system are consumers most likely to determine what goods will be produced?   (a) market economy   (b) traditional economy   (c) command economy   (d) wartime economy.

14. *Microeconomists* study questions such as   (a) What will be the effect of taxes on consumer spending?   (b) How will a decrease in the defense budget affect a nation's businesses?   (c) How will an increase or decrease in interest rates affect business spending?   (d) How will the decisions made by firm X affect consumer demand for the products produced by that firm?

15. Economists deal with *the world that is* and *the world that ought to be.*   Which of the following questions deal with *the world as it ought to be?*   (a) How would a 10 percent increase in the minimum wage affect business profits?   (b) Are minimum wage laws wise?   (c) What is the likely impact of an increase in interest rates on business spending?   (d) What would be the effect of a 3 percent increase in consumer prices on consumer spending?

16. An economic model   (a) enables economists to predict economic activity with 100 percent accuracy   (b) is a complex way of looking at an economic problem   (c) can only be expressed with graphs or mathematical formulas   (d) helps economists understand economic activity and predict changes.

Thinking Critically

1. Why is economics called a study of scarcity and choice?

2. "HOW goods are produced often affects an entire society. Natural resources, we have learned, are limited. While some natural resources can be replaced or renewed, others cannot." Discuss the implications of these statements for people who make decisions concerning the use of mineral resources, fossil fuels (oil, coal, and natural gas), forest resources, and water resources.

3. Economic decisions are likely to be influenced by the *opportunity costs* involved. Explain in terms of opportunity costs your answer to each of the following questions.   (a) Should the United States undertake a program to land astronauts on Mars?   (b) Should your community build a new hospital?   (c) Should your family

buy a new automobile? (*d*) Should the federal government give financial support to a United States Olympic team?

4. "People cannot eat machinery or factory buildings. That is why poor countries should concentrate on agriculture and leave manufacturing to the industrialized nations." Explain why you agree or disagree with this statement.

5. In the United States, a neurosurgeon's income may be ten times that of a schoolteacher. In a country with a command economy, the difference might be less than two times. How can you explain the fact that individuals doing the same work in different countries do not earn comparable salaries?

SKILLS: Analyzing the Production Possibilities Curve

The *production possibilities curve* illustrates in graphic form the economic concepts of scarcity and opportunity cost. "Scarcity" may be the most significant word in economics. It compels individuals and societies to choose from among the things they want. If they choose one combination of goods and services, they must give up another. Let us illustrate the concept of scarcity by considering an imaginary country we will call "Ravinia." A tiny nation, Ravinia produces two categories of goods: necessities and luxuries. (*Necessities* are those goods and services needed to sustain daily life. *Luxuries* are goods and services that add pleasure to life but can be done without.)

In a recent survey, Ravinian economists determined the following:

● With the labor force fully employed and producing nothing but necessities (food, clothing, and shelter), 600 million tons could be turned out in one year.

● With the labor force fully employed and producing nothing but luxuries (jewelry, yachts, and candy), 110 million tons could be created in one year.

● If Ravinia chose to turn out both luxuries and necessities, various combinations of each could be produced.

Table 1.1 shows that if Ravinia chose to produce 300 million tons of necessities in a given year, it could also generate up to 90 million tons of luxuries. Suppose, however, that the Ravinians wanted more than 90 million tons of luxuries—say, 100 million tons. Would they be able to produce the additional 10 million tons of luxuries? Yes, but in so doing they would have to take some of the resources that had been engaged in the production of necessities and shift them to luxury production. The table tells us that producing 10 million more tons of luxuries would result in a 50 percent reduction in the production of

Table 1.1   Production Possibilities in Ravinia

If necessities produced are:	The maximum production of luxuries could be:
600 million tons	0 million tons
550 million tons	40 million tons
500 million tons	55 million tons
400 million tons	80 million tons
300 million tons	90 million tons
150 million tons	100 million tons
0 million tons	110 million tons

necessities. In economic terms, the opportunity cost of producing an additional 10 million tons of luxuries would be 150 million tons of necessities.

By transferring the information in the table to a graph and connecting the plotted points, we can create a production possibilities curve, as shown in Figure 1.2. A production possibilities curve depicts the possibilities for production when all resources are fully and effectively employed. In actuality, a nation is likely to produce less than it is capable of producing.

Suppose, for example, that Ravinia's present production is at point U. At U, the nation is producing 300 million tons of necessities and 45 million tons of luxuries. These amounts are well below Ravinia's capacity, and the Ravinians have fewer goods and services available to them than the economy is capable of producing.

Figure 1.2   Production Possibilities in Ravinia

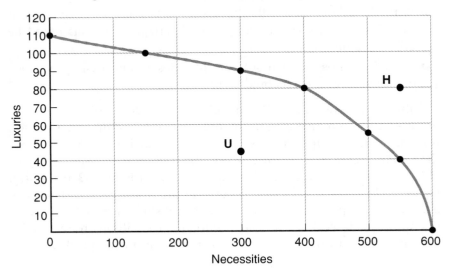

Suppose, however, that the Ravinians wanted to produce 550 tons of necessities and 80 million tons of luxuries, as depicted by point H. Would that be possible? Figure 1.2 shows that it would not be possible under present conditions to expand production to point H. The production possibilities curve indicates a limit beyond which production cannot expand using current resources. Expanding the economy beyond the production possibilities curve would require additional resources. Increasing the size of the labor force or acquiring more and better tools and equipment could lead to increased production. So too could improved management techniques or better government. For the nation's economic planners, the production possibilities curve represents a limit they must constantly strive to exceed.

1. Explain the statement that "scarcity may be the single most significant word in the field of economics."
2. Define a production possibilities curve.
3. According to the table, how many tons of luxuries could the Ravinians have produced in a year in which they turned out 400 tons of necessities?
4. What are *opportunity costs*?
5. What would be the opportunity cost to Ravinia if it chose to increase its production of necessities from 500 to 550 tons at a time when its resources were fully employed?
6. You have been asked by the Ravinian government for your opinion as to the state of its economy. Current production levels stand at 200 tons of necessities and 80 tons of luxuries a year. What would you tell the Ravinians? Explain your answer.
7. Ravinia is now producing 500 tons of necessities and 50 tons of luxuries. It would like to hold its production of necessities at current levels and increase production of luxuries to 80 tons. What are Ravinia's chances of success? Explain your answer.

Chapter 2

THE UNITED STATES ECONOMIC SYSTEM

Overview

As you walk down the aisles of a supermarket, do you ever wonder how all the packaged foods, household products, and fresh produce got there? Many of the items traveled hundreds or thousands of miles. In the winter, the store may have received its grapes from Chile, its oranges from Florida, and its tomatoes from California. In most cases, there is a constant supply of those foods and other goods. As soon as the store sells one lot of goods, a fresh supply appears as if by magic. If you choose to hold off on a purchase today, there is a good chance that the product you want or a similar one will still be available next week or a month from now. The nearest department store, too, always seems to have a wide and fairly predictable variety of items for sale.

The nation's stores and other businesses provide us with a steady stream of goods and services. Some $7 trillion worth of goods and services are produced annually by the United States economic system. Incredibly, this enormous outpouring functions without having been designed or operated by any single individual or agency. Somehow, the over 130 million people involved in running the economy are able to do so without central direction. Although our economy is not perfect, it succeeds in meeting the economic needs of many of our people. Going beyond people's needs, the economy also meets the economic wants of many Americans, making the U.S. standard of living one of the highest in the world.

How does our economic system function with no centralized management? How do the people of the United States answer the fundamental economic questions facing all societies: WHAT goods and services should be produced? HOW should they be produced? WHO should receive the goods and services produced? As you read this chapter, you will learn the answers to these and the following questions:

- ☐ What are the principles of the free enterprise system?
- ☐ Why is our economic society interdependent?
- ☐ How does a market system function?
- ☐ What are the economic goals of the United States?

PRINCIPLES OF THE U.S. ECONOMIC SYSTEM

The economic system of the United States is known as *capitalism*, or *free enterprise*. In this system, the means of production are privately owned, and the fundamental questions of WHAT, HOW, and WHO are answered by the market rather than by tradition or an economic plan. Capitalism is founded upon certain principles, the most important being free enterprise, private property, the profit motive, consumer sovereignty, and competition.

Freedom of Enterprise

The free enterprise system takes its name from the freedom people in the system enjoy to enter any legal business and conduct it as they see fit. Those who venture into the business world hope that they might be quite successful at it. They know, however, that they also risk the possibility of loss.

Freedom of enterprise has its limitations. Because *public utilities* (industries that serve the public interest, such as gas and electric companies) are often the only source of a certain product in a community, government closely regulates what they provide and how much they can charge. To protect consumers, government requires certain professions to be licensed. Most other businesses are subject to various other types of government supervision and regulation. Despite all these limitations, individuals have considerable freedom to organize and operate their businesses as they choose.

Private Property

Having the *right to private property* means allowing individuals to own property and use it in any lawful manner that they choose. The right of individuals to own the means of production (such as factories, farms, and stores) is one of the basic principles of capitalism. (In some command economies, by contrast, the means of production are owned by the government.) Like most other rights, property rights in the United States are subject to limitations. Government may, for example, tax those who own or inherit property. Similarly, the principal of *eminent domain* gives government the power to seize property it intends to use for some public purpose (such as to make room for building a road or school). Eminent domain requires, however, that government pay a fair price for the property it seizes.

Profit Motive

The main reason an individual or group of people organize a business in a market economy is to make money. The amount of money left over after subtracting business expenses from business income is *profit*. Business firms and individuals try hard to keep costs down and increase their income from sales. Of course, the better an entrepreneur succeeds at this, the higher the profits. Economists describe the desire of business owners to earn the greatest profits as the *profit motive*.

Consumer Sovereignty

Just as those in business are free to produce and sell their goods and services as they see fit, consumers are free to choose which goods and services they will buy (and which they will reject). Economists often describe this freedom as *consumer sovereignty*. Freedom of choice gives consumers the power to dictate which goods and services will be produced (and which will not).

On the one hand, if consumers are unwilling to purchase purple ballpoint pens, manufacturers will stop producing them. On the other hand, if consumers want yellow ballpoints, manufacturers will quickly produce them.

Consumers' likes and dislikes are expressed in a kind of marketplace election. Consumers "vote" for a product by buying it, and "vote" against it by choosing not to buy it. The most successful businesses are those that either can "anticipate the market" by correctly predicting what consumers will want or can successfully create a demand for their products through advertising. Four decades ago, few parents would have thought of buying disposable paper diapers for their infants. In those days, diapers were made of cloth. The development of the disposable diaper was followed, however, by huge advertising campaigns that created a demand for the product. Today, more babies are diapered with disposables than with cloth diapers.

Consumer sovereignty can be limited by government policy. If government requires much titanium for its own purposes, this scarce metal is not likely to be available for consumer products. Consumer sovereignty is also limited when there are but two or three producers of a product. Most lightbulbs, for example, are manufactured by three producers. These manufacturers can pretty much determine the size, shape, wattage, and price of their products.

Competition

The rivalry among sellers in the same field for consumer dollars is called *competition*. As we just learned, the profit motive is the driving force that pushes business firms to produce particular products or services. We also learned that consumers are free to choose what goods and services they want and from whom they wish to purchase those

In what was one of the most costly business mistakes of the decade, executives of the Ford Motor Company in 1958 assumed that the public wanted another midsized automobile. This assumption led them to produce and promote an entirely new line, which they called the "Edsel." The public, however, did not want another midsized family car. After swallowing millions of dollars of losses in only three years, Ford shut down its Edsel division. Consumer demand for 40-year-old cars is another matter. A restored and operable Edsel is worth more today than when it sat on showroom floors.

goods and services. The Ford Motor Company, for example, learned the hard way in the 1950s that consumers preferred other models of automobiles (many produced by General Motors and the Chrysler Corporation) to Ford's Edsel.

For a while, Apple Computer and IBM pretty much dominated the personal computer market. Then as others saw how profitable this market was, more companies entered it. To win a share of the personal computer business, these other firms had to offer products or services that were either better or at lower prices than those of either Apple or IBM. Competition pressures business firms to constantly try to provide the best services and to create the best products at the lowest possible prices. This is the way that companies appeal to consumer sovereignty and, thus, earn greater profits.

SPECIALIZATION AND THE ECONOMY

Jack and Mildred Green live in an apartment in a large city with their two teenage children, Ted and Laura. Jack works as a mechanic for a bus company, and Mildred is a manager in a law firm. Ted and Laura go to school. On a typical day, the Greens consume many of the same goods and services as do other families in their income bracket. They spend money for food, clothing, utilities (such as telephone service, gas, and electricity), recreation, a car, a television set, and all the many other items that go along with modern living. They also use such government-provided facilities as schools and highways.

It is likely that the Greens produce none of the goods and services that they consume. They live in a society where work is so specialized that few people are able to provide for more than a tiny fraction of their own needs. Mr. Green repairs buses, while Mrs. Green helps run a law office. In addition, both parents work at raising their children and caring for their home. How are the Greens able to obtain the hundreds of goods and services that they need and want in order to live comfortably?

The Greens, like some 270 million other residents of the United States, must count on the efforts of other people to provide them with most of their needs. This dependence on the labor of others was not always the rule in the United States and elsewhere. In the past, people relied mostly upon their own efforts and nature's abundance to provide what they needed. Frontier families in this country had to grow their own food, build their own homes, and make their own clothing. Even today in traditional agricultural societies, each family provides most of the goods and services that its members consume.

The economic independence seen in traditional agricultural societies is not possible in the United States. Instead, the U.S. economy features *specialization*. In an industrial society, jobs are highly specialized. Workers perform one specialized task and depend on other workers to provide them with the things that they need. There are many advantages to specialization. By concentrating on one activity, for example, workers produce more because they become highly skillful at what they do.

Just as individual workers become more efficient at their specialized tasks, so do companies. Many small companies produce only one type of good (such as dresses) or provide just one type of service (such as dry cleaning). Specialization encourages the efficient use of capital. If a business needs a delivery truck only twice a week, it would be wasteful for the business to purchase and maintain its own truck. The business can use its capital more efficiently by hiring the services of another company, one that specializes in making deliveries. Specialization also promotes *innovation* (new ways of doing things). Companies that produce only a few products are able to concentrate on developing new machines and production techniques that will increase production, improve quality, and lower costs for these products.

Specialization is possible only where markets are large enough to support them. In New York City, for example, there are dozens of shops that sell only handbags. Others sell only the finest grand pianos. By contrast, in driving through most small towns in Vermont, you will not find a single shop selling only pianos. The number of potential customers is too small in a Vermont town to support such highly specialized shops. In large cities, though, there are thousands of potential buyers for pianos. Such a market can support, perhaps, a dozen piano shops. Stated as an economic principle, the degree of specialization is limited by the extent of the market.

How is it that 130 million people working at thousands of different tasks are able to produce the hundreds of thousands of different goods and services that people want? And how are these goods and services distributed to where they are needed? We will try to answer these questions in the following pages.

THE CIRCULAR FLOW OF ECONOMIC ACTIVITY

People receive income from a number of sources and spend it in a variety of ways. Workers receive wages and buy consumer goods. Business owners receive profits and pay their employees and suppliers. Landlords receive rent and purchase maintenance services and fuel for their buildings. Lenders earn interest and spend part of it on new loans or other investments. No matter how money is earned, it returns to the economy when buyers purchase the things they need or want.

Economists describe the stream of funds that is constantly passing back and forth between the public and the businesses of the country as

Figure 2.1   Circular Flow of Money

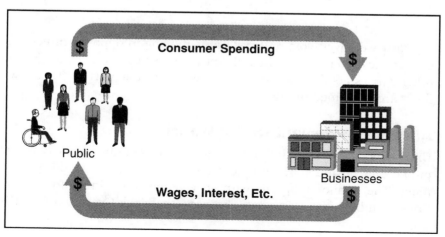

Consumer Spending

Public

Businesses

Wages, Interest, Etc.

a *circular flow*. Figure 2.1 represents this circular flow of funds. Businesses send out funds to the public in the form of wages to employees, rent to landlords, interest to banks and bondholders, dividends to stockholders, and other payments. The public, as consumers and investors, sends money back to the business community.

In addition to the circular flow of funds between businesses and the public, there is also a circular flow of goods and services. The goods and services produced by businesses are purchased by the Greens and other consumers. Consumers in turn sell their productive services to businesses—in the Greens' case, to a bus company and a law firm. The flow of goods and services is illustrated in Figure 2.2. Businesses provide goods and services to the public (consumers), and the public provides productive services (land, labor, capital, and management) to businesses.

Figure 2.2   Circular Flow of Goods and Services

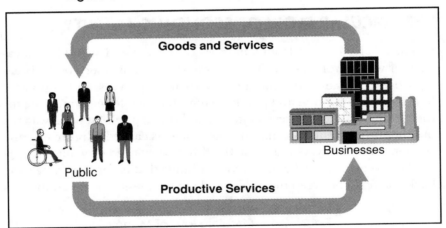

Now we have two circular streams moving in opposite directions. One carries money from the public to businesses and back again; the other carries goods and services between the same parties. These two flows are combined in Figure 2.3.

Adding Government to Our Model

Until now we have limited our discussion of economic activity to the public and business. To complete the picture, we must add government. The public's relations with government are similar to its relations with businesses. The bus company that Jack Green works for is

Figure 2.3   Circular Flow of Money, Goods, and Services

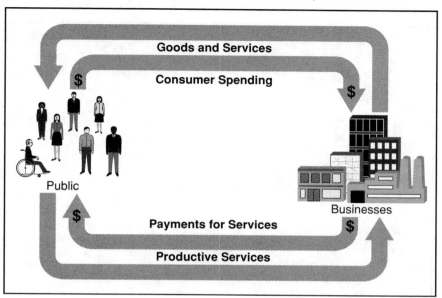

owned by the city. The city uses his productive services to provide a service to the public—in this case, transportation. The money that the public pays to the bus company in the form of fares is used by the city for wages and other payments to the public. Other city income, such as tolls and sales taxes, returns to the public in a similar way.

In Figure 2.4, the inner loop represents the money flow between the public and government. The upper portion of the inner loop represents the taxes that the public pays to provide government with the major part of its income. The lower portion of the inner loop indicates the payments that government makes to the public in the form of wages, rent, welfare, interest, and so on.

The outer loop in Figure 2.4 shows (at the top) the flow of government goods and services to the public, and (at the bottom) the flow of productive services of individuals who provide labor or other services to the government.

A similar flowchart would represent the economic exchange between businesses and government. Productive services flow from businesses to government—as, for example, if Mrs. Green's law firm were to do some legal work for a government agency. Businesses also provide government with goods, such as office furniture, paper, and helicopters. Productive services flow from government to businesses, as

Figure 2.4 Circular Flow of Money, Goods, and Services Between the Government and the Public

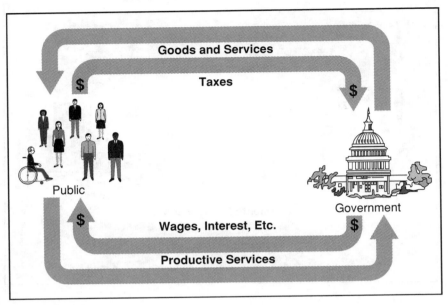

when businesses use the Postal Service to send and receive mail. Money flows from government to businesses in the form of fees (such as those charged by Mrs. Green's law firm) and other payments. Money flows from businesses to government as taxes, tolls, postage, fees, and so on.

Using the preceding information, one could construct a chart showing the circular flow of goods and services, and of money, between businesses and government. If we combine this information with the relationships described in Figures 2.1 through 2.4, we get a picture of the general flow of economic activity among the three major sectors of our economy: government, businesses, and consumers (the public). This economic activity is shown in Figure 2.5.

These circular flowcharts give us a bird's-eye view of the economy and help us to see how changes in one part of the economy may affect the other parts. For example, when we read in the newspaper that the government plans to increase spending, we will understand that this could lead to an increase in the size of the total economic flow. Similarly, a reduction in the amount of goods and services purchased by the public will reduce the amount of income received by businesses and will thus reduce the size of the total flow of spending.

Figure 2.5   Circular Flow of Economic Activity Among the Public,
Businesses, and the Government

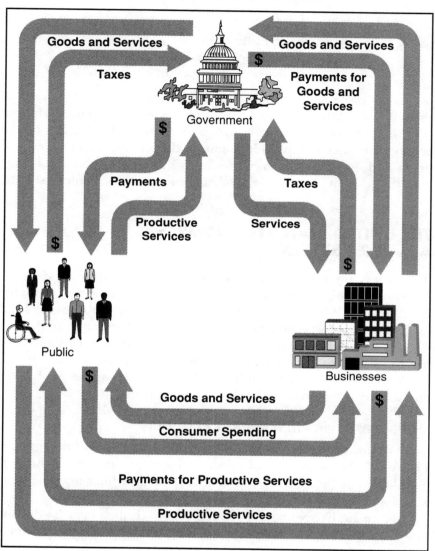

Gross Domestic Product

The size of the streams of money, goods, and services that flow between consumers, businesses, and the public is constantly changing.
Economists call the total value of the goods and services produced in a
single year the *gross domestic product* (GDP). Since the goods and
services that were produced were paid for by either consumers,

businesses, or government, the GDP can be expressed mathematically as follows:

$$C + I + G = GDP$$

where
C = consumer spending
I = business spending (investment)
G = government spending

As we discussed in Chapter 1, economists describe the study of these flows and the factors affecting them as *macroeconomics.* By contrast, *microeconomics* is the branch of economics that focuses on the economic behavior of individual units in the economy, such as a single household, firm, or industry. In other words, macroeconomics deals with the economy as a whole, while microeconomics studies its parts.

THE UNITED STATES ECONOMY IS A MARKET SYSTEM

A market is any place or circumstance in which goods or services are bought and sold. If you rent a videotape, you become part of the video rental market. Similarly, if you take an after-school job in your local grocery store, you become part of the food industry's labor market.

Since the buyers and sellers who make up a market do not have to meet face to face, markets can exist without a meeting place. In the stock market, for example, millions of shares of securities are bought and sold daily by buyers and sellers who never meet.

Dollars as Votes in a Market Economy

Circular flowcharts can illustrate the role of markets in the economy. Figure 2.6 shows the flow of goods and services between businesses and the public (households). In addition, the drawing shows the markets that are involved in the money transactions.

Figure 2.6 likens markets to an election. In the upper half of the flowchart, households "vote" for the things they want by casting their "ballots" (money) for goods and services at a certain price. Businesses put up their "candidates for office" (the goods and services they produce) so as to attract the greatest number of "votes" (dollars). The votes represent demand and the candidates represent supply. As sales are made, businesses receive the "votes" of the electorate (consumers' dollars), and their "candidates" (their goods and services) are either elected (purchased) or defeated (not purchased).

In the lower half of the flowchart, the roles are reversed: Households are the sellers and businesses, the buyers. Here the "candidates"

Figure 2.6   The Role of Markets in Our Economy

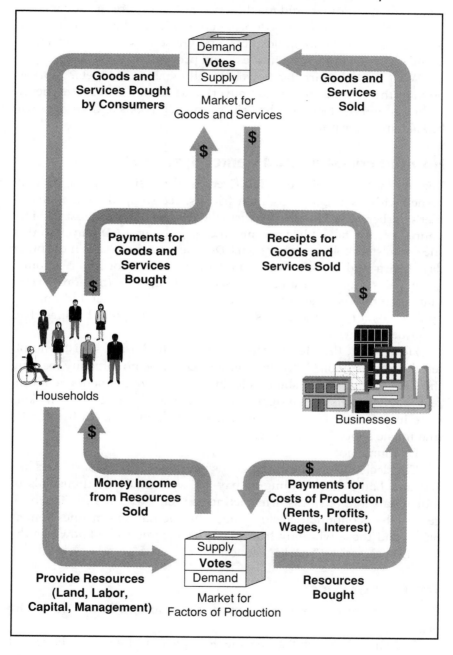

running for election are the factors of production supplied by households: labor, buildings, and machinery. The "votes" are the dollars paid by businesses for the factors of production. Money flows from firms as part of their cost of doing business, and households receive payments in the form of wages, rent, interest, and profits.

What does the circular flowchart tell us about markets? Markets provide the "polling place" for buyers and sellers. Out of the never-ending round of elections, the prices at which goods and services will be sold are determined.

How the Price-Directed Market System Works

Like many other teenagers, Ted Green and his sister Laura are concerned with keeping up with their friends. Ted stopped going to his father's barber so he can use a stylist who cuts hair in the latest fashion. Laura recently talked her parents into buying her a CD player so that she could start collecting her own CDs (compact discs). Then the other day, Laura and her mother visited their local record store, Found Sound. Mrs. Green was amazed to see how many CDs the store carried that catered to her daughter's taste. Although Mrs. Green did not recognize most of the titles, the salesclerk assured her that business had never been better.

How was it that Ted Green was able to find a hairstylist who offered the latest look? Why did Laura Green have no difficulty locating the CD titles for which she was looking? Did a government agency direct that hairstylists be assigned to neighborhoods in which their skills were in demand? Did a government supply board issue a list of CDs that music shops had to carry?

Of course not.

The decisions to supply the goods and services that consumers like Ted and Laura were willing to pay for were made by thousands of individuals and business firms acting in their own interest. Taken together, the economic decisions made by the nation's business enterprises and those who buy from them have come to be known as the "market system" or "market economy."

The Role of Prices

Some economists compare the market system to a factory fueled by prices.

Ted Green's hairstylist became very popular. Recently, she raised her price to $25 per cut. "That's too much money," Ted said to himself. "I'm going back to the barber whom Dad uses. He'll do the job for half the price. Then I can use the money I save on haircuts to buy some new clothes."

Meanwhile, Laura was excited about an ad that she saw in the morning newspaper. It seems that Found Sound was running a "One-Day-Only, Half-Off-Everything Sale!!"

"Half off everything," she exclaimed, "I can hardly wait till school's out. I'm going to buy a hundred CDs!"

"With what?" her friend Rebecca asked. "Half off doesn't mean it's free, you know."

"OK," Laura agreed, "so I'll buy one CD. And if I have enough left over, I'll buy another one, too."

Laura's and Ted's decisions to buy and not to buy were determined by the prices of the goods and services in which they were interested. As a matter of fact, almost every decision made by buyers and sellers is influenced in some way by the price of the product in which they are interested. Consumers compare the prices of goods they want to buy. Workers try to get the highest price, or wage, for their labor. Producers consider the prices, or cost, of the items needed for production and the prices they will be able to charge for the goods and services that they produce.

Indeed, price is such an important factor in the U.S. economy that economists often describe it as a "price-directed market system."

Prices Determine WHAT Goods and Services Will Be Produced. How does it happen that Found Sound had the CDs that Laura Green was seeking? With so many people willing to pay the price for its products, the store saw an opportunity to add to its profits by ordering more CDs from its suppliers. Moreover, Found Sound knew that if it did not have the recordings its customers wanted, they would simply buy them from its competitors.

What is true for Found Sound applies to all business firms. They must offer the products that customers want. They must do so at a price (1) that customers are willing to pay, and (2) at which the firm can afford to sell.

In other words, while you and all your friends might love to buy a new mountain bike for $25, your local bike shop is not likely to offer any at that price. Why? Rather than profiting from the sale, it would lose money at that price. If you and your friends, however, were willing to pay $300 for such a bike, the store would make sure that there would be plenty from which to choose.

We can see, therefore, that the fundamental economic question of WHAT goods and services are produced in a market economy is ultimately decided by the prices that consumers are willing to pay for the things they want. If customers will pay the price, they can have just about anything they want. If they are not willing to pay the price, they will have to do without.

The Effect of Prices on HOW Goods and Services Are Produced. Business firms are constantly seeking ways in which to increase their profits. Since profits represent the difference between business income and costs, a surefire way to increase profits is to reduce costs while maintaining or increasing income.

In their never-ending search for lower costs, business firms constantly seek to improve the way in which they combine the factors of production (natural resources, human resources, capital, and management). In the recording industry, for example, manufacturers have to decide how many workers are needed to package and ship compact discs. The extent to which the manufacturers can, in part, rely upon machinery for those operations affects both selling prices and profits. While machines can be expensive, in the long run using machines is usually less costly than hiring workers. Similarly, retail shops have to decide on how much of their operations they can turn over to computers. Does it make more sense, for example, to hire five employees and also use computers or have six employees doing the necessary operations without computers? Usually the use of computers will reduce the number of workers needed. Buying and maintaining computers, though, is costly. The final determination as to how to combine the factors of production will depend upon estimates as to which combination will result in the lowest cost. Since individual business firms in a competitive market have little or no control over prices, their efforts to reduce costs can spell the difference between profit and loss.

How the Market System Determines WHO Will Receive Its Goods and Services. In Chapter 1, we discussed how all economic systems must wrestle with the problem of *scarcity*. Since there is not enough of everything to go around, societies have to find ways to ration the things they produce. The U.S. economic system, like all market economies, relies on prices to ration its output. Those willing and able to pay the price asked for a good or service can obtain it. Those unable or unwilling to pay the price will simply do without.

Since we have to pay for the goods and services we want, the amount of things that we can have depends upon our income. For the most part, the income that people earn comes from the jobs they hold, their savings and investments, and (in some cases) business profits.

In most instances, the size of an individual's income determines the amount of goods and services that person can buy. Here again, price comes into play because the amount that people earn is largely a result of the price employers are willing to pay for their services and the availability of workers willing to accept that wage. There are millions of people willing to pay to see the best tennis, football, and baseball players in action. In contrast, there are only a handful of people who can perform at championship levels. Consequently, some of the highest paid people in the country are athletes.

Similarly, rents (the price of housing) in poorer sections of town are lower than rents in more prosperous areas. This difference exists because (1) people who can afford higher rents are often unwilling to live in poorer areas, and (2) landlords in poorer areas have to offer lower rents in order to find tenants.

We see, therefore, that prices provide the answer to the question: "WHO will receive the goods and services produced in a market economy?"

Evaluation of the Market System

We can gain a better understanding of the market system if we look at its advantages and disadvantages.

Advantages. Those favoring the market system (or free enterprise, as it is also known) say the following:

1. The market system is the most efficient of all economic systems. In their quest for profits, producers compete with one another for the consumers' dollars. Since consumers prefer to buy the best products at the lowest prices, producers must constantly strive to increase their efficiency. They can do this by improving their products and services and reducing their costs. Those producers who succeed are rewarded with increased sales and profits. Those who fail stand to lose money and their businesses.

2. The market system is more sensitive to consumer demand than any other economic system. Since entrepreneurs are in business to earn profits, they will do everything they can to produce or offer the things consumers "elect" to buy. They do this to increase their sales and their profits. For similar reasons, entrepreneurs will stop producing or offering certain things as soon as they realize that these goods and services are no longer wanted.

Disadvantages. The market system is not without its shortcomings. Some of the more serious of these are discussed below.

1. The market system does not provide all of the goods and services needed by society. While it is true that there are private roads, private schools, and private hospitals, it is highly unlikely that private individuals and groups would be willing or able to pay for the construction of the thousands of needed public schools and hospitals, and hundreds of thousands of miles of needed public roads.

Little in the price system insures that natural resources will be preserved or life and property protected. This is not to say that private businesses will not take measures to protect life or to attempt to restore natural resources (for example, by replanting trees). Such actions, however, are by no means certain.

Why does the market system fail to provide some essential public goods and services? The reason is that people are often only willing to buy products if they acquire the right to exclusive use of those products. They do not want to pay for goods and services that the public can also use. Food and clothing are examples of private goods and services. For the most part, they can be enjoyed only by those who pay for them. Streets, police protection, national defense, foreign relations, and public health services are *public goods and services*. They benefit us all whether we pay for them or not. But since those who use public goods and services cannot always be made to pay for the cost of providing them, private sellers will not produce them.

Therefore, where public rather than private goods and services are concerned, society must find some way other than the price system to determine WHAT things to produce, HOW to produce them, and WHO will receive them.

2. The market system does not adequately provide for the needs of all the people. Critics often point to the large number of people living in poverty in the United States. In a recent year, the figure was some 36 million persons. While the market economy generally does a good job in rewarding the most efficient and productive citizens, it does not provide adequately for all. Examples of groups often not sufficiently provided for are single-parent households headed by a woman,

From The Wall Street Journal—Permission, Cartoon Features Syndicate

children, members of many minorities, and the mentally ill. Critics of the market system maintain that all people are entitled to a decent standard of living whether or not they are capable of earning it.

3. The market system is likely to experience periods of expansion and contraction of business activity. Widespread unemployment and personal hardship often accompany the contraction of business. Unlike other economic systems in which workers are guaranteed jobs regardless of business conditions, the U.S. market economy has witnessed periods of high unemployment. In recent decades, the federal government and state governments have taken an active role in economic affairs to lessen the impact of those periods. As a result, there has been no repetition of the Great Depression of the 1930s when, in the words of U.S. President **Franklin D. Roosevelt**, ". . . one third of a nation . . ." was ". . . ill-housed, ill-clad, ill-nourished." Although government action has helped to compensate for swings in the business cycle, critics maintain that the need for such government intervention reveals weaknesses in the market system.

4. The market system cannot account for many harmful costs of doing business. Consider, for example, a coal-powered manufacturing facility that spews harmful pollutants into the atmosphere. To economists, both the coal that powers the machinery and the air currents that carry off the smoke are resources. But they are significantly different kinds of resources. Coal, on the one hand, is privately owned. It must be paid for by those who use it. Coal, therefore, is one of the costs of doing business. Air, on the other hand, belongs to all of us. Traditionally, the cost of cleaning it up does not have to be paid entirely by those who pollute it.

To economists, coal represents an *internal cost*—a cost that is part of the expense of doing business. By contrast, air is an externality, or *external cost*. *Externalities* are business costs paid for by society as a whole. Since the market system does not impose a penalty for polluting the air, the coal-powered manufacturing facility has no economic reason for changing its policies. (Manufacturers do, however, have legal reasons for not polluting. Local, state, and the federal government impose hefty fines on polluters.)

OUR NATION'S ECONOMIC GOALS

How we deal with economic issues depends upon our economic goals. Although some disagreements exist over what our country's economic goals should be, most people in the United States would include the following in their list.

Economic Freedom

Americans have guarded their traditional economic freedoms as carefully as their political freedoms. Workers in the United States take for granted their right to accept or reject a job. In some nations, workers do not have this right. U.S. workers can form labor unions that are free to strive for better working conditions—another economic freedom not enjoyed in all nations.

Economic freedom includes the right to spend or save money as one wishes and to own the goods one has purchased. It also includes the right of businesspeople to own property and make a profit. Of course, our economic freedoms (like our political freedoms) are limited by rules of law. The right of businesspeople to run their own firms does not permit them to produce or sell merchandise that would endanger the health or safety of others.

Economic Justice

Most Americans agree that all persons should have equal economic opportunity regardless of nationality, age, sex, race, or income level. There is far less agreement, however, on how to make this goal a reality. Not everyone agrees on what constitutes equal economic opportunity or on what steps should be taken to insure it.

For example, the average income of nonwhites and females in this country is far below that of white males. In an effort to raise the income of those groups, the federal government and some state governments have required that companies under government contract give preference in hiring to women and members of minorities. Critics label such programs "reverse discrimination" since the programs deny jobs solely on the basis of sex and race.

Some Americans believe that everyone should have a fair share of the nation's goods and services—that is, there should be a fairer distribution of income. Nevertheless, what constitutes "fairness" is a matter of divided opinion. The government contributes to a fairer distribution of income when it taxes wealthier individuals and groups at a higher rate and distributes some of that wealth to the needy.

Economic Stability

A period of economic stability is one in which changes in the level of prices, employment, and business activity are modest. In stable times, prices of most goods and services remain at levels that people can afford, and jobs are plentiful. An important economic goal, therefore, is to maintain stable prices and employment.

Unfortunately, there have been times when the United States has experienced economic decline or inflation. During an economic decline, business activity falls off, workers lose their jobs, and many resources lie idle. When the decline is severe, as it was during the 1930s, it is called a *depression*. A milder decline is known as a *recession*.

Inflation is a general rise in prices. During inflation, people find that unless their incomes are increasing as fast as prices, they cannot buy as much as before. Inflation is particularly cruel for people with fixed incomes, such as pensions.

The hardships resulting from depression and inflation led Congress to take action to maintain national economic stability. The **Employment Act of 1946** declared that it is the responsibility of the federal government "to promote maximum employment, production, and purchasing power." In later chapters in this book, we will discuss how our government tries to maintain the nation's economic stability.

Economic Efficiency

A nation must make the best use of its resources to provide the greatest quantity of the goods and services that its citizens want. How well it achieves that goal is a measure of the nation's economic efficiency.

Economic Security

People like to know that in times of illness or unemployment and in old age, they and their families will be provided for. They may set aside a portion of their earnings in the form of savings, insurance, and other investments for that purpose. Many business firms and labor unions provide their employees and members with insurance and retirement plans.

Because economic security is so important and many people could not otherwise obtain it, all levels of government have established programs to offset the risks resulting from loss of income. Examples of such programs are Social Security, unemployment insurance, welfare, and savings deposit insurance.

Economic Growth

Most people want more of the goods and services that make for a rising standard of living. But the society as a whole can obtain more only if it is producing more. An increasing output of goods and services is called *economic growth*. Some people question whether unlimited economic growth is desirable. For example, as production increases, pollution and the loss of natural resources also increase.

Summary

The U.S. economic system of capitalism rests upon the principles of free enterprise, private property, the profit motive, consumer sovereignty, and competition. In modern economies, people and businesses specialize. Individuals and businesses must rely on the labors of others to supply them with most of their needs. The circular flow model describes the stream of funds, goods, and services constantly passing back and forth among consumers, businesses, and government. In our market economy, prices determine WHAT goods and services will be produced, HOW they are produced, and WHO will receive these goods and services.

The market system has many advantages, including efficiency and sensitivity to consumer demands. It does not, however, provide all of the goods and services needed by society. Moreover, it does not ensure stability of production and employment.

REVIEWING THE CHAPTER

Understanding What You Have Read

1. Where is the greatest degree of economic specialization likely to be found? In a (a) traditional agricultural society (b) frontier farming community (c) poor rural area in India or Latin America today (d) an industrial society such as that of the United States.

2. Which of the following forces will be most influential in determining the number of pairs of brown as compared to black shoes a manufacturer will produce in a *market economy*? (a) government directives (b) decisions by production supervisors (c) consumer demand (d) factory workers' preferences.

3. Which statement is true of the *free enterprise system*? (a) Those who venture into the business world risk the possibility of loss. (b) There are *no* limitations placed on the freedom of individuals to organize and operate a business as they choose. (c) Government, applying the doctrine of *eminent domain*, may seize private property without compensation to the owners of that property. (d) Free enterprise and capitalism cannot exist together in the same country.

4. In an economic system operating under *capitalism*, the fundamental questions of WHAT, HOW, and WHO are answered by (*a*) tradition (*b*) the market (*c*) a government agency (*d*) congressional legislation.

5. The circular flow of spending will be affected by (*a*) an increase in business spending (*b*) a decrease in government spending (*c*) an increase in consumer spending (*d*) all of the above.

6. In the circular flow of economic activity, we see that businesses (*a*) receive money but no productive services from households (*b*) receive money from both government and households (*c*) sell more goods to government than it does to households (*d*) receive no money from government.

7. If consumers are willing to pay more for an item, it is likely that (*a*) more of that item will be produced (*b*) less of that item will be produced (*c*) producers will continue to produce regardless of production costs (*d*) the price of that item will be reduced.

8. The driving force that pushes business firms to produce particular products is (*a*) the profit motive (*b*) competition (*c*) consumer sovereignty (*d*) the needs of the public.

9. In order to earn profits, *competition* pressures business firms to (*a*) provide inferior services to consumers (*b*) appeal to consumer sovereignty (*c*) produce products of poor quality (*d*) charge high prices for products and services.

10. In a market economy, consumers can have just about anything they want if they (*a*) are willing and able to pay the price (*b*) belong to the ruling party (*c*) are famous persons (*d*) know where to go to buy that item.

11. The country's best tennis players will earn far more as professional athletes than will its best handball players because (*a*) tennis is a more strenuous game than handball (*b*) people are willing to pay more to see professional tennis than to see professional handball (*c*) tennis is more of a U.S. game than handball (*d*) tennis costs more to play than handball.

12. Which of the following statements is a major criticism of the market system? (*a*) It rewards inefficiency and waste. (*b*) It is insensitive to changes in consumer demand. (*c*) It fails to deal with certain harmful side effects of production. (*d*) It encourages the overproduction of goods and services that no one really wants.

13. Which of the following statements is said to be a major advantage of the market system ? (*a*) It is the most efficient of all economic systems. (*b*) It insures that natural resources will be preserved. (*c*) It always provides for essential public goods and services. (*d*) It provides adequately for the needs of all U.S. citizens.

Building Vocabulary

Match each item in Column A with its definition in Column B.

COLUMN A
1. capitalism
2. public utility
3. circular flow
4. profit
5. consumer sovereignty
6. competition
7. eminent domain
8. internal cost
9. external cost
10. gross domestic product

COLUMN B
a. the rivalry among buyers and among sellers in the same field
b. the power of government to seize property it intends to use for some public purpose
c. the dollar value of all goods and services produced by an economy in a single year
d. an economic system in which the means of production are privately owned
e. a cost of a business that is paid for by society as a whole
f. an industry that serves the public interest
g. a cost of business paid for by the business firm
h. the amount of money left over after subtracting business expenses from business income
i. the freedom to choose which goods one can buy
j. the stream of funds, goods, and services passing back and forth among households, businesses, and government

Thinking Critically

1. Some people claim that a command economy is more efficient than a market economy. In support of this position, they remind us that in time of war the United States government has found it necessary to assume wide economic powers. These powers have included controlling prices, wages, and hours of work, along with rationing certain goods that are in short supply. Opposing this position are those who point to the events in Europe following the breakup of the Soviet Union in 1991. The nations formed out of the USSR as well as the nations of Eastern Europe have all abandoned command economies in favor of market economies.

Answer *each* of the following questions by giving *two* reasons, with explanations for each.

   a. Why do you agree or disagree that a command economy is more efficient than our market economy?

   b. Why do you think the United States abandoned central planning after World War II?

   c. Why do you think countries that were formerly part of the Soviet Union are trying to develop market economies today?

2. Assume that three members of the nation's leading rock group were recently seen at a popular club wearing buttoned shoes. Consequently, many fashion-conscious young men and women have sought to do the same. *(a)* How would the public inform shoe manufacturers that it wanted shoes with buttons? *(b)* What economic factors would shoe manufacturers consider before deciding to produce the buttoned models? *(c)* What economic groups other than shoe manufacturers are likely to be affected by the public's decision to wear buttoned shoes? Explain.

3. HOW goods and services are produced is very much influenced by the expectation of profit. *(a)* Under what circumstances might theater owners substitute counters and salesclerks for soda-, popcorn-, and candy-vending machines? *(b)* What factors might an insurance company consider before it replaced five clerical workers with one computer system? *(c)* What factors would a dress manufacturer take into consideration in deciding where to locate a new factory?

4. Critics have charged that the market economy (1) fails to provide goods and services that are needed yet are unprofitable, and (2) imposes certain harmful effects, or "externalities," upon the public at no expense to those who caused them. *(a)* Explain these arguments. *(b)* Tell whether you agree or disagree with them and why.

5. Some observers maintain that the economic goals of the American people are impractical, unachievable, and inconsistent. They argue, for example, that economic efficiency and economic justice are frequently in conflict with each other. Explain, with examples to back up your point of view, why you agree or disagree with this statement.

SKILLS: Analyzing a Political Cartoon

Base your answers to the following questions on the cartoon below.

1. Explain the meaning of the cartoon. In your explanation, make reference to the two buildings.

2. Each of the "pillars" in the cartoon has certain limitations. For example, private property rights are limited by eminent domain.

   a. Explain how eminent domain limits one's right to own property.

   b. Identify and explain three other limitations on the "pillars" of the United States economy.

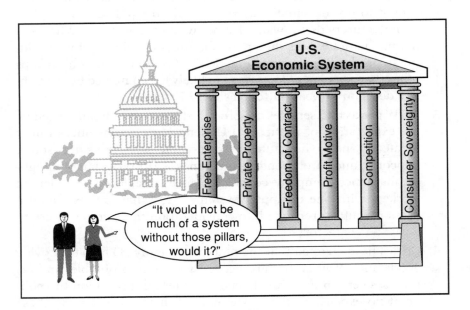

Chapter 3

SUPPLY AND DEMAND

Overview

> *"You mean you bought another watch?"*
> *"I know, I already own two watches, but at the price I simply couldn't pass this one up."*
>
> *"I just took a job at Vendors Mart."*
> *"Vendors Mart? That's a department store. I thought you were working for Gold Star Clothing."*
> *"I was until Vendors Mart offered me twice as much as I was making at Gold Star."*
>
> *"I'm looking for a new ten-speed bike."*
> *"I thought you already owned one."*
> *"I did. But Gloria offered me so much money for it that I had to sell it to her."*

There are many reasons why people decide to make a purchase, get a job, or sell something. Whatever the reasons, one element that is always present is price. If the price is too low, sellers will not sell. If the price is too high, buyers will not buy. Prices play a crucial role in our economic system. To understand how a nation's economy functions, it is necessary to have some understanding of that nation's price system.

This chapter describes the forces that determine the price of a good or service. Economists call these forces "demand" and "supply." Our discussion will consider these two forces and will then examine how they interact to establish "market price."

DEMAND

Many people would like to own a new sports car, wear designer clothes, or travel to distant lands. To the economist, these desires are merely wishes that have no economic significance. But if a person steps forward with the necessary money and says, "I will pay $30,000 for a sports car now," our economist would identify this as *demand*. Demand is the desire to purchase a particular item at a specified price and time, accompanied by the ability and willingness to pay.

Demand Schedule

The quantity demanded varies with the price of an item. Suppose, for example, that you were to survey a class of students to find out how many would like to purchase a pizza slice that would be delivered at a price of $1.50 each. Two hands might go up. Then if the price you quote is 90 cents, 23 hands might be raised. Up to a certain point, the lower the price goes, the greater the number of students who would be willing to buy. Indeed, if the price were low enough, some pizza lovers might even buy two or more slices. If we were to collect this data into a table, the demand schedule might look like this:

Table 3.1　Demand for Pizza Slices

Price	Number of Slices Students Will Buy
$1.70	1
1.50	2
1.30	6
1.10	12
.90	23
.70	45

Demand Curve

The demand schedule shown above can be illustrated with a *demand curve*. (See Figure 3.1.) This is a line graph that shows the amount of a product that will be purchased at each price. On all of the following graphs, the vertical axis measures price per unit, and the horizontal axis measures number of units, or quantity. In Figure 3.1, the demand curve D slopes downward and to the right. The points on the curve correspond to the demand schedule for pizza slices. A demand curve thus shows how much of a commodity will be sold at any given price.

The Law of Demand

The *Law of Demand* says that as the price of an item decreases, the quantity demanded will increase. Conversely, as the price increases, the quantity demanded will decrease. As the price of a product goes down, (a) more people can afford to buy the product, (b) people tend to buy larger quantities of the product, and (c) people tend to substitute the product for similar products that are either more expensive or less desirable. Similarly, as the price of a product goes up, (a) fewer people can afford to buy the product, (b) people tend to buy smaller quantities of the product, and (c) people tend to substitute cheaper products. The Law of Demand can be generalized as follows: The quantity demanded varies in the opposite direction that prices change.

Figure 3.1   Demand Curve for Pizza Slices

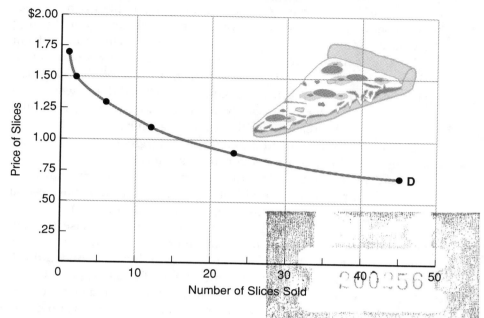

In our example, the Law of Demand determines how many pizza slices would be sold at each price. As the price of the slices is reduced, more students are interested in buying them. The lower price attracts some students who had not been planning to spend any money. Others who would have purchased one slice at a higher price buy two or more at a lower price. And still others who have been planning to buy a sandwich or a burger after class decide to eat pizza instead.

Storekeepers are well aware of the Law of Demand. That is why they lower prices when they want to clear out merchandise. Butchers know, for example, that some consumers who would not buy steak at $5.50 a pound will buy it for $4 a pound. They also know that some consumers prefer steak but also eat chicken, fish, and other foods. At $5.50 a pound, steak is more expensive than many other foods that consumers might purchase. But with steak at $4 a pound, the difference in price between steak and some alternative foods is less.

Principle of Diminishing Marginal Utility

When we conduct our pizza-slice study, we in effect make each member of the class ask the question, "Do I want to give up some of my purchasing power in order to have a pizza slice?" Anyone about to make any purchase must ask a similar question. Once you have spent a sum of money on one purchase, that sum is no longer available to you for any other purchase.

Why does a buyer choose one product instead of another? Assume, for example, that you have 75 cents with which you plan to buy either chewing gum or candy. After a few moments' consideration in front of the candy counter, you decide to buy the gum. Why gum and not candy? The economist would explain this choice in terms of utility. It is the measure of satisfaction one gets from the use of a good or service. When you chose the chewing gum, you decided that it would better satisfy your wants than a candy bar. In economic terms, the utility of chewing gum is greater than the utility of a candy bar.

Economists have devised the concept of *marginal utility* to help explain the spending patterns of consumers. Marginal utility is the degree of satisfaction or usefulness a consumer gets from each additional purchase of a product or service. (The word "marginal" has several meanings in economics. In this case, it means "additional.")

People will buy something if they expect the purchase to yield them more satisfaction, or utility, than something else. In the example of the pizza slices, many students are willing to buy a second, a third, or even a fourth slice if the price is low enough. But as the pizza is consumed, it becomes less satisfying. By the time the second or third slice is downed, the thought of still another slice has become less appealing. In economic terms, each additional slice has less utility than the preceding one. This phenomenon is summarized in the *Principle of Diminishing Marginal Utility*, which states: Each additional purchase of a product or service by a given consumer will be less satisfying than the previous purchase.

The Principle of Diminishing Marginal Utility applies to almost any product. One overcoat may be a necessity; two or three may be desirable; but what would induce you to buy four or five? Each new purchase will be less satisfying than the one before. It will have less utility. You will be less willing to give up something else to buy an additional overcoat. You may still be induced to buy another coat, but only at a lower price.

Elasticity of Demand

The Law of Demand is clear: Fewer items will be bought at a higher price than at a lower one. The Law of Demand, however, does not tell us by how much the quantity demanded will increase or decrease at different prices. If the price of milk doubles, less milk will be sold. Similarly, if the price of steak doubles, consumers will buy less steak. Nevertheless, will sales of milk and steak fall by the same percentage? For example, if milk sales drop 20 percent as the price doubles, will steak sales also drop 20 percent as the price of steak doubles? Certainly not. The population as a whole can do without steak far more easily than it can do without milk. Even at the higher price, the demand for milk will

Law of Demand. What factors will affect the demand for hot dogs at this stand?

be greater than the demand for steak, and the decline in steak sales will be far greater than the decline in milk sales.

If the prices of milk and steak drop by 50 percent, more of both products will be sold, in accordance with the Law of Demand. The percentage increase in steak sales, however, will probably be far greater than that of milk sales. The reason is that after consumers purchase what they consider a sufficient amount of milk, they will still be willing to buy more steak. Of course, in this example we are referring to the population as a whole. Many individuals will not or cannot drink milk at any price. Some people avoid red meats (such as steak), while others will not eat meat at all, at any price.

One way to measure the degree of demand is through the concept of *elasticity of demand.* This term describes the percentage change in demand that follows a price change. The more demand expands or contracts after a price change, the greater the elasticity of the demand. The demand for most goods and services may be described as either relatively elastic or relatively inelastic. When a drop in the price of an item causes an even greater percentage increase in demand, we say that the demand for that item is relatively "elastic" (the demand has "stretched" a great deal). When a drop in price results in a decrease or only a small increase in demand, we say that the demand is relatively "inelastic." The same holds true for increases in price. Demand is

Table 3.2 Demand for Milk and Steak

	Price (P)	Units Sold (Q)	Total Revenue (TR)
Milk	$1.20	200	$240.00
	.60	350	210.00
Steak	$5.00	60	$300.00
	2.50	175	437.50

considered elastic if a rise in price results in a large drop in demand, and inelastic if a rise in price results in a small drop in demand.

Elasticity of demand can also be measured by the amount that price changes affect total dollar sales. If a decrease in price of an item results in an increase in revenue, the demand for the item is said to be elastic. If, however, a decrease in price results in a decrease in revenue, the item is said to be inelastic. Similarly, if an increase in price results in a decrease in total dollar sales, the demand is elastic; and if an increase in price results in an increase in revenue, the demand is inelastic.

Suppose that your local supermarket reduced the price of both milk and steak by 50 percent. Before the sale, milk was selling for $1.20 a quart and steak at $5 a pound. At those prices, the store sold 200 quarts of milk and 60 pounds of steak each day. At the sale prices, customers bought 350 quarts of milk and 175 pounds of steak per day. This information is summarized in Table 3.2.

Table 3.2 shows that total revenue from the sale of milk fell from $240 to $210 when the price of milk was reduced. This result indicates that the demand for milk is inelastic. Total revenue from the sale of steak, however, increased from $300 to $437.50. This increase shows that the demand for steak is elastic.

What Makes Demand Elastic or Inelastic?

When we ask why some items are subject to elastic demand and others are not, we are really asking why price changes affect the purchase of some things more than of others. If one of the following conditions is present, the demand for a good or service will usually be sensitive to price changes:

1. The item is considered a luxury. Luxuries are goods or services that consumers regard as something they can live without. Consumers are less likely to buy a luxury if the price is high. They will, however, consider buying one if the price drops enough. An item considered a luxury need not be costly in dollars. For example, a person with a modest income might consider fresh flowers, a bottle of cologne, or a taxi ride as luxuries. Also, what is considered luxuries by one person (for example, plane tickets, meals in restaurants, or expensive clothes) may be normal or even necessary expenses for someone else. If a product or service is considered a luxury by a large number of consumers, it will be subject to elastic demand.

2. The price represents a large portion of the family income. Buying an automobile or a home would represent a significant portion of most families' incomes. Therefore, a rise in the price of such items will discourage many consumers from buying them. Because of the greater utility of many costly items, however, a decrease in their price will cause a significant increase in sales.

3. Other products can easily be substituted for it. Because there are many less expensive substitutes for steak, many people will shift to chicken or some other meat if the price of steak goes up. Similarly, if the price of steel rises, manufacturers and builders will substitute other materials, such as aluminum or concrete. At present, though, there are no competitive substitutes for gasoline as a fuel for automobiles. Therefore, the demand for this fuel is inelastic. Our society is trying to develop alternative energy sources that pollute less and can be produced at competitive prices. Such products include natural gas, solar-powered cells, and battery-powered electric motors.

4. The items are durable. Furniture, appliances, and automobiles are relatively long-lasting. Since they are often major household items, many consumers will purchase new ones if the prices are low enough. If prices remain high, however, people will tend to "make do" with the old ones rather than replace them.

What Is the Significance of Demand Elasticity?

The elasticity of demand for a good or service is an important factor in many business decisions. Suppose, for example, that a local bus company whose fares are regulated by the government finds itself in need of additional funds. Should the company apply for a fare increase? The answer would depend upon the elasticity or inelasticity of demand for the bus service.

Table 3.3 shows two possible results of a 20 percent fare increase. If the demand for the bus service was elastic, a 20 percent fare increase

Table 3.3 Demand for Bus Service

	If the fare is	And the number of passengers is	Total revenue will be
Present	$1.00	10,000	$10,000
Elastic Demand	1.20	7,500	9,000
Inelastic Demand	1.20	8,500	10,200

might lead to a 25 percent reduction in riders and a decrease in earnings. If the demand for the bus service was inelastic, however, a 20 percent fare increase might lead to only a 15 percent loss in riders and an increase in earnings. In order for the bus company to decide whether or not to apply for the fare increase, it must estimate the degree of elasticity of demand for its service.

What Economists Mean by an "Increase" or a "Decrease" in Demand

Certain events can make people more willing or less willing to pay a certain price for something than they once were. This change in willingness affects the demand for goods or services at all prices. If buyers are willing to buy more items at each price, we say that there has been an increase in demand. When buyers are willing to buy less at each price than they once did, we say there has been a decrease in demand. To illustrate increased demand, consider the following situation:

It is mid-July, and temperatures have been going above 90 degrees all week. Sally Simmons, a local fast-food vendor, tells us that on December 15, during a cold spell, ice cream cones that sold for $1.50 each found only 2 buyers. Now, she says, she is able to sell 9 cones a day at that price. Moreover, Ms. Simmons believes that she could sell as many as 30 cones at $1.10 each. She adds that if she reduced her prices to 70 cents each, sales would jump to 66 cones. (Some customers would consume more than one!) Let us look at a demand schedule for sales of ice cream cones on December 15 and on July 15, in Table 3.4.

This demand schedule can be plotted as a demand curve. (See Figure 3.2.) D represents the demand on December 15, while D_1 represents the demand on July 15. We can see that when demand changes, the entire schedule shifts. Because the change in this case was an increase in demand, the curve shifted to the right. Had there been a decrease in demand, the curve would have shifted to the left.

Table 3.4 Daily Demand Schedule for Ice Cream Cones

	Number of Cones People Will Buy	
Price	*On December 15*	*On July 15*
$1.70	1	6
1.50	2	9
1.30	6	18
1.10	12	30
.90	23	45
.70	45	66

Figure 3.2 Demand Curve for Ice Cream Cones
(Increase in Demand as Reflected by a Shift in the Demand Curve)

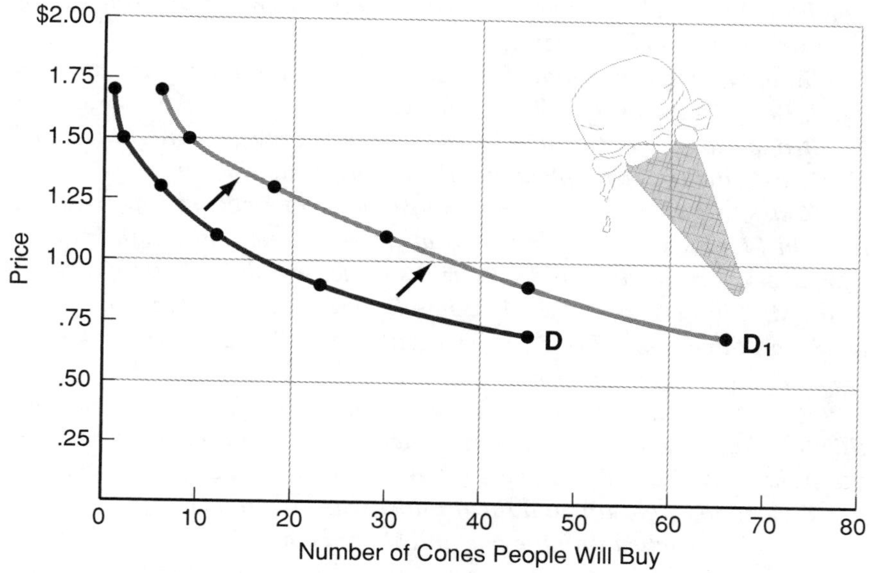

In the previous example, a rise in temperature caused an increase in the demand for ice cream cones. There are many other things that can cause a change in demand. What effect do you think each of the following situations would have on the demand for a given product?

1. An increase in the price of substitute products.
2. An increase in most people's income.
3. A change in the taste of buyers.
4. The expectation that the price of the product will soon fall.
5. The appearance of a new substitute product.
6. The fear that the nation will soon suffer a depression in which many businesses will collapse and many persons will become unemployed.

SUPPLY

Neil Simi, an economics teacher, opened the day's lesson with an experiment.

"Class, how many of you are wearing wristwatches?" Twenty-eight *hands went up.*

"You may have noticed this paper bag sitting on my desk," Mr. Simi *continued. "This bag contains $100 in one-dollar bills. I will give this*

bag of money to any one of you in exchange for your wristwatch. Will you please raise your hand if you would be willing to sell me your watch for $100." The teacher counted the raised hands and wrote the number 27 on the chalkboard.

"Brenda," Mr. Simi said, "I noticed that you did not raise your hand. Don't you want to sell me your watch?"

"No, because it cost much more than $100 only a few months ago."

"I see," the teacher replied and then peered into the bag.

"Class," he went on, "I seem to have made a terrible mistake. I thought I had $100 in this bag. Actually, it looks more like $50. Let us start over again. Who would sell me his or her watch for $50?" Once again Mr. Simi counted the raised hands, wrote the total (15) on the board, and then looked into the bag. With feigned surprise, he took a smaller bag out of the paper bag.

"Oh, this is embarrassing," he said. "I thought I had just money in this bag, but I see I had packed my lunch in it, too. I don't believe there's more than $20 here. Will anyone sell me a watch for $20?"

Five hands went up, and the number was duly noted.

Mr. Simi reached into the bag and started counting off bills. "Seven, eight, nine, ten! Well, it seems I have only $10 here. Does anyone want to sell his or her watch for $10?"

Only one hand was raised this time. The teacher placed the number 1 on the board.

"Bill," Mr. Simi said to the remaining seller, "it looks as if you have the only watch I will be buying today. Here is your $10."

"On second thought, Mr. Simi," said Bill, "I think I will hold on to my watch. You can keep the $10."

Why did Bill suddenly refuse? Perhaps it was the name "Monopoly™" printed on the money that changed Bill's mind.

Mr. Simi's experiment demonstrated the economic concept of supply. Economists use the term *supply* to describe the amount of goods or services offered for sale at a particular price. As the price that Mr. Simi offered for a wristwatch went down, fewer watches were offered for sale. Just the opposite would have happened if Mr. Simi had offered $10 to start and had increased the price: More watches would have been offered for sale.

The dress shirts worn by members of the U.S. Army are produced by several different manufacturers in accordance with specifications prepared by the military. Let us assume that a survey was taken among the manufacturers to see how many shirts each could provide at various prices. The supply schedule prepared after all of the manufacturers had submitted their bids is shown in Table 3.5.

Table 3.5   Supply Schedule for Army Shirts

At a price of	Seller will offer
$ 6	8,000
8	8,600
10	9,600
12	11,200
14	14,000

The Law of Supply

Both of the examples (wristwatches and army shirts) illustrate the Law of Supply: The quantity of a good or service supplied varies directly with its price. The number of units offered for sale increases as the price increases. There are two reasons for this. First, existing producers will increase their output at the higher price. And second, new producers will be lured into the market by the higher prices. The Law of Supply will become clearer to you as you study the supply schedule for in-line skates in the following example.

The supply schedule in Table 3.6 lists the number of in-line skates that manufacturers are willing to sell at the prices indicated. The schedule shows that at a price of $90 each, only 8,000 pairs of in-line skates will be offered for sale. At $270 each, however, 56,000 pairs will be offered. Why are sellers willing to offer so many more in-line skates at the higher price? One reason is that at a price of $270, manufacturers can afford to take on the extra help and pay for the overtime necessary to increase output to 56,000 pairs. Another reason is that manufacturers of related products such as skateboards and roller skates will find it worth their while to cease making those goods and start making in-line skates instead.

A supply schedule, like a demand schedule, can be plotted on a graph. In Figure 3.3, the supply curve S, which slopes upward to the right, summarizes the information contained in our in-line skate supply schedule for March 1.

Table 3.6   Supply Schedule for In-Line Skates on March 1

At a price of	Sellers will offer
$ 90	8,000 pair
120	20,000 pair
150	30,000 pair
180	39,000 pair
210	45,000 pair
240	52,000 pair
270	56,000 pair

Figure 3.3 Supply Schedule for In-Line Skates on March 1

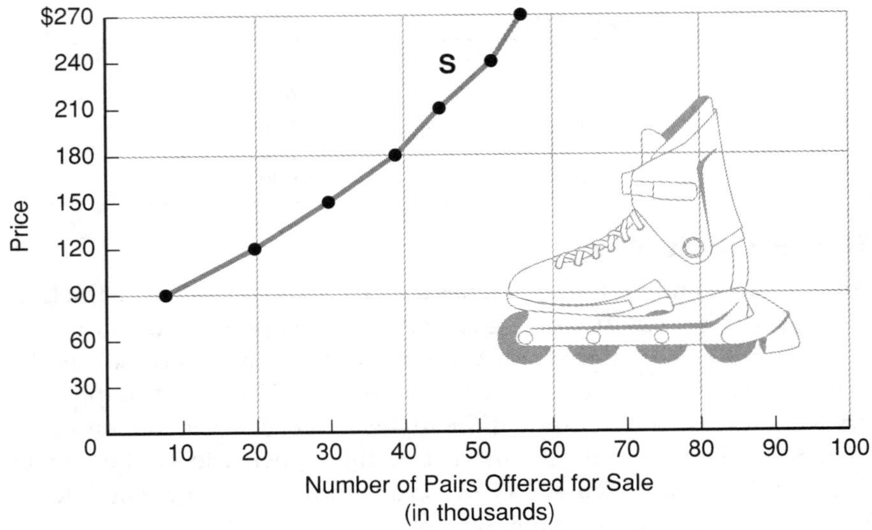

Changes in Supply

Suppose that in-line skate manufacturers discovered they could turn out the skates in a way that was less expensive and quicker. This changeover in production methods would enable producers, large and small, to increase their production so that more skates would be available for sale at each price. The supply of in-line skates would increase. Table 3.7 summarizes such a possibility. If we plot this increase on a graph, the shift from the S curve to the S_1 curve will be to the right, as in Figure 3.4.

Suppose that instead of a decrease in costs, the industry experienced an increase, such as one resulting from an increase in wages. What would happen then to the supply schedule and the supply curve?

Table 3.7 Supply Schedule for In-Line Skates on October 1

At a price of	(Percent Increase in Price)	Sellers will offer	(Percent Increase in Supply)
$ 90	(0)	12,000	(0)
120	(33.3)	30,000	(150)
150	(25)	45,500	(50)
180	(20)	55,000	(82.7)
210	(16.7)	67,000	(82.1)
240	(14.3)	78,000	(85.9)
270	(12.5)	90,000	(86.7)

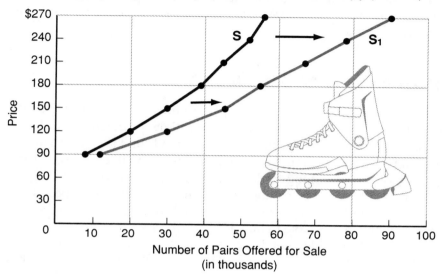

Figure 3.4 Supply Schedule for In-Line Skates on October 1 (Increase in Supply as Reflected by a Shift in the Supply Curve)

Elasticity of Supply

Like demand, supply is subject to elasticity. The supply of some commodities is more sensitive to price changes than the supply of others. If a change in price brings about a larger percentage change in supply, the supply is said to be elastic. If a change in price produces a smaller percentage change in supply, the supply is said to be inelastic.

The supply of in-line skates in our example is elastic. It is elastic because as the price for a pair of in-line skates increases from $120 to $150 (a 25 percent increase), the quantity of in-line skates offered for sale at that price increases by 50 percent.

Manufactured goods generally are subject to greater supply elasticity than goods provided by nature. In-line skate manufacturers might be able to increase their output by asking their employees to work overtime. Dairy farmers, however, could not expect such cooperation from their herds. Therefore, an increase in milk production would take longer to achieve than an increase in in-line skate production.

The amount of natural resources available is usually limited. While some resources, such as trees and wildlife, can eventually be replaced through reforestation and conservation, these measures take many years. Some additional land can be made fit for farming by draining swamps or through irrigation. For the most part, though, we have to make do with the land we have. Minerals such as petroleum, iron, and copper also are subject to relatively inelastic supply. The output of these minerals is limited by the expense of the equipment needed to extract them, the size of the known deposits, and the uncertainty of discovering new sources.

HOW PRICES ARE DETERMINED

Our discussion of demand and supply has thus far concentrated on the number of items buyers and sellers are willing to consider at different prices. We have seen that the amount of goods and services that buyers and sellers are willing to exchange fluctuates with changes in price. What people are willing to do, however, is not always what they are able to do. You may be willing to buy a new, imported ten-speed bicycle for $50, but since no one is likely to sell you one at that price, you will probably not be able to buy it.

The price at which goods and services may actually be bought or sold is called the "market price." The following discussion describes how market price is determined.

Supply, Demand, and Market Price: Bringing It All Together

In describing how the forces of supply, demand, and price come together, we will be dealing with a model of *pure competition*. Under pure competition, the following conditions exist:

- There are many buyers and sellers acting independently. No single buyer or seller is big enough to influence the market price.
- Competing products are practically identical, so that buyers and sellers of a given product are not affected by variations in quality or design.
- All buyers and sellers have full knowledge of prices being quoted all over the market.
- Buyers and sellers can enter and leave the market at will. That is, buyers are free to buy or not to buy; sellers are free to sell or not to sell.

In the discussion that follows, we will assume that these conditions exist so that we can see how prices of goods and services are set in the United States market system.

How Supply and Demand Determine Price

As the price increases, the number of items offered for sale (the supply) increases, but the quantity that buyers are willing to buy (the demand) decreases. There is only one price at which demand and supply are

Equilibrium Price. What part do supply and demand play in determining the price a store charges for sneakers?

equal. On a graph, this price is shown by the point where the demand and supply curves intersect. Because it is the price at which supply and demand are equal, the price at which goods are sold is sometimes called the *equilibrium price*. Because this price is established in the market, it is also called the *market price*.

To summarize: The price at which sales take place is the price at which the amount demanded is equal to the quantity supplied.

Table 3.8 shows the demand for in-line skates on March 1. If we add the supply schedule for this day, we will have Table 3.9. The demand and supply schedule in Table 3.9 shows that at a price of $150, the number of in-line skates offered by manufacturers is equal to the number that buyers are willing to buy. This information is illustrated graphically in Figure 3.5. Point M, which lies at the intersection of D and S, identifies the market or equilibrium price. The figure shows that this price is $150 and that 30,000 pairs of skates can be sold at this price. As long as demand and supply do not change, this is the only price at which all the skates produced can be sold. At any higher price, there will be sellers with leftover in-line skates that they can sell only by lowering the price. At a price lower than the market price, buyers unable to find any skates but willing to pay more will bid the price up

Table 3.8 Demand Schedule for In-Line Skates on March 1

At a price of	*Buyers will take*
$ 90	48,000 pairs
120	36,000 pairs
150	30,000 pairs
180	24,000 pairs
210	17,000 pairs
240	11,000 pairs
270	7,000 pairs

Table 3.9 Demand and Supply Schedule for In-Line Skates on March 1

At a price of	Buyers will take	Sellers will offer
$ 90	48,000 pairs	8,000 pairs
120	36,000 pairs	20,000 pairs
150	30,000 pairs	30,000 pairs
180	24,000 pairs	39,000 pairs
210	17,000 pairs	45,000 pairs
240	11,000 pairs	52,000 pairs
270	7,000 pairs	56,000 pairs

until they too are satisfied. All sellers willing to sell at the market price or less will be satisfied, and so will all buyers willing to pay that price, or more.

What about those buyers who will not (or cannot) pay more than $120 per pair of skates, and those sellers who will not sell for less than $180? They will neither buy nor sell because the market price is too high for the buyers and too low for the sellers. At the equilibrium or market price, the "market is cleared"—that is, all possible sales are made. For any new price to be established, there will have to be a shift in supply, demand, or both.

Effect of a Change in Demand Upon Market Price

Suppose that a panel of distinguished doctors announced that in-line skating was the key to good health and long life. Suppose also that this

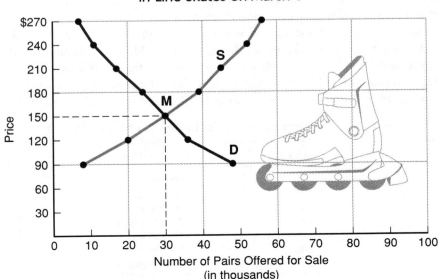

Figure 3.5 Demand and Supply Schedule for In-Line Skates on March 1

report received nationwide publicity and that prominent people in all walks of life were soon observed in-line skating to and from work and social activities. Many thousands of people might now be willing to pay more than in the past to take up the hobby. The demand for in-line skates would increase dramatically. The new demand schedule is illustrated by line D_1 in Figure 3.6. The new demand curve intersects our supply curve S at a higher point, M_1, and the new market price is $175.

Suppose, however, that our panel of doctors announced that in-line skating was harmful to one's health. Very likely then the demand for in-line skates would fall off, and the demand curve would shift to the left. In Figure 3.7, curve D_2, which intersects S at M_2, represents the new, lessened demand for in-line skates. The curve shows that as demand decreases, market price also decreases. Common sense tells us that this will be so. Manufacturers must sell what they have produced. If fewer people want a product while its supply remains constant, suppliers must lower the price to attract buyers. We can express this principle in general terms: Price varies directly with changes in demand.

Effect of a Change in Supply Upon Market Price

How is market price affected if supply increases or decreases while demand remains constant? Earlier in the chapter, we described how an improved way of making in-line skates might result in an increase in supply. The effect of such an increase was to make more skates available for sale at every price and to shift the supply curve to the right. In Figure 3.8, S_1 represents an increase in supply. The new market price, M_1, is lower than the old price, M.

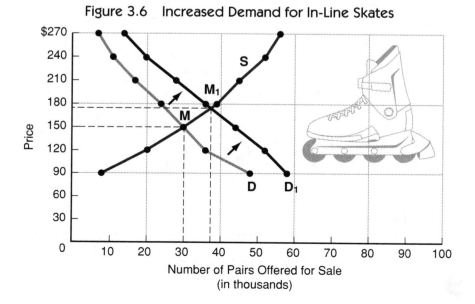

Figure 3.6   Increased Demand for In-Line Skates

Figure 3.7 Decreased Demand for In-Line Skates

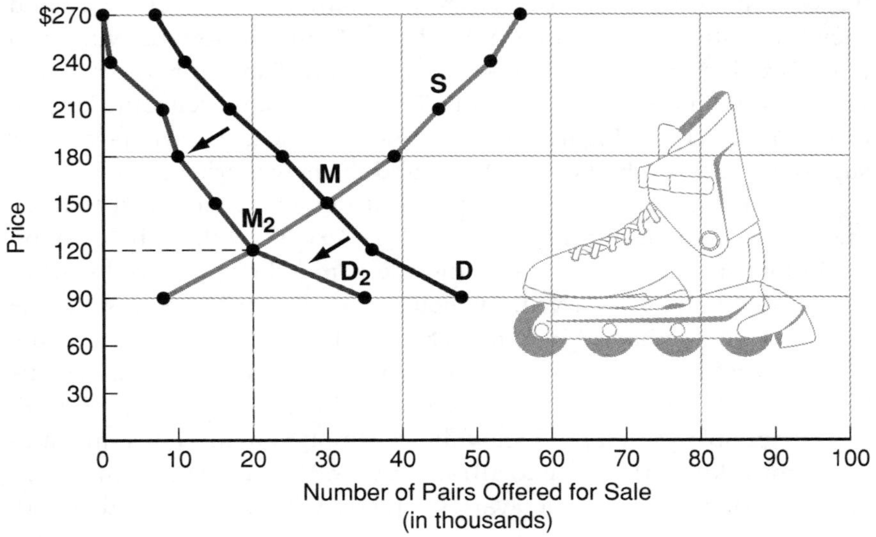

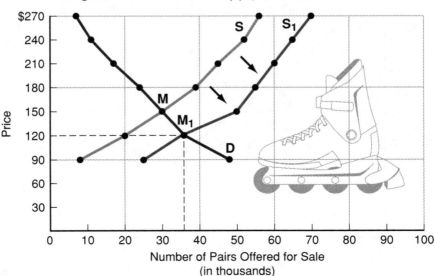

Suppose that the price of wheels rose sharply and there was a decrease in the supply of in-line skates. In Figure 3.9, S_2 represents the new supply schedule. The curve has moved to the left, and M_2, the new market price, is higher than M. Again common sense tells us that if fewer items are available for sale, the price per item will increase.

The same principle applies to any product or service. If large quantities of diamonds were suddenly discovered and made available for

Figure 3.8 Increased Supply of In-Line Skates

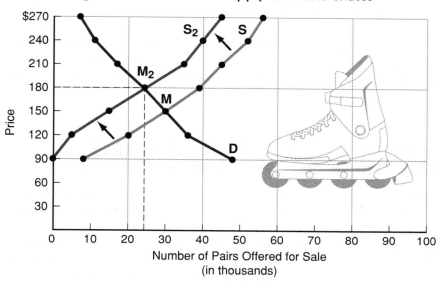

Figure 3.9   Decreased Supply of In-Line Skates

sale, the price of diamonds would fall. When certain fruits and vegetables are in short supply, their prices rise. Thus, price increases when supply decreases, and price decreases when supply increases. In general terms: Price varies indirectly with changes in supply.

To What Extent Do Supply and Demand Affect Price?

So far our discussion of market price has been based on a model of pure competition in which price is determined entirely by supply and demand. Our model has the following characteristics: (1) there are many buyers and sellers; (2) similar products are assumed to be identical; (3) all buyers and sellers have full knowledge of market conditions; and (4) buyers and sellers can enter and leave the market at will.

In an actual economy, however, these conditions are met very seldom. The supply of an item may be controlled by only one company or by a handful of firms. Similar products are often not identical. Even when they are virtually identical, advertising and other factors influence consumers to prefer one product over another. Buyers may not know that they can get the same or similar item for less under a different brand name or at the store next door. For these and many other reasons, the laws of supply and demand do not operate in real life the way they do in the model.

If pure competition is a laboratory concept that rarely exists in real life, why do we discuss it? The reason is that in spite of its limitations, competition does give us an insight into some of the forces that control prices. Although in the actual economy we may never see all four conditions of pure competition, we may see one or two. In those instances, supply and demand will affect prices. Prices are important because they keep the market functioning, and the market system is at the heart of our economy.

So far we have discussed supply, demand, and price determination in an open, competitive market. Now let us take a look at what happens to supply and demand when government (and not the market) sets prices.

WHEN GOVERNMENT CONTROLS REPLACE THE LAWS OF SUPPLY AND DEMAND

We have seen that the equilibrium price "clears the market." That is, the number of items offered for sale at the market price equals exactly the quantity demanded. Consequently, all buyers willing to pay the price will be satisfied, and no goods will remain unsold. Any price other than the equilibrium price results in either surpluses or shortages. That is, at a price higher than equilibrium, more goods will be offered for sale than buyers are willing to accept, thereby creating a surplus. Similarly, at a price lower than equilibrium, shortages will appear because there will be more buyers than there are sellers.

Sometimes governments attempt to control the market by imposing *ceilings* (maximums) on the price that a seller can charge for a product. Such actions are more common in command economies than in free-market economies. Prior to its collapse in 1991, the Soviet government set the maximum price of bread artificially low so as to keep consumers happy. The effect of such price ceilings can be illustrated as in Figure 3.10.

In this illustration, the demand curve *D* and the supply curve *S* intersect at *e* (at a market price of $5). Government, however, has established a *ceiling price* at *c* ($4). But at that price, buyers would be willing to take the number of items at point *a* (6 units), whereas sellers would only supply the number at point *b* (4 units).

The difference between the two points (6 – 4 = 2 units) represents the shortage of the product offered for sale at the government-set price of $4.

We have seen that when the price of something is less than its equilibrium price, demand outruns supply. In these circumstances people will wait on line, sometimes for hours, in order to buy the things they want. Or they may try to buy what they want in the illegal *black market,* places where items are sold illegally, usually for more than the ceiling price. In the Soviet Union under communism, both long lines and the black market were common. We will learn more about command economies in Chapter 23.

Alfred Marshall

As the 19th century drew to a close, the world described by Adam Smith and other economists had undergone considerable change. The **Industrial Revolution** had transformed England from a primarily agricultural society into an industrialized nation whose very survival was dependent upon its international trade. Political power, which in Smith's day was totally in the hands of the landed aristocracy, was now shifting to the middle class of the world of business, industry, and finance.

In the world of economics, critics of classical theory asserted that it failed to reflect these changes. Others, whom we would now describe as "socialists" and "Communists," called for the replacement of the existing order with a new kind of economic system. The publication by **Alfred Marshall** of his *Principles of Economics* in 1890 came as a tonic to the "silent majority" of the day who were looking for a restatement in modern terms of the theoretical basis of their economic order.

Alfred Marshall (1842–1924), whose work became a bible for what came to be known as "neoclassical" economics, was a member of the faculty of Cambridge University from 1885 until his death. He became a legend in his own time, and his lecture hall the center of economic thought and education for the English-speaking world. Even before the publication of his *Principles*, it was said that at least half the professors of eco-

nomics in England's universities had been his pupils. Marshall's influence spread even wider as universities in England and the United States made the *Principles* required reading. Not until the 1940s was the *Principles* supplanted by other works.

What Marshall had accomplished was a revitalization of the classical economics of writers like Smith by modernizing it and fleshing out areas of weakness in its theoretical framework. For example, Marshall developed the concept of elasticity of demand in order to explain price behavior.

For many years, too, classical economists had been debating whether supply or demand was the more important determinant of price. Marshall's introduction to his position on this issue is worth quoting as an example of his skill at slicing through complex issues with easy-to-grasp logic. "We might as reasonably dispute whether it is the upper or the under blade of a pair of scissors that cuts a piece of paper, as whether value is governed by utility or cost of production (demand or supply). It is true that when one blade is held still, and the cutting is effected by moving the other, we may say with careless brevity that the cutting is done by the second; but the statement is not strictly accurate and is to be excused only so long as it claims to be merely a popular and not a strictly scientific account of what happens."*

Although today's economic students are no longer required to read the *Principles*, Marshall's theories and methods are reflected in the works of all modern textbook authors and are part of the education of practicing economists.

* *Source*: Alfred Marshall, **Principles of Economics**. Third Edition (NY: Macmillan, 1948), p. 348.

Figure 3.10   Government Ceiling Prices Result in Shortages

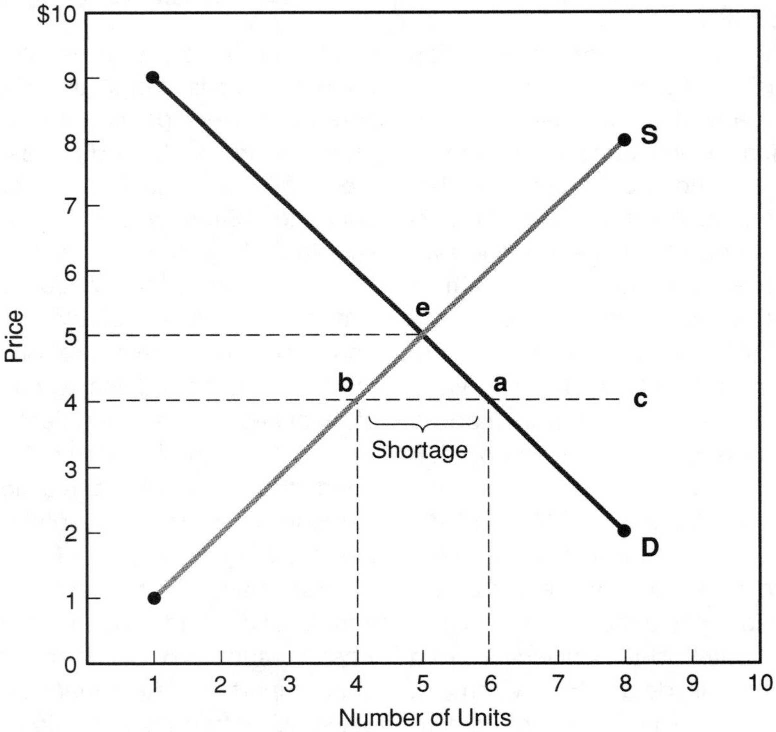

Price Floors in U.S. Agriculture

Sometimes the United States government moves to prevent agricultural goods from being sold below a specified level. Decades ago, the government set up *price floors* as a way of helping farmers receive higher prices for their produce. A price floor is an established price for a farm commodity, below which farmers have no incentive to sell. Farmers are guaranteed sales at the floor price by the government.

Government-imposed price floors have often resulted in surpluses of farm products. Too many farmers are willing to sell at the floor price. The reason for these surpluses is discussed in Chapter 6 on pages 131–134.

Summary

Price is determined by the forces of supply and demand in a market economy. The quantity demanded varies inversely with the price, and this relationship can be indicated with a demand curve. Demand increases when prices fall and decreases when prices rise. The percentage change in demand that follows a price change is the elasticity of demand. An increase or decrease in demand at all prices is known as a shift in demand.

The quantity of a good or service supplied varies directly with price. More goods and services will be offered for sale as price increases, while fewer will be offered for sale as price decreases. A supply schedule can be indicated on a graph as a supply curve. The percentage change in the amount supplied brought about by a change in price is the elasticity of supply.

The price at which a sale takes place is the price at which the amount demanded is equal to the quantity supplied. This can be shown on a supply and demand curve as the point where the two curves intersect. Government sometimes sets limits to either supply or price. The price that is established may be higher or lower than the market price.

REVIEWING THE CHAPTER

Understanding What You Have Read

1. When the supply of a commodity increases while the demand remains the same, the market price will   (*a*) rise   (*b*) fall   (*c*) stay the same   (*d*) vary directly with the change in supply.

2. Which of the following would probably lead to an increase in the demand for bricks?   (*a*) an increase in the price of lumber, which can be used as a substitute for bricks   (*b*) a decrease in the income of potential home builders   (*c*) an increase in the wages of bricklayers   (*d*) an increase in the price of bricks.

3. Which of the following would *not* have the *same* effect as the other three on the amount of beef consumed? (*a*) a rise in the price of lamb (*b*) a fall in the price of beef (*c*) an effective advertising campaign on the part of pork producers (*d*) an effective advertising campaign on the part of beef producers.

4. Which of the following is subject to the greatest elasticity of demand? (*a*) postage stamps (*b*) bread (*c*) personal computers (*d*) chewing gum.

5. When described in connection with supply and demand schedules, an increase in demand means that (*a*) the price will fall (*b*) buyers will take a larger quantity at all prices than before (*c*) the demand for the product has become more elastic (*d*) the demand curve slopes downward.

6. In an industry that has many competing firms, an increase in demand may be expected to result in (*a*) a decrease in production (*b*) no change in production (*c*) an increase in production (*d*) the elimination of inefficient firms.

7. In which of the following commodities is supply most elastic? (*a*) eggs (*b*) plastic toys (*c*) gold (*d*) corn.

Base your answers to questions 8–10 on Figure 3.11.

Figure 3.11

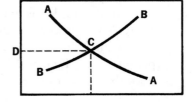

8. In the graph, A represents
   (*a*) the supply curve
   (*b*) the demand curve
   (*c*) equilibrium
   (*d*) the market price.

9. In the graph, D represents (*a*) the supply curve (*b*) the demand curve (*c*) the demand schedule (*d*) the market price.

10. In the graph, B represents (*a*) the supply curve (*b*) the demand curve (*c*) equilibrium (*d*) the market price.

11. Suppose federal laws required that all the wheat grown in the United States had to be sold for $3 per bushel. Which of the following illustrations would portray this situation?

Figure 3.12

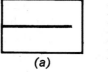
(a)

(b)

(c)

(d)

12. The price of product X increased at the same time that the quantity of the product sold decreased. Which of the following could have accounted for the price increase?   (*a*) an increase in supply   (*b*) an increase in demand   (*c*) a decrease in supply   (*d*) a decrease in demand.

13. Both the price and the quantity sold of product Y fell during the past year. Which of the following could have accounted for this decline?   (*a*) an increase in supply   (*b*) an increase in demand   (*c*) a decrease in supply   (*d*) a decrease in demand.

Building Vocabulary

Match each item in Column A with its definition in Column B.

COLUMN A	COLUMN B
1. demand	*a.* the price at which the amount demanded of a good or service is equal to the quantity supplied
2. demand curve	
3. supply	*b.* a line on a graph that shows the number of a particular item that will be sold at each price
4. supply curve	
5. law of demand	*c.* a line on a graph that shows the number of a particular item that will be purchased at each price
6. law of supply	
7. marginal utility	*d.* the extent to which supply changes following a change in price
8. elasticity of demand	*e.* the quantity of a product or service that would be purchased at a particular price
9. elasticity of supply	
10. market price	*f.* the idea that the quantity of a good or service demanded varies inversely with changes in price
	g. the quantity of a good or service offered for sale at a particular price
	h. the idea that the quantity of a good or service supplied varies directly with its price
	i. the extent to which demand changes following a change in price
	j. the degree of satisfaction from each additional purchase of a product or service

Thinking Critically

1. For each of the five possible events described below, tell (*1*) how the event would affect either the supply of or the demand for the italicized product and (*2*) how the event would affect the price of the product. (*a*) Yields decline as *corn* crop is hit by mysterious blight. (*b*) The wearing of *hats* is again becoming fashionable among men in the United States. (*c*) Only two days are left to buy a *turkey* for Thanksgiving, and food markets have many unsold turkeys. (*d*) Manufacturers of U.S. *automobiles* show great interest in the rise in European wages. (*e*) Midwestern drought forces ranchers to rush their *cattle* to market.

2. Explain the difference in prices for each of the following pairs of goods in terms of the laws of supply and demand: (*a*) natural diamonds and zircons (human-made diamonds), (*b*) a loaf of bread baked today as compared with day-old bread, (*c*) roses in January and roses in June.

3. A clothing store will usually reduce the price of smoke-damaged merchandise following a fire. Explain why some customers will buy this clothing even though it smells of smoke.

4. In a certain town, there were five bakeries and five florists. Last year, however, one firm bought out all the bakeries and another firm bought out all the florists. Both of the remaining companies have now decided to increase their prices. Which will be able to increase prices the most, the bakery or the florist? Explain.

SKILLS: Graphing Supply and Demand

Price	$16	14	12	10	8	6	4	2
Quantity	6	10	16	24	30	40	50	80

1. Construct a graph based on the data in the chart above. You may use graph paper for more precise plotting of points.
2. Does the graph show a demand or a supply curve?
3. Why does the curve slope downward?
4. On the same graph, construct another curve using the following:

Price	$16	14	12	10	8	6	4	2
Quantity	48	44	40	36	30	20	0	0

5. Does this curve represent supply or demand?
6. Why does this curve slope upward?
7. What is the equilibrium or market price?

The Role of
Business

Chapter 4

BUSINESS ORGANIZATIONS

Overview

Perhaps the most distinctive feature of the American free enterprise system is the extent to which means of production are privately owned. In socialist and Communist economies, the government owns a good proportion of the means of production. In the United States, 85 percent of the goods and services produced come from its over 20 million privately owned business firms. These companies come in all sizes. Some, such as IBM and General Motors, can be classified as "big businesses." Each employs thousands of workers and has annual sales running into billions of dollars. Big businesses tend to dominate their industries. Nine out of ten firms in this country, however, are "small businesses." They have relatively few employees, and their annual sales run into the thousands or millions of dollars.

Washington Graphics is an example of a small business. A few years ago, Frank and Rose Washington decided that it was time to go into business for themselves. Both previously had worked for other people. Now they wanted to work for themselves so that they would be their own bosses and be able to earn more money.

By combining their savings and taking out a few loans, Frank and Rose were able to put together the $30,000 needed to buy a computer graphics company in Lincoln, Nebraska. They were not deterred by the fact that this company had fallen on hard times and had just recorded an unimpressive $70,000 in yearly sales. The purchase price provided the Washingtons with necessary equipment and a list of customers. They found other customers by joining the local chapter of the Minority Development Council, a group of minority businesspeople.

Under Frank and Rose's leadership, business boomed. The company created art designs and put these designs on all types of fabrics, including T-shirts, sweatshirts, caps, jackets, and bags. Within three years, annual sales at Washington Graphics had grown to over $1.5 million.

In this chapter, we will see how U.S. businesses, both large and small, organize to produce and sell their products. As we read, we will learn about the principal forms of businesses: the sole proprietorship, partnership, and corporation. We will learn something about the advantages and disadvantages of each.

THE SOLE PROPRIETORSHIP

After being employed for four years, Wilma Jones decided to use her savings to go into business for herself. She rented a store in her old neighborhood and set up a small grocery. Although she was able to hire a clerk to help wait on customers and stack the shelves, Jones was always busy. Since she was the owner, responsibility for the success of the business rested upon her shoulders. She was there when the store opened in the morning and when it closed at night. She did all the ordering, kept the books, and often waited on customers. Because the business was hers alone, however, there were certain advantages. She did not have to share her profits with anyone. Moreover, she was her own boss.

The kind of business that Jones ran was a *sole proprietorship*, a business that is owned by one person.

Advantages of the Sole Proprietorship

Because of their advantages over other forms of business organizations, about 74 percent of all firms in the United States are sole proprietorships. As we will see, there are three major advantages of this type of business organization.

Easy to Form. The most important advantage of sole proprietorships is that they are easy to form. Aside from meeting some local license

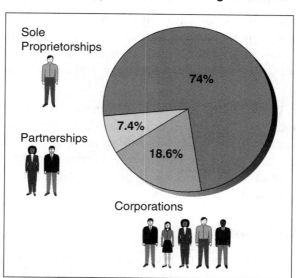

Figure 4.1   Types of Business Organizations

requirements, all Jones needed to do to start her business was to open her doors and sell groceries.

"You're the Boss." Another advantage of the sole proprietorship is the appeal of working for oneself. Although Jones might have found a job in a grocery store, she would not have been her own boss. As a proprietor, however, Jones is free to run the business her own way. She can try out her ideas on improving sales, and she does not have to take orders from others.

Potential Profits. As the sole owner, Jones does not have to share profits with anyone. She knows that were she working for someone else, she would receive a wage that was more or less fixed. There are no limits, though, to the amount of profits that a successful business can earn. Jones finds that possibility very attractive.

Disadvantages of the Sole Proprietorship

The success or failure of this type of business falls on one person: the sole proprietor. The owner often has to work long hours and forgo vacations. Running a business can cut into one's time spent on recreation or with one's family. Other disadvantages of the sole proprietorship are:

Unlimited Liability. While there are no limits to the amount of profits that Jones might earn as the sole proprietor of her business, there are also no limits to the amount she could lose. Economists describe this dire possibility as *unlimited liability*. Given that two out of three new businesses fail within four years of opening, you can see that the risk of loss is quite real.

Limited Capital. Another disadvantage of the sole proprietorship is that the amount of *capital* (or money) that the owner can raise is limited. That is, the most money that a proprietor can put into the business depends upon the size of his or her savings and that person's ability to borrow.

Limited Life. If Wilma Jones decides to go out of the grocery business (or is seriously injured or dies), the proprietorship will end. Thus, we say that sole proprietorships have a *limited life*. For that reason, it is often more difficult for proprietorships to borrow money than it is for other forms of business. Banks may be reluctant to lend to firms that may no longer exist in a few years.

THE PARTNERSHIP

Wilma Jones was growing tired of the long hours and responsibilities of her business. Although she now had two people working for her, she

How can a small business like this compete with a large supermarket?

still had to be there when the store opened in the morning and when it closed at night. Although business had been getting better, it was not getting any easier. One day, Fred Cruz, one of Jones's oldest and closest friends, dropped by to say hello. In recent years, Cruz has been working as a cook at a resort hotel. During the conversation, Cruz told Jones that he had saved some money with which he was hoping to open a small restaurant.

"Hey, that gives me an idea, Fred," Jones exclaimed. "Why don't you come into business with me? The store next door is available. We could expand in there and add a take-out food section."

"You might have something there, Wilma," Cruz replied. "I was getting nervous about going into business on my own. This way we'd be able to help each other out."

After some further talk in which they worked out the details, Jones and Cruz drew up an agreement and formed a *partnership*. It replaced Jones's sole proprietorship. A partnership is a business organization owned by two or more persons, who are known as "partners." Partners may share the responsibilities and profits in any way they choose. Under the terms of Jones's and Cruz's agreement, Cruz put up some cash, and the two agreed to share the profits equally. Soon thereafter, they began work on the store expansion. They put up a new sign in the window announcing the creation of the "C&J's Food Emporium."

Advantages of the Partnership

As with a sole proprietorship, there are several advantages to a partnership.

Additional Capital. A principal advantage of a partnership over a sole proprietorship is that the available capital (that is, money) is increased by whatever amount the additional partners bring into the business. In this instance, C&J's Food Emporium was able to expand because of the additional funds that Cruz invested in the business.

"Two Heads Are Better Than One." Partners can share the problems and responsibilities that go with owning a business. Jones now may have more free time than when she was the sole boss. Partners may also bring special talents or skills into the firm. Fred Cruz's talents as a cook enabled the business to add a lunch counter to its operations.

Easy to Organize. Finally, partnerships, like sole proprietorships, are fairly easy to organize.

Disadvantages of the Partnership

What are the negative aspects of partnerships?

Limited Life. One disadvantage of the partnership is that its life is limited. When a partner dies or resigns, a new partnership must be created.

Partners May Disagree. Another disadvantage of partnerships is the possibility of conflict among the partners. When partners disagree, the business is likely to suffer. In fact, studies have shown that disagreement among partners is a frequent cause of business failure.

Difficult to Sell. It can be difficult for one partner to withdraw from a partnership. Besides the problem of finding someone willing to pay a fair price for a share in the partnership, the buyer and the price have to be acceptable to the other partner or partners.

Limited Capital. Partnerships can raise but a limited amount of capital. That is, the amount of capital that a partnership can raise is limited by the wealth of the partners, the business's earning power, and its ability to borrow. While the addition of new partners is a possible source of new capital, many people are reluctant to enter into partnerships that make them personally liable for the debts of the business.

Unlimited Liability. Finally, the principal disadvantage of the partnership can be summed up in two words: unlimited liability. That is, each partner is personally liable for all the debts of the business. Since there is no limit to the amount of money that the business could lose, the possibility of loss for each of the partners is similarly unlimited.

Table 4.1   Forms of Business Organization

Form of Business	Advantages	Disadvantages
Sole proprietorship	Ease of formation "You're the boss" Potential profits	Unlimited liability Limited capital Burden of responsibility on owner Limited life
Partnership	"Two heads are better than one" Ease of formation Additional capital	Limited life Partners may disagree Difficult to sell Unlimited liability Limited capital

Some time after forming their partnership, Jones and Cruz approached their former classmate and friend Yvette Miller to ask her for money to modernize their store. Miller agreed to invest $15,000 in exchange for a 10 percent share in the partnership. Because she was busy running her own dress shop, however, Miller would not have time to spend at C&J's Food Emporium. She made the investment with the understanding that she would be a "silent partner." Although she would get 10 percent of the profits, the management of the firm would be left to Jones and Cruz.

Unfortunately, the store soon fell upon hard times. Sales declined drastically. Unable to pay their debts, Jones and Cruz had to close their doors and go out of business. By this time, the company owed its creditors $20,000, and neither Jones nor Cruz had any money of their own. Yvette Miller, however, had about $25,000 in savings. Even though she was only a 10-percent partner, her status as a partner made her fully liable for its debts. The creditors were paid off by Miller, whose savings were reduced by $20,000.

THE CORPORATION

We have seen that the advantages of the sole proprietorship and partnership are offset by a number of serious disadvantages for each. For that reason, many businesses turn to a third type of organization: the corporation.

What Is a Corporation?

A *corporation* is a business organization licensed to operate by a state or the federal government. A corporation's license is called a *charter*. It gives the firm the right to do business and to issue a specified number of *shares of stock* (certificates representing ownership in a corporation). Anyone holding one or more shares of stock is a part owner of the corporation. If, for example, a corporation issued only 1,000 shares of stock, anyone holding 100 shares would own 10 percent of the business. Those who own shares in a corporation are called *shareholders* or *stockholders*.

A unique feature of the corporation is its separation from the people who own it. Corporations can enter into contracts, sue or be sued, and pay taxes. For that reason, corporations are often described as "artificial persons." Thus, a musician who signs a contract with a recording company is, in a legal sense, entering into an agreement with the corporation rather than with the people who own it.

Let us return to the time when Cruz and Jones invited Miller to invest in C&J's Food Emporium. Suppose that instead of coming into the business as a partner, Miller had asked that the company be reorganized as a corporation. Under the terms of her proposal, Cruz and Jones would each keep 45 percent of the stock. Meanwhile, Miller would be given 10 percent of the stock in exchange for her $15,000 investment.

The partners liked Miller's proposal enough to ask their lawyer to apply for a charter from the state. After they obtained the document, they changed the sign over the store to read: "C&J's Food Emporium, Inc."

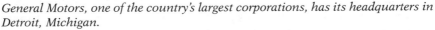

General Motors, one of the country's largest corporations, has its headquarters in Detroit, Michigan.

Advantages of the Corporation

Why had Miller insisted on incorporating before she agreed to invest in the business? She did this because of the special advantages of the corporate form of business.

Limited Liability. Because the corporation is legally separated from those who own it, the shareholders cannot be held liable for its debts. Therefore, if the business should fail, the most that any shareholder could lose (that is, their liability) would be limited to whatever they had paid for their stock. This *limited liability* is arguably the most important advantage of the corporation over other forms of business enterprise. For that reason, British corporations use the term *Ltd.* (Limited) to identify their corporations rather than our *Inc.* (Incorporated).

Returning to the tale of C&J's Food Emporium, Inc., let us again suppose that the company failed, leaving $20,000 in unpaid debts. Let us suppose, too, that Yvette Miller had $25,000 in her savings account. In this instance, her savings would be safe. The most that Miller could now lose would be her original $15,000 investment.

Because the possibility of personal loss is limited, it is easier to interest people to invest in a corporation than in a partnership. This advantage is especially important to businesses that would like to expand. They can do so by selling shares of stock.

Unlimited Life. Unlike businesses that end when the owners withdraw or die, corporations can go on forever. This situation makes it easier for corporations than for unincorporated businesses to borrow money for long periods of time.

Ease of Transfer. Buying in or selling out of a corporation is relatively easy. To buy, all one needs to do is find someone with stock to sell. To sell one's ownership in a corporation, all one needs to do is find a buyer for the shares that one owns.

Disadvantages of the Corporation

What are some of the disadvantages of forming a corporation?

Difficulty and Expense of Organizing. Organizing and operating a corporation is a complex process. It usually requires the services of a lawyer and an accountant—services that can add thousands of dollars to the cost of doing business.

Double Taxation. One of the reasons that people invest in a corporation is to receive *dividends*, profits that are distributed to shareholders. Like any other income, dividends are subject to *personal income taxes*. But even before dividends are distributed to shareholders, corporate profits are subject to *corporate income taxes*. (Various types of taxes will be discussed in Chapter 12.)

Many people have long argued that this double taxation is unfair. Nevertheless, except for the S Corporation (discussed below), double taxation remains as the major disadvantage of the corporate form of business enterprise.

S, the Corporation for Small Businesses

In an effort to aid certain small businesses, Congress added Subchapter S to the Internal Revenue Code. This law allows the owners of corporations with 75 or fewer stockholders to be taxed as though they were sole proprietorships or partnerships. Thus, owners of *S corporations*, as the businesses are called, enjoy limited liability and the other advantages of the corporation while, at the same time, they avoid double taxation.

How Large Corporations Are Organized

Corporations account for 90 percent of the business generated in this country. Although they vary in size from small, family-operated businesses to huge enterprises employing tens or even hundreds of thousands of workers, it is the largest firms that play the most important role in our economy. In one recent year, for example, the oil company

Table 4.2   Forms of Business Organization

Form of Business	Advantages	Disadvantages
Sole proprietorship	Ease of formation "You're the boss" Potential profits	Unlimited liability Limited capital Burden of responsibility on owner Limited life
Partnership	Two heads are better than one Ease of formation Additional capital	Limited life Unlimited liability Partners may disagree Difficult to sell Limited capital
Corporation	Unlimited life Ease of transfer Limited liability	Double taxation Difficulty and expense of formation
S Corporation	Limited liability Unlimited life Ease of transfer Avoid double taxation	Difficulty and expense of formation

Exxon (with more than 100,000 employees and 700,000 stockholders) ran up sales totaling nearly $80 billion. That same year, the 500 largest industrial corporations accounted for $2 trillion in sales, or 41 percent of the nation's GDP.

Giant corporations like Exxon have organizational and operational problems quite different from those faced by smaller corporations. Although each of its 700,000 stockholders are part owners of the company, it would hardly make sense for all of them to attempt to run the company. Instead, large corporations look to their officers and boards of directors to run the businesses on behalf of the shareholders.

The Officers. The officers, selected by the board of directors, run the corporation. Typically, officers include the president, a number of vice presidents, a secretary, and a treasurer (see Figure 4.2). The officers hire the personnel and conduct whatever operations are necessary to the functioning of the firm.

Figure 4.2   Organization of a Typical Corporation

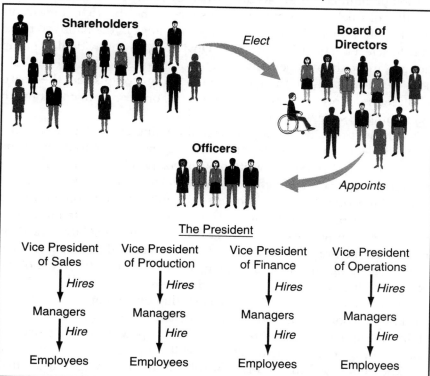

The Board of Directors. Shareholders elect the *board of directors*, including its chairperson. Unlike political elections that follow the "one person, one vote" rule, shareholders are entitled to one vote for every share of stock they own. Consequently, a person with 25,000 shares of stock in a corporation in which 100,000 shares were issued would be entitled to cast 25,000 votes (one quarter of the total).

Typically, the board of directors sets long-range goals for the corporation but leaves day-to-day operations to its officers. Two of the board's principal areas of concern, however, are long-term financing and the distribution of profits. When, for example, the company needs additional funds for expansion, the board of directors will decide whether to borrow the money or sell additional shares of stock. Similarly, the board will decide how much of the firm's profits will be distributed as dividends and how much will be reinvested in the business.

The board also keeps shareholders informed of significant developments, prepares certain financial reports, and conducts periodic elections to seats on the board.

The Separation of Ownership and Control

Although giant corporations are owned by many stockholders, only a handful of stockholders own enough shares to be able to influence corporate policy. In a large corporation, control lies in the hands of those able to select the board of directors. Obviously, any individual or group holding more than 50 percent of a corporation's stock would have absolute control because the individual or group could select the board of directors. More often than not, however, one can gain control with something less than 50 percent of the stock.

How is it possible for an individual holding only a fraction of the total shares to control a corporation? The answer has to do with the use of proxies. A *proxy* is a written authorization by a shareholder giving another person the right to vote one's shares of stock at a shareholders' meeting. Most stockholders are reluctant to become involved in the details of a corporation. They do not know or care to know how the business functions. For this reason, they will usually give their proxies to the present management when requested to do so. As long as management can gather enough proxies to control 50 percent of the votes cast, it can remain in power indefinitely.

Some people have criticized the fact that ownership and control in the large corporation are so widely separated. They argue that it is not right that individual stockholders are almost powerless to change the course set by management. Others, while conceding that individual stockholders have little, if any, control over their company, argue that this is as it should be. Modern-day businesses are so complex that only experts can make intelligent decisions pertaining to them. Thus, most people investing in a large corporation willingly turn over control of their investment to management in exchange for the opportunity to share in the profits and growth of the company. Sometimes, however, groups of stockholders get together in an attempt to oust management. While these undertakings are usually very difficult, they have on rare occasions been successful.

OTHER FORMS OF BUSINESS ORGANIZATION

Besides the more common sole proprietorships, partnerships, and corporations, we will look at other forms of business organization, some of which are variations of the three major types.

Government-Owned Corporations

While most businesses in the United States are privately owned, some are government owned. That is, they are owned and operated by a local or state government or by the federal government. Atlanta's Metropolitan Area Rapid Transit Authority (MARTA) is a corporation owned by local government. It operates a regional bus and subway system. Similarly, the Pennsylvania Turnpike Authority and the U.S. Postal Service are examples respectively of state and federal government-owned corporations.

In many instances, government ownership has developed because private interests have been unable or unwilling to supply needed services. The reluctance of private utilities to provide electric service in some rural areas in the 1930s explains why the federal and state governments went into that business then.

The Trend Toward Privatization. Since the 1980s, there has been some movement away from government ownership of businesses. The trend, known as *privatization*, seeks the transformation of publicly run businesses into privately operated and owned ones. In some communities, for example, privatization has led to the establishment of privately operated prisons and fire departments.

Not-for-Profit Corporations

The American Red Cross, the United Way, and the Boy Scouts of America are examples of *not-for-profit businesses*. So, too, are most other public service, charitable, and religious organizations. Unlike businesses that distribute profits to their owners, anything earned beyond costs by a not-for-profit business is put back into the organization to further its work. For this reason, not-for-profits are generally exempt from the payment of income taxes.

Corporate Raiders

How much stock does one need to own to take over a large corporation? One needs far less than 50 percent.

Control of a large corporation rests in the hands of its board of directors. Board members are elected to office by the shareholders. But since most shareholders fail to vote or turn their right to vote over to others (by giving them their proxy), the selection of directors is usually in the hands of a small group of shareholders who own substantially less than 50 percent of the corporation's stock. In other words, those who control a large corporation do so because they can muster more than 50 percent of its voting power.

Of course, what is true for insiders who control a corporation is equally true for the outsiders who would like to replace them. News reporters use the term *corporate raiders* to describe these outsiders.

Sometimes a raider buys up large blocs of a corporation's stock with no intention of taking over the corporation. The raider will, however, hint to the firm's board of directors that he or she does intend to take over the corporation, elect new directors, and oust the management. In an effort to block such a takeover, some boards have offered to buy back the raider's stock, at an enormous profit to the raider. In exchange for this, the raider

In 1984, Saul P. Steinberg threatened to take control of Walt Disney Productions and then oust its management. He seemed to have the power to do this even though he had purchased only 11 percent of the corporation's stock. In the end, the only way Disney's management could prevent the takeover of the corporation was to buy back the stock at an inflated price. In exchange for a $32 million profit, Steinberg sold his share and pledged not to buy Disney stock again for the next ten years.

agrees to abandon efforts to take over the company. The similarities between this practice and blackmail led to the use of the word *greenmail* to describe the corporate raiders' actions. (*Blackmail* is the threat of public exposure to extract money or favors from someone.)

Cooperatives

Cooperatives (or "co-ops") are associations of individuals or organizations. Co-op members band together to buy or sell more efficiently than they could as individuals. The most common types of cooperatives in this country are consumer cooperatives, producer cooperatives, and cooperative apartment buildings.

A *consumer cooperative* is a retail business owned by some or all of its customers. Co-ops in which only members can make purchases sell their products at lower-than-average prices. Those that are open to the public usually have somewhat higher prices. They might distribute profits to their members in proportion to the amount of purchases each member makes during the year.

Producer cooperatives are organizations of producers who cooperate in buying supplies and equipment and in marketing their products. Ocean Spray cranberries, Sunkist oranges, and Blue Diamond almonds are well-known examples of products sold by producer cooperatives.

Cooperative apartment buildings are run by corporations whose capital stock is owned by its tenants. As stockholders, co-op tenants receive many of the benefits normally associated with landlords, such as tax deductions and reduced rents.

Summary

Perhaps the most distinctive feature of the U.S. free enterprise system is the existence of so many privately owned businesses. Most of these business firms are organized in one of three ways: as a sole proprietorship, partnership, or a corporation. The first is a business owned by one person, while a partnership is a business association of two or more owners. A corporation is a business owned by its stockholders. Since it is impractical for stockholders to maintain hands-on control of large corporations, they elect a board of directors to represent them. The board of directors, in turn, hires officers to manage the corporation.

Besides the three basic forms of business enterprises in this country, other forms, such as government-owned corporations, cooperatives, and not-for-profit corporations, also exist on limited bases.

REVIEWING THE CHAPTER

Building Vocabulary

Match each term in Column A with its definition in Column B.

COLUMN A	COLUMN B
1. sole proprietorship	*a.* the status of being personally responsible for all the debts of a company
2. partnership	*b.* money
3. corporation	*c.* the trait of a business that it will close upon the death of an owner
4. S corporation	*d.* an unincorporated business owned by one person
5. unlimited liability	*e.* a document that authorizes another person to vote one's stock
6. capital	*f.* a type of business with fewer than 76 stockholders
7. proxy	*g.* a business chartered under state or federal law and owned by its stockholders
8. stockholder	*h.* a government license to form a business
9. limited life	*i.* an unincorporated business owned by two or more persons
10. charter	*j.* an owner of a corporation

Understanding What You Have Read

1. Which form of business organization is most numerous in the United States? (*a*) sole proprietorships (*b*) partnerships (*c*) corporations (*d*) cooperatives.

2. Which of the following is the most attractive feature of the sole proprietorship? (*a*) the ease with which it can be organized (*b*) its ability to expand across state borders (*c*) the ease with which ownership can be transferred (*d*) its limited liability.

3. Which of the following is a disadvantage of most corporations? (*a*) limited life (*b*) unlimited liability (*c*) limited capital (*d*) double taxation.

4. As a rule, who has voting rights in a corporation? Its (*a*) officers (*b*) stockholders (*c*) board of directors (*d*) employees.

5. Stockholders in a large corporation generally do not (*a*) receive a share of the profits (*b*) elect the board of directors (*c*) manage the everyday affairs of the business (*d*) own the business.

6. Limited liability, unlimited life, and a charter are characteristics of (*a*) sole proprietorships (*b*) partnerships (*c*) all businesses in the United States (*d*) corporations.

7. Ownership and control in a large corporation is often separated. This means that (*a*) a few stockholders own enough shares to control the corporation (*b*) stockholders do not want to participate in managing a corporation (*c*) stockholders do not share in the profits of a corporation (*d*) stockholders are not capable of managing a large corporation.

8. A proxy (*a*) is the head of a corporation (*b*) gives shareholders the right to choose company officers (*c*) transfers a stockholder's voting rights to someone else (*d*) is a stockholder's share of corporate profits.

9. How do the stockholders of a giant corporation like Mobil Oil or IBM manage their companies? They (*a*) elect a board of directors by casting one vote for every share of stock they own (*b*) elect a board of directors in accordance with the principal of "one person, one vote" (*c*) take turns serving on the stockholders' committee that runs the corporation (*d*) organize a group of workers to represent the interests of the stockholders at directors' meetings.

10. Why might a small corporation organize as an S corporation? An S corporation (*a*) does not have to issue stock (*b*) is not subject to the corporate income tax (*c*) is the only form of business organization that offers limited liability (*d*) is the only form of business organization that provides unlimited life.

11. "Double taxation" refers to the fact that (*a*) corporations have to pay both state and federal taxes (*b*) the part of a corporation's earnings not distributed as dividends is subject to excess profits taxes (*c*) corporations pay both income taxes and sales taxes (*d*) corporations pay income taxes on their earnings, and the earnings that they distribute as dividends are subject to personal income taxes.

12. The Girl Scouts of America is an example of a (*a*) consumer co-op (*b*) sole proprietorship (*c*) not-for-profit corporation (*d*) government-owned corporation.

Thinking Critically

1. You have saved enough money to start a shoe repair business in your neighborhood. A friend who has business experience suggests that you start your operation as a single proprietorship. Another experienced businessperson tells you to incorporate. Whose advice would you take? Explain your answer.

2. Upon graduation from electronic repair school, Harriet Zoltan opened a small shop as a sole proprietor. A few years later she was approached by an old friend, Bill Paseo, who offered to put $5,000 into the business in exchange for 50 percent interest. Zoltan agreed, and they formed the partnership of Zoltan and Paseo.

   a. Explain *three* factors that might have led Zoltan to start her business as a sole proprietorship.

   b. Explain *three* reasons why Zoltan might have been willing to take Paseo into the business.

3. Suppose, because of business losses, Zoltan and Paseo decide to call it quits. After selling all the tools, furnishings, and inventory in the shop, they are still $10,000 in debt. Bill Paseo tells Harriet Zoltan that he is broke because every penny he had was invested in the business. Harriet replies that all she has is the $10,000 in the bank—money that she has been saving to buy a new car.

   a. How much, and from whom, will Zoltan and Paseo's *creditors* (the people to whom the $10,000 is owed) receive?

   b. Suppose that instead of organizing as a partnership, Zoltan and Paseo had formed a corporation. How would you then answer question (*a*)?

   c. If Harriet and Bill had decided to incorporate, do you think that they should have formed an S corporation? Explain your answer.

4. The stockholders are the owners of a corporation. However, giant corporations with thousands of stockholders have organizational and operational problems quite different from those faced by small, closely held corporations.

   a. What is the role of the *board of directors* in a large corporation? How are board members elected?

   b. What is the function of the *officers* of a large corporation? How are the officers selected?

   c. What is meant by separation of ownership and control in large corporations?

   d. In a recent election for the board of directors of a large corporation, the efforts of a group to unseat the existing board failed. The reelected board stated that the election represented "corporate democracy in action." The losers said that the election simply demonstrated how difficult it is to defeat the "insiders." Explain both points of view.

SKILLS: Completing and Analyzing a Table

Table 4.3 Business Organizations and Their Receipts, 1993

Number (millions)	Percent of Total	Business Organizations	Receipts (billions)	Percent of Total
15.848		Sole Proprietorships	$ 757	
1.467		Partnerships	627	
3.965		Corporations	11,814	

1. Complete the table by calculating and filling in the percentages of total number and total receipts for each type of business organization. Use the information contained in the completed table and in your text to answer the following questions.

2. According to the chart, how many sole proprietorships are there? Partnerships? Corporations?

3. Compare the earnings of those three types of business organizations. Which has the greatest earnings? The smallest?

4. How would you explain the fact that with such a small percentage of the total number of business firms, corporations account for such a large percentage of business earnings?

Chapter 5

BUSINESS FINANCE

Overview

Louise and Bob White formed Quail Hill Window Cleaning Service about a year ago. Working together, they washed windows of downtown stores, as well as of a number of private homes and apartments. Last weekend, Louise and Bob gathered their financial records together. They looked to see if the year's efforts had been worthwhile.

"So, what do you think?" Bob asked after all the results had been tallied.

"Darn good, I'd say. We've paid for our supplies and cleaning equipment, and never missed a payment on our truck loan."

"See, I told you the truck would be a good idea," Bob continued. "Now, if we could just afford to hire one or two helpers, we could take on more jobs and make more money."

"That's true, but what would happen if we hired a couple of people and business fell off?" Louise asked. "You miss a couple of payments on the truck loan, and it's bye-bye truck."

"You know what it boils down to, Louise? Money! If the cash keeps flowing, we'll be able to hire more workers, and have more time for ourselves."

"And if it doesn't," Louise interjected, "Quail Hill will become a dead duck."

WHY DO BUSINESS FIRMS NEED MONEY?

We sometimes call money the "lifeblood of business." Like its red equivalent, the flow of funds enables business firms to meet their day-to-day obligations, and to grow. If something were to interrupt the flow of money, the firm would wither, and eventually die.

Businesses need money to:

- meet their everyday expenses, such as payroll, rent, and utilities
- replace and expand their *inventory* (the goods they sell and the materials used in their manufacture)
- expand and grow through the purchase of additional plant and equipment
- meet the interest payments on their debts.

Figure 5.1 The Flow of Company Funds

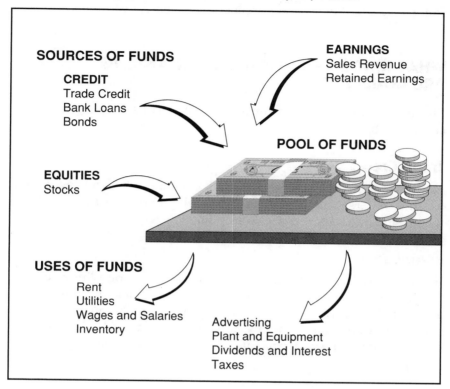

Normally, funds needed to meet a firm's daily expenses come out of its *revenues* (that is, income from the goods or services that the firm sells). When revenues are not sufficient to meet a firm's needs, it will resort to one or more of the following:

- dip into its savings
- borrow money
- sell some more of its stock.

SHORT VS. LONG-TERM FINANCING

When businesses run short of cash and need to finance operations, they use short-term financing to make up the difference. The term *short-term financing* applies to loans that need to be repaid in less than a year. *Long-term financing* applies to loans and other financial strategies that are made for periods of a year or more. In most instances, businesses use long-term financing to pay for things like major renovations, new buildings, and purchases of expensive equipment.

WHAT KINDS OF SHORT-TERM FINANCING ARE AVAILABLE?

The most frequently used forms of short-term financing are trade credit and bank loans.

Trade Credit

Business suppliers frequently give their customers 30 to 60 days to pay for their orders. This kind of payment delay, known as *trade credit*, is the most common type of short-term financing.

Bank Loans

Banks generally extend credit as a promissory note or a line of credit. A *promissory note* is a written promise to repay a loan, plus interest, at a specified date. A *line of credit* is a loan arrangement in which a bank allows a business to borrow any sum, up to a specified limit, whenever it needs the money. Terms of repayment would be part of this arrangement.

WHAT LONG-TERM FUNDS ARE AVAILABLE?

As you might expect, funds for the day-to-day operation of most businesses come from the businesses' earnings. But where do the firms get the money they need to replace worn-out or obsolete buildings and equipment or to expand the scope of their operations? There are three sources for such funds: retained earnings, loans, and the sale of shares of stock.

Retained Earnings

Profits that are not distributed to the owners of a business are called *retained earnings*, or *undistributed profits*. Corporations rely on retained earnings as the major source for their new funds. A major advantage of retained earnings, as compared to borrowing, is that they are interest-free. Retained earnings enjoy an advantage also over the sale of new stock as a means of raising capital. With the issue of more stock, ownership in the corporation increases. It follows, therefore, that a company will divide profits among a larger number of shareholders.

Leverage in Action

The use of borrowed funds to finance business operations is called *leverage*. Leverage can increase the rate of return earned on an investment. The following example illustrates this concept.

Last year, Frankie and Ernie each opened a newspaper stand at the local airline terminal. The two businesses, which competed with each other, were virtually identical. Frankie and Ernie (1) both sold newspapers and magazines to airline passengers, and (2) each invested $50,000. There was a major difference between the two businesses, however. Ernie paid cash to open his business, while Frankie put up only $5,000 of her own funds. She borrowed the rest at 15 percent interest. At the close of one year in business, Frankie and Ernie reported their financial results as follows:

Table 5.1

Frankie's Investment		Ernie's Investment	
Cash	$ 5,000	Cash	$50,000
Loan (at 15%)	45,000	Loan	- 0 -
	$50,000		$50,000
First-Year Earnings			
Earnings	$15,000	Earnings	$15,000
Less interest		Less interest	
payments	6,750	payments	- 0 -
Profit	$ 8,250		$15,000
Return on investment	$\frac{\$8,250}{\$5,000} = 165\%$		$\frac{\$15,000}{\$50,000} = 30\%$

By year's end, both Frankie and Ernie had earned $15,000. Since Ernie had no interest to pay, he kept his entire $15,000. This represented a return of 30 percent on his initial investment.

After paying the interest on her loan, Frankie was left with a profit of $8,250. In this case, however, the return was 165 percent on her investment!

As long as earnings exceed the cost of borrowing, leveraging will increase the return on an investment. When they fall below that point, they magnify the loss.

Alas, second year earnings for both Frankie and Ernie fell to $5,000. Note how this affected the return on their investments.

Table 5.2

Frankie's Investment		Ernie's Investment	
Cash	$ 5,000	Cash	$50,000
Loan (at 15%)	45,000	Loan	- 0 -
	$50,000		$50,000

Second-Year Earnings

Earnings	$ 5,000	Earnings	$ 5,000
Less interest payments	6,750	Less interest payments	- 0 -
Profit (loss)	($1,750)		$ 5,000
Return on investment	$\frac{(-)\ 1,750}{\$\ 5,000} = (-35\%)$		$\frac{\$\ 5,000}{\$50,000} = 10\%$

By the end of the second year, both had earned $5,000. Since Ernie had no interest to pay, he kept the entire $5,000. This figure represented a return of 10 percent on his initial investment.

After paying the interest on her loan, Frankie was left with a loss of $1,750, or 35 percent of her investment.

Long-Term Loans

Those who borrow for a year or more usually have to both pledge some form of collateral and make periodic payments over the life of the loan. *Collateral* is any item of value that the lender may seize should the borrower fail to make loan payments as promised.

Equity Financing

You may have heard of *stock exchanges*, places where shares in the nation's major corporations are bought and sold. Daily newspapers and radio and television programs carry reports on the doings of the stock exchanges.

In terms of the amount of money raised by corporations, *equity financing* (a corporation's selling of its stock) is the least important source. In a recent year, for example, the sale of stock accounted for only 4 percent of the funds raised by corporations. To those corporations that rely on the sale of stock to finance their operations, however, equity financing is extremely important. It is important also to the millions of people who, for reasons described below, are buying or selling shares of stock.

The fortunes of the *stock market* (a term that includes all places where stocks are bought and sold) often mirror how the people of the United States view their economy. Indeed, economists often look to stock market trends to help them assess the nation's mood. When the public is feeling good about the future, stock purchases increase and stock prices rise. When the public is feeling pessimistic, stock sales fall, along with stock prices.

One thing that sets a corporation apart from an unincorporated business is the corporation's ability to sell stocks and bonds. Unlike stocks (which represent ownership in a corporation), *bonds* are certificates issued in exchange for a loan. Thus, stockholders are part owners of a business, whereas bondholders are among its creditors.

Stocks: Common and Preferred. Most stocks are *common stocks*. They entitle their owners to a voice in the selection of the board of directors. Holders of common stock may also share in the profits of the company whenever the corporation's board of directors decides to pay dividends.

Let us suppose that a corporation's directors set aside $3 million of profits for distribution to shareholders. If the corporation had sold 1 million shares of stock, stockholders will receive $3 for every share they own. If the business should be dissolved for any reason, holders of

Common Stock Certificate. Why would anyone want to own one of these certificates?

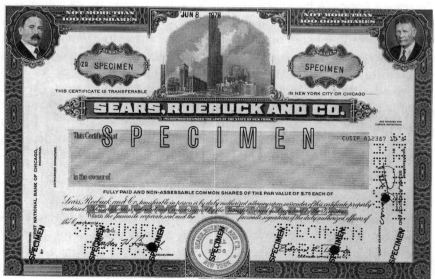

common stock would receive their share of whatever remained, if anything, after all debts had been paid.

While all corporations issue common stock, some also distribute *preferred stock*. Holders of preferred stock usually have no voting rights. They are, however, entitled to a fixed dividend whenever the board of directors votes to pay it. Holders of common stock cannot receive dividends until the holders of preferred stock have received theirs. In a similar situation, should the business fail, the holders of preferred stock are in line to share in its assets ahead of the holders of common stock. Some companies have stock that is "cumulative preferred." This term means that if a corporation fails to pay dividends during one year, it must make up the missed payments in succeeding years to owners of cumulative-preferred stock before common stockholders can receive any dividends.

The Miracle Lantern Company's motto, "If it works, it's a Miracle!" made the company a household name. The company has issued 100,000 shares of cumulative-preferred stock that pays annual dividends of $1 per share. In addition, it has issued 1 million shares of common stock. In 1995, the company paid no dividends. In 1996, though, the board of directors set aside $700,000 in profits for payment to stockholders. The company paid dividends to the cumulative-preferred stockholders of $2 per share: $1 for 1996 and $1 for 1995 (when no dividends had been paid). Only $500,000, or 50 cents a share, was left for distribution in 1996 to the holders of common stock.

Corporate Bonds. A bond is a kind of IOU. It is a promise by a corporation to repay a specified sum (the face value of the loan, or *principal*) at the end of a specific number of years, along with annual interest. Since bonds represent a debt of a corporation, bondholders are among its creditors. If it declares *bankruptcy* (unable to pay its debts), the company will pay off its bondholders and other creditors first. Then (if there is any money left) the company will pay off its stockholders.

Many investors assume that bonds are always safer investments than stocks. This is not always true. The safety of any security depends upon the company that issues it. The common stock of a well-established, profitable corporation is likely to be safer than the bonds of a newly organized gold-mining enterprise that has yet to find any gold.

Government Bonds. You may be familiar with the Series EE savings bonds issued by the U.S. government. The most popular of these bonds sells for $25. It pays $50 after being held for a period of time. Like corporate bonds, government bonds are evidences of debt. When we purchase a savings bond, we are lending money to the federal government. In exchange for the loan, the government promises to return our principal plus interest on a specified date.

All levels of government—federal, state, and local—sell bonds from time to time. Depending on the type of bond, methods of payment, interest rates, and denominations differ. All bonds are issued in exchange for a loan and thus represent a promise to repay the loan with interest.

HOW STOCKS AND BONDS ARE SOLD TO THE PUBLIC

When a corporation needs to sell its stocks or bonds to the public, it usually goes to an *investment bank,* a bank that specializes in this kind of activity. The investment bank *underwrites* the issue: it buys the entire issue of some corporation's stocks or bonds and then sells the securities to the public at a price that will yield a profit. The corporation can use the funds it receives from the bank without any further concern over whether all the stocks or bonds are sold.

State and local governments also use investment banks to market their bonds. In contrast, the federal government sells its bonds through the Federal Reserve System, which is discussed in Chapter 16.

Those who buy stocks and bonds from underwriters are free to sell them any time they choose. But neither the issuing corporation nor the initial underwriter is likely to buy them back. Hence, there is a need for organized markets in which stocks and bonds may be sold. Stock exchanges fill some of that need. They provide places where stocks can be traded at a moment's notice.

Stock Exchanges

The stocks of the nation's largest corporations are generally traded in one of the stock exchanges. The largest of these is the **New York Stock Exchange**, and the second largest is the **American Stock Exchange**, both located in New York City. There are other exchanges in major cities around the country, but the New York Stock Exchange is by far the most important. Indeed, the total value of its sales is greater than the combined total of the stock sales in all the other exchanges. Figure 5.2 on page 108 explains how stock exchange transactions are reported in a daily newspaper.

In the nation's stock exchanges, stocks are bought and sold through an auction system. Brokers representing the buyers and sellers offer their wares to the highest bidder and call out their own bids in an attempt to acquire stocks for their clients at favorable prices.

In order to qualify to have their stocks listed on the national exchanges, firms must meet certain standards regarding size and financial security. Not all firms seeking to sell their stocks to the public meet these standards. Accordingly, many corporations sell their stocks either in the regional exchanges or over-the-counter (described below).

Over-the-Counter Market

The *over-the-counter market* consists of the many brokerage firms throughout the nation that buy "unlisted" stocks from special dealers and sell them to investors. The over-the-counter market handles the stocks of relatively small firms and of most banks, insurance companies, and mutual funds. It also handles the sale of stocks being offered to the public for the first time. The stocks of more than 40,000 firms may be bought and sold over-the-counter. In contrast, the stocks of fewer than 3,000 firms are traded on the floors of the New York and American stock exchanges.

As with the stock exchanges, over-the-counter transactions are publicly reported the instant they take place. Some of these stocks are reported by the National Association of Securities Dealers Automated Quotations, or **NASDAQ**. NASDAQ has a computerized system that enables investors interested in the over-the-counter market to keep informed of the availability and selling price of securities.

Why do securities markets exist? One reason is that investors would not be willing to buy stocks or bonds if there were no easy way to sell them later. Corporations would then find it excessively costly to sell their securities.

Another reason stock markets are needed is that they enable us to know the value of stocks. This knowledge is indispensable to investors who own or are thinking of buying stocks. Stock markets are also important to the economy as a whole. They serve to withdraw funds from areas where money is no longer needed and transfer these funds to areas where money is needed. For example, suppose that the outlook for new-car sales is poor at a time when there is an increasing demand for personal computers. During this time, the value of automobile-industry stocks will probably decrease, while the value of computer-industry stocks will increase. Firms in the computer industry will then have an easier time than auto firms in raising new money through the sale of stocks.

Brokerage Firms

People who wish to buy or sell stocks or bonds must use the services of a *brokerage firm*, a company of sales specialists known as *brokers*. Brokers buy and sell *securities* (stocks and bonds) on behalf of their clients and receive a commission, or fee, for their work. When a customer

New York Stock Exchange. Why do stock prices go up and down?

places an order for a stock listed on an exchange, the broker relays the order to the brokerage firm's representative on the floor of the exchange. There the broker's representative meets with others who are trading the same security and buys according to the customer's instructions.

The price at which a security is bought and sold depends upon the supply of and the demand for that security. If the demand for the security rises, its price will be pushed up. If the demand for the security falls, so too will its price. Similarly, if few people want to sell a security, the short supply will push prices up. If many want to sell, the oversupply will push prices down. Whatever the price, none of the money that changes hands after the first sale goes to the corporation that issued the security.

Why People Buy Stocks

Stock ownership in the United States is not confined to the wealthy. Members of one in five American families own shares of stocks. In addition, millions of Americans who have insurance policies or are participants in pension funds own stocks indirectly. The insurance companies and pension funds invest in stocks and bonds to build up their reserves of money. Why do so many people and institutions invest in the stock market? Most do so for one or more of the following reasons:

Dividends. Each year, a corporation may distribute to its shareholders *dividends*, a part of the company's profits. Many individuals and institutions invest in stocks in order to receive these dividends.

Capital Growth. The value of a stock is not fixed. Instead it fluctuates with changes in supply and demand. Many people invest in stocks because they expect that in time these stocks will be worth more than what they paid for them. Such an increase in value is called *capital growth*.

Stocks increase in value for a number of reasons. One reason is business performance. If a corporation's sales and profits increase, its value and the value of its stock will rise. The value of a stock also increases because of public expectations. If investors expect a corporation to do well, the demand for its shares will increase and so will the value of those shares.

Still another reason why individual stocks increase in value has to do with the value of stocks in general. At times when the stock-buying public is feeling optimistic about the economy, the prices of securities tend to rise. When they are feeling pessimistic about the economy, stock prices tend to fall.

Speculators. People who buy and sell stocks for the reasons listed above (for dividends and capital growth) are called *investors*. Another category of buyers and sellers of stocks are known as *speculators*. Unlike investors (who hope to share in a company's profits and growth over the long term), speculators hope to turn a quick profit.

Because the prices of stocks fluctuate from day to day, speculators can profit if they can correctly predict the price movements. Depending on whether they predict a rise or fall in prices, speculators will either "buy long," or "sell short."

Buying Long. Investors who believe that the price of a given stock will rise are called *bulls*. They hope to profit from this by *buying long*—that is, by buying the stock now and selling it later at a higher price. A general rise in prices of stocks is known as a *bull market*.

Clara Ferdinand is bullish on Xerxes, a computer software company whose stock is currently selling at a price of 24½. (Stock prices are quoted in dollars and fractional eighths of a dollar. Thus 24½ = $24.50 per share. Had the price been 24⅜, it would have been equal to $24.375 per share.)

Clara bought 200 shares of Xerxes for $4,900 (200 x $24.50 = $4,900). Three months later, Xerxes had risen to 30¼, and Clara sold. This left her with a profit of $5.75 per share, or $1,150 (less brokerage fees and taxes). Of course, if instead of increasing, the price of Xerxes stock had fallen, Clara Ferdinand would have lost money.

Selling Short. *Bears* is the name given to investors who are expecting the price of a specific stock to decline. In such circumstances, they normally would sell any of this stock that they own in hopes of buying it back later at a less expensive price. Some bears hope to profit by *selling short.*

To sell short is to sell stock that you do not own (that you borrow from a broker) in the hope of buying the stock back later at a lower price. When you return the stock to the broker, you keep the difference between what you sold the stock for and what you paid for it.

Frank Jones feels that the stock of Maypak Corporation is overvalued and that its price will soon fall. Jones does not happen to own any Maypak stock. Since he expects its price to fall, it would not be profitable for him to buy the stock. So instead of actually buying Maypak stock, Jones borrows the stock from his broker.

Jones orders his broker to sell 100 shares of Maypak short at the current market price of 50¼. (Remember, he does not own any Maypak stock.) Jones's broker lends the stock to Jones, sells it for him, and credits Jones's account for $5,025. A week or so later, Jones proves correct in his prediction. The price of Maypak falls to 43. Jones then orders his broker to settle his Maypak account. The broker withdraws $4,300 from Jones's account and uses the money to buy 100 Maypak shares (the number of shares that was "lent" to Jones) at the new, lower price of 43. Jones returns the 100 shares to his broker. This leaves Jones with a gross profit of $725. From this sum, the broker will deduct brokerage fees, taxes, and a rental fee for the borrowed stock.

Of course, it is also possible to lose money in this kind of transaction. Indeed, in a short sale there is no limit to the amounts speculators can lose if they are wrong, because there is no limit to the prices to which their stocks could climb. For example, if the price of Maypak stock in the previous example climbed to 80, Jones would have to pay $8,000 for 100 shares for which he received only $5,025—a loss of $2,975.

The Role of the Broker. Brokers act as intermediaries between "bulls" and "bears" and earn fees and/or commissions from each transaction. For every "bull" who is buying there must be a "bear" who is selling.

Margin. People may purchase stocks partly on credit, an action called *buying on margin.* In the past, though, too many people invested with stock bought on credit, and the stock market crashed. To prevent future crashes, the Federal Reserve Board (discussed in Chapter 16) sets the *margin* (percentage that a buyer has to put up in cash). Since 1934, the margin has fluctuated between 40 and 100 percent.

Buying and Selling Bonds. Like stocks, bonds may be sold in organized exchanges or over-the-counter. A majority of bonds (including all municipal bonds) are not listed on the exchanges. As with stocks, the price is determined by how much buyers are willing to pay and how little sellers are willing to accept. Figure 5.3 on page 109 illustrates how bond market transactions are reported in a daily newspaper.

The price of a bond is influenced chiefly by two factors: its safety and its rate of interest. If the public has any doubts about the ability of the issuer of the bond to pay either the principal or the interest, the bond's price will tend to fall. The price will also tend to fall if the rate of interest of the bond is less than the rate of interest prevailing in the economy. For example, in order to sell a $1,000 bond that paid 4 percent interest at a time when the prevailing rate on other bonds was 8 percent, one would expect the price to be considerably less than $1,000.

Similarly, the interest paid on newly issued bonds reflects both how safe the investment is and current interest rates. The interest paid on bonds issued by a local electric power company (a safe investment) is likely to be less than that paid by a newly organized oil-drilling corporation (a risky investment, because the corporation's income depends upon its ability to find oil).

In the 1980s, individuals seeking to buy out corporations raised huge sums through the sale of *junk bonds*. These are highly risky investments that offer extremely high rates of interest. The issuer has to

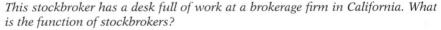

This stockbroker has a desk full of work at a brokerage firm in California. What is the function of stockbrokers?

pay high rates because of its poor credit rating. Some investors still buy junk bonds, but they are not as popular as they were in the 1980s.

Junk bonds are issued by companies with heavy debt or other financial problems. Therefore, these bonds carry higher yields to compensate investors for the risk that the company issuing the bond might not be able to repay its debts. Because of their high yields, many individuals, companies, and local governments carry a percentage of junk bonds in their *portfolios* (groups of investments that an investor might own).

SPECIALIZED MARKETS

Similar to securities exchanges, markets also exist for selling and buying commodities such as wheat, barley, rye, coffee, tin, and silver. If you examine the financial pages of your local newspaper, you will probably see these specialized markets listed. Because trading in these markets requires far more specialized knowledge than trading in the securities of large corporations, the specialized markets are not as popular with the public.

SECURITIES AND EXCHANGE COMMISSION

The **Securities and Exchange Commission (SEC)** was created by an act of Congress in 1934. Its purpose is to protect the public against deception or fraud in the selling of securities.

Caveat Emptor

The SEC does not say what it thinks of a particular investment. Rather, it subscribes to the principle of *caveat emptor*—"let the buyer beware." It would be inappropriate for a federal agency to either endorse or condemn any particular corporation's securities. But just as important, trading in securities is subject to so many variables of interpretation and chance that no single body could safely set itself up as an authoritative source of advice for investors.

The SEC requires that most companies wishing to sell their securities to the public register with the SEC by filing certain financial information. Failure to do so, or the publication of false or misleading information by a corporation, is punishable by fine, imprisonment, or both. It is up to investors to examine the financial reports of companies in which they wish to invest. If a mining company with worthless stock informs the public of the true facts in its financial statements, then people who lose their money by investing in the company would have no one to blame but themselves.

How to Read Financial Tables

Figure 5.2 How to Read a New York Stock Exchange Table

52-Week High	Low	Stock	Div	Yld %	P/E	Sales 100s	High	Low	Last	Chg
70	391/2	TJX pfCcld	3.13	...	...	56	641/4	631/2	641/4 —	1
195	1523/4	TJX pfE		...	...	4	188	186	186 —	4
285/8	163/8	TNP	.98 f	3.8	8	62	261/8	257/8	26	...
83/4	33/8	TRC	...	...	dd	45	4	37/8	37/8 —	1/4
97	641/8	TRW	2.20 a	2.4	14	551	925/8	913/4	925/8	...
113/8	61/8	TVX Gld	...	...	80	5698	81/4	8	8 —	1/4
273/4	201/4	Tadiran	.20 e	0.8	8	60	237/8	231/2	237/8+	3/8
111/2	81/4	TaiwanE	.31 e	2.9	q	156	103/4	103/4	103/4	...
253/8	191/2	Taiwan	.03 e	0.1	q	238	233/4	233/8	235/8+	1/4
401/2	231/2	Talbots	.36	1.0	19	2073	35	343/8	341/2+	1/8
93/4	61/2	Talley	...	...	dd	156	77/8	75/8	73/4—	1/8
53	36	Tambd	1.84	4.4	18	1203	423/8	413/4	421/4+	1/2
151/4	83/8	Tandem	...	...	cc	1862	11	103/4	11	...
643/8	341/8	Tandy	.80	1.8	19	4120	441/2	431/4	443/8+	7/8
93/8	51/8	Tndycft	...	...	dd	119	65/8	61/2	65/8	...
263/8	225/8	Tanger	2.08	8.7	17	39	237/8	233/4	237/8+	1/8
231/2	193/4	Tangr pf	1.80	8.2	...	4	22	22	22 +	3/4

Columns 1 and 2 list the highest and lowest prices at which the stock traded during the past 365 days (but not including yesterday). Prices are quoted in dollars and fractions of dollars per share (note that ⅛ equals 12½ cents). During the year, Tandy Corporation ranged in price from $34.125 to $64.375 per share. The name of the company issuing the stock (Column 3) is followed by the annual dividend (Column 4), here $.80 per share. (Listings are of common stock unless the letters *pf*—meaning preferred—follow the stock's name.) *Yield* (Column 5) is the percentage return in the form of dividends due to an investor who purchased the stock at the day's closing price. Thus, $.80 (the annual per share dividend) is 1.8 percent of $44.375 (the closing price of one share of stock). Column 6, *Price Earnings Ratio*, is the number of times by which the company's latest 12-month earnings per share must be multiplied to obtain the stock's current selling price. (The PE ratio is 19.) In Column 7, the number of shares sold during the reported trading day is listed in hundreds (in this case, 4120 equals 412,000 shares). Columns 8–10 (*High, Low,* and *Last*) refer to the trading price range during the day. In this case, the high was $44.50 per share, the low was $43.25, and the closing price was $44.375. *Change* (Column 11) is the difference between this day's closing price and the previous day's closing price. Here the closing price of $44.375 was ⅞, or 87.5 cents, *less* than the closing price on the previous day.

Figure 5.3 How to Read Bond Market Quotations

Company	Cur.Yld	Vol	Price	Chg
GenEl 7⁷/₈06	7.0	15	112¹/₂	− ¹/₄
GnHost 8s02 cv	...	12	88	...
GnHost 11¹/₂02	11.4	38	100⁵/₈	+ ¹/₂
GSignl 5³/₄02	5.5	5	104³/₄	− ¹/₄
Genesco 10³/₈03	11.5	23	89⁷/₈	+ ³/₈
Genrad 7¹/₄11 cv	...	30	91	+1¹/₂
Gerrity 11³/₄04	...	75	94³/₄	+ ⁵/₈
GPA Del 8³/₄98	...	81	92³/₄	− ⁵/₈
Grancre 6¹/₂03	...	90	88¹/₂	− ¹/₂
Gulfrd 6s12	6.3	61	96	+ ¹/₄
GulfMo 5s56f	8.4	20	59¹/₂	−1
Hallwd 7s00	...	1	74	...
Halwd 13¹/₂09	30.4	1	44³/₈	...
Halwd 13¹/₂09A	32.9	1	41	+1¹/₂
HlthSo 5s01	...	10	166	
HlthSo 9¹/₂01	...	5	107¹/₈	− ³/₈
ICN Phrm 8¹/₂99	...	81	107¹/₂	...
IllPow 8s23	...	30	103¹/₈	+ ¹/₈

In Column 1, the name of the firm issuing the bonds (General Electric) is listed in abbreviated form (GenEl), followed by the bonds' rate of interest (7⅞) and the year in which they mature (06, which stands for 2006). These GE bonds pay 7.875 percent of their $1,000 face value, or $78.75, in interest yearly. When they *mature* (come due) in the year 2006, the bonds will be worth $1,000 each (their *face value*) to their holders. Column 2 lists the *current yield* (Cur. Yld), the rate of return on investment based on the purchase price. Newspaper quotations use the closing (or last) price in calculating the current yield. Since the closing price was $1,125.00 (from Price, in Column 4, explained below) and the bonds paid $78.75 in interest, the yield was 7.0 percent (because 78.75 / 1,125 = .07 = 7 percent). Column 3 (Vol.), tells us the number of units worth $1,000 in face value that changed hands. In this instance, 15 GE bonds worth a total of $15,000 in face value (15 x $1,000) were sold. Closing bond prices are found by multiplying the published figures in Column 4 by $10. Thus, the closing price was $1,125 (112½ x $10). Net change (Chg in Column 5) is the difference between the previous day's closing price and the closing price on the day reported. Here the closing price of 112½ (or $1,125) was ¼ of $10, or $2.50, less than the closing price of 112¾ on the previous day.

The SEC has also set certain procedures designed to prevent any person or group from manipulating stock prices. For example, the SEC will fine investors who buy or sell stocks in companies about which they have information that has not been released to the general public. Such illegal actions are called *insider trading*. An example of insider trading would be if an officer of a company sold his or her stock just before the company released to the public a financial report whose contents would cause the price of the stock to go down.

Financial Statements: Required Reading for Investors.

We can learn about the operations and finances of *public corporations* (corporations whose stock is bought and sold by the public) by reading documents known as prospectuses and annual reports. A *prospectus* describes the operations of a company that is issuing new securities. An *annual report* provides financial information about a company whose securities are traded on an exchange.

The most important financial statements in these documents are the balance sheet, income statement, and statement of cash flows.

Balance Sheet. Financiers often compare the *balance sheet* to a snapshot because it presents a kind of picture of a business at a particular time. Included in the balance sheet are three areas of information: assets, liabilities, and net worth.

Assets represent anything of value that is owned by a business, including cash on hand or in the bank, plant and equipment, merchandise, and furniture and fixtures.

Liabilities represent the obligations, or debts, of a company. These include unpaid bills and salaries, borrowed money, and mortgages on the building or equipment.

The difference between what a firm owns and what it owes is its *net worth*, or *owner's equity*. The concept may be stated as:

$$\text{Assets} - \text{Liabilities} = \text{Net Worth}$$

For convenience, accountants *transpose* (transfer) liabilities from one side of the equal sign to the other when drawing up the balance sheet, in the following manner:

$$\text{Assets} = \text{Liabilities} + \text{Net Worth}$$

Table 5.3 illustrates a typical balance sheet.

Income Statement. If we think of a balance sheet as a snapshot of the financial condition of a business, then the *income statement* is like a

**Table 5.3   SUNSHINE LAUNDERETTE BALANCE SHEET
DECEMBER 31, 199_**

Assets		Liabilities and Net Worth	
Cash	$ 7,000.00	Accounts payable	$ 1,480.00
Machinery	12,200.00	Unpaid taxes	1,000.00
Supplies	350.00	Total liabilities	2,480.00
Truck	2,400.00	Owner's equity	19,470.00
Total	21,950.00	Total	21,950.00

motion picture. This is because an income statement (also known as a *profit and loss statement*) summarizes financial activities of a firm over a period of time.

The principal purpose of an income statement (as in Table 5.4) is to show profitability. It does this by summarizing the items of (1) income, (2) expense, and (3) subtracting expenses from income to determine profit or loss.

Statement of Cash Flows. Regardless of how wealthy a firm may be, it has to be able to pay its bills. Even though a department store may own a building worth $10 million, it might become bankrupt if it is unable to pay a $100,000 bill (or an even smaller amount). For that reason, those thinking of investing in a firm will also want to examine its *statement of cash flows*. This statement summarizes a firm's sources and uses of cash over a period of time.

Limitations of Financial Statements

Financial statements are useful, but they have limitations. Some of the more important limitations are:

1. Financial statements are a record of past events, not a forecast of the future. Past success does not guarantee a successful future.

**Table 5.4   PRECISE STATIONERY COMPANY INCOME STATEMENT
FOR THE YEAR ENDING DECEMBER 31, 199_**

Sales	$141,000.00	
Cost of goods sold	84,500.00	
Gross profit on sales	56,500.00	
Other income	750.00	
Gross income		57,250.00
Operating expenses	35,930.00	
Other expenses	240.00	
Gross expenses		36,170.00
Net income		$21,080.00

The South Sea Bubble

Americans invest surplus funds in a variety of ways. They buy stocks and bonds; contribute to savings and insurance programs; own real estate; and participate in a variety of financial opportunities. Unfortunately, too many lose their money to swindlers, those who push financial schemes that have little possibility of making money for anyone other than themselves.

For as long as there have been investment opportunities, there have been swindles. One of the most famous of these from the past is known as the *South Sea Bubble.*

In the early 1700s, Great Britain was wrestling with the burden of its national debt. This problem prompted the Earl of Oxford to make an unusual proposition, which the British government soon accepted. The Earl offered to create a firm (to be called the "South Sea Company") that would assume payment of a portion of the national debt. In exchange, the British government would grant the South Sea Company the exclusive right to trade in Central and South America. The name "South Sea" referred to the South Atlantic and Pacific, where much of the trading would take place.

In the belief that the South Sea Company would soon be bringing in gold and silver from Mexico and Peru, hundreds of British people rushed to buy shares in the South Sea Company. Share prices jumped from 130 to 300 *pounds* (British unit of currency) in March 1720, and went to 900 pounds by May of that year.

It was not long before people began to notice that, despite the run-ups in prices, the South Sea Company was not trading goods in the South Sea or, for that matter, anywhere else. As prices began their downward fall, sellers rushed to rid themselves of their shares. Their actions pushed prices down still further, and faster. In time, hundreds who had put their money in this "South Sea Bubble" lost their life's savings. The British politicians who had started it all (by making their agreement with the Earl of Oxford) fell from power.

Swindles such as the South Sea Bubble continue to occur. The motto of the story, then, is to beware of any scheme that promises a "fast buck." More likely than not, you will not make money quickly on one. Instead, you will probably lose money quickly.

**Table 5.5 HOME 'N OFFICE PRINTING CO.
STATEMENT OF CASH FLOWS (YEAR ENDING DECEMBER 31, 199_)**

Receipts:		
Outside jobs	$86,400	
Inside jobs	28,800	
Total receipts		$115,200
Payments:		
Wages	$69,600	
Rent	14,400	
Utilities	2,520	
Office expense	1,080	
Insurance	4,500	
Taxes	13,560	
Equipment	1,200	
Total payments		$106,860
Cash at end of period		$ 8,340

2. Financial statements may not reflect the changing value of money that results from inflation or deflation.

3. Some of the figures in the statement may be based on opinion, not on fact. For example, some companies may assign a dollar value to their name because experience has shown that a good reputation attracts customers. This dollar value will show up as "goodwill" in the asset section of the balance sheet.

The figure for "total assets" is supposed to give some idea of what the firm would be worth if it were forced to *liquidate* (sell off its assets and go out of business). If items in the inventory were valued at a higher price than they could actually be sold for, the figure would make the firm appear to be worth more than it is.

As stated earlier, the sale of stocks has a great impact on investors and on the economy in general. For that reason, corporations are required by law to make certain financial information available to the general public. Investors can find this information in the corporation's income statement and balance sheet. The wise investor will obtain and carefully study these statements before risking money in an investment.

Summary

All businesses need money to meet their day-to-day expenses and to grow. They obtain their funds by dipping into savings, borrowing money from suppliers and banks, or selling stocks or bonds.

When people buy stocks in a corporation, they become part owners of that business and have votes on certain matters regarding the corporation. Bondholders, by contrast, are creditors of a corporation and have no voting rights. People often buy stocks and bonds through stockbrokers. Investors buy stock in expectation of periodic dividends and an eventual rise in value of the stock. The main appeal of bonds is the interest that they pay.

Investing in stocks and bonds of businesses is risky. Before investing in a corporation, one should read its financial statements. Moreover, one should not invest more than one can afford to lose.

REVIEWING THE CHAPTER

Building Vocabulary

Match each term in Column A with its definition in Column B.

COLUMN A	COLUMN B
1. retained earnings	a. the use of borrowed funds to finance ownership of something
2. inventory	b. any item of value owned by a business
3. bull	c. one who buys stock expecting its price to rise
4. bear	d. profits of a business that are not distributed to its owners
5. equity financing	e. the sale of a corporation's stock as a means for the business to raise additional capital
6. asset	f. a summary of the financial activities of a company over time
7. investment bank	g. an institution that buys an entire new issue of a corporation's stock or bonds for resale to the public
8. net worth	h. one who buys stock expecting its price to fall
9. income statement	i. the difference between what a firm owns and what it owes
10. leverage	j. the goods a business plans to sell and the materials used in their manufacture

Understanding What You Have Read

1. Corporations obtain most of the funds that they need for expansion from   (a) the sale of stocks   (b) the sale of bonds   (c) short-term borrowing   (d) their undistributed profits.

2. The holder of one share of stock in a corporation is   (a) a creditor of the corporation   (b) a debtor of the corporation   (c) an owner of the corporation   (d) an officer of the corporation.

3. The holder of a corporate bond is   (a) a creditor of the corporation   (b) a debtor of the corporation   (c) an owner of the corporation   (d) an officer of the corporation.

4. Preferred stock is like   (a) a bond in that the dividends must be paid regularly   (b) a bond in that the holder of the stock is a creditor of the corporation   (c) common stock in that dividends will increase as profits increase   (d) common stock in that there may be times when the board of directors decides to pay no dividends.

5. A corporation pays a dividend on its common stock   (a) every year   (b) when the interest becomes due   (c) whenever its board of directors votes to do so   (d) whenever it earns a profit.

6. Which statement is true?   (a) Every time people buy Microsoft stock, Microsoft receives money for new capital investment.   (b) Preferred stock is better than common stock.   (c) The main function of the SEC is to prevent stockholders from losing money on stock purchases.   (d) The higher the margin rate, the more difficult it is to buy stocks with borrowed funds.

7. To "buy on margin" means   (a) to buy long   (b) to buy over-the-counter   (c) to buy stocks in the hope of selling at a profit in the near future   (d) to buy stocks with borrowed funds.

8. When a corporate security is registered with the Securities and Exchange Commission, this means that   (a) the SEC has approved the security as a safe investment   (b) certain financial information has been filed with the SEC   (c) the SEC may act as a broker for the corporation   (d) the public may inquire of the SEC as to its opinion of the advisability of purchasing the security.

9. All of the following information is contained in a balance sheet, except   (a) assets   (b) liabilities   (c) net worth   (d) total sales.

10. Which information is contained in a corporation's income statement?   (a) net income   (b) accounts payable   (c) value of the firm's factory   (d) total liabilities.

Thinking Critically

1. Explain why you agree or disagree with the statement, "The fortunes of the stock market mirror how the people of the United States view their economy."

2. What arguments can you give for and against buying each of the following securities: (*a*) common stocks (*b*) preferred stocks (*c*) corporate bonds (*d*) government bonds.

3. When they are not selling new issues, those who sell Bell Atlantic, Gillette, and Sears Roebuck stocks on the New York Stock Exchange do not add new funds to these companies. Why, then, are the officers of these corporations concerned about fluctuations in the prices of their corporation's stock sold on the exchange?

4. Why is the over-the-counter market important in how corporations raise funds?

5. Some people invest for dividends, while others invest for capital growth. Explain the differences between the two types of investing and the advantages and disadvantages of each to an investor.

6. Why is it important for the wise investor to carefully study a corporation's financial statements before investing in that corporation? What are the limitations to the information in a corporation's financial statements?

SKILLS: Understanding Stock Market Transactions

1. On January 12, the following transactions took place:
   - Robert Allison, convinced that Dr. Pepper stock was undervalued, instructed his broker to buy 200 shares of it.
   - Margo Bromley, believing that Tenneco stock was undervalued, purchased 100 shares.
   - Patrick Chin thought that Wal-Mart was in for a bad year and ordered his broker to sell short 100 shares of its common stock.

   These transactions took place at the closing price for January 12:

Dr. Pepper	12¾
Tenneco	97½
Wal-Mart	35

   Three months later, Allison, Bromley, and Chin closed out their stock transactions at these prices:

Dr. Pepper	18½
Tenneco	90¼
Wal-Mart	70

a. Identify the bulls and the bears in these transactions.

b. How much money did each of the three speculators earn or lose? (Ignore commissions and taxes in calculating your answers.)

2. The Boswash Computer Company, Inc., has the following securities outstanding:

   $1 million in 10 percent bonds, due 2005

   2 million shares of common stock

Last year, the company's profits totaled $1.75 million after all interest payments had been made, including debt on the bonds. The board of directors voted to distribute $1 million to the common stockholders as dividends. (a) How much was paid in interest to the bondholders? (b) How much did a holder of 100 shares of common stock receive in dividends? (c) In connection with the bonds issued by the corporation, explain the meaning of "due 2005." (d) Suppose that next year Boswash Computer fails and the company is liquidated. After all the corporation's debts are paid, $1.2 million remains. How will this sum be divided?

Chapter 6

PRODUCTION AND PRODUCTIVITY

Overview

"*Oh, I remember when I was your age. Those were the good old days.*"

How often have you heard your grandparents or other older adults speak lovingly of times gone by as "the good old days"? To hear them tell it, the days of their childhood were ones of simple pleasures and abundance.

Perhaps things were better for some at an earlier time. Today, though, most people in the United States are living longer and enjoying more goods and services than the earlier generations ever did. We can illustrate this as follows:

☐ In 1914, the average factory workweek was 55 hours. Workers then were earning less than $16 per week (equivalent to approximately $239 today). Factory workers now work about 40 hours per week, for an average wage of more than $500.
☐ In the 1920s, it took an average factory worker more than 275 hours to earn enough to buy a clothes-washing machine and about 400 hours to buy a refrigerator. Today's factory worker earns enough to pay for a washing machine in about 40 hours and a refrigerator in about 50 hours.
☐ One hundred years ago, half the nation's population lived on farms. Today, fewer than 2 percent do so. Yet our farms are able to feed and clothe us, and much of the outside world as well.
☐ With a Gross Domestic Product of over $7 trillion, the United States is the world's greatest producer of goods and services.

In this chapter, we will discuss the meaning of production and productivity, how a firm organizes for production in order to maximize productivity, and the relation among production, productivity, and profit. We will also discuss how the U.S. economy's ability to outproduce other countries is a result of two economic factors: (1) the quantity and quality of its resources, and (2) its productivity. Finally, we will concentrate on farm productivity, and its consequences.

THE QUANTITY AND QUALITY OF PRODUCTIVE RESOURCES

In Chapter 1, we learned that the resources that go into the production of goods and services are land, labor, capital, and entrepreneurship. The United States is an incredibly wealthy nation and has an abundant supply of these resources.

Wealthy as it is, however, the U.S. economy cannot produce everything it needs. For that reason, nearly 20 percent of the goods and services we consume comes from abroad. Meanwhile, as the nations of the industrialized world increase their output, world supplies of natural resources have shrunk. This situation has made it increasingly important for all nations to find ways to get more out of those resources. Or, as economists prefer to say: to increase productivity.

Productivity measures the efficiency with which we produce goods and services. Because of increased farm productivity, 20th-century agricultural workers can produce over ten times as much food as their 19th-century counterparts. Similarly, productivity increases have enabled today's factory workers to produce more, in fewer hours, than did factory workers in years gone by.

Measuring Productivity

Productivity is the efficiency of a factor of production, measured in terms of units of output for every unit of input. For example, batting

Figure 6.1   People Fed by One U.S. Farmworker

1900	7
1950	16
Today	80

What does this graph say about productivity?

averages measure a baseball player's productivity as a hitter. A ball player whose batting average is .300 has made three hits (output) for every ten times at bat (input). By comparison, a .200 hitter made only two hits for every ten times at bat.

The measure most frequently used to gauge economic efficiency is *labor productivity*. This term is often expressed as the output per worker per hour.

Blair Chair Company manufactures folding chairs that are commonly used for picnics, barbecues, and other outdoor activities. The factory employs five workers and had been producing on average 160 chairs in an eight-hour day.

Under these circumstances, labor productivity at Blair Chair was four chairs per worker per hour. We have arrived at this figure with the following two mathematical operations:

- *160 chairs ÷ 8 hours = 20 chairs/hour*
- *20 chairs/hour ÷ 5 workers = 4 chairs/hour/worker*

Last week, executives of Blair Chair Company rearranged its plant's manufacturing process to make it more efficient. They found that they could improve productivity by 50 percent. What the Blair executives discovered was that under the new arrangement, the same number of workers could produce 240 chairs in an eight-hour day, or 6 chairs per worker per hour. Three mathematical operations showed this:

- *240 chairs ÷ 8 hours = 30 chairs/hour*
- *30 chairs/hour ÷ 5 workers = 6 chairs/hour/worker*
- *6 is 50 percent greater than 4 (6 ÷ 4 = 1½ = 150 percent of 4).*

ORGANIZING FOR PRODUCTION

As we discussed in Chapter 1, entrepreneurs bring together the factors of production in order to create a business enterprise. Since organizing and launching a business is costly, time-consuming, and difficult, one might ask, "Why do it? Why risk time, effort, and money in a venture that might very well fail?"

The answer can be summed up in one word: profits. Entrepreneurs do what they do (launch business ventures) in the hope that they will succeed and earn profits. Profits represent the difference between revenues and costs. For that reason, entrepreneurs try to combine the factors of production in such a way as to earn the greatest revenues at the least cost. Some of the things they need to consider in that effort are described in the following case study.

Lucille Miracle is an entrepreneur. She gathered together a group of wealthy investors who, along with her, put up enough money to set up a factory to manufacture a line of lanterns. (Customers use these battery-powered lanterns outdoors at night to cast a strong beam of light.) The venture became known as the "Miracle Lantern Company."

Lucille thought about the things she needed to get production under way. On a sheet of notepaper, she wrote:

THINGS TO CONSIDER

- *Factory: should we rent or buy?*
- *Machinery: given our budget, should we get the latest models (requiring a few highly skilled workers) or less complicated equipment (requiring a greater number of workers but who need not be so skilled)?*
- *Raw materials: should we buy enough to carry us through for a few years or reorder from week to week?*
- *Products: should we manufacture plastic and/or metal models? How many different models will we offer?*

After deciding which products to produce and where and how to produce them, Lucille remembered two more questions that needed to be added to her list:

- *Diminishing returns: when will they set in?*
- *Economies of large-scale production: when will "bigness" become a disadvantage?*

Law of Diminishing Returns

When we add additional factors of production such as workers or machinery, productivity usually increases. Eventually, though, we reach a point where the addition of inputs (in this instance, workers or machinery) has the opposite effect. That is, output per worker or machine will begin to decline. Economists describe this phenomenon as the *Law of Diminishing Returns.* The following example illustrates this law or principle.

With one worker, Miracle Lantern was able to produce 50 lanterns a day. By adding a second worker, total output grew to 110 lanterns. This increased output prompted the company to hire a third worker, with the result that 180 lanterns were completed. The production is summarized in Table 6.1.

Table 6.1 LANTERN OUTPUT WITH ONE TO THREE WORKERS

Number of Workers	Output per Day	Net Increase From Each Additional Worker	Output per Worker
1	50	50	50
2	110	60	55
3	180	70	60

As additional workers were added, both the total number of lanterns produced (output per day) and productivity (output per worker) increased. Let us see what happened when the company continued to add workers to this production line.

The Miracle Lantern Company continued the experiment by adding a fourth, fifth, sixth, and finally a seventh worker to its production line. The results were tallied and assembled in Table 6.2.

We can see from the tables that although the fourth worker increased total output from 180 to 240, average production per worker (i.e., productivity) remained unchanged at 60 lanterns. When the fifth worker was added, something different happened. Although total output continued to increase, output per worker declined to 56 units. This was Miracle Lantern Company's point of diminishing returns. Once diminishing returns began to set in, each additional worker added less to total output. Eventually, the continued addition of workers resulted in negative returns. This occurred with the hiring of the seventh worker. Then total output fell from 300 to 280 for the day—a reduction in total output.

Diminishing returns set in because as more and more variable

Table 6.2 LANTERN OUTPUT WITH FOUR TO SEVEN WORKERS

Number of Workers	Output per Day	Net Increase From Each Additional Worker	Output per Worker
4	240	60	60
5	280	40	56
6	300	20	50
7	280	-20	40

resources are added, less of the fixed resources are available for sharing. In the case of the Miracle Lantern Co., as more workers (the variable resource) were added, less of the fixed resources (machinery, tools, floor space, etc.) was available to each worker. Or, to put it another way: as more and more workers were added, the need to share machinery and tools resulted in a decline in productivity.

THE ECONOMICS OF "BIGNESS"

Maximum production under existing conditions at the Miracle Lantern factory was 300 units per day, as we can see in Table 6.2. To expand production beyond that would require additional resources, such as new or additional equipment or floor space.

In thinking about adding to its *capacity* (potential output), a firm must consider both the advantages and disadvantages of expansion or, as economists sometimes say, the *economies and diseconomies of scale*.

Advantages of Expansion

The principal reason for increasing a firm's output is to reduce unit costs or, to put it another way, to increase productivity. The following factors may contribute to increased output for larger companies.

Division of Labor, or Specialization. It is a rare factory worker who has a hand in the manufacture of a product from beginning to end. Were you to visit most large plants today, you would likely see workers involved solely in one or two stages of the total production process. For example, if you visited a plant that manufactured gasoline-powered lawn mowers, you might see one group of workers preparing motors for installation. A second group might be doing the electrical wiring, while a third might oversee the stamping and painting operations. Final assembly and packaging might be the responsibility of two other groups.

This breakdown of the total production process into a series of simpler tasks is known as *division of labor*, or specialization. Among the many advantages of specialization are the following:
(a) A worker need be trained to perform only one operation or process. Therefore, with this training, a worker can soon become highly skilled at one job.
(b) Because the task has been subdivided, it is easier to perform. In a television assembly factory, only a highly trained worker would be able to assemble an entire set. By dividing the tasks, however, the firm is able to hire less-skilled workers at lower wages.

(c) Supervisory and management responsibilities may also be subdivided with specialization. Like other workers, supervisors and managers will be able to attain a higher level of expertise in a few specialized tasks than they would if they were responsible for all production from beginning to end.

Quantity Discounts. Large firms can frequently obtain their raw materials at lower cost than small ones can. Suppliers are especially eager to keep their biggest customers and may offer discounts for quantity purchases.

Availability of Specialized Machinery. Large-scale production and the division of labor makes more practicable the use of specialized machinery. Large firms can more easily afford to purchase such machinery. For example, large automobile companies can afford to buy very expensive laser equipment to weld joints on automobile body frames. A small firm, however, cannot afford to do so.

Easier Access to Credit. Big businesses find it easier to borrow than do small ones. One reason is that the large firms are better known, and consequently lending institutions and the public are often more will-

What advantages of expansion do you see in this picture of a 19th-century Westinghouse foundry?

ing to lend them money. Also, their size makes them appear to be less of a risk. This easy access to capital funds makes it easier for large firms to expand their operations.

Research, Development, and By-Products. As businesses grow, they can afford to hire the best brains available to conduct elaborate research programs. Research has led to the development of many new products and methods of production. In addition, research leads to the discovery and development of *by-products*. These are goods produced along with the major items of production, often from materials that once may have been considered waste. For example, companies that process orange juice formerly discarded the orange peel. After industrial researchers discovered that orange peels could be made into fertilizer and feed, the juice industry began selling a profitable by-product. Big businesses are better able to invest in the equipment needed to produce by-products than are smaller ones. Large meat-packing companies, for example, have been able to produce glue, fertilizers, and soap by-products that smaller meat-packing firms could not afford to produce.

When Firms Get Too Big

As a firm grows, it may pass the point where the economies of large-scale production (the economies of scale) are effective. It reaches a point of diminishing returns. That is, the increase in income resulting from the firm's expansion will be less than its increased cost of operation (economists sometimes call this the *diseconomies of scale*).

Many of the giant firms in the United States—including General Motors, IBM, and AT&T—experienced the disadvantages of being too large in the early 1990s. General Motors, partly because of its size, had become inefficient and was spending more than many of its competitors to produce an automobile. In 1992, GM announced that it was going to reduce the size of its operations by closing plants and laying off workers. As a result of this downsizing and measures to reorganize and divide operations, GM once again became competitive. What GM and many other large companies realize is that they can expand only to the point where *unit production costs* (the average costs of producing an item) stop decreasing and begin to increase. This is the point where diminishing returns set in. In order to reverse this trend and bring down unit production costs, firms are likely to reorganize and divide operations. GM followed this course. By 1994, it had become a leaner but more profitable company.

Costs, Revenues, and Profits in the Process of Production

The principal goal of any business firm is to earn profits. For that reason, when given a choice of two or more production alternatives, a firm will select the alternative that it believes will result in the largest profits for the company. Economists describe the efforts to earn the greatest profits as *profit maximization.*

In order to maximize profits, one of the first things a firm must determine is the best level of production. "Why," you might ask, "doesn't a firm simply produce all it can?" The reason is that although profits are likely to increase for a time as output is increased, eventually a point will be reached at which profits will begin to decline.

In the discussion that follows, we will analyze (1) the reasons why the level of production affects profits, and (2) how economic analysis helps business managers determine the level of production that will give a company the greatest profit.

Recently, the management of Miracle Lantern Company became unhappy with company earnings. In an effort to increase profits, Miracle engaged a firm of economic consultants to analyze its operations and make recommendations for improvements.

The consultants found Miracle's production process to be a fairly simple one. A specially designed machine at one end of the assembly line stamped out lantern cases. After that, a conveyor belt moved parts past workers who assembled and prepared the finished products for shipment. An office staff attended to administrative chores (payroll, advertising, sales, etc.).

As indicated by Table 6.3 (Columns 1 & 2), output depends upon the number of workers employed on the assembly line. With one worker, the factory could produce 200 units a week. With two workers, output increased to 500 lanterns, and so on until a maximum of 1,490 units were turned out by eight workers. Beyond that number, output declined.

Consultants determined that Miracle's capacity is 1,490 units. A plant's *capacity* is the maximum number of units it can produce in the short run. To an economist, a *short run* refers to a period of time during which a factory operates with existing equipment. A *long run* is a period of time during which any or all of the factors of production could vary. For example, a factory could enlarge its plant and/or buy additional equipment. Under such new circumstances, Miracle could increase production beyond its present capacity. This process, however, would take some time to accomplish.

Table 6.3 also illustrates the effect of the law of diminishing returns. As we can see in Column 3, the addition

Table 6.3 COST, REVENUE, AND PROFIT POSSIBILITIES

MIRACLE LANTERN COMPANY

Laborers	Output	(Net Increase)	Total Fixed Costs	Total Variable Costs	Total Costs	Average Unit Costs Fixed	Average Unit Costs Variable	Average Unit Costs Total
Column 1	Column 2	Column 3	Column 4	Column 5	Column 6	Column 7	Column 8	Column 9
0	0	(0)	$2,000	$ 0	$2,000			
1	200	(200)	2,000	500	2,500	$10.00	$2.50	$12.50
2	500	(300)	2,000	1,000	3,000	4.00	2.00	6.00
3	900	(400)	2,000	1,500	3,500	2.22	1.67	3.89
4	1,150	(250)	2,000	2,000	4,000	1.74	1.74	3.48
5	1,275	(125)	2,000	2,500	4,500	1.57	1.96	3.53
6	1,375	(100)	2,000	3,000	5,000	1.48	2.22	3.70
7	1,450	(75)	2,000	3,500	5,500	1.38	2.41	3.79
8	1,490	(40)	2,000	4,000	6,000	1.34	2.68	4.02
9	1,480	(−10)	2,000	4,500	6,500	1.35	3.04	4.39

of the first, second, and third worker resulted in a net increase of 200, 300, and 400 units respectively. When a fourth worker was added, however, the increase in output diminished from previous increases. We can see, too, that the addition of a ninth worker marked the onset of negative returns, or losses.

At one point, the consultants examined Miracle's costs of production—both its fixed costs and its variable costs. *Fixed costs* are those that remain unchanged regardless of the number of units produced. These include rent, real estate taxes, and interest on loans. Miracle's fixed costs, those that the company had to meet whether it produced one lantern or a thousand, totaled $2,000 a week.

Variable costs are those that increase or decrease with the level of production. Variable costs include things like wages (because workers can be laid off when business is slow and rehired when it picks up again), raw materials, and electrical power to operate equipment. A detailed account of Miracle's variable costs, along with a number of other findings, is summarized in Table 6.3. Let us take a closer look at these figures.

Column #2 shows output—the total number of units produced weekly by the workers listed in Column #1. Total fixed costs are listed in Column #4. Variable costs, averaging $500 per worker, are summarized in Column #5. Total costs (Column #6) represent the sum of the variable

and fixed costs (listed in Columns #4 and 5).

Columns #7, 8, and 9 list the *average unit costs* of production. These were calculated by dividing the fixed, variable, and total costs of production by the number of units produced at each level of input.

Thus far, all we have been looking at has been the company's costs of production. As we have noted, however, a firm's primary goal is to earn a profit. Thus, the question uppermost in management's thoughts must be, "What level of production will yield the greatest profit?"

To answer that question, Miracle's consultants (and most economists) turn to *marginal analysis*. It is simply a way of looking at what happens to profits when a firm adds one more unit to the production process. In this instance, the consultants analyzed the effect of the addition of one more assembly-line worker on output, costs, and profits. As long as adding workers also adds to profits, it pays to do so. When the point is reached where adding a worker results in a reduction in profits, however, this person should not be hired.

In fact, a company will increase production only as long as the revenue that production generates is greater than what it costs the company to produce the additional output. Economists would say it this way: As long as marginal revenue remains greater than marginal costs, expanding output will add to a company's profits. *Marginal revenue (MR)* is the

Table 6.4 COST, REVENUE, AND PROFIT POSSIBILITIES

MIRACLE LANTERN COMPANY

Laborers	Output	Total Fixed Costs	Total Variable Costs	Total Costs	Average Unit Costs			Marginal Costs	Price (Marginal Revenue)	Total Revenue	Profits
					Fixed	Variable	Total				
Column 1	Column 2	Column 3	Column 4	Column 5	Column 6	Column 7	Column 8	Column 9	Column 10	Column 11	Column 12
0	0	$2,000	$ 0	$2,000							
1	200	2,000	500	2,500	$10.00	$2.50	$12.50	$ 2.50	$5.00	$1,000	(–)$1,500
2	500	2,000	1,000	3,000	4.00	2.00	6.00	1.67	5.00	2,500	(–)500
3	900	2,000	1,500	3,500	2.22	1.67	3.89	1.25	5.00	4,500	1,000
4	1,150	2,000	2,000	4,000	1.82	1.82	3.63	2.00	5.00	5,750	1,750
5	1,275	2,000	2,500	4,500	1.57	1.96	3.53	4.00	5.00	6,375	1,875
6	1,375	2,000	3,000	5,000	1.48	2.22	3.70	5.00	5.00	6,875	1,875
7	1,450	2,000	3,500	5,500	1.38	2.41	3.79	6.67	5.00	7,250	1,750
8	1,490	2,000	4,000	6,000	1.34	2.68	4.02	12.50	5.00	7,450	1,450

income from the production of one more unit. *Marginal cost (MC)* is the addition to costs resulting from the production of one extra unit.

Now we can answer the question, "What level of production will yield the greatest profit?" The answer is: the point at which marginal revenue equals marginal cost.

We can illustrate this concept in the case of the Miracle Lantern Company by referring to Table 6.4. The price at which Miracle sells its lanterns is $5 each. (See Column #10.) Since each additional lantern produced adds $5 to the firm's income, we can say that $5 represents the firm's marginal revenue. Its marginal costs, the costs of producing the *additional* lanterns, are summarized in Column #9.

We know that the Miracle Lantern Company is in business to make money. We have also learned that the company can produce 1,490 lanterns with its present equipment. If the company can sell whatever quantity it chooses to produce up to its present capacity, what level of production would you expect management to target?

If you said 1,275 units, you would be correct, because at that level the firm would earn the greatest profit. Table 6.4 shows that at an output of 1,275 lanterns, marginal costs are $5 and marginal revenue is also $5, giving Miracle a profit of $1,875. Now suppose Miracle were to increase production by hiring additional workers. What would happen to the company's profits? By looking at Table 6.4 once again, you can see that a sixth worker increases marginal costs to $6.67, while marginal revenue remains at $5. The result is that profits have not increased even though output and sales have. Adding still more workers will result in lower profits.

PRODUCTIVITY IN THE UNITED STATES

A country's standard of living improves when its supply of goods and services increases faster than its population. There are two ways a country can increase its supply of goods and services: (1) Its businesses can employ more factors of production, such as labor and capital; and (2) Its businesses can increase the productivity of the factors of production.

For years after 1870, the United States experienced increased productivity averaging about 2.25 percent. In the 1950s and 1960s, though, productivity grew much quicker—about 2.7 percent. Since 1973, however, the U.S. productivity increases have began to slip, sometimes dropping below 1 percent a year. It recovered somewhat—to about 2 percent a year—in the economic recovery of the 1990s, but economists are worried that it will decline again the next time the economy goes flat. Many economists believe that the United States will never regain the average levels of increases in productivity that it achieved in earlier decades.

Economists trying to understand why U.S. productivity increases are sometimes low believe that the reason is the low rate of capital investment in the United States as compared, for example, to rates of investment in Japan, Germany, and France. Capital investment encourages technological changes that can lead to improvements in productivity. It must be added that investment in "human capital" through education and training of the workforce will also contribute to increased productivity. In fact, the two go together: investing in technological change assumes also investing in workers capable of utilizing technological advances.

FARM PRODUCTION AND PRODUCTIVITY

Since 1929, the number of people working on farms has shrunk by two thirds, yet output has increased by more than 60 percent. Or, to put it another way: in 1940, the average farmer produced enough to feed 12 people. Today, one farmer produces enough to feed 80.

The increase in farm productivity is the result of advances in science and technology. Highly specialized equipment performs tasks that until recently could only have been performed by hand. As a result, modern farm workers can cultivate far more acreage than their predecessors. Similarly, improvements in fertilizers, pesticides, and seeds have enabled farmers to increase their output per acre (see Table 6.5).

Table 6.5 OUTPUT PER ACRE AND PERCENTAGE INCREASE FOR SELECTED CROPS

Crop	1946–1950 Annual Yield per Acre	1990 Yield per Acre	Percentage Increase
Wheat	16.9 bu	39.5 bu	116
Corn	37.0 bu	118.5 bu	220
Sorghums	19.2 bu	63.1 bu	229
Soybeans	20.4 bu	34.0 bu	67
Cotton	273 lbs.	656 lbs.	140
Potatoes	132 lbs.	293 lbs.	122

How does this photo explain why the farm population has declined?

Farmers, Profit Maximization, and the Level of Production

A company will increase production as long as marginal revenue remains greater than marginal costs. Earlier in this chapter, for example, we learned that the Miracle Lantern Company is capable of producing 1,490 lanterns but earns the greatest profit at a production level of 1,275 units. Thus, the management of Miracle Lantern will stop producing lanterns at 1,275 units. A farmer is an entrepreneur and, of course, is interested in maximizing profits. Unlike the management of Miracle Lantern Company, though, an individual farmer cannot control production so as to appreciably affect supply, demand, and price. There are reasons why this is true for farmers.

Inelastic Demand. Although people will buy more farm products at a lower price than at a higher one, there is a limit to how much any of us can eat (or would be willing to buy) at a particular time. For that reason, the demand for farm products is relatively inelastic. That is, the percentage change in quantity of food demanded will be less than the percentage change in price. For example, it is unlikely that your family will buy twice as much bread, milk, or lettuce if the prices for those products were reduced by half. Your family is likely to buy more bread, milk, and lettuce, but not enough to make up for the price decreases to farmers. For farmers, this has meant that in years when harvests were abundant and prices fell, so, too, did their incomes.

Inelastic Supply. When sales slump, manufacturers can reduce production by laying off workers and shutting down plants while, at the same time, maintaining prices. Similarly, when demand for products increases, manufacturers can increase their output accordingly. Farmers do not have these options. Once their crops are planted or the size of their herds established, there is little that farmers can do to increase or decrease production until the next season. For that reason, the supply of farm products are relatively inelastic.

As a result, farm prices often follow a boom or bust pattern. For example, with wheat prices unusually high at the end of a poor growing season, farmers are likely to increase their wheat acreage the following year. But if that year is also accompanied by good weather, yields will be higher than needed to satisfy demand, and prices will plummet.

Adding to their woes is the inability of individual farmers to affect prices. Wheat farmers have little choice but to plant as much as they can, even when prices are high. If they do not plant the corn, the prices will fall anyway because individual production decisions do not affect market prices. By not planting, the farmers would simply deny themselves a share of the wheat market.

Government and the Farmer

With much of Europe devastated by the First World War (1914–1918), U.S. farmers expanded production to feed the people of the affected countries. After the war ended, however, Europeans returned to their farms and fields and thereby increased agricultural production. Soon, U.S. farmers found themselves growing more than they could profitably sell. With the supply of farm products outrunning demand, farm prices fell in the 1920s.

The decline in farm prices continued until 1933 when the newly elected administration of President Franklin D. Roosevelt pushed through Congress a number of federal programs to help the farmer. Help came in the form of price supports, supply restrictions, and subsidies.

Price Supports. In the 1920s and 1930s, many farmers complained that the prices they were receiving for their products were too low. Thus, the federal government introduced a program of price supports for some (but not all) of their products. With *price supports*, the government set a floor on the selling price of selected farm products by offering to buy these products at the set prices. (Technically, the price supports involved a government loan to the farmers, but since the government often forgave the loans, the government's action constituted a purchase.)

Because the value of money fluctuates, fixed prices were helpful for a limited time only. Suppose, for example, that the government put a floor of $1 per bushel for corn during a period when the value of the dollar declined by 25 percent. By the end of this period, the $1 per bushel price would have declined in purchasing power by 25 cents. For that reason, government support programs tried to protect purchasing power rather than prices. This was achieved through the concept of *parity*, the price for commodities that would give farmers the purchasing power that farmers had during the years 1909–1914.

By way of illustration, let us assume that the average price of wheat between 1909–1914 was 50 cents a bushel. Let us also suppose that by 1990 the cost of living had increased by seven times. In those circumstances, it would have taken a wheat price of $3.50 a bushel in 1990 to equal its purchasing power in 1909–1914.

In most instances, the federal government supported prices at something less than 100 percent of parity. If in the above example government had chosen to support prices at 80 percent of parity, farmers would have been guaranteed $2.80 per bushel for their wheat that year ($3.50 x .80 = $2.80).

Look at Figure 6.2. Notice that the floor set by the government was usually higher than the equilibrium price. Because of this factor, farmers usually produced more than they could sell. This created surpluses. When this happened, the government stepped in to purchase and store the surplus products. Since the storing of farm surpluses was very costly, the government developed several programs to give the food away to the needy both at home and abroad.

Supply Restrictions. We have just learned that price supports often created surpluses. The easiest way to increase agricultural prices without creating surpluses was to reduce the supply of farm products. *Supply restrictions* were carried out through strategies such as acreage control and import restrictions.

1. Acreage-Control Programs. In the 1930s, the federal government began paying farmers who grew certain crops to withhold a specified number of acres from planting. In this way, it was hoped, production of those crops would decrease and prices would rise. By 1983, this program had become so large that U.S. farmers were withholding more acreage than all the farmers of Western Europe were planting.

Figure 6.2 Government Price Floors Result in Surpluses

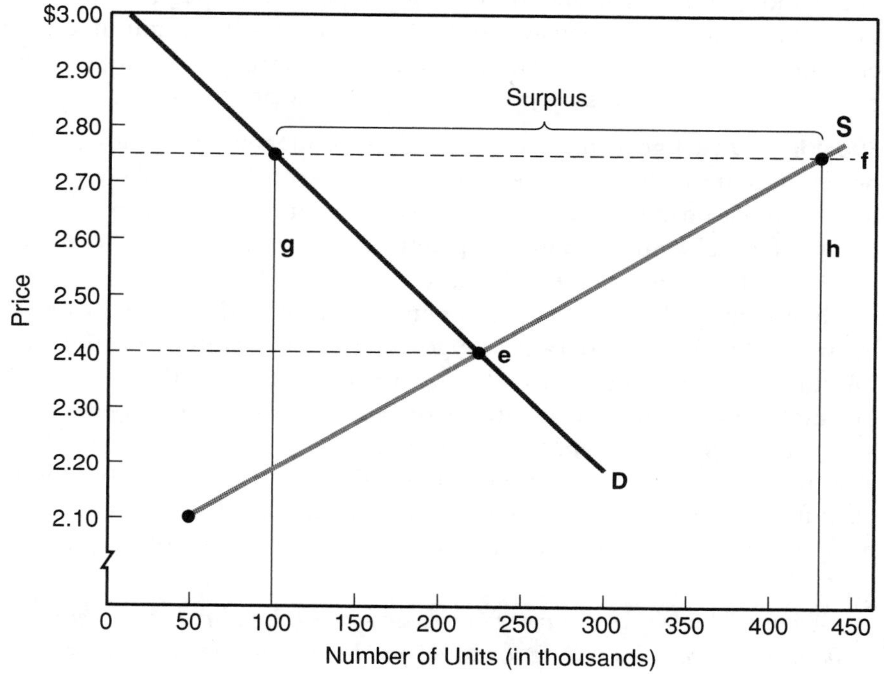

The U.S. Government has set a floor price of $2.75 per bushel (f). This price is well above the equilibrium price of $2.40 (e). At $2.75, sellers will provide 430,000 bushels (h), but buyers will only take 100,000 bushels (g). The difference between the two, 330,000 bushels (h minus g), represents the surplus of unsold products. Since there will not be enough demand to clear the market, the U.S. government will have to buy up the farm surplus at the floor price.

2. Import Restrictions. The supply of farm products is also limited through *import restrictions*. The federal government sets a limit, or possibly an outright ban, on the importation of certain foreign farm products. With these restrictions, the government forces U.S. consumers to purchase mainly domestic farm products. In this way, consumers help reduce the accumulation of farm surpluses in the United States. This policy, however, has a downside for U.S. consumers. It keeps prices for those products produced at home artificially high.

One of the biggest beneficiaries of import quotas and price supports has been the sugar industry. The world price of sugar is about half of that paid to U.S. growers of sugar cane and sugar beets. Were it not for the protection afforded by import quotas and support prices, sugar growing would all but disappear as an industry in the United

States. Industrial users of sugar in the United States, such as soft drink and candy manufacturers, oppose supporting U.S. sugar growers. Since sugar is more expensive in the United States, U.S. manufacturers who use sugar in their products claim that they are at a competitive disadvantage with overseas producers of similar products.

Subsidies. Direct government payments to producers of certain goods or services are called *subsidies*. The U.S. government has used subsidies to assist farmers in a variety of ways. In one program, for example, the federal **Department of Agriculture** reimbursed farmers for a portion of their fertilizer expenses.

For a while, the federal government used *target pricing* to subsidize farmers. Under this program, the government guaranteed participating farmers a minimum price for their crops. Farmers then sold the products to the public at whatever price the market would bear. The government paid farmers the difference, if any, between the market and the target price. A major advantage of target pricing was that total output was sold in the open market. Consequently, government did not have to deal with the expenses of storing and disposing of surpluses.

Assume that the target price of wheat was $4.35 a bushel. At the same time, wheat was selling for $2.95 per bushel on the open market. Farmer Jones sold 10,000 bushels of wheat on the open market, for which he was paid $29,500. Jones also received a check from the government for $14,000 to make up for the difference between the target and market prices.

Farming in the 1980s and 1990s

In the 1930s, 25 percent of the U.S. population lived on farms, but farming accounted for only 10 percent of the GDP. Farmers were among the poorest segment of the population. By way of helping farmers, the federal government enacted the programs just described.

In the 1980s and 1990s, changing conditions on the farm and different political priorities prompted many Americans to call for a revision of the government's agricultural policies. It was time, they said, for "market forces" (i.e. supply and demand) to replace government intervention in the market for farm products. What were the forces that prompted the call for government's new agricultural policies?

Budget Deficits. As we will learn in Chapter 19, by the early 1990s the national debt had gotten very high. Politicians from all political camps were calling for balanced federal budgets. They looked at the costly federal agricultural programs as one area where spending cuts could be made.

Figure 6.3   Changes in U.S. Farming

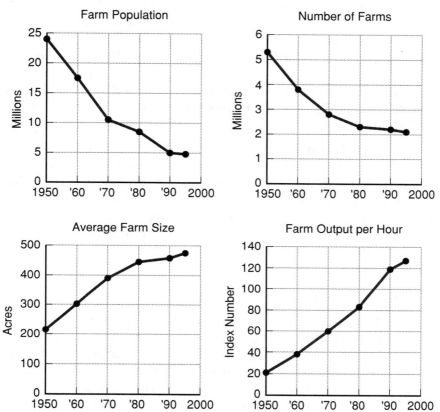

Agriculture's Declining Clout. When 25 percent of the population lived on farms, farmers (and the people who did business with them) had much political clout. By the 1990s, less than 2 percent of the population lived on farms, and farming accounted for less than 2 percent of the GDP. Moreover, only a small fraction of the 2.1 million farms accounted for almost all farm production. These are large operations that are run as large-scale business enterprises.

Growth in International Trade. Productivity gains in agriculture fueled enormous growth in exports. In the 1930s, only 8 percent of U.S. wheat production was exported; by the mid-1990s, over 50 percent of this crop was exported. Similarly, corn exports have gone from less than 2 percent of production to more than 25 percent. But exports are highest in a climate of free trade, which means fewer restriction on the importation of foreign agricultural products and reduced levels of price supports given to products sold abroad.

The Average Farmer Is No Longer Poor. In the 1930s, farmers earned about one-third less than other Americans. Price-support programs were intended to raise the incomes of farmers. By the mid-1990s, however, those farmers receiving government benefits were better off than the average American. Moreover, two-thirds of farm benefit programs went to the largest 18 percent of farms—even though their average income was triple that of the typical U.S. household. Only a small fraction of the 2 million farms accounted for most of the total farm production.

Environmental Concerns. The environmental costs of farming have increased. Modern farmers use more artificial fertilizers and pesticides, which often run off the soil and pollute waterways. The pollutants also enter underground sources of drinking water. Agricultural expansion has also been a major cause of wetlands losses. Wetlands protect regions against floods, help purify water, and are important places for wildlife to live.

New Legislation

In 1996, Congress passed a revolutionary new farm bill that seeks to reduce drastically the extent of government intervention in farming by the year 2002. First of all, the new law replaces fluctuating payments to farmers (price supports) with a fixed subsidy that will run out in 2002. Regardless of what happens to the price of farm crops, affected farmers will receive a predetermined subsidy for seven years.

Secondly, the act, labeled "Freedom to Farm," gives farmers a number of options. They will no longer have to keep land idle or grow a specific crop in order to qualify for subsidies. Instead, they can grow the crops of their choice, grow nothing at all, or turn their farmland into pastures. The new law rewards farmers for diversifying their planting in response to market demand. The act calls for the market, rather than government, to dictate what crops are planted.

A third aspect of the new law is the elimination of the big grain reserves that have been characteristic of previous farm programs. Opponents of the new law point out that grain storage saved producers (and, indirectly, consumers) billions of dollars by making grain available at reasonable prices for cattle feed and cereal production during periods of drought.

While there is much support for such reforms, many Americans worry that, after 2002, farmers will have a hard time meeting expenses. If so, farm families might experience a general decline in their incomes. Under pressure from rural constituents, Congress may have to revert back to the price support programs of earlier years.

Summary

The United States is able to produce so much because it is fortunate to have abundant resources. In addition, resources in the United States are used efficiently. Productivity, the ability to use resources, is measured in terms of units of output for every unit of input. Entrepreneurs try to combine the factors of production in order to earn the greatest profits. Often, increasing output results in increased productivity. At some point, however, diminishing returns set in. Profit maximization depends on the level of production and productivity. Economists make use of marginal analysis to determine the most efficient level of production in terms of maximizing profits.

REVIEWING THE CHAPTER

Building Vocabulary

Match each term in Column A with its definition in Column B.

COLUMN A	COLUMN B
1. capacity	*a.* the breaking down of production into simpler tasks
2. variable costs	*b.* the maximum amount that can be produced in the short run
3. labor productivity	*c.* a price that will give farmers the same purchasing power from the sale of crops that farmers had during the years 1909–1914
4. division of labor	
5. parity	
6. Law of Diminishing Returns	*d.* efforts to earn the greatest profit
	e. a way of looking at profits when a firm adds one more unit to the production process
7. fixed costs	*f.* output per worker per unit of time
8. marginal analysis	
9. profit maximization	*g.* costs that increase or decrease with the level of production
10. marginal revenue	*h.* the point beyond which adding variable inputs to fixed resources results in decreased productivity
	i. the income from the production of one more unit
	j. costs that remain unchanged regardless of the number of units produced

Understanding What You Have Read

1. As a result of our nation's increasing productivity, (a) most goods are cheaper than they were years ago (b) more goods are available per person than years ago (c) goods are made better by machine than they were by hand (d) output per employee per hour has decreased.

2. Before modernizing, the Chelsea Video Games Company employed 20 workers and produced 200 games a day. After modernizing, the company laid off 5 workers and is now producing 300 games a day. As a result of modernization, productivity at the Chelsea plant (a) doubled (b) increased by 50 percent (c) remained the same (d) declined.

3. Which of the following is *least* likely to result in increased productivity? (a) efficient use of natural resources (b) employee training programs (c) improved machinery (d) working overtime.

4. When the point of diminishing returns is reached as workers are added to a production line, (a) total revenue will decline (b) output per employee will decline (c) total profits will decline (d) the factory should hire more workers.

5. The best way to increase productivity in a plant is to (a) employ all the factors of production more efficiently (b) keep hiring more workers (c) keep hiring more plant managers (d) increase output.

6. Which of the following is an example of a fixed cost? (a) rent (b) electricity to power machinery (c) commission on sales (d) raw materials.

7. In industries with high overhead costs, increasing production tends to lower (a) return on investment (b) total variable costs (c) overhead cost per unit (d) total operating costs.

8. The Kilroy Bicycle Company has fixed annual costs of $100,000 and variable costs of $10 per bicycle. If output is increased from 5,000 to 10,000 bicycles per year, the total cost of producing each bicycle will be reduced from $30 to (a) $25 (b) $20 (c) $15 (d) $10.

9. The Clamalot Seafood Company was considering the purchase of an additional automatic packaging machine for its frozen fried clams line. Studies revealed that the new machine would increase output but would also increase the cost per package. The company would most likely (a) purchase the machine because it would require fewer workers (b) not purchase the machine because it would result in increased costs per package (c) purchase the machine because it would result in increased output (d) not purchase the machine because it increased productivity.

10. Which of the following is an example of a disadvantage to a company of getting too big? A company (*a*) goes out of business because of decreased demand for its product (*b*) becomes so large that it has to expand into new quarters (*c*) finds that it is spending more on new managers than it is earning in additional profits (*d*) is receiving more orders than it can fill.

11. With respect to agriculture in the United States, which one of the following was the cause of the other three? (*a*) parity payments to farmers (*b*) scientific and mechanized methods of farming (*c*) overproduction of farm products (*d*) decline in the farm population.

12. When harvests are good, farmers may experience difficulty in selling their crops because (*a*) prices will rise and consumers will therefore buy less (*b*) the reduction in prices might not result in a corresponding increase in the consumption of farm products (*c*) consumers buy less when the prices of farm products fall (*d*) the demand for farm products is highly elastic.

Thinking Critically

Table 6.6 AUTOMOBILE BATTERY PRODUCTION

Number of Workers	Output per Day	Output per Worker	Net Increase From Each Worker
1	50	50	50
2	120	60	70
3	210		
4	260		
5	300		
6	330		
7	350		
8	360		
9	351		

1. After acquiring the equipment for the production of automobile batteries, a manufacturer hired one worker to operate it. This resulted in a day's production of 50 batteries. The next day, the manufacturer hired a second worker, and total output rose to 120 batteries. Continuing the procedure, the manufacturer found that three workers could produce 210 units. Eventually, the manufacturer hired a total of nine workers. Table 6.6 gives partial data on the company's productivity. (*a*) Complete the table. (*b*) At what number of workers did the operation reach the point of diminishing returns? (*c*) At what number of workers did the manufacturer reach negative returns? (*d*) What additional information

would be necessary in order to determine how many workers the manufacturer should employ?

2. A manufacturer of motorcycle batteries has a plant capacity of 100,000 batteries per year. Overhead costs are $500,000 per year, in addition to which there are variable costs of $10 for each unit produced. Sales have been running at 50,000 units per year at a wholesale selling price of $25. Recently, a large mail-order department store offered to purchase an additional 50,000 batteries a year, which it would market under its own name. The store offered to pay the manufacturer $20 per battery. (*a*) Assuming that 50,000 units continue to be sold to the other customers at $25 each, should the manufacturer accept the offer? Explain. (*b*) Suppose that the department store offered to buy the entire output of 100,000 batteries at $15 per battery. Should the manufacturer accept the offer? Explain.

3. The federal government's program of farm assistance has long been a source of discussion and debate. (*a*) Explain *three* reasons that were advanced to justify federal assistance to farmers. (*b*) Explain *three* arguments advanced in criticism of these programs. (*c*) Explain why Congress passed a "Freedom to Farm" bill in 1996.

4. Sugar growers in the United States argue that they need protection from overseas sugar producers. Candy, soft drink producers, and other industrial users of sugar disagree, arguing that sugar prices in this country are kept artificially high. High sugar prices here make it difficult for U.S. firms that use sugar in their products to compete with foreign producers. Similar arguments might be heard about other farm products. Explain why you agree or disagree that farmers should be protected from overseas competition.

SKILLS: Interpreting Tables and Working With Data

1. According to the data contained in Table 6.3 on page 127, (*a*) when did Miracle reach the point of *diminishing returns*? (*b*) what happened to average fixed costs per unit as output increased from 900 to 1,450 lanterns?

2. According to the data given in Table 6.4 on page 129, (*a*) how many workers would be needed to give Miracle the greatest profit? (*b*) what would happen to profits if output were increased from 900 to 1,275 lanterns per week? (*c*) what would happen to profits if output were increased beyond 1,275 lanterns per week?

3. What would Miracle Lantern Company have to do if it wanted to increase output while maximizing profits beyond 1,490 lanterns per week?

Chapter 7

COMPETITION AND MONOPOLY

Overview

"I do not believe it. I don't care if she is my teacher."

"You don't believe what?"

"My economics teacher said that eggs and breakfast cereals are sold in different kinds of markets. C'mon—it just so happens that I work in a supermarket after school, and I know that we sell breakfast cereals and eggs. She's wrong. They're sold in the same market."

"You know what the problem is? You're talking about a store. She's talking about an economic market."

Perhaps some of us, too, are confused about the term "market." It might become somewhat clearer if we understand that a market is simply any place or process in which buyers and sellers exchange goods and services. For example, farmers, wholesalers, and retailers are engaged in the production and distribution of eggs—from hens to people—in the egg market. Similarly, those employed in the manufacture, storage, and sales of breakfast cereals comprise the market for breakfast cereals.

All markets are similar in one respect: they are made up of buyers and sellers. But the numbers of buyers and sellers (and their ability to control prices) differ from one market to another.

In this chapter, we will discuss the range of situations between *pure competition* (with its many buyers and sellers and a free flow of information) and *monopoly* (in which one supplier controls the entire output of a good or service). We will also discuss types of business combinations (past and present), laws that regulate business combinations and encourage competition, and some of the pros and cons of big business today.

TYPES OF MARKETS

In Chapter 3, we described pure competition. In this largely theoretical situation, market price is determined exclusively by the forces of supply and demand. While the concept of pure competition provides us with a useful framework for understanding market situations, it does not describe most everyday buying and selling activities. The prices we pay for food, clothing, entertainment, and everything else that goes into daily living are not set in a fully competitive market. Instead, they are subject to some kind of competition.

The kinds of markets that exist vary all the way from pure competition, in which there are many buyers and sellers, to monopoly, in which there is but one seller. A market in which there is but a single buyer is known as a *monopsony*. For example, as the sole buyer of certain kinds of military hardware, the U.S. government exercises monopsony power in that market.

The term *market power* refers to the power of buyers and sellers to influence prices. In a perfectly competitive market such as the egg market, there are so many buyers and sellers that no one buyer or seller has the power to set the prices. However, in a market where there is but one major producer of a product, sellers have considerably more market power.

Economists use the term *imperfect competition* to describe markets where there is neither pure competition nor pure monopoly. Imperfect competition may be further subdivided into (1) *monopolistic competition* and (2) *oligopoly*. The following pages show the range of markets extending from perfect competition to monopoly.

Pure Competition

In Chapter 3, we discussed how the interaction of supply and demand affects prices. The laws of supply and demand apply only to the market structure of pure competition. All the following conditions must prevail in order for pure competition to exist:

- There are many buyers and sellers acting independently. No single buyer or seller is big enough to affect the market price.
- Competing products offered for sale are virtually identical, so that buyers do not care from whom they buy.
- Buyers and sellers are fully informed about prices, quality, and sources of supply.
- Firms can enter and leave the market at will.

The market for eggs resembles pure competition for the reasons just cited. In this market, there are many buyers and sellers; competing products are almost identical; buyers and sellers are well informed; and it is relatively easy to go into the egg business.

Those who sell in competitive markets are sometimes called *price takers*, because they take whatever price they can get. They have no control over the price they receive for their wares. Once suppliers begin to exercise control over prices, imperfect competition exists.

Monopolistic Competition

Most people who own motor vehicles are likely to prefer to use one service station above all others. The quality of the service, the location, or some other reason may account for their preferences and willingness, perhaps, to pay a little more for the service. What is true for service stations for some people may also apply to restaurants, shoe stores, local grocery stores, and other local retail shops. That is, these businesses offer goods or services that are available elsewhere, at similar (but not necessarily identical) prices.

Gasoline service stations, groceries, and shoes are but a few of the goods and services sold under conditions of *monopolistic competition*. Monopolistic competition contains the following characteristics:

- Product differentiation
- Many sellers who produce similar products that the buyer believes differ in some qualities.

It is fairly easy to start a business selling haircuts, shoes, or groceries. For that reason, there are many of these businesses. Nevertheless, despite the competition (and the fact that the products or services they sell are nearly identical to those of their competitors), these sellers have some control over prices. In each of these examples, *product differentiation* gives suppliers the power to influence prices.

Product differentiation refers to whatever it is that gives buyers the impression that virtually identical products are different. Brand names, advertising campaigns, packaging, and the quality of services are the kinds of things that make one product more attractive to buyers than another virtually identical product. In addition, consumers may prefer one product over a similar product because of family tradition or personal loyalty.

As an example of product differentiation, let us consider aspirin. Because all companies that make aspirin use the same general formula, one brand is about the same as another. Yet supermarkets and drug stores regularly stock a half dozen or so brands of aspirins. The best-selling brand of aspirin is often the most expensive. Apparently more people believe that Brand X will relieve their aches and pains better than any other brand will, even though all brands are essentially the same. In this example, a brand name gives Brand X product differentiation from all other brands of aspirin sold. The producers of Brand X are able to charge more than their competitors because they have, in effect, a minor monopoly with their product. Through advertising, they have been able to convince consumers that their product is unique. Of course, what is true in the case of aspirin is also true for other products with brand names.

Joan Robinson

When the English economist **Joan Robinson** (1903–1983) began her studies of the market system, economists generally believed that eventually all trade would take place under conditions of "perfect (pure) competition." According to the theory of perfect competition, no individual buyer or seller could become big enough to determine prices. The lure of profits, economists assumed, would always attract competition, and for that reason monopoly would not long survive.

Although the theory worked on paper, perfect competition simply did not exist in real life. Much of the world's trade was being carried on by giant monopolies and oligopolies, whose conduct did not match that of the perfect competition model. Robinson demonstrated this disparity between theory and reality in *The Economics of Imperfect Competition* (1933).

Joan Robinson wrote this book shortly after she joined the faculty of Cambridge University, where she had been a student. In outlining her theory of imperfect competition, Robinson demonstrated how product differentiation and consumer preferences gave certain companies the ability to manipulate prices despite the presence of competing firms. In other words, under imperfect competition, giant firms gained "monopolistic powers."

In Robinson's view, monopolistic competition posed a threat to society as a whole. By restricting production in order to maintain unnecessarily high prices, monopolists deprived the public of the goods and services it might otherwise have enjoyed. Worse still, she went on, fewer goods and services resulted in fewer jobs, declining income, and less consumption. In other words, the end result would be economic recession. Robinson called for vigorous regulation of the economy by the national government as a way of preventing what she viewed as abuses of the market system.

Although many economists disagreed with her conclusions, Joan Robinson continued to work on the central economic questions of the day until her death. She helped elucidate John Maynard Keynes' economic theory (discussed in Chapter 17) in her *Introduction to the Theory of Employment* (1937), discussed overall economic growth in *The Accumulation of Capital* (1956), and authored *Economic Philosophy* (1962) and *Introduction to Modern Economics* (1973).

When, because of product differentiation, consumers perceive some goods or services to be better than the competition, sellers of those items are able to charge more. How was Ivory differentiated from other brands of soap?

Oligopoly

A market in which a few sellers produce all or most of the supply of a product is called an *oligopoly*. The breakfast food industry provides an example. A handful of large corporations dominates the industry. While it is fairly expensive to build a cereal-processing plant, it takes millions more in advertising and other expenses to persuade the public to try a new cereal product. Other examples of industries dominated by oligopolies would include those that manufacture automobiles, chewing gum, electrical appliances, steel, cement, and aluminum. An oligopoly has the following characteristics:

- Few sellers that produce almost identical products (such as the aluminum, steel, and chemical industries)
- Few sellers that produce differentiated products (such as the industries that make automobiles, breakfast cereals, and soft drinks).

Competition Within Industries Dominated by Oligopolies. Industries operating under conditions of oligopoly are usually dominated by a handful of giant producers. Executives in every firm know that if they should cut prices, other firms in the industry will also reduce their prices. Therefore, all that cutting prices would accomplish is to reduce everyone's profits. For that reason, oligopolies try to avoid price competition. Instead of relying on competition, prices for products of oligopolies are the result of product differentiation and, in some instances, *collusion* and *price leadership*.

1. Product Differentiation. Industries that make cement, steel, or paper clips produce products that are virtually identical with those of their competitors. Thus, product differentiation is minimal. Still, USX Corp., for example, does try to convince buyers that its steel products are better or different from those of its competitors. Other oligopolistic industries, such as those that produce electrical appliances, automobiles, and soft drinks, do lend themselves better to product differentiation. Ford Motor Co. goes to great expense to convince the public that its automobiles are different from, and better, than those of Chrysler Corporation, General Motors, and foreign auto companies. Coca Cola, Dr. Pepper, and Pepsi do much the same in the soft drink industry, as does Maytag and General Electric in the appliance industry.

2. Collusion. Since there are so few competing firms in an oligopolistic market, there is a great temptation to limit competition by setting prices and dividing the market among these few firms. Agreements to limit competition (known as *collusion*), however, are illegal. Therefore, oligopolistic firms adopt strategies other than collusion to accomplish the same goal (to fix prices) and, hopefully, evade prosecution. One such strategy is price leadership.

3. Price Leadership. This term refers to a practice by which the most powerful company in an industry sets its price, and every other firm follows suit. Price leadership, like collusion, is illegal. As an example of price leadership, consider the following case involving eight airlines.

U.S. CHARGES 8 AIRLINES IN FARE-FIXING SCHEME

WASHINGTON, DC, Dec. 21, 1992 The Justice Department accused the country's 8 largest airlines with using their computerized reservation systems to fix air fares.

The complaint said that by listing future fare changes in the computer, other firms were able to follow suit while, at the same time, acting as if it were their idea. Without admitting or denying the accusation, several airlines agreed to end the practice.

Price leadership, you will note, is very similar to collusion. With price leadership, though, there is no need for a formal agreement to set prices among competing firms.

Monopoly

A *monopoly* is a firm that controls the entire supply of a good or service. The word also describes a market in which:

1. There is a single supplier. As the only supplier, the firm controls both the supply and the price of a product.
2. There are no close substitutes for the product that the single supplier sells. This is the case, for example, with firms that provide local electrical service.
3. It would be extremely difficult for any other firm to enter the industry for the following reasons:

- High Costs. The costs of entering certain businesses are so high as to make it extremely difficult for others to do so.
- Exclusive Ownership of a Resource. Before the 1950s, the Aluminum Company of America (ALCOA) controlled virtually all the bauxite (aluminum ore) produced in the United States. This gave ALCOA a monopoly over the aluminum market for years.
- Legal barriers (such as patents, copyrights, and public franchises).

Patents (issued by the federal government) give the inventors of new products the exclusive right to market their inventions or sell the patents. Recently, Chrysler Corporation—one of the nation's "Big Three" automobile manufacturers—was ordered to pay $18.7 million to the inventor of a time-delay windshield wiper. Federal courts ruled that Chrysler had used the electronic intermittent wiper design without properly compensating the inventor, who held a patent on it.

Copyrights give similar rights to authors, musicians, and artists. The federal government grants patents and copyrights as ways of stimulating innovation, cultural achievements, and scientific progress. By placing limits on the number of years that patents and copyrights are in effect, however, the law prevents the subsequent monopolies from becoming permanent.

Public franchises are licenses granted by governments to do business within their jurisdictions. Public franchises create monopolies because they exclude other firms from competing with the franchisees. The cable television companies serving local communities provide examples of public franchises. Other examples are public utilities (including privately owned electric, gas, and mass transit companies). These utilities do not lend themselves to competition. You can imagine the chaos that would follow if competing bus lines had to race each other to pick up waiting passengers.

Utilities and other public franchises are monopolies. For that reason, government agencies protect the public by overseeing the work these monopolies do and regulating their prices.

THE ECONOMICS OF MONOPOLY POWER

Large, unregulated monopolies have all but disappeared from the U.S. economy. *Monopoly power* remains, however. This term refers to the ability of a group of firms to behave as if it were one big monopoly. The exercise of monopoly power by big business has been a controversial issue for many years. In examining the problem of monopoly power, we will (1) explain what it is, (2) describe its impact on output and prices, and (3) summarize governmental efforts to regulate it.

Measuring Monopoly Power: The Concentration Ratio

Strictly speaking, a monopoly exists when there is but a single seller of a good or service. As a practical matter, however, most large firms operate under terms of imperfect competition. That is, they conduct business in markets in which there is at least some competition.

Monopoly power is directly related to a firm's control over supply. If two or three firms control nearly all of an industry's output, they

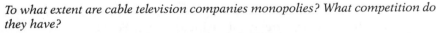
To what extent are cable television companies monopolies? What competition do they have?

have a great deal of monopoly power. Selling new automobiles, for example, is highly competitive. But because a relatively few big companies control the supply of new automobiles, they alone determine total output and, therefore, price. However, where there are many competitive firms (none of which control a large share of the market) monopoly power is not a factor.

As a way of measuring the extent to which monopoly power exists in imperfectly competitive markets, economists devised the *concentration ratio*. This ratio is the percentage of an industry's total output produced by its four largest firms. (See Table 7.1.) If an industry consists of four or fewer firms, its concentration ratio is equal to 100. This number indicates a high degree of monopoly power. In contrast, industries with a concentration ratio of 10 or less are unlikely to have monopoly power.

Some economists define oligopoly as an industry with a concentration ratio of 50 percent or more (that is, one in which 50 percent of the industry's output is in the hands of four or fewer corporations). For example, while there are some 22 manufacturers of breakfast cereals, the industry has a concentration ratio of 85 percent. In other words, the four largest producers of breakfast cereals account for 85 percent of the industry's sales. Only 15 percent of the market remains to be shared by the remaining 18 or so processors. We can say, therefore, that the breakfast cereal industry (1) falls within our definition of an oligopoly, and (2) exercises considerable monopoly power.

Similarly, economists generally classify industries with a concentration ratio of 25 percent or less as monopolistically competitive markets. With over 5,000 manufacturers and a concentration ratio of 6 percent, the women's dress industry easily falls into this category.

Concentration ratio can be misleading at times. For instance, one might think that the camera and film industry in the United States

Table 7.1 COMPETITION IN SELECTED INDUSTRIES

Industry	*Concentration Ratio*
Lead	99%
Cameras and film	98%
Razor blades	98%
Chewing gum	97%
Household refrigerators	94%
Breakfast cereals	85%
Men's and boys' shirts	19%
Book publishing	17%
Women's dresses	6%
Concrete blocks and bricks	4%

(with a ratio of 98 percent) has enormous monopoly power. This is not the case, though, because the figure excludes the powerful Japanese and German camera and film companies that sell in the United States. Because of these foreign firms, the camera and film industry in the United States is actually quite competitive.

At the opposite end of the scale is the concrete block and brick industry with a concentration ratio of only 4 percent. Although no concrete block firm dominates the national market, more often than not producers have considerable monopoly power in their local communities. Why? The reason is that shipping costs make it uneconomical for a customer to buy concrete blocks from distant suppliers.

THE EFFECT OF MONOPOLY POWER ON OUTPUT AND PRICES

Under pure competition, individual sellers cannot affect the market price. Sellers have the choice of either taking the going price for their wares or staying out of the market. If, for example, a seller owns 100 shares of AT&T stock on a day when the market price is $85, that seller would have the option to sell anywhere from 0 to 100 shares at $85 per share.

Output and Prices in Monopolized Markets

We have said that in perfectly competitive markets, sellers are "price takers." That is, they must either take the equilibrium price ($85 per share in our example) or drop out of the market. Under monopoly conditions, the opposite is true: sellers are "price setters." Since they are the sole source of supply, monopolists can select any price along the demand curve for their product simply by adjusting their output. As with any demand curve, the quantity demanded will decline as the price increases. This will now become clearer as we discuss how monopolies maximize profits.

How Monopolists Maximize Profits

What price will monopolists select? The highest they can think of? The lowest? Neither. Like everyone else, monopolists try to maximize their profits. That is, they will select the price and level of output that will yield them the greatest profit.

ABC Pharmaceuticals, Inc., holds the patent and, therefore, a monopoly on the manufacture of Itchaway. Itchaway claims to be the nation's most effective treatment for athlete's foot. After an extensive market survey, ABC's economists prepared an analysis of the demand

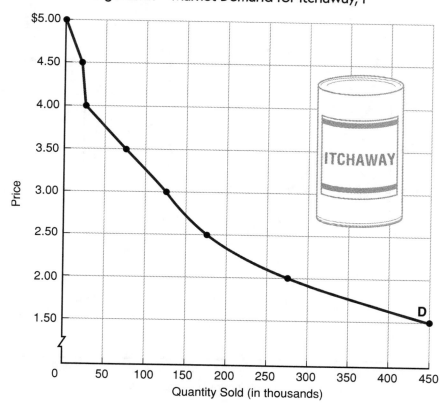

Figure 7.1   Market Demand for Itchaway, I

for Itchaway, along with a breakdown of production costs. Their find-ings are summarized in Figure 7.1 and Table 7.2.

After being given the results of the market survey and the produc-tion data, ABC's management selected a selling price of $3 per can. Why did management choose this price? By studying Table 7.2, we can

Table 7.2   ABC PHARMACEUTICALS PRICE-SALES ANALYSIS

At a price per can	we could sell this number of cans	gross income of	minus costs of	would leave us with a profit of
$5.00	5,000	$ 25,000	$ 60,000	–$ 35,000 (loss)
4.50	20,000	90,000	85,000	5,000
4.00	25,000	100,000	88,000	12,000
3.50	75,000	262,500	163,000	99,500
3.00	125,000	375,000	206,000	169,000
2.50	175,000	432,500	300,000	169,000
2.00	275,000	550,000	500,000	50,000
1.50	450,000	675,000	837,000	–162,000 (loss)

Figure 7.2   Market Demand for Itchaway, II

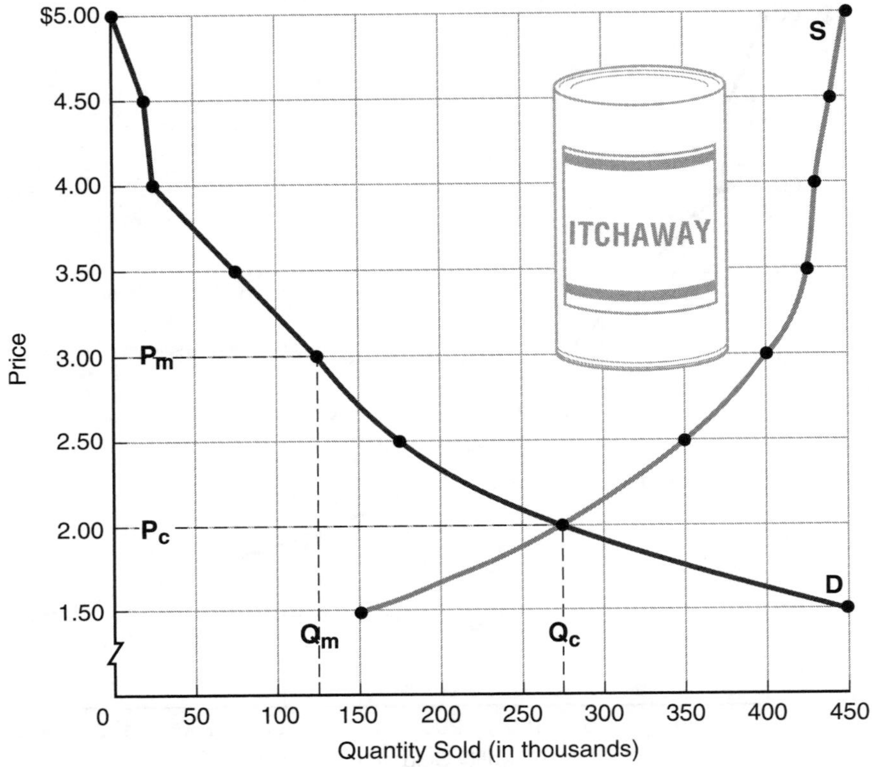

see that ABC's maximum profit—$169,000—corresponds to a price of $3 per can. Since ABC Pharmaceuticals is a monopoly, management can set production at any level it chooses. In this example, management determined that an output of 125,000 cans will result in the greatest profits.

In the following year, ABC's patent on Itchaway expired. Hundreds of new producers entered the market. We can see in Figure 7.2 that as new producers entered the market the equilibrium price dropped from $3 to $2 per can. At a price of $2, 275,000 cans will be supplied. The graph illustrates the idea that output is generally lower and prices higher in a monopoly market than in a perfectly competitive market.

BUSINESS COMBINATIONS, PAST AND PRESENT

An early form of business combination was the *pool*, an agreement between two or more firms to share the market for their products and to fix prices. A number of industries, including railroads, set up pools in the 1870s and 1880s, but pools became less popular in the 1890s. Since pools were created informally (and secretly), their agreements could not be enforced. If one or more member firms broke the rules by underselling the pool or invading another member's territory, the pool ceased to exist. Eventually, a new type of business combination emerged—the trust.

Trusts

Standard Oil became the country's first *trust* (a large business monopoly whose shareholders place control of the firm in the hands of trustees). With its power to undersell, Standard Oil was able to demand that independent firms sell out to them or face a price war they could not win. Most of these companies chose to sell. When they did, stockholders of the purchased companies turned their shares of stock over to the *trustees* of Standard Oil, the people who ran the corporation. In exchange, the former stockholders received "trust certificates" entitling them to a share of the profits in the form of dividends.

Oil was not the only 19th-century industry dominated by a trust. Trusts soon developed in other industries, including cottonseed oil, linseed oil, whiskey, sugar, lead, and cordage. By 1904, trusts controlled 50 percent or more of the production in each of 80 of the nation's largest industries. Public opposition to trusts soon resulted in action by Congress and the courts. The **Sherman Antitrust Act** of 1890 and the **Clayton Act** of 1914 outlawed trusts that were "in restraint of trade." Rulings by several state courts made trusts illegal in the corresponding states.

Holding Companies

After trusts were declared illegal, *holding companies* became the most important means by which companies combined to reduce competition. A holding company is a corporation organized for the purpose of owning or "holding" a controlling interest in other corporations. Controlling interest is ownership or control of more than 50 percent of the voting stock of a corporation. In Figure 7.3, Companies A, B, and C are

Figure 7.3   Holding Company X

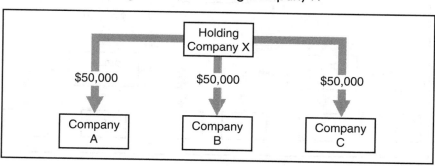

Figure 7.4 Holding Company Y

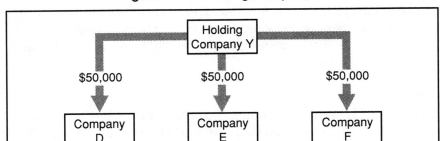

controlled by Holding Company X. If each company is worth $100,000 (as represented by 100,000 shares of stock at $1 per share), an investment of $50,001 (which we shall call $50,000) will give the purchaser control of the firm. With $150,000, therefore, Holding Company X will have acquired control of Companies A, B, and C.

Assume identical conditions for Holding Company Y and Companies D, E, and F, as shown in Figure 7.4. We now have two holding companies, each with stock worth $150,000 that controls corporations whose value totals $300,000. Suppose now that another holding company is created and that it acquires control of Holding Company X for $75,000 and control of Holding Company Y for $75,000. Figure 7.5 shows that this new holding company, which we shall call Z, has acquired control of corporations whose total value is $600,000.

We can see that control of Holding Company Z could be obtained with an investment of $75,000 and that this would mean control of $600,000 worth of corporations. The technique of building up control of corporations through several levels of holding companies is called "pyramiding." Companies X and Y, which control operating firms, are

Figure 7.5 Holding Company Z

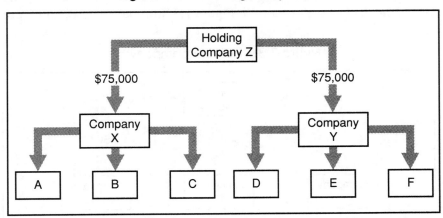

Figure 7.6   Interlocking Directorate

Corporation Y

Directors

BCD FG

Corporation X

Directors
A
BCD
E

Directors

BCD HI

Corporation Z

The Same People

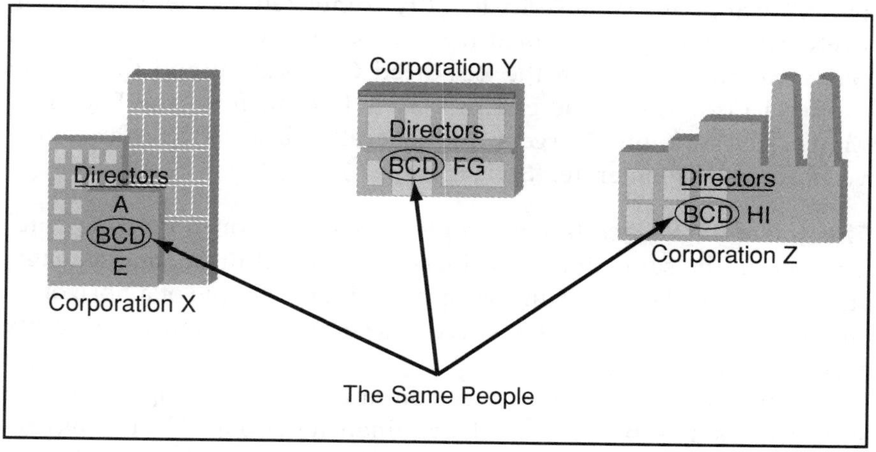

called "first-level holding companies." Company Z is called a "second-level holding company" because it holds control of first-level holding companies. In the case of public utilities, holding companies beyond the second level are illegal.

Interlocking Directorates

When the same people sit on the boards of directors of several firms, these firms have *interlocking directorates*. In Figure 7.6, directors B, C, and D sit on the boards of Corporations X, Y, and Z.

While many kinds of interlocking directorates are illegal, others are legal and are used at times to coordinate the operations of two or more companies.

Cartels

When independent firms formally agree to stop competing and work together to establish a monopoly, they have created a *cartel*. The two essential ingredients in a cartel are control of production levels and control of prices. By limiting production to an agreed level, the cartel creates a demand for a product. With increased demand, the price of the product goes up. This kind of collusion is generally illegal in the United States, but it is legal in most other countries. The world's best-known cartel is the **Organization of Petroleum Exporting Countries (OPEC)**. In the 1970s, OPEC was able to raise the world price of crude oil from $1.40 to $40 a barrel by severely limiting output.

Mergers

In recent decades, the most common form of business combination has been the *merger*. A merger occurs when one corporation absorbs another. The absorbed company may remain intact as a division of the parent firm or it may lose its identity completely. Sometimes an entirely new company is formed from a merger of two or more firms. Such was the case when the Lockheed Corporation and the Martin Marietta Corporation merged in March 1995 to form the Lockheed Martin Corporation. Mergers are generally classified as horizontal, vertical, or conglomerate. (See Figure 7.7.)

The Horizontal Merger. In a *horizontal merger*, two or more companies engaged in the same line of business are brought under one management. The Lockheed Martin Corporation is an example of a horizontal merger because both the Lockheed Corporation and Martin Marietta were producers of airplanes.

Horizontal mergers have been common in the banking industry in recent years. For example, the Fleet Financial Group (Fleet Bank) acquired NatWest Bank in 1995. NatWest had been a U.S. subsidiary of the National Westminster Bank of Britain. Another recent merger was that of the Chase Manhattan and Chemical banks. Such combinations

Figure 7.7   Horizontal, Vertical, and Conglomerate Combinations

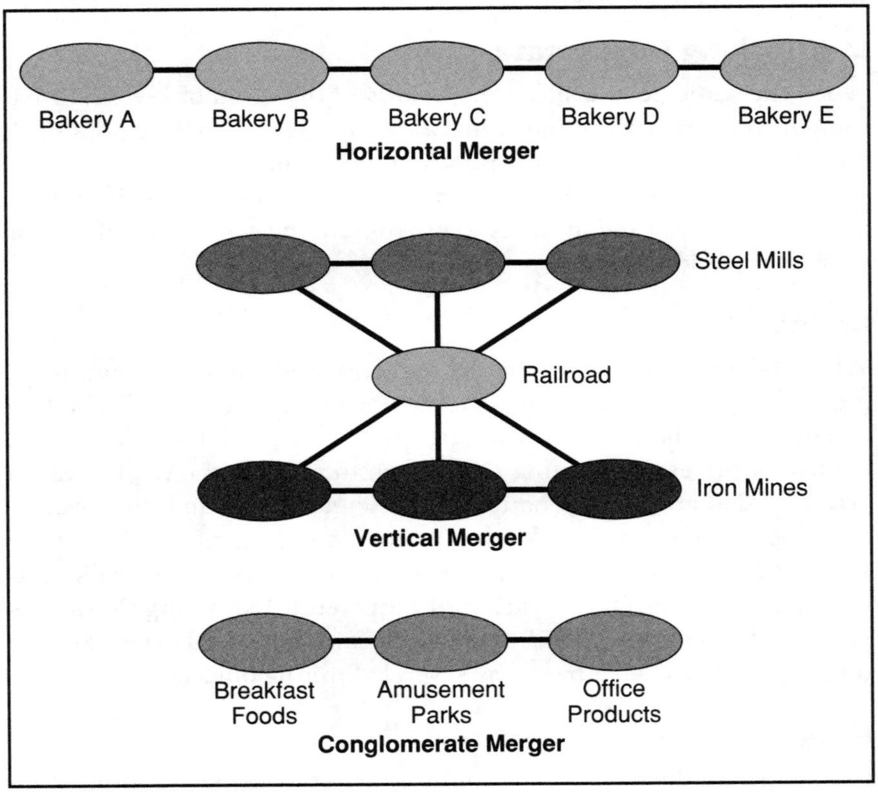

| Bakery A | Bakery B | Bakery C | Bakery D | Bakery E |

Horizontal Merger

Steel Mills

Railroad

Iron Mines

Vertical Merger

Breakfast Foods   Amusement Parks   Office Products

Conglomerate Merger

are designed primarily to reduce competition and lower certain kinds of overhead.

Competition is reduced because the firms that are combined were formerly contending with each other for business. Costs can be reduced because functions that were duplicated can now be combined. For example, Fleet Financial Group hopes to trim 1,800 jobs and close 30 branches as a result of merging with NatWest. The Chase Manhattan-Chemical Bank merger is expected to result in a reduction of 12,000 jobs.

The Vertical Merger. In a *vertical merger*, two or more firms engaged in different stages of marketing or producing the same good or service combine under a single ownership. USX Steel, for example, owns its own iron mines, shipping companies, and steel mills.

THE WALT DISNEY COMPANY

Film Production—Hollywood, Caravan, Touchstone, and Walt Disney Pictures
TV Studios—The Disney Channel
Animation Studio—Feature films and TV cartoon series
Film Distribution—Buena Vista and Miramax films; television syndication; and home
   video
Theme Parks and Resorts—Walt Disney World, Disneyland, Disneyland Paris (39%
   share), and Tokyo Disneyland (royalties)
Other Interests—The Mighty Ducks of Anaheim (hockey team); Disney on Ice shows;
   stage productions; Hyperion Publishing; and Disney Licensing

CAPITAL CITIES/ABC

ABC Television Network Group—ABC Entertainment; ABC Sports; and ABC
   Daytime
Capital Cities/ABC Broadcasting Group—10 television stations and 21 radio
   stations
Cable and International Broadcast Group—ESPN and ESPN2 (80%); A&E Television (37.5%); and Lifetime Television (50%)
International Investments—Part owner of television production companies in
   France, Germany, Britain, Japan, and Scandinavia
Publishing—Newspapers, magazines, and trade journals
Multimedia—On-line services, developing technologies.

Source: **Time**, August 14, 1995.

The merger of The Walt Disney Company and Capital Cities/ABC in 1995 brought together companies involved in one way or another with the information industry: movies, television, cable channels, books, newspapers, magazines, and radio. As a result of this combination, the Walt Disney Company's family of entertainment (such as the hockey team, ice shows, stage productions, and films) can be shown more easily on ABC television stations around the world and advertised in Disney/ABC-owned newspapers, magazines, and trade journals. What type of business combination does Walt Disney/ABC represent?

The Conglomerate Merger. A conglomerate merger combines companies producing unrelated products or services. Thus, for example, the H&R Block Company is well known throughout the United States as a business that helps individuals prepare their income tax returns. In addition to its tax preparation business, H&R Block owns CompuServe, one of the major companies providing on-line information services, electronic mail, and Internet access. Companies become conglomerates for various reasons. Some businesspeople see conglomerate mergers as a way of spreading or cushioning the impact of hard times. When business is bad for one industry in a conglomerate, it may be better for another industry in the same conglomerate.

Other reasons for conglomerate mergers include the following: (1) to gain entry into a line of business at lower cost than if the acquiring company had to start fresh; (2) to buy a company undervalued by the stock market at a bargain price; (3) to take advantage of loopholes in the tax laws; (4) to invest surplus funds; and (5) to benefit from economies of size. Recent court decisions indicate that the federal government is more likely to approve conglomerate mergers than horizontal or vertical mergers because conglomerate mergers are least likely to reduce competition.

Downsizing

A major reason for business combinations is the expectation that the merged firms will be more efficient than the separate units. Often this is the case. Some businesses found out, however, that bigness is not always better and have broken up into smaller companies. For example, the International Telephone and Telegraph Corporation (ITT) was one of the largest and oldest conglomerates. But in 1995, ITT split into three separate companies. The ITT Corporation no longer exists. In its place are the three following corporations:

- ITT Industries (auto parts, military electronics, and fluid-handling systems)
- ITT Hartford Group, Inc. (property, casualty, and life insurance)
- ITT Destinations, Inc. (Sheraton and Ciga hotel chains, Caesar's World, Madison Square Garden, the New York Knicks, and the New York Rangers).

EVOLUTION OF FEDERAL ANTITRUST LEGISLATION

As the 19th century drew to a close, public opposition to the trusts and the exercise of monopoly power led to demands for government regulation of business. Congress responded by enacting a series of *antitrust laws*.

Interstate Commerce Act (1887). The law restricted monopoly power of railroads by creating the nation's first regulatory agency, the **Interstate Commerce Commission (ICC)**. The ICC continued to regulate the railroads and other means of transportation until 1996, when it was abolished by act of Congress. The ICC's duties were taken over by other federal agencies.

Sherman Antitrust Act (1890). The act declared that ". . . every contract, combination . . . or conspiracy in restraint of trade is illegal." It provided penalties for those who violated the law by conspiring to limit competition.

At first, the Sherman Act was weak, because of the following:

● It failed to specify exactly what constituted a "restraint of trade."
● It failed to create an agency responsible for administering the law.
● The U.S. Supreme Court in 1903 held that (1) only "unreasonable" trade restraints were illegal, and (2) the law could be used to curb the power of labor unions.

Clayton Antitrust and Federal Trade Commission Acts (1914). The laws sought to correct the weaknesses of the Sherman Act by:

● Describing specific practices as "restraints of trade";
● Exempting labor unions from the provisions of the antitrust laws;
● Creating a regulatory agency, the **Federal Trade Commission (FTC)**, to administer the antitrust laws. The FTC still works to prevent unfair trade practices and false or misleading advertising.

Robinson-Patman Act (1936). This law sought to protect small stores from unfair competition by chain stores and other large retailers. The **Robinson-Patman Act** required wholesalers to offer the same discounts to both large and small retailers, unless the discounts could be justified by lower costs.

Celler-Kefauver Antimerger Act (1950). The **Celler-Kefauver Antimerger Act** prohibited mergers that would result in the creation of a monopoly.

Why Has Monopoly Power Been Restricted?

Except for legal monopolies (such as utilities), monopolies have been outlawed in the United States. This prohibition has been the result of the following accusations against monopolies:

Why do you suppose the U.S. Justice Department was interested in investigating Microsoft when this cartoon was published in 1995?

Monopolies Raise Prices. Prices are higher in industries in which monopoly power is exercised than they are in competitive markets. The only limitation on a monopolist's ability to set prices is the ease with which buyers can find substitute products. If the public can easily do without the product, demand will quickly fall as prices rise. If, however, the product is a necessity for which there are no adequate substitutes, buyers will be under greater pressure to pay the price asked.

Monopolies Reduce Output and Living Standards. Monopolists set prices by adjusting output to match the demand for their product. Since monopoly prices are higher than prices would be in a competitive market, output is lower. In this way, monopolies reduce everyone's standard of living because fewer goods are available. When consumers must pay more for these goods, they have less to spend on other things.

Monopolies Are Inefficient and Wasteful. Since monopolies do not have to worry about competition, they are under less pressure to reduce costs or to increase productivity. In this way, they waste human resources, capital resources, and natural resources.

Monopolies Are Insensitive to Consumer Demand. In a free market economic system, firms do their best to outperform the competition by

Government Regulation—Why the Controversy?

Ever notice how competitive the air travel industry is? Ads and commercials promoting special fares and discounts on flights around the country and overseas are an everyday occurrence. Ads like these were virtually unheard of in the years prior to 1978. In those days, airline travel was a regulated industry. That is, a government agency, the **Civil Aeronautics Board (CAB)**, determined who could operate an airline, what routes they could fly, and the prices they could charge.

The airline industry before 1978 had many problems. In the absence of competition in many markets, airlines had little incentive to operate efficiently. The fares they charged were high relative to today's rates. Moreover, because airline service to many small communities was not profitable, the federal government subsidized these markets.

In 1978, the federal government *deregulated* the airline industry. This meant that the federal government removed its controls over prices and routes. The Civil Aeronautics Board was phased out. Critics of this *deregulation* predicted that it would lead to higher prices, fewer communities being served, reduced safety, one or two companies with too much power, and poorer service. In the decades since deregulation, only the last of these predictions has proven true. No single airline company dominates the industry. Fares have gone down, not up. More communities are being served by airlines. Moreover, airlines are safer today than they ever were. Service, however, has suffered. In an effort to increase profits, airlines have moved aircraft seats closer together and have cut costs in meals. Many small communities that previously had large jets landing at their airport now are served by smaller planes, which generally provide bumpier rides.

In recent years, the debate over the merits of regulation vs. deregulation has been extended to the cable-TV and telephone industries. In 1993, Bell Atlantic, a major telephone company, announced that it was planning to merge with the nation's largest cable television company, Tele-Communications Inc. (TCI). This merger would create a company capable of delivering phone calls, cable-TV programs, motion pictures on demand, and home-shopping services. The debate that followed the announcement of the proposed merger sounded much like a replay of the discussions at the time the airlines were deregulated. Once again, those opposing deregulation warned of runaway price increases, the concentration of too much power in too few hands, and poorer service. Those favoring deregulation argued that government regulation inevitably leads to high operating costs, poor productivity, and higher prices.

The merger between Bell Atlantic and TCI never took place. In 1995, merger talks broke off because of "...the unsettled regulatory climate...." In other words, leaders of both firms feared that the agencies regulating their industries would make it impossible for them to earn a profit.

What is the cartoonist saying about deregulation?

giving consumers what they want, at the lowest possible prices. Where there is no competition, however, sellers can offer their wares to consumers on a take-it-or-leave-it basis.

Monopolies Engage in Unfair Competition. Monopolists prevent other firms from entering the market and destroy those already there. Powerful companies sell their products at a loss so as to force their competitors into bankruptcy. Then, with the competition eliminated, prices are restored to their original level or to a higher one.

Monopolies Help Bring on Recessions. Monopolies are often guilty of *price rigidity*—the maintenance of prices at unnecessarily high levels even when demand is on the decline. But the only way to maintain prices in the face of falling demand is to reduce output. This often leads to job layoffs, unemployment, and recession.

They Threaten Our Political System. Big companies (some of which are monopolies) spend millions of dollars on public relations, lobbying, and the financial support of politicians. In these ways, large firms seek (and sometimes get) the passage of national and state laws favorable to the special interests of these firms. Politicians who get financial support from big businesses may feel more indebted to these companies than they are to their constituents.

Is "Bigness" Necessarily Bad?

Some people believe that the antitrust laws may have gone too far in limiting the ability of U.S. firms to compete in global markets. Further, they argue, big is not necessarily bad. Their arguments are:

Economies of Scale. The economies of scale resulting from mass production serve to raise the country's standard of living. Mergers often result in reduced costs, increased productivity, and technological innovation. Thus, consumers benefit in terms of new and improved products at lower costs.

International Competition. Antitrust laws impair the ability of U.S. firms to compete in international markets. These firms may be prosecuted and found guilty of violating U.S. antitrust laws for their activities abroad. Thus, U.S. antitrust laws put U.S. firms at a disadvantage in competing with foreign firms that do not have to worry about such laws.

Antitrust laws also curtail the ability of U.S. firms to compete with foreign companies in the United States. Although the courts penalize U.S. companies for growing too big, in some cases the foreign companies with whom they are competing are even bigger. Critics of antitrust laws argue that domestic firms should be as free to compete with foreign oligopolies as the foreign companies are free to compete with U.S. firms.

Expense of Antitrust Work. Many of the antitrust cases prosecuted by the U.S. government cost too much, take too long, and should not have been started in the first place. Cases begun by the U.S. government often continue for ten years or more, cost millions of dollars to prosecute, and are sometimes dropped or end up with the government's defeat.

Effect on Consumers. Even when the government does win, it is not clear that the public benefits. As a result of an antitrust action in 1984, the nation's largest corporation, the American Telephone and Telegraph Company (AT&T), sold off its 22 local telephone companies. Some people argue that consumers are now paying more for their local telephone service than when it was all provided by AT&T.

Big Business Growth Is Natural. The population of the United States, our government, and labor unions are all bigger than they were when the major antitrust laws were enacted. Moreover, these large power blocs offset the power of big business. For example, big labor unions limit the power of big business to set wage rates for workers in their employ. Thus, the powerful giant automobile, steel, and rubber industries must all bargain with equally powerful labor unions and with one another.

Big Business Benefits Small Business. Small companies feed off the large companies and have actually increased in number rather than disappeared as a result of the growth of big business. For example, consider the vast number of auto dealerships, auto supply stores, and service stations that thrive because of the giant auto industry.

Summary

In a theoretical situation of perfect competition, prices are set in the marketplace by supply and demand. Conditions of perfect competition rarely exist, and most markets fall somewhere between perfect competition and monopoly. This imperfect competition can be further divided into monopolistic competition and oligopoly. Oligopolists rely mainly on product differentiation to set prices. The ability of an oligopoly to set prices depends upon their monopoly power in the market as measured by concentration ratio. The monopolist price is not necessarily the highest price a firm can get but it is the price that will return the maximum profit.

Monopolists have resorted to various organizations to reduce competition, including trusts, interlocking directorates, cartels, holding companies, and mergers. Because of the evils associated with monopoly power, Congress has passed antitrust laws to limit this power and to further competition. Some people argue, however, that having large corporations helps the economy and that antitrust laws may have gone too far in limiting the ability of U.S. firms to compete in a global market.

REVIEWING THE CHAPTER

Building Vocabulary

Match each term in Column A with its definition in Column B.

COLUMN A	COLUMN B
1. monopoly	*a.* to remove a government regulation
2. copyright	*b.* percentage of an industry's total output produced by its four largest firms
3. monopolistic competition	*c.* a corporation that has a controlling interest in other companies
4. product differentiation	*d.* a market that has only one supplier
5. oligopoly	*e.* a market that has only a few suppliers
6. concentration ratio	*f.* efforts to give buyers the impression that virtually identical products are different
7. antitrust law	*g.* a government grant of legal control over reproduction of a literary, musical, or artistic work
8. holding company	
9. patent	*h.* a market with many sellers offering similar products that the buyers believe differ
10. deregulate	*i.* an exclusive right given to market an invention
	j. an act that prohibits a business monopoly

Understanding What You Have Read

1. Prices are usually lowest for a product when it is produced by (*a*) only one company   (*b*) many competing companies   (*c*) a few very large companies   (*d*) a public utility.

2. In selecting their selling price, monopolists select the price that (*a*) will maximize their profit   (*b*) is the highest price they can get for their product   (*c*) is determined by consumer demand   (*d*) is determined by both supply and demand.

3. Monopolistic competition takes place when   (*a*) there are only a few buyers for a product   (*b*) only two or three firms manufacture a product   (*c*) many firms sell a similar product   (*d*) there is no competition among firms selling similar products.

4. Product differentiation enables businesses to   (*a*) charge more than they would under pure competition   (*b*) set prices as they

would under conditions of monopoly   (c) improve the quality of their product   (d) produce products completely different from those of their competitors.

5. Patents and copyrights are similar in that both   (a) provide government with important sources of revenue   (b) are issued by the boards of directors of corporations   (c) last forever   (d) grant the holder a legal monopoly.

6. Last night, the network news reported that one of the nation's largest manufacturers will increase its prices next week. The other manufacturing firms in the industry are expected to follow suit soon afterward. Even without knowing what the product is, what would you assume to be true about the industry?   (a) It produces consumer goods.   (b) It produces heavy equipment for industry.   (c) It has many manufacturing firms.   (d) It has very few firms.

7. In its effort to expand, ABC Pharmaceuticals acquired the stores of two of its competitors in the manufacture of products for the treatment of athlete's foot. In this way, ABC Pharmaceuticals was building a   (a) horizontal combination   (b) vertical combination   (c) conglomerate combination   (d) circular combination.

8. Business was so brisk for ABC Pharmaceuticals that its management bought a box-manufacturing company. This purchase enabled ABC to manufacture its own packaging materials. The new company was a   (a) horizontal combination   (b) vertical combination (c)   conglomerate   combination (d)   circular combination.

9. A few months ago, ABC Pharmaceuticals was acquired by one of the nation's largest producers of breakfast cereals. This was a   (a) horizontal combination   (b) vertical combination   (c) conglomerate combination   (d) circular combination.

10. Interlocking directories are formed when one company   (a) is absorbed by another   (b) holds controlling shares of stock in other companies   (c) has representatives on the boards of directors of competing firms   (d) absorbs another company.

11. The federal government has attempted to regulate monopolies chiefly in order to   (a) eliminate big business in the United States   (b) reduce the number of public utilities   (c) encourage competition   (d) increase the number of small businesses.

12. Which of the following laws first declared any "contract, combination . . . or conspiracy in restraint of trade" to be illegal?   (a) Interstate Commerce Act   (b) Sherman Act   (c) Clayton Act   (d) Federal Trade Commission Act.

Thinking Critically

1. In a certain city, all music stores charge the same price for their CDs. Competition, however, is quite brisk, and the stores frequently advertise on the radio. (*a*) Since all the stores are charging the same prices for their merchandise, what techniques might each one adopt to differentiate its products and services from the others? (*b*) What kind of competition does this illustrate? (*c*) Advocates of other economic systems have argued that it is wasteful for firms to compete in the sale of identical products. Give *two* arguments to counter this point of view.

2. Big businesses have developed a number of strategies to combine and coordinate the activities of what had formerly been independent firms. In the past, these strategies included pools and trusts and, more recently, holding companies and mergers.
   a. Explain how each of these business combinations may reduce competition and enable powerful firms to control prices and increase profits.
   b. How might it be argued that business combinations enable firms to increase their economies of scale, reduce their production costs, and thus reduce prices to consumers?
   c. Explain why you think that "Big Business" in the United States today is, or is not, too big.

3. Which of the following involves the most efficient use of natural resources? Explain your answer.
   A. A city with one bus company.
   B. The same city with two bus companies providing service to the same neighborhoods.

SKILLS: Interpreting a Table

Refer to Table 7.3, on page 170, to answer the following questions:

1. (*a*) Identify the *three* industries with the greatest amount of competition among those listed. (*b*) Identify the *three* industries with the least amount of competition among those listed.

2. With reference to one of the industries you identified in answer to question 1(*a*), why do you suppose this industry is so much more competitive than others?

3. With reference to one of the industries you identified in answer to question 1(*b*), what would account for the lack of competition in this industry?

4. "Concentration ratios can be a misleading measure of competition or the lack of competition." Explain this statement

Table 7.3   COMPETITION IN SELECTED INDUSTRIES

Industry	Number of Producers (establishments)	Concentration Ratio (percentage of output produced by four largest firms)
Aerospace	1,280	61
Book publishing	1,744	18
Bread and cake	3,062	33
Concrete (ready-mixed)	5,433	5
Dairy products	3,731	27
Farm machinery and equipment	264	89
Motor vehicles	322	93
Sawmills and planing mills	7,544	17
Soft drinks	2,192	75
Sporting and athletic goods	1,878	21
Telephone and telegraph	264	89
Women's and misses' dresses	6,953	8
Zinc	6	80

Source: Department of Commerce, **U.S. Industrial Outlook**

Chapter 8

THE LABOR FORCE IN OUR ECONOMY

Overview

Carmen Vargas and Celena Montgomery are friends who went to the same high school and college. One major difference between the two, however, is that when they were students, Carmen read about labor market trends and then decided to prepare for a field where there was a demand for workers. She majored in a medical assistant program. Celena, by contrast, did not learn much about future job opportunities. She loved to act, and thus majored in theater in hopes of learning how to earn a living in that field.

Just before graduating from college, the two friends went to their college employment and counseling center. There Carmen received recommendations to interview with five different employers. Soon a local medical center offered her a position as a medical assistant. Carmen accepted the offer because of the center's convenient location and the salary and benefits that went with the job.

At the college counseling center, Celena's counselor told her that the college had no requests for actors. Her drama professor, however, encouraged her to look for acting work and gave her several suggestions on how to proceed. The professor advised Celena to become involved with local community theater groups where she could get acting experience. Because most not-for-profit groups do not pay actors, Celena would still have to find a paying job to support herself. She did not give up. From time to time, small theaters gave her nonpaying parts. Finally, though, Celena had to accept a position waiting on tables at a downtown restaurant. She still hopes to obtain paid work as an actor.

What can we learn from Carmen's and Celena's experiences? Can we say that it is better to study medical assisting than theater? In terms of monetary rewards, the answer is not clear-cut. A few talented actors earn millions, but most struggle to make ends meet. Probably no medical assistant earns millions. In fact, yearly earnings for medical assistants with 11 years of experience average about $21,000. We can say, however, that it is much easier to get employment as a medical assistant than as an actor.

As we think about the kind of *career* (lifelong work) we want, it soon becomes clear that we need to become more knowledgeable about the world of work. We need to become more familiar with the overall labor market. In this chapter, we will discuss this market and how and why it is changing. We will discuss the forces that determine an individual's earnings. We will then examine what the best job opportunities are today and what they are most likely to become in the coming years. Finally, we will look further at what factors we should consider in choosing a career.

LABOR FORCE TRENDS

The *labor force* (sometimes called the *workforce*) is made up of all persons 16 years of age or older who are either working or looking for work. At present, the size of the labor force in the United States is some 135 million people (about half the total population). Significant changes are taking place in the labor force, and present trends will probably continue in coming years. Since eventually you are likely to be entering the job market as a full-time employee, you may want to think about these changes as you plan your career.

The labor force changes as the country's population changes and as the kinds of work people do change. As we examine how the population is changing, we will also study changes in the labor force and in particular occupations.

The U.S. Population Is Growing

As indicated in Figure 8.1, the U.S. population has been growing for a long time. As the country's population has grown, so too has its labor force. One reason is that an increase in population usually means that more people are looking for jobs. In addition, an increase in population often leads to the growth of the economy. As the economy grows, it creates more jobs.

Although the population of the United States has been growing, its *rate of population growth* has been slowing down in recent decades. In a similar manner, the rate of growth of the labor force also has been declining. In the period 1979–1992, the labor force increased 21 percent. Most estimates are that it will increase only 19 percent in the period 1992–2005. Despite the slowdown in its rate of growth, the total labor force population will continue to grow. Along with the growth in the labor force, we can expect to see an increase in the demand for goods and services. More people will want and need more things. The demand for workers is directly related to consumer demand for goods and services. Most likely, more workers will be needed to help produce the increased goods and services that consumers demand.

Figure 8.1   Increases in Size of the U.S. Population
and Labor Force

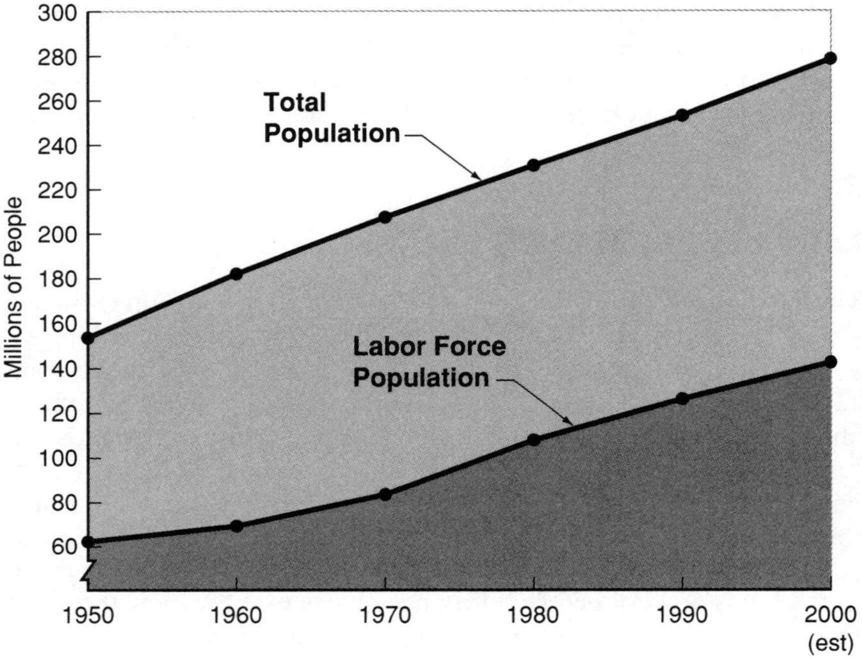

The Population Is Getting Older

The U.S. population is getting older, and the percentage of our population that is age 65 and over is expected to increase. Meanwhile, the percentage of our population that is 17 or younger is expected to remain the same. As the average age of the U.S. population gets older, so, too, does the average age of the labor force. The average age of the labor force in 1992 was about 37, and it is expected to rise to about 41 in 2005.

Earlier Retirement Age. Although Americans are living longer, retired people are getting younger. The *median retirement age* (half fall above and half fall below this level) was 66.9 for men and 67.7 for women in 1950. It dropped to 62.7 for men and 62.9 for women in 1994, and it is expected to drop still further—to 61.7 for men and 61.2 for women—in the year 2005.

Changes in retirement patterns of the population affect employment opportunities. Sometimes firms offer older workers early retirement, with benefits, in order to reduce the number of workers on these companies' payroll. As workers retire from the labor force, job opportunities open up for younger people.

Current estimates are that those 85 years and older will increase about four times as fast as the general population through 2005. This increase, in turn, is bound to add to the demand for workers in the health-care industry, already one of the fastest-growing industries in the economy. Individuals 85 and over are more likely to require medication and medical treatment than younger persons. Some elderly will require institutional care. Doctors, nurses, health aides, and other health-care workers will be in greater demand to service the growing numbers of elderly persons.

The Population Is Becoming More Varied

Increasing numbers of women are entering the labor force. In 1979, women made up only 42 percent of the labor force. By 2000, this percentage will grow to about 50 percent. In greater numbers than ever before, women have gained top management positions and jobs that once were considered almost exclusively "men's work."

Figure 8.2   Age Distribution of the U. S. Labor Force

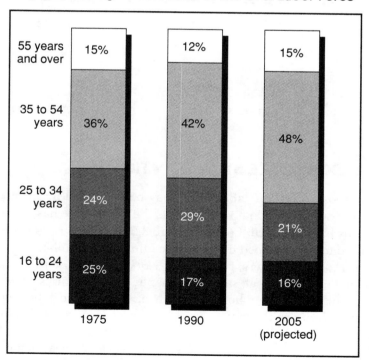

Which age groups in the labor force are expected to increase between 1990 and 2005?

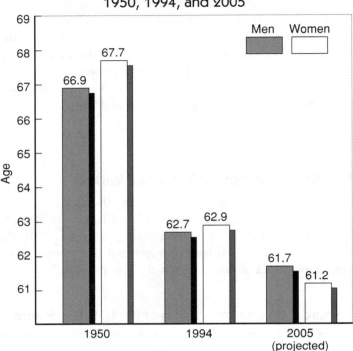

Figure 8.3   Median Retirement Age of Men and Women 1950, 1994, and 2005

Nonwhite workers are also becoming a larger part of the labor force. Figure 8.4 describes some projected labor-force changes.

THE LABOR FORCE BY OCCUPATIONS

The composition of the labor force may be examined in terms of the kinds of work people do for a living. As the labor force has grown, occupations have changed. Look at Figure 8.5. For purposes of comparison, our data are grouped under the headings white-collar, blue-collar, service, and farmworkers. *White-collar workers* are those in the professional, technical, clerical, sales, and managerial categories. *Blue-collar workers* include those who have craft, operative, and laboring jobs. *Service workers* are those who work in the service industries and include government employees, fire fighters, hospital employees, building maintenance workers, workers in restaurants, beauticians, and many more. Finally, farmers, farm operators, and farm laborers are all included under the umbrella of "farmworkers."

Figure 8.4   Projected Shifts in the Racial Composition of the Labor Force, 1992–2005

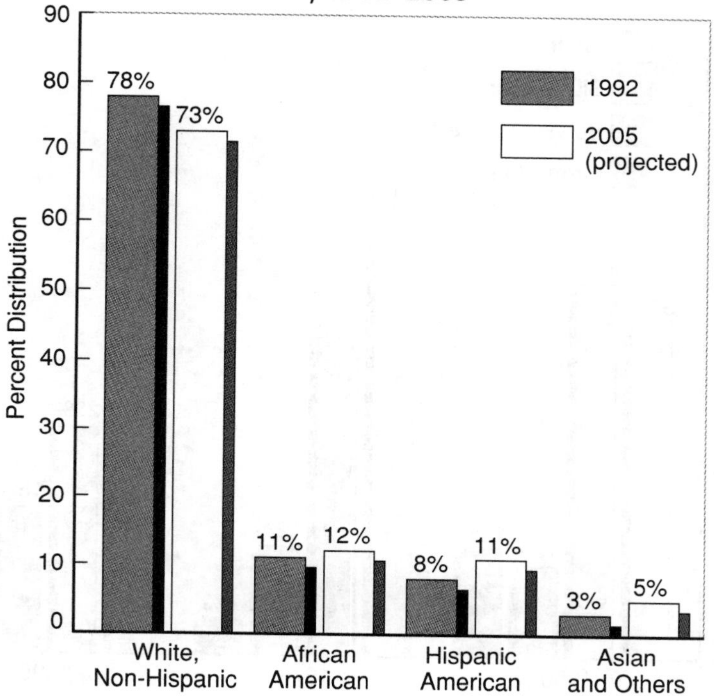

Most New Jobs Are in the Service Industries

Jobs have been shifting from goods-producing industries (manufacturing, construction, and agriculture) to the service industries (transportation, trade, finance, and government). The increasing demand for protective services and cleaning and maintenance services, and the more frequent use of restaurants, beauty salons, and leisure services have made the service workers category the fastest growing section of the labor force.

White-collar workers, once only a small proportion of the total labor force, today represent about half of all workers. As white-collar jobs have become more important, blue-collar jobs have become relatively less important.

Because of the spectacular growth of farm productivity, fewer farmers are able to feed more people than ever before. Therefore, fewer and fewer farmworkers have been needed over the years.

The trends shown in Figure 8.5 are expected to continue. Service-producing industries will account for much of the job growth that is projected to the year 2005. They are expected to provide about four out

Figure 8.5 Occupations of Employed Workers, 1950, 1970, and 1995

Figure 8.5 Occupations of Employed Workers, 1950, 1970, and 1995

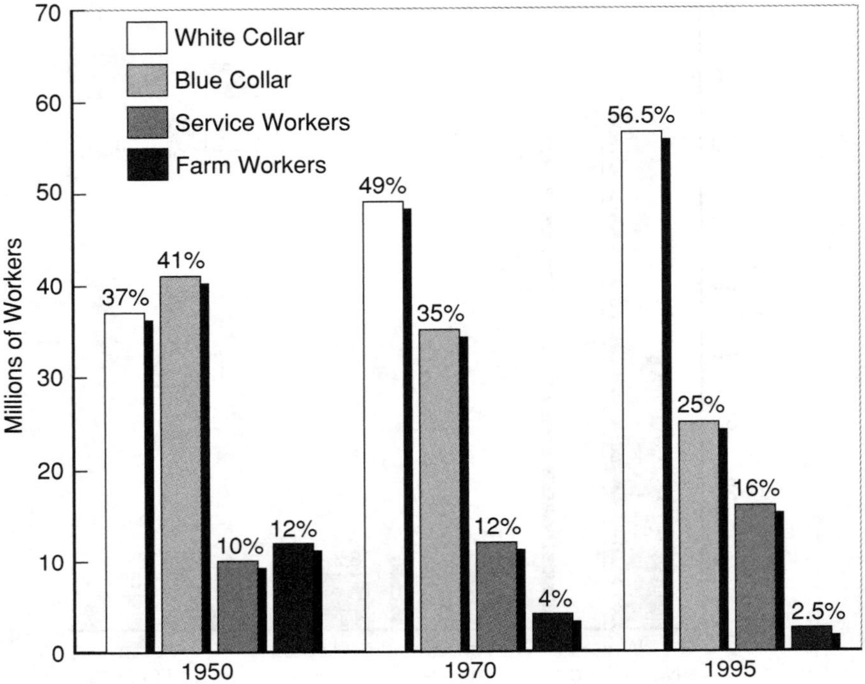

of five new jobs by the year 2005. Farmworkers will remain a small part of the workforce.

In view of the trends that we have just discussed, consider the following factors as you begin to make your plans for the future:

Occupations Are Changing

We know that in the past some industries have grown more rapidly than others. Very likely some industries will grow more rapidly than others in the future as well. Figure 8.6 illustrates where some future jobs are likely to be.

The Role of Technology

Technological revolution is a term used to describe the rapid changes in ways of producing goods and services. In recent decades, electronic machines have reduced the amount of human labor needed to produce an equal output. This revolution in technology is occurring worldwide. A few examples of changing technology include the use of computers to perform many tasks in offices and the use of robots or other automated machinery in factories. Satellites, microwave equipment, and fiber optic wires allow people to communicate more rapidly with one another than before. You probably know many more examples of technological changes.

The technological revolution has resulted in both losses of jobs and increases in jobs.

Losses of Jobs. Many workers have lost jobs because of *automation* (the use of machines to operate other machines). In some automobile manufacturing plants, for example, robots weld, paint, and test automobile frames. Fewer auto workers are now needed to build the same number of automobiles as before automation. In many bottling plants, oil refineries, and factories, similar changes have taken place. Automated machines operated by handfuls of technicians produce what had previously required hundreds of workers in each plant.

In the period 1991–1995, the 400 largest U.S. corporations reduced employment by 4 million. General Motors and IBM, facing stiff competition and poor sales, were motivated to restructure their organizations and introduce improved technology. These two giant firms were able to downsize by reducing the number of manufacturing plants, offices, and workers. For example, in the early 1980s, General Motors employed 369,000 people at 130 manufacturing facilities to make 4.5 million vehicles a year. After downsizing in the early 1990s, GM reduced its workforce to about 250,000 people at 120 facilities to produce roughly the same number of vehicles. Similarly, IBM went from

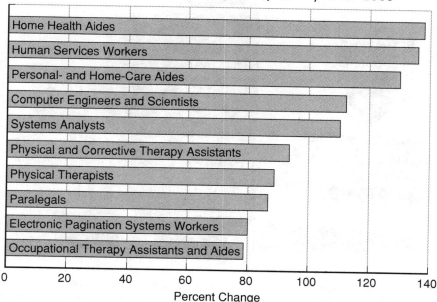

Figure 8.6   Fastest-Growing Occupations, 1992–2005

373,000 people at 34 manufacturing facilities to produce computers and computer software in the 1980s to 225,000 at 22 manufacturing facilities in 1995.

Gains in Jobs. While the technological revolution has displaced workers in some industries, it has created new jobs for other workers. Although 4 million jobs were lost among the 400 largest U.S. firms in the period 1991–1995, employment increased by 6 million nationwide in the same period. Many of these jobs are in new industries. The demand for highly specialized workers is so great in some industries that employers have difficulty filling jobs.

Highly trained people are needed to design computers and other automated machines. Other educated individuals are needed to develop the software that operates such complex equipment. And trained workers are needed to operate, maintain, and service computers and computer-operated equipment.

The Emphasis on Education Will Continue

The *educational attainment* (years of schooling) of the average worker has been increasing. In 1975, for example, 67 percent of workers between the ages of 25 and 64 had completed only four years or less of high school. By 1990, this number had dropped to 53 percent. During the same period, workers with four or more years of college increased

ROB ROGERS Reprinted by permission of United Feature Syndicate, Inc.

One of the proposed solutions to job losses caused by automation is to set up job retraining programs. What is the cartoonist's view toward these programs?

Even though an occupation is expected to grow rapidly, it may provide fewer openings than a slower growing but larger occupation. For example, paralegals *(assistants to lawyers) is a category that is expected to increase by 85 percent between 1992 and 2005. Retail sales workers, on the other hand, are expected to increase by only 24 percent in this period. Nevertheless, in 1994 there were almost 3.7 million retail sales workers and fewer than 91,000 paralegals. Thus, a 24 percent increase in the retail trade comes to 887,000 workers, while an 85 percent increase of paralegal workers comes to only 77,000.*

from 18 to 26 percent. It is fortunate that more and more people are continuing their education beyond high school because three out of the four fastest-growing occupational groups today are those that require high levels of education and job skills.

High school dropouts who manage to find jobs most likely earn the least. Also, they have the poorest opportunities for advancement. The slogan "It pays to stay in school" is true, as we can see in Table 8.1.

Table 8.1   MEDIAN INCOME AND UNEMPLOYMENT RATES BY EDUCATIONAL ATTAINMENT, 1993

Educational Attainment	Median Income	Unemployment Rate
Elementary School	$13,920	13.0 %
High School	28,700	7.3
College	56,116	3.2

WHY DO SOME JOBS PAY MORE THAN OTHERS?

If all people and jobs were exactly alike, there would be no differences in wages. We know, though, that the labor force is not homogeneous. People and jobs are different, and some jobs pay more than others. This is true for those in the same occupation as well as for individuals in different occupations. For example, some of the country's best athletes have become wealthy, while other athletes cannot earn a living at their sport. Newspaper accounts tell us of multimillion-dollar contracts signed by the nation's outstanding football, baseball, basketball, and tennis players. We do not hear similar tales about outstanding volleyball, water polo, or badminton champions. Regardless of their ability, those athletes are unpaid or paid relatively little.

What is true of professional athletics applies to every other occupation as well: some workers get paid more than others. Why is this so? Why do physicians, lawyers, and engineers earn more, on the average, than secretaries, cashiers, and child-care workers? (See Table 8.2.) To explain these differences, economists refer to: (1) the market forces of supply and demand, and (2) nonmarket forces.

Table 8.2   MEDIAN WEEKLY EARNINGS, 1996

Physicians	$1,199
Lawyers	1,149
Aerospace Engineers	1,097
Computer Analysts	891
Electricians	811
Rail Workers	740
Aircraft Mechanics	720
Secondary School Teachers	697
Secretaries	406
Janitors and Cleaners	301
Service Station Attendants	275
Waiters and Waitresses	271
Apparel Sales Workers	265
Cashiers	247
Child-Care Workers	198

Market Forces in Action: How Supply and Demand Affect Wages

Every Sunday during the football season, millions of fans are glued to their television sets or are at a stadium watching their favorite professional teams compete. Professional baseball, basketball, and hockey also have many fans. We can say that there is a great demand on the part of the public to see outstanding athletes perform. Yet there are tiny numbers of athletes capable of making the grade in these sports. The supply of and demand for outstanding athletes create a market situation that pays high wages.

What is true for athletes applies to other jobs and professions as well. We have noted that physicians earn more than emergency medical technicians and that plumbers earn more than individuals in retail apparel sales. We can use our knowledge of supply and demand (as described in Chapter 3) to explain these differences in earnings.

Figure 8.7 compares the market for plumbers with the market for retail apparel sales workers. The supply of these salespeople is far greater than the supply of plumbers (as anyone knows who tries to find a plumber in an emergency). Because of the demand for plumbers, the average hourly wage paid plumbers is greater than that of retail apparel sales workers.

The hourly wage for plumbers in the illustration is around $18 per hour at point e, the equilibrium price. At this intersection, the supply of plumbers willing to accept $18 per hour is equal to the demand for plumbers at that wage rate. In the other part of the graph, we note that 38,000 individuals are willing to accept a wage of $8 per hour as retail apparel salespeople. At a wage above the equilibrium price (e_1), the demand for sales workers would be less than the supply available. At a wage below the equilibrium price, not enough sales workers would be willing to work.

So far we have been discussing wage rates in the same terms used in Chapter 3 (supply and demand). Supply and demand as applied to people, however, requires further explanation.

Figure 8.7 Supply and Demand for Plumbers and Retail Sales Workers

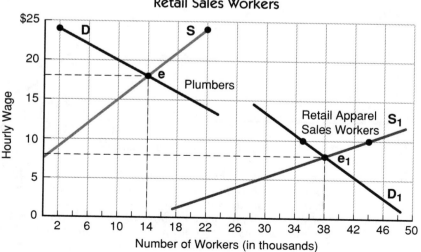

What Factors Affect the Demand for Labor?

The term "demand for labor" is the number of workers that a firm will hire at a particular wage. This, in turn, depends upon (1) the demand for the firm's products and services, and (2) the productivity of each additional worker in the firm.

Demand for Goods and Services. If consumers buy less of a good or service, the demand for workers in that industry will decline. In the 1970s, for example, U.S. consumers switched from buying domestic-made television sets and radios in favor of those made in Japan. As a result, the number of workers that the U.S. consumer electronics producers were willing to hire at any price declined. Or, as economists might say, the demand for workers in the consumer electronics industry declined. This is illustrated graphically in Figure 8.8.

When consumers buy more of a good or service, the demand for workers who produce that item or service will increase. Suppose that millions of people suddenly become fans of water polo. Increased consumer demand to follow the sport would lead to an increase in the

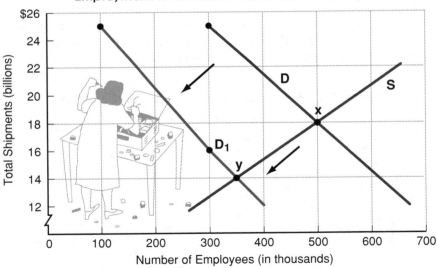

Figure 8.8   Effect of Reduction in Consumer Demand on Employment in Consumer Electronics Industry

Fewer workers are needed to produce the smaller quantity of electronic goods. In this hypothetical illustration, consumer electronics industry output is represented by curve S. With consumer demand at levels represented by D, the industry employed 500,000 workers to produce and ship $18 billion worth of goods (see point x). When consumer demand declined from D to D_1, production fell to $14 billion, and the workforce was reduced to 350,000 (see point y).

demand for professional water polo players. Other things being equal, increased demand for players would result in an increase in the wages paid to those athletes. In terms of supply and demand curves, we would say that the demand curve shifts to the right.

The number of workers that a firm hires (or fires) depends upon a firm's expected sales and output. As more goods and services are demanded, the demand for labor needed to produce those goods and services increases. As fewer goods and services are demanded, the demand for workers to produce these goods and services decreases. The demand for labor is called a *derived demand* because the demand for goods and services being produced (the primary factor) influences the number of workers employed (the derived or secondary factor).

Productivity. The second factor affecting the demand for labor is the productivity of each additional worker hired. An employer can afford to pay a new worker no more than what the worker adds to the firm's income. For example, if the addition of one worker will add $60 in income per day, the employer can afford to pay that worker any wage up to $60 daily. (For this example, a worker's wage includes taxes, insurance, and all other expenses associated with hiring and keeping that worker.) A wage above that figure will result in a loss to the firm. If, because of improved technology, the worker in this example were later able to produce $100 worth of additional income daily, the firm could then afford to pay a wage up to $100 per day.

Productivity sets only the upper limits to the amount of wages that workers are likely to earn. Employers will try to pay workers much less than the increased value of the good or service these workers produce. Suppose that if in one week a company with ten workers produces goods worth $4,000 more than the cost of raw materials, rent, and capital. The employer will not be able to pay these ten employees more than an average of $400 each. The employer would certainly be willing to pay them less than $400 because lower wages would add to the company's profits.

Economists sometimes use the term *marginal productivity* in describing the value of the output of the last worker hired by a company. In theory, a company will add workers until the point is reached where the extra income added by the last worker hired is equal to the worker's wage. Economists express this by saying that workers will be hired until marginal revenue is equal to marginal costs—that is, until the value of the additional production is equal to the cost of the last worker hired.

The demand for labor varies inversely with wages. In other words, if employers reduce wages (while leaving the other factors of production the same), employers can afford to hire more workers.

Butcher (left), forester (center), and aircraft mechanic (right). What factors affect the supply of each of the people in their job categories?

Factors Affecting the Supply of Labor

By the term "supply of labor," we mean the number of workers available to perform a particular job at a specified wage. As is the case with goods, the supply curve for labor slopes upward. The number of workers will increase as wages rise, and decrease as wages fall. This is logical because as wages in one field increase, workers in other fields will be attracted to it. If, for example, nurses in private hospitals were paid more than those in public hospitals, nurses would leave public service for the higher-paying private jobs. Similarly, if wages in one industry fall, workers in this industry will move to higher-paying jobs in other industries.

Wages alone cannot determine the total supply of labor in a particular field. Supply is subject to a number of other factors, including the following:

Attractiveness of the Job. Some jobs carry more prestige or are more appealing than other jobs paying similar salaries. Many persons prefer office work to more strenuous jobs even though office work may pay less. Also, writers, actors, dancers, and artists tend to like their work so much that they often stay in their respective field even though they could probably earn more money elsewhere.

Choosing Your Career

If you stop to think about it, almost half of your waking hours will be spent going to, returning from, or working at a job. That being the case, you will want to spend that time doing something you find satisfying. Moreover, the kind of occupation you will have will determine how much you will earn. That, in turn, will determine the kind of lifestyle you and your family can lead.

The job you want may or may not be there when you want it. Or, it may be available but not close to your hometown. Then, too, it is easier to find work when the economy of the country as a whole is doing well than when business conditions are poor. Given all of these factors, here are some ideas as to how you should go about choosing your career.

First and foremost, you should know what you want most out of your career. Is it money? Prestige? Helping people? Would you rather work with your hands or your head? Do you prefer working outdoors? Indoors? With people? Alone? What are your hobbies and other interests? Can they be transformed into an occupation?

Once you have put together your thoughts on these and other concerns, you should talk to your school guidance counselor. If one is available, you should also talk to a job counselor at a local counseling service. These trained specialists can help you to learn more about the careers that interest you.

Counselors can also help you match your abilities with possible careers. Knowing what your abilities are, though, is quite tricky. On the one hand, some people seem to be born with certain talents. On the other hand, a lot of what we call talent is really the result of hard work. A great athlete or musician must spend many hours learning and developing the skills that make that individual outstanding. So talent and skill (which together make up one's abilities) go together with effort. If you think you have a special talent, it is important that you develop it through education, training, and lots of hard work.

The amount of education and training you will need depends on the career you choose. Your first objective, though, is to finish high school. Then, you might continue with your education, go directly to work, or, perhaps, join one of the branches of the armed forces.

If you decide to continue your education, you might attend a two-year junior or community college, both of which offer programs leading to an associate's degree. You may want to go to a four-year college and receive a bachelor's degree, or to a trade or technical school to learn specific job skills.

Choosing the armed forces can open up other career choices to you. You might make the service a lifetime career or enter a training program in a specialty that you can follow in civilian life.

Entering the world of work will open up many other possibilities to you. Your first job need not be your final one. It might be merely a step up on a career ladder. In this first job, you might receive *on-the-job training* (learning a job by doing it). Or you may advance your skills by attending evening classes in subjects related to your field of interest. Remember, whatever your first job, it need not last forever. You may leave one job for another if you think the second one offers you greater opportunities. You might work for awhile, then return to school or join the armed forces. After completing your education or your hitch with the armed forces, you might return to the world of work, hopefully in your chosen career field.

There are many sources of information about careers. We have already suggested a school guidance counselor. Your teachers at school may help you too, particularly teachers in your field of interest. Do not forget those close at hand—your relatives, friends, and neighbors. Ask these people questions and listen to what they have to say. Pay particular attention to people who are already working in a field in which you are interested.

Private employment agencies and state employment offices provide good information about available job openings. Your state employment office may even offer free job counseling.

Finally, do a lot of reading. There are many books and magazines related to any number of careers. Become familiar with careers that interest you. Study the *Occupational Outlook Handbook*. This biannual, U.S.-government publication describes some 250 occupations. For each one, it tells the nature of the work, working conditions, requirements for the job, number of jobs, job locations, typical salaries, and the *job outlook*, or chances of finding work in that occupation. Much information is also available to you elsewhere—on videos, CD-ROMs, and the Internet and in books and magazines—concerning schools, colleges, job opportunities, and other career concerns. Choosing a career is not easy. It takes much time and effort, but your time and effort will be well spent.

Skill Required. Only a limited number of people have the skill or talent required for certain jobs. No matter how well the job pays, for example, not everyone can become a professional singer or ballplayer.

Required Training. Some occupations have much longer training periods than others. Young people who want to become physicians may have to spend an additional eight to ten years in school after they graduate from high school. Other professions and technical fields also require extensive training beyond high school. Many people, though, cannot afford the time or money necessary for this training. The greater the amount of training required for a particular job, the smaller the supply of workers available.

Worker Mobility. The willingness of workers to move "to where the jobs are" is described as their *mobility*. Young adults who have no family responsibilities are more mobile than others. But most people want to stay in the community where they are living. Employers in certain parts of the country may find it difficult to hire enough workers. Merely raising wages slightly may not help attract workers to this region. In the early 1980s, for example, certain computer-related industries on the West Coast experienced shortages of workers. During the same period, however, some workers in the Midwestern and Northeastern United States who possessed needed computer skills were unemployed. People are naturally reluctant to leave their friends and families or move their children from one area to another. Workers' lack of mobility accounts in part for pockets of poverty in some regions of the country.

Nonmarket Forces in Determining Wages

While supply and demand—the so-called market forces—are major factors in determining wage levels, they are not the only ones. In some instances, other factors (or nonmarket forces) also have an impact. These include the following:

Labor Unions. When labor union negotiators and company management sit down to negotiate wages, the laws of supply and demand often fade into the background. Instead of supply and demand, the relative strengths of labor and management are likely to dominate the proceedings. If, for example, union members appear to be able to weather a long strike, they might extract a substantial wage increase from the employer. If, however, the workers appear as if they could not afford the loss of income that a work stoppage would impose, the unions will be under pressure to keep their salary demands down.

Although labor-management negotiations are partly guided by nonmarket forces, both labor and management are still subject to the laws of supply and demand. Businesses must show a profit in order to survive. This factor places a limit on the amount that businesses can pay out in wages. Similarly, there is a bottom-line salary below which qualified workers will simply quit or (if not currently employed) refuse to apply for jobs. The role of labor unions is discussed in more detail in Chapter 9.

Government Legislation. Laws can affect wage levels. Regardless of the laws of supply and demand, employers must pay the minimum wage set by federal and state laws. Similarly, laws require that many workers must be paid higher, overtime rates whenever they work more than a maximum number of hours per week. Other laws limit the supply of labor by banning the employment of children in many industries and requiring that children attend school until they reach a certain age.

Civil rights laws and other government rules require that workers receive equal pay for equal work. The purpose of these laws is to prevent discrimination on the basis of race, religion, nationality, sex, or disability. The extent to which such laws are enforced will, therefore, affect the job market and wages.

Table 8.3   MEDIAN WEEKLY EARNINGS OF FULL-TIME WORKERS, 1994

White males	$547
White females	408
African-American males	400
African-American females	346
Hispanic-American males	343
Hispanic-American females	305

Discrimination. Certain groups in this country earn more than others. Studies show, for example, that African Americans and Hispanic Americans earn less than non-Hispanic whites, and that women earn less than men (see Table 8.3). Although there are a number of reasons for these differences, *discrimination* is a major cause of wage differences. Discrimination involves favoring one group over another in hiring, salary, or promotion for reasons that have nothing to do with ability to learn and perform job skills. Discrimination in employment is a violation of both federal and state laws.

Table 8.4   AVERAGE ANNUAL PAY OF WORKERS, BY SELECTED STATES, 1994

Rank	State	Annual Pay
1	Connecticut	$33,811
2	New York	33,439
3	New Jersey	33,439
4	Alaska	32,657
5	Massachusetts	31,024
46	Arkansas	20,898
47	Mississippi	20,380
48	Montana	20,218
49	North Dakota	19,893
50	South Dakota	19,255

Geography. Where people live and work affects their earnings because wages differ from one part of the nation to another. This is shown in Table 8.4, which ranks the top five and the bottom five states according to average annual pay. Just because one lives in a high-wage state (such as Alaska) does not mean, however, that one is better off. The cost of living in such states is usually much higher than that of the low-wage states.

Education. People who have completed many years of school earn more, on the average, than those who have completed fewer years. How much more the better-educated ones earn is shown in Table 8.5.

Table 8.5 MEDIAN PERSONAL INCOME, BY SEX AND EDUCATIONAL ATTAINMENT, 1970–1995

Highest Level of Education Completed	Males			Females		
	1970	1980	1995	1970	1980	1995
Elementary School	$ 5,400	$ 8,900	$11,723	$1,800	$ 4,200	$ 7,096
High School	8,800	14,600	23,365	3,400	6,100	12,046
4 yrs. College	12,100	22,200	39,040	5,400	11,700	24,065
5+ yrs. College	13,400	26,900	49,076	7,900	15,100	33,509

George Danby for the Bangor Daily News, Maine

Summary

The labor force in the United States is made up of all those 16 years of age and older who are working or looking for work. As the population of the United States has changed, so too has the labor force. More women are entering it. The average age of the labor force is getting older, but workers are retiring earlier. Technological change has brought changes in the composition of the labor force. The percentages of white-collar and service workers in the labor force are increasing, while percentages of blue-collar workers and farmworkers are decreasing. The service workers' category is the fastest-growing sector.

Some jobs pay more than others. The market forces of supply and demand help explain wage differentials. Wages are highest where the demand for workers' services is greatest and the supply of such workers is smallest. The demand for workers is influenced by the demand for the product or service with which the workers are involved. The supply of workers is influenced by the skill, training, and education needed, the attractiveness of the job, and whether workers are willing to move to accept jobs. Wages are influenced by nonmarket forces, including labor unions, government laws, and location.

REVIEWING THE CHAPTER

Building Vocabulary

Match each term in Column A with its definition in Column B.

COLUMN A	COLUMN B
1. labor force	*a.* the willingness of workers to move to where the jobs are
2. educational attainment	*b.* the added value of production by the last worker hired
3. white-collar worker	*c.* one's lifelong employment
4. blue-collar worker	*d.* rapid changes in ways of producing goods and services
5. service worker	*e.* the substitution of modern machinery for human labor in the production process
6. career	
7. automation	*f.* one employed in craft, operative, and manual labor occupations
8. worker mobility	*g.* the number of years of school completed
9. technological revolution	*h.* one employed in clerical, professional, or managerial work
10. marginal productivity	*i.* the number of people 16 years of age or older working or looking for work
	j. one employed in transportation, trade, finance, or government work

Understanding What You Have Read

1. As soon as you take some action to find a job, you (*a*) have chosen a career (*b*) enter the labor force (*c*) must leave school (*d*) cannot change your mind about your job.

2. A striking change in the labor force in recent decades has been the increase in numbers of (*a*) farmworkers (*b*) manufacturing workers (*c*) service workers (*d*) laborers.

3. There is a growing demand for workers with (*a*) a lot of talent but little training (*b*) little education and training (*c*) more education and training (*d*) much physical strength.

4. Average yearly earnings are generally highest for (*a*) elementary school graduates (*b*) high school dropouts (*c*) high school graduates (*d*) college graduates.

5. Wages are not the same for all workers because (*a*) not all people and all jobs are alike (*b*) some people work harder than others

(*c*) it is illegal to pay all workers the same wage   (*d*) some families need more money than others.

6. The demand for workers in an industry tends to rise as   (*a*) the supply increases (*b*) the demand for the goods produced decreases (*c*) the demand for the goods produced increases (*d*) productivity falls.

7. According to economic theory, it will pay employers to hire additional workers (*a*) until the point of diminishing returns is reached   (*b*) until the value of the additional production is equal to the cost of hiring the last worker   (*c*) so long as marginal costs are greater than marginal revenue   (*d*) until production exceeds demand.

8. A major concern brought on by the technological revolution is that it might result in   (*a*) a shortage of workers   (*b*) displacement of workers   (*c*) increased prices   (*d*) increased labor costs.

As the manager of a large firm, you are responsible for hiring computer analysts. Your company is willing to pay up to $22 per hour to the individual you hire. Study Figure 8.9 and then answer Questions 9–12.

Figure 8.9   Supply and Demand for Computer Analysts

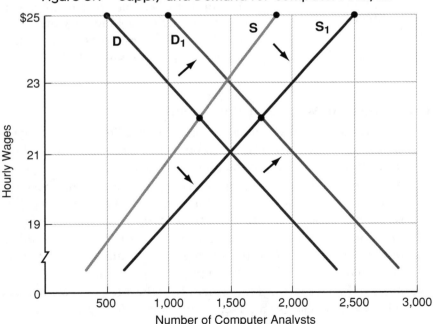

9. About how many computer analysts will be in demand at an hourly wage of $22 before demand increases to D_1? (*a*) 1,000 (*b*) 1,250 (*c*) 1,500 (*d*) 2,000.

10. About how many computer analysts are willing to work for $22 per hour? (*a*) fewer than 1,000 (*b*) 1,250 (*c*) 2,000 (*d*) 2,500.

11. What wage will you have to offer a computer analyst when the demand increases from D to D_1? (*a*) $19 (*b*) $22 (*c*) $23 (*d*) $25.

12. A large number of computer analysts graduate from engineering school, causing supply curve S to shift to the right (S_1). As a result, the number of persons willing to accept $22 per hour will most likely (*a*) increase (*b*) decrease (*c*) remain unchanged (*d*) not enough information is given to determine this.

Thinking Critically

1. "As our labor force gets older, our retirees are getting younger."
   a. Explain what is meant by that statement.
   b. Discuss why you believe that workers are retiring at an earlier age.
   c. How may the aging of the U.S. population and the trend toward earlier retirements affect employment opportunities in the United States?

2. "The labor force in the United States is becoming more varied."
   a. Discuss, with examples, the truth or falsity of that statement.
   b. What statistical evidence can you cite from the text to prove or disprove the view that employment and wage opportunities are equal for all groups in the country.

3. The technological revolution has brought about a considerable change in the composition of the labor force.
   a. How has the technological revolution affected the demand for labor?
   b. Explain why you are encouraged, or discouraged, by the impact the technological revolution has had on employment opportunities.

4. Wages are determined by both market and nonmarket forces.
   a. Explain how the forces of supply and demand of workers affect wages.
   b. Discuss nonmarket forces that affect wage payments in the United States.

SKILLS: Interpreting Double-Line Graphs

Study the graphs below and answer the questions that follow.

1. What was the average annual pay for workers in the state of
   (*a*) Connecticut (*b*) Mississippi?
2. Explain why a shift in the demand curve to the right or the supply
   curve to the left would increase the average annual pay in the state
   of Mississippi.
3. What factors might bring about a shift in the supply or demand
   curve for labor in the state of Mississippi?

Figure 8.10 Supply and Demand for Workers in Two States, 1994

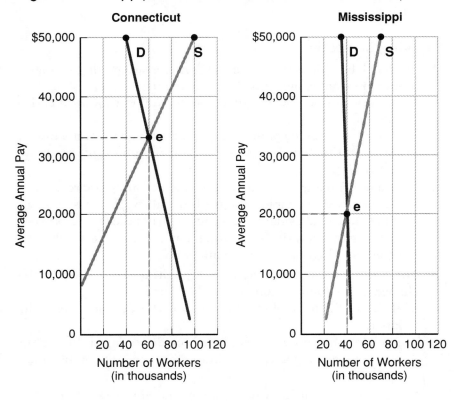

Chapter 9

LABOR UNIONS IN OUR ECONOMY

Overview

Some 16 million workers in the United States (about one worker in seven) belong to labor unions. Although this figure represents a decline from the peak years of the 1950s (when one in three workers belonged), labor unions remain a powerful force in the U.S. economy.

It was not always this way. Historically, unions have long struggled to gain strength and recognition. Most business managers have viewed unions as a threat. After all, a major goal of unions has been to pressure employers to raise wages and improve working conditions. Such demands, when granted, have added to employers' costs. From the point of view of many workers, however, unions have been a necessity, especially in workplaces where wages have been low and working conditions poor.

In this chapter, we will discuss the history of labor unions in this country from the earliest labor organizations to the present. Then we will discuss some of the basic aims of unions, including wages, non-wage benefits, and working conditions. Finally, we will examine how unions negotiate with employers, and what happens when such negotiations fail.

HIGHLIGHTS FROM THE HISTORY OF LABOR UNIONS

Labor unions existed even in the early days of the U.S. republic. These early unions were local *craft unions*, consisting of only a few members who worked in the same *craft* (skilled occupation). For example, workers in the print shops of Philadelphia joined together in 1786 to force employers to raise wages. In a similar manner, barrelmakers in Boston joined together, as did weavers in New York. Unions, however, were not yet organized on a national level, so that printers in New York and Boston did not help printers in Philadelphia when the latter were on strike.

The union way of negotiating an employment contract is known as *collective bargaining*. In collective bargaining, the union represents its members in negotiations rather than have each worker negotiate individually with an employer. Before the Civil War (1861–1865), unions were small, local, and poorly organized. They had great trouble persuading employers to negotiate with union representatives. Instead, employers usually dealt directly with each employee.

Rise and Fall of the Knights of Labor

Unions in the United States increased in size as a direct response to the increased size of businesses. After the Civil War, railroad companies spanned whole regions of the country and wielded enormous power. How could workers hope to bargain for better employment contracts from these corporate giants? One answer was to organize unions on a national scale instead of on a local basis.

The first *national union* to achieve any real success was the **Knights of Labor**, which **Uriah Stephens** founded in 1869. Unlike earlier unions, the Knights did not build upon the existing craft unions. Instead, it was "one big union." All workers, regardless of the kind of work they did, could become members. They could be skilled or unskilled. Neither race nor national origin became a consideration for membership in the Knights.

The Knights conducted several strikes against railroad companies, some of which were successful and resulted in wage increases for union members. By 1886, total membership in this national union had grown to an impressive 700,000. Then, however, the Knights were unfairly blamed for the Haymarket Riot, which resulted in the deaths of at least seven police officers and one civilian. Because of the incident, the union's reputation was damaged, and it went into a period of decline. By 1889, the Knights of Labor had almost ceased to exist.

Rise of the American Federation of Labor

In 1886, a cigarmaker named **Samuel Gompers** founded the **American Federation of Labor**, or **AFL**. It was not a union but a federation, or association, of existing craft unions. These craft unions (cigarmakers' union, carpenters' union, wheelwrights' union, and so on) maintained their separate identities within the larger organization. Only skilled workers of a particular trade were eligible for membership in the craft union that represented that trade. Thus, only a skilled carpenter could belong to the carpenters' union, a skilled cigarmaker to the cigarmakers' union, and so on. An unskilled worker (such as a clerk or janitor) in a printing shop could not join the printers' union.

The AFL became the most successful labor organization of its time. Its membership grew steadily to a peak of almost 4 million in 1920. Gompers insisted that the AFL concentrate on economic issues such as higher wages, shorter hours, and better working conditions. When political candidates of either major party (Republican or Democratic) offered to support the goals of the AFL, they, in turn, received the AFL's endorsement.

The Opposition of Business and Government

Despite the growth of the AFL, unions were still at a serious disadvantage in their dealings with powerful corporations. Before the 1930s, U.S. presidents and state governors tended to give more help to employers than to union organizers. Striking workers sometimes clashed with nonunion "strikebreakers" in battles outside factory gates. Government authorities would then send troops and militia to stop the violence by arresting union leaders. The presence of troops made it easier for business managers to crush strikes. In 1892, for example, unionized steelworkers called a strike against the Carnegie Steel Company mills at Homestead, Pennsylvania. The state governor responded to the resulting violence at Homestead by sending in state militia to restore order. This government action had the effect of breaking the strike.

In 1919, the AFL tried and failed to create a union in the steel industry. It began to organize steelworkers and called a strike. The steel companies, however, were able to keep their plants going with strikebreakers. The AFL's reputation was hurt after it ended the strike without gaining any benefits for the workers.

Mary ("Mother") Jones, left, helped organize coal miners and helped found the Industrial Workers of the World. Samuel Gompers, right, missed only one year between 1886 and 1895 as president of the AFL.

Before the 1930s, the courts' interpretation of federal laws tended to hurt unions and help business. In Chapter 7, we discussed how Congress passed the Sherman Antitrust Act in 1890 in order to regulate business monopolies. In 1903, though, the U.S. Supreme Court ruled that this law could apply to unions as well. The Court said that a striking union of hatmakers in Danbury, Connecticut, had violated the restraint-of-trade provision of the Sherman Act. The Court ordered the union to pay damages to the hatmaking company. This interpretation of the Sherman Antitrust Act prevailed until 1914, when Congress passed the Clayton Antitrust Act. This law stated that unions were not combinations in restraint of trade and, therefore, were not subject to penalties under the Sherman Act.

Existing laws, however, still allowed courts to severely limit union activities by issuing *injunctions*. An injunction is a court order that directs a person or group to stop committing certain acts. From the 1890s until 1932, state and federal courts regularly issued injunctions to stop unions from carrying out strikes. Then Congress passed laws to make it more difficult for courts to issue such injunctions.

A New Deal for Labor

The laws that most dramatically improved the status of unions were enacted during the Great Depression in the 1930s. Near the close of Herbert Hoover's administration, Congress passed the **Norris-LaGuardia Anti-Injunction Act** of 1932. This law limited the use of court injunctions in labor disputes. Franklin Roosevelt, who followed Hoover as president, thought that federal laws should protect and encourage unions. As part of his **New Deal** program, Roosevelt signed into law two acts of Congress that enabled unions to grow into extremely large and powerful organizations. One law was the Wagner Act of 1935 (also called the National Labor Relations Act). The other was the Fair Labor Standards Act of 1938.

- The **Wagner Act** helped change the balance of power between labor and management. It guaranteed all workers the right to organize and join unions and the right to bargain collectively. It defined unfair labor practices by management and created a **National Labor Relations Board (NLRB)** to enforce provisions of the law. The NLRB could conduct elections in a factory or other workplace to determine whether workers wanted to be represented by a particular union.

- The **Fair Labor Standards Act** established a national minimum wage of 25 cents per hour and a maximum workweek of 44 hours. (In a few years, the former would rise to 40 cents, while the latter would fall to 40 hours.) Workers who put in more than the maximum workweek were to be paid overtime at a rate one and a half times their normal hourly pay. Another provision of the act restricted the employment of children.

Rise of the CIO

Until the 1930s, unskilled and semiskilled workers in steel mills and other mass-production industries had been generally left out of the union movement. They could not join the AFL because they did not belong to any skilled trade group. The passage of the Wagner Act in 1935, however, made it possible for unions to organize all wage earners in an entire industry.

This was the goal of labor leader **John L. Lewis,** who in 1935 helped to form the Committee for Industrial Organization. At first, Lewis's group was only a committee within the AFL. It set out to found "vertical unions" in major mass-production industries. Such unions were to include all the workers within an industry regardless of the job they performed. The older, "horizontal unions" grouped workers of similar skills. Quarrels between Lewis and leaders of the AFL caused Lewis to break away and create, in 1938, a new federation of industrial unions. This was the **Congress of Industrial Organizations**, or **CIO**.

The CIO and the AFL competed with each other for members, and so they became increasingly alike. Like the CIO, the AFL brought in many unskilled members; like the AFL, the CIO recruited some highly skilled workers. Factory workers often quarreled among themselves about whether to be organized by the AFL or by the CIO. To avoid these troubles, the great rivals decided in 1955 to merge into one organization—the **AFL-CIO**.

By 1955, unions in the United States had gained tremendously in membership and power. There were 17 million union members then (compared to just 3 million members in 1930). Fully one-third of all nonagricultural workers in the United States belonged to a union in 1955. Since that time, the percentage of union workers in the labor force has declined significantly.

Federal Laws That Regulate Unions

Following World War II (1941–1945), Congress enacted several important laws designed to regulate unions.

Taft-Hartley Act, 1947. This law limited the activities of labor unions in a number of ways. The **Taft-Hartley Act** (1) defined certain labor practices as "unfair," and (2) outlawed the closed shop but did permit the union shop. In both shops, all workers in a workplace must belong to the union that is recognized as their bargaining agent. In a *closed shop*, which had been legal under the Wagner Act, workers were required to

Figure 9.1 Development of Labor Unions in America

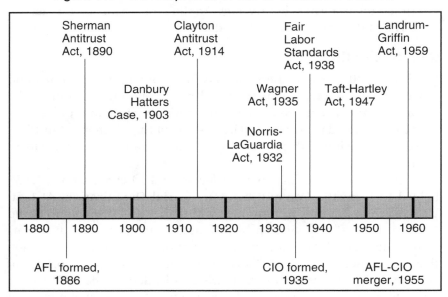

be union members before they could be hired. But in a *union shop*, nonunion workers are permitted (and are required) to join the union after they have been hired. (3) The act also required that a union give a company 60 days' notice before going on strike. Moreover, in an industry that affects the national welfare, the U.S. president can request a court injunction delaying the strike an additional 80 days. (4) As an attempt to control union corruption, the law required union leaders to submit reports on union finances to the government.

Landrum-Griffin Act, 1959. This law also sought to reduce corruption and to improve democratic procedures in unions. The **Landrum-Griffin Act** guaranteed workers the right to participate in the union's affairs and to elect their officers. The *embezzlement* (stealing) of union funds was made a federal offense.

Right-to-Work Laws. Some 19 states, located mostly in the South and Midwest, have enacted *right-to-work laws*. These laws state that workers may hold jobs without being required to join unions.

THE DECLINING POWER OF LABOR UNIONS

Union membership and power have decreased in recent decades. In the mid-1950s, 35 percent of nonfarm workers belonged to unions. By 1980, union membership had declined to 23 percent, and by 1997 it had fallen to 14.1 percent. When the millions of union members who work for federal, state, and local governments are excluded, unions represent only about 9 percent of private sector personnel. If this rate of decline continues, unions will represent a mere 5 percent of private sector workers in the year 2000. While economists disagree as to the exact reasons for the decline, most would include the following: (1) the decline of mass-production industries, (2) automation, (3) global competition, and (4) general unpopularity of unions.

Fewer Mass-Production Jobs

In our discussion of the labor force in Chapter 8, we learned that there has been a decline in blue-collar workers and an increase in service workers. It was the blue-collar workers who had flocked to the unions in the 19th and early 20th centuries. The number of blue-collar workers has been declining because mass-production industries have been declining. (*Mass production* is the making of a product in quantity, usually with machinery.) Today, there are fewer jobs in auto and textile plants and more jobs in insurance and financial services companies.

Although there are fewer factory jobs, office jobs continue to grow. Office workers have always been less likely to join unions, even though unions are spending much effort at trying to organize them. An exception is in government employment, some of which involves office work. Union membership among government employees has grown dramatically in recent decades. While in the 1960s only one non-military government worker in ten belonged to unions, by the mid-1990s this figure had grown to one in three.

Automation

The trend toward using more automated equipment to produce more goods with fewer workers is also contributing to the decline in union membership. Thus, there are fewer mechanics and line workers, both of which are professions whose members tend to join unions.

The effect of automation can be illustrated in another field of work—banking. Traditionally, bank tellers were needed to handle deposits and withdrawals. Now both of these transactions can be completed by *automated teller machines (ATMs)*. Open seven days a week, the machines are found not only at banks, but also in shopping malls, airports, and other places where people gather. Only a few individuals are needed to stock the boxes with cash and pick up the deposits. Banks have been able to reduce their staffs of tellers.

Telecommunications is another field in which automation is reducing the labor force. In 1995, for example, AT&T announced plans to install computerized telephone-operator services. This change would allow the company to eliminate one-third, or 6,000, of its operators. These workers would be replaced by "voice recognition" technology that enables callers to make telephone requests to a computer rather than to a live operator.

Global Competition

As a result of increased foreign competition, some industries (such as consumer electronics, men's and women's wear, and shoe manufacturing) have seen most of their production move abroad. To remain competitive with foreign competition, many firms still located in the United States have sought to reduce their costs of doing business. Many unions have had to accept wage reductions and reduced benefits as concessions to increased foreign competition. These retreats by labor unions have made the unions less attractive to workers.

General Unpopularity of Labor Unions

Unions are not universally popular among workers. Some workers believe that union dues cost too much and that membership in a union

Figure 9.2   U.S. Labor Union Membership

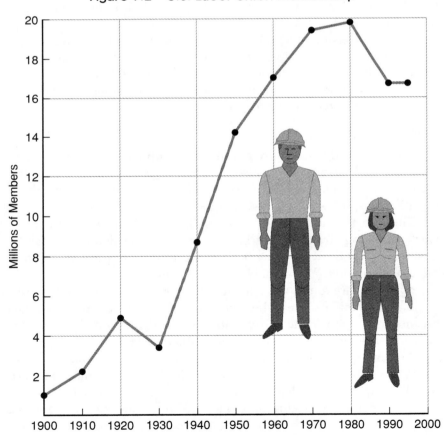

does not provide enough benefits to offset these dues. Others do not want to belong to a union because they believe that union leaders are corrupt. They get this idea because some union officials have been found guilty of pocketing money that was supposed to be used for the benefit of all union members.

In the South, unions have not been as popular as elsewhere. Thus, many employers from the Northeast and the Midwest have moved operations to that part of the country to avoid having to deal with unions. To counter this trend, unions have been trying to organize unions in the South.

Public opinion polls indicate that many union members have lost faith in their unions. Perhaps union workers see their union as being less powerful and, therefore, less important in their lives. Unions in 1995 represented only 10 percent of the nation's private sector workforce as compared to 36 percent at its peak in 1953. Or perhaps it is because the downsizing of large manufacturing companies (which were heavily union-organized) resulted in many union workers losing high-paying jobs forcing them to accept new jobs at lower pay. Workers felt powerless and ignored by their union leaders. It is very likely that both union members' allegiance to their unions and union influence in national elections will continue to decline unless there is a reversal in the decline in the strength of unions.

THE BASIC AIMS OF UNIONS

Labor unions have many goals. The major ones are higher wages, better working conditions, a union shop, job security, fringe benefits, and grievance machinery.

Higher Wages

Of primary concern to all unions are the so-called bread-and-butter issues of wages and hours. In presenting their demands for higher wages, unions usually rely on one or more of the following arguments:

Profits and Ability to Pay. Unions believe that workers are entitled to share in a company's prosperity. Thus, unions frequently claim that large profits justify wage increases.

Equal Pay for Equal Work. If workers performing identical or similar jobs in other companies are earning higher rates of pay, union leaders will argue that their members should be brought up to that level. This is fair, they claim, because if the job is worth so much to one company, it should be worth that much to another.

Productivity. Union leaders argue that if the productivity of a group of workers is increased, those workers should share in the profits that often result from increased productivity.

Rising Cost of Living. For the last five decades, U.S. consumers have experienced a general rise in prices. If prices continue to rise, workers' current wages will probably not be able to buy as much in the future as they can today. To protect their members against increases in living costs, unions frequently base their wage demands on expected changes in the price level. They may also ask for an *escalator clause* in their contract. This clause ties money wages to the cost of living in order to keep real wages constant. Thus, if the cost of living should rise by 10 percent in the course of the year, wages would automatically be raised by 10 percent. Often an escalator clause will tie wage raises to a cost-of-living index such as the Consumer Price Index, discussed in Chapter 14.

Shorter Workdays and Workweeks

Just as unions have striven to increase their members' wages, so, too, have they sought to reduce the number of hours worked. This latter effort has been directed toward the reduction of both the number of hours worked each day and the number of days worked each week. Whereas in the early 19th century, the workweek in New England textile mills averaged 72 hours, the present-day nonfarm workweek averages about 35 hours. Unions claim much of the credit for this reduction in number of working hours.

Union Shop

During collective bargaining, a union attempts to gain more than improved wages and hours. Among its primary goals is the establishment of a union shop, a workplace where only union members could be hired. For its part, management prefers an *open shop*, one in which workers are free not to join the union.

A compromise between the union shop and the open shop is the *agency shop*. Under this arrangement, nonunion workers are required to pay dues to the union as long as they work in the shop. These workers, though, do not have to join the union. In an agency shop, there are no "free riders," workers who do not pay dues to a union but who benefit from the gains won by the union.

Checkoff

Another contract provision commonly sought by unions is the *checkoff*. It provides that dues will be deducted automatically from the workers' pay and sent on to the union. This provision helps the union to stay financially solvent.

Everyone smiles when management and workers agree on a new contract because the agreements are often the result of weeks of negotiating.

Union Label

We sometimes see goods for sale that have a label that announces the goods had been made by union workers. Unions try to pressure employers to attach this union label to the goods they produce. Unions also try to induce the public to look for a union label before making purchases.

Job Security

One of the main objectives that workers expect union negotiators to achieve is job security. Union contracts usually provide that workers may not be dismissed without good reason. In anticipation of layoffs, most contracts provide that the workers with the most *seniority,* or years of service, will be the last to lose their jobs. Unions have also tried to achieve a form of guaranteed annual wage. In some contracts, this has taken the form of supplementary unemployment benefits, which are payments by the employer to laid-off workers.

Fringe Benefits

Benefits not directly connected with wages or the job are called *fringe benefits*. They include items pertaining to health, welfare, vacations, and retirement. In recent years, fringe benefits have made up an increasing percentage of the total labor costs of employers. Many employers, for example, pay the cost of health insurance programs for their employees. Although the cost of this insurance does not appear in workers' pay envelopes, it nonetheless represents added income.

Grievance Machinery

Once a labor contract is drawn up and in force, disagreements may arise between the employer and union members over many issues. A worker may feel that a supervisor has been unfair. Management may claim that union members have not been living up to their responsibilities. Whatever the dispute, most labor contracts provide for *grievance machinery*, or methods by which disputes can be resolved. This machinery usually involves hearings, with the right of appeal to a higher level. The final appeal under many union contracts is to an impartial *arbitrator*. Under the procedure of *arbitration*, an impartial third party, the arbitrator, hears both sides of the argument and renders a decision that is binding on both parties.

THE COLLECTIVE BARGAINING PROCESS

Before a shop is organized, there are usually some workers who would like to be represented by a union and others who are either uncertain or would prefer to remain independent. The situation may be further complicated if two or more unions are seeking to organize the same workers.

Achieving Recognition

Under the terms of the National Labor Relations Act, a union can ask the National Labor Relations Board to *certify* (approve) it as the official bargaining agent for a particular shop. If there is any objection, the NLRB is authorized to conduct an election to determine who, if anyone, should represent the employees. Having won a majority of the votes in such an election, a union is certified by the NLRB as the sole bargaining representative for its members. The employer is legally bound to bargain in good faith with that union.

Negotiating a Labor Contract

Once it has been designated as the exclusive bargaining agent, the union will seek to negotiate a *labor contract*. It is a written agreement between the employer and the union representing employees. The labor contract sets the conditions of employment (compensation, hours, and working conditions) and the procedure to be used in settling disputes.

Representatives of the union and management sit down to hammer out an agreement through collective bargaining. More than 90 percent of union contracts are drawn up entirely as a result of these kinds of discussions. There are times, however, when collective bargaining breaks down, and disagreements between employer and union members become difficult to resolve. Workers might go out on strike.

We read and hear more about strikes than about other types of union activities. They frequently become the focus of television newscasts and newspaper stories. This is understandable because strikes are more exciting news than labor agreements are. Nevertheless, peacefully negotiated agreements in the United States average about 300 a day, while fewer than 3,000 strikes take place in a year.

Collective bargaining usually involves talks between the officials of a single company and a union. Sometimes, however, unions bargain with more than one company at a time. Collective bargaining normally will follow one of these patterns:

Local Bargaining. Where companies in a particular industry do not normally compete outside their own community, collective bargaining usually takes place on a community basis. For example, retail food stores in Peoria, Illinois, do not compete with those in Columbia, South Carolina. Therefore, food merchants in those towns may negotiate separately with the local unions.

Pattern Bargaining. In certain industries, a few very influential companies control major portions of the market. Whatever they do will probably be followed by the other firms. Consequently, unions try to first reach an agreement with the most influential company in an industry. USX Steel, General Electric, and Ford are typical of the companies with which unions negotiate in the expectation that the agreements reached will "set the pattern" for other companies in the industry.

Industrywide Bargaining. If one trucking company could sign a union contract in which its drivers were paid less than those working for other firms, this company would be in a position to undersell its competitors. This would not take place under industrywide bargaining, in which representatives of all firms negotiate one nationwide union contract for all firms in this industry. This kind of negotiation can benefit both management and unions. Management is protected against unfair competition from companies having lower labor costs. Unions help keep competing firms in business, thus protecting the jobs of their members. (Note that an industrywide contract could include foreign companies that operate union shops in the United States.)

WHEN COLLECTIVE BARGAINING FAILS

Although the overwhelming number of union contracts are worked out through collective bargaining, there are times when this process fails

Question: Which baseball team won the 1994 World Series? (Answer: No team won.) In 1994, the baseball season was cut short weeks before the time the World Series would have been held. With salary negotiations between ballplayers and team owners deadlocked, the players called a strike on August 12th. One month later, with talks between the parties still tied up, the owners canceled the remaining games.

to bring about an agreement between management and the union. When face-to-face bargaining breaks down, the choices that remain usually involve either intervention by a third party or the application of some form of "arm-twisting" by either management or the union.

How Unions Put Pressure on Management

In seeking to achieve their goals, labor unions may use a variety of tactics.

Strikes. A *strike* is a work stoppage for the purpose of gaining concessions from management. It is labor's most powerful weapon because of the financial penalties it imposes upon the employer. Of course, a strike also costs participating workers a loss in income. Striking workers often wonder whether the potential gains from a successful strike will outweigh the expenses of lost wages.

The amount of time lost because of work stoppages is far less than the public seems to believe. In 1995, for example, the time lost because of strikes was 0.02 percent of the total time worked by all workers in the country. Indeed, as indicated by Figure 9.3, in only one year since 1945 has the working time lost because of strikes gone above one percent of the total. In this regard, union leaders remind us that the time lost because of strikes is tiny compared to the number of workdays lost through unemployment.

Despite the relatively light cost of strikes, certain industries are so closely related to the public interest that even the briefest stoppage can become intolerable. If, for example, a strike should shut off public transportation, garbage removal, or milk delivery, the public welfare is directly involved. Also, the U.S. economy is so specialized that, if one segment of it fails to function, many others will feel the pinch. A strike in the steel industry will eventually be felt by all industries that use steel. A tire strike will affect the production of all motor vehicles. A stoppage by dockworkers that shuts down the waterfront will inevitably leave its mark on many other industries and their workers. Thus, despite the relatively small number of strikes in the United States, their impact can be widely felt. Furthermore, because the public is often affected by strikes, it frequently adopts a hostile attitude toward the strikers.

As we discussed on page 202, the Taft-Hartley Act permits the federal government to obtain an injunction that can delay a strike for 80

Figure 9.3   Work Time Lost Because of Strikes Since 1945

days if the national welfare is involved. Of course, at the end of the 80-day period, the workers can go on strike. When Congress passed the act in 1947, people hoped that during this "cooling-off period" the negotiating process would continue and a strike could be avoided.

In extreme cases of national emergency, as during wartime, the government has seized and operated plants that were on strike. This is a last-resort measure that most lawyers feel is unconstitutional during peacetime.

Picketing. *Picketing* takes place when workers march outside a business carrying signs, usually to proclaim the existence of a strike. The objectives of picketing are to (1) discourage workers from entering the workplace, and (2) arouse public sympathy and urge the public not to patronize the struck business.

Boycott. A union *boycott* is a refusal to buy goods or services from a company whose workers are on strike. Unions ask their members and their families to "spread the word" to boycott the struck company's goods. They may also call upon the general public to cooperate in the action. The objective is to add to the financial pressures on the employer by reducing the company's sales. Because the pressure is being applied to the company being struck, this tactic is called a "primary boycott." When the same pressure is put on a company whose workers are not on strike (but which is doing business with the struck company), we have a "secondary boycott." If, for example, the workers of the Rifle Towel Company were on strike and they and others refused to buy Rifle towels, we would have a primary boycott. However, should the union order its members not to have any dealings with stores that sell Rifle towels, this would be a secondary boycott. Certain types of secondary boycotts have been made illegal by the Taft-Hartley and Landrum-Griffin acts.

Slowdown. When workers deliberately reduce their output in order to force concessions from their employer, this is called a *slowdown*. Since they are not on strike, however, workers can continue to draw their wages.

Political Action. Although labor has not organized its own political party, unions try to induce their members to support political candidates whose views the unions consider favorable. These activities are no different from those of business leaders who support political candidates. Also, like management, unions lobby for the passage of laws that will strengthen their position.

Illegal Methods. Unions have resorted to tactics that either were never legal or have since been declared illegal. Among the most common of these were the following:

1. Secondary Boycott. This tactic was described on the previous page.

2. Strong-Arm Methods. Unions have been known to hire thugs to coerce management into accepting their demands. The extent and nature of these illegal activities were revealed in the investigations conducted in the 1950s by the McClellan Committee of the U.S. Senate. After considering the findings of this committee, Congress passed the Landrum-Griffin Act in 1959.

3. Jurisdictional Strike. Sometimes a dispute breaks out between two unions over the question of which one has authority over a particular job. For example, should the worker who removes a part of a costume from the stage during a play be a member of the Costumers' Union or the Stagehands' Union? While at one time such disputes might have led to *jurisdictional strikes*, the Taft-Hartley Act of 1947 outlawed them as unfair labor practices.

How Management Puts Pressure on Unions

Most employers have accepted the idea of working with unions and have done their best to maintain cordial relations with them. Nevertheless, the occasional breakdowns in labor-management negotiations have led management to take certain steps against unions. The following are some of the more important management tactics.

In the 1970s, Cesar Chavez (center), of the United Farm Workers Union, organized a boycott of lettuce grown on nonunionized farms.

Lockouts. A *lockout* occurs when management shuts down a workplace in hopes of bringing the workers to its terms. Although the effect is the same as a strike (in that work is suspended), management hopes it can better afford the temporary financial losses involved. In recent decades, the lockout has sometimes been followed by a permanent shutdown of operations and a move to a region of the country where unions are weaker. The possibility of such a move puts pressure on the union to come to terms.

Injunctions. Sometimes a court will issue an injunction to halt a strike. The use of the injunction in labor disputes, however, is not common. It was sharply limited by the Norris-LaGuardia Act of 1932.

Strikebreakers. One way for an employer to break a strike is to hire workers to replace striking union members. It is legal to hire *strikebreakers,* or "scabs," as the unions call them. Some states, however, require that employers tell these new employees that they have been hired to replace workers on strike.

Political Activity. By persuading the federal government and the states to pass laws that limit the power of unions, industry has tried to maintain a strong bargaining position. Unions point to states' right-to-work laws as examples of legislation favoring management.

Public Relations. Industries have founded or supported organizations such as the **National Association of Manufacturers** and the **Chamber of Commerce of the United States**. These groups have sought to present management's point of view to the public and have lobbied for laws favorable to management. In addition, some companies buy newspaper advertisements and time on radio and television to present their side of a labor dispute.

Peaceful Ways to Settle Labor Disputes

There are a number of methods of settling disputes between labor and management that avoid strikes.

Fact-Finding. In some labor disputes, the government might appoint a "fact-finding board." This board investigates the issues, makes a report, and, in many cases, suggests solutions. Its recommendations are not necessarily binding.

Mediation. In *mediation*, a third party brings together the two parties in the dispute, listens to their arguments, and perhaps offers a solution. The compromise proposals suggested by the mediator, however, are not binding on either party. (This procedure is also called "conciliation.")

The Nobel Prize in Economics

The growing importance of economics and the influence of economists were given international recognition in 1969 with the award of the first Nobel Prize in Economic Science to **Ragnar Frisch** (left) of Norway and **JanTinbergen** of the Netherlands. They were pioneers in *econometrics*. Economists in this field develop mathematical models that are used to describe and predict changes in the economy. Since 1901, the Nobel Prizes (which are financed out of the estate of the Swedish inventor of dynamite, **Alfred Nobel**) have been given for outstanding achievement in physics, chemistry, medicine, literature, and international peace. The award for economics was the first new category

to have been added since the creation of the prize. In 1979, the Prize was shared by Theodore W. Shultz of the United States and Sir Arthur Lewis of Great Britain. Sir Arthur, the first black to win a Nobel Prize in Economics, studied the transition from agricultural to industrial society in developing nations.

Table 9.1 WINNERS OF THE NOBEL PRIZE FOR ECONOMICS

Year	Winner	Year	Winner
1969	Ragnar Frisch	1984	Sir Richard Stone
	Jan Tinbergen	1985	Franco Modigliani
1970	Paul Samuelson	1986	James Buchanan
1971	Simon Kuznets	1987	Robert Solow
1972	Sir John Hicks	1988	Maurice Allais
	Kenneth Arrow	1989	Trygve Haavelmo
1973	Wassily Leontief	1990	Harry Markowitz
1974	Gunnar Myrdal		Merton Miller
	Friedrich von Hayek		William Sharpe
1975	Tjalling Koopmans	1991	Ronald Coase
	Leonid Kantorovich	1992	Gary Becker
1976	Milton Friedman	1993	Robert Fogel
1977	Bertil Ohlin		Douglas North
	James Meade	1994	John Harsanyi
1978	Herbert Simon		John Nash
1979	Sir Arthur Lewis		Reinhard Selten
	Theodore Schultz	1995	Robert E. Lucas, Jr.
1980	Lawrence Klein	1996	William Vickrey
1981	James Tobin		James Mirrlees
1982	George Stigler	1997	Robert C. Merton
1983	Gerard Debreu		Myron S. Scholes

Arbitration. As we discussed earlier in the chapter, in the arbitration method of settling labor disputes, a third party gives a decision that is binding on both sides. Arbitration is rarely used to negotiate labor contracts. More frequently, it is used as the final step in the handling of a grievance arising out of the interpretation of an existing contract.

Grievance Committee. Where workers are represented by a union, procedures for the handling of *grievances* (complaints) are spelled out in the labor contract. Union contracts provide for hearings in which workers air their grievances or in which management explains the reasons why it wants to discipline or dismiss a worker.

Summary

Early labor unions in the United States were small, local, and associated with a particular craft. In the 19th century, the Knights of Labor organized skilled and unskilled workers on a national level into one big union. Later, the AFL created a federation of independent craft unions. In the 20th century, the growth of mass production industries gave rise to the CIO, an organization of unions of all workers in the same industry. The AFL and CIO merged into the AFL-CIO in 1955. While unions were very powerful then, they have since lost much of their power, mainly because of the decline of the mass production industries that were the major sources of union members.

Unions have as their basic aims higher wages, better working conditions, a union shop with a check-off provision, job security, fringe benefits, and grievance machinery. Collective bargaining is the process where the union negotiates a contract for its members. Both labor and management resort to various practices when collective bargaining fails. The strike is the primary weapon of unions, while the lockout is a powerful management weapon.

REVIEWING THE CHAPTER

Building Vocabulary

Match each term in Column A with its definition in Column B.

COLUMN A	COLUMN B
1. arbitration	*a.* a court order to stop a certain action
2. collective bargaining	*b.* the process of settling a dispute using non-binding decisions of a third party
3. boycott	*c.* the process of settling a dispute using binding decisions of a third party
4. closed shop	*d.* negotiations by representatives of a union and a company about the terms of a union contract
5. craft union	
6. mediation	*e.* the shutting down of a business by management to keep workers off the job
7. open shop	*f.* a workplace in which only workers belonging to a specific union may be hired
8. injunction	
9. strike	*g.* the refusal to buy goods or services from a company
10. lockout	*h.* a union action against an employer to refuse to continue working
	i. a union of skilled workers in the same trade
	j. a workplace in which the employer is free to hire either union or nonunion workers

Understanding What You Have Read

1. Labor unions in the United States have as their main goal to (*a*) create labor unrest (*b*) prevent new technology from being introduced (*c*) improve workers' wages and working conditions (*d*) make conditions difficult for employers.

2. About what proportion of the U.S. labor force belongs to unions? (*a*) more than 75 percent (*b*) between 50 and 75 percent (*c*) between 20 and 50 percent (*d*) less than 20 percent.

3. Most labor contracts are arrived at as a result of (*a*) a strike (*b*) picketing (*c*) collective bargaining (*d*) arbitration.

4. The growth of the assembly line and mass-production industries led to the organization of the (*a*) Knights of Labor (*b*) AFL (*c*) CIO (*d*) National Labor Relations Board.

5. Labor legislation was most favorable to labor unions during the period (a) 1865–1910 (b) 1910–1930 (c) 1930–1945 (d) 1945–present.

6. The first law to guarantee the right of collective bargaining was the (a) Sherman Antitrust Act (b) Wagner Act (c) Taft-Hartley Act (d) Landrum-Griffin Act.

7. The Fair Labor Standards Act of 1938 (a) set a minimum wage and maximum workweek (b) defined certain labor practices as unfair and outlawed the closed shop (c) made the embezzlement of union funds a federal offense (d) prohibited public employees from striking.

8. Which tactic might be used by union workers against management? (a) lockout (b) injunction (c) picketing (d) hiring strikebreakers.

9. Which tactic might be used by management against union workers? (a) slowdown (b) strike (c) boycott (d) lockout.

10. When a strike threatens the nation's health and safety, the president of the United States may (a) forbid the strike (b) request an injunction to halt the strike temporarily (c) impose a settlement (d) provide for government operation of plants threatened by the strike.

11. In which type of shop must workers join the union *after* being hired? (a) union shop (b) closed shop (c) open shop (d) agency shop.

12. In recent decades, unions have been affected by (a) an increase in job opportunities for unskilled workers (b) an increase in blue-collar jobs (c) a decline in service industries (d) a decline in mass-production industries.

Thinking Critically

1. The history of labor unions in the United States indicates several periods of growth. Select *one* of the following two periods: 1869–1920 or 1935–1955. Describe the labor unions and national organizations that developed during the period you selected and discuss the reasons for their growth.

2. Study Figure 9.4 and answer the questions that follow:
   a. Give *three* arguments to show that labor was at a disadvantage in the years before 1914.
   b. Give *two* arguments to show that in 1946 labor had the upper hand in its relations with management.

Figure 9.4 Balance Between Labor and Management in 1914, 1946, and Today

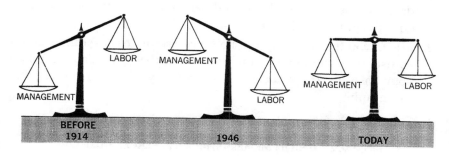

c. What events have taken place in the years since 1946 to help "restore the balance of power" between labor and management?

d. Explain why you agree or disagree that the balance of power has been restored.

3. Union power has decreased in recent decades. Some of the reasons given for this decline are *(a)* global competition, *(b)* the shift in types of jobs in the labor force, and *(c)* automation. Select any *two* of these reasons and explain, with examples, how each one chosen may contribute to the decline in the power of labor unions.

4. In recent years, there have been a number of strikes by public employees, such as teachers, sanitation workers, and air traffic controllers. In most instances, these strikes were in violation of antistrike laws. Do you believe that public employees ought to have the right to strike? If your answer is "yes," explain why. If your answer is "no," explain some procedures you might suggest for settling disputes between government and its employees.

5. Assume that the union representing the workers in a large bakery has just signed a contract with management. Summarize under the following headings some of the provisions that the agreement is likely to include: *(a)* union recognition *(b)* conditions of work *(c)* grievance procedures *(d)* wages *(e)* job security *(f)* fringe benefits *(g)* other provisions.

6. Some labor disputes are settled through arbitration. *(a)* Explain the meaning of *arbitration*. *(b)* Do you think that arbitration is a good method to settle labor disputes? Explain your answer.

SKILLS: Creating and Interpreting a Graph

1. Draw a line graph using the data given in the table below. Put dates on the horizontal axis and percentages on the vertical axis. Give the graph a title.

2. (*a*) Do you find the graph to be more useful, less useful, or about as useful as the table in understanding the given data? Explain your answer. (*b*) What conclusions can you draw from reading this graph?

Table 9.2   UNION MEMBERSHIP AS A PERCENTAGE OF NONAGRICULTURAL WAGE AND SALARY WORKERS

Year	Percent	Year	Percent
1950	31.5	1985	18.0
1955	33.6	1987	17.0
1960	31.4	1989	16.4
1964	29.5	1991	16.1
1966	28.8	1992	15.8
1968	28.4	1994	15.5
1970	28.0	1995	14.9
1978	23.6	1996	14.5
1980	25.2	1997	14.1
1983	20.1		

Chapter 10

THE CONSUMER IN THE AMERICAN ECONOMY

Overview

The subject of consumer spending is important to the whole economy. Consumers as a group buy a good percentage of all the goods and services produced and sold in the United States. Consumer spending is also important to the individuals who do the spending (that is—us). As individuals, how we spend, save, and borrow money has much to do with our quality of life.

During our lifetime, each of us will probably be receiving an income. If so, we will have to decide how much of the income we will spend and how much we will set aside as savings and investments. We will also have the opportunity to borrow in order to buy something now that we will pay for in the future. How we use future income, savings, and credit opportunities will directly affect the amount of goods and services we will be able to buy. In this chapter, we will explore the variety of ways in which consumers save and borrow money.

CONSUMER SPENDING

In our discussion of the interdependence of economic society in Chapter 2, we discussed how a flow of money is constantly passing back and forth among the public, business firms, and all levels of government. This "circular flow," as it is called, consists of consumer spending (C), business firm investments (I), and government spending (G).

The money that consumers in this country spend every year (the "C" in our equation) runs into the trillions of dollars. Indeed, better than two-thirds of the goods and services that make up our gross domestic product (GDP) is purchased by or for consumers. The remainder is purchased by business firms and government (see Table 10.1). Total spending, or GDP, equals C + I + G. Consequently, even a small shift in consumer spending is likely to be felt by the entire economy. If consumers spend less, business firms will produce less, and thus need fewer workers. If consumers spend more, production and employment will increase. In 1995, for example, a 5 percent increase in consumer spending would have pumped an additional $246 billion into the circular flow ($4,923 × .05 = $246). Naturally, a 5 percent decrease in consumer spending would have had quite the opposite effect. Total

Table 10.1   **GROSS DOMESTIC PRODUCT, 1995 (IN BILLIONS)**

Consumer Spending (Consumption)	$4,923
Business Spending (Investment)	1,068
Government Spending (Government)	1,358
GDP	$7,349

spending would have dropped by $246 billion (from $4,923 to $4,677 billion).

Looking at the circular flow chart (Figure 10.1) on the next page, we can see that the money consumers spend does more than simply pay for the goods and services they buy. Those same payments are distributed as profits to businesses, as wages to workers, and as taxes to government. Since consumer spending is so important to total spending, to earnings, and to production in the U.S. economy, it is no wonder that economists study why and how consumers spend and save their money.

The Economic Implications of Savings

In order for any society to increase its output, it must devote part of its production to the manufacture of capital goods and services. The automobile industry, for example, cannot increase its total output unless some auto companies build new machinery and tools. What is true for the automobile industry is true for all industries. New capital must be constantly produced to expand production and to replace equipment that has worn out.

To pay for capital investments, businesses might set aside part of their earnings in the form of savings, sell stock, or borrow. In other words, business investment is paid for out of the savings of businesses themselves or of others. Businesses might also borrow money from commercial banks, insurance companies, investment banks, or other financial agencies. These institutions in turn get their funds from people who put their money in these institutions.

The process of saving and investing is voluntary in our economy. No one tells consumers or businesspeople how much they may spend or save. Although the government may use its powers to influence these choices, the final decisions rest with individuals.

The sum total of millions of individual decisions whether to spend or save will ultimately affect the kind and quantity of goods and services produced. Savings are an important link in the economic process because savers, by giving up the opportunity to enjoy goods and services in the present, are making possible increased production in the future.

Figure 10.1   The Circular Flow of Economic Activity

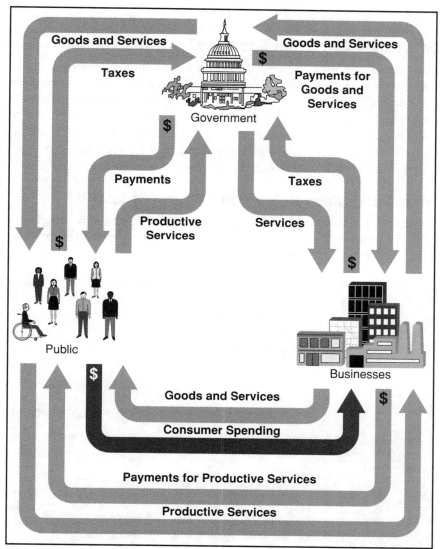

Sources of Income

People's sources of income are varied. Many people receive wages or salaries for the work they perform. Some also receive interest and/or dividends on their savings and investments. Those people who own businesses usually earn profits. Retired people might receive pension payments from their former employers or regular Social Security payments from the federal government. The government supplements some people's incomes in other ways as well, including providing several types of welfare payments.

Consumers Can Either Spend or Save Their Income

Consumers can do one of several things with their income: spend it, save it, or spend part and save the rest. In recent years, consumers have been spending about 95 percent of their *after-tax income* (income that remains after paying taxes). They have been putting the rest into savings. Economists describe the tendency to spend one's income as the *propensity to consume,* and the tendency to save a portion of one's income as the *propensity to save.*

What Determines How Much We Save or Spend?

Economists have separated five factors that determine how much consumers spend or save: income, wealth, interest rates, future expectations, and government policies.

Income. How much we spend or save is largely determined by how much money we have available to us. For low-income families, that sum depends upon how much its members regularly receive. Members of low-income families are likely to spend everything they receive just to meet the costs of living. They save little or nothing. As a family's in-

What factors determine how much this consumer spends?

come increases, though, so too will the amount its members set aside as savings.

More than any other factor, *disposable family income* (how much a family has left after paying personal taxes) determines how much a family spends or saves. In 1857, German statistician **Ernst Engel** concluded that as a family's income increases, the percentage of that income spent on food decreases. Moreover, the percentage spent on operating the household remains almost unchanged and the percentage spent on all other categories (luxuries, medical care, and personal care, for example) and on savings increases. These generalizations are known as *Engel's Law*.

Wealth. Wealth is not the same as income. Wealth is anything that has value (such as stocks, bonds, real estate, and savings). Income, by contrast, represents money that a family or individual receives (such as salary, sale of house, and dividends from stock). All other things being equal, the percentage of family income saved decreases as its wealth increases. This can be illustrated by the following example.

Two young families, the Blues and Greens, each have two young children. Both families earn identical salaries and identical incomes, but the Blues recently inherited $250,000. Since the Greens do not have $250,000 to fall back on in case of need or emergency, they (more so than the wealthier Blues) are under pressure to save for the future. It is likely, therefore, that the Greens will save a larger percentage of their income than will the wealthier Blues.

Interest Rates. A person or business usually pays interest for the use of someone else's money. Consumers who borrow money to finance a purchase will have to pay interest on the loan. Similarly, banks pay interest to their depositors in exchange for the use of the money on deposit.

When interest rates are rising, it becomes more costly to borrow. Higher costs, in turn, discourage consumer spending, particularly spending by consumers who spend with borrowed money (e.g., use credit cards). But higher interest rates encourage saving simply because individuals are being offered higher interest to put their money into a savings plan. As an individual puts more of her or his income into savings, less is available to spend.

Falling interest rates have the opposite effect: the propensity to consume increases, while the propensity to save decreases. As interest rates fall, it is cheaper to borrow. For example, if you have to pay back $8 in interest rather than $10, you would have an additional $2 to spend. In contrast, if your bank reduces interest rates on every $100 deposited from $5 to $3, you would have less of an inducement to save

Why would interest rates help determine whether this consumer buys a new car?

your money in that bank. You might decide to spend your $100 rather than save it.

Future Expectations. Consumers often base their decisions concerning how much to spend on what they feel about the future. When the general public is feeling good about the future, consumer spending tends to increase. When pessimism prevails, consumers tend to postpone some of their more costly purchases. These ideas are illustrated by the following dialogue.

"My parents were going to buy a new car, but they didn't."
"Oh yeah, what happened?"
"I don't know. Business is so bad that my Dad figured the factory where he works might have to lay off workers next year."

Government Policies. The use of government's power to tax and spend may also affect consumer spending and saving patterns. Tax increases tend to discourage spending by taking purchasing power away from consumers by an amount equal to the tax. Conversely, tax reductions stimulate spending by increasing take-home pay. Tax laws have also been used to encourage savings. For example, federal laws defer taxes on the interest earned from certain retirement savings accounts. (IRAs, or individual retirement accounts, and other retirement plans are discussed on page 236.)

Similarly, government programs such as Social Security, welfare, unemployment, and veterans' benefits can either add to or take away from consumers' purchasing power. For example, the money spent by state governments to increase benefits for unemployed workers adds to the workers' purchasing power and to consumer spending. Conversely, by withholding or reducing welfare payments, food stamps, or unemployment benefits, the individuals who would have received these payments will have less to spend.

Personal Decisions and Living Standards

We have said that consumers' decisions to save or spend affect the economy as a whole. On a more personal level, the ways in which consumers choose to save and spend will affect the quality of their individual lives. Those who choose wisely will live better than those who do not. In the pages that follow, we will review a number of things to help us choose wisely as we save and spend our money.

THE DECISION TO SAVE AND INVEST

Why do people set a portion of their income aside in savings and investments rather than spending it all? The reasons are several:

- *To prepare for the unexpected.* When an emergency (such as an accident, long-term illness, or the loss of a job) occurs, savings and investments can help soften the financial burden. That is what people mean when they say they are "saving for a rainy day."
- *To finance costly purchases.* Some purchases (such as automobiles, vacations, and computers) cost more than one's current income. Savings provide a way to afford those purchases.
- *For additional income.* Money set aside in savings accounts and investments typically earns a return in the form of interest or dividends.

Defining Savings and Investments

Most people do not immediately spend all of their income. They usually set aside some amount for use at a later time. Income that is not spent is called *savings*. Some people use their savings to buy property that they believe will increase in value. This activity is called *investing*. The properties that people purchase while investing are called *investments*. Stocks, bonds, and mutual funds are some of the popular investments that we will discuss later in this chapter.

● *For retirement.* Most people would like to retire when they reach a certain age. Probably they will be entitled to Social Security benefits. Some people are also entitled to receive benefits from their employer's pension plan. But all these benefits might not be enough to support the retired person. In order to be able to retire comfortably, an individual would be wise to establish another fund upon which he or she can draw after retirement.

● *As a hedge against inflation.* The real value of assets or income will shrink with time as the purchasing power of the dollar declines. Thus, $100 set aside in a cookie jar in 1980 did not buy as much in 1995 as it would have in 1980. If the $100 had been placed in a bank earning interest at 6 percent per year, it would have amounted to almost $240 15 years later. However, if the rate of inflation during these 15 years was greater than 6 percent per year, the $240 would have also bought less in 1995 than $100 could have purchased in 1980. Since the rate of inflation was actually about 3 percent per year during the period 1980–1995, savings earning 6 percent brought a net return (adjusted for inflation) of only 3 percent per year. But a net increase of 3 percent per year is preferable to a loss in purchasing power, which would have been the case if money had not been invested at a rate higher than the rate of inflation. From this example, we can conclude that it is wise to save or invest as a hedge against inflation.

Figure 10.2   Economic Supports for Retirees

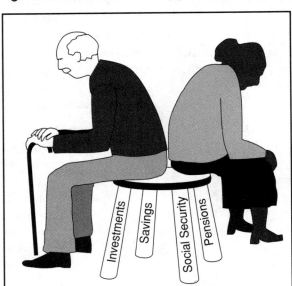

Depending upon earning money from a savings account is not usually considered the best way to hedge against inflation. At some times, for example, banks may pay interest for savings accounts at rates below the rate of inflation. Moreover, one may get a better return by investing in securities. Many people buy corporate stocks as a hedge against inflation because the value of stocks tends to rise during inflationary periods. Of course, the value of individual stocks might also fall during times of inflation (or any time). The *market risk* that the value of an investment will be low when one wants to sell is as much a concern to an investor as inflation is. The greater the market risk, however, the greater is the potential return.

Along that line of reasoning, some people invest in *real estate* (land and properties). They expect that land and property values will rise considerably faster than the rate of inflation. Such was the case through much of the 1980s. Then in the late 1980s, the real estate market collapsed. Banks and insurance companies that had invested heavily in real estate suffered great losses.

Some individuals invest in objects of art or other collectibles. Prices of specific collectible items will rise in value (or fall) depending upon demand.

Evaluating Ways to Save and Invest

Banks and stock brokerage firms spend great sums on advertising. They want consumers to entrust their money with them. In deciding which of the alternative savings and investment plans best suits their needs, wise consumers will seek answers to the following questions:

How Safe Is It? Some forms of savings are more secure than others. Money invested in U.S. Savings Bonds are as secure as the federal government itself. Similarly, bank deposits of up to $100,000 are insured by an agency of the federal government—the **Federal Deposit Insurance Corporation (FDIC).** Congress created the FDIC so that even if a bank should fail, its depositors would not lose their money.

What Are the Returns? The rate of return varies from one savings or investment instrument to another. The rate of interest one earns at a bank depends on the kind of account one opens, when one opens the account, and which bank one goes to. Corporate stocks and bonds offer the possibilities of earning more money than savings instruments. But both dividends and capital gains go up and down with the fortunes of the company that issued the stocks and bonds. Similarly, the interest offered by corporate bonds varies from one firm that issues bonds to another.

The Power of Compound Interest

Deposits in savings accounts have a mighty force working for them called *compound interest*. It is interest earned on an original deposit and on the interest already earned on that deposit. Suppose, for example, that you deposited $1,000 in a savings account that paid 5¼ percent interest compounded annually. At the end of the first year, your account would be credited with $52.50 in interest, giving you a new balance of $1,052.50. At the end of the second year, the 5¼ percent would be *compounded*, that is, it would be calculated on the basis of the new balance, with interest now amounting to $55.26. The additional dollars in interest may not sound like much now, but let us suppose that the deposit had been made by a 15-year-old who decided to leave the money in the bank until retirement at age 65. After 50 years of compounding at 5¼ percent, the $1,000 would have grown to $12,915.31. Compare this compounding process to calculating *simple interest*, a situation in which interest is earned on the principal alone. In that case, the $1,000 would have grown to only $3,625 after 50 years.

Compound interest becomes spectacular at higher levels of interest. If instead of 5¼ percent, the account had paid 12 percent in compound interest, the $1,000 deposit would have grown to $289,001.90 in 50 years!

SPECIAL NOTE: Compound interest can be computed quite easily on some pocket calculators or computers. Simply add 1 to the interest rate; multiply this sum by the principal; and strike the (=) sign once for each year to be compounded. For example, suppose that you wanted to calculate the balance after seven years of a deposit of $800 in an account that paid 9.5 percent in compound interest. This process would be entered in a calculator as follows:

$$1.095 \times 800 = \quad 876.00$$
$$= \quad 959.22$$
$$= 1,050.35$$
$$= 1,150.13$$
$$= 1,259.39$$
$$= 1,379.03$$
$$= 1,510.04$$

The final readout is the correct balance: $1,510.04.

How Liquid Is It? The ease with which a savings vehicle can be converted into cash is described as its *liquidity*. ATMs (automated teller machines) enable some bank depositors to withdraw limited amounts of funds at any time of any day. Slightly less liquid are bank savings accounts that can be withdrawn only during business hours. Some forms of savings require advance notice for withdrawals, while other types of savings must be left on deposit for a period of months or years before they can be withdrawn without penalty.

Certificates of deposits are offered with different rates of interest for different time periods. Several choices are presented on this sign in a bank window.

Ways to Save and Invest

In this section of the chapter, we will discuss a number of saving and investment methods: savings accounts, certificates of deposit, bonds, U.S. Savings Bonds, stocks, and mutual funds.

Savings Accounts. Commercial banks, savings and loan associations, mutual savings banks, and credit unions all offer one or more types of savings accounts. Savings accounts offer easy access to funds. But compared to other vehicles for saving (and compared to investment vehicles), they pay relatively low rates of interest. Some checking accounts called *NOW accounts* pay interest, and thus can be considered a form of savings account. But the interest that these NOW checking accounts pay is always quite low.

Certificates of Deposit. Since savings accounts pay so little in interest, it is advisable to leave in them only limited sums (say, the equivalent of two months' income). Additional savings (those that will not be needed until the distant future) would be better invested in vehicles with higher rates of return. One such option is the *certificate of deposit*, or *CD*. A certificate of deposit is a time deposit that the depositor agrees to keep in a bank for a specified time. CDs offer higher rates of return than do savings accounts. But depositors can withdraw their money from savings accounts whenever the bank is open. CDs, by contrast, must be held for anywhere between 3 and 72 months before they can be cashed in without penalty.

Bonds. Bonds are long-term obligations issued by governments and private corporations. With most bonds, the issuer of the bonds repays the principal at the end of a specified period of time. It also makes periodic payments of interest to the bondholders. Interest paid by state- and local-government bonds is exempt from federal income taxes, as well as from state and local taxes. Interest paid by federal bonds is exempt from state and local taxes, but not from federal income taxes.

Unlike bank deposits, corporate bonds and government bonds (with the exception of U.S. Savings Bonds) do not guarantee the return of principal before *maturity*. (Maturity is the date at which the issuer of the bond promises to redeem the bond at its face value.) If a corporation or government agency is selling a bond that has a face value of $1,000 with maturity at 2007, it is promising to pay $1,000 to the owner of the bond in the year 2007.

If the owner of the bond were to sell the bond in the open market at any time before 2007, he or she may receive more or may receive less than $1,000 for the bond. The market value of a bond depends upon many factors, including risk, quality of the bond, and interest rates.

1. Risk. In most instances, the longer the maturity of a bond, the greater is the risk. A bond that matures in 30 years, for example, is considered a greater risk than a bond issued by the same company or government that matures in 2 years. Of course, if an investor buys the 30-year bond 2 years before maturity, the risk is the same as if that bond were a 2-year bond.

2. Quality. Not all bonds are equal in quality. U.S. Treasury bonds are directly backed by the full faith and credit of the U.S. government. Thus, they are considered very safe investments and of high quality. Some states and localities, by contrast, have experienced financial difficulties. In some instances, owners of bonds issued by these governments have been able to redeem their bonds at only a fraction of their face value. State and local bond issues, therefore, are more risky (and of lower quality) investments than U.S. Treasury issues.

Similarly, not all corporate bonds are equal in quality. A bond issued by a well-known, financially stable corporation can be sold at a higher price than one issued by a lesser-known or unstable corporation.

Bonds are analyzed and classified by bond-rating services according to how likely the issuers of the bonds are to repay the principal at maturity. **Standard & Poor's Corporation** and **Moody's Investors Service** are among the best known of these services. Look at Table 10.2. Ratings at Baa (under Moody's) or BBB (under Standard &

Poor's) and above are considered *investment grade*. Bonds below investment grade are sometimes called *junk bonds*.

You may wonder why anyone would buy a junk bond. These investments, although risky, offer high rates of interest. In the 1980s, junk bonds were quite popular. People seeking to take over corporations would offer these bonds as a way of obtaining the necessary capital. Investors were attracted to the high rates of interest that junk bonds were offering and were willing to take the risks involved in these securities. Today, some investment advisors still recommend the purchase of junk bonds to improve the performance of certain individuals' portfolios. In the financial section of newspapers, you can see these risky bonds advertised as "high-yield bond funds."

3. Interest Rates. The value of bonds varies inversely with the rise or fall of interest rates: If interest rates rise, bond prices fall; if interest rates fall, bond prices rise. For example, a $1,000 face-value bond guarantees to pay $50 per year at its issue rate of 5 percent ($1,000 × .05 = $50). The $50 is the yield for this bond. (As we learned in Chapter 5, the *yield* of an investment is its rate of return based on its original purchase price.) Suppose market interest rates increase to 7 percent. In order for a $1,000 bond to pay 7 percent, the bond would have to sell for less than $1,000. In fact, it would sell for $714.29. A quick way to figure out how much a bond will sell for at various interest rates is to divide the yield by the interest rate. Thus, a $1,000 bond yielding $50 sells for $1,250 at 4 percent interest (50 ÷ .04 = 1,250). A $1,000 bond yielding $50 sells for $714.29 at 7 percent interest (50 ÷ .07 = 714.29).

Table 10.2   BOND RATINGS

Rating	Moody's	Standard & Poor's
Highest Quality	Aaa	AAA
High Quality	Aa	AA
Upper Medium Grade	A	A
Medium Grade	Baa	BBB
Predominantly Speculative	Ba	BB
Speculative, Low Grade	B	B
Poor to Default	Caa	CCC
Highest Speculation	Ca	CC
Lowest Quality, No Interest	C	C
In Default		DDD
In Arrears		DD
Questionable Value		D

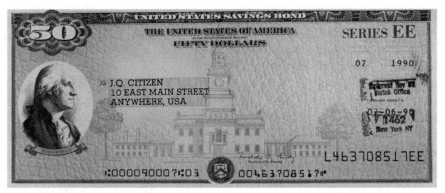

This U.S. EE Savings Bond was purchased for $25, but it will be worth $50 upon maturity.

U.S. Savings Bonds. A *U.S. Savings Bond* is a contract showing that money has been loaned to the Treasury of the United States. Buying these government-guaranteed bonds is an absolutely safe and liquid investment. The Series EE Savings Bonds are easily available for the small investor because they may be purchased for as little as $25 from many local banks. The bonds accrue interest until they are *redeemed* (cashed in) or they reach final maturity, whichever happens first. Series EE Bonds are available in $50, $75, $100, $200, $500, $1,000, $5,000, and $10,000 denominations. The purchase price of each bond is 50 percent of its face amount. For example, a $100 bond costs $50. It will be worth $100 at its maturity.

The *original maturity* of a Series EE Bond depends upon the guaranteed minimum rate of interest at the time of purchase. For example, if the government guarantees a rate at the time of purchase of 4 percent, a $100 savings bond would have an original maturity of 18 years ($50 compounded semiannually at 4 percent equals $100 after 18 years). Series EE Bonds held five years or longer earn interest on a market-based variable rate, which may be higher than the original rate offered (the minimum rate). It may never be lower than the minimum rate. Therefore, a Series EE Bond may reach maturity before 18 years from issue (assuming an original rate of 4 percent). Savings Bonds continue to earn interest (until they are redeemed) for up to 30 years from issue. Thirty years is the final maturity date.

Although we said that buying U.S. Savings Bonds is a liquid investment, they must be held for at least six months after the issue date before they can be redeemed. The benefits of purchasing U.S. Savings Bonds include safety and the absence of fees for purchasing or redeeming bonds. Some people may qualify for exclusion from federal income tax if the bondholder pays tuition at a qualified post-secondary educational institution. U.S. Savings Bonds are exempt from state and local taxes. The U.S. government guarantees the bondholder both principal and interest. If a bond is lost, stolen, mutilated, or destroyed, it can be replaced free of charge.

Common Stocks. As we discussed in Chapter 5, some people invest a portion of their savings in the stocks of publicly held corporations. Many of these stocks yield a return in the form of dividends. Investors who sell their stocks might also receive a *capital gain* if the value of these stocks has increased from the time they bought them.

There is considerable risk attached to stock ownership. A firm's ability to earn profits and grow will directly affect the size of the dividend it can afford to pay and the value of its stock. The failure of the firm either to produce a profit or to grow could, therefore, result in financial loss to those who had invested in it.

You may wish to review Chapter 5, where we discussed the purchase of stocks and how to read a corporation's financial report.

Mutual Funds. Some people invest a portion of their savings in stocks and bonds. But there are thousands of stocks and bonds from which to choose. Those investors with much money to invest often look to professional securities consultants to assist them. Most consumers, however, have neither the funds nor the skills necessary to buy and sell securities on their own. For that reason, many people have turned to *mutual funds* as a way of investing. A mutual fund is a corporation that uses the proceeds from the sale of its stock to purchase the securities of other corporations.

Mutual fund managers work with pools of funds running into millions (sometimes billions) of dollars. In this way, the mutual fund managers can spread the risk of investing over many securities. They can also afford to hire full-time analysts to manage their investments. Since most mutual fund managers will open accounts for $1,000 or less, they are within the reach of the average investor.

There are many varieties of mutual funds. The most common of these being the money market, equity, and bond funds.

1. Money Market Funds. The managers of money market funds pool the savings of hundreds or thousands of investors to purchase short-term credit instruments, such as treasury bills and short-term promissory notes. (*Treasury bills* are credit instruments representing borrowing by the U.S. government to meet its current expenses. *Short-term promissory notes* are issued by individual corporations and government agencies in order to borrow working capital from banks.) The money market funds earn interest on these securities and distribute most of the interest to the investors. Money market funds are highly liquid. Investors can withdraw their money at any time without penalty. Money market funds, unlike savings deposits, are not insured against loss by the federal government.

2. *Equity Funds*. This type of fund consists of *portfolios* (groups of investments) of corporate stocks. Typically these stocks earn both dividends and capital gains, most of which are distributed to the shareholders by the managers of the mutual funds.

3. *Bond Funds*. As the term suggests, bond funds consist of portfolios of bonds. Managers of the bond funds periodically distribute to the investors most of the interest earned on these investments.

4. *Balanced Funds*. This type of fund is made up of portfolios of both stocks and bonds. By buying into such a fund, investors hope to gain the advantages of both stock and bond ownership.

Should You Put Your Savings in a Mutual Fund? Like the securities, stocks, and bonds that the fund managers buy, the value of mutual funds fluctuates daily. For that reason, on any given day some people might find that the mutual fund shares they own are worth less than they did when they first bought them.

Moreover, mutual fund managers charge for the services they perform. In many instances, these charges make the purchase of mutual funds much more expensive than buying individual stocks and bonds. It is also true that some funds are better managed than others. For all these reasons, people thinking about investing in mutual funds should investigate and compare before making their decisions.

IRAs and 401(k) Plans. The federal government has authorized several methods to allow individuals to accumulate funds for retirement. An *IRA*, or *individual retirement account*, can be set up by individuals with earned income. An individual has many investment options with an IRA. In fact, any one or combination of the savings and investment vehicles previously discussed may make up an IRA.

A *401(k) plan* is a pension plan run by an employer for employees that allows an individual employee to contribute savings from his or her paycheck before taxes are deducted. Some employers add matching dollars to each individual's 401(k) plan. Investment options vary from plan to plan. Employees usually have some choices to make on how to invest their retirement money.

Under both the IRA and 401(k) plans, income is tax deferred. This means that that earnings from investments in an IRA or 401(k) plan can grow without being taxed until a withdrawal is made from the account. When withdrawals are made, taxes are levied only on the amount withdrawn each year. Funds remaining in the IRA or 401(k) plan continue to accumulate tax-deferred income.

BORROWING

"Neither a borrower nor a lender be." Until about 50 years ago, most people would have agreed with the advice given by a character in Shakespeare's *Hamlet*. Borrowing by individuals was looked upon as a human frailty, one with terrible, long-term consequences. Attitudes have since changed drastically. The use of credit has become a way of life for millions of U.S. consumers (see Figure 10.3). Despite credit's popularity, however, the excessive use of debt can cause personal hardship and unhappiness. For that reason, it would pay us all to learn how to use credit properly.

People use credit because it enables them to buy things now that they would otherwise have to forgo or delay buying until they had saved enough money. Consider the case of the young married couple who would eventually like to purchase their own appliances, car, and

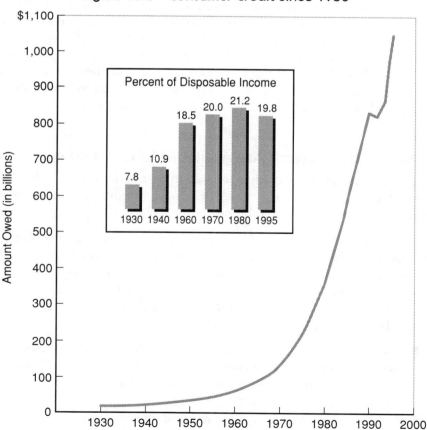

Figure 10.3   Consumer Credit Since 1930

home. They calculate that, by setting aside a portion of their income each week, they will have saved enough by the end of the year to buy the appliances they want. The car will take about three years more. But to purchase a home will take at least 20 years of saving. They decide, instead, to borrow the money to buy the appliances, automobile, and home now.

A similar decision to use credit was made by a high school graduate who elected to take a student loan to pay for a college education. And two coworkers at an insurance company used credit to "fly now and pay later" for their two-week summer vacation in Europe.

Credit, while usually costly, can sometimes save people money in the long run. One might, for example, find it less expensive to buy a car on the installment plan than to regularly rent one. Large families might find it less expensive to buy a washer and dryer on credit than to continue using the coin-operated machines to wash the family's laundry.

Consumer credit also serves to keep up the high level of consumer spending on which our economy relies to stay healthy. It is unlikely that all the goods bought with credit would have been purchased if the buyers had to pay cash. Experience has shown that people will spend far more in their lifetime when they are able to borrow against future earnings than when they have to pay out of past savings. We can see, therefore, that the availability of credit for consumers increases their total level of spending. This increase, in turn, benefits the economy as a whole.

What Kinds of Credit Are Available to Consumers?

Consumer credit is generally available in any or all of the following forms: installment plans, charge accounts, credit cards, personal loans, home mortgages, and home equity loans.

Installment Plans. Consumers use the *installment plan* (a method of purchasing something on credit with scheduled payments over time) most frequently to finance the purchase of expensive items, such as household appliances and motor vehicles. At the time of sale, installment buyers will be required to make a down payment and sign a contract. The contract will include the following:

- a statement showing the selling price of the item, the size of the down payment, all the finance charges that will be added to the selling price, and the total cost of the purchase after the charges are added to the selling price
- the number, amounts, and due dates of all payments
- the penalty for failure to make the regular payments on time.

Charge Accounts. Most large department stores, as well as some smaller stores, offer *charge accounts*. With a charge account, title to the merchandise passes to the buyer in exchange for the promise to pay. Those who pay their charge account bills on time (usually within 30 days of the billing date) do not have to pay finance charges. Late payers, however, are subject to these additional fees.

Some stores provide special kinds of charge accounts for customers who prefer not to pay the full amount of their purchases within a month. These *extended-credit accounts* or *revolving charge accounts* entitle buyers to repay on a monthly basis a portion of the outstanding balance.

Credit Cards. The little plastic cards that so many people carry to pay for all kinds of goods and services—*credit cards*—came into their own in the 1960s and 1970s. These cards permit their holders to charge purchases at thousands of stores, restaurants, and hotels—both in the United States and abroad.

Many of the nation's banks offer credit cards through the Master-Card, Discover Card, and VISA programs. Credit card holders are billed monthly. Those customers who pay their credit card bills promptly are not charged for the service. Those who pay only a portion of their bills are subject to a service charge of about 1.5 percent of the monthly balance. In addition, some banks levy an annual fee for the use of their cards.

"SO FAR, SO GOOD"

from Herblock on All Fronts (New American Library, 1980)

Why has the cartoonist shown credit cards stacked this way?

Shopping for Credit

It costs money to borrow money. Lenders charge interest on their loans. They may also levy charges to cover the cost of credit investigations, insurance, and other expenses. Since interest costs and other charges vary, it is wise to compare costs before deciding upon a particular kind of financing. The U.S. **Truth-in-Lending Law** has simplified the task of comparing the cost of loans by requiring that lenders tell borrowers the *annual percentage rate (APR)* and the *finance charge* on their loans. The APR is the percentage cost of credit on a yearly basis. The finance charge is the total dollar amount one pays to use credit.

Suppose you decide to buy a used car that sells for $7,500. You have saved $1,500 for the down payment and plan to finance the $6,000 balance with a loan. The car dealer offers to arrange the financing, as do two of your town's banks. Each lender offers somewhat different terms, which are summarized in Table 10.3.

Which of these arrangements would be best for you? The lowest-cost loan over all is available at Bank X, where you will pay back a total of $7,279.20 on a loan of $6,000. You could, however, lower your monthly cost by taking a longer-term loan from Bank Y or from the dealer. These loans, however, would ultimately be more costly than one from Bank X. A loan from Bank Y would add nearly $450 more to the cost of the loan. A loan from the car dealer would add some $600 more than a loan from Bank X.

Getting and Keeping a Good Credit Rating

Nobody has to lend you money. Creditors—the people in the business of making loans—have a right to expect to be repaid on schedule and in full for the use of their money. They also have the right to investigate applicants for loans in order to determine if they are good credit risks. Sooner or later, you are likely to need some kind of credit. Thus, it would be wise to take steps to establish your credit worthiness before that need arises.

What Creditors Look For. In looking into the qualifications of a person applying for a loan, credit investigators usually apply the "Three C's" test of

Table 10.3   CREDIT OPTIONS FOR A NEW-CAR PURCHASE

Lender	Cost	APR	Length of Loan	Monthly Payment	Total Finance Charge
Bank X	$7,279.20	13%	3 years	$202.20	$1,279.20
Bank Y	7,727.04	13%	4 years	$160.98	$1,727.04
Car Dealer	7,871.04	14%	4 years	$163.98	$1,871.04

credit worthiness: character, capacity, and capital. "Character" refers to the applicant's willingness to repay debts incurred, as indicated by a search of the applicant's *credit history* (a record of how an applicant has paid bills in the past). "Capacity" measures a person's ability to meet obligations when they fall due. It weighs current income and expected income against current and expected expenses. "Capital" refers to the financial resources (income and savings) behind the applicant's promise to repay the loan.

If you want to establish yourself as a good credit risk, a logical first step is to open savings and checking accounts in your own name. These accounts, plus a charge account at a local store, will provide you with several financial references when the need for them arises.

The rest is up to you. If you pay your bills on time and maintain a balance in your checking account, you will gain the reputation you are seeking: a person who is a good credit risk. In all likelihood, your record will be passed along to one or more credit bureaus. These institutions maintain files on virtually everyone who has ever used bank or charge-account credit in the United States. Lenders pay these bureaus for information about the people who apply for loans. If your file indicates that you are a good credit risk, you are likely to get your loan. If it does not, you may be out of luck.

Federal Laws Protect Those Who Borrow or Wish to Borrow. Creditors have the right to deny you a loan because you are a poor risk. Federal laws, however, prohibit lenders from turning you down because of your sex, race, disability, religion, national origin, marital status, age (provided that you are old enough to make a legal contract), or receipt of public assistance.

If you are turned down for a loan, the law requires that the lender notify you within 30 days and explain the reason. At your request, credit bureaus holding files on you must make the contents of those files available for your inspection. The credit bureaus must make corrections if you can show that the files contain any errors.

Credit: Master or Servant? A pamphlet written for the members of the armed forces and their families concludes with this advice:

Credit can be a powerful force in your life. If you use it with intelligence and restraint, it can help you to obtain the things you want. If you stay its master, it can serve you well.

But if you use credit carelessly, without due regard for the obligations it creates for you, credit can become your master and you its servant. You can find yourself working not for the things you want for yourself and your family, but to pay for the privilege of having used someone else's money.

—"Master or Servant?"
U.S Department of Defense, 1978

Credit cards different from the bank cards discussed on page 239 are issued by organizations such as American Express and Diners Club. Cardholders are expected to pay their outstanding balances in full at the end of each month or be subject to a finance charge. In addition, they may be charged annual fees for the use of their cards.

Consumers who wish to obtain a credit card should engage in comparison shopping. Interest rates and annual fees vary from one issuer of cards to another. Do not necessarily accept the first offer of a credit card that you receive.

Personal Loans. Banks and other lending agencies make personal loans that are secured by a customer's general credit rather than by any specific merchandise. In such cases, the lender has a reasonable assurance that the borrower can repay the loan in periodic installments out of current income. If the lender is a bank in which the borrower has a savings account, the bank may extend a low-interest loan based on the balance in the depositor's savings account.

Home Mortgages. *Home-mortgage loans* finance the single biggest investment in many people's lives: the purchase of a home. Mortgage loans are long-term loans, usually running from 15 to 30 years. *Collateral* (security) for the mortgage loan is the home that it finances. After making a sizable down payment, the new homeowner will pay equal monthly installments until the mortgage is paid in full. One portion of the payment is used to reduce the principal of the loan. The rest of the payment represents interest on the outstanding balance.

In recent years, banks have been offering variable-rate mortgages. Those who obtain such loans typically pay a lower rate of interest for the first year or so. Then, when interest rates in general are rising, the bank will raise the rate of the variable-rate mortgage. This rate will come down again when interest rates in general decline.

Home Equity Loans. Some people use their home as collateral in purchasing major consumer goods. This type of loan is a *home equity loan*. The term "equity" refers to the value remaining on a property after deducting the mortgage. If the fair market value of the home is $200,000 and the mortgage balance on this home is $125,000, then the owner would have an equity in the home of $75,000 ($200,000 − $125,000 = $75,000). Assuming that the owner has no other legal claims on the property, the owner may borrow up to $75,000 on the equity.

Home equity loans are popular for two reasons. (1) Current federal tax laws allow deductions of 100 percent of the interest on home equity loans (up to $100,000) from the sum of one's total income in determining tax liability. (2) Moreover, home equity loans can be obtained at rates lower than the prevailing rates for other types of consumer loans. As with any type of loan, there are some disadvantages to the home equity loan. One must pay back the loan in a timely manner or risk losing one's home.

Summary

The consumer is very important to the U.S. economy. Consumer spending represents about two-thirds of our gross domestic product. A decline in consumer spending can result in a decline in production and employment nationwide. An increase in spending can increase production and employment in the United States. Consumer savings is also important to the economy because it is the fund from which new capital investment is derived.

Consumers have a choice to spend or save their income. The consumers' propensity to spend is determined by income, wealth, interest rates, future expectations, and government policies. Consumers' propensity to save is influenced by such factors as the safety, return, and liquidity of the place in which they put their savings. There are a number of ways to save and invest. These include savings accounts, certificates of deposit, bonds, stocks, and mutual funds.

The use of credit is commonplace today. Credit is a form of borrowing and is costly. Consumer credit is available as installment plans, charge accounts, credit cards, personal loans, home mortgages, and home equity loans. When buying something on credit, it pays to compare different ways of obtaining this credit.

REVIEWING THE CHAPTER

Building Vocabulary

Match each term in Column A with its definition in Column B.

COLUMN A	COLUMN B
1. certificate of deposit	a. a fund into which an individual annually deposits a limited amount to have money for retirement
2. yield	
3. liquidity	b. the interest earned on the principal and on the interest already earned
4. money market fund	c. a corporation that uses its stockholders' capital to buy securities of other firms
5. mutual fund	
6. compound interest	d. a consumer loan based on the value of a home minus any legal liabilities
7. IRA	e. the ease with which a form of savings can be converted to cash
8. home equity loan	f. a savings instrument in which the buyer agrees not to withdraw his or her deposit for a period of time
9. home mortgage	
10. installment plan	g. a long-term loan secured by the home for the purchase of which the loan is made
	h. a time payment plan for borrowing
	i. a vehicle that allows consumers to invest savings in short-term securities
	j. the rate of return on an investment based on the purchase price

Understanding What You Have Read

1. Most of the nation's output of goods and services in the United States is purchased by (a) consumers (b) business firms (c) state and local governments (d) the federal government.
2. Which of the following forms of saving and investing offers the greatest liquidity? (a) savings account (b) corporate stock (c) real estate (d) certificate of deposit.
3. Which of the following types of saving and investing would consumers be most likely to use if they were interested in growth? (a) savings account (b) NOW account (c) corporate stock (d) government savings bond.
4. Which of the following forms of saving and investing offers the greatest degree of safety? (a) a mutual fund (b) corporate stock (c) real estate (d) a government savings bond.

5. Mutual funds are attractive to small investors because (*a*) the funds offer a guaranteed return on investment (*b*) the funds are insured by an agency of the U.S. government (*c*) the funds offer the opportunity to share in an investment in a variety of stocks and bonds (*d*) investors know that at the end of a specified number of years their investment will be worth more than it would have been if they had put their money into a savings account.

6. Which of the following investments paid the highest rate of return? (*a*) a corporate bond that paid $72 per year in interest and that cost $600 to purchase (*b*) a money market fund that paid 8 percent interest (*c*) a corporate stock that cost $40 to buy and that paid dividends of $2 per share (*d*) a 9.5 percent certificate of deposit.

7. Which type of bond fund is most likely to return the highest yield? (*a*) government bond fund (*b*) municipal bond fund (*c*) high-quality corporate bond fund (*d*) "junk bond" fund.

8. Some people put all or part of their savings in an "inflation hedge" because a hedge (*a*) offers the greatest liquidity (*b*) fixes the dollar value of one's savings regardless of what happens to the cost of living (*c*) helps protect people against the loss of purchasing power that accompanies inflation (*d*) is a security insured by the federal government.

9. A bond yields $100 yearly at 4 percent interest. What is its market value? (*a*) $1,000 (*b*) $1,500 (*c*) $2,000 (*d*) $2,500.

10. Which of the following is *not* a form of consumer credit? (*a*) charge accounts (*b*) installment plans (*c*) credit cards (*d*) checking accounts.

Thinking Critically

1. Explain what is meant by the statement, "Savings are essential to the nation's economic health."

2. Compare the following kinds of saving and investment alternatives by describing their advantage in one column and their disadvantages in another: (*a*) savings account (*b*) certificate of deposit (*c*) money market fund (*d*) NOW account.

3. IRAs and 401(k) plans are forms of tax-sheltered savings. Explain the similarities and differences between an IRA and a 401(k) plan in terms of (*a*) eligibility, and (*b*) tax-deferment possibilities.

4. "People who want to borrow money would be well-advised to shop as carefully for their credit as they would for costly merchandise." (*a*) Explain this statement. (*b*) What should one look for in shopping for credit?

5. Home equity loans have become popular in recent years. (*a*) Explain what a home equity loan is. (*b*) Give *two* advantages and *one* disadvantage of the home equity loan over other types of consumer loans.

SKILLS: Analyzing a Table

Study Table 10.4. Based on the table and your reading of the text, answer the questions that follow.

Table 10.4 AVERAGE ANNUAL FAMILY EXPENDITURES BY INCOME AND TYPE OF EXPENDITURES

Income Before Taxes or Assistance	Low Income $6,612	Middle Income $43,412	High Income $90,390
(+/−) Assistance/Taxes	(+)$7,454	(−)$ 3,640	(−)$ 9,066
Disposable Personal Income (DPI)	$14,066	$39,772	$81,324
Expenditures as Percent of Total Expenses			
Food	18%	13%	9%
Shelter	20%	16%	13%
Utilities	10%	6%	4%
Household Services	1%	1%	2%
Furnishings	4%	4%	4%
Other Household	2%	1%	1%
Health Care	8%	5%	3%
Apparel	5%	5%	4%
Transportation	15%	20%	13%
Auto Purchases	5%	10%	6%
Vehicle Expenses	8%	9%	6%
Public Transportation	1%	1%	1%
Entertainment	2%	3%	3%
Personal Insurance and Pensions	2%	11%	11%

1. What was the average income of each of the three categories of families *before taxes*?
2. How much did each of the three families pay in taxes or receive in assistance?
3. How is disposable personal income calculated?
4. How well does the data contained in this table illustrate the effect of Engel's Law?

The Role of Government in a Free Enterprise Economy

Chapter 11

THE IMPORTANCE OF GOVERNMENT

Overview

In earlier chapters, we learned that the U.S. economic system of capitalism relies upon market forces rather than upon government to answer the WHAT, HOW, and WHO questions: WHAT goods and services should be produced? HOW should they be produced? WHO will receive the goods and services?

Despite the system's reliance on markets, one does not have to be a detective to find evidence of government's participation in the economy. Think, for example, of your daily trips from home to school and back. What parts do the federal government and state and local governments play in that aspect of your life? Although circumstances vary, it is likely that the roads you travel have been constructed by government; the electricity you use is provided by or at least regulated by government; and the courses you take are prescribed by your state's education department.

In many ways, the economic behavior of government (local, state, and federal) is similar to the economic behavior of businesses and individuals. Government, too, must try to achieve its goals of obtaining the greatest amount of goods and services by using limited resources. The economic goals of government, however, are different from those of individuals and business firms. Whereas businesses and individuals are principally concerned with their own well-being, government is supposed to focus on the welfare of all its people.

In this chapter, we will learn more about the role of government in the U.S. economy. We will also be concerned about the following questions:

☐ Why has the participation of government in the economy grown so great?

☐ How does government raise the money it needs, and how does it budget its spending?

☐ How do government budgets transform economic goals into reality?

THE ECONOMIC ROLES OF GOVERNMENT

The government has many economic roles. One of the most obvious is the effect on the economy of the many taxes that government imposes and collects. The average family spends about 25 percent of its income on taxes. Business firms often spend a much greater percentage. Then there are the effects that raising and lowering taxes can have on economic growth. These tax-related topics will be discussed in the next chapter. In this chapter, we will concentrate on discussing the economic responsibilities of government, which include:

- safeguarding competition and the market system
- providing public goods and services
- correcting for harmful externalities, such as pollution
- maintaining economic stability
- redistributing income and wealth
- redistributing resources.

Safeguarding Competition and the Market System

Under ideal circumstances, the market system benefits us all. Competition and the quest for profits move producers to give consumers the goods and services they want. Since it is in the sellers' interest to meet or beat the competition's prices, it pays them to produce their products in the most efficient way they can. Thus, we can say that competition promotes the efficient use of scarce resources and the satisfaction of consumer wants.

The absence of competition has the opposite effect: fewer goods and services are produced and prices rise. For these reasons, federal, state, and many local governments do what they can to promote competition, and discourage those who try to restrict it. In Chapter 7, we learned about some of the antitrust laws that the federal and state governments have enacted. These laws prohibit efforts by individuals or firms to interfere with competition.

Providing Public Goods and Services

Certain things would not be provided were it not for government. Economists describe goods and services provided mainly by government as *public goods and services*.

Public goods and services are available to everyone, whether they pay for them or not. Think of a local police force. Regardless of which residents of a community pay for it, police protection is available to everyone. Similarly, there is no way that the light from street lamps could shine only for those who pay for them. Since people will not pay

What public service is shown here? Should the service be provided by private enterprises?

for things they can enjoy for free, frequently government has to provide them. The alternative, of course, is to do without some public goods and services. Indeed, many serious discussions take place in legislatures throughout the country among those who argue that government is not providing enough services and those who argue that government already provides too much. The latter argument usually involves discussion of what the government (and ultimately the taxpayers) can afford.

Correcting for Harmful Externalities and Promoting Beneficial Ones

Natural resources such as air and water are sometimes available without cost to those who produce goods and services. When that happens, some producers may waste these resources.

Consider, for example, a tractor factory whose coal-powered generator spews harmful pollutants into the atmosphere. To the economist, both the coal and the air that carries off the smoky wastes produced by the generator are resources. There is an essential difference between the two, however. On the one hand, the coal must be purchased before it can be used. Coal, therefore, makes up part of the factory's costs of doing business. For that reason, the factory will not likely waste the coal. On the other hand, air is a natural resource that belongs to all of us. The factory does not need to purchase it. Moreover, the cost of cleaning up the air often is borne by society in general, not just by those who pollute it.

To an economist, coal represents an *internal cost* of doing business. By contrast, air is an *externality*, or *external cost*. Externalities are paid for by society as a whole. The tractor factory will have to consider the cost of coal in setting its prices for tractors. In the absence of any laws prohibiting air pollution, the factory need not concern itself with the costs of cleaning the air polluted by its smoke. Of course, today there are numerous federal, state, and local laws designed to reduce pollution of air, water, and land resources. Backed by these laws, governments can fine factories that pollute the environment.

Pollution is a *harmful externality*, but not all externalities are harmful. Some office buildings are erected with plazas and courtyards available for public enjoyment. Since those who use these facilities probably did not pay for them, they can be described as *beneficial externalities*. Government can encourage beneficial externalities by awarding tax reductions or cash awards to firms that provide public facilities such as outdoor courtyards and plazas.

Government can discourage harmful externalities through regulation and taxation. Laws prohibiting harmful emissions or requiring the installation of emission controls are examples of how government regulations can be used to discourage harmful externalities. Similarly,

Why is this plaza a beneficial externality of the business that owns the land and the office building connected to it?

the levying of special taxes on those who smoke and pollute the atmosphere is an example of the use of government's powers to tax in order to reduce air pollution.

Have our legislative representatives gone too far in curbing externalities they consider harmful? This is a difficult question that legislators must wrestle with on an issue-by-issue basis. For example, are the costs of antipollution devices worth the results? Or are U.S. business firms being priced out of the global market because the nation's environmental laws are much stricter than laws elsewhere? Moreover, where do we draw the line on restricting individual rights in order to protect the general welfare of the rest of us?

Maintaining Economic Stability

Economic stability is a period in which there are only modest changes in the level of prices, employment, and business activity. History has shown that, without economic stability, we see unwanted increases in business failures and in unemployment and poverty levels.

Responsibility for maintaining economic stability has fallen to the federal government. In later chapters, we will discuss the kinds of things that the president, Congress, and the Federal Reserve Board do to try to maintain economic stability.

Redistributing Income and Wealth

Government conducts many programs specifically designed to help the poor and needy. Since much of the money to pay for programs to help people with low incomes comes from taxes paid by those better able to afford them, there is a redistribution of wealth from those paying taxes to those receiving benefits.

Some income redistribution programs generate beneficial externalities. An example would be the federal job-training program that helps the unemployed get jobs. People with jobs pay most of the taxes that pay for this program. The unemployed, who are often poor, benefit from the program by learning skills that can lead to jobs. If they do get jobs, they can climb out of poverty and become taxpayers themselves.

Redistributing Resources

Resources employed for one purpose cannot be used for another. When, for example, the nation's factories and workers are concentrating on producing military goods, production of civilian goods is sharply limited. In this example, Congress's declaration of war on a foreign nation can cause a major redistribution of resources within the economy.

Government Regulatory Agencies—When Does Regulation Become "Too Much Regulation"?

Ever since the Interstate Commerce Commission (ICC) was created in 1887, the federal government has used regulatory agencies or commissions to protect the public against many aspects of economic life. These agencies, now about 50 in number, make up what some have come to call the "fourth branch of federal government." (The legislative, executive, and judicial branches are the first three.) Some of the more well-known regulatory agencies are the Federal Communications Commission (FCC), the Securities and Exchange Commission (SEC), and the Consumer Product Safety Commission.

While many people have praised regulatory agencies' work in protecting the public interest, other people (particularly in the business community) have complained that the agencies often go too far. Overregulation, they have argued, increases the costs of doing business and leads to higher prices and lower living standards.

In response to these and other complaints, Congress has moved to *deregulate* (remove regulations from) a number of industries. With the **Air Transportation Deregulation Act** of 1978, for example, Congress removed price controls in the airline industry. The law also made it easier for

people to form new airlines. In the years that followed, the federal government reduced its regulation of the banking, trucking, bus, and railroad industries.

More recently, opponents of regulatory agencies have sought to limit the effects of the **Clean Air Act**, the **Occupational Safety and Health Act**, and other key regulatory laws. After the Republicans gained control of Congress in the 1994 elections, they announced their intention to subject government regulation of businesses to *cost-benefit analysis*. This process involves weighing the numerical costs and benefits of a regulation. Experts would question laws, for example, that require paper mills to reduce their pollution of the air by acquiring new equipment to clean the mills' emissions. If experts could show that the cost of replacing present equipment outweighs the monetary value of the cleaner air (measured in reduced health-care costs, for example), the lawmakers might abolish the regulations.

Not everyone agrees with these proposals for cost-benefit analysis. Opponents of reduced regulation of business believe that there is no reliable way to measure the benefits of clean air and water and the safety of the food and toys we buy for our families. Furthermore, opponents of cost-benefit analysis proposals argue that the American people expect their government to safeguard the products they purchase, no matter the cost to taxpayers.

Another example of redistribution of resources occurred when Congress in the 1960s decided to spend large amounts of money on space exploration. When our best scientists are using their energies for the exploration of space, they are not available to study other problems. In other words, when government decides to spend its money in one way, the resources it consumes are no longer available to produce other goods and services. In this way, government directly affects how many of the nation's resources will be used.

REASONS FOR THE GROWTH OF GOVERNMENT

Like a snowball getting ever larger as it rolls downhill, government's economic responsibilities have grown, and grown, and grown. For example, in 1929 spending by state and local governments and the federal government totaled $9 billion, or less than 10 percent of that year's Gross Domestic Product. Contrast this with 1994, when government purchased $2.2 trillion (or about 19 percent of that year's output of goods and services).

Government spending has grown over the years, especially since the 1930s when the federal government was fighting the Great Depression. Spending has grown in both real and actual dollars. (See Figure 11.1.)

Table 11.1 illustrates government expenditures as a percentage of total national output (GDP). Note that the percentage of total government purchases increased from 1930 to 1945, then decreased for a few years before increasing again. Since 1970, it has declined slightly. What is also interesting to note are the changes in the relative share of spending by the two levels of government. For example, federal spending was 41 percent of national output in 1945 (the year World War II ended), while state and local spending was only 5 percent that year. Compare those figures with the figures for 1970. We can see that the state and local government's percentage of spending increased while the federal government's percentage decreased. This trend has continued since 1970.

Table 11.1 GOVERNMENT PURCHASES AS A PERCENTAGE OF NATIONAL OUTPUT (GDP)

Year	Total Government Purchases	Federal	State and Local
1930	10	1.5	8.5
1935	11	3	8
1940	14	6	8
1945	46	41	5
1950	13	6	7
1955	19	11	8
1960	19	11	8
1965	19	10	9
1970	21	10	11
1975	20	8	12
1980	19	8	11
1985	19	8	11
1990	19	8	11
1994	19	8	11

Increased Military Spending

The United States assumed an immense financial burden in this century by fighting four major wars and by undertaking the protection of the free world in the cold war. These costs were reflected in the nation's outlays for military hardware, military personnel, and other military expenses. Even though the cold war ended by 1991, military spending has remained high. U.S. leaders still perceive the world to be a dangerous place.

Population Growth

The United States has a much larger population now than it had at the turn of the century. Since 1900, the population has grown from 76 million to over 270 million. The increased population requires more schools, police, firefighters, roads, sewers, and prisons—in short, more of everything that government provides.

Rising Expectations

Thanks to the nation's enormous capacity to produce goods and services, people in the United States expect to live better than earlier generations did. As a consequence, governmental expenditures for services have had to improve. Two-lane roads have been replaced by four-lane interstate highways in many areas. Government regulations require school districts to spend much more money on staff, equipment, and facilities than before. In these and other areas, citizens have come to expect more from their government.

Figure 11.1   Our Growing Local, State, and Federal Government

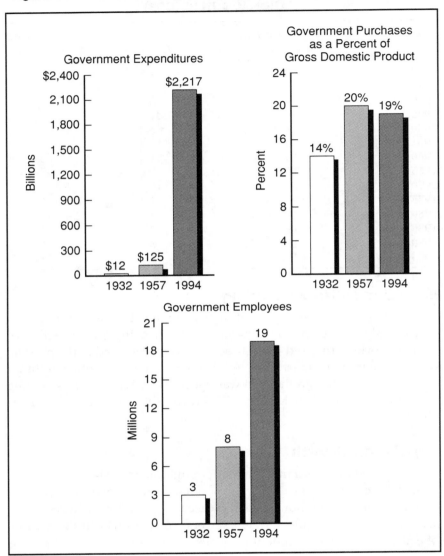

Inflation

Since 1940, prices in general have increased ten times. Thus, the government has had to pay higher costs for all the services it provides. For this reason, a substantial amount of the greater expenditures of government does not result from expanded services but from increasing costs.

Changing Attitudes Toward the Role of Government

Throughout most of the nation's history, people in the United States seemed to agree with the saying, ". . . government is best which governs least." Accordingly, government was expected to furnish little more than protection from criminals and foreign enemies and a few goods and services that could not have been profitably provided by private enterprise (such as schools, postal service, and highways).

Attitudes toward the role of government changed somewhat during the first two decades of the 20th century. Then they dramatically changed in the 1930s. During the Great Depression, unemployment and business failures achieved record highs. With the economy teetering on the brink of collapse, the public demanded that the federal government act to revitalize the economy. From that time until recent years, government involvement in the nation's economic and social well-being continued to expand.

President **Lyndon B. Johnson** in his State of the Union Address in 1965 introduced his idea for a **Great Society** program. While Roosevelt's New Deal had been a response to an emergency—the Great Depression—Johnson was promising a better life for all at a time of general prosperity. President Johnson believed that poverty could be eliminated in the United States and that it was the responsibility of the federal government to take appropriate actions to achieve this end.

Earlier, in August 1964, Congress had given Johnson some weapons to begin his "War on Poverty." It passed the **Economic Opportunity Act**, aimed at eliminating the causes of poverty. The act established (1) the **Job Corps** in urban centers to provide vocational training for young adults, (2) the **Neighborhood Youth Corps** to provide jobs for young people, and (3) the **Work-Study Program** to give financial aid to needy college students. Other weapons in the War on Poverty included **Head Start** (a preschool program for underprivileged children), **VISTA** (or Volunteers in Service to America—a domestic version of the Peace Corps), and **Manpower Development and Training** (a program to aid and retrain those workers displaced by machines).

Congress set up special redevelopment programs for specific regions of the country that were considered "pockets of poverty." For example, one program helped people in Appalachia, the coal-mining area of the Appalachian Mountains in the Eastern United States. Federal money was spent to build highways, sewage-treatment plants, hospitals, and vocational schools and to restore lands scarred by mines.

The Great Society programs were not new. They were extensions of existing programs. The tools used to achieve the goals of a Great Society were familiar: federal grants, federal loans, and (along with the loans and grants) federal controls. Today, more and more Americans believe that government, especially at the federal level, has become too large, inefficient, and corrupt. These people want the state and local governments to take over from the federal government many responsibilities, including welfare programs, with few or no controls from Washington. They would also like to see many activities that government has been involved in taken over by private charities, religious institutions, community groups, and private enterprise.

THE FEDERAL BUDGET

A *budget* is a financial plan that summarizes anticipated income and expenses. All levels of government rely on budgets to help them plan their income and expenditures. Think of the budget as a balance scale. When the planned income and expenses are equal, we say that the budget is *balanced*. When the expected income is greater than planned expenses, we say that the budget has a *surplus*. When anticipated income is less than the planned spending, we say that the budget has a *deficit*.

Establishing a Budget

A federal budget runs from October 1 of one year to September 30 of the following year. We call this 12-month period a *fiscal year*. The **Office of Management and Budget (OMB)** prepares the federal budget. This agency, which reports to the U.S. president, starts working on a budget about 15 months before the budget is to go into effect. This schedule enables the president to present a proposed budget to Congress each January, about nine months before the beginning of the fiscal year.

The budget that the president delivers to Congress is merely a recommendation. Congress has the power to make whatever adjustments it chooses in levels of income and spending. It might, for example, refuse to allocate funds for new programs requested by the president. It might decline to increase taxes as requested. Congress might increase spending for some program to levels much more than what the president wants.

Once members of Congress have agreed on the changes they want, they put them into effect by passing a series of appropriation and revenue bills. Once passed, Congress sends the laws on to the president for his or her signature.

Since federal budgets are prepared in advance of the fiscal year, they are merely a forecast of what is expected to happen, not a summary of what actually occurs. This difference is because:

Figure 11.2 Three Types of Budgets

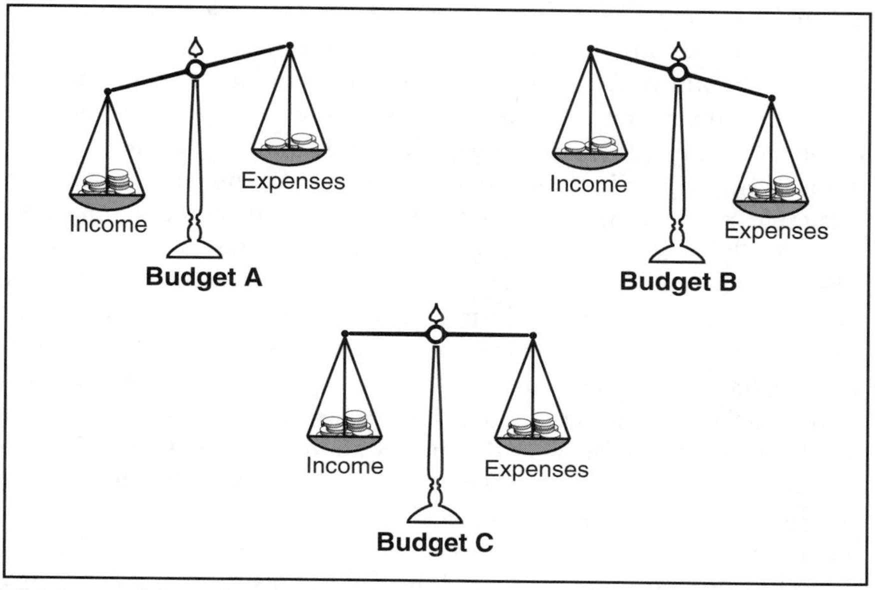

Budget A

Budget B

Budget C

Which one of these three budgets is balanced? Which has a surplus? Which has a deficit?

The Unexpected May Occur. Crises, such as the Los Angeles earthquake of 1993 or the U.S. military expeditions to Haiti in 1994, require emergency appropriations (in these cases, to provide for relief and to pay the cost of mobilizing troops).

Income Depends Upon Business Conditions. Unlike families living on fixed incomes, government income fluctuates. This happens because government tax revenues depend upon the incomes of individuals and businesses. When times are bad, business and individual incomes decline, as do tax receipts. When times are good, the opposite occurs.

Table 11.2 RECEIPTS AND OUTLAYS OF THE FEDERAL GOVERNMENT (BILLIONS OF DOLLARS)

Year	Receipts	Outlays
1955	$ 65.5	$ 68.5
1965	116.8	118.4
1975	279.1	324.2
1985	734.1	946.4
1997	1,579.0	1,601.0

In what year was the federal budget most nearly in balance? In what years was there a surplus? A deficit?

How Budgets Transform Goals Into Reality

The federal budget serves many purposes. Not only does it itemize expected revenues and intended expenses for the coming year, it also is a plan for the future. What does the government plan to spend on each program, department, and agency? And how is it going to get the money to do all of this spending? Table 11.3 summarizes the principal items of income and expense in a federal budget. As we can see from this table, most of the federal government's income comes from taxes.

We will be taking a closer look at taxes in the next chapter. Meanwhile, let us examine the expense side (*outlays*) of the budget for a few moments. The list of expenditures in the budget tells us much about what Congress and the president have agreed is important in a given year. Governments, like people, have limited resources. Agreement has to be reached among conflicting interests and groups as to (1) how much to spend, (2) for what the money should be spent, and (3) who will pay for this spending. Members of Congress often follow the wishes of their party leaders when they vote to spend, or not to spend, on various projects. The legislators, however, are looking ahead to the next election and must consider how their votes meet the needs and wants of their constituents.

By comparing the budget of one year with that of another, we can often identify those programs that seem to be growing in importance, and those that may be falling out of favor. Let us see if we can detect any such trends by comparing the 1995 budget to budgets of earlier years.

National Defense. National defense appropriations are used to support the activities of the armed forces. The level of defense spending often mirrors international conditions. During times of war or international tensions, defense spending tends to rise. When tensions decline, less money is appropriated for defense. From 1941—the year that the United States entered World War II—until 1973, national defense was the largest single item of expense in the U.S. budget. For many of these years, national resources were devoted to containing the military power and political influence of the Soviet Union.

Political and economic changes in Eastern Europe in the late 1980s led to a lessening of tensions between the Soviet Union and the United States. With the end of the cold war and the breakup of the Soviet Union in 1991, the threat of a global war had passed. People began to speak of a "peace dividend." By that they were expressing the hope that the nation could now reduce its defense outlays so dramatically as to enable the nation to spend more on other matters, such as social programs. (Actually, many people wanted to use the money saved from

Table 11.3 BUDGET OF THE FEDERAL GOVERNMENT, 1995

	Billions of Dollars	Percent of Total
Receipts		
Individual income taxes	$ 588.4	43.7%
Corporate income taxes	150.9	11.2
Social insurance taxes and contributions	484.4	35.9
Excise taxes	57.6	4.3
Estate and gift taxes	15.6	1.2
Customs duties	20.9	1.6
Other	28.6	2.1
Total budget receipts	**$ 1,346.4**	**100.0%**
Outlays		
National defense	$ 271.6	18.0%
International affairs	18.7	1.2
Income security	223.0	14.5
Health	115.1	7.5
Medicare	157.3	10.2
Social Security	336.1	21.8
Veterans' benefits & services	38.4	2.5
Education, training, employment, & social services	58.1	3.9
Commerce and housing credit	−12.0	
Transportation	39.2	2.5
Natural resources & environment	21.9	1.4
Energy	4.6	.3
Community & regional development	12.6	.8
Agriculture	14.4	.9
Net interest	234.2	15.2
General science, space, & technology	17.0	1.1
General government	14.5	.9
Administration of justice	17.6	1.1
Undistributed offsetting receipts	−41.4	
Total budget outlays	**$1,538.9**	**100.0%**

Source: **Economic Report of the President, 1995**

lower defense costs toward eliminating the federal debt.) So far, that peace dividend has not come about. Defense spending continues to be high because of perceived threats from unfriendly nations that are developing nuclear weapons and promoting terrorism.

International Affairs. The United States plays an active leadership role in international affairs because national well-being depends, in part,

Figure 11.3 National Defense as a Percentage of Total Outlays

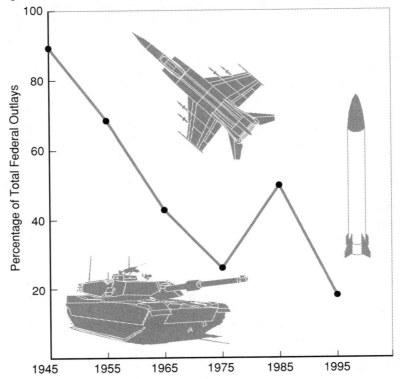

How do these expenditures reflect the nation's priorities?

upon events beyond our borders. Funding for these activities falls into four categories: (1) foreign economic and financial assistance; (2) military assistance to allies and other friendly nations; (3) administration and conduct of foreign affairs; and (4) foreign information and exchange activities. For many years, money budgeted for foreign affairs has remained between 1 and 2 percent of the total budgeted outlays. Today, however, some politicians would like to make severe reductions in foreign aid and other aspects of international affairs.

Income Security. One of the major outlays in the federal budget is *income security*, or welfare. An example in this category is the **Food Stamp Program.** In 1956, outlays in income security made up 14 percent of the total budget. In the 1980s, though, the percentage grew much higher—to above 30 percent. By 1995, budgeted income security funds had dropped to about the 1956 percentage.

Health Care. The federal government has been providing health services ever since 1798, when it created the **Public Health Service**. Now the largest health-care program is **Medicaid**, a program that provides medical care and medicines for the poor. The federal government provides the states with a good share of the funds needed for Medicaid. Then the states are required to provide additional funds and administer the Medicaid program in their state. In 1995, the government budgeted $115 billion on Medicaid and other health care programs. At 7.5 percent of total federal outlays, the health care share of the budget was about half of what it had been in 1990—14.1 percent.

Medicare. Between 1970 and 1995, outlays for Medicare increased from $7 to $157 billion. **Medicare** is a federal health insurance program for people 65 or older and certain differently abled persons. There are two parts to the Medicare program. Hospital Insurance (Part A) helps pay for care of patients in hospitals and in skilled nursing facilities, as well as for home health care and hospice care. Medical Insurance (Part B) helps pay for doctors' services, hospital *outpatient* (relating to patients who do not stay overnight) services, hospital inpatient services, durable medical equipment, and a number of other medical services and supplies that are not covered by Part A of Medicare.

The Social Security System. Every month the federal government mails more than 40 million green checks to beneficiaries of the Social Security system. **Social Security** is the nation's basic method of providing a continuing income when family earnings are reduced or stop

How the budget pie is sliced...

ROTHCO

Mike Smith/Las Vegas Sun, NV/Rothco

What is the cartoonist saying about how this budget pie was sliced?

because of retirement, disability, or death. About nine out of every ten persons working today are covered. Coverage comes in the forms:

1. Retirement Payments. Workers may start receiving retirement checks as early as age 62. Most people begin receiving benefits at age 65. In the near future, the standard age for receiving retirement checks will be 67.

2. Disability Payments. These payments are sent to workers who become severely disabled before age 65.

3. Survivors' Benefits. If a worker dies, payments go to certain members of his or her family.

4. Health Insurance. The two-part health insurance program called Medicare was discussed above. Although Medicare is part of the Social Security system, it has its own line in the budget.

5. Unemployment Insurance. Most workers who have lost their job are entitled to receive *unemployment compensation*. These benefits, which vary from state to state, are paid out of a fund created by state payroll taxes on employers and by contributions from the federal government. Benefits run for a limited time only.

Veterans' Benefits and Services. The government provides benefits to veterans and their families. It pays veterans for education, pensions, and health services. In recent years, this program has remained a small part of total outlays—about 2.5 percent. Many of the following budget lines have also maintained a constant proportion of the total budget.

Education, Training, Employment, and Social Services. These programs help individuals who need to complete their education, acquire job skills, receive career counseling, or obtain assistance in child care.

Transportation. The Department of Transportation is responsible for interstate highway planning, development, and construction; urban mass transit; railroads; aviation; and the safety of waterways, ports, highways, and oil and gas pipelines. Among the better-known agencies of this federal department are the Federal Aviation Administration, Federal Highway Administration, Federal Railway Administration, and U.S. Coast Guard. The cost of supporting all the activities of the Department of Transportation is accounted for in this budget category.

Natural Resources and Environment. Various federal programs attempt to curb pollution of the land, air, and water; conserve and develop minerals, timber, and other natural resources; and preserve natural areas, historic sites, and fish and wildlife stocks.

Financing Social Security— A Crisis?

Workers, their employers, and self-employed people pay Social Security taxes. In theory, this money pays for the administrative expenses and the current benefits of the program. In turn, when people who are presently working and paying taxes are eligible for benefits, they will receive them from taxes paid by working people at that time.

As long as the economy and the labor force are expanding, the Social Security system works. In fact, the system has long had a surplus. Congress has seen fit to increase benefit payments so that they keep up with cost-of-living increases. These increased benefits are financed out of increases in the Social Security tax rate. Taxes can also increase when the economy slows down and unemployment increases. With fewer workers employed, taxes often need to be raised to maintain benefits at current levels.

Another problem is that the number of workers eligible for benefits is growing. While in 1960 only 9 percent of the population was 65 years or older, in 1992 the proportion had reached over 12 percent. By the year 2030, it is projected to reach 21 percent. In 1995, the Clinton administration predicted that the Medicare Hospital Trust Fund (the surplus of taxes collected over expenses) would run out of money in the year 2002. Furthermore, the administration pre-dicted, Social Security trust funds would be depleted by 2029.

As early as 1983, it was clear that in order to save the Social Security system, Congress would have to enact important changes in the law. Congress chose both to increase taxes and reduce benefits. Under the terms of the new law, the tax paid by employers and employees increased nearly 2 percent, to 15.3 percent. In addition, retired people in the middle-income and upper-income brackets now had to pay income taxes on a portion of their Social Security pensions. Other changes reduced cost-of-living increases and raised the age at which today's young workers will be

This Post Office poster of the 1930s promoted what was then the new Social Security system.

eligible to receive full retirement benefits. The retirement age will gradually rise from the present 65 years to 67 years. Currently, Congress is discussing measures to induce people to work beyond the age of 67. Other proposals include a gradual increase in the payroll tax, adding public employees (the largest group still not covered by Social Security) to the tax base, reducing Medicare benefits, and investing Social Security funds in the stock and bond markets.

A potential third problem involves proposals for putting Social Security trust funds in the same pool of funds for the rest of the government's budget. This action would immediately reduce the federal debt and make it easier for Congress to come up with a balanced budget. Retired people and others looking forward to retirement in coming decades have protested this plan. They fear that Social Security funds will soon be wiped out and that they will spend their retirement years substantially poorer than they had expected.

Energy. Funding for energy programs is designed to (1) protect the security and independence of the nation's energy supplies; (2) promote energy production and conservation; (3) develop renewable sources of energy; and (4) increase the safety of nuclear power and the long-term disposal of nuclear wastes.

Community and Regional Development. The federal government sponsors a number of programs that attempt to provide housing for the nation's poor. Other programs in community and regional development assist in creating business opportunities in economically depressed neighborhoods. Still other programs provide disaster relief and insurance.

Agriculture. The major part of the money allocated to agriculture in 1995 was used to support the prices U.S. farmers receive for their products. (Price supports are discussed in Chapter 6.) Another area of the government's agricultural programs includes efforts to improve the production and marketing of farm products. Federal expenditures for agriculture have been declining in recent years because (1) farmers have been receiving relatively high prices for their products in the marketplace, and (2) federal price support programs have been drastically cut.

Interest on the Debt. Interest is the cost of borrowing money. In recent decades, the money needed to pay the interest on the national debt has reached astounding proportions. Whereas in 1900, the public debt stood at $1.3 billion (or $16.60 for every man, woman, and child in the nation), by 1995 the total was almost $5 trillion (or $19,000 per person). Nearly all the $234.2 billion set aside for interest payments in 1995 was a result of this huge debt.

General Science, Space, and Technology. The goals of these federal programs are to: (1) expand scientific knowledge through support of basic research in all fields of science; (2) promote technological innovation in industry; (3) develop a greater understanding of the solar system and physical universe through space exploration; and (4) develop and demonstrate practical, economic, and productive applications of space technology.

General Government. The funds in this category are used to carry out the everyday business of government as it is conducted by the executive, legislative, and judicial branches of government.

Administration of Justice. This category provides the funding needed to finance the activities of federal law enforcement agencies (such as the FBI), the courts system, and *correctional* (prison, parole, and probation) programs.

STATE AND LOCAL FINANCES

When economists speak of "state and local governments," they are referring to well over 80,000 units. In addition to the 50 states, these include some 3,000 counties, 19,000 municipalities, 17,000 townships, 15,000 school districts, and 30,000 special districts.

Where the Money Comes From

Income, sales, and property taxes provide large shares of revenues to state and local government. Their largest single source of money, however, is the federal government. State and local governments look to *grants-in-aid* to finance their operations. Grants-in-aid is money given by a higher government (such as the federal government) to a lower one. Grants-in-aid may be unconditional in that they can be spent in any way the recipient government sees fit. More frequently, grants-in-aid are conditional. This means that they must be spent for a particular purpose.

Suppose, for example, that a city needs additional street lighting at a time when federal grants are only available for waste disposal or rapid transit projects. In those circumstances, the city will have to finance a street lighting project out of its own funds. Meanwhile, it

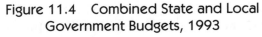

Figure 11.4 Combined State and Local Government Budgets, 1993

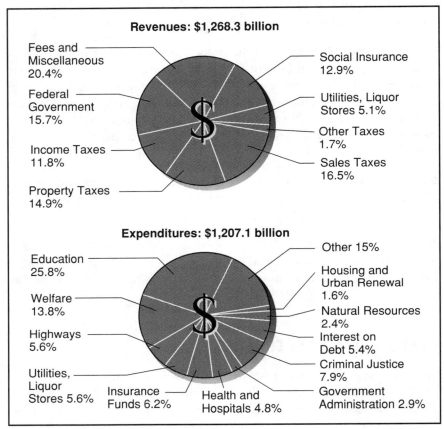

Revenues: $1,268.3 billion

Fees and Miscellaneous 20.4%

Federal Government 15.7%

Income Taxes 11.8%

Property Taxes 14.9%

Social Insurance 12.9%

Utilities, Liquor Stores 5.1%

Other Taxes 1.7%

Sales Taxes 16.5%

Expenditures: $1,207.1 billion

Education 25.8%

Welfare 13.8%

Highways 5.6%

Utilities, Liquor Stores 5.6%

Insurance Funds 6.2%

Health and Hospitals 4.8%

Other 15%

Housing and Urban Renewal 1.6%

Natural Resources 2.4%

Interest on Debt 5.4%

Criminal Justice 7.9%

Government Administration 2.9%

could also apply for federal funding of one of the other projects. Federal aid to state and local governments in 1994 totaled more than $197 billion.

States and localities seek additional revenue to meet expanding needs from sources other than those previously cited. Note in Figure 11.4 that sources other than income, sales, and property taxes and federal grants accounted for more than 25 percent of state and local revenue in a recent year. You may have heard about the "other taxes" and "fees and misc." that your state or locality imposes. You may have even complained about the costs of these other taxes and fees. These fees are collected as a percentage of bridge tolls, admissions to museums, fees for automobile licenses, fees for registration of documents, and fees for parking in a public garage.

States and municipalities can raise money in other ways as well. They can sell bonds. They can issue traffic and parking tickets. Some states run lotteries or authorize gambling establishments in order to raise revenues.

How State and Local Governments Spend Their Money

Twenty-five cents out of every dollar spent by state and local governments goes for education. Programs that aid the needy, unemployed, and differently abled are the next largest category of expenses. As you might expect, road construction and repair of roads and public transportation networks make up a fair percentage of total state and local expenditures.

States and localities have found it increasingly difficult to balance their budgets. Many state and local officials blame their problems on so-called *unfunded mandates*. These are programs and services that one level of government requires a subordinate level to provide but which get little or no funding from the higher level. The following are examples of unfunded mandates:

- In 1989, Congress forced the states to provide Medicaid to pregnant women and their children up to age six in families with incomes below 133 percent of the official poverty line. In 1990, the federal government required states to extend Medicaid coverage to all poor children under the age of 19, not just to those in AFDC families. As a result of mandates such as these, Medicaid soon made up nearly 20 percent of state government spending.

- Congress forced states to allow longer and heavier trucks onto highways within their borders. This rule added to the state's costs in road maintenance because the larger trucks caused more wear on the highways.

- Federal law now requires that mass-transit systems modify their equipment to achieve "total accessibility for the handicapped." Local governments that operate buses, subways, and trains find that this requirement has added greatly to their expenses.

Some local governments have been especially hard hit by unfunded mandates. Columbus, Ohio, for example, was ordered to clean up some discarded solvents at a municipal garage. Columbus officials calculated that this federally mandated task would add $2 million to their projected expenses. Many small communities that have volunteer firefighters have been faced with new federal requirements regarding these volunteers. The federal government has required towns to apply the same standards to volunteer firefighters that they apply to paid, professional fire departments. What with required physical examinations, individual air masks, hazardous material-training programs,

Figure 11.5 State Lottery Proceeds and Their Distribution

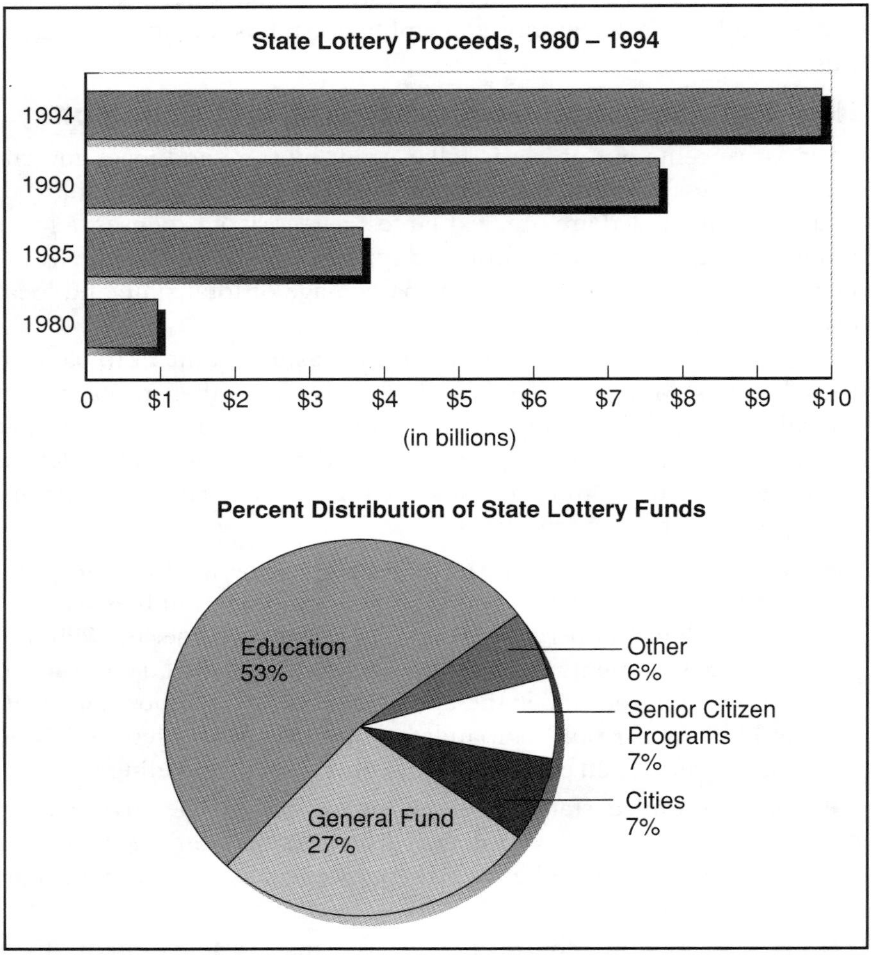

State Lottery Proceeds, 1980 – 1994

Percent Distribution of State Lottery Funds

States are realizing increasing amounts of income by running gambling operations. Do you think this is a good idea?

and the like, Indiana's Wayne Township spent more than $2 million to bring its volunteer force up to standard. This requirement created a major fiscal burden for a local government operating on a $4.5 million annual budget.

In 1995, the Republican-controlled Congress passed legislation making it more difficult for the federal government to impose rules on states and localities without providing federal money to pay for them.

In a related matter, some political leaders have urged that control over social, environmental, and safety programs be transferred to the states (and, in some instances, to charities and other private organizations). This transfer to the states could be accomplished, they say, through more use of *block grants*—sums of money that the federal government grants to the states to achieve broad policy goals. But they want these block grants to have no strings attached so that the states would have freedom to decide how to spend these grants. States, for example, would be free to use transportation block grants to fund whatever road-building or mass-transit projects they preferred. States could set their own environmental standards and set their own rules for eligibility for Medicaid and welfare funds.

This method would contrast with current methods whereby the federal government gives the states funds for specific programs with strict guidelines as to how these funds are to be used. The current methods involve much paperwork, which the reformers claim is very time-consuming and wasteful. Critics of federal programs say that states and localities know best how to solve state and local problems. They say that federal programs do not work, waste money, and often make beneficiaries lazy.

Opponents of this trend toward less federal control have raised several points:

- Along with eliminating federal controls, Congress is providing less money for affected programs. This means that either the state or local governments must raise more funds or that the programs will become weaker or be eliminated. Critics of block grants see dangers for a society that has weaker environmental laws, provides less money and health care for the poor, and spends less on building and repairing roads, bridges, and water and sewage systems.

- Problems caused by pollution and the destruction of wildlife often require national rather than state or local solutions. How, for example, could block grants prevent the destruction of forests in the Eastern part of the country by emissions from Midwestern factories?

- Why should the public believe that state and local governments will be more efficient, less wasteful, and more honest in administering programs than the federal government has been?

- Those who favor continuing federal control of many programs argue that without federal regulations and controls, there would be disparities from state to state on how well government helps its citizens.

- In response to suggestions that private charities take over some of the welfare responsibilities from the federal government, critics of this idea say that private charities are not wealthy enough or large enough to do the job.

The sides are clearly drawn. Whether the states should, or could, replace the federal government in many tasks is likely to be a matter of debate for years to come.

Summary

Government (federal, state, and local) plays important roles in the U.S. economy. Through antitrust laws, government attempts to safeguard competition and the market system. It provides public goods and services and corrects for harmful externalities. Government is concerned with maintaining economic stability. Through programs designed to help the poor and needy, government redistributes wealth.

The federal government's role in the economy grew for awhile for the following reasons: increased military spending; increases in the U.S. population; increased demands for government services; and increased costs of these services. The roles of state and local governments in the economy have been growing even faster. State and local governments together purchase more of the nation's output of goods and services than does the federal government.

The federal government and state and local governments have budgets. A budget tells us about a government's economic goals by indicating how much it will spend on various programs. By comparing budgets from year to year, we can see which programs have grown in importance and which have declined.

REVIEWING FOR UNDERSTANDING

Building Vocabulary

Match each item in Column A with its definition in Column B.

COLUMN A	COLUMN B
1. public goods and services	*a.* federal aid to state and local governments
2. externalities	*b.* the government medical and hospital insurance program for the elderly
3. economic stability	*c.* the money that a government spends
4. federal budget	*d.* the state-run medical insurance program for the poor
5. fiscal year	*e.* things provided mainly by government
6. unfunded mandate	*f.* for the federal government, the period from Oct. 1 of one year to Sept. 30 of the following year
7. expenditures	*g.* costs or benefits of an economic activity that are paid for or enjoyed by society as a whole
8. block grant	
9. Medicare	*h.* a period of modest changes in the level of prices, employment, and business activity
10. Medicaid	*i.* the nation's proposed annual plan for spending money based on anticipated receipts
	j. a program or service required by one level of government of a lower level

Understanding What You Have Read

1. Approximately what percentage of the gross national product is accounted for by government spending today? (*a*) 5 percent (*b*) 10 percent (*c*) 17 percent (*d*) 25 percent.

2. "Spending large amounts on the space program means that less money is available to spend on other areas of the economy." This statement illustrates (*a*) the superiority of government-sponsored programs (*b*) the laws of supply and demand (*c*) the effect of government spending upon the allocation of resources (*d*) the law of diminishing returns.

3. A government's budget is a (*a*) summary of the money that was spent in previous years (*b*) statement of expenditures and income that took place during the preceding year (*c*) plan of

income and expenses for the year to come (*d*) law to prevent the government from spending more than it earns.

4. According to Table 11.1, "Government Purchases as a Percentage of National Output (GDP)," total government purchases of the nation's GDP was greatest in (*a*) 1930 (*b*) 1945 (*c*) 1970 (*d*) 1990.

5. Approximately how large is the federal debt per capita? (*a*) $1,000 (*b*) $4,000 (*c*) $10,000 (*d*) over $15,000.

6. When the government expects that its income will be more than its expenditures, the budget will be described as (*a*) "balanced" (*b*) "having a deficit" (*c*) "having a surplus" (*d*) "allocated."

7. According to Figure 11.4, which item is the second principal source of revenue for state and local governments? (*a*) individual income taxes (*b*) property taxes (*c*) federal grants (*d*) fees for services.

8. One can conclude from Table 11.1 that the role of government in the U.S. economy in the period 1930–1994 (*a*) remained unchanged (*b*) generally decreased (*c*) generally increased (*d*) increased and decreased several times.

9. The largest item of state and local expenditures in recent years has been for (*a*) income security (*b*) crime prevention (*c*) highway construction and maintenance (*d*) education.

10. Those who favor transferring some of the authority of the federal government to the states and localities would most likely advocate (*a*) another War on Poverty (*b*) martial law (*c*) more unfunded mandates (*d*) more unconditional block grants.

Thinking Critically

1. Two speakers are discussing government spending and the U.S. economy. With which speaker would you agree the most? Explain your answer.

SPEAKER A: "The United States government has to decide what it wants to do first: balance the budget; eliminate poverty and homelessness in the country; or stop the spread of political tyranny abroad."

SPEAKER B: "With a seven-trillion-dollar GDP, the U.S. government can do anything it wants, provided it stops wasting its resources."

2. "That government which governs best, governs least," summarizes a popular attitude held by many Americans during the 19th century. Then the U.S. government was relatively small, and its involvement in the economy was also relatively small. During the

20th century, however, the federal government has played a much larger role in the nation's economy.

  a. With reference to *three* events or developments that took place after 1900, show why the role of the government in the economic life of the nation expanded.

  b. In your view, was this expansion of governmental activities necessary? Explain your answer with at least *two* examples.

3. Study the data in Table 11.1, page 255.

  a. Summarize the changes that took place in total government expenditures as a percentage of GDP during the period from 1930 to 1994.

  b. Compare the growth of state and local government purchases of the nation's output of goods and services with that of the federal government during the period from 1970 to 1994.

4. Social Security, Medicare, and Medicaid have all been causes of concern to economists and politicians. These programs, called *entitlements* because people are entitled to them if they meet certain qualifications, are major expenditures, which continue to rise each year. Many beneficiaries fear that the programs will run out of money and their benefits will be cut. Discuss why you agree or disagree with each of the following proposals: (*a*) Taxes should be increased to fund these programs. (*b*) Benefits should be cut across the board. (*c*) Beneficiaries with higher incomes should receive fewer benefits than poor beneficiaries.

5. The federal government has set up two major health-care programs: Medicaid and Medicare. Briefly describe each program, pointing out how Medicaid differs from Medicare.

SKILLS: Interpreting a Table

Study the "Budget of the Federal Government," on page 261. Based on the data in Table 11.3 and information given in the text, answer the following questions:

1. What was the major source of revenue for the federal government?

2. What was the major outlay of the federal government?

3. Which was greater, receipts from social insurance taxes and contributions or combined expenditures for Social Security and Medicare?

4. Was the federal budget a balanced budget? Explain.

5. What percentage of the federal budget went to pay interest? Why was this figure so high?

Chapter 12

TAXATION

Overview

> *". . . but in this world nothing can be said to be certain but death and taxes . . . ."*
>
> —*Benjamin Franklin*

Benjamin Franklin had it right: taxes are a fact of life. They are also quite costly. Tax collections by the federal, state, and local governments totaled $2.1 trillion in 1994. That averaged out to nearly $8,200 for every man, woman, and child living in the United States that year.

While the previous chapter dealt mainly with how governments spend money, this chapter focuses on taxes and taxation. We will learn about: (1) why governments levy taxes, (2) the kinds of taxes people pay, (3) various standards for a good tax, and (4) proposals to change our federal tax system.

WHY TAXES?—THE FUNCTIONS OF TAXATION

It is not news to say that few people want to pay taxes. The American colonists' objection to British taxes was one of the reasons for their revolution against the British government in 1776. In 1794, farmers in Pennsylvania who objected to a federal tax on whiskey staged a violent protest that came to be known as the "Whiskey Rebellion." If so many people have been against taxes, why do governments tax? The purposes of government taxation are several.

To Pay for the Cost of Government

The principal reason that governments levy taxes is to pay for the cost of governing. In the previous chapter, we learned that the federal government spends billions of dollars on national defense, Social Security, and other programs. State and local governments spend billions more on police, education, roads, public buildings, and other matters. Someone must pay for all these federal, state, and local expenditures. That someone is primarily the taxpayer. About 82 percent of federal income and 50 percent of the income of state and local governments come from taxes. Not surprisingly, as the responsibilities and costs of government have increased over the years, so too have taxes increased.

To Redistribute Wealth

Taxes redistribute wealth by taking money from some people and giving it to others. For example, the Medicaid program pays medical bills of poor people. Much of the funding for the Medicaid program comes from taxes collected by the federal government. These taxes are collected largely from people who have more money than the Medicaid recipients. In contrast, the poor people who are Medicaid recipients generally pay little or no taxes. Other examples of tax money being used to redistribute wealth include funds for food stamps and welfare payments. Again, the taxes paid by those who benefit from these programs are relatively minor compared to taxes paid by those with higher incomes.

To Promote Certain Industries

Some taxes, such as tariffs, are designed to benefit certain industries. A *tariff* is a tax on goods entering the country from a foreign country. The purpose of tariffs can be to raise money for the government, to raise the cost of imported goods, or to do both. We call this tax a *protective tariff* when its major purpose is to raise the cost of imports. The tariff is protective of an industry in the United States because it tends to make foreign imports more expensive than similar U.S.-made products. In this way, the tariff promotes U.S. industries. For example, suppose that Sally Smith in her Connecticut factory produces shirts that sell for $16 each. Sam Huong obtains similar shirts from a factory in Taiwan and sells them in the United States for $15 each. An import tax of 10 percent on shirts will protect Sally Smith's market in the United States. Ten percent of $15 is $1.50. An imported shirt that might otherwise sell for $15 will now cost the U.S. consumer $15 + $1.50, or $16.50. The tariff makes it possible for Sally Smith (a U.S. producer) to undersell Sam Huong (an importer).

To Influence Consumer- and Business-Spending Patterns

The level of taxation affects the amount of money individuals and business firms spend or invest. Assume that an individual with taxable earnings of $30,000 is taxed 15 percent on that salary. Fifteen percent of $30,000 is $4,500. Thus, after taxes are subtracted from $30,000, the individual will have $25,500 left to save, spend, or invest. ($30,000 – $4,500 = $25,500.) Now let us suppose taxes are increased to 30 percent. Thirty percent of $30,000 is $9,000. After paying these taxes, the individual would only have $21,000 to save, spend, or invest. ($30,000 – $9,000 = $21,000.)

Whenever government increases taxes, individuals and business firms have less to save, spend, or invest. Conversely, when government lowers taxes, individuals and business firms have more money to save, spend, or invest. There are times when it would be helpful to the economy if everyone spent less and saved more. At other times, the economy would become healthier if everyone spent more and saved less. In Chapter 19, we will describe how the federal government uses its power to tax to influence levels of spending and saving.

Local governments try to attract new business firms to their communities by offering to excuse them from paying local taxes for a time. A local government might, for example, offer to excuse a firm from paying all or part of its real estate taxes for ten years just for locating that business in the community. The business firm benefits by the amount saved in not paying real estate taxes. When the business locates in the community, it creates jobs and more taxpayers. It also increases the amount of money circulating in the local economy, thereby helping other businesses as well.

To Discourage Certain Behavior

Taxes designed to discourage what some members of society consider to be improper or unhealthy behavior are often known as "sin taxes." A government might impose these taxes on products that it wishes to discourage people from using, such as alcohol and tobacco. Imposing federal and state taxes on these products substantially increases the cost of these products for the consumer.

THE FEDERAL INCOME TAX

The individual (or personal) income tax is the principal source of revenue for the federal government. It is also perhaps the tax with which most people in the country are familiar. The income tax is a *progressive tax*. That is, the proportion of earnings subject to the tax varies directly with the taxpayer's income. People with higher incomes pay greater tax rates.

To find out how much they must pay in federal income taxes, most people refer to tax tables found in the instruction booklet accompanying tax forms. By consulting the tax table accompanying forms 1040EZ, 1040A, and 1040 for a recent year, we can see the progressive feature of the income tax in action.

As indicated in Table 12.1, a single individual with $7,000 in taxable income was liable for $1,054 in taxes; one with $28,000 in income had to pay $4,812; and a person with $49,000 in taxable income was liable for $10,692 in taxes.

Table 12.1 TAX TABLE FOR PERSONS WITH TAXABLE INCOMES OF LESS THAN $100,000

IF YOUR TAXABLE INCOME IS		AND YOU ARE			
At least	but less than	Single	Married filing jointly	Married filing separately	Head of a household
YOUR TAX IS					
7,000	7,050	1,054	1,054	1,054	1,054
7,050	7,100	1,061	1,061	1,061	1,061
7,100	7,150	1,069	1,069	1,069	1,069
7,150	7,200	1,076	1,076	1,076	1,076
7,200	7,250	1,084	1,084	1,084	1,084
28,000	28,050	4,812	4,204	5,312	4,204
28,050	28,100	4,826	4,211	5,326	4,211
28,100	28,150	4,840	4,219	5,340	4,219
28,150	28,200	4,854	4,226	5,354	4,226
28,200	28,250	4,868	4,234	5,368	4,234
49,000	49,050	10,692	8,657	11,249	9,665
49,050	49,100	10,706	8,671	11,265	9,679
49,100	49,150	10,720	8,685	11,280	9,693
49,150	49,200	10,734	8,699	11,296	9,707
49,200	49,250	10,748	8,713	11,311	9,721

The Income Tax in Our Daily Lives

Much of the responsibility for maintaining the income tax system is left to individual taxpayers. All taxpayers are expected to keep records, report income, calculate their taxes, and make payments. These tasks are made easier by the fact that employers must regularly withhold income taxes from their employees' wages. The employers, in turn, forward the collected taxes to the **Internal Revenue Service (IRS)**, the federal agency that collects income taxes. Self-employed persons (and others with non-wage income) are required to estimate their tax liability for the coming year. They then pay that amount to the IRS in four equal installments during the year.

We have seen that the amount of income taxes one pays depends upon the tax rate and the individual's *taxable income*. The key words here are "taxable income," because whatever one earns in the course of the year is more than one's taxable income. There are three reasons for this: (1) some forms of income are excluded from taxation, (2) certain exemptions and deductions can be taken against one's income, and (3) some individuals are entitled to tax credits.

Wage earners can spend many hours each year preparing their income tax forms.

Income Not Subject to Taxation. The law exempts interest earned on state and municipal bonds from federal taxation (but this interest must be reported on tax returns). Similarly, inheritances and most Social Security payments must be reported to the IRS, but all or part of

---

Progressive and Regressive Taxes

When the percentage of income paid in taxes increases as one's income increases, the tax is said to be "progressive." Best known of the progressive taxes is the federal personal income tax. In 1995, individuals with a taxable income of $23,350 or less paid a federal tax of 15 percent on this income. Incomes above that amount but less than $56,550 were taxed at a rate of 28 percent. The tax on incomes between $56,550 and $117,950 was 31 percent. Incomes between $117,950 and $256,500 had a tax of 36 percent. Finally, those with taxable income over $256,500 paid 39.6 percent.

Regressive taxes take a larger fraction of one's income as income decreases, and a smaller fraction as income increases. Sales and excise taxes (discussed on pages 284–286) are examples of regressive taxes.

this income might not be subject to tax. Welfare benefits, in contrast, need not be reported to the Internal Revenue Service, nor are they subject to taxation.

Exemptions and Deductions. Taxpayers are entitled to reduce their taxable income with an *exemption* for each of their dependents, including themselves. In 1995, the exemption was $2,500 per person. (This figure increased in 1996 to $2,550.) Thus, in 1995 a couple with three dependent children was entitled to take $12,500 in exemptions. (Three children plus two adults equal five exemptions. $2,500 × 5 = $12,500.) One effect of these exemptions is to allow the lowest-income families to avoid paying any income taxes. Also, large families are given a tax break (because they have more exemptions than a small family).

All taxpayers can reduce their taxable income by choosing to use the so-called *standard deduction*. A married couple filing a joint return in 1995, for example, could claim a standard deduction of $6,550. The standard deduction for an individual was $3,900. The amount of the deduction changes from year to year. (In 1996, it was $6,700 for a married couple and $4,000 for an individual.)

Certain expenses can be used to reduce the amount of taxable income still further. Instead of using the standard deduction, some taxpayers may choose to itemize deductions on Schedule A, Form 1040. On this form, amounts paid for state and local taxes, real estate taxes, mortgage interest, charitable gifts, and medical expenses may be deducted from one's taxable income.

Income Tax Credits. After reducing one's earnings to eliminate those items not subject to tax, a taxpayer calculates his or her income tax liability. This, too, may be reduced if the taxpayer is entitled to certain *tax credits*. These credits are offered for two purposes: (1) to promote certain activities, and (2) to help specific groups of individuals.

To help elderly persons with low incomes, for example, the law allows a married couple aged 65 or older to earn up to $13,050 before that couple must file a tax return. Certain low-income families can use the Earned Income Credit (EIC). It allows families to reduce their tax liabilities by an amount that depends upon the number of its children and the earned income of that family. If the EIC is greater than the tax that the family would ordinarily pay the IRS, the family can actually receive a check from the government in the amount of the difference.

Opinions Differ on the Income Tax

People who favor the personal income tax stress its progressive character and the effect it has on income distribution. By taking more from the wealthy and less from the poor, the income tax helps break down income differences. Also, the argument continues, the tax does not harm the economy because enough people, after paying this tax, are left with the purchasing power they need to buy the goods and services produced by the nation's industries.

Almost all taxpayers agree that the present income tax laws are too difficult to understand and that they need to be simplified. Moreover, too many people are able to avoid paying the tax. Other criticisms of the personal income tax are the following:

Favors the Rich at the Expense of the Poor. Income earned from wages and personal effort was taxed as high as 91 percent in the 1950s, 70 percent in the 1960s, 50 percent in the 1980s, and 39.6 percent in the mid-1990s. At the same time that the tax rates on high-income earners were declining, rates on low-income earners increased from 11 percent prior to 1987 to the present 15 percent. In sum, the current personal income tax is less progressive than it once was. Moreover, the argument continues, wealthy people with surplus capital to invest can afford to invest in tax-free state and municipal bonds and hire expensive tax accountants to find numerous legal tax loopholes so as to avoid paying maximum taxes. As a result, the actual percentage of income a wealthy person pays on all income—taxable and tax-free—further reduces the progressive nature of the current income tax structure.

Table 12.2   INDIVIDUAL INCOME TAXES COLLECTED BY INCOME CATEGORY, 1992

Adjusted Gross Income	Taxes Collected (in billions)	Percent of Total Collections	Tax as a Percentage of Adjusted Gross Income
Less than $7,000	$ 1.0	.21%	3.25%
$7,000 to $14,999	9.1	1.91	5.85
$15,000 to $24,999	28.7	6.03	7.6
$25,000 to $29,999	18.5	3.88	9.0
$30,000 to $39,999	43.7	9.18	10.3
$40,000 to $49,999	43.6	9.18	10.9
$50,000 to $74,999	88.5	18.58	12.4
$75,000 to $99,999	51.6	10.84	15.1
$100,000 to $199,999	67.4	14.15	18.3
$200,000 to $499,999	52.0	10.92	23.8
$500,000 to $999,999	24.8	5.21	26.0
$1,000,000 or more	47.5	9.97	26.9

How might the data in the table above be used to either support or oppose criticisms of the personal income tax?

Discourages Incentives and Investments. Some critics of the personal income tax say that it is harmful to the economy because it lacks enough deductions, exemptions, and credits that would promote individual investments in private enterprises. They want more tax advantages for investors like those for people purchasing municipal bonds. For example, these critics would like to lower or remove the tax on capital gains. This is the money one gains by selling a stock, bond, or piece of property at a price higher than what one originally paid for it. Critics of capital gains claim that more people would buy investments if the capital gains tax was much lower or was abolished.

OTHER FEDERAL TAXES

In addition to the individual income tax, the federal government imposes other major taxes, including the corporate income tax, excise taxes, estate and gift taxes, and the Social Security and Medicare taxes.

The Corporate Income Tax

About 11 cents of every dollar raised by the federal government comes from the income tax on corporations. Like the individual income tax, the *corporate income tax* is based on a simple principle: Taxes on net profits increase proportionately with the size of these profits. Defining what constitutes net profit can become quite complicated, however, and frequently requires the services of accountants and lawyers.

The corporate income tax has received the following criticisms:

- The corporate tax subjects the owners of corporations (the stockholders) to double taxation. Corporations are taxed on their profits, and also the stockholders are taxed on the dividends they receive from those profits.
- The corporate tax discourages economic growth because the money taken by government might have been used by corporations to expand their production.
- Some or all of the corporate income tax is passed on to consumers in the form of higher prices. If this happens across the country, the cost of living rises, what we call inflation.

Those favoring the corporate tax argue that the government is able to tap a source of revenue that might otherwise avoid taxation. Since corporations do not have to distribute all their profits, were it not for the corporate income tax, money that the corporations retain would not be taxed.

Excise Taxes

Taxes levied on the manufacture or sale of particular goods and services are called *excise taxes*. These taxes account for four cents out of every dollar collected by the federal government. Those who pay an excise tax usually pass its cost along to the final consumer. If competition is strong or the product is subject to relatively elastic demand, however, producers are likely to absorb some or all of the excise tax themselves.

Politicians are frequently attracted to excise taxes because people are often unaware that they are paying them. While many items are subject to an excise tax, nearly three-fifths of the government's excise receipts come from taxes on alcoholic beverages, gasoline, and tobacco. These are mass-consumption goods on which poor families spend a larger percentage of their incomes than do wealthy families. Excise taxes thus are likely to be regressive.

Estate and Gift Taxes

The *estate tax* is levied on a person's property at the time of death. Most people are not affected by federal estate taxes because the law allows a sizable exemption. Meanwhile, the truly wealthy can use a variety of legal accounting devices to reduce the impact of the estate tax.

The *gift tax* was created to prevent wealthy persons from giving their property away so that their heirs would escape paying estate

Figure 12.1   Sources of Federal Income

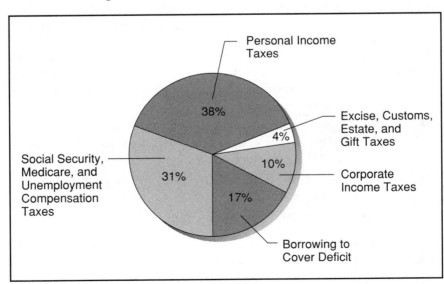

This pie chart shows the relative sizes of the major categories of federal income for fiscal year 1995.

At IRS offices, specialists check all tax returns for errors as part of the processing.

taxes. Thus, gifts in excess of specified limits are subject to federal taxation.

Social Security and Medicare Taxes

The Social Security and Medicare taxes are payroll taxes designed to pay the costs of the Social Security and Medicare programs. About 32 cents out of every dollar received by the federal government comes from these taxes. Wage earners and their employers both pay the same percentage of the workers' salaries into the Social Security system. The Social Security tax is sometimes described as an income tax in reverse. This is because it taxes income only under a certain limit ($60,600 in 1995). There is no income limit for the Medicare tax.

STATE AND LOCAL TAXES

State and local governments impose a variety of taxes.

Sales and Gross Receipts Taxes

"How much do I owe?"

"Let's see now. These items you've bought add up to $15.65. The tax on that amount is $1.25. So the total bill is $16.90, please."

Everyone who lives in a state or community that has a sales tax will recognize this dialog. Governments levy *sales taxes* on the value of certain retail sales of goods and services. These taxes are usually computed as a percentage of the sales price and added to that price. The firms that sell the taxed goods and services are responsible for collecting and forwarding the taxes to the state or local government.

Certain states and communities also levy *gross receipts taxes* on businesses. These taxes are calculated as a percentage (usually a fraction of 1 percent) of a firm's receipts from wholesale as well as retail activities. A business may or may not pass on gross receipts taxes to its customers. When these taxes are passed on to consumers, however, the buyers are unlikely to be aware that they paid the taxes.

Sales and gross receipts taxes are the principal sources of income for many states. Sales taxes are popular among the states because they are easy to collect and administer, and because they yield much money. Sales taxes are often regressive in that they impose a heavier burden on the poor than on the rich. In order to make the sales tax less regressive, many states and localities exempt from the tax certain necessities, such as food, medicine, and rent.

Property Taxes

As we saw in Figure 11.4 on page 268, property taxes are a major source of income to state and local governments. These taxes fall into two categories: *real property taxes,* which are levied upon buildings and land; and *personal property taxes,* which are levied on valuable items, such as jewelry, furniture, securities, clothing, and automobiles. Of the two, the tax on real property is by far the more widespread.

In administering the real property tax, the locality *assesses* (officially evaluates) each taxpayer's holdings. The community's total *assessment* serves as the basis for the establishment of the real property tax rate. Thus, if the community needs $1 million in revenue for the coming year and the total assessed valuation of all the taxpayers' holdings is $100 million, the tax rate for that year will be 1 percent.

The real property tax rate is usually applied uniformly throughout a community regardless of a taxpayer's ability to pay. It is, therefore, often particularly regressive. For example, if two families live in identically assessed homes, they will both pay the same tax. It is quite possible, however, that one of the two families is much wealthier than the other. The less wealthy family will find the tax to be more of a burden than the wealthier one. The tax can cause hardships for elderly people who own their own home but have limited income. Therefore, some communities will give the elderly with low incomes a break on their property taxes.

Critics of both real and personal property taxes point out the absence of a uniform method of assessing property. As a result, some property may be overvalued and some undervalued. In general, studies have shown that smaller real properties are more likely to be overvalued than larger properties. This again tends to make the tax regressive. In addition, personal property is easy to hide and therefore may go unassessed and untaxed.

Some critics also complain that the real property tax discourages home improvements because improvements increase the value of property and, therefore, the homeowners' taxes.

User Taxes

Taxes that are imposed on people who use a product or service are called *user taxes*. This category includes gasoline taxes, license and registration fees for motor vehicles, hunting and fishing license fees, and highway and bridge tolls. Highway and bridge tolls pay for the cost of the maintenance and construction of roads and bridges. State gasoline taxes help finance the construction and repair of roads and bridges. Hunting and fishing license fees pay for programs that manage wildlife.

Personal Income Taxes

Most states and some localities impose personal income taxes that are similar in concept to federal personal income taxes. These taxes currently account for about 25 percent of the tax dollars raised by the states and 6 percent of the funds raised by localities.

Inheritance Taxes

These state taxes are similar to the estate taxes levied by the federal government.

Payroll and Business Taxes

Collected in a variety of forms by state and local governments, payroll and other business taxes are often used to finance unemployment insurance programs, as well as health, disability, and retirement programs.

Corporate Income Taxes

Some states and localities impose taxes on corporations that do business within their jurisdiction. These corporate income taxes are similar to the corporate taxes levied by the federal government.

Unincorporated Income Taxes

To raise money from businesses that are not corporations (and thus do not pay corporate income taxes), some states and localities impose the *unincorporated income tax*.

Grant-in-Aid Programs

As we discussed in Chapter 11, grants-in-aid are sums given for a specific purpose by the federal government to states and localities, or by states to localities. Though not a tax, a grant is a very important source of income. In 1993, federal grants-in-aid totaled $186 billion, or about 21 percent of the total receipts of the states and localities.

The use of grants-in-aid provides another example of how the power to tax can be used to redistribute income. The grants usually go to areas that are in need. For example, federal grants-in-aid have been given to states to help them set up child-care centers, provide unemployment insurance, and aid the handicapped. Grant-in-aid programs can also stimulate states into taking action in fields that they had neglected in the past. Through "matching provisions," the federal government gives aid to the states only if the states also make matching appropriations. The **Interstate Highway Act** set up a program of this kind by matching nine dollars of federal funds for every dollar of state funds appropriated for the construction of interstate highways.

States also have grant-in-aid programs. They give financial aid to their cities, counties, townships, and special districts. In recent years, most of this assistance has been for education.

IS THE TAX SYSTEM WORKING WELL?

People frequently complain about the taxes they pay. Government spending has reached record high levels, and taxes have risen to keep up with the increased government spending.

Criticisms of Our Tax System

For some time now, critics of our tax system have claimed that (1) it has not raised enough revenue, (2) it is too complex and inefficient for its own good, and (3) too many people are able to evade paying taxes. Some people believe that certain groups are not paying their fair share of taxes and that other groups are being taxed too much.

Virtually all people in the United States would like to see improvements in the country's tax policies. Therefore, the existing tax structure is a subject of persistent study and discussion.

The Underground Economy—A Drain on Us All

"I can paint your apartment next week, but remember, I expect you to pay me in cash."

"I like buying from those guys in the street. They never charge a sales tax."

"Working for tips is great—you collect $100 and report $50."

"Isn't that illegal?"

"Of course, but who's to know?"

There is a sector of the economy whose activities are not included in official government statistics on the economy. This sector is known as the *underground economy*. Its participants conceal income from their activities because they are attempting to evade paying taxes on this income, because the activities themselves are illegal, or for both reasons.

Figure 12.2   The Underground Economy

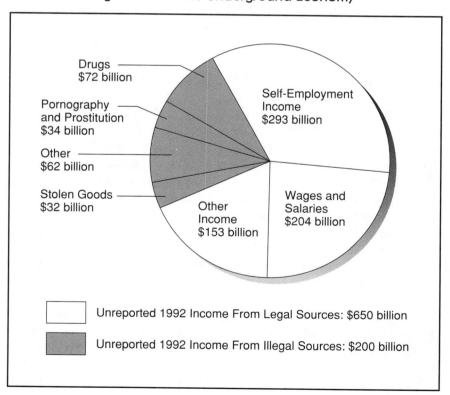

Drugs
$72 billion

Pornography
and Prostitution
$34 billion

Other
$62 billion

Stolen Goods
$32 billion

Self-Employment
Income
$293 billion

Other
Income
$153 billion

Wages and
Salaries
$204 billion

☐ Unreported 1992 Income From Legal Sources: $650 billion

▨ Unreported 1992 Income From Illegal Sources: $200 billion

Who are these income producers in the "underground economy"? Some are hardened criminals whose unlawful activities will land them in jail once they are caught. Far more of them, however, are people from many walks of life who have found ways to conceal from the government the financial details of their otherwise legal activities. Shopkeepers who fail to ring up cash sales and professionals who fail to report cash payments fall into this category. So, too, do those who fail to report their tips or who trade one thing of value for another and fail to report these transactions.

How large is the underground economy? Any estimate as to the size of unreported and illegal transactions must remain just that, an estimate. Government economists, though, have arrived at some figures that are astounding. Starting with the assumption that all underground activity relies upon the use of cash, they have compared the amount of currency required to conduct the reported volume of business with the amount actually in circulation. The excess of cash provides the basis for the estimates of the size of the underground economy and amounts to between 10 and 15 percent of the reported Gross Domestic Product, or $700 billion to $1,050 billion a year. That figure would put the total value of the U.S. underground economy at something more than the GDP of Turkey, Greece, Iceland, New Zealand, Norway, and Portugal combined.

"What," we might ask, "has all this got to do with us? Why should we care if some people are getting away with not paying their taxes?"

We should be concerned because the underground economy hurts us all. For one thing, the taxes we pay are higher than they would be if all taxpayers paid their fair share. Based upon IRS estimates that the underground economy represents 10 to 15 percent of GDP, it is fair to assume that in 1995 roughly $130 billion in taxes were lost to the underground economy. Had those funds been collected, our taxes might have been much lower.

The underground economy gives government planners and others a distorted picture of the economy as it actually exists. This distortion affects us all. For example, the federal government relies upon certain data when deciding whether to increase or decrease the nation's money supply. (How and why the government does this is discussed in Chapter 18.) If, because of the $700 billion or more in the underground economy, the government were to err in its economic planning, a recession that might otherwise have been ended will be extended.

Another problem with the underground economy is that a large sector of the labor force may be more interested in money they can earn there than in money they can earn in the legitimate economy. The money that is escaping taxation may be valued more highly by its producers than is taxable income. If this is true, productivity may be adversely affected. If, for example, an assembly-line worker pays less attention to a daytime job than to an after-hours, cash-only appliance-repair business, the worker's daytime efficiency may be affected.

Most people in the United States report their earnings and pay their taxes in full when they are due. But these people have to carry the burden of paying for those who are not meeting their obligations.

1. What is meant by the "underground economy"?
2. According to the pie chart (Figure 12.2), what were the sources of income in the underground economy?
3. Why is the underground economy sometimes described as a "drain on us all"?
4. "Any estimate of the amount of money circulating in the underground economy will always be more a guess than a fact." Explain this statement.
5. How does the underground economy complicate the government's job of monitoring our nation's economy?
6. In what way does the underground economy pose a threat to U.S. productivity?
7. What do you think should be done about the underground economy? Explain your answer.

What Are the Ingredients of a Good Tax System?

In his *Wealth of Nations* (1776), British economist Adam Smith set forth three criteria or standards for judging a nation's tax system. To this day, economists refer to these standards in their evaluation of taxes.

Fairness. The first standard Smith set forth was that taxes should be fair and that taxpayers should believe the taxes are fair. For this reason, Smith called for governments to require the payment of taxes in proportion to one's income.

Clarity and Certainty. Everyone should be able to understand what the rate of the tax is and how the tax is to be paid. Smith felt that people would be more willing to pay their taxes if they knew what was expected of them. If, in contrast, the tax was whatever the tax collectors felt like charging, as was frequently the case in 18th-century Europe, people would be tempted to avoid it.

Simplicity and Efficiency. If the cost of collecting a tax was more than its yield, there would not be much point to levying the tax. Taxes should be easy to collect, difficult to evade, and inexpensive to administer.

To this list of Smith's standards, modern economists have added the following, which they consider another essential ingredient of any tax system:

Flexibility. Taxes should adjust to economic conditions. In times of general prosperity, people can afford to pay taxes that at other times might be a hardship. Business taxes that at one time are reasonable might at another time (and at the same rate) be oppressive.

Ideally, taxes should adjust themselves automatically to the state of the economy. In reality, however, few taxes are able to do this. The income tax leans in the right direction. When business activity booms and people's earnings increase, the people's and businesses' income taxes increase automatically. Similarly, during periods of recession and business decline, the taxes are automatically reduced because people are earning less.

Fairness in Taxation

Everyone agrees that taxes need to be "fair." But then what makes a tax fair? Or to put it another way: Who should pay taxes? And how much? Responses to these questions usually involve one of two principles of taxation: (1) benefits received, and (2) ability to pay.

Benefits-Received Principle. The suggestion that taxes ought to be paid by individuals in proportion to the benefits they receive from the government is called the *benefits-received principle*. A gasoline tax whose proceeds are used to finance the construction and maintenance of highways is an example of a benefits-received tax. Why? Because the tax is paid "at the pump" by motorists who will directly benefit as roads are improved.

Benefits-received taxes are limited in usefulness. For example, a tax whose proceeds will be used to aid people living in poverty could not be financed by the poor. Nor could public education function well if its costs were borne only by those with children attending public schools.

Ability-to-Pay Principle. The most widely supported principle of taxation is that people should be taxed in accordance with their ability to pay. The *ability-to-pay principle* suggests that those who earn more should pay more in taxes; those who earn less should pay less, regardless of the benefits they receive from government programs.

Tax Proposals Whose Time May Have Come

Proposals to improve the existing tax system are many. We will discuss three: the value-added, energy, and flat taxes.

The Value-Added Tax

A tax levied on the value added to a product is known as a *value-added tax* or *VAT*. It is widely used by the European Union countries. VATs resemble sales taxes in that they are collected by sellers, who transmit the levy on to the government. But unlike sales taxes, which are collected only at the time of the final sale to the individual consumer, value-added taxes are levied at every stage of production and distribution.

The following scenario might occur if, for example, Congress were to pass a 7 percent value-added tax.

Captain Pearl earns his living dredging oysters in Chesapeake Bay. The Captain has just sold $1,000 worth of oysters (the amount equal to the wages, profits, and other costs incurred by Captain Pearl in harvesting the oysters) to Shelley's Wholesale Fish Company. Shelley's paid Pearl $1,000 plus a 7 percent VAT. Captain Pearl will turn 7 percent of $1,000—or $70—over to the government.

The next day, Shelley's sold the oysters to the Simply Seafood Market for $1,500 plus $105 VAT ($1,500 × 7 percent = $105). Shelley's sent only

$35 of the $105 collected on to the government, and pocketed the remaining $70.

Why did Shelley's forward only $35 of the $105 in VAT that they collected on the sale? Because the value that Shelley's added to the oysters in terms of wages, profits, and other costs was only $500, and 7 percent of $500 equals $35. The $70 that Shelley's retained represented the VAT Shelley's had already paid when the company bought the shipment from Captain Pearl.

Now if Simply Seafood adds $200 in labor, profit, and other costs to the production process, a VAT of $14 (7 percent of $200) must be sent to the government.

How much will the customer pay for the oysters? Add $1,000 + 7 percent, + $500 + 7 percent, + $200 + 7 percent = $1,819. This amount includes the total of the value added at each stage of production ($1,700) plus the total VAT ($119).

VATs: The Advantages. Supporters of value-added taxes say that the principal advantages are:

- They are levied at every stage of production.
- Value-added taxes are easy to collect and difficult to evade.
- The VAT could make it easier for U.S. firms to compete abroad because VATs are usually levied only

on sales inside the country that imposes the VAT. Let us look more closely at VATs.

In pricing their merchandise, U.S exporters need not factor in VATs. In most instances, U.S. exporters do not have to pay value-added taxes on sales abroad. Those exporters who do pay the VAT can apply for rebates. Similarly, U.S. tourists abroad can receive refunds for any value-added tax that they may have paid while buying goods in foreign lands.

While touring New Zealand, Frank Blue, a U.S. citizen, purchases a sweater for $100. Included in the price was a $20 VAT. Blue will be refunded the $20 when he leaves the country (if he fills out the proper forms and shows his sales receipt).

VATs: The Disadvantages. Those opposing the VAT say that, like the sales tax, a VAT is regressive. It increases the costs of all goods and services. Its burden falls more heavily on those least able to afford it.

Let us suppose that Francine earns $500 a week in New Zealand, while Terisa earns $350. Let us also suppose that both bought a New Zealand sweater costing $100, and that this price included New Zealand's $20 VAT. The VAT cost each purchaser the same in dollars ($20), but the percentage of each individual's weekly income was not the same. The VAT constituted 4 percent

of Francine's income ($20 divided by $500 equals .04), but made up 5.7 percent of Terisa's income ($20 divided by $350 equals .057).

Determining the value added at each stage of production is not an easy task. Businesses have to spend much time and money on paperwork to accomplish the task.

Many nations with VATs will *rebate* (return) the VAT to foreign buyers. Since U.S. producers cannot rebate sales taxes to foreign buyers, those foreign competitors with VATs have a trade advantage.

In a previous example, Frank Blue received back the $20 VAT on the sweater he purchased in New Zealand. The $100 sweater actually cost Frank $80. If New Zealanders purchase sweaters in the United States, however, they will not get back the sales taxes they pay.

Energy Taxes

Some reformers would like to see a federal *energy tax*. This would be a tax on products such as oil, coal, gasoline, natural gas, and other resources that produce heat, power, electricity, or fuel for air, land, and sea vehicles. Such an energy tax would have two goals: (1) to raise revenue, and (2) to reduce the consumption of energy. We have already discussed why the federal government wants to raise more money. Some people want to reduce Americans' consumption of energy to make the United States less reliant on foreign sources of oil. Others want to reduce energy consumption because of fears that it is contributing to a *global warming*. That is a long-term increase in the surface temperature of the earth. Global warming, if it indeed is happening, would cause major climatic changes and would disrupt agricultural activities around the world.

The United States has long had an excise tax on the consumption of gasoline, natural gas, and other fuels. This tax, however, is designed mainly to raise revenue. An energy tax would have the added benefit of regulating the consumption of energy.

Tax rates for an energy tax could be based on the amount of energy required to produce goods or services. Another approach would tax the carbon content of fuels. In that way, the carbon fuels that contribute most to global warming, such as coal and oil, would be hit harder than less polluting alternatives, such as natural gas and methyl alcohol (produced from corn).

The principal disadvantage of the energy tax is that it would put the heaviest burden on those least able to afford it. In other words, it would be regressive.

An alternative to an energy tax is to continue to use energy tax credits. The federal government and many states give tax credits to business firms that use alcohol as a fuel, that produce electricity using renewable sources of energy, and that use electric-powered vehicles. Unlike energy taxes designed to discourage energy use, energy tax credits are designed to encourage the use of cleaner and safer energy sources than coal, gas, oil, and nuclear power. Those in favor of an energy tax agree that an energy tax credit is a step in the right direction. They would prefer, however, to see the reduction of energy use that would come about with an energy tax.

The Flat Tax

Much of the controversy surrounding the federal personal income tax results from the complex loopholes, deductions, credits, and incentives that have crept into the system over the years. Most of these methods to reduce taxes would be eliminated by the *flat tax*, a proposal that has attracted considerable attention. Simply stated, a flat tax applies a single rate—20 percent is one suggestion—to all incomes above a certain level. Depending on the plan, few or no deductions or exemptions would be permitted. Since people would be taxed on a greater amount of their earnings, tax rates could be significantly lower than they are now. A flat-rate system, its supporters claim, would discourage many existing schemes (some legal, some not) to avoid paying taxes. Filing income taxes would become much simpler. Some reformers suggest that the form could fit on the back of a postcard.

Opposition to the flat-tax proposal comes from people or groups who benefit directly from the deductions and loopholes in the present laws. Charitable organizations, for example, fear losing income if contributions are no longer tax-deductible. State and local government officials worry about what will happen to their borrowing ability if the interest on their bonds is no longer exempt from taxation. People in the real estate industry foresee a decline in home sales and construction if mortgage interest payments can no longer be deducted from taxes.

Similarly, people who claim to represent the interests of the middle class are critical of the flat tax. Remember that a flat tax applies a single rate on all incomes above a certain level, with few or no deductions or exemptions allowed. The elimination of exemptions for each dependent would be a hardship on large families with wage earners but limited incomes. In addition, homeowners, many of whom are middle class, would be hurt if the deductions for interest on mortgage payments and property taxes were eliminated as part of the flat-tax program.

Some critics of the flat tax believe that the wealthy would be its main beneficiaries. While the wealthy would lose many deductions, these losses would be more than offset by the sharp reductions of their tax rates (in some cases from 39.6 to 20 percent).

By permission of Mike Luckovich and Creators Syndicate

Progressive, Regressive, and Proportional Taxes

We learned earlier about progressive or regressive taxes. Depending on people's income levels, the two taxes take different proportions of their incomes. In contrast to these two, a tax that requires all persons to pay the same percentage of their total income in taxes is a *proportional tax.*

Progressive Taxes. When the percentage of income paid in taxes increases as one's income increases, the tax is said to be progressive. As we learned earlier, the federal personal income tax is a progressive tax.

Regressive Taxes. Regressive taxes take a larger fraction of one's income as income decreases, and a smaller fraction as income increases. Sales and excise taxes are examples of regressive taxes. We can illustrate how regressive a sales tax is in the following example:

> *The sales tax on a new automobile is the same regardless of whether one earns $20,000 or $200,000. Suppose, for example, that the sales tax on a new car is $1,000. One thousand dollars is 5 percent of the earnings of a person whose yearly income is $20,000, whereas it is less than 1 percent of the earnings of a person earning more than $100,000. Since the individual with the lower income pays a higher percentage of that income in sales taxes than does the individual with a higher income, the sales tax is said to be regressive.*

Proportional Taxes. Proportional taxes take the same share of one's income at all levels. By way of illustration, let us suppose that everyone was subject to an income tax rate of 20 percent. In those circumstances, an individual earning $15,000 would pay $3,000 in taxes, while a person with $150,000 in earnings would pay $30,000. Some people would argue that this is a fair tax because it takes ten times as much in taxes from someone earning ten times more in income. Others, however, cite Engel's Law (first discussed in Chapter 10) to show that proportional taxes discriminate against low-income families.

Ernst Engel was a 19th-century German economist who pioneered in studies of consumer behavior. From these studies, Engel developed a theory that came to be known as "Engel's Law." It states that the proportion of family expenditures for necessities (basic food, clothing, and shelter) increases as income decreases, while the proportion of expenditure for luxuries (expensive clothes, furs, cars, jewelry, expensive houses, and so on) decreases as income decreases. Thus, a family of four earning $15,000 a year might have to spend 90 percent of its income on food, clothing, and housing. That would leave it with but $1,500 for life's luxuries. In those circumstances, a $3,000 tax takes all the funds a family has for luxuries plus $1,500 of the money the family needs to buy necessities.

"Of course, it won't do the economy any good, but it'll be fun to hike taxes on the rich."

By contrast, a family earning $150,000 might need to spend only 30 percent of its income for the same necessities. The remaining 70 percent (or $105,000) could be spent on luxuries. For this family, a $30,000 tax would simply reduce the funds they had available for savings or luxuries from $105,000 to $75,000.

The Social Security program is financed in part by a kind of proportional tax. All workers pay the same percentage (6.20 percent) of their income, up to a certain limit. Earnings above that limit are not subject to the Social Security tax.

TAX INCIDENCE: WHO REALLY PAYS A TAX?

CUSTOMER: "Gee, that's a nice pair of jeans. Let's see, they're my size, and they're on sale for $15. I've got $15. I'll take them."

CASHIER: "Yes, that's a nice pair of jeans. That will be $16.20, please."

CUSTOMER: "I think you are mistaken, these jeans were marked down to $15. Oh, I forgot—you also charge sales tax."

CASHIER: "Hey, we don't charge the sales tax, we just collect it. The extra $1.20 goes to the state."

In many instances, those who pay taxes to a government can pass the cost along to someone else. Sales tax laws require merchants to put aside a percentage of their sales and send this amount on to the state or local government. But these sales taxes are really paid by customers, who find the tax added to their bills.

The process of transferring the burden of a tax from those upon whom it is levied (in many cases, the merchants) to another individual or business is known as *shifting*. The *incidence* of a tax refers to those on whom the burden of a tax finally falls. Thus, one might say, "The incidence of a sales tax is shifted from retailers to their customers."

Direct and Indirect Taxes

Taxes that cannot be shifted fall into the category of *direct taxes*. Those that can be shifted are classified as *indirect taxes*.

Direct Taxes. Taxes that are levied on people and that cannot be shifted are called "direct taxes." Examples include income taxes (which are levied on people's earnings and other income) and inheritance or estate taxes (which are levied on heirs).

Indirect Taxes. Taxes that can be shifted to others are called "indirect taxes." Such taxes are usually levied on goods and services rather than on people. Excise taxes, sales taxes, and tariffs are indirect taxes because the one on whom the tax is levied can shift the burden on to another. A real property tax is usually a direct tax. It becomes an indirect one, however, when a government taxes a building owner, who in turn passes the tax on to the renters in the building in the form of higher rents.

What does this picture tell us about the shifting *and* incidence *of taxes on parking a car?*

Although sales taxes are added to the posted prices of goods and services, excise taxes and tariffs are not. Instead, the latter two taxes are included in the selling price. Thus, a Peruvian sweater selling for $40 may include a $5 tariff in its selling price. The wholesaler who imported the sweater from Peru recovered the $5 by adding it to the price she charged the retailer. For his part, the retailer shifted the tax along to the consumer by including the $5 tariff in his selling price.

Taxes that are included in the selling price of an item without the buyer knowing about them are often described as *hidden taxes*.

The Effects of Tax Incidence

The question of tax incidence is one of the first things legislators consider when thinking about changing tax laws or introducing new taxes. Suppose, for example, that Congress wanted to levy an excise tax on wheat. Before enacting such a law, however, the lawmakers would want to investigate the incidence of the new tax. For example, they might ask:

● Will the tax be passed on to consumers in the form of higher bread prices? Or,

● Will farmers absorb the tax with lower profits? Or,

● Will millers and bakers absorb the tax by reducing their profits, or by requiring their employees to absorb some or all of the tax in the form of reduced wages?

● What effect will the tax on wheat have on the market for substitute products, such as rye or oats?

Summary

The federal government and state and local governments all impose taxes. Taxes are necessary in order to pay for the many government services, such as police, armed forces, schools, roads, health care, and welfare programs. As government expenditures increase, government income to meet these increasing costs must also rise.

While taxes are the main source of income for governments, taxes also have other uses. They may be used to redistribute wealth in our economy. They may be used to promote certain industries. Taxes are sometimes passed to influence consumer and business spending.

The major tax of the federal government is the personal income tax. Social Security taxes, Medicare taxes, and corporate income taxes are also major sources of federal income. State and local governments rely on revenue largely from sales and property taxes, and to a lesser extent from personal and corporate income taxes. Another major source of revenue for states and localities are grants-in-aid.

When considering the fairness of a tax, one might discuss the benefits-received and the ability-to-pay principles. One should also consider whether a tax is progressive, regressive, or proportional. Finally, whether a tax is direct or indirect is important in evaluating it.

Proposals to change the tax system in the United States are many. They include, but are not limited to, a value-added tax (VAT), an energy tax, and a flat tax.

REVIEWING THE CHAPTER

Building Vocabulary

Match each term in Column A with its definition in Column B.

Column A	Column B
1. ability-to-pay principle	*a.* a tax whose burden cannot be shifted
2. benefits-received principle	*b.* a federal tax levied on a person's property at the time of death
3. progressive tax	*c.* a tax that takes a larger proportion from low-income people than from high-income people
4. proportional tax	*d.* a tax designed to discourage certain behaviors
5. regressive tax	*e.* the idea that taxes should be paid by those who benefit from the way the money will be spent
6. flat tax	*f.* the idea that people who are best able to afford to pay taxes should pay more than others
7. VAT	*g.* a tax whose rate increases as the taxpayer's income increases
8. direct tax	*h.* a tax with a single rate that is applied to all income above a certain level
9. "sin tax"	*i.* a tax that has the same rate of tax applying equally to all persons regardless of income
10. estate tax	*j.* a tax paid on the value added to a good at each stage of production

Understanding What You Have Read

1. Last year, A earned $5,000, B earned $50,000, and C earned $500,000. Under the terms of a special tax passed that year, A paid $50, B $500, and C $5,000. What kind of tax did they pay? (*a*) regressive (*b*) progressive (*c*) proportional (*d*) none of these.

2. Suppose that instead of paying the taxes described in Question 1, A paid 10 percent of income, B 25 percent, and C 50 percent. The tax would now be described as (*a*) regressive (*b*) progressive (*c*) proportional (*d*) none of these.

3. Suppose that instead of the taxes described in Questions 1 and 2, the government announced that all families would have to pay the same tax, $100, regardless of income. Such a tax would be (*a*) regressive (*b*) progressive (*c*) proportional (*d*) none of these.

4. Which type of tax falls most heavily on families with low incomes? (*a*) personal income tax (*b*) inheritance tax (*c*) sales tax (*d*) bridge and highway tolls.

5. Which of the following types of revenue is based upon the benefits-received principle? (*a*) income tax (*b*) sales tax (*c*) property tax (*d*) bridge and highway tolls.

6. The property tax is regressive because (*a*) it is terribly old-fashioned (*b*) it is based upon assessed valuation, not income (*c*) the rich pay heavier taxes on their homes than the less wealthy (*d*) property assessors do not allow for changes in the cost of living.

7. In the United States, taxation is used to accomplish all of the following, *except* to (*a*) redistribute income (*b*) reduce purchasing power (*c*) discourage the consumption of specific goods (*d*) promote the purchase of a particular brand of merchandise.

8. Which of the following is the best example of an ability-to-pay tax? (*a*) income tax (*b*) sales tax (*c*) property tax (*d*) bridge and highway toll.

9. The incidence of taxation refers to (*a*) the size of a tax (*b*) the importance of a tax (*c*) the group responsible for collecting a particular tax (*d*) the group that actually pays a tax.

10. The process of passing taxes on to others is called (*a*) incidence (*b*) shifting (*c*) buck-passing (*d*) a nuisance tax.

11. A tax that cannot be passed along to someone else is called (*a*) an indirect tax (*b*) a direct tax (*c*) an excise tax (*d*) a tariff.

12. The tax yielding the most revenue to cities, towns, and villages is (*a*) the income tax (*b*) the sales tax (*c*) the property tax (*d*) an excise tax.

Thinking Critically

1. Benjamin Franklin said that we can always be certain of death and taxes. But why are taxes necessary? Give *three* reasons with explanations for each.

2. Select *one* of the taxes imposed by the federal government. Explain why you favor or oppose this tax.

3. According to Adam Smith and others, a good tax should have the following features: (*1*) fairness, (*2*) clarity and certainty, (*3*) convenience of payment, (*4*) ease of administration, and (*5*) flexibility. With reference to these criteria, evaluate either the   (*a*) sales tax, or   (*b*) real property tax.

4. In recent years, states and localities have had increasing difficulty in meeting the rising cost of government.   (*a*) By comparing their sources of income with those of the federal government, discuss the reasons why they are having these financial difficulties. (*b*) What proposal would you suggest that would help states and localities obtain adequate revenues?

5. There is much talk today about grants-in-aid. Some people object to the federal controls that come with these grants. Others fear that localities have become dependent on federal "handouts" instead of looking for economies and fending for themselves. What do you think about this issue? Give reasons for your answer.

SKILLS: Completing a Federal Income Tax Form

Most people who have a job and/or receive interest income must file a federal income tax return. Moreover, it can be to people's advantage to fill out such a return to see if they qualify to receive a refund from the Internal Revenue Bureau. The law requires that employers withhold a portion of their employees' wages in each pay period, and send these sums to the government. When individuals file their returns, they calculate how much they owe in taxes on the previous year's income. The difference between the amount withheld and the amount owed is either returned to the taxpayer (if there is an overpayment) or paid to the government (if the amount withheld is not sufficient to cover the total amount of taxes owed).

Although preparing an income tax return can be quite complicated, it is usually a simple matter for single people with part-time jobs. In most instances, the return that they use will be the 1040EZ form. (See Figure 12.3.)

In 1995, Jean LaRue had a part-time job at a local supermarket. In the course of the year, Jean earned $6,240 at the supermarket and paid

$936 in withholding taxes. Jean also had a savings account that paid $184 in interest.

Write the numbers 1–12 down the left side of a blank piece of paper. Put your answers to the following instructions on this paper instead of writing in Figure 12.3.

1. Enter Jean's wages on line 1.
2. Enter the interest Jean earned on her savings account on line 2.
3. Since she received no unemployment compensation, we put nothing on line 3.
4. Add lines 1, 2, and 3. This is Jean's *adjusted gross income*. Enter this amount on line 4.
5. In accordance with the instructions written on the back of the 1040EZ form, Jean received a standard deduction of $3,900. Enter this amount on line 5.
6. Enter the total earnings subject to tax (line 4 minus line 5) on line 6. This is Jean's *taxable income*.
7. Enter the amount of federal income tax withheld on line 7.
8. You should leave line 8 blank since Jean is not eligible for Earned Income Credits.
9. Add lines 7 and 8. These are Jean's *total tax payments*.
10. The amount of tax Jean owes on her taxable income is found in the tax table accompanying the 1040EZ instruction booklet. Determine Jean's tax from Table 12.3. Enter the amount of tax Jean owes on her taxable income on line 10.

Table 12.3 PARTIAL TAX TABLE

At least	But less than	Single	Married filing jointly
2,500	2,525	377	377
2,525	2,550	381	381
2,550	2,575	384	384
2,575	2,600	388	388
2,600	2,625	392	392
2,625	2,650	396	396

11–12. Calculate the difference between Jean's total tax payments (line 9) and the amount you entered on line 10. Enter this amount—either a refund or an amount owed—on the proper line (either line 11 or line 12).

Great! You have completed Jean's 1040EZ tax form. Note that the preparer must sign and date the return. When it is time for you to fill out a tax form, be sure to read the declaration that you are asked to sign.

Figure 12.3 1040EZ Federal Tax Form

Form **1040EZ**

Department of the Treasury—Internal Revenue Service

Income Tax Return for Single and Joint Filers With No Dependents (L) **1995**

OMB No. 1545-0675

Use the IRS label here

Your first name and initial: JEAN — Last name: LA RUE

If a joint return, spouse's first name and initial — Last name

Home address (number and street). If you have a P.O. box, see page 11. Apt. no.

1563 MAIN STREET, N. W.

City, town or post office, state, and ZIP code. If you have a foreign address, see page 11.

OGDEN, UT 84403

See instructions on back and in Form 1040EZ booklet.

Your social security number 462 05 1397

Spouse's social security number

Presidential Election Campaign (See page 11.)

Note: *Checking "Yes" will not change your tax or reduce your refund.*

Do you want $3 to go to this fund? ▶ ✓

If a joint return, does your spouse want $3 to go to this fund? ▶

Income

Attach Copy B of Form(s) W-2 here. Enclose, but do not attach, any payment with your return.

1 Total wages, salaries, and tips. This should be shown in box 1 of your W-2 form(s). Attach your W-2 form(s). 1

2 Taxable interest income of $400 or less. If the total is over $400, you cannot use Form 1040EZ. 2

3 Unemployment compensation (see page 14). 3

4 Add lines 1, 2, and 3. This is your **adjusted gross income.** If less than $9,230, see page 15 to find out if you can claim the earned income credit on line 8. 4

Note: *You **must** check Yes or No.*

5 Can your parents (or someone else) claim you on their return?
✓ **Yes.** Do worksheet on back; enter amount from line G here.
☐ **No.** If **single,** enter 6,400.00. If **married,** enter 11,550.00. For an explanation of these amounts, see back of form. 5

6 Subtract line 5 from line 4. If line 5 is larger than line 4, enter 0. This is your **taxable income.** ▶ 6

Payments and tax

7 Enter your Federal income tax withheld from box 2 of your W-2 form(s). 7

8 **Earned income credit** (see page 15). Enter type and amount of nontaxable earned income below. 8

9 Add lines 7 and 8 (don't include nontaxable earned income). These are your **total payments.** 9

10 **Tax.** Use the amount on **line 6** to find your tax in the tax table on pages 29–33 of the booklet. Then, enter the tax from the table on this line. 10

Refund or amount you owe

11 If line 9 is larger than line 10, subtract line 10 from line 9. This is your **refund.** 11

12 If line 10 is larger than line 9, subtract line 9 from line 10. This is the **amount you owe.** See page 22 for details on how to pay and what to write on your payment. 12

I have read this return. Under penalties of perjury, I declare that to the best of my knowledge and belief, the return is true, correct, and accurately lists all amounts and sources of income I received during the tax year.

Sign your return

Keep a copy of this form for your records.

Your signature: Jean La Rue — Spouse's signature if joint return

Date: 3/25/96 — Your occupation: CLERK — Date — Spouse's occupation

For Privacy Act and Paperwork Reduction Act Notice, see page 7. Cat. No. 12617R Form 1040EZ (1995)

Chapter 13

ECONOMIC GROWTH AND THE QUALITY OF LIFE

Overview

Economic growth—the ever-increasing output of goods and service—may be society's oldest economic goal. It is hardly a surprising goal since the dream of a better tomorrow seems to be part and parcel of the human condition. For that reason, economists have long studied and written about the process of economic growth. Moreover, every U.S. president in modern times has supported policies and programs to promote growth.

In recent years, however, questions have been raised about some of the basic assumptions of economic growth. As evidence of the relationship between production and environmental decay continues to mount, some people question whether society can afford to pay the price of growth. The controversy has yet to be resolved.

In this chapter, we will discuss aspects of economic growth, including:

- [ ] What this growth is
- [ ] Why growth is important to our economy and to the global economy
- [ ] The ingredients of economic growth
- [ ] The role of government in promoting growth
- [ ] The debate between those who would limit economic growth and those who advocate few restrictions on it.

WHAT IS ECONOMIC GROWTH?

Economic growth refers to an increase in the output of goods and services over time. It is most commonly measured in terms of changes in the dollar value of the gross domestic product (GDP). All other things being equal, if the GDP in one year is greater than that of the preceding year, we could say that economic growth has taken place. But all other things are not necessarily equal. We know, for example, that the value of the dollar is constantly changing. If the GDP increases by 5 percent in a year in which the purchasing power of the dollar declines by 10 percent, fewer goods and services are actually produced that year. For that reason, economists prefer to use the GDP as expressed in

Table 13.1 GROSS DOMESTIC PRODUCT, 1929–1994 (IN CURRENT AND CONSTANT (1987) DOLLARS)

	CURRENT DOLLARS		CONSTANT (1987) DOLLARS	
	Total (billions)	Per Capita	Total (billions)	Per Capita
1929	$ 103.1	$ 846	$ 821.8	$ 6,743
1940	100.0	757	906.0	6,857
1950	287.0	1,892	1,418.5	11,453
1960	513.4	2,840	1,970.8	10,903
1970	1,010.7	4,928	2,873.9	14,013
1980	2,708.2	11,892	3,776.3	16,584
1990	5,546.1	22,189	4,897.3	19,238
1994	6,736.9	25,840	5,342.3	20,490

constant dollars (or *real GDP*). This method eliminates yearly changes in the value of the dollar from the measurement of economic growth.

Population change is another variable affecting economic growth. While real GDP enables us to compare the economy's total output of one year with that of another, it does not tell us much about living standards. For example, if the population were to increase by 10 percent while the GDP was increasing by 5 percent, there would be fewer goods and services available *per capita* (for every person). Thus, despite the increase in output, living standards as measured by per capita GDP would have decreased. For that reason, economists developed a second gauge of economic growth: *real GDP per capita*. This measure eliminates both fluctuations in the value of the dollar and population differences as factors in comparing the output of one period of time with that of another.

We can now refine our definition by saying that economic growth is the increase over time in either real GDP or real GDP per capita.

WHAT IS THE IMPORTANCE OF ECONOMIC GROWTH?

In the 18th century, English economist **Thomas Malthus** predicted that the world's population would outgrow the food supply. He believed that many people would starve to death unless wars and diseases killed them first. His theories have not yet proven correct. The world's population has increased tremendously since the 18th century, along with tremendous growths in food supplies. What has happened is that the productive capacity of industrialized nations has increased

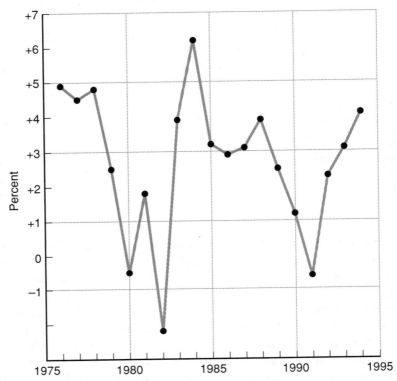

Figure 13.1   Real Gross Domestic Product
(Annual Rates of Change)

How does this graph illustrate economic growth? Which year or years shown do not show growth?

at a rate faster than the increase in population. Economic growth has made this possible. In many of the developing countries, however, economic growth has not increased at a faster rate than the increase in population. Thus, the dire predictions of Malthus are of real concern in these countries. (The many obstacles to growth in the developing nations are discussed in Chapter 24.) Economic growth has been largely responsible for the following: (1) higher living standards, (2) high employment levels, (3) income security, and (4) a strong national defense. We will discuss each topic.

Higher Living Standards

Economists attribute the improved living standards in the industrialized nations of the world over the past 200 years to economic growth. As we have said, economic growth is an increase in goods and services per capita over a period of time. Whenever real GDP per capita increases, there is more of everything to go around. This increase in goods and services has resulted in higher living standards in the past and is likely to do so in the future as well.

High Employment Levels

If we are to maintain high employment levels, our economy must grow. We must create new businesses to compensate for the ones that are cutting back on numbers of employees and those businesses that are folding. The economy must expand to create over a million new jobs each year.

Income Security

Economic growth enables the nation to maintain its Social Security system and programs to assist the needy, such as food stamps. Millions of Americans depend on funds from these programs. As we learned in Chapter 11, the United States spends hundreds of billions of dollars each year on income security and poverty programs. Without economic growth, the country would have difficulty funding these programs.

Strong National Defense

Because of its tremendous output of goods and services, the United States has been able to build a powerful national defense force and still meet its other needs. From the late 1940s until 1991, the United States was considered the leader in the free world's confrontations with the Soviet Union and its allies. Now that this cold war has ended, U.S. leaders believe that they still need to maintain heavy spending on national defense. They fear that instability in various regions of the world might endanger U.S. interests. They also fear that several unfriendly nations are developing nuclear weapons and are promoting terrorism.

Economic growth has made it possible for the United States to maintain its leadership role in world politics. The United States provides high levels of economic assistance to countries in various parts of the world. It participates in numerous UN-sponsored peacekeeping missions. In recent years, for example, the United States has sent armed forces to help restore order in Somalia, Haiti, and Bosnia. Costly as these efforts are, it is possible for the government to undertake them without reducing living standards at home. The United States does this by drawing on the surplus created by its expanding economy.

Figure 13.2 Real GDP and Real GDP per Capita in 1950, 1970, and 1994

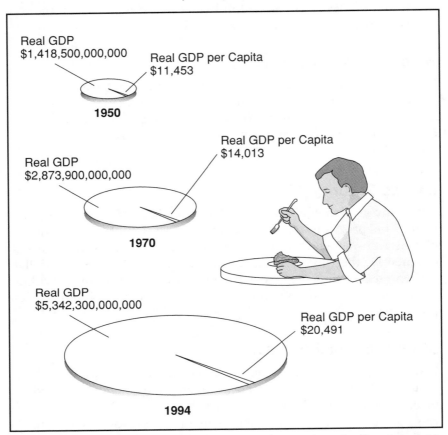

Real GDP
$1,418,500,000,000

Real GDP per Capita
$11,453

1950

Real GDP per Capita
$14,013

Real GDP
$2,873,900,000,000

1970

Real GDP
$5,342,300,000,000

Real GDP per Capita
$20,491

1994

As economic growth (the pie) increases, the size of the "slice of pie" each individual receives also grows. How may an increasing real GDP per capita in a country affect the quality of life in that country?

WHAT ARE THE INGREDIENTS OF ECONOMIC GROWTH?

Like any good recipe, it takes a number of ingredients to produce economic growth. These are: (1) an ever-increasing ability to produce goods and services; (2) expanding demand; and (3) a favorable business climate.

Ever-Increasing Productive Capacity

Economic growth requires a long-term increase in real output per person. There is a limit, however, to the amount of goods and services the economy can produce at any point in time. Exactly what this limit is will depend upon the economy's supply of productive resources and society's ability to use them—that is, its *productive capacity*.

As we discussed in Chapter 6, productive resources such as raw materials, labor, management, and capital are limited. Once these resources are fully employed, output cannot be increased unless a new supply of resources is made available or new and more efficient production techniques are applied. Therefore, in order to continue economic growth, our nation must be able to increase its ability to produce more goods and services. Thus, an ever-increasing productive capacity is essential to economic growth.

Expanding Demand

Regardless of what the economy is capable of producing, actual production will depend upon how much consumers, businesses, and governments are willing to buy. The total of this willingness to buy is called *aggregate demand*. To stimulate economic growth, aggregate demand needs to be maintained. On pages 312–313, we will discuss how the federal government attempts to do this.

Favorable Business Climate

Economic growth is more likely to occur in a climate favorable to businesses. Among the more important features of such a favorable business climate are the following:

Political Stability. Businesses are more likely to flourish in politically stable countries (nations whose rulers come to power through legal means and whose government is capable of maintaining order). In such an atmosphere, businesses are more inclined to accept the risks of business expansion. In a politically unstable atmosphere, by contrast, businesses are less likely to accept the costs and risks of expansion and growth.

Government Concern for the Needs of Business. There is much that government can do to assist businesses and thereby promote economic growth. We will discuss these measures on pages 312–315.

A Willingness to Save and Invest. Capital formation—the acquisition of tools, machinery, and plants—is essential to increasing productivity and stimulating growth. This capital cannot be acquired, however, unless there is a sufficient amount of money in the economy available for investment. Often this money comes from individuals who save and invest their money. Some societies are so poor that people cannot afford to save any money. The funds that should be set aside to invest instead is used to clothe, house, or feed people. Frequently, those few people with money available to invest prefer to do so abroad, where the financial returns are more certain. Other rich individuals may choose to use their wealth to acquire houses or luxuries, neither of which will add to a nation's productive capacity.

Japan, one of the leading industrial nations of the world, has a high rate of savings. Many economists attribute Japan's industrial development to the Japanese people's propensity to save. Because of Japan's high savings rate, Japanese businesses can make extensive long-term investments. The United States has a savings rate only about one-third of Japan's. But its savings rate is still high compared to that in many developing countries.

GOVERNMENT AND ECONOMIC GROWTH

The federal government has a special role to play in fostering economic growth. It does this by using its powers to (1) influence aggregate demand; (2) promote employment; (3) support research, education, and training; and (4) promote savings and investment.

Influencing Aggregate Demand

Through various means, the federal government strives to maintain a healthy balance among business demand, consumer demand, and gov-

Serving under President Bill Clinton as Secretary of Commerce, Ronald Brown vigorously promoted the interests of U.S. businesses abroad. Here Brown was visiting the Great Wall while on a trip to China in 1994.

Table 13.2 SAVINGS RATES IN DEVELOPED COUNTRIES, 1985–1994

Country	Average Rates of Household Savings
Japan	14.9%
France	12.7%
Germany	12.4%
Canada	9.9%
Great Britain	9.3%
United States	4.9%

ernment demand. If the economy is to grow, aggregate demand must keep pace with its productive expansion. Failing that, prices will fall, workers will be laid off, and expansion will grind to a halt. There is a danger, however, if aggregate demand increases faster than the economy's ability to satisfy it. In that case, prices will rise in what could become a growth-killing inflationary spiral. We will discuss the federal use of monetary and fiscal policies to influence aggregate demand in Chapters 18 and 19.

Promoting Employment

Full employment has been a goal of the federal government for over 50 years. Government advances this goal by stimulating business activity, promoting the education and training of the workforce, reducing discrimination in the workplace, and helping unemployed workers find jobs.

Government officials do not expect that every person willing and able to work will be able to find a job. Instead the government tries to keep unemployment rates down to between 4 and 6 percent. In fact, some economists believe that if the unemployment rate were to get too low (say, below 5 percent), workers would be in demand and could command higher wages. If this would happen all over the country, the economists think, then high rates of inflation might result.

Supporting Research, Education, and Job Training

Increasing productivity is a key to economic growth. As output per worker increases, total national output is likely to follow. One source of increased productivity comes from the invention of new machines. Another follows as businesses develop new and improved ways of producing goods and services. From its earliest days, the federal government has stimulated inventions and innovations. In some instances, government has been directly involved in research and development projects, such as the NASA space program. The Defense Department grants money to some businesses doing research that might have applications in the area of national defense. Indirectly, government fosters research by awarding patents and by granting tax concessions to businesses for research and development projects.

Government aids all levels of education to help provide an educated workforce. It also has several job-training programs. The idea behind all of these programs is to increase the productive capacity of people to bring them or keep them out of poverty. Examples of such programs include the Job Corps, which provides vocational training to young adults, and the Neighborhood Youth Corps, which hires young people. Another federal effort is the **Job Training Partnership Act (JTPA)**, which funds job training for the economically disadvantaged, dislocated workers, and others who have difficulty getting work.

Promoting Savings and Investment

The savings of individuals and families are the source of investments and capital formation that business firms need to expand. Anything the government can do to increase incomes in the United States will encourage individuals to save more and, thus, allow business firms to invest more. We know that taxes take income away from individuals and businesses. Thus, lowering taxes results in increased income to individuals and businesses. This additional income becomes available for spending, savings, and investment.

In Chapter 12, we discussed the progressive income tax and proposals for a flat tax. Progressive income taxes tend to discourage sav-

These young adults are enrolled in a job-training program that is government funded and that may help them get better jobs.

ings and investment because those with the highest incomes (and thus the ones who would most likely save the most) are the ones who have to pay the highest rates of taxes. In contrast, a flat tax would encourage savings among the wealthy because it would reduce taxes for this group. According to some proposals for the flat tax, the government would not tax income from savings, investments, or capital gains, but it would tax income from wages and salaries. The lower taxes resulting from enacting a flat tax would encourage wealthy people and businesses to save and invest. Of course, as previously discussed in Chapter 12, there are good arguments against the flat tax and in favor of the progressive income tax.

Government has other ways to increase savings and investing. If capital gains taxes are decreased, individuals are likely to invest more. If corporation taxes are lowered, businesses are likely to invest more. Finally, businesses are likely to invest more when interest rates (the costs of borrowing) are low. As we will learn in Chapter 18, the federal government has ways of influencing these interest rates. In sum, government policies can do much to promote savings and investment.

ECONOMIC GROWTH AND THE ENVIRONMENT

We have heard numerous praises of economic growth. But economic growth also has its critics. These critics caution that growth has been a principal cause of the depletion of our natural resources and environmental decay.

Depletion of Natural Resources

The ever-increasing output of goods and services, which we call "economic growth," consumes inputs of human, capital, and natural resources. Some of these resources are said to be "renewable" because, although consumed, they can still be replaced. Lumber is a renewable resource because cleared forests can be replanted. So, too, are fish and wildlife renewable resources because they can reproduce. With proper management, reduced animal and plant populations can be returned to higher levels.

Nonrenewable resources (such as petroleum, coal, and copper) are those that cannot be replaced once they have been consumed. Given the absolute limit in the supply of any nonrenewable resource, there is a danger that one day its supply will be exhausted. How long the depletion process takes depends upon the rate at which the resource is consumed and the available supply.

Supplies of renewable resources could also be exhausted were society to fail to apply the kind of conservation techniques required to

Reforestation Project. Tree farming requires planning and care. Here some trees have been left after cutting a forest so as to protect the soil from erosion. Soon seedlings will be planted between the remaining trees.

preserve them. In the early 1990s, for example, stocks of striped bass (an important sport and food fish) all but disappeared from the East Coast because of the pollution in Chesapeake Bay and the Hudson River. In the Northwest today, industrial development along the Columbia River threatens the salmon fishing industry with extinction. Greenpeace International estimates that 69 percent of the world's fish stocks are either overfished or depleted. This organization and others urge international cooperation to limit fishing around the world.

Is Economic Growth to Be Blamed for Environmental Decay?

Pollution is not a new phenomenon. First-century Romans, 15th-century Parisians, and 19th-century Londoners all complained about the foul wastes created by animals, households, and industries of their time. Never before, however, have the problems and dangers of pollution reached the point that they have today.

At one level, littered parks and highways are unsightly and deprive us all of the enjoyment they might otherwise provide. More serious is the air and water pollution that causes illness and even death. We know, for example, that prolonged inhalation of certain minerals and dusts (such as coal and asbestos) can cause lung disease and cancer.

Most ominous, however, are those forms of pollution that threaten the survival of the planet itself. A case in point is the *greenhouse effect* created when carbon emissions from numerous automobiles, factories, and power plants combine with water in the atmosphere. The effect creates a mantle of carbon dioxide around the globe. This mantle acts as a kind of giant greenhouse. A garden greenhouse allows the sun's light rays to come in and then be reflected out, while holding in the sun's heat. On a global basis, the warming created by the greenhouse effect threatens to change climate patterns and melt the polar ice caps. Scientists disagree whether or not the greenhouse effect has led to global warming or whether we are entering a period of colder conditions that might lead to another ice age. There is agreement, however, that should the polar ice caps melt, the action would release so much water as to raise ocean levels and force the abandonment of many of the world's coastal communities.

Given the relationship between economic output and pollution, some critics of continued economic growth have suggested that there should be *zero economic growth*. That is, they say that the GDP should increase only enough to accommodate population growth. This zero economic growth, they say, would reduce pressure on the environment and protect global supplies of natural resources.

Economic Growth Has Its Defenders

Quite the opposite is argued by those who say that economic growth should be allowed to follow whatever course the market dictates. They remind us that throughout history there have been those who foresaw doom and gloom in every period of change. In each instance, they point out, humankind found a way to overcome the threat. For example, Thomas Malthus, who predicted that world population growth would outstrip the food supply, has thus far been proven wrong. Malthus failed to foresee that a technological revolution would increase farm productivity and that millions of acres of new farmland would be opened in the Americas and elsewhere.

In the same way, we are unable today to predict what discoveries later generations will make to solve their problems. Furthermore, the defenders of economic growth argue, we are a long way from exhausting supplies of natural resources. They say that new sources will be found or new technologies developed by industries when needed.

Another important argument is that industries provide jobs, and that jobs and people are more important than the existence of certain species of plants and animals.

Thomas Robert Malthus

Adam Smith and many other writers of the 18th century saw a world in which natural forces were working everywhere to benefit humanity. Indeed, the underlying justification for *laissez-faire* policies was to allow people to do, in Smith's words, "...that ... which is advantageous to the society." In 1798, however, a work titled *An Essay on the Principle of Population* was published in Great Britain. Written by Thomas Robert Malthus, an English minister, its views served to mark economics as the "dismal science."

Malthus's central thesis was that a population always increases more rapidly than the food supply. With not enough food to go around, large sections of the population are doomed to go hungry or starve. The reason for this dilemma, Malthus explained, is that the population increases in a *geometric progression* (a sequence of numbers in which the ratio of one number to its predecessor is always the same). For example, a married couple (two people) might have two children; each of these two children might have two children, increasing the number at this generation of the family to four. The next generation might have eight; the following generation, 16; and so on in geometric progression. The food supply, in contrast, is limited by the amount of available land and the quantity of seed, fertilizer, and labor applied to it. Although the total food supply could be increased in time, it would do so in an

arithmetic progression, as for example: two, four, six, eight, and ten (or one, two, three, four, and five). Figure 13.3 illustrates the Malthusian Theory.

With population increasing at a faster rate than the food supply, there comes a point when the number of people is greater than the amount of food available to feed them. What happens once the population outstrips the food supply? Malthus foresaw a "season of distress" when the shortage of food would push prices to such a high level that many people would go hungry or starve. Malthus predicted that in the wake of the famine, disease, and war that would surely follow, fewer people would marry, and, as a consequence, the birthrate would decline. Meanwhile, an abundant supply of cheap labor combined with high food prices would encourage farmers to increase their output. In time, therefore, the supply of food would be equal to the needs of the population, and marriage and

birth rates would return to normal. And then what? Population growth would once again surpass the food supply, and the dreary cycle would be repeated.

Was Malthus correct? Is Earth doomed to a perpetual state of overpopulation? Are famine, disease, and death unavoidable consequences?

History at first seemed to refute Malthus's predictions. Using the biological and technological advances of the Industrial Revolution, farmers in Canada, Australia, New Zealand, the United States, and Europe were able to provide more than enough food for their countries. Meanwhile, changing social attitudes in the industrialized nations slowed population growth.

These two developments enabled the industrialized nations to escape Malthus's predictions.

But many of the nonindustrialized countries around the world have not been so fortunate. A recent study predicted that the world's population will jump from 5 billion in 1987 to 6 billion in 1998, and then to 7 billion in 2009. Most of this growth will take place in the poorest, nonindustrialized countries. No doubt malnutrition will prevail there, and some famines will break out.

Some 200 years ago, Malthus wrote: "The power of population is infinitely greater than the power in the earth to produce subsistence for man." Do you think that Malthus's viewpoint is still valid?

Figure 13.3 Food Supply and Population Growth According to Malthus

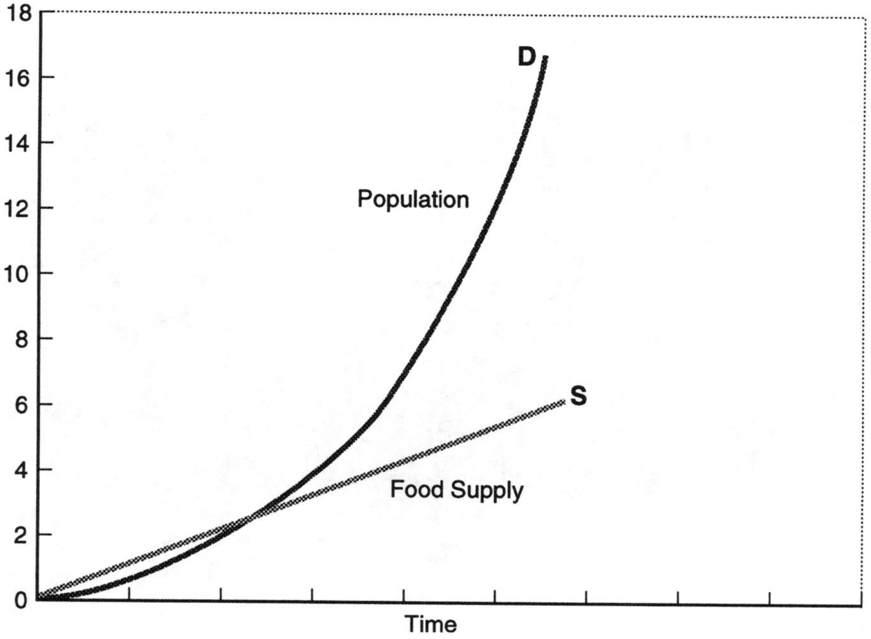

Somewhere between the two positions (unlimited economic growth and zero growth) lies a middle ground occupied by those advocating what they call *sustainable economic growth*. Advocates of this theory argue that every generation should pass along a stock of "net resources" to future generations. Net resources would include natural resources, along with knowledge, technology, and physical and human capital. Thus, if part of a forest were harvested to build a school, the actions would fall into a definition of sustainable growth because future generations would benefit from the school building.

Those who support growth say that a growing economy makes it possible to improve living standards for the poorest segments of society as well as for the wealthy. The wiser course, their argument continues, is to pursue economic growth while at the same time to seek ways to avoid the dangers that accompany the growth. **Robert Solow**, who won the Nobel Prize for Economics in 1987, put it this way:

> *My real complaint about the Doomsday school (those who predict the worst) is that it diverts attention from the really important things that can actually be done to make things better. The end of the world is at hand—the earth, if you take the long view, will fall into the sun in a few billion years anyway, unless some other disaster happens first. In the meantime, I think we'd be better off passing a strong sulfur-*

"I HEAR A GOVERNMENT PANEL HAS DECIDED TO PROTECT AN ENDANGERED SPECIES--EMPLOYED LUMBERJACKS......"

By William Costello for Newspaper Enterprise Association

emissions tax, or getting some Highway Trust Fund money allocated to mass transit, or building a humane and decent floor under family incomes, instead of worrying about the generalized "predicament of mankind."

"Is the End of the World at Hand?" **Challenge,** March 1973.

Summary

Economic growth is the increase in output of goods and services over time. Its most useful measurement is in terms of real GDP per capita. Economic growth helps the nation improve its living standards, maintain high levels of employment, continue its income security programs, and maintain a strong national defense.

Economic growth requires an ever-increasing productive capacity, expanding demand, and a favorable business climate. Government can contribute to economic growth in many ways. It can influence aggregate demand; promote employment; support research, education, and training; and encourage savings and investment.

Some people have criticized economic growth as having a negative impact on the environment. They say it helps deplete nonrenewable resources, causes pollution, and adds to the "greenhouse effect." Others argue that these environmental concerns are either unfounded or exaggerated, and that new resources and new technologies will be found to meet our needs. Those favoring economic growth argue that people's livelihoods are more important than the environmental concerns expressed. In between unlimited growth and zero growth are those who favor sustainable growth, which would provide for economic progress while still showing concern for the environmental impact of such progress.

REVIEWING THE CHAPTER

Building Vocabulary

Match each term in Column A with its definition in Column B.

COLUMN A	COLUMN B
1. economic growth	*a.* the total of purchases by consumers, business, and government
2. GDP per capita	*b.* the idea that every generation should pass on a stock of net resources to future generations
3. productive capacity	
4. aggregate demand	*c.* the trapping of the sun's heat by atmospheric gases
5. greenhouse effect	*d.* the increase over time in real GDP per capita
6. productive resource	
7. constant dollar	*e.* a job for every person willing and able to work
8. geometric progression	*f.* the amount of goods and services the economy is able to produce at a given time
9. full employment	
10. sustainable growth	*g.* the output of a nation divided by its population
	h. a sequence of numbers in which the ratio of one number to its predecessor is always the same
	i. the value of the currency adjusted to eliminate the effects of inflation or deflation
	j. a resource that is necessary for production

Understanding What You Have Read

1. Economic growth may be defined as a change in   (*a*) personal income   (*b*) population   (*c*) the amount of goods and services produced   (*d*) the money supply.

2. If the population of the nation should grow at the rate of 5 percent per year while production increases at the rate of 4 percent, (*a*) living standards are likely to increase   (*b*) living standards are likely to decrease   (*c*) living standards will remain the same   (*d*) inflation is inevitable.

3. Which of the following is the most reliable measure of economic growth?   (*a*) total GDP in current dollars   (*b*) GDP per capita in current dollars   (*c*) total GDP in constant dollars   (*d*) GDP per capita in constant dollars.

4. According to Table 13.1, real GDP per capita increased during the period 1990–1994 by   (*a*) $1.2 billion   (*b*) $3.7 billion   (*c*) $545 million   (*d*) $1,252.

5. Figure 13.2 demonstrates that   (*a*) economic growth varies directly with population growth   (*b*) real GDP per capita varies directly with real GDP   (*c*) real GDP per capita increases as long as GDP increases   (*d*) economic growth cannot occur if there is an increase in population.

6. Economic growth may be expected to provide a nation with all of the following, *except*   (*a*) more consumer goods and services per citizen   (*b*) the ability to continue aiding foreign nations   (*c*) more unemployment   (*d*) the ability to reduce poverty at home.

7. All of the following are necessary ingredients in economic growth, *except*   (*a*) increased productivity   (*b*) reduction of aggregate demand   (*c*) stable government   (*d*) a highly motivated workforce.

8. Savings are important to economic growth because   (*a*) when everyone saves there is less wasteful spending   (*b*) savings provide investment capital that can be used to increase future production   (*c*) consumers can use their savings to buy the things they really need   (*d*) when savings are ample, the government can afford to reduce its expenditures.

9. Advocates of zero economic growth favor   (*a*) an increase in the GDP   (*b*) a reduction in the GDP   (*c*) a freeze in real GDP per capita   (*d*) a rapid increase in real economic growth.

10. If aggregate demand declines while the nation's productive capacity is unchanged,   (*a*) economic growth will decline   (*b*) economic growth will increase   (*c*) prices will increase   (*d*) unemployment will decline.

11. Which of the following proposals seems to offer the best hope of reducing the depletion of nonrenewable natural resources?   (*a*) increase the production of natural resources   (*b*) increase the rate of economic growth   (*c*) seek ways to substitute renewable natural resources for the nonrenewable ones   (*d*) increase government subsidies for the cleanup of toxic-waste sites.

Thinking Critically

1. (*a*) In describing economic growth, economists most frequently speak of "per capita GDP in constant dollars." Summarize the reasons why this phrase is preferable to the phrase "total GDP in current dollars." (*b*) "GDP per capita as expressed in constant dollars is not a perfect measurement of the nation's economic

health for there are things that are important to economic well-being that are not reflected in the GDP." Explain this statement.

2. (*a*) What benefits can economic growth offer the nation as a whole? (*b*) How does its economic growth put the United States in a position to help the world's developing nations? (*c*) Show why *each* of the following has been a necessary ingredient in U.S. economic growth: (*1*) increasing productivity, (*2*) increasing aggregate demand, and (*3*) political and social stability.

3. "One of the key ingredients in economic growth is investment." (*a*) Explain this statement. (*b*) Identify and explain two steps that the government might take to promote investment. (*c*) Why is the shortage of investment capital more of a problem for developing countries than for the world's developed ones?

4. Read the selection below and answer the following questions:

If the present growth trends in world population, industrialization, pollution, food production, and resource depletion continue unchanged, the limits to growth on this planet will be reached sometime within the next one hundred years. The most probable result will be a rather sudden and uncontrollable decline in both population and industrial capacity.

—D.H. Meadows, *et. al.*, **The Limits to Growth** (New York: Universe Books, 1972).

a. Why do the authors of the book from which this selection is taken say that there is a limit to growth?
b. Do you agree with the authors? Explain your answer.

SKILLS: Analyzing Readings

Read the selections below and answer the questions that follow.

Selection I

. . . the Peabody Holding Company, the nation's largest coal producer, shut down the Tygart River Mine and dismissed all 368 workers last December, making it one of hundreds of mines to close in a landscape altered by a single provision of the Clean Air Act of 1990. . . .

Conditions across most of the Eastern coal country are the bleakest since the Great Depression, largely because the coal here is too high in sulfur to easily meet the clean air requirements. Mines are thriving in the West and in eastern Kentucky and southern West Virginia, all producers of low-sulfur coal. But they are closing through most of Appalachia and in other coal-mining areas east of the Mississippi, and their loss is leaving huge gaps in the surrounding communities. It is the anguished human face of policies that even miners acknowledge have purified the air they breathe and the streams they fish in.

Since 1990, according to the National Coal Association, nearly 1,000 coal mines have closed in the United States, nearly all east of the Mississippi, leaving 2,500 [still operating].

Source: "East's Coal Towns Wither in the Name of Cleaner Air," by Peter T. Kilborn, **The New York Times**, February 15, 1996. © 1996 by The New York Times Co. Reprinted by Permission.

Selection II

At the 1993 "Timber Summit" in Portland, Oregon, workers called on President Clinton to end logging restrictions in the old-growth forest. . . . The controversy over protecting the habitat of the spotted owl is much more than a "jobs versus the environment" debate. Most of the 40,000 timber jobs that have disappeared since 1979 have done so for reasons that are unrelated to protection of the old growth. Nevertheless, some 20,000 jobs may ultimately be lost to preserve the ancient forest.

Is such a trade-off typical or unique? The conventional wisdom is that, like death and taxes, a fundamental and widespread conflict be-tween jobs and the environment is a regrettable fact of life. In a Wall Street Journal *poll, an astounding one-third of the respondents thought it somewhat or very likely that their own jobs were threatened by envi-ronmental regulation. While the poll also confirmed strong support for aggressive environmental protection measures, clearly there is broad ac-ceptance of at least one of two major trade-offs between jobs and the en-vironment: Trade-off #1 is that environmental regulation is a significant cause of the nation's high unemployment rate. Trade-off #2 is that, even if environmental protection measures have not cost the economy jobs overall, they have nevertheless generated widespread plant shutdowns and relocations and have led to massive layoffs.*

Based on evidence presented in a recent Economic Policy Institute Report. . . , both of these propositions are myths. At the national level, claims of a trade-off between jobs and the environment are completely without substance. Instead, the facts of the case are:

- *The great majority of economy-wide studies show a small positive ef-fect of environmental regulation on overall employment;*
- *very few shutdowns of manufacturing plants have resulted from en-vironmental protection;*
- *the so-called pollution haven effect—in which industrial firms relo-cate to poor countries to take advantage of lax environmental regula-tion—has seldom been observed.*

We should not minimize the real personal and social costs of job loss and unemployment, whether arising from environmental protection measures or a more common cause. The dramatic decline of our manufacturing base over the last twenty years has had profound, negative consequences for working people in this country. More job loss appears likely, as a result of corporate downsizing, import competition, and defense cutbacks. Policy measures to foster re-industrialization and to provide high-paying jobs for high school graduates are essential, if we seek to recapture the American dream. But, while we face this grim challenge, there is also some good news: The question—"jobs or the environment?"—is simply irrelevant. . . .

Plant Shutdowns?

Perhaps the most serious economic charge leveled against environmental protection has been that it has accelerated the decline of U.S. manufacturing and has helped to cause the disappearance of more than 3 million blue-collar jobs over the last fifteen years. Environmental protection expenses alone are simply not large enough to cripple an otherwise healthy plant. However, stringent pollution regulations might serve as the straw that breaks the camel's back—making production at certain locations unprofitable.

Industrial Flight to Pollution Havens?

Workers are primarily concerned about the threat of layoffs and shutdowns, because these impose high personal and community costs. But critics have charged that EP spending has had a more insidious and long-term negative effect on U.S. manufacturing job growth, by encouraging new investment abroad. Rather than experiencing shutdowns, one might expect new investment to occur in poorer countries with less strict pollution regulations. How serious is this problem of capital flight to so-called pollution havens? A study by H. Jeffrey Leonard of the impact of the federal water and air pollution regulations of the 1970s suggests that such effects were localized to a very few industries. . . .

Why were the effects not greater? First, pollution-control costs appear to be a small portion of total business costs (typically 1 to 2 percent). Second, costs are only one factor influencing business-location decisions. Factors as diverse as access to markets and the quality of life are important components of business-location decisions. For these reasons, at the end of 1991, 79 percent of all U.S. manufacturing investment abroad occurred in other developed countries. The country with the second highest share of U.S. investment—Germany—is also the country with the most stringent pollution control requirements outside the United States.

While manufacturing investment in poor countries remains relatively small, capital flight to low-wage countries has clearly had a major impact on several U.S. industries. Critics of NAFTA, in particular, have expressed concern that lax environmental enforcement, along with close proximity and low wages, might attract investment to Mexico that would otherwise occur in the United States.

This hypothesis has recently been tested in the Maquiladora region of Mexico—an area within one hundred kilometers of the U.S. border— from which plants can import and export products freely. While these plants are required, in theory, to meet U.S. federal environmental standards, in practice, the underfunded Mexican government has not vigorously enforced the law. As a result, air and water pollution problems have become quite serious in the region.

However, a comprehensive look at investment in the Maquiladora region by Gene M. Grossman and Alan B. Krueger confirms the earlier insight: . . . Industries with higher than pollution-abatement costs are not overrepresented among the Maquiladoras, while those with higher labor costs are. At this point, the direct costs associated with pollution control have not been a major factor in influencing plant-location decisions. Highly polluting industries are relocating to poor countries; but the reason, overwhelmingly, is low wages.

From False Trade-Offs to Real Issues

In the mining and logging industries, local job loss from environmental protection can clearly be significant. Yet, even here, new jobs are generated in providing substitute products for the timber or minerals preserved, in fishing and tourism, as well as in industries seeking high "quality of life" for their employees. Generally, these job gains will balance job losses in the long run. . . .

However, most environmental regulation does not have this kind of significant local impact on jobs. Two decades of research on the question of jobs and the environment has established that at the economy-wide level, there simply is no trade-off between employment and environmental protection. If anything, environmental regulation has led to a small net increase in jobs, while clearly providing employment disproportionately weighted to traditional blue-collar sectors. Moreover, layoffs from regulation have been startlingly small, and the so-called pollution haven hypothesis has seldom been observed.

Source: "Job or the Environment? No Trade-Off" by Eban Goodstein, **Challenge**, Jan.–Feb. 1995. Reprinted by permission from M.E. Sharpe, Inc., Armonk, NY 10504.

1. What impact of environmental regulations does Selection I, from an article by Peter T. Kilborn, portray?

2. In what ways does Professor Eban Goodstein, in Selection II, challenge commonly held views on the impact of environmental regulations on employment levels and industrial flight to other countries?

3. Which of the two points of view, Kilborn's or Goodstein's, is reinforced by the cartoon on page 320? Explain your answer.

4. Some people believe that national environmental policy should focus on improving environmental quality and should not be driven by concerns for jobs either created or destroyed. Do you agree or disagree with these views? Explain your answers.

5. Based on these readings and any other information you might have, explain why you think that environmental regulation does or does not hamper economic growth.

Money and Banking

Chapter 14

MONEY IN OUR ECONOMY

Overview

We are all interested in money. We use money to buy the things we want. We save money for something we want in the future. Almost anything we have of value we measure in money. In earlier chapters, we spoke in money terms when we discussed supply and demand, the federal budget, and our Gross Domestic Product. Without money, the economy as we know it could not function. Why is this so? What is money?

In this chapter, we will discuss these matters. We will also discuss the following questions:

- ☐ Why did money replace the barter system?
- ☐ What are the functions of money?
- ☐ What are the characteristics of money?
- ☐ What kinds of money do we use in the United States?
- ☐ How is currency produced and distributed?
- ☐ How do we measure the nation's money supply?
- ☐ Why does the value of money fluctuate?

MONEY REPLACES THE BARTER SYSTEM

Suppose that a modern-day Robinson Crusoe were to find himself on a desert island, completely out of touch with civilization. Suppose also that in his search for food and water, he were to come upon a chest containing a million dollars in United States currency. Would his situation be improved? Hardly. What could he buy on an uninhabited island? Our Robinson Crusoe would have learned a fundamental lesson in economics: Money has value only when it can be exchanged for goods and services. With no one from whom to buy (and with nothing to buy), a million dollars would be worthless.

If money did not exist, the only way that a person could acquire things would be to exchange something else of value for the desired items. Such an exchange is called *barter*.

The barter system works well on a simple level when, for example, someone with a hunger for fish and a rabbit to swap can find a person with a fish and a yearning for rabbit stew. Barter, though, has serious shortcomings. Consider, for example, the case of the farmer with a hog to swap. Suppose the farmer wants a dozen eggs, which are worth much less than a hog. How will the egg seller make change? What will the farmer do if the egg seller does not want a hog at all?

The problems associated with barter were eliminated with the invention of money. *Money* can be anything, yes, anything, as long as it is generally accepted in payment for goods and services. Now a person with a rabbit to sell and an appetite for fish need only find a buyer for rabbit. With the money received from the sale of the rabbit, the shopper can buy a fish from any seller.

MONEY: HISTORICAL BACKGROUND

Many things have served as money in the past. The ancient Romans used salt. The Aztecs in Mexico used cacao beans. Fishhooks, arrowheads, and shells were money to some Native Americans, as were furs and tobacco to the European explorers and colonists in the Western Hemisphere. During World War II, U.S. prisoners of war developed a mini-economy based on the use of cigarettes as a kind of money. When used as money, fishhooks, shells, and many other commodities served as mediums of exchange. That is, they enabled people to exchange one good or service for another. In colonial times in North America, ferry operators accepted fur pelts in payment for moving people and goods

People of the Pacific islands of Yap once considered huge stone discs such as these to be money.

across rivers. They did so knowing that they could pay for the things they needed with those same pelts. In this example, fur served as a kind of money. If, however, the purpose of the exchange was to give the ferry operator a means of keeping warm, the exchange would be described as barter.

Because money was generally more acceptable if it was durable and easy to carry, metallic money became popular early in the history of civilization. Around the year 2500 B.C., ancient Egyptians produced one of the earliest kinds of metallic money in the form of rings. About 400 years later, the Chinese began using gold cubes as money. The first metal coins were struck in the 8th century B.C. by the Lydians, a people who lived in Asia Minor.

The first people to develop paper money were the Chinese. Italian traveler Marco Polo reported on its use in China in the late 1200s. During the late Middle Ages in Europe, merchants and other travelers sought to protect themselves from highway robbers by exchanging their gold coins (which the robbers wanted) for goldsmiths' receipts (which the robbers found useless). The receipts could be exchanged back to coins by designated goldsmiths in other cities. In time, the receipts became so popular that people used them to pay debts without bothering to exchange them for coins.

FUNCTIONS OF MONEY

If money is doing its job, it will perform the functions of a medium of exchange, standard of value, and store of value.

Medium of Exchange

With money, a woodcutter who wants shoes does not have to find a shoemaker who wants wood. Or, to use a more modern example, a welder who wants shoes does not have to find a shoe-store owner who needs some welding done. The welder can sell his services to anyone, because the money that he receives in payment will also be accepted by the owner of the shoe store, who can then exchange it for the things she wants. In this way, money serves as a medium of exchange.

Standard of Value

Money provides a convenient standard with which we can express the value of different items. Thus, a paperback book selling for $6 is equal in value to ten candy bars selling for 60 cents a piece. All goods and services can be measured by the yardstick of their monetary value.

Store of Value

Because money can be saved for future use, it provides a means of storing value. Thus, our egg merchant can save the money earned from the sale of eggs and use the savings at a later date to buy an expensive item.

CHARACTERISTICS OF MONEY

We have already indicated that anything can be called money if it is generally accepted by society. Experience has shown, however, that good money will possess the following characteristics:

- *Durability*. Money should have the ability to stand up under use.
- *Portability*. Money should be light enough to be carried.
- *Divisibility*. Unlike an egg, money should be capable of being divided into change.
- *Uniformity*. Every unit of money should be similar to every other unit of that denomination.
- *Ease of Recognition*. Money should be identifiable as such by everyone who sees it.
- *Relative Scarcity*. In order to be usable, money should be scarce. If it is too easily obtainable, people will be able to pay whatever price is asked. If that happens, prices will continue to rise until money becomes worthless.
- *Stability*. Money's value should not rapidly change.

Gresham's Law

In the 16th century, English financier **Sir Thomas Gresham** observed that when two or more kinds of money having the same nominal value circulate, the one considered more valuable is hoarded and disappears from circulation. Since that time, the principle that "cheap money drives out dear [expensive] money" has been known as *Gresham's Law*.

During and immediately following the Revolutionary War (1775–1781), American colonists saw Gresham's Law in action. People saw their silver and gold coins as having value and hoarded them. Soon this metallic money all but disappeared from circulation. To pay for goods, the colonists spent the distrusted paper dollars that were issued by the Continental Congress.

In the late 1950s, the rising world demand for silver as an industrial metal began pushing up its price. By the 1960s, prices had risen to the point where U.S. coins were worth more in terms of their silver content than of their face value. Once again, Gresham's Law swung into action as silver-based coins and currency began to disappear from circulation. More and more people chose to hoard their dimes and quarters (or sell them to metals traders) rather than use them for money.

Gresham's Law also affected paper currency during this period. In the 1950s and 1960s, U.S. paper currency consisted mostly of Federal Reserve notes and, to a lesser extent, of *silver certificates*. Unlike holders of Federal Reserve notes, holders of silver certificates had the right to exchange them for silver from the **U.S. Treasury Department**. Soon silver certificates disappeared from circulation. The public either hoarded them or sold them to speculators for more than their face value.

As more and more silver certificates and coins disappeared from circulation, Congress moved to eliminate silver from the money supply. Between 1965 and 1970, that metal was replaced by an alloy of copper and nickel in all coins except pennies. Moreover, Congress authorized the Treasury Department to stop redeeming silver certificates. As one economist put it, "Congress finally moved to repeal Gresham's Law."

WHAT KINDS OF MONEY DO WE USE?

Money is money. We probably do not think of what form of money we have. But money does come in different formats, including coins, paper currency, checkbook money, and traveler's checks.

Currency

Currency is money issued by the federal government. Anyone else or any other group or organization attempting to produce money is guilty of *counterfeiting*, which is a serious crime. All United States currencies are *legal tender*. This means that they must be accepted in payment for debts. Thus, if you owe a store $1,000, it does not have to accept your jewelry or even your check in payment. It must, however, accept the currency you offer it.

All forms of U.S. currency are known as *fiat money*. This money has value because the government says it does, not because of its natural value. Thus, a dime consists of copper and nickel that would be worth far less than ten cents if the dime were melted down for its metallic content. Similarly, the paper upon which a $5 bill is printed is hardly worth anything at all. While there once was a time when the "melt value" of coins was close to their face value and there existed a certain quantity of gold- and silver-backed paper currency, this is no longer the case. (See pages 341–342 for a further discussion of this topic.)

There are then two kinds of currency presently in use in the United States: coins and paper currency.

Coins, or "Fractional Currency." The government produces pennies, nickels, dimes, quarters, and half-dollars, our *fractional currency*, primarily for the convenience of making change. In addition, it produces a small number of coins worth $1. All U.S. coins now are *token money*, so-called because their metallic value is far less than their face value. In all, coins make up about 8 percent of the nation's money supply.

Paper Currency. Virtually all the paper currency in circulation today is in the form of *Federal Reserve notes*. These notes are issued by the 12 banks of the Federal Reserve System (discussed in Chapter 16). Figure 14.1 is a drawing of a typical $10 bill. We can identify it as a Federal Reserve note by the name that appears on the top line and in the black seal, and by the green serial numbers.

In the illustration, we note the words identifying the Federal Reserve note as legal tender immediately below and to the left of the country's name. Federal Reserve notes are printed by the Bureau of Engraving and Printing of the Department of the Treasury. The Bureau's name does not appear on the notes, but the Department of the Treasury's seal is located to the right of the portrait of Alexander Hamilton. The round seal that appears to the left of the Hamilton portrait designates the issuing Reserve bank by name and by an alphabet letter. The district's number is located about an inch from each corner.

On rare occasions, you might come across *United States notes*, bills issued by the Treasury Department. They have red serial numbers, a

Figure 14.1 $10 Bill

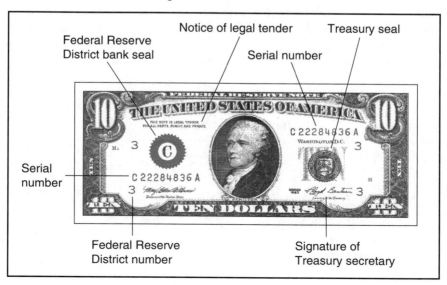

red seal, and the name "United States note" printed at the top. United States notes had their origins as the "greenbacks" that the Union (the North) began issuing during the Civil War (1861–1865). The federal government still prints and circulates a small quantity of these notes.

Paper currency makes up about 19 percent of the money supply.

"Nineteen percent? Wait a minute! Didn't you say that coins make up about 8 percent of the money supply? Nineteen plus 8 percent equals 27 percent. Where does the remainder of the money supply come from?"

The answer, very simply, is "checks." Most transactions are paid for by checkbook money.

Checkbook Money

Although we tend to think of paper currency and coins as money, they represent but a fraction of the total money in circulation. Indeed, if the nation's total currency supply were equally divided, it would come to only $1,400 for every person in the country. Most transactions are paid for by check. Technically, checks are orders written by individuals or firms directing banks to pay specified sums to their legal holders. People who have money on deposit in accounts that offer check-writing privileges can order banks to make payments. These accounts are known as "checkable" ones or, more familiarly, as checking accounts. Accounts with check-writing privileges are also available from mutual savings banks, savings and loan associations, and credit unions.

Most checkable accounts (over 50 percent of the total) are held in demand deposits in the nation's commercial banks. A *demand deposit* is a deposit in a bank that promises to pay on demand an amount of money specified by the customer who owns the deposit. Unlike demand deposits, which pay no interest, some checkable accounts offer interest on part or all of the balance in the account. The best-known interest-bearing checking account is the negotiable order of withdrawal (NOW). (See pages 358–361 for a fuller discussion of banking services.)

Table 14.1 MONEY SUPPLY, 1995
(BILLIONS OF DOLLARS)

Currency		$ 367.1
Coin	$113.8	
Paper currency	253.3	
Checkbook money		769.1
Demand deposits	389.6	
Other checkable deposits	379.5	
Traveler's checks		8.9
Total money supply		$1,145.1

Maintaining a Checking Account

Some day you may want to open a checking account. Or you may already have one. The following explanations will help you to write and endorse checks and record transactions.

About Checks

A check is a written order directing a bank to pay a specified sum of money to a designated person or institution. The person making the demand has money deposited in the bank with the understanding that the bank will follow his or her orders.

There are three parties to a check: (1) the person writing the check, or *drawer*; (2) the bank upon which the check is drawn, or *drawee*; and (3) the person to whom the check is payable, or *payee*.

Maureen Kane purchased a pair of roller blades for $59.95 from Mort's Sports, Inc. Maureen paid for the purchase by check, as illustrated in Figure 14.2.

About Endorsements

Endorsements pass title to a check on to another party. Mort's Sports will deposit Maureen's check in Mort's Sports's bank account after endorsing it on the reverse side, as indicated in Figure 14.3.

In addition to transferring owner-

Figure 14.2 A Typical Check

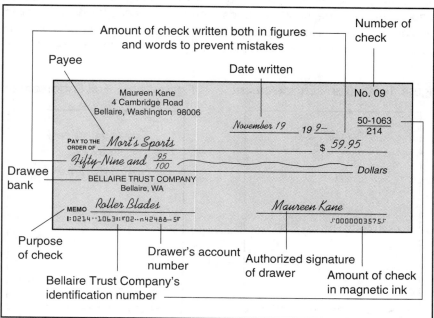

Amount of check written both in figures and words to prevent mistakes

Number of check

Payee

Date written

Maureen Kane
4 Cambridge Road
Bellaire, Washington 98006

No. 09

November 19   19 9—

50-1063
214

PAY TO THE ORDER OF *Mort's Sports* $ 59.95

Fifty-Nine and 95/100   Dollars

Drawee bank

BELLAIRE TRUST COMPANY
Bellaire, WA

MEMO *Roller Blades*   *Maureen Kane*

I:0214··1063I:ˮ02··ɳ42488··5ˮ   .ˮ0000003575.ˮ

Purpose of check

Drawer's account number

Authorized signature of drawer

Amount of check in magnetic ink

Bellaire Trust Company's identification number

Figure 14.3 Restrictive Endorsement

For deposit only
Merchants National Bank
Mort's Sports, Inc.
01336315

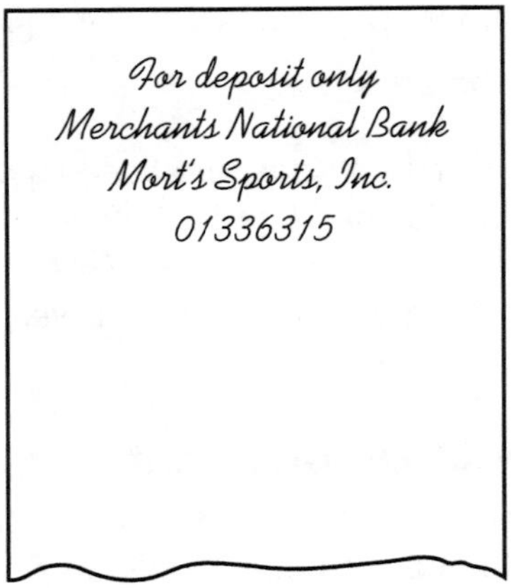

ship, an endorser guarantees that he or she will make good on a check if there is something wrong with it.

Endorsements can be made in a variety of ways. Figure 14.3 illustrates a *restrictive endorsement*. Such endorsements describe how the funds are to be used. In this instance, Mort's Sports has passed title to the check on to its bank with the understanding that the funds will be deposited in its account.

In Figure 14.4, Maureen Kane has simply signed her name on the reverse of a check written to her. This action is known as a *blank endorsement*. Such an endorsement transfers title to a check to anyone holding the check.

In Figure 14.5, Maureen has used a *full endorsement* to transfer a check made out in her name to her brother Arlo. Such an endorsement transfers title to a check to a specific party.

Keeping Records

One needs to know the amount of money in one's account before writing a check. Banks will not honor a check unless there are sufficient funds to cover it. For that reason, people with checking accounts need to maintain accurate records of both the deposits they make and the checks they write.

Figure 14.4 Blank Endorsement

Maureen Kane

Figure 14.5 Full Endorsement

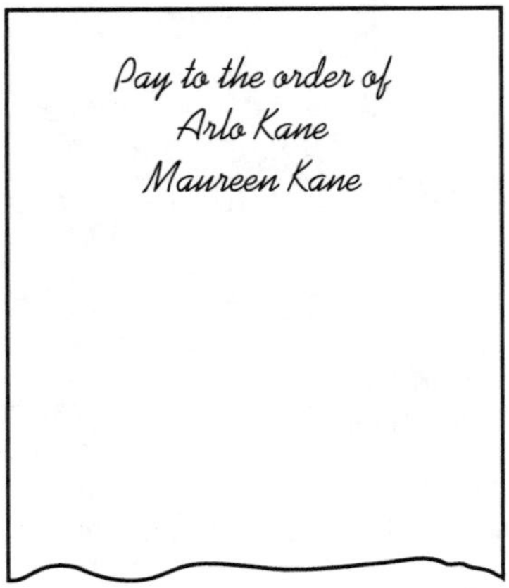

Pay to the order of
Arlo Kane
Maureen Kane

Figure 14.6 Check Register

No.	Date	Issued to or Description of Deposit	Amount of Check			Amount of Deposit		Balance Forward
								672 31
108	11/17	To Myra Maple	25	15				−25 15
								647 16
	11/18	Deposit Paycheck				358	49	+358 49
								1,005 65
109	11/19	To Mort's Sports	59	95				−59 95
								945 70
110	11/20	To CASH	98	36				−98 36
								847 34

Banks simplify the task of record keeping for checking accounts by providing their depositors with a check register. Figure 14.6 illustrates how Maureen Kane recorded transactions in her checking account.

Traveler's Checks

Travelers typically do not like to carry large sums of money with them, yet they might have difficulty in cashing personal checks. For that reason, some people purchase *traveler's checks*, which are widely accepted both at home and abroad. Traveler's checks are issued by a few large banks and certain specialized firms (such as American Express and Thomas Cook) and can be purchased at most banks. Since traveler's checks are as usable as checkable accounts, they are included in Federal Reserve data as a component of the money supply.

The money supply of the United States in 1995 is summarized in Table 14.1.

HOW CURRENCY IS PRODUCED AND DISTRIBUTED

Did you ever wonder how the paper currency and coins that you have in your pocket are produced? One of the more fascinating visits that you can make in Washington, D.C., is to the **Bureau of Engraving and Printing**. There you can see the elaborate process by which our

The Bureau of Engraving and Printing designs, prints, and finishes a variety of security products, including Federal Reserve notes, U.S. postage stamps, and Treasury securities.

paper money is printed. Although the **Bureau of the Mint** also has its offices in Washington, you will not be able to see any coins being produced there because coins are *minted* (manufactured) elsewhere—at mints in Philadelphia, Denver, and San Francisco.

The Bureau of Engraving and Printing does everything it can to prevent counterfeiting. Each feature of a bill (such as the portrait, lettering, and ornamental scroll work) is prepared by a separate engraver. Engravers cut the individual features of a note's design into steel dies. These are assembled in a series of operations into plates for use in the printing process. The Bureau uses distinctive, specially produced paper and manufactures its own inks according to secret formulas.

The question that might well come to mind at this point is, "How do these coins and this paper money get into the hands of the public?" This is accomplished by the nation's banks, which act as intermediaries between the government and the public in the distribution of the currency. Individuals obtain currency from their banks either by cashing checks or making withdrawals from their accounts. "Well," you ask, "how do banks get the currency?"

Just as individuals maintain bank accounts upon which they can draw when they are in need of funds, so too do many commercial banks. For their part, however, commercial banks keep their "savings," or reserves, in the Federal Reserve bank in their district. Whenever a private commercial bank runs short of currency, it can draw upon its account with the Federal Reserve and replenish its stock. The Federal Reserve banks get their supplies of coins and paper money from the Treasury Department's Bureau of the Mint and Bureau of Engraving and Printing.

MONETARY STANDARDS IN UNITED STATES HISTORY

We have seen that any number of things can be (and have been) used as money. Grains, shells, glass, stones, arrowheads, furs, and precious metals have all been adopted at one time or other for that purpose. Whatever commodity or definition a society chooses to use for its money is known as its *monetary standard*.

From its earliest days until 1900, the United States was on a *bimetallic monetary standard*. Two metals—gold and silver—served as the basis for our monetary system. The value of the dollar was expressed in terms of specific quantities of gold and silver. A dollar could be exchanged for either of those metals.

From 1900 until 1933, the United States was on the *gold standard*. This meant that the dollar was defined in terms of gold (about $21 for one ounce of gold), and that the government stood ready to buy or sell gold at this price. Under terms of the gold standard, institutions or individuals could convert their gold at any time into dollars, or could convert their dollars into gold at the official price.

During the Great Depression of the 1930s, most of the world (including the United States) went on a modified gold standard. While the value of the dollar and other currencies would continue to be based on gold, individuals and private institutions could no longer own that precious metal. In the United States, people were directed to convert their gold holdings into paper dollars, or face jail terms. The government also raised the official price at which it would buy gold from $21 to $35 an ounce. Foreign governments could either buy or sell dollars at this price, and the Federal Reserve System was required to hold some gold as a reserve or "backing" for the dollars it circulated.

This modified gold standard came to an end in August 1971, when the United States announced that it would no longer sell its gold for dollars even to foreign governments. In the United States, gold is now treated like any other commodity (such as wheat, rubber, or tin). Both private individuals and the federal government may buy or sell gold at will at a price determined in the marketplace. The U.S. government, however, does not guarantee to buy back dollars for gold at a set price, as was the case when the United States was on the gold standard. The U.S. dollar is no longer backed up by gold or any other precious metal. U.S. currency has value because the government says it has value— that is, by fiat—and because people are willing to accept the dollar for payments. Economists call this system a *paper money* or *fiat currency standard*.

In the absence of precious metals upon which to base its value, to-day's U.S. dollar is often measured in terms of its purchasing power. But purchasing power is subject to change. Sometimes it increases, and sometimes it decreases.

THE VALUE OF MONEY FLUCTUATES

"No, sir, a dollar just isn't worth a dollar anymore."

"You're telling me? Do you know what I just paid for a pack of chewing gum? I mean, chewing gum!"

"Don't tell me about chewing gum. When I was your age, we could buy a whole pack of gum for a dime, and when Grandma was your age, she bought a pack for a nickel."

"A nickel? I heard a comedian on a talk show last night say that prices are so high these days even a nickel costs a quarter."

When people complain that "a dollar isn't worth a dollar anymore," they are not suggesting that there is something less than 100 cents in every dollar. What they are really saying is that most things cost more than they once did. We see, therefore, that although there will always be 100 pennies and four quarters in a dollar, its value or purchasing power will *fluctuate* (move up or down).

Economists describe a period of generally rising prices as "inflation." The value of the dollar falls during periods of inflation because it buys less than it once did.

On rare occasions in its past history, the United States also experienced periods of generally falling prices, or *deflation*. Since during a period of deflation the dollar can buy more than it once did, its value increases.

Measuring Purchasing Power With Index Numbers

When we speak of rising and falling prices, we are referring to the general price level rather than to prices of one or two goods or services. Those who measure changes in the price of goods and services often express the results of their findings in terms of an index number.

An index number expresses percentage change from a base year. The index number most frequently used to measure changes in the value of the dollar is the *Consumer Price Index (CPI)*. The CPI assigns a value of 100 to the average of prices from 1982–1984. In 1990, the CPI was 130.7. That meant that prices had increased by 30.7 percent between the base years and 1990 (because 130.7 – 100 = 30.7).

Sometimes the value of money is expressed in terms of its *purchasing power*. This is a way of expressing the cost of living in terms of dollars and cents. Thus, if the cost of living has doubled since the base years, one would say that the value of the dollar stands at $.50. Or, to put it another way, it would now take $20 to purchase what could have been purchased for $10 during the base period. Figure 14.7 and Table 14.2 illustrate what happened to the value of the dollar after 1950.

How Inflation Affects the Economy and People's Lives

Although money may increase as well as decrease in value, there has not been a long-term period of deflation since the 1930s. Inflation, however, has been a fact of life for as long as most people can remember. With the exceptions of 1949 and 1955 (years when living costs actually declined), consumer prices have risen in every year since 1939. Prior to 1965, however, the annual cost of living increase was rarely more than 1.5 percent. Although even in those years people grumbled about rising prices, most Americans seemed to accept a modest inflation rate as the price of economic growth and relative prosperity. Beginning some time around 1965, however, inflation began to accelerate. Consumer prices increased at a 4 percent annual rate between

Table 14.2   CONSUMER PRICES AND PURCHASING POWER, 1950–1995

Year	Consumer Price Index (1982–84 = 100)	Purchasing Power of Dollar (1982–84 = $1)
1950	24.1	$ 4.15
1960	29.6	3.37
1970	38.8	2.57
1980	82.4	1.22
1990	130.7	.77
1995	151.7	.66

Figure 14.7   Purchasing Power of a 1982 Dollar in Selected Years

1965 and 1970, and this rate increased by 7 percent per year from 1970 to 1975 and to 9 percent from 1975 to 1980. In 1974, the nation experienced its first "double-digit inflation" (when the cost of living increased by 11 percent). Double-digit inflation struck again in 1979 and in 1980, when the inflation rate reached 13.5 percent.

In its more extreme forms, inflation can wreck an economy and even an entire society. The experiences of Germans in the years following World War I (1914–1918) stand as a terrible example of the consequences of runaway inflation. In 1913, the year before the war began, 4 *marks* (the German unit of currency) could be exchanged for a dollar. By 1923, it took 4,000,000,000,000 (that is 4 trillion) marks to buy a dollar. The cost of living in Germany had increased a trillion times. So, for example, the price of a pound of butter had climbed to 1.5 million marks and that of a loaf of bread to 200,000 marks. Newspapers printed photographs of people with wheelbarrows and baby carriages on their way to market to buy bread. Why the wheelbarrows and carriages? To carry the money needed for their purchases.

Not everyone is adversely affected by inflation, however. Depending upon their circumstances, some people may actually profit from it. Here is a summary of inflation's likely impact upon a variety of people in your community.

1. Savers and Investors. For a wide variety of reasons, people set aside a portion of their incomes as savings. Some save for a "rainy day" when

Germany was beset by inflation in the 1920s. This woman in Berlin used German currency to light her stove because the money was almost worthless.

the unexpected will put special demands upon the family purse. Others save for a new car, a musical instrument, or a college education. Whatever our reasons, we all would like to feel that our savings are secure and are earning a nice return in the form of dividends or interest. If the cost of living should increase at a rate higher than the return on our savings, however, the money we withdraw will be worth less than it was when we deposited it. Suppose, for example, that in 1979 Ygenna deposited $1,000 in a savings account that paid 6 percent interest. Two years later, in 1981, she withdrew the deposit along with $123.60 in accumulated interest, for a total of $1,123.60.

"Not bad," she thought. "I put in $1,000 and got back $1,123.60. Not bad at all."

But wait. The inflation rate during those years averaged 12 percent a year. This rate meant that in 1981 it took $1,254 to buy as much as $1,000 bought in 1979. But Ygenna, the saver, received only $1,123.60 in principal and interest. She was, therefore, worse off by about $130.

Because money loses its purchasing power during inflationary times, people with surplus funds frequently look for investments that will increase in value as fast as or faster than the cost of living. Among the most popular hedges against inflation have been real estate, gold, and precious gems. For similar reasons, rare postage stamps, antiques, and works of art have also enjoyed popularity as vehicles for anti-inflationary investment. There are no guarantees accompanying these investments, though. As many people discovered when the time came to sell, many so-called inflation hedges were worth less than their initial costs.

2. People on Fixed Incomes. The income from some pension plans is fixed, meaning that affected retired people receive the same amount of pension payments each year. Those who depend on such "fixed incomes" for financial support suffer during periods of inflation. When prices go up, there is nothing that people on fixed incomes can do but spend less.

The income from annuities is also fixed. *Annuities* are funds purchased for a fixed sum in order to provide income at a later time. This money (with accumulated interest or dividends) provides for payments of money from an agreed-upon date (usually when one plans to retire) for the remaining lifetime of the owner of the annuity. An annuity differs from life insurance, which pays the beneficiary at the time of the insured person's death.

In recent years, Social Security benefits have risen automatically with rises in the cost of living. This relationship has meant that as the Consumer Price Index increases, so too do Social Security payments. There is no guarantee that this federal policy will continue, however. Social Security income may become fixed.

3. Business Firms. The extent to which individual firms are affected by inflation depends upon a firm's ability to cover its increased costs. Suppose, for example, that as a result of an inflationary trend a firm is able to raise its selling prices by 20 percent without any loss in its volume of sales. If, at the same time, the firm's costs of doing business have increased by less than 20 percent, it will be better off than it was before the inflation began. If the increased cost of doing business cannot be offset by higher prices, however, the firm will be hurt by the inflation.

4. People Who Owe Money. *Debtors* (people who owe money) will generally profit from inflation if the value of the money they repay is less than the amount of their loans. Suppose that you had borrowed $1,000, which you promised to repay in two years. Suppose also that inflation averaged 10 percent per year over those two years, for a total of 20 percent. You would be able to repay your $1,000 loan with dollars that had the purchasing power of only $800 (because $1,000 – 20 percent of $1,000 = $800). As one economist aptly put it: "It's rather like borrowing steak and repaying the loan with hamburger."

You may recall from your study of U.S. history that certain groups, such as farmers, traditionally favored inflationary, or "cheap-money," policies. The farmers relied heavily on borrowed funds to finance their businesses. Moreover, they saw inflation as a means of easing their burden of debt because they repaid their loans with money that had less purchasing power than when they took out their loans. During some recent decades, however, many farmers suffered from inflation when the cost of borrowing increased even faster than the cost of living.

5. People Who Lend Money. Lenders can be hurt by inflation for the same reason that borrowers may profit: the value of the money that lenders lend is worth more than the value of the money that borrowers repay. Lenders can, and frequently do, protect themselves from the impact of inflation by putting that cost into their interest rates. So, for example, if the average cost of a loan was 20 percent over a period of time when the inflation rate was 8 percent, lenders would continue to earn a profit.

What Are the Causes of Inflation?

Economists offer a number of reasons why we have inflation. Virtually all of these reasons fall into one of two categories: demand-pull and cost-push.

1. Demand-Pull. *Demand-pull inflation* is brought on when the demand for goods and services outpaces the economy's ability to produce them. In this situation, prices will necessarily increase. One economist may have best described demand-pull as a situation in which "too much money was chasing too few goods."

What, you may ask, is the source of all this excess demand? One source is the federal government. Sometimes, the government spends more than it earns in taxes and other revenues. The net effect of excess spending is to leave the public with more money and greater purchasing power than it had before the government acted.

The government also has the power to increase the money supply through the Federal Reserve System. The Fed issues virtually all the paper money that passes through our hands. If, as a result of Federal Reserve policies, the supply of money is increased fast enough, the excess demand that results will lead to a general rise in prices.

The federal government, though, is not the only source of demand-pull inflation. Changes in the spending habits of individuals and business firms can also result in "too much money chasing too few goods." A classic example of this process followed the end of World War II (1941–1945). Although personal income was high during the war, production was geared toward military goods. As a result, there were few consumer goods for people to buy. Since savings were viewed as both practical and patriotic, most people set aside a portion of their earnings toward the day when consumer goods would again become more readily available. After the war ended, people rushed to buy new appliances, cars, and homes as fast as they became available. As a result, consumer prices, which had risen by only about 10 percent during the four war years, quickly escalated by an additional 30 percent over the following three years.

Still another source of demand-pull inflation is a psychological factor that is sometimes called "public expectations." If consumers and managers of business firms believe that prices will be rising in the near future, they may rush to buy today what they might otherwise have postponed buying until a later time. Ironically, if a large enough section of the public acts on this expectation, the prophecy will be fulfilled. Why? Because the rising demand will lead to an increase in prices.

2. Cost-Push. Not all inflation can be explained as "too much money chasing too few goods." The inflation of 1979–1981, for example, saw prices increasing at a record rate at a time when U.S. industries were operating at barely 80 percent of capacity and one worker out of fourteen was out of work. In other words, people did not have "too much money." The U.S. economy could have produced many more goods and services if there had been more demand. And yet the country experienced inflation. Economists use the term *stagflation* in describing

"YOU CAN'T WIN -- EVERY TIME WE GET TO EARN A LITTLE OVERTIME,
IT GETS EATEN UP BY INFLATION!"

an economy experiencing inflation at the same time as its resources are underutilized, as was the case during 1979–1981. According to economists, the cause in this and some other recent rising price spirals was *cost-push inflation*. This name describes the run-up in prices that results as sellers raise their prices because of increases in their costs.

Cost-push inflation occurs because large segments of the nation's economy do not operate under conditions of pure competition. Thus, some labor unions can achieve wage increases without increasing their members' productivity. And producers in certain key industries have the power to increase prices even though shortages do not exist.

Management and labor are frequently at odds as to which is the first cause of a period of cost-push inflation. Management is likely to charge that the principal causes of inflation are unions' demands for wage increases that outrun productivity. In the absence of additional output, businesses are compelled to offset higher wage costs with price increases. For their part, unions are likely to argue that their wage demands are merely efforts to make up for increases in the cost of living. "Don't blame us," unions might say. "Businesses raised their prices first."

Some liken the question to the age-old puzzle about which came first, "the chicken or the egg." Without attempting to settle the argument, we can say that the *wage-price spiral* has led to a series of inflationary price increases in the past and is likely to do so again in the future.

In recent years, the type of cost-push inflation that has been most troublesome is known to economists as *commodity inflation*. This term identifies run-ups in the prices of certain key commodities as the source of general price increases. The most dramatic example of commodity inflation in the 1970s took place in the petroleum industry. Foreign suppliers operating through the Organization of Petroleum Exporting Countries (OPEC) were able to use their monopoly power to push prices from under $4 a barrel in 1973 to $40 in 1980–1981. As the price increases radiated out to gasoline and other petroleum by-products, the inflationary spiral seemed to affect virtually every one of the U.S. economy's goods and services.

MEASURING THE NATION'S MONEY SUPPLY

A proper supply and flow of money is vital to the survival of the economy. For that reason, economists closely follow the total quantity of money in circulation and the number of times it changes hands (its rate of flow). It is not easy, however, to accurately determine the rate of flow of money. To make matters worse, there are several definitions used by economists when discussing the money supply. Let us now consider some of the problems in defining money supply and some of the compromise solutions reached.

There is no question that paper currency and checkable accounts are generally acceptable in payment for goods and services and so fall within our definition of money. Problems arise, however, over the status of other assets that are easily converted into cash. For example, a shopper cannot walk into a store, plunk a bankbook down on the counter, and ask the clerk to wrap up an article worth $100. The shopper could, however, withdraw $100 from a bank savings account and pay for the item a short time later. People with money market accounts at a bank can quickly withdraw whatever they need to make a purchase by simply writing a check. At many banks, a service charge is made for each check drawn from a money market deposit account. Some people buy (from a broker) money market mutual funds that have check-writing privileges. Most of these funds require that checks drawn on an account cannot be below a specified dollar value, for example, $500. (We discussed money market mutual funds in Chapter 10.)

Since assets such as government bonds, bank savings accounts, and money market funds are so easily converted to cash, economists

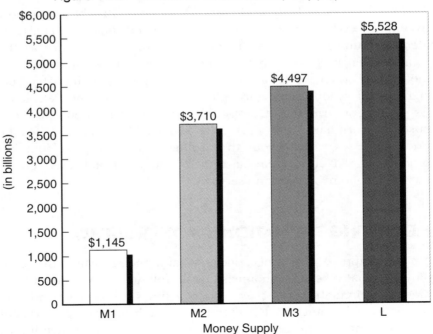

Figure 14.8 Measures of the Money Supply, 1995

Table 14.3   MONEY SUPPLY, 1995
(BILLIONS OF DOLLARS)

M1	
Coin	$113.8
Paper currency	253.3
Traveler's checks	8.9
Demand deposits	389.6
Other checkable deposits	379.5
Total M1	$1,145.1
M2 (M1 plus:)	
Money market deposit accounts and savings deposits	$1,091.2
Small time deposits	921.0
Money market funds	441.5
Other funds	111.6
Total M2	$3,710.3
M3 (M2 plus:)	
Large time deposits	$397.9
Large money funds	212.4
Other funds	176.3
Total M3	$4,496.9
L (M3 plus:)	
Other liquid assets	$1,031.4
Total L	$5,528.3

Source: **Survey of Current Business**

include them in their definition of money supply. Because some forms of money can immediately be used to make a purchase, while others might take a day or two (or longer) to convert to cash, economists apply four different measures of the money supply to distinguish one from others. These are M1, M2, M3, and L.

M1

M1 measures that portion of the money supply most easily used as a medium of exchange. This includes paper currency and coin, checking accounts, and traveler's checks. M1 is the measure most frequently referred to by economists and others when they discuss the money supply.

M2

By adding savings accounts, money market funds, money market deposit accounts, and small certificates of deposit to M1, we arrive at M2. These additions are less easily converted into cash than those included in M1.

M3

M3 is the total of M2 plus large denomination certificates of deposit ($100,000 or more) and other large funds. The additions require a little more time to convert to cash than M2 does.

L

L is the broadest measure of the money supply. It consists of M3 plus savings bonds, short-term Treasury securities, banker's acceptances, and commercial paper. (All corporate stocks and bonds and other commercial securities that mature in more than 18 months are not considered part of the money supply.)

Summary

Money can be anything that most people are willing to accept in payment for goods or services. Long ago, money replaced the barter system and is now used in all societies. Money provides a medium of exchange, a way of calculating value, and a store of value.

The principal kinds of money used in the United States are paper money, coins, and checkbook money. Paper money and coins are issued by the federal government. Checks constitute about three-fourths of the nation's money supply. The nation's money supply is measured in terms of M1, M2, M3, and L. M1 is the total amount of currency, checkbook money, and traveler's checks in circulation on a given day. M2 adds individual savings accounts, money market funds, and small CDs to the M1 total. M3 adds large CDs to the M2 total. L adds other liquid assets, such as savings bonds, to the M3 total.

The value of money changes. Inflation is a rise in the prices of most goods and services. Deflation is the opposite of inflation. Inflation hurts some groups of people more than others, but continued inflation hurts the economy as a whole. The purchasing power of the dollar is measured by the Consumer Price Index (CPI), which compares one year's prices to prices in a base year.

REVIEWING THE CHAPTER

Building Vocabulary

Match each item in Column A with its definition in Column B.

COLUMN A	COLUMN B
1. barter	*a.* M1 plus individual savings deposits, small CDs, and money market funds
2. stagflation	*b.* a rise in the level of prices caused by an increase in demand
3. demand-pull inflation	*c.* the total of all currency, checkbook money, and traveler's checks in circulation on any given day
4. Consumer Price Index	
5. deflation	*d.* the exchange of one person's goods or services for another person's goods or services
6. cost-push inflation	*e.* a rise in price level caused by increases in costs of doing business
7. Gresham's Law	*f.* M2 plus large CDs and other large funds
8. M1	*g.* a period of both recession and inflation
9. M2	*h.* a general decline in the price level
10. M3	*i.* a series of index numbers that shows the percentage change in prices from a base year
	j. the idea that cheap money tends to drive good money out of circulation

Understanding What You Have Read

1. Each of the following is an example of currency, *except* (*a*) a dime (*b*) a $1 bill (*c*) a check for $5 (*d*) a penny.

2. During the Revolutionary War, many American colonists spent their paper money, which had been issued by the Continental Congress, and hoarded their metallic currency. This activity was an illustration of (*a*) barter (*b*) legal tender (*c*) Engel's Law (*d*) Gresham's Law.

3. Under what circumstances might peacock feathers be called "money"? (*a*) if they were very rare (*b*) if they were all identical in size and shape (*c*) if everyone accepted them in payment for goods and services (*d*) if they could be easily divided into equal parts so as to "make change."

4. Money provides a "store of value" because it (*a*) can be used to buy valuable goods in stores (*b*) is easily carried (*c*) may be

saved for future use   (d) packs a great deal of value into a small volume.

5. Which of the following best describes the U.S. monetary system at the present time?   (a) paper money standard   (b) silver standard   (c) gold standard   (d) bimetallic standard.

6. During periods of inflation, the value of the dollar   (a) decreases   (b) remains the same   (c) decreases for a while and then increases   (d) increases.

7. The purchasing power of the dollar   (a) tells us the price of a good or service   (b) is the same as the foreign exchange rate of the dollar   (c) compares the value of the dollar in one period with its value in another period   (d) never changes.

8. If the Consumer Price Index today stands at 125, this means that (a) prices have risen by 125 percent this year   (b) prices have risen by 25 percent this year   (c) there has been a decrease in the cost of living   (d) the cost of living has increased by 25 percent since the base period.

9. An increase in average weekly income does not result in a higher standard of living if it is caused by   (a) increased purchases of consumer goods   (b) increased private investment   (c) rising prices   (d) increased productivity.

10. Which groups generally would find inflation advantageous? (a) banks with 80 percent of their deposits invested in mortgage loans   (b) retired workers living on pensions   (c) investors whose holdings are mostly in bonds   (d) farmers repaying long-term debts.

11. Traveler's checks and demand deposits are described as M1 because they   (a) are closely connected with banks   (b) can easily be converted into cash   (c) can be used as legal tender   (d) can be used as security for loans.

12. In totaling the value of the nation's money supply, which of the following items would *not* be included?   (a) paper currency   (b) demand deposits   (c) traveler's checks   (d) corporate stocks and bonds.

Thinking Critically

1. During the early Roman era, the merchants of Rome frequently traveled beyond the empire's borders to trade with other peoples. Summarize the trading difficulties that probably arose in the barter economies they encountered.

2. During World War II, U.S. prisoners of war used cigarettes as a form of money. Cigarettes were used to purchase anything that

was for sale in the prison camps. Practically, however, money should possess the qualities of durability, portability, divisibility, uniformity, ease of recognition, and scarcity. In terms of these six criteria, discuss the advantages and disadvantages of cigarette money in this prison economy.

3. Throughout history, the most popular form of money has been gold.

    a. Give *three* reasons why gold has been such a popular form of money.

    b. What would happen to the value of gold if people discovered that it could easily be made at home from inexpensive materials? Explain your answer.

    c. Suppose that a nation's money supply consisted of copper, silver, and gold coins, and paper currency. Let us also suppose that the worldwide value of gold began to increase dramatically. Explain what holders of gold could be expected to do with their gold coins.

4. Exactly what constitutes the nation's money supply has been a matter of disagreement among economists and among government officials.

    a. Define what money is.

    b. Why do economists and others have difficulty in measuring the nation's money supply?

    c. What difference does it make how much money is in circulation at any particular time?

    d. Explain the differences among M1, M2, M3, and L.

SKILLS: Interpreting a Table

Study Table 14.2 on page 343 and then answer the following questions.

1. (*a*) What information is given in Column 2, "Consumer Price Index"? (*b*) What is meant by the notation "1982–84 = 100"?

2. What information is given in Column 3?

3. Explain how the price changes indicated in the table affected each of the following:

    a. a schoolteacher who retired on a fixed pension in 1980.

    b. a couple who sold their home in 1995 that they had purchased in 1965.

    c. a family with two children with money invested in a savings account starting in 1985.

    d. a farmer who borrowed money for a new tractor in 1990 that had to be repaid by 1995.

Chapter 15
BANKS AND BANKING

Overview

Most of us have or will have a bank account. It might be a savings account or a checking account or both. Those of us who have such bank accounts take for granted that a bank will accept our money for safekeeping and that we can withdraw this money from our account when we wish. We are all familiar with checks. Probably all of us have received a payment for something by check. We hardly give it a thought when we accept a piece of paper with a promise to pay a certain amount. If we open a checking account, we have a mechanism for making payments as well as a place to hold our money. Banks serve other purposes besides offering checking and savings accounts. People and businesses borrow from banks—actions that are very important in keeping our economy growing. Moreover, banks provide many other services, such as selling traveler's checks and renting out safe-deposit boxes.

In this chapter, we will discuss the services that banks provide. We will also discuss:

☐ The origins of banking
☐ The difference between commercial banks and thrift institutions
☐ How banks do business
☐ How banks create money
☐ How we keep our banks safe.

THE ORIGINS OF BANKING

As money replaced the barter system in the ancient world, the development of banking inevitably followed. History's earliest written records inform us that the people of ancient Babylonia (in what is now Iraq in Western Asia) developed an early form of currency and banking. The units of Babylonian currency were the *shekel, mina,* and *talent*. A shekel was roughly equal in value to a half ounce of silver. A mina equaled 60 shekels, and a talent equaled 60 minas.

As early as the 20th century B.C., wealthy private citizens and priests of Babylonia granted loans and held funds for safekeeping. Records show that depositors in this ancient culture could draw on their balances held for safekeeping by writing drafts (a kind of check). Like bankers today, Babylonian bankers exacted interest on their loans. Government regulations, however, imposed severe penalties on those who charged more than the legal limit.

Scientists have found similar evidence of banking in studying the ancient civilizations of India and China and the Mayan, Aztec, and Incan civilizations. As trade and commerce increased in these cultures, certain individuals and families held funds of others for safekeeping. They also made loans and, in some cases, exchanged one country's coins for another country's. Our story of banking will stress developments in Western Europe, because U.S. financial institutions are largely of Western European origin.

With the expansion of trade during the late Middle Ages, several large banking houses were established in Italy, Germany, and the Netherlands. Taking the lead were the Italians, who developed elements of banking as early as the 13th century. At that time, European trade was centered in the Mediterranean and was dominated by the Italian city-states of Genoa, Venice, and Florence. In time, the Italian bankers extended their operations beyond the Alps to France, the German states, and England. In these places, they made loans, invested in hotels, in shipping, and in the spice trade, and financed military campaigns. The Italian bankers developed some of the practices of modern banking. They accepted deposits, made loans, and arranged for the transfer of funds. They are also credited with developing double-entry bookkeeping and selling insurance on cargo being shipped by sea.

Modern banking came to England in the 17th century through the efforts of the goldsmiths of London. Because there were no police departments in those days, the *goldsmiths* (people who make articles of gold for a living) had to provide for their own security. Then, because goldsmiths had this protection, other merchants eventually offered to pay the goldsmiths to hold their gold and other valuables for safekeeping. In exchange for their deposits, the merchants were issued receipts entitling them to the return of their property on demand.

At first, merchants looked upon the goldsmiths' shops as a kind of safe-deposit box or warehouse. That is, they expected to get back the same bag of gold that they had left on deposit. In time, however, those merchants who held goldsmiths' receipts accepted the idea that it really did not matter which gold they received as long as it was of equal value to the amount deposited. Then other merchants—those who did not have gold on storage at the goldsmiths—began to accept the goldsmiths' receipts in payment for goods and services. When that happened, goldsmith receipts became a kind of paper currency.

Somewhere along the way, the goldsmiths discovered that they did not need to keep all of the gold on reserve. It was unlikely that all their customers would withdraw their deposits at the same time. It followed, therefore, that the goldsmiths could add to their profits by

The development of modern banking began in Italy in the 13th century. On the right side of the painting, a man makes a deposit. On the left, the banker shows customers the ledger books.

lending out a portion of these reserves. The profits would be in the form of interest, or a percentage of the amount loaned.

To attract additional deposits (and thus add to their profits), goldsmiths began to pay interest to their depositors. Of course, in order to earn a profit, the interest the goldsmiths paid on deposits had to be less than what they charged for the loans.

Banking as developed by the goldsmiths was a primitive institution, serving the interests of the wealthiest people in Europe. Nevertheless, the practices that the goldsmiths developed provided the basis for our modern banking system.

Like the goldsmiths, today's bankers accept deposits and make loans. When things go as planned, banks earn more in interest on their investments and loans than they pay on deposits. When things do not go well, the opposite occurs: banks earn less interest and (like the goldsmiths of old) suffer losses.

MODERN BANKING

Did you ever visit a bank and wonder what all those people were doing there?

Most customers in a bank are making deposits to, or withdrawals from, their savings or checking accounts. Others may be applying for loans, purchasing certificates of deposit, or paying utility bills. Then there are those who have come to the bank to visit their safe-deposit boxes or buy foreign currency, money orders, traveler's checks, or bank drafts. Some banks maintain trust departments for those who want the banks to manage their wealth. For example, a person might name a commercial bank as trustee of an estate. While that person is living, the bank would invest the client's money and, in some cases, pay that person's bills. Upon the individual's death, the bank would distribute his or her money and property in accordance with the terms of a will.

Modern banks offer so many services that it is little wonder that they have been called "financial supermarkets." Banks that directly serve the public fall into two categories: commercial banks and thrift institutions (or "thrifts").

Commercial Banks

With some $4.3 trillion in assets, *commercial banks* are the nation's most important financial institutions. One reason for their dominance

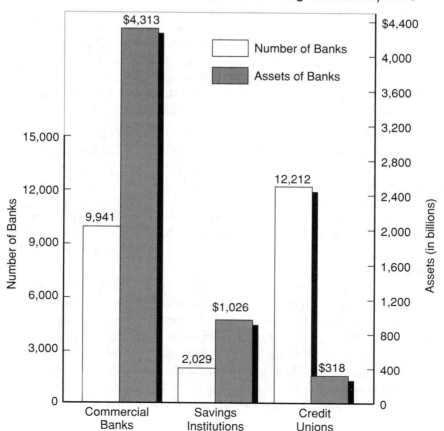

Figure 15.1 Number and Assets of Banking Institutions, 1995

is that they provide business firms with checking accounts. Although the thrifts offer checking accounts to individuals and nonprofit organizations, they are prohibited from extending them to business firms. Consequently, virtually every business firm has a checking account with a commercial bank.

The second reason for the dominance of commercial banks is that they make high profits by extending loans to businesses. Commercial banks also grant loans to consumers to purchase motor vehicles, appliances, and homes and to remodel homes.

Thrift Institutions

The term *thrifts* refers to three types of institutions: savings and loan associations, mutual savings banks, and credit unions.

Savings and Loan Associations. The largest of the thrifts in terms of assets are the *savings and loan associations (S&Ls)*. A savings and loan association is interested primarily in home financing. Therefore, virtually all its loans are in the form of long-term mortgages. A *mortgage* is a loan that is secured by the property that was purchased with the borrowed money. Dividends or interest are paid to depositors out of the earnings generated by the S&Ls' loans and other activities.

While the services offered by savings and loan associations are not as extensive as those offered by commercial banks, they go well beyond simple savings and home-loan activities. As part of their array of financial services, many of the S&Ls now offer interest-bearing checking accounts, credit cards, and Individual Retirement Accounts as well as traveler's checks, government bonds, and consumer loans.

Mutual Savings Banks. Depositors in a *mutual savings bank* are part owners of the bank. Theoretically, this gives them a voice in the management of the bank and a claim against its assets in the event of its liquidation. In practice, mutual savings banks are operated by professional managers with very little direction from their depositors.

The principal function of mutual savings banks is to accept deposits and use those funds to make loans. Depositors entrust their savings to these banks for safekeeping and for income, which is paid in dividends and interest.

In recent years, mutual savings banks have entered into competition with commercial banks by offering many of the services that were once the commercial banks' alone. For example, mutual savings banks now offer both regular and interest-bearing checking accounts to individuals and nonprofit organizations. Although the bulk of their lending is still in the form of long-term real estate mortgages, they also offer short-term consumer loans, financial services (such as investment and retirement accounts), credit cards, and safe-deposit boxes.

Credit Unions. Some 64 million Americans are members of the nation's 12,000 *credit unions*. Like mutual savings banks, credit unions are owned by their depositors. But unlike mutual savings banks, credit unions limit membership to those who belong to a particular group, such as workers at a business establishment, members of a labor union, or employees and students of a university. Credit unions accept savings deposits from members, who thereby become entitled to borrow when the need arises and, in some cases, open checking accounts. Credit unions are nonprofit organizations. This status serves to reduce operating costs and exempt credit unions from taxes. It also enables credit unions to pay higher rates of interest on their deposits and charge less for their loans.

THE BUSINESS OF BANKING

As we discussed in Chapter 5, everything of value owned by a business is known as an asset. Anything that it owes is a liability. Since a bank owns the loans and investments it makes, they are assets. Bank deposits, in contrast, represent money loaned to a bank by its depositors. Therefore, deposits represent liabilities. The difference between a bank's assets and its liabilities is its net worth.

A financial statement that summarizes assets, liabilities, and net worth is known as a balance sheet. Table 15.1 represents the balance sheet of the New City National Bank on June 19th.

Early-morning customers wait for a local credit union to open in Washington, D.C. What is a credit union?

Assets

The assets of the New City National Bank totaled $13.2 million. These assets consisted of the following:

Cash in Vault. A *vault* is a protected storage area. Bank vaults hold the bulk of the bank's cash (some cash is kept in the tellers' drawers), securities, and other valuables. Thus, *cash in vault* represents the money the bank has on hand to use. Banks need to keep a quantity of currency and coin on hand to meet the needs of their customers. The amount of cash in vault fluctuates from day to day with changes in public demand for paper currency and coins.

Reserve Account With Federal Reserve Bank. Bankers know that on any given day, some people will withdraw funds, while others will make deposits. By the day's end, a bank may have a net increase in deposits, or it may have a net decrease. Either way, it is evident that a bank need keep only a fraction of its total deposits on hand to meet withdrawal demands. The rest can be used to make loans or investments.

The funds that a bank sets aside to meet withdrawal demands is known as its *reserves*. How much of its deposits a bank holds depends upon the *reserve ratio*. This ratio is the percentage of deposits that banks are required by law to hold on reserve. Suppose, for example, that a bank held $100 million in deposits, and the reserve ratio was 15 percent. In that case, the bank would be required to set aside $15 million in reserves. It could lend or invest the balance—$85 million.

Banks keep most of their reserves in special accounts at a district Federal Reserve Bank. (We will study the Federal Reserve System in Chapter 16.) As indicated by its balance sheet, New City had some $1.6 million in its reserve account. Taken with the $200,000 cash in its vaults, the bank held a total $1.8 million in its reserves.

Loans. Loans are classified as assets because they are owned by the bank and represent obligations payable to the bank. Most of a bank's

Table 15.1   NEW CITY NATIONAL BANK BALANCE SHEET
JUNE 19, 199–

Assets		Liabilities and Net Worth	
Cash in vault	$ 200,000	Demand deposits	$ 6,200,000
Reserve account	1,600,000	Time deposits	4,200,000
with Federal		Total deposits	10,400,000
Reserve Bank		Net worth	2,800,000
Loans	8,200,000	Total	$13,200,000
Securities	2,800,000		
Building and fixtures	400,000		
Total assets	$13,200,000		

profits are earned from its loans. In addition to business loans, banks lend money to consumers to help finance major purchases, such as automobiles, major appliances, and real estate. New City had $8.2 million in loans outstanding on June 19th.

Securities. Banks cannot afford to allow funds for which they can find no borrowers to lie idle. Instead, banks invest those sums in relatively safe, interest-bearing securities, such as government bonds. New City's investments totaled $2.8 million that day.

Building and Fixtures. The premises in which New City National Bank conducts its business was estimated to be worth $400,000.

Liabilities and Net Worth

In a balance sheet, the sum of the liabilities and net worth equals assets.

Demand Deposits. Deposits are a bank's principal obligations. As we discussed in Chapter 14, demand deposits are those that can be withdrawn at any time, such as checking accounts. Deposits in New City's checking accounts totaled $6.2 million.

Time Deposits. Another term for savings accounts is *time deposits*. Such funds are usually left in banks for longer periods of time than demand deposits. Savings deposits are subject to advance notice of withdrawal, but as a rule they are available to customers whenever they choose to withdraw them. They are a liability of a bank because they represent funds owed to depositors.

Net Worth. The difference between a bank's assets and its liabilities is its net worth. In the case of New City, this amounted to $2.8 million.

How Banks Create Money

When a bank grants a loan, typically the funds are deposited in a checking account. Since checks are a form of money, the loan represents an addition to the nation's money supply created by the lending bank. We can illustrate this process with the following case study.

John Spratt owns a small toy store. In anticipation of the next Christmas shopping season, Mr. Spratt would like to add to his inventory of toys and games. He figures that if he could borrow $25,000 before the end of June, it would enable him to get his buying done well in time for the Christmas shopping rush, which begins in November.

Mr. Spratt discussed his problem with Nancy Hubbard, the lending officer at New City National, his local bank. Ms. Hubbard and other bank officers have been doing business with Mr. Spratt for many years.

Figure 15.2   Promissory Note

$25,000.00	Monroe, UT	June 15, **19** 97

Eight months   **AFTER DATE**   I   **PROMISE TO PAY TO**

THE ORDER OF   New City National Bank

Twenty-Five Thousand and 00/100 ———— **DOLLARS**

PAYABLE AT   New City National Bank

FOR VALUE RECEIVED WITH INTEREST AT   10%

DUE February 15, **19** 98   *John Spratt*

Confident that he would be able to sell his merchandise and pay off his loan, they approved his request.

Meanwhile, Spratt was happy because he would have the capital he needed that summer. For its part, the bank was also pleased because it needs to make loans in order to earn a profit.

On June 15, Spratt signed a promissory note (a legal IOU) at the New City National Bank in the amount of $25,000. As stated on the note, the principal was payable in eight months at an interest rate of 10 percent. Meanwhile, the bank credited Spratt's checking account for $25,000.

Eight months later (on February 15), Spratt drew a check in the amount of $26,875 to repay his loan. Of this total, $25,000 was the principal amount of the loan, while $1,875 represented the interest. Interest is expressed as the rate per year. The equation for calculating interest (I) is:

$$I = P \times R \times T$$

where   P = principal (amount borrowed)
R = rate (of interest per year)
T = time (in years or fractions of years)

The moment that Spratt's account was credited for his loan, the nation's money supply increased by $25,000. Why? Because demand deposits are a form of money, and that sum did not exist until the bank granted the loan and credited the account.

Money Grows

Banks create money by granting loans that wind up as demand deposits. The amount of money that an individual bank can create is limited by its deposits and the reserve ratio. As we discussed earlier, the reserve ratio is that percentage of a bank's deposits that must be held on reserve.

By way of illustration, let us assume that at the very moment a new bank opened its doors, Mary Perkins walked in to open a checking account. As her first transaction, Mary deposited a check for $10,000 that she had just received from the City Central Insurance Company for damages to her home caused by recent floods. The deposit will appear on the bank's balance sheet as follows:

ASSETS		LIABILITIES	
Reserves	$10,000	Deposits	$10,000

When these events took place, the reserve ratio was 20 percent. That meant that the bank had to add at least $2,000 (20 percent of $10,000 = $2,000) to its reserves. The remaining $8,000 was available for loans.

As luck would have it, the very next customer to enter the bank, John Scope, president of Scope's Hardware, applied for, and was granted, an $8,000 business loan. Mr. Scope needed the money to improve dock facilities at his hardware store. The amount ($8,000) was credited to the firm's checking account and was reflected in the bank's balance sheet as follows:

ASSETS		LIABILITIES	
Loans	$ 8,000	Deposits	$18,000
Reserves	$10,000		

Let us pause for a moment to see what happened.

Acting on a fundamental assumption of banking—that not all depositors will ask for their money at one and the same time—the bank lent the bulk of its first customer's deposit. Reserves still totaled $10,000 because, for the time being, no withdrawals have been made. Scope's Hardware has a credit of $8,000 in its checking account, which it will soon spend. Deposits, which totaled $10,000 before the loan, are now $18,000, even though no one brought in an additional $8,000.

Where did the additional $8,000 come from? It appeared when the bank granted the loan. Could the bank have loaned $9,000? No, because the reserve ratio at that time was 20 percent. (The bank could have loaned $9,000 if the reserve ratio had been 10 percent.) We see, therefore, that an individual bank can expand deposits by an amount

Deposits and Balance Sheets. A bank customer is making a deposit using an ATM. How will this deposit affect the bank's balance sheet?

equal to its *excess reserves* (the reserves held by a bank over and above its required reserves). But that is not the end of the story. As the borrowed money is spent and redeposited, the money supply expands still further. The funds continue to travel through the nation's banking system.

How the Banking System Expands Deposits

Scope's Hardware, the business that borrowed the $8,000, paid Hickory Dock, Inc., that amount to improve its dock facilities. Hickory Dock deposited the check in its account at a second bank. The second bank's balance sheet will reflect the $8,000 deposit as follows:

ASSETS		LIABILITIES	
Reserves	$ 8,000	Deposits	$ 8,000

The first bank's balance sheet will now look like this:

ASSETS		LIABILITIES	
Loans	$ 8,000	Deposits	$10,000
Reserves	$ 2,000		

The second bank will now be able to lend out an additional $6,400 (80 percent of $8,000). When added to the borrower's (of the $6,400) checking account, the loan will be reflected with the following additions to the bank's balance sheet:

ASSETS		LIABILITIES	
Loans	$ 6,400	Deposits	$14,400
Reserves	$ 8,000		

Just as the original loan moved on to a second bank, this second loan could be deposited in a third bank, which could then lend up to $5,120 of the $6,400 deposited (80 percent of $6,400 = $5,120). Theoretically, this loan could move through the banking system until the last cent was set aside in reserve. At this point, we would observe that a total of $40,000 had been lent as a result of the initial $10,000 deposit, and that total deposits had expanded to $50,000. We should also note that, although no one bank lent out more than its excess reserves, the banking system as a whole expanded deposits by five times the original deposit. Table 15.2 summarizes the progress of the $10,000 deposit as it moved through the banking system.

We can see that the reserve ratio affects the money supply. If, on the one hand, the ratio were 25 percent, then an initial deposit of $10,000 could have been expanded to only $40,000. On the other hand, a 10 percent reserve ratio would have permitted the deposit to expand to $100,000. In the next chapter, we will see how the government uses the reserve ratio as a tool to keep the money supply healthy.

When Deposits Contract

Just as a deposit of cash can lead to a great expansion of deposits throughout the banking system, so the withdrawal of funds can have the opposite effect. If a bank has no excess reserves and some money is withdrawn, it has to replace the reserves by either calling in loans or selling securities. If the funds that were withdrawn from one bank are placed in another, then the banking system as a whole does not lose. However, if the money is not deposited in another bank, then the total of all deposits in the economy is reduced. If the reserve ratio is 20 percent, then total deposits are reduced by $5 for every dollar withdrawn.

Table 15.2 PROGRESS OF $10,000 THROUGH THE BANKING SYSTEM

Bank	Deposits	Required Reserves	Loans
First	$10,000.00	$ 2,000.00	$ 8,000.00
Second	8,000.00	1,600.00	6,400.00
Third	6,400.00	1,280.00	5,120.00
Fourth	5,120.00	1,024.00	4,096.00
Fifth	4,096.00	819.20	3,276.80
Sum of Remaining Banks	16,384.00	3,276.80	13,107.20
Total	$50,000.00	$10,000.00	$40,000.00

KEEPING OUR BANKS SAFE

The Great Depression of the 1930s was the most dreadful period in U.S. economic history. For many, the most psychologically painful memories of those times were the numbers of people without jobs, and the many failed banks. During the worst of those times, in 1933, 25 percent of the labor force was unemployed and half the nation's banks failed. We will focus on unemployment in Chapter 20. For now, let us think about what it must have been like to learn that the bank in which one's life's savings had been deposited had failed.

Failure of a savings institution meant that the bank would no longer be able to meet withdrawal requests from its depositors. Later (perhaps months later, perhaps years later), depositors might receive a fraction of their savings. Some received 10 cents on the dollar. Others received nothing. With so much to lose if one's bank failed, even the faintest rumor of trouble resulted in lines of depositors hoping to withdraw their money before disaster struck.

Widespread bank failures destroyed public trust in the banking system. They also left people fearful of spending or investing their money. This fear and uncertainty was bad for business. In addition, high unemployment levels made the situation even worse because people without jobs did not have money to save and invest, and little money to spend.

Deposit Insurance

To restore confidence, one of the first efforts of newly elected President Franklin D. Roosevelt was to get Congress to pass laws concerning deposit insurance. Accordingly, in 1933, Congress set up the **Federal Deposit Insurance Corporation** (**FDIC**). The following year, Congress created a similar organization, the **Federal Savings and Loan Insurance Corporation** (**FSLIC**), to insure people's deposits in savings and loan associations.

Eventually, the FDIC and FSLIC guaranteed deposits in insured banks and S&Ls for up to $100,000. Funding for the insurance came from the insured institutions, which paid a percentage of their deposits to the insuring agencies. Secure in the knowledge that even in the event of bank failures their deposits were secure, people regained their confidence in the banking system.

Events in more recent years, however, again raised questions about the ability of banks and thrifts to protect their depositors.

The Thrift Crisis. In the 1980s, disaster struck the nation's banks and thrifts. Bank failures, which had averaged fewer than 3 per year between 1943 and 1974, reached 42 in 1982, 120 in 1985, and 203 in

1987! Even harder hit was the savings and loan industry. In 1988, one in three S&Ls was losing money, and one in six was in danger of folding.

A principal cause of the problem was the sharp increases in interest rates that had taken place during the early 1980s. The increases forced the S&Ls and other thrift institutions to pay higher and higher rates to attract deposits. Meanwhile, most of the thrifts' investments were in the form of long-term real estate loans. Since the loans had been made before the interest rate run-up, the thrifts received much lower interest payments than those for more recent loans. The thrifts' income from these loans did not keep up with rising costs. Many of the savings institutions were either barely breaking even or losing money. In an effort to increase their profit margins (and knowing that insurance would protect their depositors from loss), the thrift institutions made many risky loans.

Through it all, the nation's depositors were unworried, since they had been told that federal deposit insurance guaranteed their savings accounts. What the public failed to understand, though, was that the funds held in deposit insurance reserves were limited. With losses running so high, neither the FDIC nor the FSLIC had enough in their reserves to guarantee the deposits of all the failed institutions. That left it to the federal government to come up with the billions of dollars needed to guarantee the threatened savings accounts. By 1995, this need amounted to about $200 billion. Over a thousand thrift institutions had to close or merge with another.

From The Wall Street Journal. Permission, Cartoon Features Syndicate

As a first step toward resolving the crisis in the thrift industry, Congress enacted the **Financial Institutions Reform, Recovery, and Enforcement Act (FIRREA)** of 1989. The principal goals of the act are to: (1) bolster the enforcement powers of the agencies that regulate thrift institutions, and (2) strengthen the deposit insurance programs. In addition, the FSLIC was dismantled and replaced by the FDIC, which is now responsible for all deposit insurance programs.

Some critics of FIRREA complained that the law does not do enough to eliminate the sloppy banking practices that got the thrifts into financial trouble in the first place. Others argued that the real cause of the thrift crisis was deposit insurance. Deposit insurance, they explained, lulls depositors into accepting poor banking practices because savings are guaranteed. Moreover, the argument continued, when savings are insured, bankers are almost encouraged to engage in reckless ventures with their customers' money.

Summary

The origins of banking can be traced back to ancient times. Certain individuals or families accepted money for safekeeping, made loans, charged interest, and exchanged foreign and local coins. Commercial banks today make loans and provide checking accounts to both businesses and individuals. Moreover, they offer many other services to their customers, including savings accounts and safe-deposit boxes.

Thrift institutions include savings and loan associations, mutual savings banks, and credit unions. The thrifts offer to individuals many of the same financial services offered by commercial banks, but they are mainly depositories for savings and places for individuals to obtain home mortgages and other loans. Unlike commercial banks, they do not offer services to businesses.

Banks earn money by making loans. When a bank grants a loan, the loan fund is deposited in a checking account. Since checking accounts are a form of money, the loan adds to the nation's money supply. The amount of money that an individual bank can create is limited by its deposits and the amount the bank must keep in reserves (the reserve ratio). The higher the reserve ratio, the less money that banks can create.

Bank failures during the Great Depression of the 1930s led to the creation of two federal agencies to insure deposits—the FDIC and the FSLIC. In 1989, Congress strengthened the deposit insurance system and dismantled the FSLIC, making the FDIC responsible for all federal deposit insurance programs.

REVIEWING THE CHAPTER

Building Vocabulary

Match each item in Column A with its definition in Column B.

Column A	Column B
1. FIRREA	a. a pledge of property as security for a loan
2. commercial bank	b. a savings institution owned by depositors
3. savings and loan association	c. the percentage of deposits a bank is required by law to hold to meet withdrawal demands
4. FDIC	d. a law that strengthened existing deposit insurance programs
5. reserves	e. money that a bank has on hand to use
6. mortgage	f. a business that provides both individuals and firms with checking accounts and loans
7. cash in vault	g. a term that includes S&Ls, mutual savings banks, and credit unions
8. reserve ratio	h. a business that mainly provides home mortgages
9. mutual savings bank	i. the funds a bank sets aside to meet withdrawal demands
10. thrifts	j. an institution that insures bank deposits

Understanding What You Have Read

1. Which of the following statements is true? (*a*) Banking developed at the same time as the barter system. (*b*) Early civilizations in India, China, and the Middle East lacked any of the characteristics we associate with banking. (*c*) Banking houses were established in Italy, Germany, and the Netherlands during the late Middle Ages. (*d*) English goldsmiths in the 17th century held gold for safekeeping but did not lend out any of the gold deposited with them.

2. A basic assumption on which banks operate is that (*a*) not everyone is entitled to withdraw deposits at the same time (*b*) all depositors may be required to give advance notice of their intention to withdraw their deposits (*c*) deposits are the property of the bank and are therefore carried as "assets" on the balance sheet (*d*) depositors will not withdraw all their deposits at the same time.

3. Which of the following is <u>not</u> classified as a thrift institution? (*a*) a commercial bank (*b*) a credit union (*c*) a mutual savings bank (*d*) a savings and loan association.

4. The principal characteristic of a commercial bank is that it (*a*) lends money for home mortgages (*b*) provides businesses with checking accounts and loans (*c*) sells traveler's checks (*d*) sells stocks and bonds.

5. The major source of income for banks is (*a*) service fees charged on their deposit accounts (*b*) fees from the sale of government bonds (*c*) income from services such as safe-deposit boxes, life insurance, and notary fees (*d*) interest earned on their loans.

6. The section of a balance sheet in which a bank's deposits are summarized is the (*a*) capital stock (*b*) assets (*c*) liabilities (*d*) net worth.

7. Lila Gallo borrowed $10,000 from her bank to build up the inventory of her stationery store. The loan was payable in six months at 12 percent interest per year, which the bank deducted in advance. How much money did Lila actually receive? (*a*) $10,000 (*b*) $8,800 (*c*) $9,400 (*d*) $9,600.

8. Most bank reserves are kept in (*a*) the vaults of other banks where they can earn interest (*b*) a Federal Reserve bank (*c*) miscellaneous investments so as to earn income (*d*) very safe, long-term government bonds.

9. With a reserve ratio of 25 percent and deposits of $4 million, what is the total amount of money that a commercial bank is permitted to lend? (*a*) $3 million (*b*) $8 million (*c*) $1.6 million (*d*) $1 million.

10. The Federal Deposit Insurance Corporation guarantees (*a*) all funds deposited in all financial institutions (*b*) funds deposited in commercial banks only (*c*) funds of any depositor who buys a special insurance policy (*d*) deposits of up to $100,000 in all banks and thrift institutions in the United States.

Thinking Critically

1. The origins of banks and banking can be traced way back in history.

   a. Describe *three* functions of a modern bank that can be traced back to activities performed by individuals and families in ancient civilizations.

   b. Describe *three* major practices developed by London goldsmiths that have been incorporated into modern banking.

2. Briefly describe the *three* types of thrift institutions.
3. Suppose that banks were required to keep 100 percent of their deposits on reserve. How would banking differ from the way it is currently practiced in the United States?
4. The expansion of bank loans affects the nation's money supply.
   a. Explain how a bank loan creates money.
   b. Explain why the amount of money that an individual bank can create is limited by its deposits and the reserve ratio.
   c. Explain, with reference to Table 15.2, how it is possible for the banking system as a whole to expand money by several times the amount of excess reserves in the system.

SKILLS: Analyzing a Balance Sheet

The balance sheet of the Third National Bank for December 31 is summarized in Table 15.3.   (*a*) Explain the meaning of *each* of the balance sheet entries (numbered 1–8).   (*b*) In the week after December 31, cash deposits that were kept on hand increased by $10 million. In addition, the bank increased its loans by $7 million, all of which was credited to deposit accounts. Create a new balance sheet that shows the changes that took place as a result of these transactions.

**Table 15.3   BALANCE SHEET, THIRD NATIONAL BANK
DECEMBER 31, 19—**

Assets		Liabilities and Net Worth	
(1) Cash in vault	$ 7,500,000	(6) Deposits	$24,000,000
(2) Reserves	12,500,000	(7) Capital stock	5,500,000
(3) Loans	9,750,000	(8) Surplus and profits	10,000,000
(4) Securities	8,500,000		$39,500,000
(5) Other assets	1,250,000		
	$39,500,000		

Chapter 16

THE FEDERAL RESERVE SYSTEM

Overview

Bankers assume that on most days deposits will more than offset withdrawals. That being the case, banks need only set aside a portion of their deposits to satisfy withdrawal demands. Banks are free to use the rest of the deposits to make investments and loans. On the rare occasions when withdrawals outrun deposits and vault cash begins to run low, banks can replenish supplies by drawing upon their reserves at their district Federal Reserve Bank. Although the banking system works well enough today, it did not in the years before 1913. That was the year Congress created the Federal Reserve System.

In this chapter, we will discuss the role of the Federal Reserve System in our economy. We will also discuss:

☐ Why did U.S. leaders decide that there was a need for the Federal Reserve System?
☐ How is the Federal Reserve System organized?
☐ What does the Federal Reserve System do?

HISTORICAL BACKGROUND

The chief weakness of the banking system in the United States prior to 1913 was the lack of a central bank. A *central bank* is a national institution that has the responsibility for: (1) supervising every other bank in the country, (2) controlling the volume of bank credit, and (3) regulating the money supply. A central bank deals mainly with other banks and the national government rather than with the general public. That is why central banks are referred to as "bankers' banks."

Before 1913, the United States lacked a central bank but had a **National Banking System**. This was a system of federally chartered banks (still not quite a central bank) authorized to issue notes backed by U.S. government bonds. It was created by Congress in the **National Bank Act** of 1863.

Federally chartered banks were allowed to issue national banknotes worth up to 90 percent (later changed to 100 percent) of the amount of government bonds they held. Each federally chartered bank was required to redeem its own notes in gold or silver. These notes were uniform in design, and they were sound because they were backed by government bonds. By the end of the Civil War, in 1865,

Before the creation of the National Banking System, state banknotes such as this one were common.

state banknotes were no longer in circulation. The United States had, for the first time, a uniform currency.

Weaknesses of the National Banking System

Despite the new system, in the years following the Civil War the nation experienced a number of financial panics (in 1873, 1884, 1893, 1903, and 1907). Many people blamed the national banking system for these panics. They pointed to the following four weaknesses in the system:

1. Inflexibility of Bank Credit. Banks could lend only up to the limit permitted by their reserves. Once that limit was reached, however, new lending stopped. There was no central agency to help banks that needed more cash to lend or to provide additional reserves. Thus, credit became tight.

2. Inelastic Money Supply. The amount of national banknotes was relatively fixed. The National Banking Act provided no mechanism for increasing the money supply when more money was needed or reducing the money supply when less money was needed.

3. Inefficient System of Clearing and Collecting Checks. Clearing checks under the National Banking System was inefficient and slow. It often took weeks to clear checks drawn against out-of-town banks. A check *clears* when payment is made to the final recipient of the check and the check is deducted from the account of the person who wrote the check. (Later in this chapter, we will discuss how this process of clearing checks may now be completed much more quickly.)

4. The Uncontrolled System of Redeposited Reserves. Before 1913, it was the custom for small town and rural banks around the country to deposit their reserves in big city banks that offered high interest rates.

Naturally, the big city banks used the deposits of the other banks to extend loans.

Problems arose during hard times when business activity declined. With their profits falling, business firms around the country withdrew their funds from local banks to meet expenses. Other business firms, unable to repay their bank loans, were forced into bankruptcy. As word spread about the heavy withdrawals and business failures, nervous depositors lined up to withdraw their savings. This compelled the smaller banks to call upon the city banks to return some or all of their reserves.

But the city banks were soon in much the same fix as the country banks. Whenever bank depositors believe that their bank is unable to convert their deposits into cash, there can be so many withdrawals that the bank's cash reserves are depleted. Large withdrawals by many depositors at the same time is called a *run on a bank*. During such a run, the bank might refuse to pay out currency. This happened in 1907 as many banks suspended payments and then collapsed. Historians refer to this breakdown of the banking system as the **Panic of 1907**. As banks suspended payments, various substitutes for currency came into use and, in fact, many people had to resort to barter to acquire the things that they needed.

In the wake of this panic, Congress began an investigation of the U.S. banking system. Its study concluded that to avoid future panics, the country needed: (1) an elastic currency, and (2) a central bank.

An *elastic currency* is one that expands and contracts with the needs of business. For example, suppose that Sally Jones needs money to meet the operating expenses of her furniture store in Texas. Sally goes to her bank—the National Bank of Amarillo—for a loan and receives cash. Sally's bank sends the promissory note that Sally had signed to a central bank. The central bank accepts the note (for a fee) and gives the National Bank of Amarillo cash. When Sally repays her loan to the National Bank of Amarillo, this bank (1) returns the currency to the central bank, and (2) buys back Sally's promissory note. Thus, cash is available when it is needed by business (when Sally receives cash) and withdrawn when it is no longer needed (when Sally returns the cash).

The congressional study of 1907 found that nearly all countries that had an elastic currency also had some form of central banking. Created by a federal government, a central bank: (1) provides banking services to the government and to private banks, (2) supervises private banks, and (3) coordinates the nation's supply of money and credit. Although other major nations had long recognized its advantages, the United States was without a central bank from 1836 until 1913.

ORGANIZATION OF THE FEDERAL RESERVE SYSTEM

Congress created the Federal Reserve System with the passage of the **Federal Reserve Act** of 1913. Commonly known as the **Fed**, the **Federal Reserve System** functions as this nation's central bank. The Fed is composed of a Board of Governors located in Washington, D.C., and 12 District Reserve Banks, each serving a different geographic region. Congress chose a decentralized system that was unlike the central banks set up in other countries. Congress chose this unique system because it wanted to: (1) avoid placing too much power in the hands of a single bank, and (2) meet the special needs of the regions.

Each District Reserve Bank is owned by the member banks in its district. All of the member banks are required to purchase the stock of its District Reserve Bank. Control of the Federal Reserve System remains, however, in the hands of the federal government. The Reserve banks earn a profit every year. They do this because they acquire in the course of their operations large quantities of income-producing government securities.

The organization of the Federal Reserve System can be compared to a pyramid. (See Figure 16.1.) At its highest point is the seven-member Board of Governors. Below this board are the 12 Federal Reserve Banks and their 25 branches. At the base stand the approximately 39,000 depository institutions that make up the bulk of the system.

Figure 16.1   Structure of the Federal Reserve System

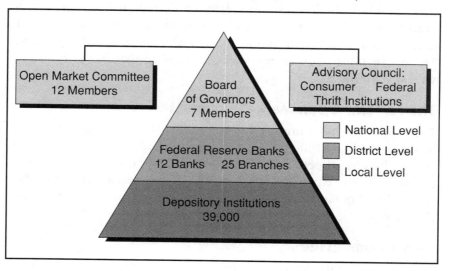

The Board of Governors

The **Board of Governors** supervises the many activities of the Federal Reserve System. In addition, the board establishes and oversees the nation's *monetary policies*—that is, the Fed's programs to regulate the country's supply of money and credit. The seven members of the Board of Governors are appointed by the president of the United States subject to the consent of the Senate. The term of their appointment is 14 years. The chairperson of the board is appointed from among the members by the president for a four-year term.

The District Reserve Banks

The 12 District Reserve Banks are "bankers' banks" in that they are primarily concerned with servicing the member banks within their districts. All but two of the District Banks maintain branches, each of which meets the needs of member banks in its particular part of a district.

Member Banks

By law, all national banks (those holding charters from the federal government) must be members of the Federal Reserve System. Many of the larger state banks as well as some smaller ones have also joined. Now about 40 percent of the nation's 12,000 banks are members. These banks hold approximately 70 percent of the banking system's demand deposits.

Before 1980, only those banks that were members of the Federal Reserve System were subject to its regulations and services. Since then, however, the law has been changed so that all *depository institutions* (businesses that hold people's deposits)—including S&Ls, mutual savings banks, and credit unions—are now subject to Fed regulations. The distinctions between member and nonmember banks have been virtually eliminated.

The Federal Open Market Committee

The **Open Market Committee** is the most important policy-making group of the Fed. It directs the purchase and sale of government securities, thereby affecting the nation's supply of money and credit. Members of the Open Market Committee include the seven members of the Board of Governors and five of the twelve District Reserve Bank presidents.

Other Committees

With so many complex responsibilities, the Federal Reserve looks at a number of other committees to undertake major tasks. Among these, for example, is the **Federal Advisory Council,** a 12-member commit-tee of bankers that meets several times a year to advise the Board of Governors on matters of current interest.

FUNCTIONS OF THE FEDERAL RESERVE SYSTEM

The Federal Reserve System has several key functions.

The Fed Supervises Individual Banks

Every day somewhere in the United States, one or more Federal Re-serve examiners are going over the books or examining the procedures of a local bank. The examiners visit local banks to ensure that the banks conduct their business in a safe and legal manner. The Fed also supervises banks to ensure that consumers are treated fairly when they borrow money from the banks. The Fed oversees the nation's banking system in the following ways.

Figure 16.2   Districts of the Federal Reserve System

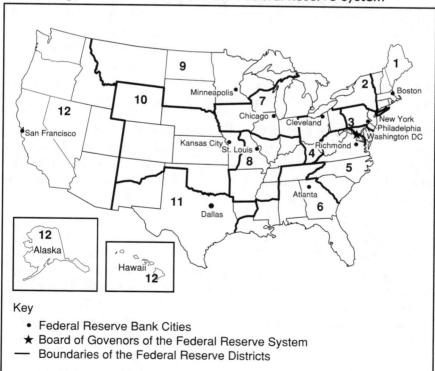

Key
* • Federal Reserve Bank Cities
* ★ Board of Govenors of the Federal Reserve System
* — Boundaries of the Federal Reserve Districts

What is the number of the Federal Reserve District in which you live?

District Banks Hold the Nation's Reserve. In our last chapter, we discussed how banks are required by law to keep a percentage of their deposits in reserves. The percentage of deposits a bank is required to keep in reserves is called the reserve ratio. Banks hold their required reserves either as cash in their vaults or as deposits in the Federal Reserve Bank in their district. If withdrawal demands are more than a bank's reserves can handle, the bank can borrow additional funds from their District Reserve Bank.

Supplies the Nation's Currency and Coin. All new money printed or minted by the U.S. Treasury is put into circulation by the Federal Reserve System. The paper currency issued by the Fed are Federal Reserve notes. The public's need for money changes from day to day. More cash is needed during the days before a holiday, a weekend, and during the summer season than at other times.

The Fed introduces paper currency and coin to the public through the banking system. Banks maintain accounts at the Federal Reserve Bank in their district. As supplies of currency and coin run low, local banks order additional amounts from their District Bank. After a holiday, local business firms deposit excess cash in local banks. As local banks deposit the excess funds to their accounts at their District Bank, the cash finds its way back to the Federal Reserve System.

In the above example, we see how the Federal Reserve System provides an elastic currency, that is, one that expands and contracts with the needs of business. Currency that is made available for a holiday season is withdrawn when the currency is no longer needed.

The Federal Reserve System Clears Checks. Nine out of every ten dollars that Americans spend are in the form of checks. Nearly all of these are submitted to the District Reserve Banks for clearance and collection. The following describes the system for check clearance used during most of the 20th century.

Let us suppose that Brown gave Jones a check for $100 drawn upon the First National Bank of Middletown, New York, in which Brown had an account. Jones deposited the check in the People's National Bank of Newburgh, New York, which is located in the same Federal Reserve district as Middletown. Jones's account was credited with $100.

At this point, we see that the People's National Bank of Newburgh had given Jones $100 in exchange for a check. It then wanted to get its money back by presenting the check to the First National Bank of Middletown for payment. This could have been accomplished by mailing the check to Middletown. However, this would have been hardly a practical procedure since the First National Bank probably received hundreds of *checks from dozens of banks on any business day. The paperwork involved in settling with each bank individually would have been staggering. What the bank did instead was to send the check to the clearinghouse at the Federal Reserve Bank in its district. Here the account of the People's National Bank of Newburgh was credited with $100, and the amount was deducted from the account of the Middletown bank. The check was then forwarded to Middletown, where the bank deducted the sum from Brown's account and sent Brown the canceled check.*

Electronic Funds Transfer. The process as described above worked fine for many years. Today, however, with billions of checks going through the system every year, the Fed now uses an electronic system. It allows the transfer of funds between financial institutions anywhere in the nation in a matter of minutes. For example, a bank in Jacksonville, Florida, wishes to transfer $1 million to a bank in Anaheim, California. There is no need to physically transport the $1 million. All that the

The Board of Governors meets in this building in Washington, D.C.

Florida bank needs to do is to enter the amount of the transaction ($1 million) into its computer. The Florida bank's computer is connected by telephone lines to its District Bank in Atlanta, Georgia. The Atlanta Federal Reserve Bank deducts $1 million from the account of its member bank (the Jacksonville bank) and by computer notifies the District Bank in San Francisco to add $1 million to the account of the Anaheim bank. The bank in Anaheim, California, now has a $1 million deposit credited to it at the District Bank of San Francisco.

The Fed Is a Banker for the U.S. Government

The Fed maintains the world's largest bank account—that of the federal government. Virtually all government checks are drawn on accounts maintained by the government at the District Reserve Banks. Similarly, most tax receipts are deposited into those accounts. The District Banks also sell and redeem government securities such as Treasury bills and U.S. savings bonds.

MONETARY POLICY AND THE FED

If it is true that the price level (P) is determined by the amount of money (M) and the quantity of goods (Q), it follows that increasing or decreasing M or Q will affect prices. Therefore, if the government is to control inflation in our economy, it needs to regulate the amount of goods produced, the money supply, or both. The question then is how can the government control production and money supply.

The government cannot directly control output of goods and services. The decision to produce goods and services in the U.S. economy is mostly in private hands.

The amount of money that individuals and business firms can spend depends in part upon how much they can borrow. When credit is readily available at a reasonable price, spending and business activity increase. When credit is tight (that is, less available), spending and business activity decreases.

The Fed can regulate the level of economic activity through its control over the money supply. There are times when the economy as a whole could benefit from an increase in the money supply. At other times, a decrease is required. The Federal Reserve System has a number of tools that it uses to regulate the supply of money and credit. These tools are: (1) the reserve ratio, (2) the discount rate, and (3) open market operations. Monetary policy refers to the use of these tools to regulate the economy.

The Equation of Exchange

In Chapter 14, we studied how fluctuations in the supply of goods affects prices. We can use the equation of exchange, described below, to better understand how the amount of money in circulation also may influence prices.

The relationship between the money supply and prices is summarized in the *equation of exchange*. The equation is written as:

$$MV = PQ$$

where M = money supply
         V = velocity
         P = average price paid
             for goods and services
         Q = quantity of goods
             and services produced

To find the total spending by all Americans over a year, it is necessary to multiply the money supply (M) by the number of times those funds were spent (V). Money changes hands as it is spent. That $5 bill you used to rent a video was given in change to another customer, who used it to buy groceries. In similar fashion, the $5 continued to duck in and out of circulation. By year's end, the $5 bill had changed hands 100 times. This process added $500 to total spending in the economy that year.

The dollar value of the goods and services purchased in the economy in a year is equal to the number of goods and services produced by the economy (Q) multiplied by the average price (P) paid for these goods and services. But the dollar value of all the goods and services produced by the economy in the course of the year is the Gross Domestic Product (GDP). Therefore, PQ is the same thing as GDP, or PQ = GDP.

We can write the equation of exchange ($MV = PQ$) in terms of price: $P = MV \div Q$. (We get this new formula by dividing both sides of the original equation by Q.) The new formula tells us that the average price is equal to the money supply (M) multiplied by the number of times those funds were spent (V) divided by the number of goods and services produced in the country (Q).

To find out what happens to average prices when (1) the supply of goods and services changes, and (2) the money supply changes, answer the following questions. (Assume velocity remains the same.)

1. What is the average price when M = $1 million; V = 10; and Q = 100,000?
2. What happens to the average price when Q doubles? When Q declines by half?
3. What will happen to the average price if the money supply is increased from $1 million to $2 million? If money supply is decreased to $500,000?
4. Since the Fed controls the nation's money supply, how can the Fed influence average prices in the U.S. economy?

Reserve Ratio

The major functions of banking are to receive deposits and make loans. Indeed, interest earned on loans is the principal source of income for most banks. We discussed in Chapter 15, however, that banks must keep a portion of their depositors' funds on hand as reserves to meet their withdrawal demands. Required reserves are expressed as a ratio of a bank's deposits (the reserve ratio). Thus, with a required reserve of 15 percent, a bank that has total deposits of $1 million must maintain $150,000 in reserve ($1,000,000 × .15 = $150,000).

Reserve ratios are established by the Board of Governors of the Federal Reserve System. When the Board increases the reserve ratio, a bank's ability to lend is decreased because the bank must keep a larger share of deposits on hand. When the reserve ratio is reduced, the bank's ability to lend is increased. For example, with $100 million in deposits and a reserve ratio of 15 percent, the Second National Bank will be free to lend up to $85 million (100 percent − 15 percent = 85 percent or .85. Therefore, $100 million × .85 = $85 million). The remaining $15 million will be held on reserve in its account at a District Federal Reserve Bank, or in its own vaults. Now assume that the Fed increases the reserve ratio to 20 percent. Second National will then have to limit its loans to $80 million (80 percent of $100 million), thereby reducing its lending ability by $5 million.

The effect of a change in reserve requirements is magnified as deposits travel through the banking system. In Chapter 15, we saw how a reserve ratio of 20 percent enabled a deposit of $10,000 to expand to $50,000 as it traveled through the banking system. We also noted that if the required reserve ratio was increased to 25 percent, a $10,000 deposit could be expanded to only $40,000.

The impact of changes in the required reserve ratio is reflected in the *deposit multiplier*. It tells us the number of times deposits could be increased by the banking system for every dollar in reserves. The deposit multiplier is equal to 100 divided by the reserve ratio. For example, with a reserve ratio of 25 percent, the deposit multiplier would be 4 (because 100 ÷ 25 = 4). A new deposit of $1 million could potentially add $4 million to bank deposits and the money supply. Now suppose that the reserve ratio were reduced to 10 percent. The deposit multiplier would then go up to 10 (100 ÷ 10 = 10) and a new deposit of $1 million could add as much as $10 million to bank deposits and to the money supply.

The Fed can use its power to set reserve ratios to increase or decrease the money supply. By increasing required reserves, the ability of banks to lend money is reduced, thereby reducing the money supply. When the reserve ratio is decreased, the opposite occurs.

The Discount Rate

When their reserves run low, member banks can replenish them with loans from their District Federal Reserve Bank. At one time, the interest on these loans was *discounted* (deducted in advance). Although loans are no longer discounted, the interest charged by District Banks on loans to member banks is still referred to as the *discount rate*. This rate is determined by the Fed.

Like any business, banks must profit in order to survive. For that reason, they need to charge more for the money they lend to their customers than those funds cost to borrow from the Fed. The discount rate that banks pay to the Fed is reflected in the interest rate that banks charge their customers. Thus, if the discount rate is 5 percent, a bank might charge its customers 5¼ percent. If the discount rate were to increase to 5¼ percent, the banks might charge their customers 5½ percent.

Since banks and other lenders adjust their loan rates to meet changes in the discount rate, the Fed can regulate the economy by making changes in the discount rate. For example, if the Fed wanted to increase the money supply, it could do so by reducing the discount rate. Similarly, by increasing the discount rate the Fed could reduce the supply of money and credit.

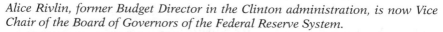

Alice Rivlin, former Budget Director in the Clinton administration, is now Vice Chair of the Board of Governors of the Federal Reserve System.

Open Market Operations

The most important of the Fed's monetary tools are *open market operations*, the buying and selling of government bonds by the Federal Open Market Committee (FOMC).

- When the Fed buys securities, its payments are usually deposited in the sellers' bank accounts. This action increases bank reserves, thereby making more money available for the bank to loan. The Fed gets individuals and institutions to sell securities by offering whatever price is necessary to convince holders of securities to sell.

- When the Fed sells securities, the payments it receives reduces the balances in the buyers' accounts. This action reduces bank reserves, thereby decreasing the amount of money the banks can loan. The Fed gets individuals and institutions to buy securities by lowering the asking price of the securities it wishes to sell so as to make these securities attractive to buyers.

We know that the lending power of banks is limited by the requirement that they maintain adequate reserves. When reserves are reduced, the lending power of banks is reduced. When they increase, the opposite occurs. Therefore, when the Board of Governors decides that it is time to increase the money supply, it may do so by ordering the FOMC to buy securities in the open market. When the Fed decides that it is time to reduce the money supply, it can do so by ordering the Open Market Committee to sell securities.

Like changes in the reserve ratio, the effect of open market operations is magnified by the deposit multiplier. (The deposit multiplier, you will recall, is equal to 100 divided by the reserve ratio. See page 384.) With, for example, a reserve ratio of 20 percent, the deposit multiplier would be 5 (because $100 \div 20 = 5$). In those circumstances, the purchase of $100 million in government securities by the Open Market Committee could add as much as $500 million to the money supply.

For similar reasons, the sale of securities by the FOMC has the opposite effect on the money supply. The sale can shrink bank deposits and reduce the money supply by the deposit multiplier. We will learn more about open market operations and monetary policy in Chapter 18.

Summary

The Federal Reserve System was established in 1913 to provide the United States with a central bank and an elastic currency. The Federal Reserve System consists of 12 district banks, each one in a different part of the country. A seven-member Board of Governors supervises the 12 Federal Reserve District Banks, which, in turn, supervise the 12,000 member banks. The Federal Reserve System serves as the central bank of the country. The Fed issues paper currency (Federal Reserve notes) and places into circulation all new money printed or minted by the U.S. Treasury. Member banks maintain accounts at their district bank. They can withdraw cash from their accounts as needed and return cash to the accounts when the funds are no longer needed.

The Federal Reserve System provides a mechanism for efficient collection and clearance of checks; serves as the banker for the U.S. government; holds the deposit accounts of the U.S. government; and regulates the supply of money and credit in the U.S. economy through its powers to establish the reserve ratios, the discount rate, and open market operations

REVIEWING THE CHAPTER

Building Vocabulary

Match each item in Column A with its definition in Column B.

COLUMN A	COLUMN B
1. run on a bank	a. the institution that supervises the activities of the Fed
2. elastic currency	b. the Fed's programs to regulate the country's supply of money and credit
3. monetary policy	
4. Board of Governors	c. the number of times deposits can be increased by the banking system
5. depository institutions	d. large withdrawals by many depositors at a time
6. discount rate	e. the interest rate the Fed charges member banks
7. Fed	f. the U.S. central banking system
8. open market operations	g. currency that increases or decreases in response to needs of business
9. deposit multiplier	h. banks, savings and loan associations, and credit unions
10. District Bank	i. one of 12 Federal Reserve banks
	j. the buying and selling of government bonds by the Fed

Understanding What You Have Read

1. Central banks are "bankers' banks" because they (*a*) deal mainly with banks and the national government (*b*) are located in large cities (*c*) deal primarily with the general public (*d*) are chartered by the states.

2. The Federal Reserve System was created in (*a*) 1789 (*b*) 1836 (*c*) 1863 (*d*) 1913.

3. Where are member banks of the Federal Reserve System required to keep reserves against their deposits? (*a*) entirely in the bank vault (*b*) partly in their own vault and the remainder at any other larger bank (*c*) entirely in a central bank (*d*) partly as cash-in-vault and the remainder at their District Federal Reserve Bank.

4. When output (*Q*) cannot be increased, an increase in the money supply (*M*) will result in (*a*) decreased output (*b*) lower prices (*c*) higher prices (*d*) greater price stability.

5. Federal Reserve notes are an "elastic currency" because (*a*) their total value is fixed by Congress in accordance with the needs of business (*b*) their supply automatically expands and contracts with fluctuations in the GDP (*c*) the Board of Governors can expand or contract the supply as needed (*d*) their value is automatically adjusted to the Consumer Price Index.

6. The Federal Reserve System acts as a fiscal agent for the U.S. government by (*a*) supervising the collection of income taxes (*b*) maintaining a part ownership in all the nation's commercial banks (*c*) receiving deposits and making payments on the government's behalf (*d*) printing all the nation's paper money.

7. Monetary policy refers to the Federal Reserve System's power to (*a*) provide currency to commercial banks (*b*) supervise the practices of the member banks (*c*) regulate the nation's supply of money and credit (*d*) clear checks.

8. When commercial banks expand the value of the loans they make, the effect upon the economy is (*a*) a reduction in the money supply (*b*) an increase in the money supply (*c*) an increase in interest rates (*d*) a lowering of bank reserves.

9. The Federal Reserve System can expand the money supply in the United States by (*a*) raising reserve requirements (*b*) selling government securities in the open market (*c*) lowering the discount rate (*d*) reducing the ability of banks to lend money.

10. Federal Reserve notes are (*a*) interest-bearing securities (*b*) redeemable upon demand in gold (*c*) paper currency issued by the Fed (*d*) manufactured with an elastic consistency.

11. Which of the following determines the maximum amount of money a commercial bank can create? The amount that the bank has on hand of (*a*) excess reserves (*b*) Treasury bonds and notes (*c*) cash in its vault (*d*) gold and silver.

Thinking Critically

1. Explain why the National Banking System was unable to respond to the public demand for currency and credit during the Panic of 1907.

2. The amount of money that individuals and business firms can spend depends in part upon how much they can borrow.
   a. How does availability of credit affect business activity?
   b. When would the economy as a whole benefit from an increase in the supply of money and credit?
   c. When would the economy as a whole benefit from less money and credit?

3. The Federal Reserve System controls the supply of money and credit in the U.S. economy. Explain how each of the following actions taken by the Fed will affect the supply of money and credit.
   a. lowering reserve requirements of member banks
   b. raising the discount rate
   c. buying securities in the open market.

4. "Bank reserve requirements affect the size of the nation's money supply."
   a. Prove this statement by showing the effect on the money supply of an increase in the reserve ratio from 10 percent to 20.
   b. Describe the effect on the money supply if a person were to withdraw $100,000 from a commercial bank account and bury it in his or her backyard. For purpose of illustration, assume a reserve ratio of 25 percent.

SKILLS: Working With the Reserve Ratio and the Deposit Multiplier

1. Complete the chart below by filling in the missing data. Note that the deposit multiplier is equal to 100 divided by the reserve ratio. The maximum expansion of the original deposit is equal to the deposit multiplier multiplied by the amount of the excess reserves in bank.

2. Using data in the chart, explain what action you would recommend to the Fed if you wanted it to: (*a*) expand bank deposits; (*b*) reduce bank deposits.

3. Explain why an increase in bank deposits increases the money supply, while a decrease in bank deposits reduces the money supply.

4. What conclusions can you infer from your answer to Question 2 concerning the relation between the reserve ratio set by the Fed and the supply of money in the U.S. economy?

Reserve Ratio (Percent)	Deposit Multiplier	×	Excess Reserves in Bank	=	Maximum Expansion of Deposits
10	$100 \div 10 = 10$		$10 \times \$100,000$	=	$1,000,000
10			$1,000,000	=	
12.5			$100,000	=	
20			$100,000	=	
			$100,000	=	$100,000
25				=	$4,000,000

Managing the Economy

Chapter 17

OUR FLUCTUATING ECONOMY

Overview

The economic history of the United States has been marked by both good times and bad. In good times, jobs are plentiful, stores are busy, and the nation's factories hum with activity. In bad times, just the opposite is true. Jobs are scarce, business is slow, and factories and machines stand idle. The rise and fall of prices, production, consumption, employment, and investment is called the business cycle. Fluctuations in economic activity are not new. Economists have long debated what to do about them. Some believe that the economic fluctuations in the business cycle are governed by automatic forces with which government should not tamper. Other economists believe that intelligent government efforts to control economic fluctuations are both possible and desirable. After reading this chapter, you will understand why economic fluctuations occur. You will be able to explain each of the following:

- ☐ The four phases of the business cycle
- ☐ Theories on the causes of business cycles
- ☐ The relation between demand, employment, and prices
- ☐ How economists measure the nation's economic performance.

THE BUSINESS CYCLE: THE UPS AND DOWNS OF THE ECONOMY

The periodic ups and downs in the level of economic activity are collectively known as the *business cycle*. Figure 17.1 summarizes fluctuations in economic activity since 1905. The straight horizontal (0) line depicts what statisticians determine would have been an average level of activity during those years. The jagged line indicates the extent to which actual economic activity was above or below the norm. For example, you will note that the jagged line is considerably below the horizontal (0) line during the period of the Great Depression and well above that line during the period of World War II.

The graph also shows that although no two cycles have been identical in either duration or intensity, there has been a consistent up-and-down pattern through the years. Economists studying business cycles have identified four phases through which each cycle passes. These

Figure 17.1   United States Business Activity Since 1905

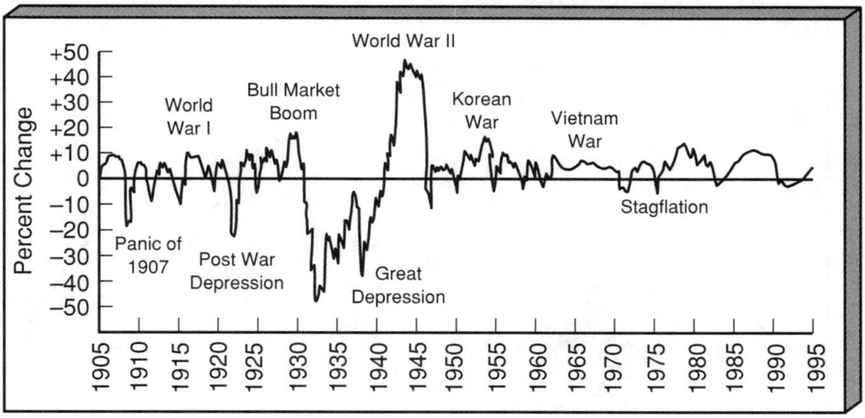

Source: **AmeriTrust,** Cleveland, Ohio
The ups and downs in the graph portray the economic history of the United States. The percentages indicate the percentage change from the norm.

are: (1) contraction or recession, (2) trough, (3) expansion or recovery, and (4) peak. We will take a closer look at each of these phases, which are illustrated in Figure 17.2.

Contraction or Recession

During a *contraction*, economic activity goes into a decline. Consumers buy fewer goods and services. Retailers and wholesalers cut back on their orders, and the pace of manufacturing is slowed. As business goes into a decline, workers are laid off. The fall in earnings further reduces consumer spending and business profits. If the contraction is so severe that it continues for six months or more, economists will describe it as a *recession*.

Trough

Sooner or later, a contraction or recession will bottom out into what is described as the *trough* of the cycle. When a contraction or recession is mild and short-lived, the trough will be reached before the levels of unemployment and business shrinkage become serious. At other times, a recession might extend for a long period of time and be known as a *depression*. The most famous depression was the *Great Depression* of the 1930s. Exactly when a recession becomes a depression is vague.

Bad as things may be in terms of unemployment and business failure, when the trough is reached we can start to be optimistic. The nation's economic health will soon begin to improve.

Figure 17.2 Phases of a Business Cycle

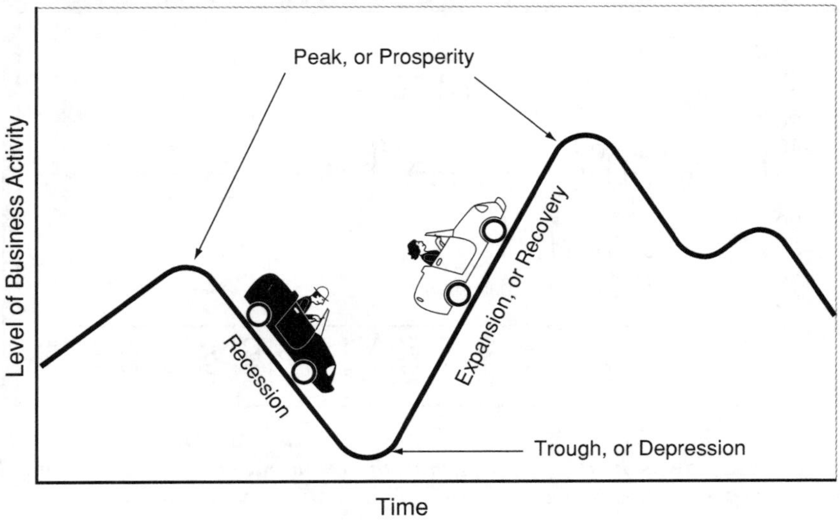

Expansion or Recovery

As the economy advances out of the trough of the business cycle, it begins its period of *expansion*. When feelings of optimism spread, consumer spending (along with production and other business activity) increases. As more and more workers find jobs, the increase in earnings fuels still more spending by consumers and businesses.

When the expansion follows a contraction severe enough to have been classified as a recession, it is called a *recovery*.

Peak

The *peak* is the highest point in the roller-coaster-like ride of the business cycle. Increasing sales prompt firms to expand operations and reopen idled or underutilized factories. At the peak, the economy may close in on its capacity. When that happens, shortages of productive factors or goods and services may lead to generally higher prices.

THEORIES ON THE CAUSES OF BUSINESS CYCLES

For as long as economists have been aware of the periodic ups and downs of the economy, they have searched for reasons to explain and predict them. **W. Stanley Jevons**, a noted British economist, created quite a stir in 1878 with his announcement that business cycles were caused by sunspots. These dark patches on the sun, Jevons believed, affected global weather patterns, which, in turn, had a direct influence on crops. Worldwide crop failures raised food prices, lowered living standards, and triggered recessions and depressions. It was an interesting idea, but the science of astronomy later proved that Jevons' theory had little basis in fact.

External Causes

Since Jevons' day, there has been no shortage of theories and explanations for the causes of business cycles. The most widely accepted explanations focus on two categories of causes—external and internal. External causes are those that are generated by events outside the economy. Sunspots would be an example of an external cause of fluctuation in the business cycle—if the stated theory on sunspots' effects were true. Other (more realistic) examples of external causes fall into the categories of innovations and political events.

Innovations. Some economists have attributed the development of certain innovations as a principal cause of fluctuations in the economy. The shift from hand labor to machine labor in the textile industry, a process that opened the Industrial Revolution in England, is a case in point. Similarly, the introduction of the "horseless carriage" (the automobile) in the early 1900s and the computer in the 1950s both set off a series of events that changed the direction of the U.S. economy.

Because innovations involve new ways of doing things, the theory goes, they require investments to pay for new capital (plant and equipment). These new investments put additional income into the hands of businesses and their employees. This income leads to additional business and consumer spending, which, in turn, stimulates expansion and prosperity. In time, the expansion fostered by the innovations comes to an end, leading to a leveling off of business activity, a contraction in consumer spending, and (possibly) a recession.

Political Events. Major political events, such as a war or an economic boycott, can so affect a nation's economy as to reverse its course. Perhaps the most dramatic case in recent years was the successful effort by the Organization of Petroleum Exporting Countries (OPEC) to increase the price of crude oil. Within a few years starting in 1973, OPEC pushed the price of oil up from $2 to more than $20 a barrel by enacting an *embargo* (prohibition) on oil shipments to the United States. The immediate effect of this 1,000-percent price increase was to pay foreign oil suppliers billions of dollars that would otherwise have been in the hands of U.S. companies. With so much less business- and consumer-spending power available, the sales of goods and services in this country declined sharply. This decline in sales, in turn, led to the nation's most serious recession since the 1930s.

The Great Depression

Values have shrunk to fantastic levels; taxes have risen; our ability to pay has fallen; government of all kinds is faced by serious curtailment of income; the means of exchange are frozen in the currents of trade; the withered leaves of industrial enterprise lie on every side; farmers find no markets for their produce; the savings of many years in thousands of families are gone. More important, a host of unemployed citizens face the grim problem of existence and an equally great number toil with little return. Only a foolish optimist can deny the dark realities of the moment.

These words, which described the worst economic crisis ever faced by the United States, were spoken by President Franklin D. Roosevelt during his Inaugural Address in March 1933. He hardly exaggerated. With 13 million workers unemployed (representing one out of every four persons in the labor force), with 4,000 banks failing, with other business failures at an all-time high, and with production at its lowest point since 1900, times were hard indeed.

The Great Depression of 1929–1939 profoundly disturbed economists. Some explanation had to be found for those awful years. True, swings from good to bad times were nothing new. You may have heard about Joseph's Egypt and the seven fat and seven lean years. Those economic fluctuations, though, were brought about by obvious physical causes, such as droughts and plagues. No such cause could be identified for America's miseries in the 1930s. Although the production of goods and services had fallen by one-third from 1929 to 1933, the nation's capacity to produce was at an all-time high. Why then should a nation rich in resources and technology be so stricken? What remedial measures could be taken to restore the prosperity of the 1920s? What could be done to prevent the recurrence of such a depression?

In seeking the answers to these questions, economists tried to develop a better understanding of economic forces and their impact upon human well-being. Several theories as to the causes of economic fluctuations were formulated, along with the steps that might be taken to keep them under control. The quest for answers to those questions did much to shape current thinking about: (1) macroeconomic problems (economic problems that affect the economy as a whole), and (2) what government could, and should do, to solve them.

Because of a gas shortage caused by OPEC's oil embargo, drivers had to wait in long lines to fill their vehicles with gasoline.

Internal Causes

Internal causes of fluctuation in business cycles relate to factors within the economy that are likely to trigger either an expansion or a contraction of business activity. Some of the more widely held theories on internal causes are described below.

Psychological Factors. If businesspeople believe that conditions are going to improve, these beliefs will lead to a series of events that will make the prophecy come true. For example, if in the expectation of increased sales most firms increase their investment in new plant, equipment, and merchandise, their actions will add to employment and personal income. With more to spend, consumers will, in fact, spend more, thereby stimulating additional business investment and personal income. Thus, as the economy expands, businesspeople will enjoy the fulfillment of their prophecy.

If, on the contrary, businesspeople believe the future to be bleak, firms are likely to reduce production and lay off workers. This belief too could become a self-fulfilling prophecy. For with reduced employment, consumer spending will decline and businesses will continue to contract.

Psychological theory can also be applied to the behavior patterns of consumers. When they believe that hard times are approaching, consumers are likely to postpone major purchases and spend less money. The business community will then have to reduce the level of its operations. As unemployment increases and personal income declines, the recession will gain momentum. Consumers will witness the fulfillment of their prophecy. Consumer optimism, in contrast, will have the opposite effect. Increased spending will trigger increased business activity, employment, and earnings, and the business cycle will swing into its recovery phase.

Underconsumption. A situation in which consumer expenditures lag behind output can be classified as *underconsumption*. According to the theory of underconsumption, recessions result when consumer expenditures fall behind the production of goods and services. As unsold inventories increase, business firms reduce their output and lay off workers. With unemployment on the rise, consumption (consumer spending) declines still further, more workers lose their jobs, and the recession deepens.

MEASURING THE NATION'S ECONOMIC PERFORMANCE

Good motorists know that they need to look from time to time at their vehicle's dashboard gauges. By monitoring speed, fuel supply, and engine performance, motorists can often prevent trouble before it occurs. Just as motorists keep an eye on their dashboard instruments, so do economists and others monitor the nation's economic performance.

Although there is no such thing as an "economic dashboard," there are certain widely published statistics that inform us about the state of the economy. Best known and most widely published of these, of course, is the gross domestic product (first discussed in Chapter 2). In addition to the GDP, there are dozens of other *economic indicators* (sets of data about the performance of a segment of the economy) that economists rely upon to help them monitor the business cycle.

Economic Indicators

As a matter of convenience, economists place economic indicators into three categories: (1) leading, (2) coincident, and (3) lagging indicators.

Leading Indicators. These economic indicators move ahead of the economy. One sees *leading economic indicators* going up and down some time before one sees the peaks and troughs of the business cycle. Economists have discovered that soon after an increase in the construction of new homes, the entire economy seems to improve. Similarly, an increase in employment in manufacturing is likely to be followed by an upturn in business in general. By contrast, a decline in new housing or

Figure 17.3   Where Are We Going From Here?

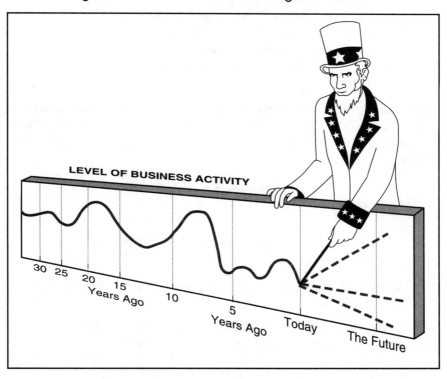

LEVEL OF BUSINESS ACTIVITY

30 25 20 15 10
Years Ago

5
Years Ago   Today   The Future

manufacturing is often a sign that the economy as a whole will soon decline. Indexes of building permits, factory employment, and new orders for manufacturing of consumer goods are some of the more closely followed leading indicators.

Coincident Indicators. These indicators move up and down along with the economy. *Coincident economic indicators* let one know where the economy is in the business cycle. The *industrial production index* (which measures changes in output in the nation's factories, mines, and utilities) is a closely followed coincident indicator. So, too, are employee payrolls, GDP, and personal income. Personal income is discussed on page 408.

Lagging Indicators. Measurements that seem to move behind general economic trends are *lagging indicators*. They reach their highs and lows later than the business cycle. So, for example, an increase in the unemployment rate tends to follow the beginning of a recession. The unemployment rate will not decline until the recovery is well under way.

The Gross Domestic Product

As we learned in Chapter 2 and later chapters, the Gross Domestic Product (GDP) is the value of all the goods and services produced in the United States in a single year. Statisticians have two ways to tally the Gross Domestic Product: (1) the expenditures approach, and (2) the income approach.

GDP: The Expenditures Approach. The total output of goods and services (GDP) is purchased by consumers, business, and government, and by international buyers of U.S. goods and services. Economists often state this mathematically as

$$C + I + G + X = \text{GDP}$$

where C = consumption
I = investment
G = government expenditures
X = net exports

This way of calculating GDP is called the *expenditure approach*, which is illustrated in Table 17.1.

Personal Consumption Expenditures. This category is made up of all consumer spending. Personal consumer expenditures include *durable goods* (long-lasting items, such as automobiles, refrigerators, and furniture), *nondurable goods* (quickly consumed items, such as food, clothing, gasoline, and medicine), and services (such as medical care and recreation). Consumer expenditures typically account for about two-thirds of the GDP. (In 1995, personal consumption expenditures of $4,923.4 billion divided by a GDP of $7,247.7 billion equaled 67.9 percent.)

Gross Private Domestic Investment. The statistic *gross private domestic investment* constitutes the sum of spending by businesses for new equipment, construction, and changes in business inventories of raw materials, partially finished goods, and finished goods. Gross private domestic investment amounted to $1,067.5 billion in 1995.

Table 17.1   PURCHASERS OF THE GDP, 1995 (IN BILLIONS)

Personal Consumption Expenditures		$4,923.4
Gross Private Domestic Investment		1,067.5
Government Purchases		1,358.5
Exports	$804.5	
Imports	906.2	
Net Exports		−101.7
Gross Domestic Product		$7,247.7

Government Purchases of Goods and Services. In 1995, government purchases accounted for less than 20 percent of the GDP ($1,358.5 ÷ $7,247.7 = 18.7 percent). Government purchases include spending by all levels of government—federal, state, and local—for such things as national defense, income security, interest on debt, health care, highway construction, and much more. (The importance of government spending is discussed in Chapter 11.)

Net Exports of Goods and Services. We have learned that GDP measures U.S. production of goods and services. But not all the goods and services purchased by consumers, business, and government are produced in the United States. Nor, for that matter, are all the purchasers of U.S. goods and services living in the United States. *Imports* represent U.S. purchases of foreign goods and services, while *exports* represent the sale of U.S. products and services to foreigners. The difference between those two items is carried as *net exports*. Net exports is included (along with consumption, investment, and government purchases) in the final GDP tally. (If imports are greater than exports for a year, then the number appears as a negative one.) In recent years, imports have been greater than exports. This was the case in 1995 when exports totaled $804.5 billion, while imports amounted to $906.2 billion. The difference (-$101.7 billion) was included as net exports in the GDP of that year.

GDP: The Income Approach. We have just calculated the GDP by tallying the money spent by consumers, business, and government for the goods and services produced in the United States in a given year. We called this method the "expenditures approach." There is another way to calculate GDP, however—the *income approach.* In using this method, we identify the recipients of those expenditures and then tally all these receipts to find the GDP. In other words:

EXPENDITURES	=	GDP	=	INCOME
(total spent on year's output)		(total market value of goods and services)		(total income received by those in the production process)

Table 17.2 summarizes the amounts received as income by the recipients of the GDP in a recent year.

Compensation of Employees. Most of the income flow goes to employees in the form of wages, salaries, and other benefits (health insurance, retirement plan, etc.). In 1995, employee compensation totaled over $4 trillion.

Table 17.2 GROSS DOMESTIC PRODUCT, 1995 INCOME FLOWS (IN BILLIONS)

Compensation of employees	$4,209.4
Proprietors' income	477.9
Corporate profits	615.2
Rental income	122.2
Net interest	401.3
Capital consumption	825.8
Indirect taxes	695.9
Gross Domestic Product	$7,247.7

Proprietors' Income. This figure is the profits earned by owners of the nation's unincorporated businesses. In 1995, proprietors' income totaled $477.9 billion.

Corporate Profits. This figure shows what corporations earn in a year. For 1995, corporate profits came to $615.2 billion.

Rental Income. This category includes payments to landlords for the use of property, *royalty payments* to individuals (such as inventors and songwriters) for the use of their creative works, and payments to corporate holders of patents and copyrights. Rental income added some $122 billion to the GDP in 1995.

Net Interest. Most businesses borrow money, and some lend money also. The term *net interest* represents the difference between the total interest received and that paid out by the business sector in a given year. In 1995, net interest was about $400 billion.

Capital Consumption. This category, also called "depreciation," represents sums that businesses have to set aside to replace plant and equipment worn out in the course of producing the GDP. Depreciation is largely a bookkeeping entry and does not actually represent a current income flow. Funds set aside for depreciation will enter the flow of income as they are spent for new investment. In 1995, capital consumption was some $825 billion.

Indirect Taxes. The sales and excise taxes that we pay for our purchases are not kept by the businesses collecting them. Instead, they are passed on to the federal, state, and local governments. In 1995, indirect taxes totaled $695.9 billion.

Measuring GDP Can Be a Difficult Chore. The Gross Domestic Product is the primary measure of U.S. production. In using GDP, economists have to (1) find a way to tally the millions of goods and services going into the GDP without counting the same item more than once, and (2) make it possible to compare GDP from one year to the next without having to worry about fluctuating dollar values. The answers to these two problems are found in the concepts of *final goods* and constant dollars.

Why Only Final Goods Are Included in the GDP. In order to avoid counting the same product more than once, only the final price of an item is included in the GDP. See the example below.

Last year, the Warm Sweater Company spent an average of $7 in materials and labor to produce each sweater. The company sold its sweaters to wholesalers for $10 each. Retail stores paid $14 apiece for the sweaters, which they sold to consumers for $20. How much did Warm Sweater add to the GDP for every sweater they produced last year?

If your answer is $20, you are correct.

In the example above, the $7 paid by the manufacturer, the $10 paid by the wholesaler, and the $14 paid by the retailer are all included in the price paid by consumers. Therefore, only the final price—$20—is added into the GDP.

Used goods are also not included in calculating the GDP. Suppose, for example, that after a month or so you decided that you no longer liked your Warm Sweater and sold it to a friend for $10. That sum would not be added to the GDP because, like other used goods, it adds nothing to the nation's wealth.

Why are sales of used books not included in the GDP?

John Maynard Keynes

The ideas of economists and political philosophers are more powerful than is commonly understood. Indeed, the world is ruled by little else. Practical men, who believe themselves to be quite exempt from any intellectual influences, are usually the slaves of some defunct economist.

In these words from the final pages of his most famous work, *The General Theory of Employment, Interest, and Money,* **John Maynard Keynes** (pronounced Kay-NZ) correctly anticipated the impact of his own writings on later generations. Keynes' *General Theory* now stands with Smith's *Wealth of Nations* and Marx's *Kapital* as one of the most influential statements of economic philosophy in the modern age.

Keynes was born into academic surroundings in Cambridge, England. His father was an economist at Cambridge University, and his mother was one of its first women graduates. At Cambridge, Keynes was considered Alfred Marshall's most brilliant student. (See page 69 for a discussion of Marshall.) After graduation and a brief stint with the British civil service, Keynes joined the Cambridge faculty.

He left the university in 1915 to undertake a successful career in the British Treasury. In 1919, Keynes attended the Versailles Peace Conference that followed World War I. His dismay with the direction in which those talks were taking led him to resign his post in protest. Keynes warned that the reparations the Allies were imposing on Germany would bankrupt the country and force it to take up arms again. As the chief British representative to the Bretton Woods Conference following World War II, Keynes helped shape the course of international trade for decades.

His *General Theory,* published in 1936 during the Great Depression, heralded what has come to be known as the "Keynesian Revolution." Prior to the appearance of the *General Theory,* most economists held that, left to its own devices, the economy would achieve equilibrium (a state of balance) at full employment. This theory was in accord with the ideas of French economist **Jean Baptiste Say** (1767–1832), who had suggested that supply creates its own demand, that is, whatever the economy produced would be purchased. Moreover, prices would seek whatever level was necessary to bring about this supply-demand relationship and full employment. If there was unemployment at any point in time, it existed only because wages were too high. In such circumstances, market forces could be expected to drive wages down to whatever level was necessary to enable employers to hire all those willing and able to work. Naturally, it followed from Jean Baptiste Say's reasoning that the worst thing a government could do would be to interfere with the economy, for to do so would prevent market forces from restoring a full-employment equilibrium.

In the 1930s, however, many people concluded that Say's theory simply did not work. Millions of workers then were unable to find jobs, while factories lay idle for want of orders. Similarly, farm products rotted unsold in the midst of worldwide hunger. Keynes pointed out that the economy had indeed reached equilibrium, but it had done so at a point well below full employment. There simply was no self-correcting mechanism that would, in the short run, put people back to work.

"Perhaps not," said many economists. "But in the long run, the system will come into balance and unemployment will disappear."

"In the long run," Keynes replied, "we are all dead."

The key ingredient in Keynes' analysis was "aggregate demand," the collective spending by all elements of the economy. (This term is introduced in Chapter 13.) There is, he argued, a level at which aggregate demand will support full employment. Anything below that level would simply result in less than full-employment equilibrium. At levels higher than full employment, there would be inflation.

The challenge, then, in times of unemployment and idle capacity was to find ways to increase aggregate demand. Keynes' solution called upon governments to "prime the pump" of consumer spending and business investment through certain taxing and spending policies.

This program was a revolutionary break with the *laissez-faire* thinking of the time, which vigorously opposed government intervention in economic affairs. Indeed, Keynes ignited a controversy that continues to this day between those who favor government participation and those who oppose it.

One of those influenced by Keynes' ideas was President Franklin D. Roosevelt. His New Deal program marshaled the resources of the United States economy in an unprecedented effort to fight the Great Depression. Following World War II, the Employment Act of 1946 made the participation of government in efforts to stabilize the economy part of the overall economic policy of the United States.

Constant Dollars: Correcting for Changes in the Price Level. In Chapter 13, we discussed how the value of the dollar (in terms of what it can buy) is subject to change. A dollar may not buy as much in one year as it did in the previous year. For that reason, comparisons of the GDP from one year to the next can be misleading. For example, let us suppose that in two successive years, the nation's output of goods and services were identical. The number of autos, electric trains, haircuts, and everything else that goes into the GDP remained exactly the same. Suppose, too, that during the second year, prices had risen by 10 percent. GDP the first year was $4 trillion. Since output the second year was identical to the first, the 10 percent increase in prices pushed the GDP up to $4.4 trillion, or an additional $400 billion. This increase occurred despite the fact that production had not increased at all.

While current dollars state actual prices of each year, constant dollars express the value of dollars in terms of their purchasing power of an earlier base year (presently 1987). We can illustrate this concept with the following example:

In 1987, Product X sold for $100. Over the next five years, prices increased by 20 percent. The selling price of Product X in 1992 was $120 in current dollars. In constant dollars its selling price was $100. Why $100? Because 1987 was the base year and Product X sold for $100 in 1987.

The GDP in current and constant dollars for a number of years are summarized in Table 17.3.

Per Capita GDP and Its Uses. *GDP per capita* is often used to compare productive output and living standards of two or more nations. (*Per capita* means *per person*.) Other things being equal, the nation with the

Table 17.3   GROSS DOMESTIC PRODUCT FOR SELECTED YEARS, 1959–1994

Year	Current Dollars (billions)	Constant Dollars (billions, 1987 dollars)
1959	$ 494.2	$1,928.8
1966	769.8	2,616.2
1973	1,349.6	3,268.6
1980	2,708.0	3,776.3
1987	4,539.9	4,539.9
1989	5,250.8	4,838.0
1992	5,950.7	4,922.6
1994	6,737.4	5,342.3

Can you explain why 1987 is the only year shown in which GDP in current and constant dollars are identical?

greater GDP per capita will have more goods and services available for its citizens. Per capita GDP is found by dividing a nation's GDP by its population.

Limitations of the GDP. Although the GDP is the most talked-about measure of a nation's economic activity, it has its limitations. Two of the most serious defects of the GDP are its failure to include transactions that take place outside the market economy and its inability to measure the economic well-being of the nation in qualitative terms.

1. Failure to Include "Nonmarket" Economic Activities. While the GDP is supposed to represent the total value of all goods and services produced by the economy, a large chunk is not included. For example, homemakers who spend their days caring for children, cleaning their home, and cooking for their family are performing services whose value is not included in the GDP. Meanwhile, the services of paid housekeepers, cooks, cleaning service workers, and other household help are included in the GDP. Similarly, the earnings of gardeners are included in the GDP, whereas the value of the labor performed by those who take care of their own gardens and lawns is not.

In addition, there is an entire category of illegal and unrecorded economic activity that is not included in the GDP. Known as the "underground economy" (discussed in Chapter 12), these transactions include activities like narcotics sales and illegal gambling, as well as purchases, sales, and employment that people fail to report to the government.

2. Failure to Measure Economic Well-Being. Although the GDP tells us whether total output is increasing or decreasing, it does not tell us anything about the quality of that output. So, for example, $1 billion worth of cigarettes and $1 billion worth of grain receive equal value in the GDP totals, even though the former product may be harmful to people's health.

Table 17.4   GROSS DOMESTIC PRODUCT OF SELECTED COUNTRIES, 1995

	Total GDP (millions)	*Per Capita GDP*
Japan	$4,963,587	$39,640
United States	7,100,007	26,980
Sweden	209,720	23,750
France	1,451,051	24,990
Spain	532,347	13,580
Greece	85,885	8,210
India	319,660	340
Rwanda	1,128	180

Why is Japan listed above the United States in this table?

Table 17.5 NATIONAL INCOME, 1995 (IN BILLIONS)

Compensation of employees	$4,209.4
Proprietors' income	477.9
Corporate profits	615.2
Rental income	122.2
Net interest	401.3
National Income	$5,826.0

Similarly, the production of things that we all want often leads to the production of harmful byproducts that we do not want (such as pollution). In these circumstances, GDP will count the "good things" but it will not include the bad ones. When increased factory output leads to a greater quantity of goods and services, these totals are included in the GDP. If, however, the output creates a greater amount of environmental pollution, the cost of that pollution is not reflected in the GDP.

Other National Income Accounts. Three other measures of income often reported on by the news media are: national income, personal income, and disposable personal income.

National Income. You might recall from Chapter 10 that earnings come in a variety of forms. Employees earn salaries and wages, property owners earn rent, corporations earn profits, and many people earn returns in other forms, such as interest and dividends. The sum total of all these earnings are included in that part of the Gross Domestic Product known as the *national income.* In 1995, national income came to $5,826 billion.

Personal Income. The total of income received by individuals and families before they pay their income taxes is personal income. In addition to wages, dividends, interest, and rent, some people received *transfer payments.* These are government payments to individuals in exchange for which no goods or services were produced. Social Security benefits and unemployment compensation are examples of transfer payments. Table 17.6 lists sources of personal income.

Disposable Personal Income. Individuals' income remaining after personal income taxes have been paid is called *disposable personal income.* In 1995, people in the United States paid $794.6 billion in income taxes. They were left with a total of $5,306.4 billion in disposable personal income ($6,101.0 − $794.6 = $5,306.4).

Table 17.6   PERSONAL INCOME, 1995
(IN BILLIONS)

Wages and salaries	$3,419.7
Other labor income	404.9
Proprietors' income	477.9
Rental income	122.2
Personal dividend income	214.8
Personal interest income	714.4
Transfer payments	<u>1,022.6</u>
Personal Income	$6,101.0

AGGREGATE DEMAND, FULL EMPLOYMENT, AND THE PRICE LEVEL

The nation's total output of goods and services—its gross domestic product (GDP)—is purchased by three principal groups: consumers, producers, and government. (For purposes of this discussion, we have included net exports with business spending.) As we discussed earlier, economists refer to the total sum as "aggregate demand." In this chapter, *full employment* refers to the total amount of goods and services that the economy could produce if its resources were fully employed. The level of aggregate demand as compared to that of full employment goes a long way toward explaining why the economy is undergoing a period of recession, expansion, or inflation.

For example, during periods of recession, aggregate demand declines so that the spread between it and full employment increases. As factories, stores, and offices close, workers are laid off and total income falls.

The reverse happens during periods of recovery. At these times, consumer, business, and government demand is greater than current production levels. Producers expand their activities, leading to more employment, increased purchases of raw materials, and expanded production facilities.

As aggregate demand increases, it may exceed the capacity of the economy to satisfy it. If the nation's factories, shops, and workers are fully employed, increased spending would not add to employment or production. With "too much money chasing too few goods," prices would probably increase. Conversely, a reduction of aggregate demand in those circumstances is likely to lead to lower prices rather than to a reduced output of goods and services.

In its efforts to stabilize the economy and promote its growth, the federal government will seek to adjust aggregate demand at levels sufficient to keep the economy fully employed without promoting

Aggregate Demand and Full Employment

Figure 17.4 illustrates the economic importance of aggregate demand and its relationship to full employment. In this hypothetical illustration, we have assumed that with its resources fully employed the economy will be able to produce $7 trillion worth of goods and services at current prices.

In Case I, aggregate demand stands at $6 trillion. This level will leave the nation with unused capacity in the form of idle plants, shops, and, of course, workers. Economists refer to the $1 trillion spread between the actual GDP and its potential as the *recessionary gap*. How would you describe economic conditions at this time?

In Case II, aggregate demand exactly equals the economy's ability to produce at full employment. How would you describe economic conditions at this time?

In Case III, aggregate demand is running at $8 trillion. This level is 25 percent greater than the economy's ability to produce at full employment. Economists refer to the $1 trillion spread as the *inflationary gap*. How would you describe economic conditions in these circumstances?

Figure 17.4   Aggregate Demand and Its Significance

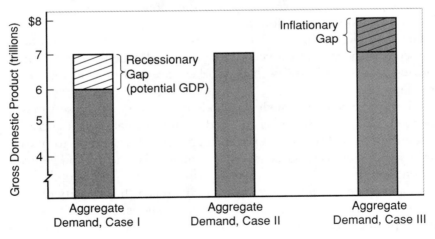

inflation. Toward that end, economists have spent a great deal of time studying the gross domestic product and its components in an effort to discover ways in which to turn the government's dream into a reality. As recent history has shown, much remains to be done before that goal can be achieved. Nevertheless, a number of significant discoveries have been made.

ECONOMIC FLUCTUATIONS MAY BE CUMULATIVE

Frequently, economic fluctuations feed upon themselves: Expansion creates further expansion, and recession begets more recession. One explanation for these effects can be found in the multiplier.

The Multiplier

Two weeks ago Friday was your lucky day. You received a birthday gift of $1,000 from rich Uncle Louis. You had no difficulty deciding what to do with the money. You put $200 in the bank and spent the remaining $800 on the video recording and playback equipment you had wanted for a long time. WAM Electronics, from which you bought the equipment, used $640 of your money to have its store painted, and banked the rest. Meanwhile, painter Paul Carmino used $512 of the $640 he received for his work to pay for a week's vacation at the shore. The remaining $128 went into Paul's money market fund.

Let us freeze the action right here because something interesting has been happening. Uncle Louis's $1,000 gift has already led to total spending of $1,952 (because $800 + $640 + $512 = $1,952). Moreover, let us assume that as the process of spending and saving goes on, people will continue to spend 80 percent of their additional income. If this happens, another $3,048 in income will be generated. This will bring the total amount of spending begun by Uncle Louis's $1,000 to $5,000. Economists refer to the increased national income generated by additional spending as the *multiplier effect*, or simply, the *multiplier*. Since in this instance total spending was increased to $5,000, the multiplier will be said to have been 5. ($1,000 × 5 = $5,000.)

The size of the multiplier depends upon the public's inclination to spend. If, on the average, people spend 75 percent of any additional income that comes their way, the multiplier would be higher than it would be if their inclination to spend or, as the economists put it, their *marginal propensity to consume* were only 50 percent.

Suppose, for example, that a state government plans to build a new length of highway at a cost of $1 million. As the work progresses, the sum will be disbursed to workers, suppliers, contractors, and others. Let us also suppose that during the course of construction the marginal propensity to consume is 50 percent. Accordingly, the recipients of the $1 million in construction funds will spend $500,000 of that amount and save the rest. Those receiving the $500,000 will then spend half that amount, as will those receiving the $250,000, and so on down the line until there is nothing additional remaining to be spent. By that time, some $2 million will have changed hands. Since the $2 million is twice the original $1 million, the multiplier is 2.

Had buyers been willing to spend three-quarters of their additional income, the multiplier would have been 4, and the $1 million that went into building the highway would have added $4 million to national income.

The multiplier also works in reverse. A decrease in spending will reduce total income by a multiple of the amount of the reduction. Thus, if total spending were to decrease by $50 billion when the multiplier was 3.5, national income would decline by $175 billion.

Aggregate Demand and the Government

While the amount spent by consumers and business is the result of millions of private decisions, government spending can be planned and controlled in such a way as to benefit society as a whole. For example, when the economy is functioning at less than full employment, the government can increase its spending in order to increase aggregate demand. Similarly, the government can deliberately curtail the level of its spending to reduce aggregate demand during a period of inflation. In either case, the government's efforts will be aided by the multiplier, which will magnify the impact of the increase or decrease in spending.

The government can also affect aggregate demand through its power to tax. Tax increases reduce the ability of consumers and business to spend, while tax cuts have the opposite effect. In Chapter 19, we will take a closer look at these and other techniques available as part of the U.S. government's efforts to regulate the economy.

The Paradox of Thrift

"A penny saved is a penny earned." —*Benjamin Franklin*

A paradox *is a statement that is seemingly contradictory or opposed to common sense and yet is perhaps true.* **—Webster's Collegiate**

We have mentioned that when the economy is producing at a level below its capacity, any increase in spending will result in a still greater increase in output. But suppose that, instead of increasing its spending, society as a whole were to apply Benjamin Franklin's advice and increase its savings. Since more savings would reduce total spending, the multiplier would serve to decrease production by an even greater amount. This sequence would add to unemployment, reduce earnings, and compel some people to dip into their savings in order to survive. In other words, by increasing its savings, society as a whole would have less to save. But, as everyone knows, an increase in savings is frequently a desirable course for individual families to follow. Were society as a whole to do the same, however, it would reduce the amount available for savings. This concept, which defies the common-sense proposition that saving is a worthy activity for every individual, is described by economists as the *paradox of thrift.*

The Multiplier and the Accelerator

When the economy is operating at something less than full employment, small changes in spending by consumers (consumption) or business (investment) lead to much larger changes in production and employment. The multiplier and the accelerator effect (or more simply, the accelerator) help us to understand why this is so.

As people earn additional income, they can do one of two things with their earnings: spend it or save it. We have seen that the marginal propensity to consume (MPC) describes the public's inclination to spend. Economists express the MPC as a fraction of an additional dollar of income that people would spend on additional goods and services. Thus, a marginal propensity to consume of .8 would indicate that $100 of additional income would increase spending by $80. The balance of $20 (or .2) would go into savings.

Economists describe the public's willingness to save as the *marginal propensity to save (MPS)*. Since income not spent is considered to be savings, it follows that MPC + MPS = 1, or 1 − MPC = MPS.

Lola Montes has been promised a $2,000 raise in her yearly salary. She will spend $1,800 of that amount on her wardrobe and put the rest into a bank. Since $1,800 is 90 percent of $2,000, we see that Lola's MPC is .9 and that her MPS is .1. (Remember that MPC plus MPS equals 1.)

The Multiplier

The multiplier is expressed mathematically as the *reciprocal* (reverse the numerator and the denominator of a fraction) of 1 minus the marginal propensity to consume:

$$\text{multiplier} = \text{reciprocal of } \frac{1-\text{MPC}}{1} = \frac{1}{1-\text{MPC}}$$

But since 1 − MPC = MPS, the multiplier can be expressed as $\frac{1}{\text{MPS}}$.

Thus, if the marginal propensity to consume were 90 percent, the multiplier would be 10 because:

MPC = .90; MPS = 1 − .90 = .10; the reciprocal of $\frac{1}{.10} = 10$.

If, however, people were spending less so that the MPC were 80 percent, the multiplier would be 5 because: MPC = .80; MPS = (1 −.80) = .20; and the reciprocal of 1 divided by .20 = 5.

The Acceleration Principle

The *acceleration principle* states that small changes in the demand for consumer goods generate a much greater change in the demand for investment goods (and inventory) needed for the production of these goods. If the demand for consumer goods increases, there is a much greater demand for investment goods. And if the demand for consumer goods decreases (or remains the same), there is a much greater decrease in the demand for capital goods.

The *accelerator* describes the effect of changes in spending upon business investment (the purchase of new plant and equipment). Consumer demand has a great impact on this investment in capital goods. As consumer demand increases, a point will be reached when business firms will need to purchase additional equipment, build new plants, or add to their existing facilities in order to increase output. The significance of the acceleration principle is that it explains why changes in consumption lead to proportionately greater changes in investment. Table 17.7 demonstrates this effect by examining the impact of changes in lawn mower sales on the industry that makes engine blocks for power lawn mowers.

In our example, each lawn mower is fitted with one engine block. Let us assume that 100 milling machines are needed to manufacture 100,000 lawn mower engine blocks and that 10 milling machines wear out each year and must be replaced.

According to the table, 100,000 mowers were sold in 1991 and 1992. The engine blocks for these mowers were manufactured with the help of 100 milling machines, but 10 of these milling machines had to be replaced each year. Therefore, as indicated in the table, there was no increase in the number of milling machines in either 1991 or 1992 from the previous year even though 10 replacements were purchased in each of these two years. What happens in 1993 when lawn mower sales increase to 110,000 units? The engine-block milling-machine industry needs 110 machines to produce 110,000 engine blocks. The industry must purchase 20 additional machines in 1993 to meet the demand for 10,000 more engine blocks. Why is this true? Because 10 milling machines are needed as replacements plus 10 additional milling machines are needed to produce 10,000 additional engine blocks.

How does the increased demand for lawn mowers in 1994 and 1995 impact on the milling-machine industry? In 1994, 120 milling machines

Table 17.7   IMPACT OF LAWN MOWER SALES UPON THE ENGINE-BLOCK MILLING-MACHINE INDUSTRY, 1991–1995 (HYPOTHETICAL)

Year	Mowers Sold (Consumption)	Milling Machines Required	Additional Machines Purchased	Percent Change From Previous Year
1991	100,000	100	10 (replacements)	0
1992	100,000	100	10 (replacements)	0
1993	110,000	110	20 (10 replacements + 10 additional)	+100
1994	120,000	120	20 (10 replacements + 10 additional)	0
1995	120,000	120	10 (replacements)	−50

were needed to produce 120,000 engine blocks. The industry already had 110 milling machines. Therefore, 20 additional milling machines (10 for the added production and 10 as replacements) were needed. But 20 milling machines were all that were needed in 1993. Thus, the number of milling machines purchased in 1994 is the same as in 1993.

In 1995, the demand for lawn mowers is 120,000, the same as it was the previous year. How many additional milling machines were needed to meet this demand? Only the number of machines needed to replace the worn out milling machines (10 in our illustration). As a result, the production of milling machines in 1995 declined by 50 percent from 20 in 1994 to 10 in 1995 (20 − 10 = 10; 10 ÷ 20 = 50 percent). In our illustration, even though consumer demand remained unchanged, the impact on a capital goods industry was quite severe. Capital-goods industries (such as the milling-machine plant in our example) need an ever increasing demand for consumer goods just to remain stable. But like everything else, consumer demand will fluctuate. When it does, it will trigger still wider swings in capital-goods industries.

Interaction of the Multiplier and the Accelerator

Just as two or more members of the same family can pass a cold back and forth in a cycle of illness, so can the multiplier and the accelerator feed upon each other. Thus, a recession will be aggravated, and economic expansion will be promoted.

As a result of the multiplier effect, a small increase in spending will increase total income by a greater amount. This effect will generate an even greater increase in investment as producers respond to increased consumer demand. The investment increase generated by the accelerator will lead to another round of additions to income, spending, and multiplier effects, and the economy will continue to climb toward prosperity, full employment, and (if the trend should continue) inflation.

On the downside, a leveling off of consumer demand will result in a still greater decline in the capital-goods industries. The reduction in investment and the decline in income that result will lead to a reduction in consumer spending. National income will be reduced by a multiple of the initial reduction in spending, and the recession will pick up momentum.

Summary

Aided by the multiplier and the accelerator, the business cycle feeds upon itself. As consumer demand declines, business cuts back on production and reduces its labor force. The resulting worker layoffs reduce consumer demand still further, and the recessionary process worsens. At its extreme, uninterrupted recession has led to widespread unemployment, poverty, and depression. On the recovery side, business expansion increases earnings. This, in turn, fuels demand and price increases, which can lead to inflation.

The economic behavior of consumers and business firms feed the ups and downs of the business cycle. Government, though, has the ability to moderate those swings. It does this through the application of its monetary and fiscal powers. Monetary powers relate to government's ability to regulate the money supply. Fiscal powers come from its ability to tax and spend. In the chapters that follow, we will describe how the federal government uses its monetary and fiscal powers to regulate the economy for the common good.

REVIEWING THE CHAPTER

Understanding **What You Have Read**

Questions 1–3 are based upon Figure 17.5.

Figure 17.5

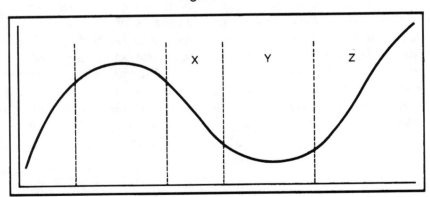

1. Phase X represents the (*a*) peak (*b*) trough (*c*) recovery (*d*) recession.
2. Phase Y represents the (*a*) peak (*b*) trough (*c*) recovery (*d*) recession.

3. Phase Z represents the (*a*) peak (*b*) trough (*c*) recovery (*d*) recession.

4. Which of the following groups accounts for almost all purchases of the nation's total output? (*a*) government, business, and farmers (*b*) business, consumers, and government (*c*) households, consumers, and business (*d*) government, consumers, and foreign buyers.

5. When is the economy most likely to operate at less than full employment? (*a*) during periods of inflation (*b*) when there are shortages of unskilled labor (*c*) when total spending is falling (*d*) when consumer spending is increasing.

6. One way to avoid counting an item in the GDP more than once is to (*a*) count only the wholesale cost of the item (*b*) include only the final retail price of the item (*c*) deduct the capital consumption allowance (*d*) count each resale only once as the item passes from producer to retailer.

7. According to the *General Theory* of John Maynard Keynes, (*a*) left to its own devices, an economy would achieve equilibrium at full employment (*b*) unemployment exists only because wages are too high (*c*) the worst thing that government can do would be to interfere with the economy (*d*) in times of unemployment and idle capacity, government should "prime the pump."

8. Economists refer to the sum total of consumption, investment, and government spending as (*a*) the multiplier (*b*) the acceleration principle (*c*) the sunspot theory (*d*) aggregate demand.

9. If aggregate demand declines as compared to the productive capacity of the economy as a whole, which of the following events is likely to occur? (*a*) Employment will increase. (*b*) The growth rate will decline. (*c*) Prices will rise. (*d*) Tax receipts will increase.

10. As a stabilizing influence, the most important component of the GDP is government spending because it (*a*) is the largest component (*b*) fluctuates the least (*c*) is the only component that can be deliberately adjusted in the public interest (*d*) is the smallest component of the GDP.

11. Changes in the level of spending by any sector of the economy (consumers, business, or government) will be magnified in their effect upon the total economy. One explanation for this is contained in (*a*) the law of diminishing returns (*b*) Engel's Law (*c*) the theory of the multiplier (*d*) the innovation theory.

12. The size of the multiplier is directly affected by (*a*) government spending (*b*) business spending (*c*) business inventory (*d*) the marginal propensity to consume.

Building Vocabulary

Match each item in Column A with its definition in Column B.

COLUMN A	COLUMN B
1. business cycle	*a.* the expansion phase of a business cycle
2. recessionary gap	*b.* a set of statistics about the performance of a sector of the nation's economy
3. trough	*c.* the effect of increased spending on national income
4. recovery	*d.* ups and downs in the level of a nation's economic activity
5. peak	
6. multiplier	*e.* the rate at which the public spends as national income goes up
7. accelerator	*f.* the lowest point in a business cycle
8. economic indicator	*g.* the rate at which the public saves as national income goes up
9. marginal propensity to consume	*h.* the upper turning point of a business cycle
10. marginal propensity to save	*i.* the effect of changes in consumer spending upon investment
	j. the amount by which aggregate demand falls short of the total needed to sustain full employment

Thinking Critically

1. In comparing the economies of two nations, economists frequently use per capita GDP figures. (*a*) Why is per capita GDP rather than total GDP used? (*b*) What other indicators are important in comparing economies?

2. In the midst of a deep recession, the president of the United States calls upon the nation's consumers to "spend their way" out of the slump. What does the president mean?

3. Assume that the nation has just reached the bottom of a long recession. Summarize the probable effect of the recession upon: (*a*) prices, (*b*) wages, (*c*) employment, (*d*) investment, and (*e*) profits.

4. In its efforts to stabilize the economy, the federal government frequently attempts to influence the level of aggregate demand.

    a. Explain how government may affect aggregate demand by reducing taxes.

    b. Explain how government may affect aggregate demand by reducing government spending.

    c. Prove that $\dfrac{1}{1-\text{MPC}} = \dfrac{1}{\text{MPS}}$

    d. Explain how the multiplier and the accelerator can magnify the impact of government efforts.

SKILLS: Analyzing a Line Graph and a Bar Graph

Answer the following questions based on your analysis of Figure 17.1 (page 393) and Figure 17.4 (page 410).

1. How would you describe the level(s) of economic activity in the United States in the period 1905 through 1995?

2. How would you describe the levels of economic activity during World War I, World War II, the Korean War, and the Vietnam War?

3. During periods of war, workers and industries are fully employed and consumer demand is strong. Which example in Figure 17.4 would correspond to these periods of war—Case I, Case II, or Case III? Explain your answer.

4. Why is there a recessionary gap in Case I, Figure 17.4?

5. Which years in Figure 17.1 would correspond to Case I? Explain your answer.

Chapter 18

MANAGING THE NATION'S ECONOMY: MONETARY POLICY

Overview

Looking at the front page of your local newspaper, your eyes catch a small headline, "Fed Passes on Cutting Interest Rates." Reading a bit of the accompanying article, you wonder why the author says that stock and bond market analysts were "... anxiously waiting to see whether the Fed would cut rates to promote growth in the economy." The author points out that the discount rate (the rate the Federal Reserve Board offers banks for overnight loans from its own reserves) was raised in February 1995 to 5.25 percent because then the economy appeared to be growing too rapidly. Later in the article, you read that the discount rate had been only 4.0 percent in September 1994. Then in the winter of 1994–1995, the U.S. economy grew at a rate of 5.1 percent. Fearing inflation, the Fed policy makers continued to raise the federal funds rate (the rate for overnight loans that banks make among themselves) from 4.29 percent until it reached 6.0 percent. Increasing interest rates, the article's author said, would slow the economy, hopefully without pushing it into a recession.

As a result of the Fed's action in raising interest rates, the economy did slow down—to 2.7 percent in the first quarter of 1995. Now the fear was that the Fed might have gone too far. Therefore, it started to cut rates in July 1995.

Probably you are now a bit confused. How could an economy grow too rapidly? Did we not learn in other chapters that economic growth creates jobs and provides greater output for everyone? More to the point, what did the Fed have to do with economic growth, employment, and inflation? We will try to answer these questions in this chapter.

We begin with a discussion of the goals of U.S. economic policy. Next we discuss the problems of unemployment and inflation. Then we examine how the Federal Reserve System uses monetary powers in order to solve these economic problems. In the next chapter, we will discuss how the fiscal powers of government are used to manage the economy.

THE GOALS OF ECONOMIC POLICY

The **Employment Act of 1946** made the federal government responsible for maintaining economic stability. It charged the government with promoting ". . . maximum employment, production, and purchasing power." The act also created a **Council of Economic Advisers.** This three-member body studies economic conditions, recommends courses of action to the president, and submits a yearly report to Congress. In 1978, Congress enacted the **Humphrey-Hawkins Act**, which modified the Employment Act by defining how much unemployment and inflation was acceptable. Despite the Employment Act of 1946 and the Humphrey-Hawkins Act of 1978, the U.S. economy has been subject to business cycles that include recurring unemployment, reduced production, and inflation.

Since maximum employment, maximum production, and maximum purchasing power have been identified as goals of U.S. economic policy, let us see what they mean.

Maximum Employment

The Employment Act of 1946 committed the federal government to promote "maximum employment." To some people, *maximum employment* means that everyone willing to work will be able to find a job. Most economists believe, however, that some unemployment is

In March 1998, President Clinton announced that the nation's unemployment rate was the lowest in 24 years—4.6 percent. With Clinton were Budget Director Franklin Raines, Chief of Staff Erskine Bowles, and Janet Yellen, Chair of the Council of Economic Advisers.

inevitable and acceptable. What percentage of unemployment Congress considers "acceptable" was spelled out in the Humphrey-Hawkins Act of 1978, which specified a 4 percent or lower unemployment rate as the equivalent of maximum or full employment.

Maximum Production

As we discussed in Chapter 6, entrepreneurs try to combine the factors of production (land, labor, and capital) in order to earn the greatest profits. From the standpoint of the individual firm, *maximum production* is the level at which entrepreneurs believe that it is no longer profitable to add more workers, land, or capital to the production process. In Chapter 6, we learned that this comes at the rate of output where marginal revenue equals marginal costs.

While entrepreneurs can fairly easily figure out their own maximum production levels, economists in the federal government have much difficulty discovering when the level of maximum production has been reached on a national level. They try to find out when the economy is producing the most goods and services of which it is capable. For that purpose, economists assume that rising employment levels will lead to increased output. When that happens, increasing demand (relative to supply) will lead to higher prices. Thus, economists generally assume that maximum production has been reached when further increases in employment bring on inflation.

Maximum Purchasing Power

Most people would like to feel that the money they set aside in savings will be able to buy as much tomorrow as it could today. That is, they hope that the purchasing power of their dollar will remain more or less constant. Consumers achieve *maximum purchasing power* when the general price level is maintained so that the purchasing power of the dollar remains stable. Assume that you saved money for a year to buy a dirt bike advertised for $200. You would hope that when you have accumulated the $200, the price of the dirt bike will not have increased.

Experience tells us, however, that some decrease in the value of the dollar and some increase in prices are inevitable. How much inflation is acceptable? Once again, Congress set policy guidelines in the Humphrey-Hawkins Act of 1978, which set national goals at an inflation rate of 3 percent or less.

PROMOTING MAXIMUM EMPLOYMENT

Maximum employment has been a primary goal of government for over 50 years. Since unemployment often has multiple causes, the government has tried a number of ways to relieve the problem. Econo-

After losing a job, the first step toward receiving unemployment compensation is to file a claim.

mists have identified three types of unemployment: frictional, structural, and cyclical.

Frictional Unemployment

When is unemployment not unemployment? When it is *frictional unemployment*. The term describes the status of workers who have left one job and are likely to find another soon. The jobs these workers are seeking are available, and it is only a matter of time before they will be employed again. Since frictional unemployment is a normal (often voluntary) event, some economists allow for it in their definition of full employment. Exactly how many workers are frictionally unemployed at any time is uncertain. Most economists, however, would agree that frictional unemployment of 4–6 percent of the labor force is a reasonable estimate.

Since frictional unemployment is seen as a normal economic condition, the federal government has not done much to reduce it. Most states maintain offices that assist both employers and employees in job placement. But unemployment levels vary from state to state. It is possible that there may be a shortage of workers in a few states at the same time there are high levels of unemployment in other states. To deal with this problem, a nationwide network of state job service agencies has been set up. It is designed to reduce frictional unemployment by speeding up the process by which people find jobs (and employers find workers) in states other than their own.

Structural Unemployment

Unlike frictional unemployment, *structural unemployment* refers to workers who have lost their jobs because of changes in technology, consumer preferences, or the movement of job opportunities from one region to another. These workers are not likely to be rehired in the near future at the types of jobs they had before.

Structural unemployment is caused by changes in the nature or location of employment opportunities. It may occur in certain parts of the labor force when new technology makes certain skills obsolete, as when farmhands are replaced by automatic harvesting machinery, and clerical workers are replaced by computers. Or structural unemployment may occur on a regional or sectional basis, as when much of the textile industry left New England for the South earlier in the 20th century. Prejudice and discrimination, which make it more difficult for some Americans than others to find jobs, are additional causes of structural unemployment. (See Figure 18.1.) The relationship between discrimination and unemployment is discussed in more detail in Chapter 20.

The reduction of structural unemployment is extremely difficult and costly. At the least, it requires:

● Retraining workers whose skills are no longer in demand

Figure 18.1   Unemployment Rates for Selected Groups, 1995

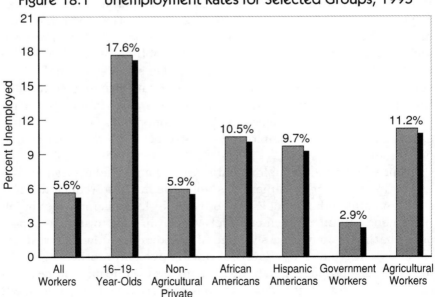

- Moving people to where the jobs are or enticing industry to move into areas of high unemployment
- Changing the social values of those who would discriminate against others because of their race, age, religion, sex, or disability.

Cyclical Unemployment

The name given by economists to unemployment that results from downturns in the business cycle is *cyclical unemployment*. It is caused by insufficient demand, that is, when the demand for goods and services is running at something less than the economy is capable of producing. In such instances, businesses will operate at less than capacity, and workers who might otherwise be employed will be laid off. In its efforts to reduce cyclical unemployment, government will rely upon its fiscal and monetary powers to maintain aggregate demand at maximum employment levels.

THE PROBLEM OF INFLATION

Inflation has been described as "the cruelest tax of all." It is "tax-like" because the payment imposed by inflation cannot be escaped. Inflation is "cruel" because it affects mostly those who can least afford its costs, such as people on fixed incomes.

The Causes of Inflation

A continuing period of rising prices (that is, "inflation") occurs when the rate of growth of the money supply is consistently greater than the rate of growth of the economy's output. When the money supply grows much more quickly than does the output of goods and services, inflation is high. When it grows only slightly faster than output, inflation is low. And when the growth of money supply decreases relative to output, there is deflation. During periods of deflation, prices fall, as they did during the Great Depression of the 1930s.

Although the underlying causes of inflation are fairly well understood, it continues to plague countries around the world, including our own. Why does inflation persist? What are the obstacles to bringing it under control? To answer these questions, let us review three causes of inflation: government printing presses, demand-pull, and cost-push.

Government Printing Presses and Inflation. In some countries, inflation occurs because the nation's leaders finance budget deficits mainly by printing money. Unwilling or unable to increase taxes or borrow money to balance their budgets, they resort to the printing press. That is what the government of Argentina did in 1989. It created as much money as it needed to make up for the difference between its income and its expenditures. As a result, a candy bar that had sold for 6 *australes* (the Argentine unit of currency) in January 1989 had increased to 250 australes by September of that year.

Many other nations around the world have had similar experiences. Inflation has been brought under control in those places only when the underlying budget deficits were finally reduced and the printing of new currency was brought under control.

The United States has not had to resort to printing money to finance its budget deficits. Instead, it has been able to make up the difference between income and expenditures through borrowing.

Demand-Pull Inflation. This type of inflation occurs when the total demand for goods and services exceeds the available supply. Or, as some economists describe it, demand-pull is a situation in which "too much money is chasing too few goods."

Federal Reserve policies that expand the money supply too rapidly can trigger demand-pull inflation. So, too, can sudden increases in spending by consumers, businesses, or the government. Government spending during the Vietnam War (1965–1973) caused a serious round of inflation. As the war escalated, the Lyndon Johnson administration raised military spending. At the same time, the government continued high levels of domestic spending on the social programs of the "Great Society." As a result, the budget deficit grew from $1.4 billion in 1965 to $25.2 billion in 1968. While unemployment fell during this period, aggregate demand increased and inflation became a problem.

Still another source of demand-pull inflation is a psychological factor often described as "public expectations." When, for example, individuals or firms believe that prices will be rising in the near future, they may rush to buy today what they might otherwise have postponed to a later date. Ironically, if a large enough sector of the public acts on this expectation, the prophecy will be fulfilled. Why? Because the rising demand will lead to an increase in prices.

Cost-Push Inflation. Some more recent periods of inflation in the United States cannot be explained in terms of "too much money chasing too few goods." During 1979–1981, for example, prices increased at a record rate at a time when industry was operating at less than 80 percent of capacity and 1 worker out of 14 was unemployed. In short, Americans did not have "too much money." The economy could have produced more goods and services. Despite the recession, prices were climbing. Economists call this phenomenon "stagflation." The term describes a period that combines economic recession (stagnation) and inflation.

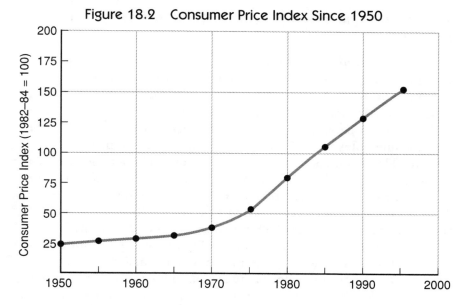

Figure 18.2   Consumer Price Index Since 1950

In searching for an explanation for stagflation, economists came up with the theory of cost-push inflation. As suggested by its name, this type of inflation refers to a period in which sellers raise their prices because of an increase in their costs. Cost-push inflation occurs because large segments of the nation's economy do not operate under conditions of pure competition. For example, some strong labor unions can achieve wage increases without any increase in the productivity of their members. Thus, the production costs of the workers' employers rise, and the employers raise the prices of the goods and services they produce.

Fighting Inflation

Controlling or eliminating inflation has been a goal of the federal government ever since World War II. Most of this effort has been aimed at the principal causes of inflation: demand-pull and cost-push.

Curing Demand-Pull Inflation. Efforts to cure demand-pull inflation can have both positive and negative effects.

First, the Good News. Demand-pull inflation can be moderated with monetary and/or fiscal policies. On the monetary side, the Fed can use its powers (described later in this chapter) to slow the rate of growth of the money supply.

Fiscal policies are the responsibility of the president and Congress, and include the powers to spend and tax. Any combination of reduced spending and increased taxes will reduce the spending power of consumers and businesses. With less to spend, demand will fall, along with prices.

And Now the Bad News. While reductions in consumer and business demand will take the pressure off price increases, reduced demand is likely to add to unemployment. This effect follows because with declining sales, business firms tend to lay off workers and reduce inventories. As unemployment rates increase, sales will decline still further because unemployed workers will have less money to spend.

The relationship between the inflation rate and unemployment can be represented graphically by a *Phillips Curve*. It was named in honor of **A.W. Phillips**, the British economist who developed it. In Figure 18.3, unemployment increased from 1 percent of the labor force to 10 percent as the inflation rate fell from 12 percent to 2 percent.

Another piece of bad news concerning the fight against demand-pull inflation has to do with the Fed's tactic of raising interest rates. This Fed action places a special burden on industries that rely heavily on borrowed funds, such as housing construction. Since virtually all housing is built at least partly with borrowed funds (in the form of mortgages), efforts to raise interest rates make borrowing more difficult. As a result, many people are unable to buy new homes because they cannot obtain or afford mortgages. Meanwhile, as the number of new housing starts plummets, building contractors, suppliers, and construction workers experience a reduction in earnings.

Curing Cost-Push Inflation. While monetary and fiscal policies can fight demand-pull inflation by cooling aggregate demand, they are not ef-

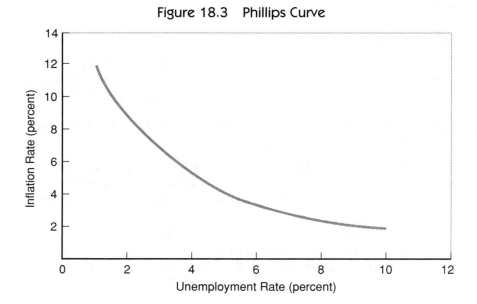

Figure 18.3   Phillips Curve

fective against the cost-push variety of inflation. To fight cost-push inflation, government applies what are known as incomes policies. These policies seek to stem the wage and price increases associated with cost-push inflation with one or more of the following: voluntary controls, direct controls, antitrust laws, and aiming at inflation from the "supply side."

Voluntary Controls. In the 1970s, presidents Nixon, Ford, and Carter called upon labor leaders and heads of industry to limit voluntarily their respective wage demands and price increases. The government issued guidelines for what it considered proper percentage increases. These efforts to obtain self-regulation generally failed. Many company executives and labor leaders were fearful that even if they followed the presidents' requests, others would not, and these others would benefit.

Direct Controls. During World War II and parts of the Korean and Vietnam wars, the federal government imposed wage and price controls across the country. These controls established maximum prices on many items, and also fixed wages. Direct controls were generally effective during World War II because that war was a popular one and the U.S. public supported controls then. During other, less popular wars, however, controls have not been so well received. Many Americans regard price and wage controls as inconsistent with a democratic society and a free enterprise system. These controls are also very costly to administer because thousands of people have to be hired to enforce them.

Antitrust Legislation. Cost-push is most likely to occur in those industries in which management or labor is so strong that it can dictate prices. For example, if a powerful union forces an industry to grant union workers a 10 percent wage increase, businesses in that industry very likely will increase prices by at least 10 percent, which can add to inflationary pressures. Similarly, a monopolistic firm may try to maximize profits by limiting output and raising prices. By contrast, in a competitive environment prices are less likely to increase and the pressure of inflation is reduced. That is why the government tries to control the powers of both labor and management through antitrust laws.

Aiming at Inflation From the "Supply Side." Market price, you may recall from Chapter 3, is a function of both demand and supply. In the 1970s, a group of economists suggested that price increases could be limited even if the output of goods and services were increased. As these economists saw it, the biggest hindrances to increased output were federal taxes, which were so high as to discourage investment and production. Their key to reducing inflation was to reduce taxes. The increase in take-home pay that would result from reduced taxes,

Kirk Anderson

According to the cartoonist, to what does a low unemployment rate lead? Do you agree with this view? Explain.

they reasoned, would enable consumers to increase both their spending and savings. The increased spending would then encourage businesses to expand. Meanwhile, the increased savings would add to the pool of funds available for investment. As investment increases, so, too, does output, that is, the supply of goods and services. As you know from your study of the laws of supply and demand, all other things being equal, an increase in supply will result in a *decrease* in prices. Thus, the supply-siders concluded, reducing taxes would result in reducing inflation, because it would stimulate investment, increase output, and lower prices. The ideas proposed by these economists, named *supply-siders*, created a sensation. Heretofore, a tax cut had been regarded as a way to increase, not decrease, prices. (See the feature on supply-side economics on pages 447–449.)

Fighting Inflation in the 1980s. The federal government used a combination of monetary policy and supply-side techniques to combat a very serious inflation in the early 1980s. Results of the effort were mixed. By limiting the growth of the money supply (monetary policies) and reducing taxes (a supply-side strategy), cost-of-living increases were slowed to the lowest rate in nearly 20 years. Unemployment, however, climbed to nearly 10 percent of the labor force, its highest level since the Great Depression. By 1989, though, the unemployment level had declined to 5.3 percent.

MONETARY POLICY

As we discussed in Chapter 16, the efforts of the Federal Reserve System to stabilize the economy by regulating the supply of money and credit is called "monetary policy." The availability and cost of credit affects both the money supply and business activity. When loans are easily obtained, spending will increase (along with the money supply, business activity, and prices). When loans are harder to come by, the opposite occurs: sales decline (along with the money supply, business activity, and prices).

The Tools of Monetary Policy

To reverse trends in the business cycle, the Fed makes use of a number of monetary tools that either increase or decrease the money supply. The most important of these tools are reserve requirements, the discount rate, and open market operations, all of which we first discussed in Chapter 16.

Reserve Requirements. A major part of a bank's income comes from the interest it earns on the loans of its depositors' money. Banks, however, cannot lend unlimited sums. They are required instead to keep a percentage of their deposits on reserve. This percentage, or reserve ratio, is set by the Federal Reserve Board of Governors. When the Fed increases the reserve ratio, the lending ability of banks is curtailed. When reserve ratios are reduced, the opposite happens.

With the reserve ratio at 15 percent and $1 million in deposits, the First National Bank could lend up to $850,000. ($1,000,000 × .15 = $150,000; $1,000,000 − $150,000 = $850,000.) If the Fed increased the required reserve ratio to 20 percent, First National's lending ability would be reduced to $800,000. ($1,000,000 × .20 = $200,000; $1,000,000 − $200,000 = $800,000.)

The effect of a change in reserve requirements on the banking system as a whole is even more dramatic. In Chapter 15, we discussed how with a reserve ratio of 20 percent, a deposit of $10,000 could lead to an expansion of deposits totaling $50,000 as the deposit traveled through the banking system. With a reserve ratio of 25 percent, the same $10,000 deposit could be expanded to only $40,000 in deposits.

We see then that during periods of expansion (when resources are fully employed and prices are moving into inflationary levels) the Fed can move against these trends by increasing the reserve ratio.

During recessions the Fed can take the opposite tack. It can reduce the reserve ratio—an action that enables banks to make more loans. By making more loans, the banks can in turn add to the money supply and aggregate demand.

The Discount Rate. When their reserves get low, member banks can replenish them with loans from the Federal Reserve Bank that services their district. The interest paid on those loans is known as the "discount rate." Since banks are in business to earn a profit, they charge their loan customers something more than this rate.

The amount of money that the public borrows is affected by prevailing interest rates. As the cost of loans increases, borrowing decreases. We see then that the Fed can use its power of increasing or decreasing the discount rate to affect the volume of loans and the quantity of money and credit in circulation.

As it did during the mild inflation of the early 1990s, the Fed may choose to increase the discount rate when it wants to tighten up on credit and slow the growth of the money supply. A slower growth of the money supply, in turn, puts downward pressure on prices and inflation.

During recessions, the Fed could choose to reduce the discount rate. As banks follow suit by reducing their interest charges, business and consumer loans would increase. The increased loans, in turn, would kick off increased business activity, consumer spending, and employment.

Open Market Operations. The most important of the Fed's monetary tools are called "open market operations." These operations involve

Alan Greenspan is the Chair of the Federal Reserve's Board of Governors.

M. Thompson/Rothco

the purchase and sale of government securities (bonds, bills, and notes) by the Fed's Open Market Committee. When this committee buys or sells government securities, it adds reserves to or subtracts reserves from the nation's banking system.

Assume, for example, a mutual-fund company buys $1 million worth of Treasury bills. It pays for them by check. This purchase reduces the deposits in the mutual fund's bank account by $1 million, and the reserves of the bank in which the deposits were held are reduced by $1 million. Remember from Chapter 16 that because of reserve requirements, a reduction in deposits is magnified as it travels through the banking system. The banking system as a whole expands or contracts deposits by an amount equal to the reciprocal of the reserve ratio. Therefore, if the reserve ratio is 10 percent (10 percent = 1/10), a reduction in bank deposits of $1 million will reduce the opportunity of the banking system to expand deposits by $10 million (the reciprocal of 1/10 = 10; 10 × $1 million = $10 million) or by ten times the amount of the reduced deposit.

Now let us suppose that the mutual-fund company sells the government securities that it owned. As the money from the sale is deposited, bank reserves and loans expand (along with the money supply and aggregate demand).

If the Fed called upon the Open Market Committee to bring prices down and reduce the threat of inflation, the Committee would direct its agents to sell securities to the public. The sale would be achieved by lowering the offering price of Treasury securities (bills, notes, and bonds) to whatever point was necessary to attract the funds that the government wanted to take out of circulation.

During periods of recession, the Open Market Committee would follow the opposite course: buying government securities. The purchases would add to bank reserves because the sellers of the securities would deposit to their accounts the proceeds from the sale. Banks would be able to increase their loans (based upon the increased funds deposited with the banks). In addition, the money supply could expand to as much as ten times the amount of the purchase (if the reserve ratio is 10 percent). Hopefully, as money and credit is more readily available, business activity would increase.

Monetary Policy in Action

Depending upon economic conditions, monetary policies generally follow one of three scenarios.

Scenario 1: Things Are Going Well. With full employment and price stability, the Fed will try to maintain the present state of affairs. It does this by allowing the money supply to grow at exactly the same rate as the growth of the GDP.

Scenario 2: The Economy Is in a Recession. With unemployment on the increase and business activity in a decline, the Fed might adopt an *easy-money policy* (that is, it might increase the money supply). This policy allows the money supply to grow faster than the GDP, and stimulates aggregate demand.

In a recession, the Fed will (1) reduce reserve requirements to increase the lending power of the banking system, (2) lower the discount rate to enable member banks to charge lower interest rates for loans and, hopefully, stimulate borrowing, and (3) direct the Open Market Committee to buy securities. When the Fed buys securities, the sellers of the securities deposit the proceeds in their accounts (adding to the deposits held by banks and increasing the banks' lending capacity).

Scenario 3: Inflation Threatens. With prices increasing at an unacceptable rate, the Fed is likely to follow a *tight-money policy* (that is, slow the growth of the money supply). This policy will: (1) slow the rate of increase in the money supply to something less than the increase in the GDP, and (2) dampen aggregate demand.

With its trusty monetary tools, the Fed in inflationary times could be expected to do one or more of the following:

Increase Reserve Requirements. By requiring that local banks hold a larger portion of their deposits on reserve, the lending ability of banks will be reduced, along with the money supply.

Raise the Discount Rate. Since higher rates cost local banks more to borrow from the Federal Reserve System, they will have to increase the interest rates they charge their customers. This increase will, in turn, discourage borrowing, slow the growth of the money supply, and reduce aggregate demand and prices.

Direct the Open Market Committee to Sell Securities. When the Open Market Committee sells government bills, bonds, and notes to the public, the payments from the sale of these securities are received by the Federal Reserve System. The sales reduce bank reserves, the lending ability of the banking system, and the money supply.

Monetary Policy Has Its Limitations

We have described how the Fed uses its monetary tools to regulate the economy. How well the Fed can achieve its goals depends upon a number of factors, the most important of which are:

● The ability of the Fed to forecast trends and time its responses
● The business cycle
● New banking laws
● The global economy.

Table 18.1   MONETARY POLICY SUMMARIZED

Recession and High Unemployment	*Inflation and Full Employment*
1. Lower the reserve ratio	1. Raise the reserve ratio
2. Buy securities	2. Sell securities
3. Lower the discount rate	3. Raise the discount rate
4. Lower margin requirements	4. Raise margin requirements

Forecasting and Timing Difficulties. The success of monetary policy depends upon how quickly and accurately the Fed is able to recognize economic trends. Though economists are able to describe in general terms how well or poorly the economy is doing, no one has discovered how to predict the future of the economy with certainty. If economists cannot be certain, how can the Fed know exactly how much to raise or lower the money supply? Furthermore, there is a time lag before monetary policies impact on the business community. In retrospect, some economists might argue that monetary measures came too soon, too late, or were not necessary to begin with.

Business Cycle. Monetary policy is least effective at either end of the business cycle. During the depths of a recession, the Fed will lower interest rates. This action alone, however, may not be enough to overcome the fears created by a period of job layoffs and business failures. For that reason, business and consumer spending may remain at low levels despite the reduced cost of loans.

Similarly, as the business cycle climbs toward the upper reaches of a recovery, the effectiveness of monetary policy wanes. In these times, we can expect the Fed to increase interest rates so as to: (1) discourage loans, (2) slow the growth of the money supply, and (3) lower prices. But with business prospects looking good (as they do during peak recovery periods), firms will continue to borrow and expand on the theory that increased sales will more than offset the higher costs of money. When this happens, prices will continue to rise despite the Fed's efforts to reverse the trend.

New Banking Laws. There was a time when consumers placed the bulk of their savings in bank accounts and the interest offered by savings institutions was limited by law. More recently, however, Congress gave banks the right to determine the interest they would pay depositors.

While the deregulation of interest rates has allowed banks to become more competitive, they have also made the banks less responsive to policy shifts by the Federal Reserve System. For example, in the days before deregulation, the Fed could direct the banks to reduce the interest rates they paid on their deposits as a way of discouraging

Table 18.2   UNITED STATES INTERNATIONAL TRADE (IN BILLIONS)

	1974	1997
Exports of goods and services	$148	$ 931
Imports of goods and services	137	1,045

savings. Today, however, bankers need not follow the lead of the Fed if, in their opinion, it would be more profitable to do otherwise.

The Global Economy. As indicated in Table 18.2, U.S. participation in the global economy has grown enormously over the years. One result of this trend is that foreign individuals hold many more dollars than they once did. As we will discuss in Chapter 22, the U.S. dollar holdings of foreign governments has an effect upon prices in the United States. But as we have seen, prices directly affect economic activity. While the Federal Reserve Board has a great deal of control over the supply of dollars in this country, its ability to regulate how dollars in foreign hands are used is limited. For that reason, U.S. firms' increasing involvement in world trade has lessened the ability of the Fed to regulate the value of the dollar, the level of prices, and the business cycle.

Summary

The federal government has the responsibility to maintain maximum employment, maximum production, and maximum purchasing power. It attempts to do so by maintaining appropriate levels of aggregate demand. When aggregate demand equals the economy's ability to produce, the economy is at full employment. When aggregate demand is below this capacity, a recessionary gap exists. By contrast, an inflationary gap occurs when aggregate demand is greater than the economy's capacity to produce.

During periods of recession and inflation, the government attempts to correct imbalances in aggregate demand through the use of fiscal and monetary policies. The Federal Reserve System administers the country's monetary policy. It regulates the nation's supply of money and credit by virtue of its power to regulate reserve requirements, the discount rate, and open market operations. In the next chapter, we will discuss fiscal policy.

REVIEWING THE CHAPTER

Building Vocabulary

Match each term in Column A with its definition in Column B.

COLUMN A	COLUMN B
1. frictional unemployment	*a.* a graph illustrating the tradeoff between inflation and unemployment
2. fiscal policy	*b.* the status of workers who lose their jobs because of insufficient demand for goods and services
3. structural unemployment	*c.* a three-member body that reports to the U.S. president
4. Council of Economic Advisers	*d.* the use of the federal government's taxing and spending powers to regulate the economy
5. easy-money policy	*e.* the status of workers who lose their jobs and are soon likely to find a similar one
6. tight-money policy	*f.* the status of workers who lose their jobs because of changes in the nature or location of job opportunities
7. cyclical unemployment	*g.* a Fed policy to expand the money supply
8. supply-side economics	*h.* an unemployment rate of 4 percent or below
9. Phillips Curve	*i.* a Fed policy to slow down the growth of the money supply
10. maximum employment	*j.* the idea that emphasizes production as the key to reducing prices and increasing employment

Understanding What You Have Read

1. The statement that the federal government has the responsibility to use its powers to promote stability, growth, and full employment is contained in the   (*a*) U.S. Constitution   (*b*) Employment Act of 1946   (*c*) Social Security Act of 1935   (*d*) National Labor Relations Act.

2. When certain jobs disappear in one region and reappear in another, the unemployment that results is referred to as   (*a*) normal   (*b*) structural   (*c*) cyclical   (*d*) frictional.

3. Unemployment is likely to increase when   (*a*) aggregate demand is high   (*b*) there is a period of moderate inflation   (*c*) the

demand for goods is less than the economy is capable of producing (*d*) workers voluntarily leave their jobs in search of new ones.

4. Which step might be taken to stimulate business activity during a recession? (*a*) lower the discount rate (*b*) increase margin requirements (*c*) decrease spending for public works (*d*) raise corporate income tax rates.

5. Which combination of conditions would generally have a tendency to create inflation? (*a*) low wages and a surplus of consumer goods (*b*) a limited supply of money and an expanding population (*c*) a high rate of employment and a shortage of consumer goods (*d*) an increase in taxes and a decrease in government spending.

6. When prices are forced upward because there is "too much money chasing too few goods," economists describe this as (*a*) spiraling deflation (*b*) demand-pull inflation (*c*) cost-push inflation (*d*) push-pull inflation.

7. A major problem in the government's efforts to control inflation is that (*a*) people do not like to see government increase its level of spending (*b*) efforts to reduce prices often add to unemployment (*c*) such efforts require a reduction in taxes (*d*) no one knows how to measure inflation.

8. During periods of inflation, the value of the dollar (*a*) decreases (*b*) remains the same (*c*) decreases for a while then increases (*d*) increases.

9. An increase in average weekly income does not result in a higher standard of living if it is caused by (*a*) increased purchases of consumer goods (*b*) increased private investment (*c*) rising prices (*d*) increased productivity.

10. Monetary policies are administered by the (*a*) Treasury Department (*b*) U.S. president (*c*) Federal Reserve System (*d*) Congress.

11. The term "open market operations" refers mainly to (*a*) speculation in stocks and bonds by members of the stock exchange (*b*) the purchase and sale of government securities by Federal Reserve Banks (*c*) discounting of notes by Federal Reserve Banks (*d*) regulation of margin requirements by the Federal Reserve's Board of Governors.

12. A major effect of the lowering of reserve requirements for member banks by the Board of Governors of the Federal Reserve System would be (*a*) a decrease in margin requirements for stock purchases (*b*) a decrease in the supply of checkbook money (*c*) an increase in commercial bank loans (*d*) an increase in "tight money."

13. When the Federal Reserve raises the discount rate, member banks usually raise their interest rates because (*a*) as members they must go along with the wishes of the Federal Reserve (*b*) they are required to do so by law (*c*) it will now cost them more to borrow the funds that they will be lending out (*d*) they want to take the opportunity to increase their volume of loans.

14. The use of monetary policy to combat inflation has been criticized because it (*a*) calls for additional government spending (*b*) places too heavy reliance upon the Treasury Department (*c*) calls for higher taxes (*d*) discriminates against certain industries, such as the home building trades, that rely most heavily upon consumer borrowing.

Thinking Critically

1. The federal government has been given the responsibility "to use all practical means . . . to promote . . . *maximum employment, production*, and *purchasing power*."

    a. Briefly explain maximum employment, maximum production, and maximum purchasing power.

    b. Should the government manage the economy? Explain.

2. Inflation may be of the *demand-pull* or *cost-push* variety.

    a. Explain the meaning of each type of inflation. Which do you think is easier for the government to deal with—demand-pull or cost-push inflation?

    b. Why might workers oppose government measures to combat inflation?

3. Occasionally, the assertion is made that "full employment is not possible without inflation."

    a. Explain the meaning of this statement.

    b. Do you agree with it? Why or why not?

4. Assume that the nation has entered a period of recession and that the Fed has decided to use its monetary tools to deal with the problem.

    a. Explain *three* ways in which the Fed could use its monetary tools to reverse a recession.

    b. Assume that the tools used to reverse the recession worked and the economy seems to be heading for an inflationary period. Explain *three* tools the Fed could use to reduce inflationary pressures in the economy.

    c. Why is it difficult for the Fed to know when to implement corrective measures?

SKILLS: Researching and Writing About Economic Problems

During a period of inflation, the Fed is likely to adopt monetary measures to reduce aggregate demand. Efforts to reduce demand, however, are also likely to lead to increased unemployment.

1. Research in annual reference books such as **Economic Report of the President, Statistical Abstract of the United States,** and **World Almanac** for statistics on unemployment rates and inflation rates in recent years. Then find current unemployment and inflation rates in a newspaper or magazine.

2. Survey adults in your community (including some who are currently working or who own a business) on the subject of unemployment and inflation. Ask each adult whether he or she thinks either inflation or unemployment is a major problem in the United States today.

3. Based on your results from activities numbers 1 and 2, write a short essay on whether you think that the Fed should tighten money and credit at this time.

Chapter 19

MANAGING THE NATION'S ECONOMY: FISCAL POLICY

Overview

Some of the most important government efforts to regulate the economy involve the application of *countercyclical* fiscal policies. Fiscal policy is the use of government's power to tax and spend in order to increase or decrease aggregate demand. Fiscal policies are "countercyclical" because they attempt to reverse (or counter) the course of the business cycle. The government tries to increase aggregate demand during recessions and decrease aggregate demand during periods of inflation.

Politicians find it difficult to cut spending because some voters will lose income from each cut. Politicians also find greater voter approval for tax cuts than for tax increases. Consequently, the U.S. government usually spends more than it earns, and thus has long been in debt.

In this chapter, we will examine fiscal policies and how these policies are sometimes used to manage the economy. We will also discuss alternative proposals from supply-siders for managing the economy. This discussion leads into the topics of deficit spending and the national debt.

FISCAL POLICIES

We encounter examples of fiscal policies whenever we hear members of Congress or the president talking about the benefits of tax cuts or spending cuts (or tax increases or spending increases). Those who apply fiscal policies are targeting aggregate demand. As we discussed in Chapter 10 and elsewhere, aggregate demand is equal to the total spending of consumers (C), business (I), and government (G), or simply $C + I + G$. Consumer spending depends upon the size of consumer income and the marginal propensity to consume. Because the marginal propensity to consume is fairly constant, consumer spending will rise or fall mostly due to increases or decreases in consumer income. Business spending is far less predictable. The level of business spending will be affected by many variables, such as the expectation of increased sales, anticipated price changes, tax laws, and government regulations.

Changing the level of government spending (*G*) while other components remain constant directly affects aggregate demand. An increase in government spending will lead to an increase in aggregate demand when *C* and *I* are constant. Similarly, a decrease in government spending will have the opposite effect: Aggregate demand will decline.

The power to tax gives governments indirect influence over aggregate demand. When taxes are reduced, both consumers and businesses have more to spend, and their spending increases aggregate demand. Tax increases have the opposite effect. With less to spend, C and I will fall along with aggregate demand.

Changes in aggregate demand are magnified by the multiplier. All other things being equal, with a multiplier of 5, an increase of $1 billion in government spending will increase aggregate demand (total spending) by $5 billion. Consider the following hypothetical situation.

Government economists have determined that at full employment the economy could produce $4 trillion in goods and services. Presently, aggregate demand is running at $2.8 trillion, with a multiplier of 4. The recessionary gap, therefore, is $1.2 trillion ($4 trillion – $2.8 trillion = $1.2 trillion).

In the face of a recessionary gap, Congress votes (and the president approves) spending increases totaling $200 billion and tax decreases of $100 billion. In combination with the multiplier, the $300 billion increase in purchasing power ($200 + $100) increases aggregate demand by $1.2 trillion ($300 billion × 4), and eliminates the recessionary gap.

"Free gifts to every kid in the world?—Are you a *Keynesian* or something?"

Limitations on Fiscal Policies

Political leaders have found that there are limitations to fiscal policies.

Forecasting and Timing Difficulties. The success of fiscal programs depends upon how quickly and accurately the government is able to recognize economic trends. One problem is that business trends cannot be measured with absolute accuracy. Though economists are able to describe in general terms how well or poorly the economy is doing, no one has discovered how to predict the future of the economy with certainty. If, for example, we are in a recession, who can really say that the next day will not bring an upward turn? If that happens and recovery sets in before the government recognizes the shift, any effort to increase total demand (such as a tax cut or a spending program) could prove to be inflationary.

An additional problem is created by the sometimes agonizingly slow pace of the democratic process. In many instances, Congress takes so long to act that necessary legislation is passed too late to achieve its fiscal goals.

Political Considerations. During periods of recession, the government might lower taxes and increase spending. These actions can be quite popular politically because voters almost always favor lower taxes, and many persons benefit directly from government spending. A problem arises, however, during periods of boom and inflation when opposing actions are called for—higher taxes and decreased spending. Members of Congress do not like to associate themselves with higher taxes. Nor is it politically helpful to reduce or eliminate spending programs that would have benefited the people "back home." For this reason, fiscal policy is more popular when it is used to combat recession than when it is used against inflation.

Inflexibility of the National Budget. Ideally, government spending should increase during periods of recession and decrease during inflation. Currently, however, about one-third of the budget goes for national defense and interest on the national debt. Defense needs and interest payments must be met regardless of economic conditions, as must many other expenditures that pay for essential government services. After paying for these expenses, lawmakers have but a fraction of the total budget that they can manipulate to stabilize the economy.

Lack of Coordinated Fiscal Policies. In the best of all possible worlds, state and local governments would mesh their budgets with that of the federal government so as to launch a coordinated attack on the nation's economic woes. In practice, quite the opposite is likely to take place.

During periods of inflation, state and local tax receipts will increase, as will spending by the state and local governments. Increased spending, though, is the opposite of what is called for by fiscal theory. During times of inflation, the government should decrease its spending so as to reduce total demand.

During recessions (when tax receipts are on the decline), states and localities often reduce their levels of spending. But in times of recession, fiscal theory says, government spending should be increased as a way of increasing aggregate demand. More government spending, in turn, would lead to increased spending by consumers and businesses.

While state and local governments might like to increase their spending during hard times, they face major obstacles. First, unlike the federal government, states and localities do not have the power to print money. Second, they often find borrowing difficult during recessions. They are left with little choice other than to do their heaviest spending during times when their economies are flourishing. Unfortunately, inflationary periods are just such times.

Automatic Fiscal Policies

The tax and spending programs used by the federal government for the purpose of regulating the economy are sometimes labeled *discretionary fiscal policies*. They are "discretionary" because they are used as Congress (often with the prodding of the president) deems necessary—in other words, at the discretion of Congress.

There is another type of government measure that goes into effect automatically so as to increase or decrease taxes and spending in accordance with the needs of the economy. These changes in the level of taxes and spending occur without Congress making them. These changes occur because of the existence of a number of *automatic stabilizers*—taxes and expenditures in the federal budget that automatically change in such ways that steady the economy. Three of the best-known automatic stabilizers are unemployment insurance programs, welfare programs, and the income tax.

Unemployment Insurance. Through unemployment insurance programs, states provide income to qualified workers who have lost their job. Funding for these state programs comes from taxes paid by employers. During a recession, a time when large numbers of workers are laid off, the number of people receiving unemployment insurance payments automatically increases. In this way, additional funds are pumped into the economy exactly when they are needed most. Also

Workers collect unemployment compensation when they are laid off during a recession. How does this help the economy to recover?

during a recession, the total amount that employers pay in unemployment taxes decreases because fewer workers are employed.

During the recovery phase of the business cycle, just the opposite happens: employment increases and state government payments automatically decrease. At the same time, tax collections for the state programs increase.

Welfare. Welfare programs provide both financial and in-kind assistance to poor individuals and families. *Financial assistance* comes in the form of cash payments. *In-kind payments* come in the form of goods or services (e.g., food) rather than money. Certain payments to welfare recipients fall somewhere in between payments in-kind and financial assistance. For example, *food stamps* can be used in much the same way as money. But unlike money (which may be used to purchase almost anything), food stamps may be used only to purchase food products. Some communities make rent payments directly to a welfare recipient's landlord; other communities give poor families a monthly rent allowance. Whatever the form of welfare payment, the economic impact is the same. Welfare payments tend to increase aggregate demand.

Like unemployment benefits, welfare payments increase during downswings in the business cycle because more people apply for welfare as jobs become scarce. Also, as with unemployment benefits, welfare payments decline during recoveries because jobs become more plentiful. Thus, welfare programs automatically add to aggregate demand during recessions and shrink aggregate demand during expansions.

Income Tax Programs. The federal government and some state and local governments impose income taxes. The amount that individuals and corporations pay in income taxes varies with their earnings. During periods of expansion (as business activity, employment, and prices increase), earnings increase. Therefore, income tax collections also increase. These increased tax payments dampen the ability of businesses and individuals to increase their rate of spending, thereby keeping a lid on the boom.

Just the opposite takes place during a recession. As incomes fall, so too do income tax payments. Reduced income tax payments leave consumers and business firms with an increasing share of their income that they could spend. Any increased spending, of course, would help to restore aggregate demand.

THE DEBT AND THE DEFICIT

The United States is in debt because the federal government often spends more than it earns and makes up for the difference by borrowing. In 1997, for example, budget receipts totaled $1,579 billion, but expenditures ran to $1,601 billion. The additional borrowing necessary to cover the $22 billion deficit has brought the national debt up to about $5.5 trillion. U.S. leaders are projecting that the deficit will decline or perhaps there will be a surplus in 1998 and the following years.

How much is a trillion dollars? Statisticians tell us that it would take a stack of $1,000 bills 67 miles high to reach that sum. Put another way, a $5.5 trillion debt divided equally among every man, woman, and child in the United States would amount to over $19,000 per person.

The United States has spent more than it has earned in 43 out of the last 50 years. Indeed, one has to go back as far as 1969 to find a year in which there was last a surplus in the federal budget. Why has the United States often spent more than it has earned? Is there something ominous about an ever-increasing national debt? Or are there sound economic reasons for deficit financing, and if so, what are they? (This discussion is continued on page 450.)

Supply-Side Economics

The efforts of the federal government to stabilize the United States economy were for many years based upon the theories of British economist John Maynard Keynes (featured on pages 404–405). Keynes had identified fiscal and monetary policies as keys to both ending recessions and bringing inflation under control. According to Keynes, in times of recession the government uses its monetary and fiscal powers to increase spending by consumers, business, and itself. In times of inflation, the government follows an opposite course in order to reduce spending and bring down prices.

Keynesianism worked well enough during those years in which either recession or the rise in the price level was troublesome. In the 1970s, however, the nation found itself in the midst of both recession and inflation. Economists coined the term "stagflation" (for economic stagnation plus inflation) to describe those times. Most economists, however, seemed at a loss to suggest how the government could deal with both problems at the same time.

There was, though, one group of economists (including **Arthur B. Laffer** of the University of Southern California and **Paul Craig Roberts** of the Institute for Political Economy) who claimed to have found a solution to the dilemma. These economists were dubbed the "supply-siders" because they saw production (that is, supply) as the key to ridding the nation of stagflation. The goal of the supply-siders was to "unleash free enterprise" so as to increase investment and production. If production were increased, they argued, prices would have to come down. Meanwhile, the additional investment in new equipment and enterprises would put the unemployed back to work, increase personal and business earnings, and bring the recession to an end.

In the supply-siders' view, there were three obstacles to achieving these goals. These were:

- Income taxes were so high that they discouraged capital investment in new plant, equipment, and business enterprises.

- Government-sponsored welfare programs discouraged individual initiative. Why, the supply-siders asked, would people look for work if they knew that they could have as much money simply by going on welfare?

- Government regulatory agencies discouraged innovation and creativity because rules were pervasive and strictly applied.

The supply-side economists proposed these remedies:

- Reduce income taxes, particularly for those in the upper-income brackets. This reduction would leave businesspeople and others with additional after-tax income, which could be invested in productive enterprises. Moreover, rich people would have greater incentive to earn more money.

- Reduce government spending for social programs so as to limit assistance to the "truly needy." This provision would encourage the less needy to find jobs.
- "Get government off the backs of business" by reducing the number and powers of the regulatory agencies. Fewer government regulations mean less work for business owners and managers and, thus, lower costs for businesses.

Critics of supply-side economics said that the tax proposals would serve only to enrich the wealthy. There was no guarantee that people with additional after-tax income would actually invest the money in business enterprises. Supply-siders were also accused of being indifferent to the needs of the millions of people in the United States sorely in need of government assistance. And some critics said that supply-siders were wrong in their assessment of the value of regulatory agencies.

Ronald Reagan (1981–1989) was the first U.S. president to apply supply-side economics to programs. During his administration, income taxes were reduced, government participation in many social programs was cut back, and the activities of a number of regulatory agencies were narrowed. The results of the efforts are still being debated today. Some economists have argued that supply-side pro-

One prominent supply-sider, Jack Kemp, ran for vice president along with presidential candidate Bob Dole on the Republican ticket in 1996.

grams brought under control what had been one of the most serious episodes of inflation in U.S. history. Critics have argued that by reducing taxes and increasing spending (the latter is not a tenet of supply-side economics), the administrations of presidents Ronald Reagan and George Bush increased the national debt by more than had all previous administrations combined (from that of George Washington to that of Jimmy Carter).

Supply-side economics got a new boost with the Republican campaign in the presidential elections of 1996. Once again the Republican party leadership proposed reducing: (1) taxes as a means of stimulating the economy, (2) government spending on social programs, and (3) government interference in the affairs of business.

1. (*a*) What is "stagflation"?   (*b*) Why do the supply-side economists believe that production (or supply) is the key to fighting stagflation?   (*c*) Compare the Keynesian approach to correcting a recession to that advocated by supply-side economists.

2. With respect to the following, explain the policies favored by supply-side economists and their reasons for those policies: (*a*) income taxes (*b*) welfare programs (*c*) the regulatory agencies.

3. (*a*) Summarize the information contained in the Laffer Curve, Figure 19.1. (*b*) Why do supply-side economists use the Laffer Curve to support their positions?

4. Critics of supply-side policies say that they (*a*) discriminate against the poor, (*b*) favor the rich, and (*c*) lead to record deficits in the federal budget. Evaluate each of these criticisms.

Figure 19.1   Laffer Curve

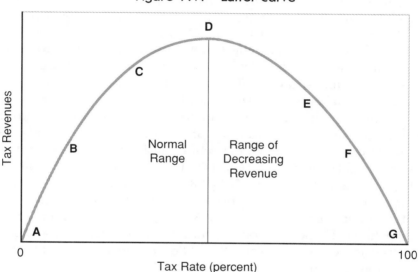

Cut taxes yet increase revenues? Absolutely, argued Arthur Laffer, who demonstrated the proof of this seeming paradox with a graphic model, the now famous "Laffer Curve." At point A, the income tax rate is zero; consequently, the government earns no revenue. As tax rates are levied and increased at B, C, and D, government revenues also increase. But something happens beyond point D, People begin to find taxes so high that they look for other uses for what had been their working time. Some people will work fewer hours, some may drop out of the labor force, while others may look for ways to hide all or part of their income from the tax authorities. At point E on the scale, we see that revenues are less than they were at C and D. At F, revenues are the same as they were at B. At 100 percent (G), revenues are again back to zero, since no one would work if all earnings were taken in taxes.

Laffer concluded from this study that as long as taxes remained within the normal range, increased rates of taxes would earn the government additional income. But beyond that lay a region of decreasing revenue. Within that broad range, government could increase its income tax revenue only by reducing tax rates.

Why Has the National Debt Been Increasing?

The national debt has been increasing because the government has run a deficit in all but eight of its last fifty budgets. The two principal causes of deficit spending have been wars and recessions. Since 1776, the U.S. government's wartime economic policy has been to spend whatever was necessary to win wars, and worry about paying for them later. As a result of the Civil War (1861–1865), the U.S. debt topped $1 billion for the first time. U.S. participation in World War I (1917–1918) brought the national debt up to what was then the unheard of total of $27 billion. Participation in the Second World War (1941–1945) added $200 billion to the total.

During the Great Depression of the 1930s, the U.S. government for the first time used its powers to tax and spend to fight a recession. Remember that fiscal solutions to the problems created by a recession call for increasing aggregate demand through tax reductions and/or increased government spending. Government expenditures for New Deal programs such as the Civilian Conservation Corps (CCC), Works Progress Administration (WPA), the Tennessee Valley Authority (TVA), and the Social Security System added $30 billion to the national debt.

The largest increase in the national debt—some $2 trillion worth—occurred during the Reagan and Bush administrations (1981–1993). During this time, however, the debt explosion was not war-related. It was brought on instead by efforts to fight the recession of 1980–1982, by the massive tax cuts of 1981–1984, and by heavy defense spending throughout the 1980s. The debt continued to rise during the early years of the Clinton administration (1993–1997). Expenditures for U.S. participation in UN peacekeeping operations in Somalia, Haiti, and Bosnia as well as increasing costs for Social Security, Medicare, and Medicaid contributed to the budget deficits during the Clinton presidency.

How Large Is the National Debt?

When we speak of the national debt, we are talking about the bonds, notes, and other securities issued by the federal government when it borrows money. In 1998, this totaled over $5.5 trillion. Of that amount, about 75 percent was owed to private institutions and to individuals. The remainder, about 25 percent, was owed to itself (more exactly, to various agencies of the federal government). For example, the Federal Reserve System holds government securities that it buys and sells as part of its open market operations. Then, too, the Department of Health and Human Services maintains trust funds for the Social Security programs. These funds are invested in U.S. Treasury securities, and therefore represent a debt that the federal government owes to its agencies.

Figure 19.2   Trends in Federal Debt Held by the Public

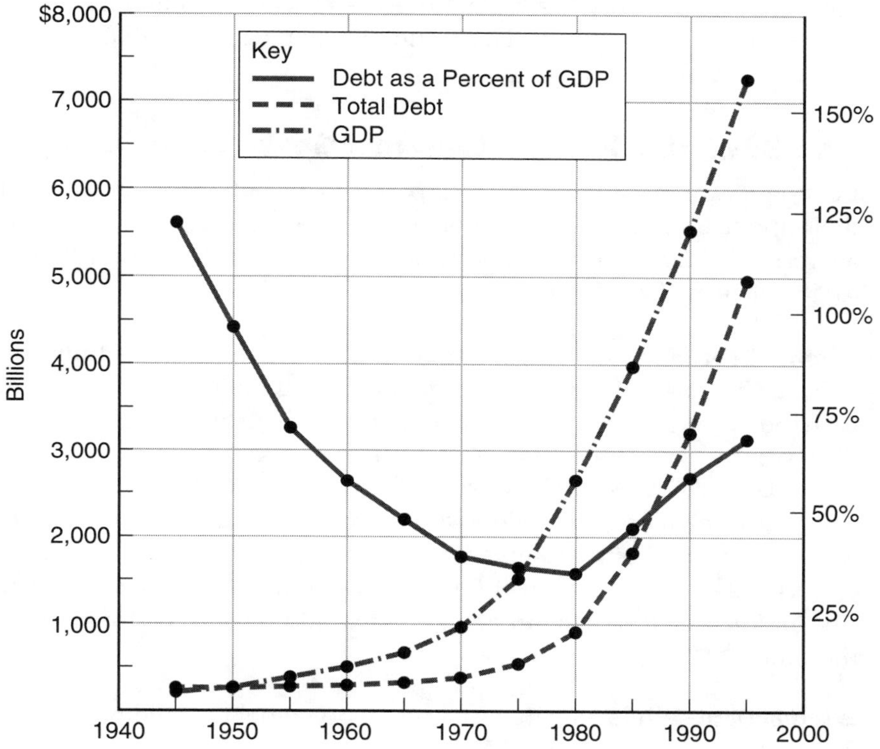

Is a $5.5 trillion debt too large? To a young person whose only income is a $15-a-week allowance, even a $200 debt might seem unmanageable. If that person has a part-time job with a weekly income of $90, however, he or she might be able to carry a $200 loan. Similarly for a family with an annual income of $20,000, a $10,000 auto loan could be out of reach. Those with an income of $50,000 might not find such a loan burdensome. In order to answer the question whether a $5 trillion debt is too large, we might consider the ability of the nation to carry such debt. Study Figure 19.2 to see what debts the country has carried in the past.

At the end of the Second World War in 1945, the GDP stood at $212 billion. That year's national debt was $260 billion, or 123 percent of the GDP. The debt declined somewhat in the five years after the war. After 1950, the national debt continued to climb, but the debt as a percent of GDP declined. This happened because the economy grew at a much faster rate than the debt. In 1980, for example, the national debt of

$909 billion represented only 34 percent of that year's GDP of $2.6 trillion. The rapidly growing budget deficits of the 1980s and 1990s reversed the 30-year trend. The national debt again increased as a percent of GDP.

Who Bears the Burden of Internal Government Debt?

Economists analyze the burden of government borrowing in terms of their opportunity costs. The opportunity cost of a federal bond issue is expressed in terms of the goods and services that the nation had to forgo because of the issue.

Internal Debt. Suppose that at a time when the economy was fully employed, the government chose to finance a $10 billion naval program with borrowed funds. Suppose, too, that the debt was an *internal debt*—that is, the money was borrowed from institutions and citizens of the United States. If there was full employment at the time, some shift out of civilian production would have to occur in order to build the warships and other items wanted by the navy. In other words, the opportunity cost of the naval-building program would have been the $10 billion worth of civilian goods that would have to be forgone for the time.

External Debt. While 86 percent of the national debt is held by U.S. individuals and institutions, the remainder is held by foreigners. This latter category is called an *external debt*.

Loans from foreign sources (that is, the external debt) might impose a burden on future generations of Americans, or they might not. An external national debt does impose a burden on future generations in the following example. Taxes collected in the future from U.S. residents to make the interest payments on those foreign loans will go to foreigners. In addition, when at some time in the future foreigners who hold U.S. government bonds choose to redeem them, dollars will flow out of the United States.

External debts will benefit future generations of Americans in the following way. When government spending is financed by foreign loans, it enables the United States to obtain goods from abroad without reducing domestic production. This situation occurs because if the government does not borrow from foreign sources, the government would have to borrow from internal sources. And as we discussed in Chapter 18, government borrowing through its sales of government securities reduces aggregate demand, which, in turn, reduces domestic production.

THE DEBATE ON DEFICIT FINANCING

Debate on budget imbalances has played a major role in presidential election politics. In 1988, Republican presidential candidate George Bush had pledged "No New Taxes." Later, as President, Bush approved a tax increase. Thus, in 1992, many people who might have voted to re-elect President Bush either stayed home, cast their votes for Bush's main opponent, Bill Clinton, or voted for a third-party candidate, Ross Perot. Budget deficits and the national debt also played a decisive role in the election of 1994. By promising to reduce taxes and balance the budget by 2002, the Republican party won control of both houses of Congress for the first time in 40 years. The national debt and budget deficits continued to be central to national political debates in the following years, including during the 1996 presidential election campaign.

The Arguments Against Deficit Financing

One often hears the following arguments in connection with the rising national debt:

The Government Is Setting a Poor Example. "If I continue to spend more than I earn, sooner or later I'll be unable to pay my debts, and I'll be forced into bankruptcy. Now, the same is true for a business and for the federal government. . . ." Statements such as this one are often used to criticize deficit spending. Many Americans believe that the federal government is living beyond its means by borrowing year after year. They feel that eventually the government will have to face the consequences and pay all its debts, as individuals and businesses have to do. Otherwise, they say, it will go bankrupt or stop operating.

Interest Payments on the National Debt Are Getting Out of Control. As the national debt has mounted, it requires heavy interest payments. In 1995, it was about $234 billion or 15 percent of the yearly budget. Critics of high debts fear that this percentage could easily grow to a point where taxpayers could never repay the debt.

The Burden Will Be on Future Generations. "The money that the federal government borrows has to be repaid by somebody. You know who that somebody will be? Our children and grandchildren, that's who. We're making future generations pay for our excesses." Arguments such as this are very frequently heard. The debts we contract today will add to the tax burden of future generations. Americans today pay about 31 percent of their gross income to taxes (local, state, and federal). Most Americans already think that this percentage is too great.

Dick Adair. Honolulu Advertiser/Rothco

They worry that when their children become taxpayers, the burden may be even greater.

The Federal Government Is Too Large. Many Americans think that the U.S. government is too large. Some say it is inefficient and bureaucratic. A leaner government, they believe, would work more efficiently and save money also. Other critics of the federal government dislike certain of its policies, whether it be the environmental laws, foreign aid, or other programs. Some Americans want many of the powers that the federal government now has turned over to the states. Such a transfer would shrink the size of the federal government.

Americans who want a smaller government usually support a balanced federal budget and a reduction in the national debt. They see the reduction of budgets for the various federal departments and agencies as a quick way to reduce the size and/or power of the U.S. government.

Budget Deficits Cause Inflation. Many people believe that there is a direct relationship between budget deficits and inflation. If inflation is to be kept under control, they say, the government must balance its budget. At a time of full employment of the nation's productive resources, deficit spending adds to the money supply. There is more money competing for the same quantity of goods and services. Thus, prices simply have to go higher. We can see this by using the formula $P = \dfrac{MV}{Q}$ introduced in Chapter 16. P (prices for goods and services) equals M (the amount of money in circulation) times V (how many transactions a dollar makes in a period of time) divided by Q (the quantity of goods and services our nation produces). Thus, if Q remains unchanged and M increases, P will increase.

Borrowing Redistributes Income Unfairly. Interest payments on the national debt are mostly financed out of income tax receipts. Since the largest holders of government bonds and notes are financial institutions and wealthy individuals, the effect of interest payments going to these institutions and individuals is to transfer wealth from middle-class taxpayers to wealthier ones. Those who believe this say that if the government did not have to make interest payments, more money would be available to provide services to those in need, or, alternately, to reduce taxes for middle- and low-income individuals.

Controlling Deficits Will Help Curb Waste. Many spending items passed by Congress can be viewed as wasteful in the sense that they serve a relatively small number of people or businesses. Members of Congress have traditionally proposed spending laws that benefit only certain people and businesses in their district. Sometimes these proposals become law because lawmakers gain support for their proposals by promising to support those of their colleagues. If passed, such spending laws are called *pork-barrel legislation* (or sometimes just *pork*). If lawmakers become serious at passing a balanced budget, the argument goes, then pork-barrel legislation would become more difficult to pass (and there would be less government waste).

The Arguments in Favor of Deficit Financing

Many economists believe that deficit financing can be a useful tool of government, at certain times. Moreover, they believe that a large national debt is not all that dangerous. Can a large debt bankrupt the nation? Does government borrowing impose an unfair burden on future generations? Let us look at these questions separately.

Can a Large Debt Bankrupt the Nation? Bankruptcy occurs when an individual or business can no longer pay its debts. The federal government, however, is not likely to go bankrupt because existing debt can be refinanced over and over again. Furthermore, the federal government has the power to tax and print money. No private individual or business can do this. In other words, the federal government can increase taxes or print as much money as it needs to meet its obligations. Of course, there is a possible danger if taxes are raised too high. Taxpayers might get angry and vote sitting lawmakers out of office. Moreover, if too much money is printed, the result might be severe inflation.

Future Generations Will Benefit From Today's Debts. Many economists concede that the debts we contract today will add to the tax burden of future generations. But, the economists say, these debts can also benefit future generations. They will benefit when they use the roads, bridges, schools, and hospitals that are now being built using borrowed money. They will benefit from the debt if deficit financing is used to fight a recession. They will benefit from current peacekeeping operations if these actions prevent a greater war.

Nevertheless, the same logic that justifies deficit financing during recessions would also call for balanced budgets during times of full employment and stable prices. Balanced budgets during these times help to stabilize the economy. A budget in balance would neither increase nor decrease aggregate demand and, therefore, would not contribute either to an inflationary gap or to a recessionary gap.

The Question of Inflation. Many economists concede that budget deficits will fuel inflation during times of full employment. At other times—such as during a recession, however—these economists see a role for deficit spending. By borrowing and incurring budget deficits during a recession, the government adds funds to the economy, stimulating production and employment.

For similar reasons, some economists call for *budget surpluses* as a way to fight inflation. A budget surplus is created when expenditures are less than receipts. Budget surpluses are extremely rare. There have been only eight since 1930, and one has to go back as far as 1969 to find the most recent example.

In order to create a surplus in the federal budget, Congress would need to enact some combination of tax increases and/or spending reductions. But tax increases and spending reductions are politically unpopular, and budget surpluses are not likely to occur in the foreseeable future.

The Need of Governments to Borrow. Many economists recognize that government debt is a necessity since certain programs cannot be paid for with the income that a government takes in during the course of one year. The basic facilities upon which the nation's economy, commerce, and industry depend is known as its *infrastructure*. Each of the following would be included in an inventory of the infrastructure: highways, aircraft control system, armed forces bases and equipment, and space exploration equipment. Since each of these can be expected to last for many years after production or construction, some economists think that it is appropriate for the federal government to spread their costs over time by borrowing to finance them. (On a local level, infrastructure would include roads, water and sewage systems, schools, hospitals, and police and fire stations. Local governments often borrow to pay for these facilities.)

Efforts to Reduce the National Debt

Ever since the deficit soared in the early 1980s, Congress and U.S. presidents have made a number of attempts at reducing budget deficits and the national debt. Democrats and Republicans, though, have differed in their focus on this matter. The Democrats have sought deficit reduction through increased taxes, while the Republicans have favored great reductions in spending for social programs and reduced taxes.

Gramm-Rudman-Hollings Act. In 1985, Congress enacted the **Gramm-Rudman-Hollings Act**, which called for year-by-year reductions in budget deficits and, by 1993, a balanced budget.

The act's goals were not met (see Table 19.1). Instead of declining, budget deficits grew during the years 1990–1993. The reasons for Gramm-Rudman-Holling's failure were both political and economic. In terms of politics, U.S. representatives and senators feared the wrath of their constituents if they were to approve the kind of spending cuts and tax increases necessary to reduce the deficit. In terms of economics, the country was going through a recession in the early 1990s. Fiscal policy during recessions require some combination of tax reductions and increased government spending. To have followed the Gramm-Rudman-Hollings guidelines (that is, increasing taxes and/or reducing spending) would have probably added to the economic decline.

Table 19.1   BUDGET DEFICITS, 1985–1997 (IN MILLIONS)

Year	Deficit
1985	212,334
1986	221,245
1987	149,769
1988	155,187
1989	152,481
1990	221,384
1991	269,169
1992	290,403
1993	255,140
1994	203,169
1995	163,900
1996	107,330
1997	22,600

The Proposed Balanced-Budget Amendment

In the wake of the 1994 congressional elections, the Republican party gained control of both the House and the Senate. Shortly thereafter, the Republican leadership introduced a measure that they claimed would eliminate future deficits in the federal budget: a Balanced-Budget Amendment to the U.S. Constitution.

As proposed, the **Balanced-Budget Amendment** would require that, starting in the year 2002, annual federal spending be limited to federal income.

Those favoring the Balanced-Budget Amendment argue as follows:

1. Individuals and business firms (as well as state and local governments) must live within their means. No less should be expected of the federal government.

2. Unless something is done to compel the government to live within its means, it will continue to spend more than it earns. The record shows that despite repeated promises to control its spending habits, Congress has shown a budgetary surplus in very few of the past 50 years. In all the other years, we have had deficits, which now total over $5 trillion.

3. Persistent annual budget deficits have pushed the national debt to an all-time high. As a result, 15 cents out of every dollar spent by the federal government now goes to pay the interest on its debt.

The U.S. Chamber of Commerce (a private association of U.S. businesses) summarized the consequences of this as follows:

"Escalating federal deficits necessitate large tax packages that sap the nation's savings, displace capital investment, slow economic growth and job creation, and weaken the competitiveness of U.S. firms. . . ."

4. With the budget in balance and the national debt shrinking, the burden of interest payments and the taxes needed to pay them will be lightened.

Those opposing the Balanced-Budget Amendment make the following points:

1. There are times when it is wrong not to borrow. If individuals were prevented by law from borrowing, it might cut down on gambling losses, but it would also prevent people from buying homes. By borrowing, one is able to spread over a long period of time the costs of major purchases. Similarly, a government has to be able to spread over a long period of time the cost of the assets it invests in major purchases. Similarly, government should be able to spread the cost of costly investments in assets that will benefit future generations, through long-term loans.

Improvements in the nation's transportation system, health care, recreational facilities, and armed forces are but a few examples of investments that are properly financed through long-term borrowing.

2. Government's power to spend and borrow is one of its most powerful weapons in the struggle to regulate the economy. Experience has shown, for example, that deficit spending is one of the most effective ways to propel the economy out of a recession.

3. Sooner or later, the government will probably have to borrow to meet some essential needs. If that happens, those opposed to the borrowing could sue on the grounds that the borrowing is in violation of the Balanced-Budget Amendment. Thus, the courts, rather than Congress, would become the final arbiters of government spending. This shift in powers would weaken the separation of powers principle that is built into the U.S. Constitution.

Budget Enforcement Act. President George Bush and Congress made another attempt at limiting the growth of the national debt by enacting the **Budget Enforcement Act** of 1990. This law was designed to limit spending. Yearly limits were set on spending for defense, international affairs, and domestic discretionary spending. It also introduced pay-as-you-go rules for Social Security and Medicare. With these rules, any proposals for new spending on these programs would have to be offset by cuts in other programs or by raising taxes. Despite this Budget Enforcement Act, the deficit continued to rise, mainly because of the automatic fiscal policies discussed earlier in this chapter. The recession of the early 1990s resulted in reduced tax collections and increased spending on unemployment and welfare programs. Adding to the deficit was the fact that federal spending for health care was also growing.

The Clinton Administration. In 1995–1996, members of Congress and President Clinton debated provisions of a bill to balance the budget by the year 2002. While the Republican-dominated Congress and the Democratic president did agree that deficit spending should be eliminated by that year, they disagreed on how to achieve the goal. Most Republicans wanted deep cuts in domestic spending along with tax cuts. Most Democrats wanted cuts in the defense budget, only minor cuts in domestic programs, but no tax cuts.

Summary

Congress and the president may attempt to reverse the course of the business cycle by increasing aggregate demand during recessions and decreasing it during periods of inflation. They can do so through discretionary fiscal policies—-the use of government's power to tax and spend. Unemployment insurance, income taxes, and welfare programs are automatic stabilizers—programs that automatically steady the economy without instructions from Congress.

The federal government has spent more than it has earned for many years. It has made up for the difference with borrowing and, therefore, is in debt. Government deficits usually rise during wars and recessions. The size of the national debt has been an issue in congressional and presidential elections. Critics of a large debt argue that the debt will fuel inflation, promote government waste, and saddle future generations with the obligation to pay for current excesses. Proponents of budget deficits argue that the debt is largely owed to ourselves, that government can always print more money or increase taxes to pay for the debt, and that deficit spending to improve the nation's infrastructure, to fight a war, and to fight a recession are all worthwhile.

REVIEWING THE CHAPTER

Understanding What You Have Read

1. Discretionary fiscal policies   (a) depend upon the skills of the Federal Reserve System for their success   (b) are more effective during periods of inflation than during recessions   (c) call for the adjustment of interest rates on loans to businesses   (d) require accurate forecasting and timely application to be effective.

2. Which of the following is the best example of a discretionary stabilizer?   (a) a tax increase   (b) a welfare program   (c) unemployment compensation   (d) Social Security payments.

3. The federal government's fiscal policies differ from its monetary policies in that its fiscal policies are concerned mostly with   (a) taxing and spending   (b) reserve ratios and discount rates   (c) economic stability in the short run   (d) the management of "checkbook money."

4. Fiscal tools have been more effective during recessions than during periods of inflation because   (a) people like to see the government reduce its spending   (b) Congress finds it is easier to reduce

taxes and increase spending than to adopt the opposite course of action   (c) the Open Market Committee finds it easier to buy bonds than to sell them   (d) a tax increase is relatively easy for the president to obtain.

5. An increase in government spending during periods of full employment would most likely result in   (a) price increases   (b) unemployment   (c) increased production   (d) increased employment.

6. Government spending that creates a deficit in the federal budget is most desirable when   (a) business profits are too high   (b) the cost of living has gone up   (c) there is rapid expansion in private spending   (d) there is a threat of a depression.

7. Which statement is true of the national debt?   (a) About one-quarter of it is held by the government itself.   (b) It declined after 1945 as a percentage of the GDP.   (c) It has passed the $4 trillion mark.   (d) All of the above.

8. The burden of the public debt on the taxpayer increases when   (a) interest rates fall   (b) both the public debt and the population are increasing at the same time   (c) the size of the debt is increasing proportionately more rapidly than national income   (d) national income is increasing and prices are relatively stable.

9. Who holds the largest portion of the national debt of the United States?   (a) foreign governments   (b) U.S. citizens and private institutions   (c) foreign private institutions and businesses   (d) the U.S. government.

10. Those who favor balanced budgets argue that deficit financing   (a) distributes wealth more equally   (b) sets a good example for individuals   (c) fuels inflation   (d) will benefit future generations at the expense of current taxpayers.

Thinking Critically

1. Assume that the nation has entered a period of inflation and that the federal government has decided to bring fiscal tools to bear upon the problem. (a) Explain *two* fiscal policies that the government might adopt to reverse the trend. (b) List and explain *three* built-in stabilizers that would automatically serve to slow down inflation.

2. Events in the late 1980s and early 1990s showed that neither monetary nor fiscal policies can guarantee full employment, a stable dollar, and economic growth. Identify and explain *four* reasons why monetary and fiscal policies may fail to achieve their goals.

3. The national debt passed $5 trillion in 1996, bringing the average debt to about $19,230 for every man, woman, and child in the country. This huge amount of debt has sparked a bitter controversy. Some people regard the debt as an evil that should be reduced and eventually eliminated. Others argue that the debt is necessary to the nation's economic health. Identify and explain *two* of the arguments advanced for *each* point of view.

4. The Balanced-Budget Amendment has been proposed as a measure that would eliminate future deficits.

   a. Prepare a chart indicating the pros and cons of the Balanced-Budget Amendment.

   b. Using the information you gathered in your chart, explain why you favor, or oppose, such a constitutional amendment.

Building Vocabulary

Match each item in Column A with its definition in Column B.

COLUMN A	COLUMN B
1. countercyclical	a. basic facilities upon which a nation's economy depends
2. automatic stabilizer	b. the total of all money owed by the federal government
3. discretionary fiscal policy	c. the money the federal government owes to U.S. institutions and citizens
4. national debt	d. spending by legislators for political reasons rather than for public necessity
5. in-kind payment	e. reversing the actions of cyclical trends
6. internal debt	f. an action that the federal government may use to regulate the economy
7. external debt	g. a proposed requirement that federal government spending be limited to its income
8. Balanced Budget Amendment	h. loans to the federal government from foreign institutions and people
9. infrastructure	i. a government program that automatically compensates for changes in the business cycle
10. "pork"	j. the giving of a good or service by a government

SKILLS: Interpreting a Statistical Table

Table 19.2   TRENDS IN FEDERAL DEBT (DOLLAR AMOUNTS IN BILLIONS)

Year	National Debt	GDP	Debt as a Percent of GDP
1945	$ 260.1	$ 212.0	122.7%
1950	256.9	265.8	96.6
1955	274.4	384.7	71.3
1960	290.5	504.6	57.6
1965	322.3	671.0	48.0
1970	380.9	985.4	38.7
1975	541.9	1,509.8	35.9
1980	909.1	2,644.1	34.4
1985	1,817.5	3,967.7	45.8
1990	3,206.6	5,522.2	58.5
1995	4,961.5	7,247.7	68.5
1996	5,181.9	7,484.7	69.2

Study Table 19.2. Based on the information given in the table and your reading in this chapter, answer the following:

1. Describe what happened to total debt in the period 1945–1996.

2. Describe what happened to total debt as a percent of GDP during the period 1945–1996.

3. In which year shown was debt as a percent of GDP the greatest? The lowest?

4. How do you explain why total debt was higher in 1975 than it was in 1950 while debt as a percent of GDP was lower in 1975 than it was in 1950?

5. Based upon the figures in the table and your readings of this chapter, explain why you believe that the size of the total debt is or is not a serious problem today.

Chapter 20

ECONOMIC CHALLENGES: POVERTY AND HEALTH CARE

Overview

The market system has worked well for most Americans, but we all know that a free market does not provide for the needs of all people. There are some individuals in the United States who are powerless to provide adequately for themselves and their families. Can our nation with its huge budget deficits provide financial support for all people who need help? Some will ask whether society should be responsible for the economic support of its members. They will say instead that it is each individual's responsibility to care for oneself and one's family? Even those who agree that society is responsible for the welfare of others disagree over what organizations within society should shoulder the responsibility—the federal government, the states, or the local governments? Or perhaps charities and other private organizations?

In addition to wondering about poverty in the United States, you may also wonder why many American families cannot afford the costs of doctor visits, drugs, and dental care and why they are not covered by any medical or dental insurance program. Other Americans, who may have such insurance, are concerned that medical and drug costs are rising so fast that their insurance premiums may increase and they will no longer be able to afford health insurance. Then, too, there are those Americans who are concerned that programs to provide medical coverage for the elderly and the poor may become too burdensome to U.S. taxpayers.

In this chapter, we will discuss two major challenges facing the United States today: poverty and health care. We begin with a discussion of poverty, what it is, how it is measured, and who are the poor.

POVERTY IN THE UNITED STATES

The distribution of income in the United States—and in every other country, for that matter—is unequal. We find poverty in the midst of plenty. Why is this so? Can we (and should we) do anything about it? First, let us see who the poor are.

Figure 20.1   Americans Living Below the Poverty Line

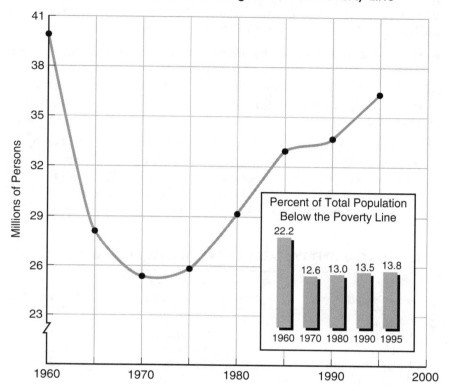

Percent of Total Population Below the Poverty Line

Who Are the Poor?

According to the U.S. Census Bureau, in 1996 approximately 36 million people in the country (or 13.7 percent of the population) were poor. By government definition, the poor are people whose cash incomes fall below certain set minimums. These minimum income levels, or *poverty levels* (also called *poverty thresholds*) are adjusted from year to year to account for changes in prices. In 1996, the poverty threshold was $7,995 for an individual living alone and $16,036 for a family of four.

The third column of Table 20.1 lists *poverty rates* (percentages of people below the poverty level) for various groups. As the table indicates, certain groups suffer a much higher rate of poverty than the national average.

Members of Some Minority Groups. In 1996 (when 11 percent of the nation's families were classified as poor), the poverty rates for African-American and Hispanic families were 26.1 percent and 26.4 percent respectively. Compare these percentages with the poverty rate for white families that year. You might note that the poverty level of white individuals (11.2) was also much smaller than that of African-American individuals (28.4) and persons of Hispanic origin (29.4).

Family Households Headed by Women in Which There Is No Husband Present. Families in which the head of the household is a woman and there is no husband present show a significantly high incidence of poverty. In 1996, some 32.6 percent of the families in those circumstances were poor.

The Young. Approximately 40 percent of all individuals living below the poverty level are under the age of 18. As indicated by Table 20.1, the poverty rate was greatest among persons under 18 (20.5 percent) followed by persons 18 to 24 years of age (17.9 percent). In comparison, the poverty rate was lowest among persons 45 to 54 years of age (7.6 percent).

Table 20.1 POVERTY STATUS OF INDIVIDUALS AND FAMILIES, 1996

Category	Number Below Poverty Level	Poverty Rate
Total Persons	36,529,000	13.7
White	24,650,000	11.2
African American	9,694,000	28.4
Hispanic origin*	8,697,000	29.4
Asian and Pacific Islander	1,454,000	14.5
Age		
Under 18 years	14,463,000	20.5
18 to 24 years	4,466,000	17.9
25 to 44 years	9,436,000	11.2
45 to 54 years	2,516,000	7.6
55 to 59 years	1,086,000	9.4
60 to 64 years	1,134,000	11.5
65 years and over	3,428,000	10.8
All Families	7,708,000	11.0
White	5,059,000	8.6
African American	2,206,000	26.1
Hispanic origin	1,748,000	26.4
Type of Family		
All Married Couples	3,010,000	5.6
White	2,416,000	5.1
African American	352,000	9.1
Hispanic origin	815,000	18.0
All Female Householders, No Husband Present	4,167,000	32.6
White	2,276,000	27.3
African American	1,724,000	43.7
Hispanic origin	823,000	50.9

*Persons of Hispanic origin may be of any race.

The Distribution of Income

Some people earn more than others. In Chapter 8, we discussed how market and nonmarket forces affect wage earnings. In addition to wage income, however, many individuals receive all or part of their income from non-wage sources (such as from government payments, interest on savings accounts or bonds, dividends, rents, insurance income payments, and pension funds). The amount of income that different individuals receive from non-wage sources varies considerably. An individual's total income, therefore, includes earnings from wages and non-wage sources.

Measuring Income Distribution. A commonly used measure of *income distribution* (the percentage of total income received by various groups) ranks household earnings from the lowest to the highest incomes. The total number of families is divided into equal fifths, and the total income earned by each group is tallied. Statisticians then calculate what percentage of the total income for each group total. These percentages are illustrated in Table 20.2.

As we look at Table 20.2, we can see changes in income distribution patterns in the United States during the period 1950–1996. For example, the lowest fifth received an increasing percentage of total income during the period 1950 to 1970, but their relative situation deteriorated after 1970. The second fifth's percentage of total income remained stable from 1950 to 1970, but declined thereafter. The middle fifth's and fourth fifth's shares of total income did not change much over the years, while that of the highest fifth declined slightly during the period 1950–1980 (and has more recently skyrocketed). What can we conclude (from Table 20.2) regarding the equality of income distribution in the United States? First, we might say the obvious—that income is not equally distributed. A second response might be that during the period 1950–1970, income distribution tended toward greater equality. But in the period since 1970, the trend has gone toward greater inequality.

Table 20.2 PERCENT OF INCOME RECEIVED BY EACH FIFTH OF FAMILIES

Income Rank	1950	1960	1970	1980	1990	1996
Lowest Fifth	4.5	4.9	5.5	5.3	4.6	4.2
Second Fifth	12.0	12.0	12.0	11.6	10.8	10.0
Middle Fifth	17.4	17.6	17.4	17.5	16.6	15.8
Fourth Fifth	23.5	23.5	23.5	24.0	23.8	23.1
Highest Fifth	42.6	42.0	41.6	41.6	44.3	46.8

Figure 20.2   The Lorenz Curve

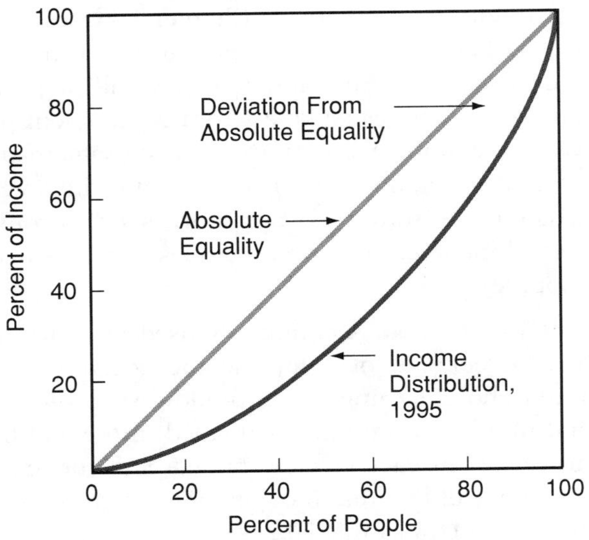

This graph portrays the theoretical and actual income data in a Lorenz Curve. The closer the Lorenz Curve approaches the 45° diagonal line, the greater is the degree of equality of income distribution. The further the Lorenz Curve moves from the 45° diagonal line, the greater is the degree of inequality of income distribution.

The Lorenz Curve

Economists and statisticians often use the *Lorenz Curve* to illustrate income distribution graphically. The Lorenz Curve shows how much of total income goes to each portion of the nation's population. In Figure 20.2, the vertical and horizontal dimensions are scaled in units of 20 percent, up to a total of 100 percent. The horizontal axis represents individuals in a given year, while the vertical axis represents the share of total income that the individuals received.

In Figure 20.2, a diagonal line at a 45° angle to the horizontal axis represents perfectly equal income distribution. At any point along this 45° line, the percentage of the population is exactly equal to the percentage of the total income earned. Thus, 10 percent of the population is shown as earning 10 percent of the income, 30 percent of the population as earning 30 percent of the income, and so on. Plotted against this theoretical line is the Lorenz Curve, which shows the actual distribution of income. The distance between an equal distribution and the actual distribution illustrates the deviation from absolute equality (or the *degree of inequality*) in income distribution that year.

The Growing Problem of Homelessness

One of the most visible problems of cities is their growing numbers of homeless people. In all major U.S. cities, the sight of people sleeping in doorways, parks, playgrounds, bus stations, and the like has become common. Homelessness has also become a problem in the suburbs, and in other towns and small cities as well. While the exact number of homeless people is difficult to measure, the federal government estimates the total at almost 500,000.

Why Does Homelessness Exist?

In an effort to establish why people become homeless, experts have come up with a number of causes.

Lack of Affordable Housing. Changes in urban housing patterns have been a cause of homelessness. Rising rents, rising costs of houses, and the rejuvenation of downtown areas of cities have displaced low-income people. The availability of the boarding houses and single-room hotels that had been typically used by poor, single adults dwindled because landlords found them unprofitable. Landlords were unable to raise rents to meet rising costs of operating such facilities. In many cases, the landlords abandoned their properties. In other cases, they sold the buildings, which were then converted to some other use. Unable to afford available rentals and having nowhere else to go, poor individuals and families have tried to find make-shift shelter wherever they can. We are all aware of homeless people staying in abandoned cars, railroad and subway stations, beach areas, parks, and on the streets. We may, though, be less aware that many homeless people have moved in with relatives. But these arrangements are often only temporary. Crowded conditions often lead to disputes, which can lead to the same people becoming homeless again.

Long-Term Joblessness. Figure 20.3 illustrates yet another reason why the homeless ranks have been growing. People who have been jobless for six months or more are classified by the U.S. Labor Department as *long-term unemployed*. As indicated by the graph, long-term unemployment has been increasing over the decades. Unable to find jobs or to afford housing, numbers of the long-term unemployed have either chosen or been forced to live on the streets.

Mental Disability. About 500,000 Americans were residents of state mental hospitals up until the early 1960s. But the costs of hospital care were high. That factor, coupled with the widely accepted viewpoint that keeping individuals in institutions did more harm than good, led to the release of most mentally ill patients. Since the 1960s, the number of people who have

Figure 20.3 Unemployment Rates and the Long-Term Unemployed

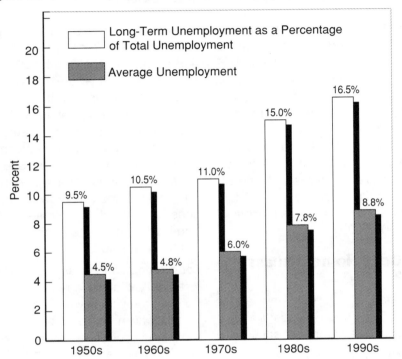

been institutionalized has fallen from some 560,000 to fewer than 100,000.

In the 1960s, experts thought that communities would open local clinics for follow-up treatment of the mentally disabled. But many Americans were unwilling to allow facilities for the mentally ill to be set up in their neighborhood. Also, economic recessions made it difficult for local governments to fund outpatient mental health clinics. Thus, few of these facilities were actually provided. Unable to cope with the stresses of modern life, many of the mentally disabled joined the ranks of the urban homeless.

Drug and Alcohol Abuse. Many of the homeless are alcohol and/or drug abusers. As such, they often cannot hold jobs. Some will go to extremes in order to get money to support their abusive habit. The easy availability of dangerous, addictive drugs such as crack and heroin has made it that much more difficult for homeless people to regain control of their lives and get off the streets. Without money for virtually anything but drugs or alcohol, addicts cannot afford proper housing. Instead, they use abandoned buildings, the streets, parks, and alleyways as their living quarters.

Teenage Pregnancy. Still another cause of homelessness is a rise in teenage pregnancy. Of course, not all (or even most) teenage young mothers are homeless. But they are much less likely to complete school than those who defer parenting. And without schooling, they find it difficult to get jobs. Studies show that many teenage mothers become homeless within four years of the birth of their first child.

What Is Being Done to Help the Homeless?

Various charities and religious organizations attempt to help the homeless. For the most part, though, programs to help the homeless have been the responsibility of state and local governments. They run shelters, soup kitchens, and various counseling services.

Not until the late 1980s did the federal government accept responsibility to assist the homeless. The **McKinney Act** of 1987 was the first law authorizing federal expenditures on emergency food, shelter, and counseling for the homeless. This was followed by the **HOPE (Home Ownership and Opportunity for People Everywhere) Act** of 1990. The HOPE program combines financial assistance in paying rent with certain services, such as counseling, to help homeless persons to live in (and eventually purchase) their own home.

PROGRAMS TO FIGHT POVERTY

At one time, dealing with poverty was a local concern. Religious groups, private charities, and individuals helped the poor in their neighborhoods. Some state and local governments gave assistance to the poor, the sick, and the aged. Not until the 1930s (during the Great Depression) did the federal government begin to assume the major responsibility for programs to deal with poverty and the poor. These efforts were part of the "New Deal" legislation of the 1930s. The government later expanded its responsibilities in this area, especially with the "Great Society" programs of the 1960s.

Government programs to fight poverty have sought either to transfer enough income to the poor to raise them above the poverty line (*income-maintenance programs*) or to attempt to reduce poverty by addressing those factors that contribute to poverty in the United States (*labor-market strategies*).

Income-Maintenance Programs

A poor person, by federal government definition, is one whose income falls below the poverty threshold. With income-maintenance programs, the government attempts to provide income to an individual or family to move the person or family above the threshold. Some income-maintenance programs provide money, while others offer in-kind payments of goods and services. Income maintenance may be in the form of social insurance or public assistance.

Social Insurance. Social Security and unemployment compensation are the government's principal social insurance programs. Like private insurance plans, these programs provide money benefits paid out of premiums. While workers and their employers both regularly pay a tax that supports the Social Security system, the employer alone pays for unemployment insurance. (See Chapter 11 for a discussion of the Social Security and unemployment compensation programs.)

Public Assistance. In contrast to social insurance programs (which protect those who have earned coverage during their working years) are welfare programs. They help the millions of needy people who, for one reason or another, are not covered by social insurance. The most important welfare programs are Supplemental Security Income, Food Stamps, Medicaid, and (until recently) Aid to Families With Dependent Children.

1. Supplemental Security Income (SSI). The SSI program is administered by the Social Security Administration and provides cash benefits aimed at assuring a minimum monthly income to needy people who are 65 or older, blind, or disabled and who are not otherwise covered by Social Security programs. Eligibility for SSI is based on one's income plus assets, such as savings accounts or home ownership. Eligible parents with disabled children under the age of 18, for example, receive payments averaging $400 a month under the SSI program. In 1995, over 6,400,000 people received SSI benefits.

2. Food Stamps. The federal food-stamp program provides noncash benefits to eligible recipients. It issues food stamps (which are coupons) to needy persons, who can exchange them for food at food stores. Over 25 million people in the United States received food stamps in 1996. The value of the stamps received by the average beneficiary amounted to $73 per month. The food-stamp program cost the federal government over $22 billion that year.

3. Medicaid. Many persons in the SSI program, as well as certain other needy persons, are eligible for health care under the Medicaid program. Medicaid, like the food-stamp program, is a noncash benefit program because recipients receive services but not cash payments. Since each state designs its own Medicaid program, the requirements for coverage and the benefits vary. In general, Medicaid pays for both medical and hospital care as well as for a variety of health-related services. Some states also provide dental care, eye-glasses, and physical rehabilitation for Medicaid recipients. Medicaid costs are shared by the federal government and the states and localities.

4. Aid to Families With Dependent Children (AFDC). This was the largest and costliest of the welfare programs whose benefits were paid in cash. The federal government set the general standards of eligibility for AFDC and contributed more than half of the program's funds. The administration of the program itself, however, was in the hands of the states. The benefits available to recipients varied from state to state. In 1996, maximum monthly AFDC payments for a family in the United States ranged from $118 in Mississippi to $731 in Alaska. The national average monthly per-family benefit was $372. In 1996, Congress abolished AFDC and replaced it with block grants to the states. Congress imposed several rules regarding these grants, including provisions that encourage welfare recipients to take a job.

The food-stamp program, set up in 1964, is administered by the U.S. Department of Agriculture. About 10 percent of the U.S. population receives food stamps.

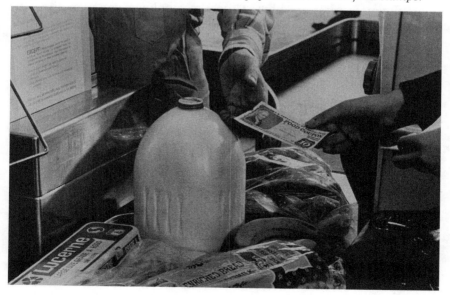

Other Noncash Programs. In addition to the government programs already described, poor individuals often receive assistance in the form of federal *rent subsidies* (partial payment of rents) or low rents in public housing. Local communities, private charities, and religious institutions also help the poor by providing food, clothing, subsidized housing, and other services.

Labor-Market Strategies

We have just described programs that attack the symptoms of poverty by transferring additional cash and noncash income to the poor. Most of the money spent by government to fight poverty has gone to these so-called transfer programs. These programs transfer money from one group (those who paid taxes to government) to others—in this case, the poor. Other strategies have sought to reduce the causes of poverty. These are called *labor-market strategies*.

Efforts to Promote Economic Growth. Poverty can result from being unemployed. Thus, the number of poor people rises during periods of national economic troubles when businesses are letting workers go. During the late 1970s and early 1980s, the U.S. economy experienced high rates of unemployment. Employment improved as the economy soared during the mid-1980s, but unemployment increased again as the economy slowed down in the late 1980s and early 1990s. Unemployment declined as the economy improved in 1994–1998.

In Chapters 18 and 19, we discussed various monetary and fiscal policies that the federal government uses to correct the economy. Both fiscal and monetary policies are used to fight a recession, a time when unemployment rates are high. Thus, these policies can sometimes be considered labor-market strategies to fight poverty.

Government Hiring of the Unemployed. Americans' prosperity suffered a serious decline during the Great Depression of the 1930s. At least one sixth of the population was then receiving some form of welfare assistance and thousands of unemployed were roaming the countryside. New Deal theorists hoped that all those who could not work would be cared for by the states but that unemployed people capable of working would be put to work. One New Deal program that provided the unemployed with work was the **Works Progress Administration (WPA)** of 1935. It hired many destitute artists, musicians, writers, and actors. Another New Deal program, the **Civilian Conservation Corps**, hired 2 million young people in conservation work. They planted trees, dug drainage ditches, set up forest-fire control systems, and constructed reservoirs.

In recent decades, the federal government has not run any major works projects. Some Americans have called for a revival of the Civilian Conservation Corps, but opponents of the idea have cited the huge

The U.S. government's Head Start program tries to fight poverty by providing instruction and activities to preschool children from disadvantaged families.

costs of such an undertaking. Many local governments today have public works programs.

Education and Job Training. "Human capital" is the economists' term to describe the physical and mental skills of the labor force. One of the chief problems faced by the poor is that they frequently have fewer marketable skills and less education than the rest of the population. For this reason, federal, state, and local governments have sponsored programs to improve the job skills and education of the labor force in general and to target programs for the poor in particular.

In 1982, Congress passed the **Job Training Partnership Act (JTPA).** The act funded job-training programs for (*a*) the economically disadvantaged, (*b*) dislocated persons, and (*c*) others with barriers to employment. Some of the funded programs provide classroom training. In other programs, individuals receive on-the-job training. In still other programs, an individual is placed temporarily with an employer in order to become acquainted with the world of work. In vocational exploration and apprenticeship training, individuals learn trade skills while working for an employer.

Health Programs. The physical and mental health of the labor force is an important ingredient in human capital. In the United States, the poor generally have below-average health. Since disability and illness reduce an individual's ability to earn a living, the government's efforts to improve the nation's health and safety also help to reduce poverty, days lost from work, and unemployment. Medicare, Medicaid, and the public health services represent the government's commitments to these goals. While permanent disabilities cannot be undone, many can be prevented. Congress created the **Occupational Safety and Health Administration (OSHA)** in an effort to prevent job-related injuries and illnesses. OSHA representatives inspect workplaces that they think might be unsafe. Employers can be fined for safety violations found by OSHA.

Efforts to Reduce Discrimination. As we can see from Table 20.1, poverty is greatest among certain minority groups and among families headed by women. Discrimination has been a major cause of this poverty.

Discrimination is illegal. Federal civil rights acts prohibit discrimination for reasons of race, color, religion, national origin, sex, or disability where the effect of such discrimination is to affect access to jobs. The **Equal Employment Opportunity Commission (EEOC)** enforces provisions of these laws. Many state and local governments have similar laws.

Figure 20.4 Median Weekly Earnings of Male and Female Workers

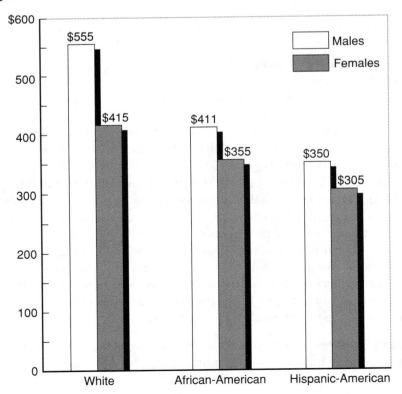

Another approach that the government uses to reduce discrimination is known as *affirmative action*. Some affirmative action plans set a quota of women and minority persons who must be hired as jobs are filled. The federal government has required some of its contractors to maintain affirmative action programs. The effect of affirmative action is to allow some minority members and women to obtain jobs that would otherwise have been given to white males.

Critics of affirmative action have termed it "reverse discrimination" on the grounds that less qualified persons may displace more qualified ones solely because of race or sex. Those favoring affirmative action say that the programs serve to correct centuries-old racist and sexist practices.

Raising the Minimum Wage. The **Fair Labor Standards Act** of 1938 established minimum wages and maximum hours for workers and prohibited child labor in industries engaged in interstate commerce. The minimum wage was set at $.40 per hour. Although this is a low figure today, in 1938 $.40 an hour was above what the market was offering low-wage workers. Forty hours was set as the maximum workweek. After 40 hours, a worker was to receive time-and-a-half pay. The 1938 act accomplished several goals. By placing a floor under wages, wages rose higher than they would have if left to market forces alone. Furthermore, employers tended to hire more workers rather than pay overtime to a smaller workforce. The provisions of the act that restricted child labor tended to expand the employment of adults.

The minimum wage has been increased several times since it was originally set at $.40 per hour in 1938. In 1996, Congress increased the federal minimum wage from $4.25 to $5.15 an hour (to be achieved in two incremental steps by September 1997). There are arguments for and against raising the minimum wage above its present rate. Those who favor increasing the minimum wage argue that the present minimum does not provide a worker with a living wage, particularly if the worker is supporting a family. Those who oppose a higher minimum wage argue that it would lead employers to lay off some workers since the employers' costs would be going up. Furthermore, foreign competitors who did not have corresponding minimums would have lower labor costs and, thus, a competitive advantage over domestic producers.

Medicaid and Medicare Reforms. Members of Congress have proposed saving millions of dollars now being spent on Medicaid and Medicare programs by restricting eligibility rules and cutting benefits. For example, they would drop the existing rule that gives all SSI recipients eligibility to receive Medicaid.

The cost of government-sponsored health-care programs are a major political issue. As part of their effort to balance the budget by 2002, the Republicans in Congress have proposed to reduce expenditures for the Medicare and Medicaid programs by some $270 billion. Those who support the cutbacks explain that cuts are needed to prevent the Medicare and Medicaid systems from bankruptcy.

Medicaid is a joint state-federal program for the poor. Republicans in the House and Senate are proposing to cut federal financing of Medicaid. At the same time, however, the states are also trying to cut back their expenditures on Medicaid, which amounted to some $69 billion in 1995. Among the proposals either being considered or implemented in various states to reduce Medicaid costs are the following:

- Reduce reimbursement rates paid to hospitals, nursing homes, and other care providers
- Require Medicaid recipients to join managed-care programs
- Scale back long-term care benefits for the elderly
- Reduce a wide array of health services, such as dental care for the poor.

More Block Grants to States. Some critics of existing welfare programs believe that the federal government is too large, too bureaucratic, too unresponsive, and too expensive to properly administer antipoverty programs. Instead, they would like to have the federal government give block grants to each state to spend on such programs as they wished.

Relying on Private Initiatives. Some critics of welfare would prefer to see the responsibility to help the poor given to charitable and religious organizations.

PERSONAL RESPONSIBILITY AND WORK OPPORTUNITY ACT

In 1996, Congress passed a major overhaul of the nation's welfare laws, the **Personal Responsibility and Work Opportunity Act**. Politicians were responding to a widespread criticism of the existing welfare system. Many people said that welfare compounded the problem of poverty.

Most people in the United States in 1996 associated welfare with AFDC (Aid to Families With Dependent Children). Individuals and single parents who were poor *and* were taking care of one or more children qualified for AFDC. The number of people receiving AFDC assistance was about 15 million. Two-thirds of that number were children. Contributing to the rapid increase in the number of children living in poverty in the United States was the great increase in single-parent families and children born out of wedlock (one child in three). The poverty rate for children in single-parent families (55 percent) was four times greater than the rate for children living in two-parent families. A profile of long-term welfare recipients indicated that a large share of chronic welfare mothers bore children while they were in their teens, never graduated from high school, had never been married, and had little or no work experience. Under the AFDC rules, the more children a woman had, the more cash she collected. Since the jobs available to most AFDC recipients generally paid less than the package of food stamps, cash handouts, and health coverage to which they were entitled, there was little reason for recipients to take a job. As a result, critics of AFDC concluded, generations of poor Americans came to look upon welfare as an acceptable way of life.

A New Welfare System

In a dramatic break with the past, Congress abolished AFDC in 1996. They replaced it with a work-orientated, time-limited system run largely by the states. Instead of a federal entitlement to monthly checks and other benefits, poor people will be given help by the state and local governments, but only for a limited time. Most will be expected to find a job and work.

Among the more important features of the 1996 welfare reform act are:

- The federal guarantee of welfare payments was replaced with lump sum payments, or block grants, to the states. The total amount for all such block grants—$16.4 billion—will remain the same until the year 2002.
- In exchange for the block grants, states accept the responsibility to design and administer welfare programs. Although the states have to follow federal guidelines, they have much latitude to experiment with programs that are different from ones in other states. The purposes of the experiments are to reduce welfare costs and get recipients to be self-supporting.
- States receiving block grants are required to impose work requirements on people seeking welfare benefits. States that do not meet these requirements may lose some of their federal grants.
- Individuals are limited to receiving welfare benefits for no more than five years.
- The heads of families receiving welfare are required to find work within two years. Failure to do so could result in a loss of benefits for the whole family.

- Childless adults ages 18 to 50 are limited to three months of food stamps during any three-year period.
- Unmarried teenage mothers are required to live at home and stay in school to be eligible for benefits.
- Cash aid and food stamps will be denied to anyone convicted of a felony drug charge.
- Food stamps and some welfare benefits will be denied to noncitizens (both legal and illegal immigrants).
- Immigrant arriving in the future may be ineligible for most other government benefits as well. States will be allowed (but not required) to cut off cash assistance, Medicaid, and other benefits during an immigrant's first five years in the United States.

Those favoring the new law said that the old system was a horrible failure because it trapped people in a cycle of dependency. President Clinton summed up the argument in favor of welfare reform by saying that it would "...strengthen incentives for the poor to find jobs, fend for themselves, and enjoy the self-respect that self-reliance offers."

Criticisms of Welfare Reform

While the 1996 welfare reform law was quite popular, advocates for the poor found much to criticize.

- Advocates for immigrants questioned the harsh provisions of the new law as they affect immigrants, both legal and illegal ones.
- Some economists argued that there are not enough jobs for all the welfare recipients to fill even in times of a strong economy. In a recession, the difficulty of finding work for the nation's poor will become much more difficult.
- Some state officials claimed that the 1996 law is too complex and some of the new welfare rules are too vague. They said that the new state welfare systems will be difficult to administer.
- Opponents of the bill questioned the wisdom of placing responsibility for administering welfare into the hands of state officials. They fear that since the poor have little political power in state governments, the temptation among state officials will be to neglect the poor.
- Local officials are concerned that as people are eventually dropped from state welfare roles, they will become the responsibility of county, city, and town governments, which do not have the funds to care for large numbers of poor people.

Opposition to Radical Welfare Reform

The problems of the poor cut across state and local lines. Therefore, opponents of radical changes in welfare programs say that the federal government must have a role in running welfare programs throughout the country. Moreover, they say, only the federal government can ensure that poor people living in different states and localities receive adequate assistance. They say that it would be unfair for welfare recipients in one state to receive much more or much less aid than those in other states.

The critics of radical welfare reform argue that churches, synagogues, and other private charitable institutions cannot deal well with the wide range of problems faced by the poor. Some Americans say that many welfare reforms would increase, not decrease poverty. These reforms will fail, say the reform critics, because they are based on widely held, but mistaken claims about the poor. Among these claims are the following:

Claim. People living on welfare are likely to pass on welfare dependency to their children.

Rebuttal. Recent studies indicate that two out of three young people whose parents received welfare did not receive it as adults.

Claim. Poverty is a lifelong affliction.

Rebuttal. Studies show that one in five poor people in any given year are not poor the following year.

Claim. Welfare costs are a burden for middle-class families.

Rebuttal. In 1994, the share of taxes going to federal programs to aid the poor came to $617 annually for families with incomes of $50,000. At the same time, families in that income category received benefits averaging about the same or slightly more than the amount paid in taxes.

Those opposed to radical welfare reforms summarize their position as follows:

● Poverty in the midst of plenty is morally wrong. It would be wrong, therefore, for the world's most powerful nation to do anything less than it is able to help its poor.

● By far the largest share of the nation's welfare benefits flows to children. While it might be argued that some adult poor are "undeserving" of assistance, who would want to deny decent food, housing, and clothing to the very young?

● Welfare programs provide a kind of insurance for the risks associated with a market economy. Today's well-paid worker may discover, for example, that the industry he works in has suddenly been downsized, and that the skills he developed over the years have suddenly been made obsolete by new technology. Similarly, the middle manager may suddenly find that her recently reorganized company no longer needs her services. Illness, widowhood, and divorce are other hazards of life that can lead to poverty. It is not hard to imagine how virtually anyone could suddenly find himself or herself numbered among the nation's poor. The security of knowing that help will be available if the worst happens makes the welfare programs worth their costs.

Some Puzzling Questions

Can poverty be eliminated in America? If so, will people in the United States be willing to bear the cost of whatever it takes to achieve that goal? If not, how much poverty will the nation be willing to accept? And who will decide which groups will receive assistance, and which will not? While most people agree that these and similar questions need to be discussed, finding answers is certain to generate a long and bitter debate.

Table 20.3   HEALTH AND HEALTH CARE IN SELECTED INDUSTRIALIZED NATIONS, 1995

	Health Care Expenditures		Life Expectancy (years)	Infant Mortality Rate (per 1,000)
	Percent of GDP	Per Capita		
Australia	8.6%	$1,741	77.8	7.1
Canada	9.6	2,049	78.3	6.8
France	9.8	1,956	78.4	6.5
Italy	7.7	1,507	77.9	7.4
Japan	7.2	1,581	79.4	4.3
Sweden	7.2	1,075	78.4	5.6
United Kingdom	6.9	1,246	77.0	7.0
United States	14.2	3,701	76.0	7.9

THE HEALTH-CARE CRISIS

Health care in the United States is in crisis. It is a crisis characterized by high costs for employers and government and by too many people unable to afford medical care.

How High the Cost?

Compared to other industrialized countries, the United States devotes a larger share of its GDP to health care (see Table 20.3). Moreover, individual Americans pay more for health care than the people of the other industrial countries listed. For Americans, the costs seem to go up every year. Many fear that they might be unable to afford medical care when they become old—just when they need it most.

The federal government has found it increasingly difficult to balance its budget because of, among other things, the high cost of health care. State governments and some local governments are also burdened by high medical expenditures.

U.S. businesses have been affected by rising health-care costs. About 65 percent of private health insurance is paid for by employers. But the rapidly increasing insurance costs have made it difficult (if not impossible) for many business firms to continue to provide the same level of coverage for their employees. Many firms have put some or all of the burden of paying health insurance premiums on the shoulders of their employees.

There are great discrepancies in what type of health care various Americans get. For those who can afford to buy what is available, most experts agree that health care in the United States is the best in the world. But not everyone gets high levels of care. Statistics in Table 20.3

Figure 20.5 The Rise in Health-Care Costs

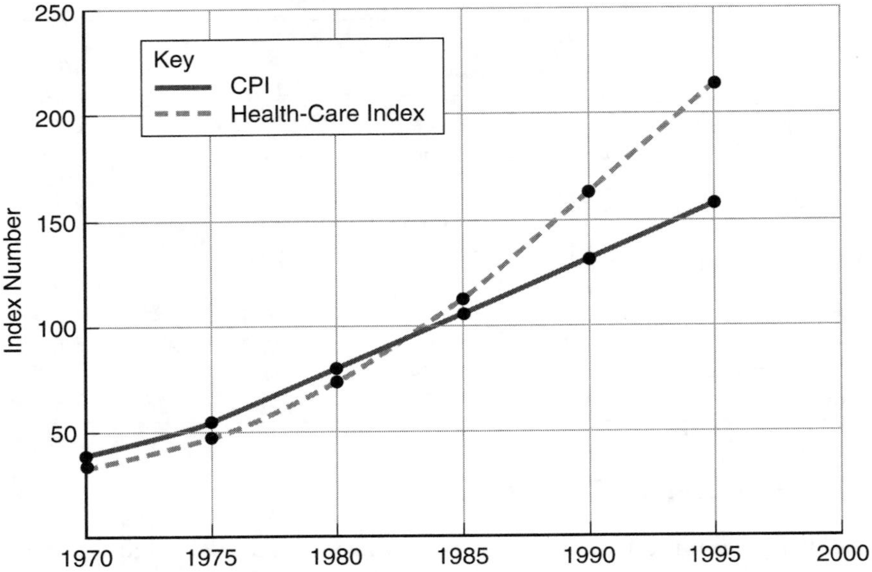

Prior to the 1980s, health-care costs increased at roughly the same rate as the Consumer Price Index. After the 1980s, the health-care component of the CPI exploded. By 1992, medical-care prices were increasing at more than twice the inflation rate.

show that people in the United States die younger and lose more of their infants than the residents of many other industrialized nations. To some extent, the nation's poor showing is due to the fact that some 42 million Americans are without health insurance. Thus, they are unable to afford adequate health care.

Why Have Health-Care Costs Been Increasing?

The rapid increase in health-care costs can be explained in terms of demand and supply.

Factors Tending to Increase the Demand for Health Care. A number of factors tend to increase the demand for health-care services and also add to the price of those services. In the United States, these factors include (1) health insurance and its effects, (2) our aging population, (3) lifestyle changes, and (4) environmental changes.

1. Health Insurance and Its Effects. It seems hard to believe that few Americans had health insurance prior to the 1960s. Most people then accepted the fact that one would have to pay out of one's pocket (or go to a public clinic) if one required health care. Today, however, health insurance is often included as one of the fringe benefits of employment. It is virtually always included in union-negotiated contracts. Workers, both union and nonunion, have come to expect that their employer will provide them with some form of health insurance. In 1965, Medicare extended health care coverage to most individuals over 65, and Medicaid began reimbursing health-care costs for the poor. The result of all these trends is that today most Americans believe that they are entitled to health insurance.

The increase in numbers of people with health insurance, in turn, has increased the demand for health care. This has happened partly because of our tax laws. It works this way. The dollar value of employer-provided health insurance is exempt from income taxes and payroll taxes (such as Social Security). This exemption encourages employees to take part of their pay in the form of health insurance. Most employees, however, do not think of their health insurance coverage as part of their wages. As a result:

● The demand for health insurance is greater than it would be if its dollar value were taxed as ordinary income. Suppose, for example, that an individual is in the 15 percent tax bracket and receives health insurance that costs the employer $1,000. The employee saves $150 ($1,000 × .15 = $150) that would have been paid as taxes if the $1,000 had been considered part of the employee's income.

● Millions of Americans work for employers who do not provide health insurance. To buy health insurance, these workers have to pay much higher premiums than do employers who can buy insurance for their employees at group rates. Moreover, the employee who buys his or her own health insurance can deduct only part of these payments from income taxes and only if the cost of the health insurance and the employee's payments for medical expenses exceed 7.5 percent of adjusted gross income. As a result of these factors, many non-covered employees go without health insurance.

Another reason why health insurance may increase the cost of health care results from the fact that health insurance entitles people to get medical and hospital services at little or no out-of-pocket expense. This is a good-news/bad-news situation. The good news is that with insurance, people can afford to pay for the health care they need. The bad news is that having this insurance often encourages unnecessary spending. Many consumers do not think twice about their health-care costs because someone else (i.e., the insurance company) is paying the bills.

Despite the arguments that health insurance may increase health-care costs, the alternative to health insurance could be much worse. People who have no health insurance are more likely to go without proper medical care. Such individuals are less likely to be healthy than those who do receive adequate health care.

2. Our Aging Population. Older people require more medical services, on the average, than younger people. With people living longer than ever before, the average age of the population increases, and so, too, does the demand for medical services. As the demand for doctors and other medical providers increases, medical costs go up.

3. Lifestyle Changes. The way people live affects the cost of health care. This is reflected in the increasing numbers of people requiring treatment for substance abuse, sexually transmitted diseases, and AIDS. U.S. government data for a recent year indicates that the following numbers of Americans required treatment: 1,000,000 for alcohol-related problems and 600,000 for problems related to drug abuse. In the same year, there were 500,000 reported cases of sexually transmitted diseases and an estimated 100,000 cases of AIDS.

4. Environmental Changes. The quality of the environment also plays a role in health-care costs. Problems with air and water quality have often proven to be hazardous to the public's health. Fumes from our

Many Americans over age 80 reside in a nursing home for a time. Why are nursing homes so expensive?

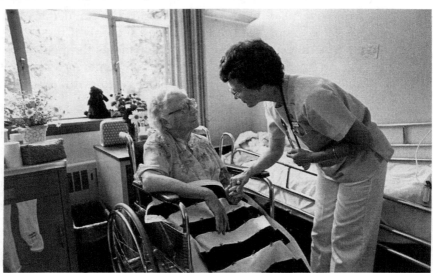

nations' industries and automobiles pollute the air. Factory and agricultural wastes enter the nation's rivers and lakes and contaminate our drinking water. Indices of lung cancer and breathing disorders have increased. Although much has been done to improve air and water quality, pollution remains a major problem. Environmental pollution contributes to the demand for and the costs of health-care services.

Factors Affecting the Supply of Health Care. While the supply of health-care services has been increasing, it has not increased rapidly enough to keep up with increased demand. This situation, too, has added to the cost of health care. Among the factors most frequently cited as affecting the supply of health-care services are (1) health-care worker productivity, (2) the supply of physicians, (3) a lack of information among consumers, and (4) an emphasis on technology.

1. Productivity. Productivity gains among health-care workers would serve to increase the supply of health-care services and push down prices. But increases in productivity have been slow in happening. Perhaps this is because profits of many health-care providers have been so great that they have not had to worry about productivity.

2. Supply of Physicians Is Limited. Despite a large number of applicants, the number of seats available in medical schools is limited. This limitation, in turn, has helped limit the supply of physicians, and kept the costs of their services high.

In addition, increased specialization among doctors has increased the variety of services that doctors offer. For example, in addition to family doctors, there are the internists, cardiologists, neurologists, oncologists, surgeons, hematologists, urologists, pediatricians, and many more specialists. The relative abundance of medical specialists has encouraged patients to consult them for routine medical problems. In many cases, these problems could have been treated by general practitioners (family doctors) at lower costs. For example, an individual suffering chest pains might visit an internist, pulmonary specialist, cardiologist, and radiologist only to be told that the problem was indigestion—a problem easily treated by a family doctor. In this instance, if a patient had visited a family doctor first, this doctor could have determined whether the patient required the services of a specialist.

3. Lack of Information Among Consumers. The health-care market is one of the few areas where most consumers are generally uninformed about the purchasing decisions they need to make. Because medical information is so specialized, consumers often have no knowledge as to whether the treatment prescribed for a given illness is necessary. Furthermore, many consumers purchase medical care infrequently.

The introduction of expensive machinery, such as the magnetic resonance imaging installation here, has contributed greatly to rising costs in medical care.

Consequently, they do not know whether the price for a particular procedure is in fact a good price. Since advertising of prices is not common in the medical profession, it is very difficult for consumers to develop even a slight understanding of the costs of the system.

4. *Emphasis on Technology.* The United States has been a leader in the development and use of high-technology medical equipment and treatment. This trend may be due, in part, to the willingness of insurance companies to pay for most medical procedures without regard to their costs. Since medical technology can be extremely expensive, it is often cited as one of the principal factors adding to the cost of U.S. health care.

Who Are the Uninsured?

About 70 percent of the population has some form of private health insurance. In addition, over 12 percent are covered by Medicaid. More than 2 percent are covered by some other form of government insurance. About 15 percent of the population (about 39 million Americans) have no health insurance coverage. In most instances, those who have no health insurance fall into one of the following categories:

Employees in Firms Where There Is No Health Insurance. While most employed individuals receive health insurance from their employers, 30 percent of them do not. Left to find health-care insurance for themselves and their families, many are unable or unwilling to pay the costly premiums.

Individuals Considered Poor Risks. Some people can afford to buy health insurance but cannot obtain it because insurance companies refuse to sell them any. These people are considered poor risks because of their medical history. That is, they have a pre-existing medical condition that makes it likely that they will be needing expensive health care. For example, people with chronic back problems, heart disease, diabetes, or AIDS are often unable to find a company willing to sell them health insurance. Some 2.5 million people fall into the poor-risk category.

The Unemployed. People without a job or other source of steady income generally cannot afford health insurance. Moreover, they cannot afford to go to a doctor very often. They may, however, be eligible for Medicaid, discussed on page 473.

PROPOSALS FOR IMPROVING HEALTH CARE

Proposals to improve our health-care system generally fall into one of the following categories: reform of existing insurance laws, "play-or-pay," compulsory health insurance, national health insurance, managed competition, and managed care.

Reform of Insurance Laws

Many of our country's leaders believe that health insurance should not be denied to any individual seeking such insurance. In 1996, Congress passed a law that makes it possible for individuals with health insurance from one place of employment to carry that insurance with them to any other place of employment. The law makes it easier for a worker (and his or her dependents) to get medical coverage during a period of transfer or unemployment. Another reform makes it easier for individuals who are considered poor insurance risks to get and keep insurance. This reform applies as well to individuals who are terminally ill.

Insurance companies warn that forcing them to insure poor-risk individuals will cause insurance premiums in general to increase dramatically. Supporters of the reform reply that insurance companies overestimate the added costs. Moreover, they say, the moral issue (the belief that it is unfair to deny an individual insurance protection) overrides economics of costs: Consumers should be willing to pay higher premiums so that more people are covered.

"Play-or-Pay"

Some Americans want to extend health-care insurance to all employed persons. They advocate *"play-or-pay" proposals* that would require employers to either: (1) "play" by purchasing health care insurance for all their employees, or (2) "pay" a payroll tax whose proceeds would be used to pay for government-sponsored health plans. Those Americans not covered by an employer's health plan would be enrolled in a government one.

Critics of "play-or-pay" proposals argue that requiring employers to buy health insurance adds to the cost of doing business. Consequently, many employers would try to reduce those costs by either hiring fewer employees or laying off workers, thereby adding to the nation's unemployment rates. In addition, critics fear that if the payroll tax (the "pay") is less costly than private health insurance premiums (the "play"), many employers would simply choose to abandon their private insurance plans in favor of the public program. This, in turn, would add to the total cost of the public insurance system (because more people would now be covered), and possibly reduce its efficiency (because it would become larger and possibly more difficult to manage). Critics argue further that forcing employers to pay into government-sponsored health-care programs would be contrary to principles of free enterprise.

Compulsory Health Insurance

Some proposed laws would require individuals and families to purchase their own health insurance in much the same way that states require automobile owners to carry liability insurance. Those who could not afford health insurance would be given tax credits and/or direct subsidies with which to purchase it. Meanwhile, Medicaid would continue to provide for the health care of the poorest people. Medicare would continue as a primary medical insurance program for those 65 years and older.

Supporters of compulsory individual insurance argue that requiring consumers to purchase their own health insurance would tend to limit health-care cost increases through careful shopping by consumers. Inasmuch as the consumer (not an employer or government agency) would have to select and pay for health insurance, the consumer would be more aware of costs and benefits. For example, consumers would soon find that it is more costly to purchase an insurance policy with a $100 deductible than one with a $200 deductible. (A *deductible* is the amount of a years' medical bills that a patient must pay before her or his insurance company begins paying.) Consumers would find that a policy which provides dental and eye care is more costly than a policy that does not provide such benefits.

Critics of compulsory insurance proposals argue that free-market competition cannot operate in the health-care field. In matters of life and death (which is often the case in health care), people will pay any price they can afford to get the service they want. Moreover, the critics say, most consumers are unable to make intelligent choices regarding medical treatment and insurance.

National Health Insurance

National health insurance is any system whereby a national government assumes responsibility for paying for the country's health-care costs. Most national health insurance proposals are variations of the Canadian system. In Canada, the provision of medical services is in private hands, but the government pays the bills. Meanwhile, the Canadian government is responsible for setting fees for doctors and hospitals and deciding what new equipment doctors and hospitals can purchase. These arrangements give the Canadian government the leverage needed to control health-care costs.

Critics of the Canadian system say that because the Canadian government limits the purchase of the most sophisticated equipment to only a few hospitals, patients often have to wait months for tests and procedures that would be immediately available to individuals living in the United States. For example, in 1992, when the United States had 2,000 hospitals with *magnetic resonance imaging machines (MRIs)*, Canada had only 15 such hospitals. Moreover, Canadians typically have to wait up to six months for CAT scans, and a year for major orthopedic work, such as hip replacements. In contrast, U.S. patients with health insurance can usually obtain these procedures on demand.

Other critics raise the question of costs: higher federal taxes would be needed to pay for a Canadian-type system. Raising taxes in the United States now would be difficult since many politicians are calling for lower taxes and a balanced federal budget.

Critics also raise the question of medical research. Drug companies and makers of medical equipment would have less incentive to research new products with a Canadian-type system. This is because private companies in the United States engage in research and development only in expectation of making high profits from the products invented. With national health insurance, profits would be limited.

Those favoring national health insurance say that it would be fairer than the system currently in place in the United States. Moreover, the new system would bring down most health-care costs. Under a Canadian-type system, they say, all those living in the United States would be treated equally, regardless of wealth. Care would be provided without the usual deductibles or *copayments* (the amount of a medical bill that many patients with insurance must now pay). Consumers would be able to choose their own doctors and other health-care providers.

Managed Competition

Placing the responsibility for providing health care in the hands of local or regional health-care networks is called *managed competition*. While some networks would consist of groups of many individuals and many small business firms, a giant corporation might operate a network of its own. Health-care networks would offer a full range of health-care services—from treatment of the common cold to open-heart surgery. Included in the networks would be the full range of health-care facilities, including clinics, doctors' offices, nursing homes, pharmacies, medical-equipment suppliers, and hospitals.

Under managed competition, everyone in the United States would be offered a choice of health-care benefits. The costs of the programs would be shared by the government, individual beneficiaries, and employers. Through Medicaid, the government would pay for poor patients to belong to a network. The self-employed would have the opportunity to join a health-care network, but would have to pay their own premiums. So too would those unemployed people who were not eligible for Medicaid.

By permission of Chuck Asay and Creators Syndicate

Those favoring managed competition argue that it would slow down or put an end to the inflation in the costs of health care. Managed competition promises to reduce costs because:

- Given their purchasing power, health-care networks would be able to pressure medical providers to offer their services at reduced prices.

- Network members would be given a fixed sum (set by Congress) to spend on the health-care plan of their choice. Since the difference between the cost of the service and their allotment would have to be made out of their own pockets, people would be likely to select plans that give them the most health-care coverage for the money (or, possibly, the cheapest plan offered to them).

- Patients would be expected to pay a nominal fee for each visit to a doctor or hospital. It is expected that charging a fee for each visit would discourage unnecessary visits, and, therefore, reduce costs to the network.

- Most health-care networks would pay medical providers a fixed fee regardless of the number of patients they treat or services they perform. Since providing more services to patients does not add profits to the network, networks are unlikely to prescribe unnecessary medical procedures. At the same time, groups that keep their patients healthy are rewarded because it costs less to treat healthy patients than patients who are sick.

Critics of managed competition argue that:

- It has never been tried, so that any claims regarding its likelihood of success are pure speculation.

- Managed competition would enrich a handful of the nation's largest insurance companies. The large insurance companies already have managerial and technical experience in the health insurance industry and, therefore, the critics predict, these companies would be operating most of the health-care networks.

- If imposed by the federal government, managed competition may involve the government in medical and other aspects of health care to an extent that most Americans would regard as excessive. The federal government may impose numerous regulations and establish bureaucracies to oversee the operations and management of the health-care networks. To the many individuals seeking less government involvement in their lives, managed competition suggests even more government involvement.

Managed-Care Plans. Closely associated with managed competition are managed-care plans, such as *health maintenance organizations*

(HMOs). These plans, which involve prepaid, coordinated care, are already an option for many Americans. HMOs have sprung up across the country, and some reformers would like to see everyone belong to one.

An individual who joins an HMO (or that person's employer) pays a fixed monthly premium. With some HMOs, the member also makes a small copayment for each visit to a doctor-member of the HMO. Some HMOs may offer benefits such as preventative care, dental care, hearing aids, and eyeglasses. By joining an HMO, the individual becomes a member of the group and must use the doctors and other medical providers in that group. An individual who wishes to use a doctor who is not a member of the HMO must pay in full for the doctor's services. One advantage of an HMO is that a member receives comprehensive medical care at relatively low cost. A disadvantage of joining an HMO is the limited ability to choose one's physician and other medical providers. HMOs receive a flat fee per enrollee. Therefore, in order to maximize profits, HMOs may limit the use of costly specialists and high-tech medicine.

Summary

In this chapter, we discussed two major challenges facing America today—poverty and health care. Poverty affects the lives of some 36 million people in the United States. Certain groups, such as African Americans and Hispanics and single-parent households headed by women, have high incidences of poverty. Government programs to fight poverty include welfare, social insurance, food stamps, and labor-market strategies. Dissatisfied with the welfare system, Congress reformed it by reducing benefits and setting time limits and work requirements. Congress shifted much of the burden of dealing with poverty from the federal government to state and local governments.

Health-care costs are expensive and are increasing for the federal government, for employers, and for individuals. Our population is living longer and demanding more health services. We have witnessed increased alcohol and drug abuse and the further spread of sexually transmitted diseases. Doctors and hospitals are providing more advanced and more expensive services. Health care varies in quality for different groups of people in the United States. There is disagreement on which of several proposed reforms of the U.S. health-care system is best.

REVIEWING THE CHAPTER

Building Vocabulary

Match each item in Column A with its definition in Column B.

COLUMN A	COLUMN B
1. affirmative action	*a.* cash and non-cash benefits provided to the poor
2. poverty rate	*b.* the provision of health care by a local or regional network
3. income maintenance	*c.* a system whereby the national government pays for a nation's health-care system
4. poverty level	
5. income distribution	*d.* the percentage of total income received by various groups in society
6. managed competition	*e.* the active hiring and promotion of members of a group who had been discriminated against
7. HMO	
8. "play or pay"	*f.* a group of providers who offer prepaid, coordinated health care
9. national health insurance	*g.* a graph that compares equal income distribution with real income distribution
10. Lorenz Curve	*h.* a yearly income figure below which one is considered poor
	i. a proposed law that would require employers to either buy health insurance for their employees or pay a payroll tax
	j. the percentage of a group whose income is below the poverty level

Understanding What You Have Read

Refer to Table 20.1 on page 466 to answer questions 1–3.

1. The household *least* likely to be poor in the United States is a household headed by (*a*) a woman in which there is no husband present (*b*) a white couple (*c*) an African-American couple (*d*) a Hispanic couple.

2. The percentage of poor persons is greatest among those in the age group (*a*) below 18 (*b*) 18–24 (*c*) 25–44 (*d*) 65 or older.

3. How many female householders with no husband present were there below the poverty level in 1996? (*a*) 4,167,000 (*b*) 3,010,000 (*c*) 1,724,000 (*d*) 2,276,000.

Figure 20.6   A Lorenz Curve

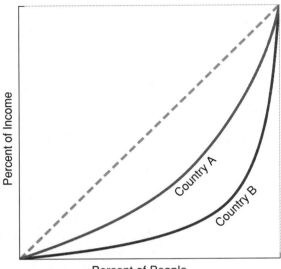

Percent of People

4. A Lorenz Curve is used to demonstrate (*a*) the tradeoff between unemployment and the inflation rate (*b*) the relation between education and income (*c*) inequality in income distribution (*d*) the number of households at the poverty level.

5. According to Figure 20.6, (*a*) income is more equally distributed in Country A than in Country B (*b*) Country A is wealthier than Country B (*c*) income is more equally distributed in Country B than in Country A (*d*) Country B is wealthier than Country A.

6. Which of the following is generally *not* considered a cause of homelessness? (*a*) increased numbers of soup kitchens (*b*) lack of affordable housing (*c*) rise in number of the long-term unemployed (*d*) increased drug and alcohol abuse.

7. Which program provided Sam Jones's family with *income-in-kind* rather than cash? (*a*) Aid to Families With Dependent Children (AFDC) (*b*) Supplemental Security Income (SSI) (*c*) Unemployment Insurance (*d*) Food Stamps.

8. The rising cost of health care in the United States can be partly explained by (*a*) the fact that some 39 million Americans are without health insurance (*b*) the low rates of infant mortality in the United States compared to those of many developing countries (*c*) improved productivity in the health-care field (*d*) increased specialization and new technology in medicine.

9. About 65 percent of the costs of private health insurance is paid for by (*a*) those receiving the benefits of the insurance (*b*) employers (*c*) doctors (*d*) the federal government.

10. Which of the following is *not* a factor likely to increase the demand for health care in the United States? (*a*) increased demand for health insurance (*b*) an aging population (*c*) increased specialization among doctors (*d*) reduced benefits for Medicare and Medicaid.

Thinking Critically

1. Existing federal programs to help the poor generally seek to redistribute income or to eliminate or reduce the causes of poverty. Many of these programs, particularly welfare, have come under attack. Agree or disagree with each of the following statements and present *at least one* argument to support your position in each case. (*a*) Private groups can do more than the federal government to end poverty. (*b*) Programs to help the poor should be dealt with on the state and local rather than on a national level. (*c*) Time limits, a work requirement, and a reduction in benefits should be imposed on all welfare recipients.

2. Explain what role, if any, you think discrimination plays in causing poverty among some groups of Americans.

3. Homelessness is a serious problem facing America today. Proposals to deal with the homeless often depend upon what one believes are the causes of homelessness, who should be responsible for the homeless, and the costs involved.

   a. List *three* typical reasons why people may become homeless.

   b. Do you believe that our society has a moral responsibility to provide food and shelter for those who cannot do so for themselves? Explain your answer.

   c. Some of the homeless prefer living in make-shift shelters on the street, in public parks, bus and rail stations, alleys, and elsewhere rather than in a public shelter. They claim that the shelters are dangerous. Many other people consider homeless people unsightly, a nuisance, or a danger. Some people insist that homeless people be removed from public places and, if necessary, be forced to stay at public shelters. What is your opinion on this subject?

4. Mary, 23 years old, is a single-parent mother of two children. She receives about $950 each month in state welfare benefits plus some non-cash benefits in the form of food stamps. Assume that the poverty level for a family of three is $11,940. Also assume that Mary has been offered a job at $5.15 an hour for 40 hours a week. If she took the job, she would no longer be eligible for

state benefits. Moreover, she would have to hire a sitter for her children.

   a. Would Mary earn more in the job than she now receives from state welfare benefits?

   b. How much would Mary have to earn an hour to equal the poverty level for a family of three?

   c. Do you think that Mary should accept the job offer? Explain your answer.

5. Even though the federal minimum wage was raised recently, antipoverty groups argue that it is still not high enough to bring a family above the poverty level. Do you think that the federal minimum wage should again be substantially raised? Why or why not?

6. "Although the United States has the best system of health care in the world, health care in the United States is in crisis." (*a*) Explain why you agree or disagree with this statement. (*b*) Explain in terms of demand and supply why health costs in the United States have been increasing.

7. Select *one* of the following four proposals for improving health care in the United States: compulsory health insurance, national health insurance, "play-or-pay" programs, and managed competition. For the proposal you have chosen, explain (*a*) how it is supposed to work, and (*b*) why you think it will or will not help solve the health-care problem in the United States.

SKILLS: Interpreting a Cartoon

Look at the cartoon on page 492 and then answer the following questions.

1. The cartoonist has drawn two scenes showing patients seeking medical treatment. Describe each scene.

2. Why has the cartoonist drawn so many people in the right-hand frame?

3. Refer to the proposals for improving health care discussed on pages 489–494. Would any of these proposals create a situation similar to the one in the cartoon that shows "free" medical care? Explain your answer.

4. What title would you give to this cartoon?

5. This cartoon is known as a *political* or *editorial cartoon* because it deals with a topic of public interest. Which type of medical system do you think the cartoonist favors—for-profit medical care or "free" medical care? Explain.

UNIT VII
The Global
Economy

Chapter 21

INTERNATIONAL TRADE

Overview

Most of us think of ourselves as active participants in the U.S. economy. We consume goods and services, and many of us have jobs as well. We rarely think, however, that we are also part of a much larger unit: the *global economy*. This economy includes the economies of all the nations of the world. In this century, countries have become increasingly interdependent. Many of the goods and services that we consume come to us either in part or in their entirety from foreign lands. Similarly, people in the rest of the world have looked to the United States for many goods and services.

Consider the case of a candy bar that can be purchased over the counter at a local store. Let us suppose that the candy bar is one of the chocolate-coated varieties with almonds. On examining the paper and aluminum foil wrapper, we see that the candy bar was produced by a *multinational corporation,* a giant firm that operates its business in two or more countries. As for the paper, it was manufactured from wood pulp produced in Canada. The aluminum foil was made of bauxite mined in Jamaica and processed in a U.S. factory. Sugar, the principal ingredient in the candy bar, was produced out of Filipino cane, while the chocolate had its origins in cacao beans that were grown in Ghana. The almonds came from southern Italy. In the candy-making process, many cargo ships brought the ingredients to the United States. One of these ships, built in a Japanese shipyard for a Greek company, sailed under Liberian registry with a mainly Indonesian crew.

In this chapter, we will discuss our global economy and why trade takes place between nations. We will explore why international trade promotes economic specialization and how specialization increases total world output. We will then discuss the evolution of U.S. trade policy and some of the current problems in global trade. We will also examine the arguments for and against protectionism.

ECONOMIC SPECIALIZATION

Two hundred years ago, British economist Adam Smith wrote that the wise head of a household will never attempt to make at home that which can be bought outside the home for less. Smith went on to explain that it made more sense for people to work at whatever they do best, and to use their earnings to buy the things they want.

Smith's advice for households and individuals to specialize in some economic activity applies equally well to localities and to nations. Consider, for example, trade between New York State and Kansas. Much of the clothing sold in Kansas was made in New York, just as many of the wheat products consumed in New York had their origin in Kansas. The reason is that, among other things, New York has extensive facilities for the manufacture of clothing and a large and experienced labor force. Meanwhile, Kansas has the necessary soil, climate, capital, and labor to produce wheat. For similar reasons, West Virginia is a major producer of coal; Florida, of citrus fruits; and California, of semiconductors.

As with states, nations tend to specialize in the production of certain goods and services. Brazil concentrates on the production of coffee beans; Honduras, on bananas. Japan has a sizable electronics industry, while the United States produces much of the world's computer software. Meanwhile, U.S. airlines and British insurance companies provide further examples of the kinds of service exports that are concentrated in certain countries.

Nations specialize in the production of certain goods and services for a number of reasons. These are related to the uneven distribution of resources, absolute and comparative advantage, and political considerations—topics that we will now discuss.

Uneven Distribution of Resources Around the Globe

Just as individuals differ in size, strength, talent, and ability, so do nations and regions differ in their resources. These differences (which limit the kinds of economic activities in which nations can successfully engage) include climate, factor supply, and demand.

Climate. The effect of climate upon the economy of a nation is, in many cases, quite apparent. Because of its climate, certain goods cannot be grown in the United States and, thus, have to be imported. The cacao beans that are used in many candy bars, for example, are imported from Africa. Coffee is another example of a product that needs to be imported. Coffee is produced in large quantities in Brazil (among other places) because the moderate temperature and heavy rainfall of

Coffee beans are harvested by hand since not all the beans on a plant ripen at the same time. This coffee plantation is in Colombia.

certain regions of Brazil favor its growth. Rubber trees, also not grown in the United States, require a damp, hot climate, as in Indonesia.

Some crops can be grown in only parts of the United States. Citrus trees need frost-free areas, such as Florida, while grains thrive in cooler climates, as in the Great Plains of the United States. Many fruits and vegetables rely on the alternating cool-damp, hot-dry type of Mediterranean climate, as in California.

Certain services are economically viable only in specific areas. For example, the terrain and cool climate of mountainous areas are most conducive to skiing, while the warm beaches encourage tourists seeking sun and sand.

In recent years, climatic factors have lost much of their former importance in determining the course of a nation's economy. Clothing manufacturers now use synthetic fibers as substitutes for natural products (such as silk and cotton) that can be produced only in certain climates. Farmers now grow new types of wheat with a very short growing season in regions formerly considered too cold for wheat production. Some farmers now grow quality tomatoes under climate-controlled conditions in "hot houses." Similarly, farmers in Israel and elsewhere with arid climates have developed elaborate irrigation programs that enable agricultural activities even in desert regions. Climatic factors, however, still continue to affect international trade. The costs of maintaining an artificial climate to develop certain industries are prohibitive. For this reason, nations will generally continue to produce goods and services for which their climate and geography is most suitable.

Factor Supply. The factors of production (land, labor, capital, and management) are not equally distributed around the world or even within most countries. This distribution helps explain, for example, why some parts of our country tend to specialize in the production of farm products, while other areas lean toward manufacturing. Texas, with its ample supply of land in relation to its population, can afford to allow cattle to roam over thousands of acres of range. Illinois, in contrast, is more densely settled. Its major city, Chicago, has many industries, including food-processing facilities and factories that manufacture machines.

On the international scene, too, the factors of production are unevenly distributed. Argentina and Australia are similar to Texas in that the ratio of people to land is relatively low. As a result, these nations can engage in extensive cattle and sheep grazing. By contrast, Great Britain and Japan, with their relatively concentrated populations, have developed manufacturing industries that rely upon ample supplies of labor and capital.

The quality of labor also varies from one nation to another. Japan, the United States, and the nations of Western Europe have relatively more skilled labor than other nations. These countries are therefore able to support industries requiring highly trained workers and complex technology. Many developing nations (such as Pakistan, China, and Mexico) are still developing their labor resources.

Capital in the form of plant and equipment (and money to invest in plant and equipment) is also unevenly distributed throughout the world. The countries with the highest concentration of capital per worker tend to have the greatest productivity. Abundant capital enables these nations to concentrate on producing goods that lend themselves to mass production. For this reason, Sweden (with a relatively small population) was able to develop an automobile industry. For the same reason, Japan (with little or no iron ore) is competitive with the rest of the world in producing finished steel. Meanwhile, countries with limited industrial capacities, such as Costa Rica, Ghana, and Sri Lanka, must emphasize preindustrial activities such as farming. In recent years, however, business firms have been investing capital and establishing factories in developing countries in order to take advantage of low labor costs. We will consider the impact of such investments in Chapter 24, "Economics of Development."

Management, too, is a vital ingredient in production. Those nations that lack an adequate supply of industrial-managerial talent tend to concentrate on the production of agricultural goods. This concentration explains, in part, the difficulties that many less developed nations have had in industrializing. These nations have been short of managerial personnel and, therefore, have had to either delay their programs or recruit managers from abroad.

Demand. Even if a wondrous genie were to provide Sierra Leone, Honduras, and Nepal with automotive factories, it is unlikely that many cars and trucks would be produced in these countries. The relatively small and poor populations of those lands could not afford to buy enough of the output to take advantage of the economies of scale. (It is more likely that foreign automotive companies might establish factories to manufacture some automotive parts in some of these countries.) Mass production can proceed only if there is a market for its output. The need for a market explains why only a small handful of nations produce commercial aircraft. Usually only a nation with markets large enough to support an aircraft industry can afford to have one. To get around this problem in Western Europe, groups of nations formed consortiums to produce airplanes (the *Concorde*, produced by France and Britain, and the *Airbus*, produced by a group of European nations).

Absolute Advantage and Comparative Advantage

When one nation can produce a good or service at a lower cost than another, the former is said to have an *absolute advantage* in that item. Therefore, nations would do well to specialize in the production of those things in which they have an absolute advantage. Furthermore,

Developing nations often have some heavy industries. This steel foundry is located in Helwan, the hub of Egypt's steel industry.

they should use the surplus from the sale of these things to buy other goods and services from nations that have absolute advantages in different items. Consider the examples of trade between the United States and Indonesia and trade between the United States and Bolivia. We know that Indonesia has an absolute advantage in producing spices, Bolivia has an absolute advantage in producing tin, and the United States has an absolute advantage in producing refrigerators. Thus, the United States buys spice from Indonesia and tin from Bolivia, and sells its refrigerators to both countries.

Under certain circumstances, however, it pays for a nation to import goods and services from abroad even though they could be produced more cheaply at home. The principle of *comparative advantage* helps us to understand why this is so.

First stated early in the 19th century by the English economist **David Ricardo** (featured on pages 508–509), the Law of Comparative Advantage may be summarized as follows:

If two nations have different opportunity costs in the production of two goods or services, the nations should (1) specialize in the one in which their opportunity costs are lower, (2) leave the production of the alternate item to the other country, and (3) trade with each other.

The concept of comparative advantage might be more easily understood if we consider the following example. Let us suppose that Lisa McBride, MD, is deluged with paperwork. Suppose further that Dr. McBride is highly proficient at typing, a skill she learned as a college student. She is considering hiring a part-time typist to ease her burden. She estimates that a typist, who would be paid $75 a day, would be needed two days a week.

At the same time, Dr. McBride knows that she could probably handle all the typing work herself in somewhat less than two-days' time and thereby save the expense of a typist. But she also knows that each hour that she would spend typing would be an hour that she would lose in earnings as a medical doctor. Dr. McBride estimates that she could earn several times a typist's salary by attending to her medical practice on the days she would have devoted to typing. Should the doctor do her own typing or hire a typist? What do you think?

Economists would recommend that Dr. McBride hire the typist. They would explain the logic of this choice in terms of comparative advantage and opportunity costs. Opportunity costs, you may recall, are the amount of goods and services one must forgo to obtain more of something else. To Dr. McBride, the opportunity cost of doing her own typing was the loss of income from one- or two-day's medical practice. These earnings were far greater than the $150 salary she would have to pay the typist for two days' work. Since the opportunity cost of doing her own typing was greater than that of attending to her practice, we

Table 21.1 COMPARATIVE ADVANTAGE I

Product	United States	Japan	Total Dollar Output
Bulldozers	3 × $100,000	2 × $100,000	$500,000
VCRs	1,000 × $200	1,200 × $200	$440,000
Total	$500,000	$440,000	$940,000

say that the physician had a comparative advantage in medicine even though she enjoyed an absolute advantage in both fields (she could both type and practice medicine better than the typist).

To illustrate how the Law of Comparative Advantage applies to nations, suppose that the United States is more efficient than Japan in the production of both VCRs and heavy earth-moving equipment, such as bulldozers. Even if the United States were able to produce both products more cheaply than Japan, it would pay the United States to produce the bulldozers and buy the VCRs from Japan. The reason for this is that the United States has a greater margin of efficiency over Japan in producing heavy equipment than it does in producing VCRs. The opportunity cost to the United States of producing VCRs would be the cost of diverting resources from producing heavy equipment.

To make this imaginary situation simpler, let us suppose that bulldozers and VCRs are the only two items each nation produces and that no other country produces these items. With a given quantity of land, labor, and capital, the United States can produce three bulldozers and 1,000 VCRs while Japan can produce two bulldozers and 1,200 VCRs. Suppose further that a bulldozer sells for $100,000 and a VCR sells for $200.

In the example above with equal factor inputs, the United States produces $300,000 worth of bulldozers and $200,000 worth of VCRs. Japan produces $200,000 worth of bulldozers and $240,000 worth of VCRs. Now let us suppose that the United States produces only bulldozers and Japan produces only VCRs.

Both nations profited when the United States specialized in producing bulldozers and Japan produced only VCRs. Total output in-

Table 21.2 COMPARATIVE ADVANTAGE II

Product	United States	Japan	Total Dollar Output
Bulldozers	6 × $100,000	0	$600,000
VCRs	0	2,400 × $200	$480,000
Total	$600,000	$480,000	$1,080,000

creased from three to six bulldozers ($500,000 to $600,000) in the United States and from 1,200 to 2,400 VCRs ($440,000 to $480,000) in Japan. World output, therefore, increased by one bulldozer and 1,200 VCRs or in terms of dollars, by $140,000 ($1,080,000 − $940,000). We may conclude that international trade and specialization increases total world output.

In terms of opportunity costs, both the United States and Japan gain by specializing in the production of those goods in which they were most efficient—the one in which they have a comparative advantage. Both Japan and the United States could use their gain to produce additional goods and services, thereby raising the standard of living in each nation. It therefore follows that if all countries produced those things at which they were most efficient, the world's output would be raised to the greatest possible level. Thus, everyone's living standards would rise.

Political Considerations

Despite the benefits of international trade, the decision to trade or not to trade is sometimes based on political rather than economic reasons. At one time, Cuba was our leading source of sugar and a major market for our exports. Then after the Cuban revolution of 1959, Communists came to power there. Because of Cuba's Communist policies, the United States stopped trading with that nation. Also for political reasons, the United States has virtually no trade with North Korea, Iran, or Iraq.

By contrast, we sometimes go out of our way to trade with some other nations simply because we want to support their governments. When it appeared that the Polish Communist government was preparing to introduce democratic reforms in the 1980s, the United States government encouraged private U.S. banks to make loans to Poland. In 1995, when it appeared that Mexico was in great financial difficulty, President Bill Clinton issued an executive order making $20 billion in credit available to the Mexican government. For decades, our government encouraged U.S. businesses to trade with South Korea but prohibited trade with North Korea. For many years, trade with the Chinese Nationalist government on Taiwan was encouraged, while trade with the Chinese Communist government on the mainland was prohibited. U.S.-Chinese trade policy changed after more normal diplomatic and trade relations were established in the 1970s between the United States and mainland China. Even today, however, many restrictions on trade between China and the United States remain in effect for political reasons.

David Ricardo

The economic order first described by Adam Smith was studied and enlarged upon by those to whom we now refer to as economists of the classical school. Second only to Smith in importance among classical economists was David Ricardo (1772–1823). The son of an affluent London stockbroker, young Ricardo opened his own brokerage firm and was so successful in this endeavor that by the time he was 35 he was able to retire a rich man. In later years, Ricardo went on to become a large landholder and member of Parliament. His most important work, *The Principles of Political Economy and Taxation*, is generally regarded as the best theoretical statement of classical economics.

Two topics that received special attention in the *Principles* were income distribution and economic growth. Income, Ricardo said, was distributed to landlords, workers, and businessowners in the form of rents, wages, and profits, respectively. Left to their own devices, businessowners would expand their operations to the fullest in order to earn the greatest profits. This investment (business spending) would create jobs for workers, whose wages would be pushed up to whatever level was required to attract the needed supply into the labor market. With their wages rising, workers could afford to marry and have families. In that way, they would create their own competition by adding more people to the labor force. The addition of these new workers would push down wages to that point where workers would earn just enough to survive.

Meanwhile, the population growth would have induced farmers to open their less productive land to cultivation. This would increase food prices and, of necessity, wages, since workers had to be paid enough to subsist. Unfortunately for the entrepreneurs, wage increases would have to come out of their profits. For their part, entrepreneurs could be expected to expand their operations as best they could through their investment in additional capital. This would lead them to employ additional workers at still higher wages, and the cycle would be repeated.

What a dismal picture Ricardo painted! Here were workers, bound to a life of bare subsistence by what came to be called the "iron law of wages," doomed because of their propensity to have children. Here, too, were entrepreneurs standing by helplessly as rising food prices pushed up the wages they had to pay at the expense of their hard-earned profits. Only the landlords seemed to benefit, for as the population grew so too did the prices they could charge for their crops and the rents they earned on their lands.

One way out of the dilemma for the business owners (there was no way out for the workers, in Ricardo's view) was to bring down food prices by importing less expensive grain from other European countries. Unfortunately, this remedy could not be applied because Great Britain's Parliament was controlled by the landowning nobility, whose primary source of income was from agriculture. In the early 19th century, by way of protecting themselves from foreign competition, they sponsored a series of laws (the so-called **Corn Laws**) that levied high taxes on grain entering Great Britain. The effect of these taxes was to make the price of imported grain higher than the price of British grain.

In the midst of this dilemma, Ricardo's work provided the theoretical ammunition needed by the middle class, which wanted these laws repealed. What Ricardo did was to introduce the Law of Comparative Advantage. This law, which is often cited by economists in defense of free trade, states that under certain circumstances two nations can benefit from trade even if one of them produces everything at lower costs than the other. In a well-known example, Ricardo demonstrated that it was to the mutual advantage of Great Britain and Portugal for Britain to export wool to Portugal and to import Portuguese wine in return, even though Portugal could produce both wool and wine at lower cost. Over the years, the strength of the British middle class grew so that by 1846 it was able to bring about the repeal of the hated Corn Laws.

The passage of time has made obsolete much of what Ricardo had to say about the economy. Nevertheless, many of his theories and methods were employed by later economists as the starting point for the development of their own ideas, and his place in history is assured.

BARRIERS TO WORLD TRADE

From what we have said thus far, you might think that nations would be eager to promote international trade and take advantage of the benefits of specialization and comparative advantage. We know, however, that all nations, including our own, have imposed restrictions on imports, and sometimes on exports. In the discussion that follows, we will examine ways in which governments apply these restrictions.

For years, Japanese-made cars have been popular in the U.S. market. Now, U.S.-made Japanese cars, such as these Toyota station wagons, are being shipped to Japan.

Tariffs

The most common form of restriction on foreign trade is the tariff. The importer usually adds all or part of this tariff to the selling price of the goods. If this tax brings the price of the item to a point where it is more expensive than an identical domestic product, consumers may hesitate to purchase the imported item. In this instance, the duty is described as a *protective tariff*, because it serves mainly to protect the domestic industry from the competition of foreign goods.

Tariffs designed primarily to raise money for the government are called *revenue tariffs*. With these types of tariffs, the increased price resulting from the duty is still lower than that of the goods produced at home. Suppose, for example, that sweaters imported from Scotland sell here for $50 each and similar sweaters produced in the United States sell for $65 each. A tariff of 10 percent would raise the price of the imported sweater by $5 (from $50 to $55). The Scottish sweater, however, would still be cheaper to buy than the one produced in the United States. In this illustration, the U.S. government receives $5 per sweater as a result of the revenue tariff imposed.

Tariffs are also classified by the manner in which they are computed. A *specific tariff* assesses a certain amount of money per unit, such as $2 per ton. An *ad valorem tariff* is expressed as a percentage of the value of the goods.

Quotas

A limit on the quantity of a particular good that may enter a country in a particular year is a *quota*. Once that limit is reached, no more of the product may be imported until the following year. The U.S. government, for example, has set a quota on imported sugar and Japanese cars. In fact, every nation in the world today has quotas, in one form or another, on goods or services entering from another nation. Regional trading blocs, discussed later in this chapter, remove quotas among member nations but retain import restrictions on goods from non-member countries. One such trading bloc, the European Union, limited the import of Japanese cars into the European market in 1995 to a little over 1 million units.

Currency Controls

In order to import goods from a particular country, the importer usually must have some of that country's currency. Thus, for example, a Moroccan importer usually must pay in francs when buying French perfume. By limiting the amount of foreign currency that importers may buy, the government can limit trade with other nations.

The U.S. dollar, however, is recognized as an international currency (as is, to some extent, the German mark and the Japanese yen). Therefore, in many countries the U.S. dollar is as freely accepted in exchange for goods and services as is the local currency. In some instances, the U.S. dollar is preferred to the local currency.

Foreign Government Interference With Trade

Sometimes called the "invisible tariff," *administrative red tape* refers to the practice followed by some governments of making the process of importing so complicated as to discourage foreign businesses from attempting to sell goods from abroad. By requiring the filing and processing of complicated forms, governments can discourage trade as effectively as they can by levying a protective tariff. Mexico's tire regulations provide one example of administrative red tape. Mexico appears willing to allow U.S. tires to be sold in Mexico, but these U.S. imports must be inspected in the laboratories of competing companies in Mexico. This inspection takes time and involves conflicts of interest on the part of Mexican tire companies.

Sometimes a government works hand-in-hand with a national company to keep a foreign firm from competing in the home market. For example, Eastman Kodak charges that Fuji Photo film and the Japanese government have conspired to prevent Kodak from enlarging its 9 percent share of the market for camera film in Japan. If you were to enter any large photography store in the United States, you very likely could buy film manufactured in the United States (Kodak), Japan (Fuji), or Western Europe (Agfa). In most photo supply stores in Japan, however, only Fuji products are sold.

Export Controls

Export controls comprise another way to restrict trade. Certain kinds of goods cannot be sold unless an export license is first obtained. In this way, strategic materials such as high-technology weapons can be prevented from reaching specific nations. Moreover, the United States today forbids most trade with a few nations, including North Korea and Cuba.

Collaboration Among Firms

In addition to trade restrictions imposed by governments, large companies within a country can get together to control the home market and keep out foreign competition. In Japan, this arrangement is called the *keiretsu*—a closely knit corporate network of firms somewhat similar to interlocking directorates. The U.S. company Kodak has had difficulty selling its film in Japan, due in part to a *keiretsu* that protects one of Kodak's major competitors, Fuji Film.

Operated very much like the Japanese *keiretsu*, the electric power industry in Germany is dominated by three large German utilities. These three firms subcontract all work to a handful of German-owned or German-based suppliers. Two large U.S. firms, General Electric and Westinghouse, have been unable to sell even one heavy generator in Germany. These companies insist that their inability to compete in the German market is due to the unfair collaboration that exists among German utility firms.

EVOLUTION OF OUR TRADE POLICY

In studying the history of our nation, we can find that trade policies played important roles. Before the American Revolution (1776–1781), Great Britain closely regulated the trade of its American colonies. The British Parliament passed laws that required colonists to export their raw materials only to British ports. It prohibited the manufacture of certain goods in the colonies. Moreover, it required that imports and exports be carried only in British or colonial ships, and not in ships of rival powers, such as Spain or France. A major purpose of these laws was to enable the colonial power, Great Britain, to have a *favorable balance of trade*—an excess of exports over imports. This concept is part of *mercantilism*, a doctrine popular in Europe from the 16th through the 18th century. According to mercantilism, the wealth of a nation could be measured by the amount of gold and silver it possessed. A favorable balance of trade would increase this wealth because colonists would pay for the home country's exports with gold and silver. Thus, these precious metals would pile up in the home country.

Other European countries also followed mercantilist policies. Accordingly, Great Britain, France, and other nations that were committed to mercantilism resorted to protective tariffs and other restrictions to limit imports. For the same reason, these powers did whatever they could to help domestic industries compete for foreign markets in order to increase exports.

Colonial powers found that their colonies were quite important. The British colonies, for example, furnished Great Britain with raw materials and precious metals at relatively low cost. In addition, they provided markets for British finished products. Great Britain forced its colonies to purchase finished goods only from Great Britain and to sell its raw products only to the home country.

After the United States won its independence from Great Britain, the new U.S. leaders had to concern themselves with trade issues. In 1791, Secretary of the Treasury **Alexander Hamilton** issued his *Report on Manufacturers* in which he recommended that the U.S. government take steps to develop the country's industries. Specifically, Hamilton urged Congress to offer cash payments to those who would start new industries or improve existing ones. He also wanted Congress to levy protective tariffs against competing foreign products. In an early application of Hamilton's advice, Congress in 1798 awarded a contract for 10,000 *muskets* (a type of heavy rifle) to the then struggling young inventor, **Eli Whitney**. While Congress could have bought muskets from manufacturers outside the United States, the deliberate government effort to help Whitney enabled this U.S. manufacturer to perfect his production methods. Whitney helped establish one of the United States' first mass-production industries—musket making.

Tariffs have provoked many political battles through the course of U.S. history. The country's first protective tariff, enacted in 1816, had widespread support. During the War of 1812, newly started industries (sometimes called *infant industries*) developed in the United States. These industries were protected by U.S. laws prohibiting trade with Great Britain during the conflict. After the war ended in 1815, the British again began selling their manufactured goods in the U.S. market. They could sell at prices much lower than those of comparable American-made goods. Owners of U.S. industries that had developed during the War of 1812 (such as New England cotton mills, Pittsburgh iron foundries, and wool producers in Vermont and Ohio) cried for

Tariffs helped some U.S. industries in the 19th century to survive against foreign competition.

protection against British and other foreign manufacturers. Thus in 1816, Congress passed the country's first protective tariff.

Nevertheless, U.S. industries continued to clamor for higher protective tariffs. Through the rest of the 19th century, the protectionists generally had their way. U.S. tariff rates were raised in 1824, and again in 1828. From 1832 to 1857, tariffs were lowered slightly, but they remained mostly protective.

The tariff issue was a major cause of sectional conflict between the Northern states and the Southern states before the Civil War. Since most U.S. industries were concentrated in the North, many Northerners insisted on tariff protection. People in the South, which was largely agricultural, feared that high U.S. tariffs would lead to retaliation by the nations of Europe. This would mean that tariffs would be raised on U.S. exports, thereby making it more difficult to sell cotton and tobacco abroad. In addition, Southerners preferred to buy the less expensive, European-manufactured goods over the competing goods manufactured in the northern United States. If tariffs were raised, then the European-manufactured goods would become more expensive.

Protectionism reached its peak in the early 1930s during the Great Depression. In an effort to protect domestic jobs and increase sales by reducing foreign competition, Congress passed the **Hawley-Smoot Tariff Act** of 1930. It raised duties to an all-time high. Instead of promoting U.S. industries, though, Hawley-Smoot nearly destroyed them. Because foreign nations were no longer able to sell to the United States, they lacked the dollars to buy U.S. products. Moreover, the high United States tariffs so outraged our trading partners that many retaliated by raising their own tariffs. High foreign tariffs thus led to a decline in U.S. exports (particularly of farm products and machinery) and increased unemployment and business failures.

The protectionist trend was reversed after the 1932 landslide election of President Franklin D. Roosevelt and a Democratic Congress. In 1934, Congress passed the **Reciprocal Trade Agreements Act**. This law permitted a U.S. president to lower tariffs by up to 50 percent for imports from any nation that would grant similar concessions to the United States.

The Act contained a *most-favored-nation clause*. Briefly, this clause said that each signatory nation would extend to the other the same preferential tariff and trade concessions that it may in the future extend to nonsignatories. Suppose, for example, the United States and Japan sign a most-favored-nation clause as part of a trade agreement.

Figure 21.1   Tariffs in U.S. History

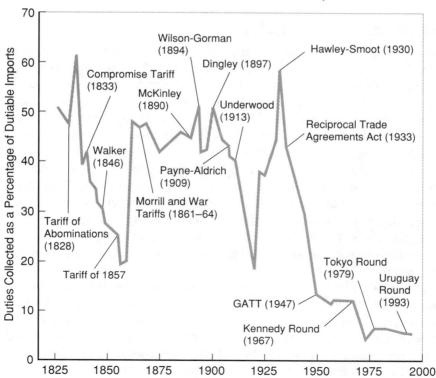

Suppose further that Indonesia did not sign this agreement. Should the United States later grant Indonesia a tariff reduction that was not part of its trade agreement with Japan, the United States would, nevertheless, be required to grant Japan (as a "most-favored-nation") the same favorable tariff terms given to Indonesia. Should Japan, in turn, grant a trade concession to Germany, the United States would (as a "most-favored-nation") be entitled to the same treatment that Japan gave to a nonsignatory (Germany).

The General Agreement on Tariffs and Trade (GATT)

After World War II ended in 1945, the United States and the other victorious powers vowed to avoid one of the mistakes of the past by promoting trade between nations. Toward that end, 23 of the world's trading nations created the **General Agreement on Tariffs and Trade (GATT)** in 1948. The organization grew to about 124 members in 1994.

Unlike the Reciprocal Trade Agreements Act, which provided for *bilateral* (two-nation) negotiations, GATT established the machinery for *multilateral* (many-nation) negotiations. Since 1948, some nine "rounds" of negotiations have dismantled the tariff barrier system of the 1930s. As a result, tariff levels today are far lower than they were half a century ago.

World Trade Organization

The signatories to GATT formed the **World Trade Organization (WTO),** which began operating in early 1995. This oversight body enforces trade agreements made by its members. All members pledge to reduce tariffs and eliminate import quotas. The WTO protects patents, trademarks, and copyrights. If a conflict arises between member countries on trade matters, any member can appeal the matter to the World Trade Organization for settlement.

One of the keys to the WTO's early success has been its ability to handle trade disputes among its members. Under its rules, if one WTO member nation accuses another of unfair trade practices, the nations are expected to attempt to settle the dispute among themselves. Should that fail, the WTO can be asked to decide the matter. Then, if found to be guilty of an accusation, the offending nation has to mend its ways or face trade sanctions.

In 1995, WTO panels were formed to investigate (1) Canada's complaints about French restrictions on the Canadian scallop trade, (2) charges brought by the European Union, Canada, and the United States against Japan for levying tariffs on imported alcohol, and (3) Venezuela's complaints about U.S. rules restricting pollutants in gasoline. That same year, three other disputes were settled even before a WTO panel had met. Supporters of the WTO took this as a sign that fear of losing a WTO case often prompts nations that violate trade rules to mend their ways.

The European Union and Other Regional Trade Groups

Tariffs and other trade barriers have long been some of the major sources of friction between nations. The search for a permanent peace in the years following the Second World War led many Western Europeans to look for ways to eliminate these barriers. A regional trade agreement, they argued, might lessen tensions among Western European nations. In addition, they believed that a free trade agreement would increase living standards of all nations that participated in the agreement. Thus, Western Europeans took a number of steps that eventually would lead to the present-day **European Union**.

Historical Background. The European Union had its origins in 1951 when France, Italy, West Germany, Belgium, Netherlands, and Luxembourg created the European Coal and Steel Community. The purpose of this organization was to increase productivity in the member countries by reducing tariffs and other barriers to trade in the coal and steel industries. Coal and steel production increased dramatically, thereby encouraging the six nations to expand the range of their cooperation.

U.S. Trade Representative Charlene Barshevsky often deals with knotty trade questions as she negotiates with her foreign counterparts.

This was achieved in 1957, when the six nations signed the Treaty of Rome. The agreement created the **European Economic Community (EEC),** whose principal aims were to: (1) preserve and strengthen peace; (2) create a region in which the free movement of goods, people, services, and capital was guaranteed; and (3) provide for some kind of political unity. Membership in the EEC (or as it was soon popularly called, the **Common Market**) grew to 12 in number after the United Kingdom, Ireland, Denmark, Greece, Spain, and Portugal joined.

The Common Market later became known as the **European Community (EC)** and is now (with even more members) known as the "European Union (EU)." Tariffs between member nations were eliminated by 1968, and for a time, their economies flourished. But a number of nontariff barriers to trade continued to slow the movement of goods across national borders. For example, member states were subject to differing sales and excise taxes, along with differing safety and health standards on machinery and agricultural products.

The European Union Today and Tomorrow. Today, goods and workers can easily cross borders between any two EU member nations. The countries have established uniform trade regulations and manufacturing standards. To further the goal of economic integration, proposals have been made to establish a single European currency and a uniform system of taxation. The currency, the *euro*, will be issued by the EU's central bank beginning in 2002. The euro will replace the currencies of the majority of EU nations. By eliminating virtually all remaining trade barriers, the EU has managed to weld its membership into a single market. With a combined population of 320 million, and a GDP close in size to that of the United States, the EU constitutes one of the world's largest and wealthiest markets.

Effects of the European Union on the United States. As long as EU markets remain open to all nations (including nations that are not members of the EU), integration benefits U.S. firms for the following reasons:

- The absence of physical barriers between EU countries (such as border controls for goods, services, and workers) reduces transportation bottlenecks and other costs of U.S. firms doing business within Europe.
- The uniformity of trade regulations makes it easier to achieve economies of scale in production and distribution. Previously, for example, Great Britain and Germany had different requirements for importing cars. In order for U.S. automobile manufacturers to sell automobiles to both countries, U.S. workers had to assemble cars differently for each country. Now with one standard in all EU

Figure 21.2 Top Purchasers of U.S. Exports and Suppliers of U.S. General Imports, 1994

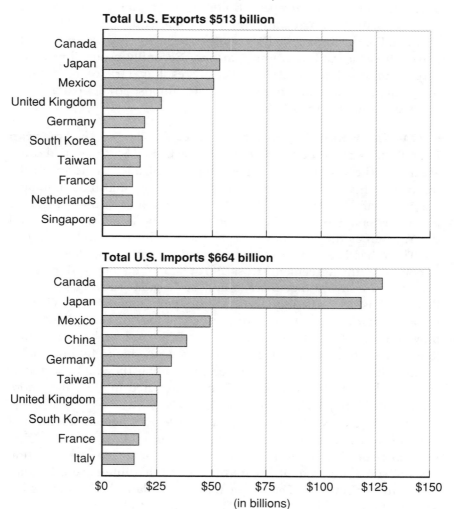

Total U.S. Exports $513 billion

Canada
Japan
Mexico
United Kingdom
Germany
South Korea
Taiwan
France
Netherlands
Singapore

Total U.S. Imports $664 billion

Canada
Japan
Mexico
China
Germany
Taiwan
United Kingdom
South Korea
France
Italy

$0 $25 $50 $75 $100 $125 $150
(in billions)

Which of our major trade partners (those listed) are members of the EU?

countries, however, the U.S. manufacturer need only produce automobiles to meet the one standard requirement.

● Subsidiaries of U.S. firms based in any European Union country have the right to buy and sell goods and services throughout the EU. Thus, General Motors, for example, has trade access to the EU equal to that of its European competitors because it has full or partial ownership in three European automobile companies.

While access to this large, barrier-free market has opened up wonderful possibilities, they can be realized only if EU markets remain open. If, instead, the European Union adopts a plan of erecting trade barriers against foreign competition, the consequences could be devastating. For one thing, the EU countries together constitute one of the two or three largest U.S. trading partners. Secondly, protectionist measures, if imposed by the EU, could easily result in a trade war in which the United States and other countries impose trade barriers on member-nations of the EU.

NAFTA—The World's Largest Free-Trade Zone. The **North American Free Trade Agreement (NAFTA)** links the United States, Canada, and Mexico in the world's largest free-trade zone. Under the terms of the treaty, which went into effect in 1994, all tariffs (and most nontariff barriers) will be lifted over the following 15 years. In the absence of trade barriers, goods will be as free to move between the Yukon and the Yucatán as they can now move between Chicago and Sheboygan.

There has been some heated opposition to NAFTA. One political opponent of the agreement, **Ross Perot**, stated his opposition rather colorfully by saying that there would be "a giant sucking sound" as jobs and businesses fled the United States and Canada for the cheaper resource markets of Mexico. In fact, a number of U.S. plants have moved to Mexico and, as a result, some U.S. workers have lost their jobs. Even though many of these workers were able to find new jobs, usually the new ones were at lower wages than they had previously earned. The U.S. Department of Labor estimated in 1995 that more than 42,200 U.S. jobs had been lost due to NAFTA.

Defenders of NAFTA respond that the NAFTA agreement was not the reason that U.S. plants have left the country. In some industries, high costs of production in the United States and lower production costs in some other countries are the factors that influence U.S. companies to go elsewhere. They argue that if U.S. plants had not moved to Mexico, they would have moved their facilities to low-wage countries in Asia or elsewhere. Since U.S. plants are going to leave anyway, NAFTA defenders reason, it is to the advantage of the United States that the plants relocate nearby in Mexico.

Those favoring NAFTA argue that the elimination of artificial barriers to trade will benefit all three nations. They claim that, in the absence of trade barriers, the law of comparative advantage will enable the United States, Canada, and Mexico to allocate their resources more efficiently. NAFTA will thus result in more jobs, more trade, greater output, and higher living standards throughout North America. Most economists believe that it is still too early to fully evaluate NAFTA.

When Congress was debating ratification of NAFTA, some labor unions staged protests against the treaty. This rally took place in San Francisco in 1993.

Other Regional Trade Blocs. The European Union and NAFTA are examples of *regional trade blocs*. Others are in operation in Latin America, Africa, and Asia. The most significant of these are the following:

- The **Caribbean Common Market (CARICOM)** links most of the Caribbean islands (plus Belize and Guyana) in a kind of common market. CARICOM is working toward the elimination of trade barriers among member states.

- The **Central American Common Market** promotes trade links among Guatemala, Honduras, El Salvador, Nicaragua, and Costa Rica. Although the bloc has proclaimed its intention to eliminate trade barriers between its members, many quotas and other obstacles remain.

- The **Asia-Pacific Economic Cooperation Forum (APEC)** was founded in 1989 to provide a meeting place for member nations to promote trade within the region and with the rest of the world. Eighteen Asian and Pacific nations and the United States have set free and open trade as an overall goal. To date, APEC's greatest achievement has been its ability to bring the nations Taiwan and China to the bargaining table to discuss trade problems.

521

Today's Debate on Protectionism

The 1996 campaign for the Republican presidential nomination rekindled the age-long debate between protectionists and free traders. At the heart of the issue lay the question as to which course (protectionism or free trade) was more likely to increase jobs and improve living standards.

The Arguments of Protectionists

Those favoring government trade restrictions argue for a *favorable balance of trade*, a situation whereby the dollar value of merchandise exports is greater than imports. The protectionists' arguments are as follows:

- When merchandise imports are greater than exports, the unfavorable trade balance results in a net outflow of dollars.

- As foreigners acquire more dollars, their value in terms of foreign currencies decreases, making it more expensive for Americans to import foreign produce.

- Higher prices and falling dollar values contribute to inflationary pressures in the United States.

- Inflation leads to higher interest rates, thereby increasing the cost of credit. Since government interest payments represent about 15 percent of the federal budget, higher interest rates also contribute to budget deficits, and add to the national debt.

- The goods imported from abroad are made by foreign workers. Had those same goods been purchased from U.S. manufacturers, they would have been made by U.S. workers. It therefore follows that imports take jobs away from workers in the United States. Imports also take away potential profits from U.S. manufacturers.

- By the same token, imports keep down the wages of U.S. workers. When U.S. workers ask for a raise, they might be told by their employer that the work can be taken abroad and done by workers who are willing to work at a fraction of the going U.S. wage.

- Another argument for trade barriers is to promote economic development by protecting "infant industries." According to this argument, newly developed industries should be given time to grow and become efficient. These new industries grow only if the government keeps foreign competition out of the country.

- From time to time, U.S. military leaders have argued that certain industries are so vital to our nation's defense that their preservation is a matter of national security. Thus, for many years, foreign petroleum was subject to a protective tariff. Such a tax was thought necessary to guarantee the existence of the domestic oil industry and, thus, assure adequate supplies in wartime. For similar reasons, the U.S. ship-building industry has been supported through direct subsidies and special regulations requiring that U.S.-owned ships carry certain goods destined for export. Those in favor of supporting the U.S. shipbuilding industry believe that, in the event of a national emergency, the nation's fleet of merchant ships should be assured.

● Finally, tariffs can provide the federal government with an important source of income. In 1800, for example, total federal income was $10.8 million. Nearly 85 percent of this total, or $9.1 million, came from customs duties. Tariffs provided almost one-half of the federal government's income as recently as 1907. Even today, some foreign governments rely on revenue tariffs as a major source of income. Tariffs are sometimes popular because they are paid for only by foreign exporters.

The Arguments of Free-Traders

Most economists believe that protective trade rules are harmful. They say that these restrictions waste resources by protecting less efficient domestic producers from foreign competition. This protection, in turn, results in higher prices because less efficient producers charge more for their products. Free trade, in contrast, gives firms access to the large international market, allowing them to increase output and lower their average cost. Meanwhile, foreign competition forces domestic monopolies or oligopolies to lower prices, and imported goods provide consumers with greater choice.

Mexican electronics workers just south of the U.S. border in Tijuana assemble components at wages far lower than those of their U.S. counterparts.

Other arguments of free-traders are the following:

- International trade allows each country to concentrate on its most efficient activities. Because of the principle of comparative advantage, two nations will gain from a goods exchange to an extent that they could not have enjoyed had they both attempted to produce the same items on their own.

- It is true that U.S. wages are higher than those paid to workers in most other (but not all) nations of the world. It is also true that, because of labor-cost differences, certain goods can be produced abroad for less than they can in the United States. If those items were allowed to enter the country freely, some U.S. entrepreneurs might be forced out of business and some U.S. workers might lose their jobs. It is not true, however, that all U.S. industries will be unable to compete with foreign producers. Labor is only one of the factors of production. Even though U.S. farmers, for example, are among the best paid in the world, the United States is a leading exporter of food. Similarly, U.S. machinery, transportation equipment, and office systems are major export items, and U.S. workers in those industries are well paid even by U.S. standards.

- Some U.S. industries with well-paid workers can compete in international markets because of their workers' high productivity.

- Trade restrictions lower living standards because, with a given amount of money, consumers purchase fewer goods at the higher prices. Imposing tariffs and other restrictions compels domestic consumers to purchase domestic goods at higher prices. This situation benefits a few manufacturers and their employees at the expense of the many consumers. Although certain persons benefit from this protection, consumers have to pay more for the goods they buy and, therefore, consumers cannot afford to buy as much. Free-traders say that in some cases it would be preferable to let industries that are unable to meet foreign competition disappear and to assist the displaced workers in finding new jobs in more efficient industries.

- Supporters of free trade argue that since not all U.S. workers benefit from free trade, it is the responsibility of the federal government and state governments to find ways of helping workers whose lives are affected negatively by foreign competition. These governments should set up training programs to teach unemployed workers marketable skills. Special unemployment compensation should be made available to prevent some of the financial hardship resulting from the loss of jobs.

- Critics of the "need to protect infant industries" argument have pointed out that in the United States today "infants" rarely are protected because industries just starting up usually cannot put the necessary pressure on Congress to obtain protection. Those industries that are protected turn out not to be "infants." Instead they have been in business a long time and are willing to spend the money needed to lobby Congress to pass protective trade laws.

● Most people agree that industries directly associated with the national defense should be closely protected and regulated. Clearly, they say, the manufacture and sale of the weapons of war ought to be conducted in such a way as to assure the nation of the sup-

plies it needs. It is not always clear, however, which industries are absolutely necessary for national defense. Many businesses will use the national defense argument to justify protecting themselves even if their industry is not directly involved in or necessary for the national defense.

● The argument that tariffs are a good source of governmental income is no longer valid. In 1995, just slightly over 1 percent of federal tax receipts came from this source. Moreover, although tariffs appear to be paid only by foreign exporters, in reality U.S. consumers end up paying for the taxes with higher prices of consumer goods.

CHANGES IN INTERNATIONAL TRADE

At one time, international trade was conducted by sellers of goods or services produced in one country to business firms in foreign lands. For example, a U.S. firm might produce automobiles in the United States to be sold to dealers in other nations. Since the end of the Second World War, however, international trade has become increasingly global. That is, more and more of it is being conducted as if national boundaries hardly existed at all. U.S. automobile manufacturers have production facilities in many nations outside the United States, including, for example, Canada, Mexico, Brazil, Great Britain, and Thailand. Japanese automobile manufacturers also have plants in many nations, including a fair number in the United States.

Much global trade today is in the hands of multinational corporations (MNCs). It is not unusual for a multinational corporation to have factories in many countries, be owned by shareholders in two or more countries, engage in research and development projects in several countries, and employ key executives of various nationalities.

The Rise of Multinational Corporations

Why have multinational corporations grown so much since the end of World War II? The reasons are several:

Barriers to Investment and Trade Have Been Falling. We have seen how regional trading blocs and international agreements like NAFTA, the European Union, and GATT have promoted trade between nations. By eliminating or reducing financial and investment barriers and tariffs, trade between nations has become much more profitable than it once was. Profitable trade and the ability to invest and build facilities in foreign countries has contributed to the growth of MNCs.

Telecommunication and Transportation Costs Have Tumbled. An electronic revolution has made it possible for us to communicate with people or witness events anywhere in the world. In today's world, it is easy to transmit messages and pictures from and to virtually anywhere in the world. At one time, it was expensive and time-consuming to deliver a portfolio of pictures and plans from, say, one part of Asia to a remote corner of Latin America. Such an operation today can be accomplished in moments at a cost of a few dollars. Reduced shipping and communication costs have promoted the growth of multinational corporations. Thus, even though the multinational corporation Asea Brown Boveri has some 208,000 employees in 140 countries, operating units can easily communicate among themselves and with headquarters in Zurich, Switzerland.

It Is Easy to Make Payments in International Trade. In an earlier chapter, we discussed money as the lifeblood of business. By making the movement of funds from one country to another as easy as, say, a transfer of funds from Miami to Minneapolis, the breath of life has been pumped into all forms of global trade. The ease by which funds are transferred globally facilitates the operations of a multinational corporation. Asea Brown Boveri, for example, can readily transfer funds between its operating units regardless of where in the world they are located.

Why Do Large Firms Become Multinational?

We have described how technological changes and the lowering of trade barriers made it possible for business firms to operate globally. But why would a firm want to become a multinational corporation? Or, to put it another way, what is in it for them?

Corporations go global (or multinational) for a number of reasons, including the following: (1) to avoid protective tariffs and quotas, and (2) to reduce costs.

Avoiding Protective Tariffs and Quotas. Shortly after its creation in the 1950s, the Common Market enacted an 18 percent tariff on farm

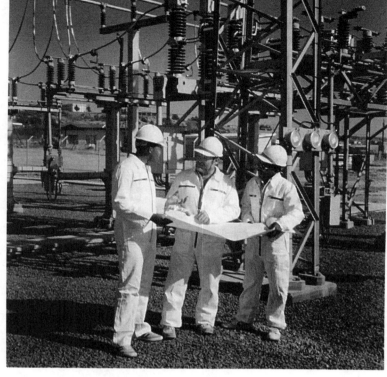

Asea Brown Boveri (ABB) is a global corporation. It was created out of the merger of two of the world's largest electric-power equipment manufacturing corporations: ASEA of Sweden and Brown Boveri of Switzerland. After its creation in 1988, ABB acquired a number of large companies, including Combustion Engineering, in the United States. Headquartered in Zurich, Switzerland, and led by a Swedish chief executive officer, ABB has factories in over 50 countries throughout the world. Despite the company's origins, its official language is English and its accounts are kept in U.S. dollars.

equipment imported from nations that were not Common Market members, including the United States. As a result, U.S. firms that manufactured farm equipment were kept out of the Common Market. In order to get around the tariff, one U.S. farm-equipment manufacturer, John Deere, built a number of production facilities in Western Europe. Farm equipment produced in John Deere's Western European factories and sold in Western Europe were not subject to a tariff and, therefore, could more easily compete with farm equipment produced by Western European competitors.

Similarly in 1991, when NutraSweet (a brand name of a popular sugar substitute) was hit with high Common Market duties, its parent company, Monsanto (a U.S. corporation), entered into a joint venture with Ajinomoto (a Japanese corporation) to build an artificial-sweetener plant in France. As multinationals, the U.S. and Japanese corporations were able to market their products in Western Europe

Figure 21.3   Total of Exports by All Nations Since 1960

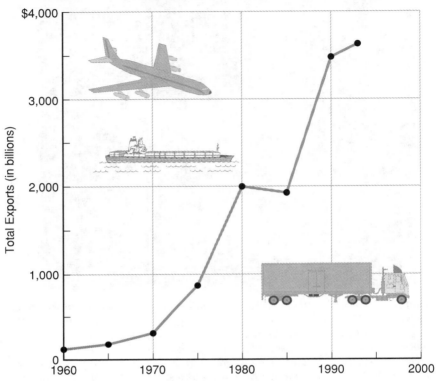

Why have exports generally grown since 1960?

almost as easily as their European competitors. By forming multinationals, corporations are able to enter markets that discriminate against firms from certain countries. For example, Japanese firms have often discriminated against Canadian companies in favor of U.S. ones. Thus, since Northern Telecom (a Canadian telecommunications company) has subsidiary companies located in the United States, it conducts business with Japan through its U.S. subsidiaries rather than from Northern Telecom's main office in Canada.

Reducing Costs. Corporations become multinationals to move their operations abroad as a way of reducing production costs. In the 1980s, Nike, an Oregon-based footwear company, closed the last of its U.S. plants and moved all production to its factories in South Korea. The shift enabled Nike to reduce labor costs from an average of $6.94 per hour it was paying its U.S. production workers to something under 50 cents per hour. Then in the 1990s, Korean wages increased. Therefore, Nike closed its Korean operations and set up new ones in Indonesia, where the going rate for shoe workers was $1.03 per day.

Table 21.3   THE WORLD'S LARGEST MULTINATIONAL CORPORATIONS (IN BILLIONS OF U.S. DOLLARS)

Company	Home Country	Sales	Profits	Assets	Market Value
Ford Motor	U.S.	$128.4	$5.3	$219.4	$ 29.9
General Motors	U.S.	155.0	5.7	198.6	52.9
General Electric	U.S.	60.1	4.7	194.5	98.9
Toyota Motor	Japan	109.0	1.2	116.3	72.2
Royal Dutch/Shell	Neth.	94.9	6.2	108.0	107.6
Hitachi	Japan	76.4	1.1	102.3	31.7
EXXON	U.S.	99.7	5.1	87.9	88.7
IBM	U.S.	64.1	3.0	81.1	54.5
British Petroleum	UK	50.7	2.4	48.6	38.8
Mobil	U.S.	59.0	1.8	41.5	39.4
Nestle	Swiss.	41.6	2.4	34.5	40.7

Source: **Forbes**, July 17, 1995

Summary

International trade is the exchange of goods and services among people and institutions of different countries. This trade takes place because nations differ in factor resources. A nation has an absolute advantage when it can produce more of a product or service with the same amount of resources than another nation. A nation has a comparative advantage when it can produce a product or service at a lower opportunity cost than another nation. International trade promotes greater specialization, which, in turn, increases total world output. Global economic interdependence has been hastened by technological change in computerization, communication, and transportation.

Nations establish trade barriers to restrict the free flow of goods, services, investments, and people. These barriers include tariffs, quotas, currency controls, administrative red tape, and export controls. Free trade among nations benefits worldwide living standards in the long run. But in the short run, some groups are likely to be hurt by international competition. Arguments in favor of trade barriers include the quest for a favorable balance of trade; the need to protect U.S. workers from cheap, foreign workers; the need to protect U.S. "infant industries"; national security; and the fact that tariffs are a source of revenue.

Tariffs have been an issue throughout the course of U.S. history. At first, protectionism dominated U.S. tariff policy, but then this protectionist trend was reversed with the Reciprocal Trade Agreements Act of 1934, which provided for bilateral negotiations to reduce tariffs between the United States and any nation that would grant similar concessions to it. In 1948, the United States and 22 other nations signed the General Agreement on Tariffs and Trade, which provides for multilateral negotiations to reduce trade barriers. In 1995, GATT created the World Trade Organization, a permanent organization that works to break down trade barriers. Along with the development of the WTO has been the formation of a number of regional trading communities, such as the European Union and NAFTA. These associations provide for various degrees of barrier-free trade among member nations

REVIEWING THE CHAPTER

Understanding What You Have Read

Base your answers to questions 1 and 2 on Table 21.4.

Table 21.4   OUTPUT PER WORKER PER DAY (IN POUNDS)

Country	Fish Output	Fowl Output	Ratio of Fish to Fowl Output
A	200	100	2:1
B	80	20	4:1

1. According to the information contained in the table,   (*a*) Country B has an absolute advantage in the production of both fish and fowl   (*b*) Country B has an absolute advantage in the production of fowl only   (*c*) Country A has an absolute advantage in the production of both fish and fowl   (*d*) absolute advantage cannot be determined because there is no mention of price.

2. According to the Law of Comparative Advantage,   (*a*) trade should not take place between Countries A and B   (*b*) Country A should buy its fish from B and raise only fowl   (*c*) Country A should buy fowl from B and devote all its energies to fishing   (*d*) Country B should buy both its fish and fowl from A.

3. When nations specialize in certain products and engage in international trade to obtain other products,   (*a*) the total output of goods and services will be increased   (*b*) fluctuations in the business cycle will be eliminated   (*c*) the likelihood of worldwide unemployment will be increased   (*d*) the living standards of wealthy nations will be lowered.

4. A protective tariff is most effective in (a) allowing a nation to make the best use of its economic resources (b) increasing the export of goods to foreign nations (c) safeguarding the interests of particular domestic industries (d) raising the national standard of living.

5. Which of the following has an effect different from that of the other three? (a) reciprocal trade agreements (b) import quotas (c) currency controls (d) protective tariffs.

6. Who ultimately bears the cost of a tariff? (a) the retailer (b) the government of the exporting country (c) the importer (d) the consumer.

7. If the United States were to abolish its tariffs, what would be a probable result? (a) There would be fewer job opportunities in U.S. exporting industries. (b) The U.S. standard of living would be considerably lowered. (c) Some workers in presently protected industries would lose their jobs. (d) Most farmers would be hurt.

8. In the mythical country of Varthia, in-line skates can be produced and sold for $110 per unit, while the mythical country of Macir can produce and sell them for $90 each. The major exporting country, Chartin, can deliver in-line skates to Varthia and Macir for $75 per unit. Both Varthia and Macir have levied a $30-per-unit tariff on imports of in-line skates. What kind(s) of tariff did Varthia and Macir levy? (a) Both countries levied a protective tariff. (b) Varthia levied a revenue tariff; Macir levied a protective tariff. (c) Both countries levied a revenue tariff. (d) Varthia levied a protective tariff; Macir levied a revenue tariff.

9. From 1816 until the 1930s, America's tariff policy could best be described as (a) one of free trade (b) protectionist (c) reciprocal (d) nonexistent.

10. All of the following have brought about the reduction of tariffs between nations, *except* the (a) World Trade Organization (b) General Agreement on Tariffs and Trade (c) Hawley-Smoot Tariff Act (d) European Common Market.

11. An economic common market has all of the following advantages, *except* that it (a) lowers trade barriers among its member nations (b) allows workers from one member nation access to jobs in another member nation (c) permits nonmember nations unlimited trading advantages (d) develops economic policies for the economic advantage of all its members.

Building Vocabulary

Match each item in Column A with its definition in Column B.

COLUMN A	COLUMN B
1. global economy	a. a newly developed industry
2. multinational corporation	b. having to do with two nations
	c. an excess of imports over exports
	d. an excess of exports over imports
3. absolute advantage	e. a tax on imports calculated as a percentage of their value
4. Law of Comparative Advantage	f. the combined economies of all nations
5. infant industry	g. a business firm that operates in two or more countries
6. unfavorable balance of trade	h. having to do with many nations
7. ad valorem tariff	i. a situation whereby a nation can produce a good or service at a lower cost than another nation
8. bilateral	j. the idea that a nation should produce products and services in which its opportunity costs are lowest and import all other goods and services
9. favorable balance of trade	
10. multilateral	

Thinking Critically

1. Economists frequently cite the Law of Comparative Advantage to show why nations should engage in international trade. (*a*) State the law. (*b*) Is it possible for one nation to have an absolute advantage in the production of all goods and services? Explain. (*c*) Is it possible for one nation to have a comparative advantage in everything? Explain your answer.

2. A U.S. appliance manufacturer recently told a friend, "When Japanese manufacturers undersell my fans, I have to lay off some of my workers. What's more, the profits that I lose because of this foreign competition and the salaries that my former workers lose are lost forever from the U.S. economy. The only answer to this problem is to raise tariffs on Japanese goods." (*a*) Should U.S. appliance manufacturers be protected against foreign competition that undersells them here? Give *two* arguments to support your point of view. (*b*) Assuming that the manufacturer quoted above was located in Peoria, Illinois, why would the manufacturer not likely use these arguments against a competitor in Denver? (*c*) Under what circumstances would you say that governments are most justified in protecting domestic producers?

3. "To many people in the United States, the European Union represents both a triumph and a challenge. On the one hand, the long-sought-after goal of European unity has been brought a giant step closer. On the other hand, the EU has become a formidable competitor in U.S. markets." (*a*) Why do many people in the United States regard the European Union as an important instrument of international unity and peace? (*b*) How has the EU become a "formidable competitor in many U.S. markets"?

SKILLS: Debating a Two-Sided Issue

Assume that you are a member of a debating team. The topic to be debated is, "Resolved that the United States withdraw from NAFTA." Prepare written notes to back either the pro or con side in the following debate:

● **Pro—***Resolved that the United States should withdraw from NAFTA.*
● **Con—***Resolved that the United States should not withdraw from NAFTA.*

Your notes will help you if you are called upon to participate in an actual debate. To help you develop your arguments, three major issues involving NAFTA are presented in the form of questions followed by background information you might feel is useful for the debate. You will probably want to do additional research on the subject in magazines, newspapers, and books. If you are not called upon to participate in the debate, write a one-page essay that defends either the pro or con position.

1. How has NAFTA affected U.S. workers?

The U.S. Department of Labor said that as of September 1995, 42,221 jobs were lost because of NAFTA. This figure may be low because it includes only those affected workers who had applied for government assistance in job training and finding new jobs. In addition to causing job losses, NAFTA is depressing some wages in the United States. For example, workers earning $8.50 an hour who lost jobs in apparel factories in Los Angeles that moved to Mexico often had to accept new jobs at $6.25 an hour. The Key Tronic Corporation, which manufactures computer keyboards in Spokane, Washington, laid off 227 U.S. workers and moved their plant to Ciudad Juárez, Mexico.

In addition to lower wages and losses of jobs, there have been benefits from NAFTA for the U.S. economy. Because of its lower manufacturing costs in Mexico, Key Tronic was able to lower the prices of its products. And because of lower prices for Key Tronic's products, the company's sales increased. Since the Key Tronic computer keyboard assembled in Mexico uses components that are made in plants near Spokane, overall employment in Spokane rose to keep up with the increased demand for component parts.

Zenith Electronics manufactures television picture tubes in Illinois and sends them to Mexico for assembly into television sets. These sets, in turn, are shipped back to Texas for distribution in the Eastern United States. Some 1,300 new jobs have been created in the United States by this procedure (not all at Zenith Electronics).

McDonald's, the U.S. food chain, has nearly 100 restaurants in Mexico and plans to double that number by the year 2000. The company will ship beef from the United States to Mexico, thereby increasing the demand for U.S. beef and benefiting U.S. cattle ranchers.

2. How do economic conditions in Mexico affect the U.S. economy?

In December 1994, Mexico devalued its currency (the peso) and the Mexican economy soon went into a severe recession. As the peso fell in value, it became more expensive for Mexicans to buy U.S. goods and cheaper for U.S. buyers to purchase Mexican products. (In Chapter 22 we discuss how the value of a nation's currency affects its trade with other nations.) The standard of living of most Mexicans plummeted because most goods and services became more expensive.

In February 1995, the Clinton administration gave Mexico $20 billion in loans and loan guarantees to shore up the Mexican economy. Clinton's critics called the action an expensive bailout of Mexico—a bailout that would have to be paid by U.S. taxpayers. The critics claimed that if NAFTA had not been concluded, the United States would not likely have loaned Mexico so much money. The Mexican government has begun to pay back the $20 billion.

Both the fall of the peso and the recession that followed in Mexico put at risk some 700,000 export-related jobs in the United States. Because U.S. industries that sell to Mexico suffered losses, fewer workers employed in these industries were needed. The Ford Motor Company increased imports (from Mexico) of cars it produced in Mexico, but sales of Ford cars in Mexico fell dramatically. Similarly, sales of Chrysler cars and trucks in Mexico declined 75 percent in the first five months of 1995 compared with a similar period in 1994. But like the Ford Motor Company, Chrysler Corporation produces cars in Mexico that it can sell in the United States and elsewhere. It can also sell in

Mexico cars and parts manufactured in its U.S. plants. Officials at the Chrysler Corporation believe that the Mexican economy will improve and, thus, its sales to Mexicans will improve.

3. Has NAFTA given Mexico an unfair trade advantage with the United States?

Mexico's peso devaluation, the lowering of tariffs by NAFTA, and Mexico's traditional low wages give Mexican products an advantage over goods produced in the United States. Mexican exports to the United States include cars, winter tomatoes, frozen strawberries, flat glass, and other products. By the end of July 1995, Mexico had sold to the United States almost $9 billion more in merchandise than it had bought from this country. NAFTA, some will argue, is responsible for this U.S. trade imbalance with Mexico.

Other people argue that NAFTA cannot be held solely responsible for the U.S. trade imbalance with Mexico. The problem, defenders of NAFTA argue, is with the Mexican economy and not with NAFTA. After the start of NAFTA in early 1994 and prior to Mexico's economic crisis of late 1994, U.S. exports to Mexico had increased considerably.

Defenders of NAFTA go on to say that because of NAFTA, Mexico has liberalized its foreign investment laws to enable U.S. companies to invest heavily in almost every part of the Mexican economy. The massive involvement of U.S. firms in Mexico might strengthen the Mexican economy. Furthermore, the peso will eventually increase in value so that U.S. products will become less expensive to Mexican buyers. As the Mexican economy improves, employment in Mexico will increase. Along with increased employment, there will be an increased demand for goods, including imports from the United States. NAFTA will ultimately have the effect of making the trade terms between the United States and Mexico much more even and, possibly, to the advantage of the United States.

Chapter 22

FINANCING INTERNATIONAL TRADE

Overview

"Hey, welcome back. How did your Latin American vacation go?"

"It was fantastic. I just loved visiting all those countries and seeing the sights. But wherever we went, we had to use a different kind of money: cruzieros, sucres, pesos. I had some time understanding prices."

United States citizens traveling abroad soon learn that they have to exchange their U.S. dollars for the money of the country they are visiting. Stores, restaurants, and hotels in other countries often do not accept U.S. dollars. To them, the dollars are foreign money. On their return home, tourists from the United States can convert their unspent foreign money back into U.S. dollars. Individuals and firms doing business in countries other than their own also must exchange the currency of their country for the currencies of the nations in which they do business.

In this chapter, we will study exchange rates and how the rate of exchange of one currency for another is determined. We will learn how gold was once used in settling international accounts, how payments in international trade are made today, how these payments are recorded, and the importance of balance of payments accounts.

EXCHANGE RATES

How much local currency people from the United States receive for their dollars in the countries they visit depends upon the exchange rate. The *exchange rate*, or *rate of exchange*, is the price of one currency in terms of another. If, for example, you had been visiting Mexico on February 22 in a recent year, you might have learned that a dollar was equal to about 5½ pesos on that day. Or, to put it another way, one peso equaled about $.18 (1 ÷ 5½ = .18). Table 22.1 on page 538 summarizes the exchange rates of the world's principal currencies on one specific day—February 22, in a recent year.

Like stocks and bonds, the prices of foreign currencies are constantly rising and falling. Indeed, because of its resemblance to the rising and falling motion of a ship at sea, economists often describe the process as *floating exchange rates*. An exchange rate table usually sum-

Figure 22.1   Floating Exchange Rates

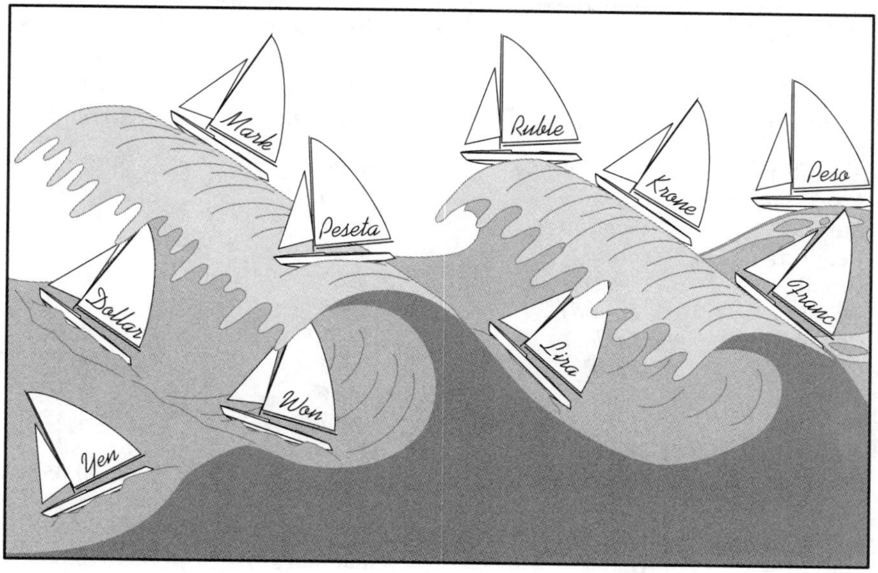

marizes exchange rates at the close of a business day. Rates can vary from one day to the next, and sometimes from morning to afternoon.

Exchange rates play a crucial role in international trade. Suppose that the rate of exchange for Norwegian kroner was to change from 6.5 kroner to the U.S. dollar to 10 kroner to the dollar. This change would make Norwegian goods less expensive to Americans because Americans would be able to buy more kroner for their dollars. As a tourist in Norway, for example, Americans could buy a 300-kroner sweater for only $30 with the latter exchange rate (300 ÷ 10 = 30). Meanwhile, dollars and U.S.-made goods would become more costly to Norwegians.

To illustrate this, let us assume that at the old rate of exchange, Norwegians could have purchased a $200 cellular telephone for 1,300 kroner (200 × 6.5 = 1,300). At the new exchange rate of 10 kroner to the dollar, the same telephone would cost 2,000 kroner (200 × 10 = 2,000).

What Determines the Rate of Exchange?

Why on the same day is the Japanese yen worth about $.01, the British pound $1.58, and the Mexican peso $.17? Why are exchange rates constantly "floating" up and down? And why do currencies sometimes plunge? An understanding of the laws of supply and demand will help us answer these economic questions.

The Demand for a Nation's Products and Its Currency. Like securities in a stock exchange, the price of one currency in terms of another varies

Table 22.1 FOREIGN EXCHANGE RATES, FEBRUARY 22, 199—

Country	Foreign Currency	How Much One Unit of Foreign Currency Equals in U.S. Dollars	How Much $1 U.S. Equals in Foreign Currency
Argentina	(Peso)	1.0000	1.00
Australia	(Dollar)	.7390	1.35
Austria	(Schilling)	.0969	10.32
Belgium	(Franc)	.0329	30.43
Brazil	(Real)	1.1905	370.07
Britain	(Pound)	1.5885	.63
Canada	(Dollar)	.7161	1.39
Chile	(Peso)	.0024	414.35
China	(Yuan)	.1186	8.43
Colombia	(Peso)	.0017	854.35
Denmark	(Krone)	.1713	5.84
Ecuador	(Sucre)	.0004	2400.05
France	(Franc)	.1948	5.13
Germany	(Mark)	.6818	1.47
Italy	(Lira)	.0006	1620.60
Japan	(Yen)	.0103	96.81
Mexico	(Peso)	.1724	5.80
Norway	(Krone)	.1538	6.50
Peru	(New Sol)	.4545	2.20
Russia	(Ruble)	.0002	4384.00
So. Korea	(Won)	.0012	790.00
Spain	(Peseta)	.0077	128.95
Switzerland	(Franc)	.8032	1.24
Taiwan	(NT$)	.0379	26.36
Venezuela	(Bolívar)	.0059	169.87

Calculate the cost in dollars of a Norwegian sweater selling for 325 kroner.

directly with changes in demand. Other things being equal, an increase in the demand for yen will increase its price in terms of dollars and other currencies. Similarly, a decrease in the demand for Japanese currency will have the opposite effect, that is, the value of the yen in terms of dollars and other currencies would fall. The main reason that people outside of Japan would want to own yen is to buy Japanese goods. In other words, the demand for yen depends upon the demand for Japan's goods and services. Therefore, if the demand for goods made in Japan were to increase, the need to pay for those imports would increase the demand for Japanese currency. The increased demand for Japanese goods and Japanese currency would also be followed by an increase in the price of the yen in foreign exchange markets.

The Supply of a Nation's Currency. Like demand, changes in the supply of a currency in foreign exchange markets affect the currency's ex-

U.S. tourists in London examine that day's exchange rates to see what they can get for their dollars. Are the rates more favorable or less favorable than those cited in Table 22.1?

change rate. Other things being equal, an increase in the supply of *lire* (plural for lira) would reduce the price of this Italian currency in foreign exchange markets. A decrease in the supply of lire would have the opposite effect—-that is, the price of lire would increase in foreign exchange markets.

The supply of a country's currency in foreign exchange markets depends largely upon that nation's imports. Suppose, for example, U.S. firms were to import many goods and services from Italy. When U.S. companies purchase goods or services from Italy, payment will have to be made in lire. The U.S. dollars used to purchase the Italian currency will increase the supply of dollars in foreign exchange markets and, other things being equal, push down the price of the U.S. dollar.

Similarly, if Italians were to import fewer goods and services, the supply of lire in foreign exchange markets would decline. As the supply of lire falls, it becomes more costly to exchange foreign currency for lire. Meanwhile, Italians would find it less costly for them to import goods and services because of the increased purchasing power of the lira.

Table 22.2   EFFECT OF CHANGES IN SUPPLY AND DEMAND ON THE PRICE OF A FOREIGN CURRENCY

As Demand for Italian Goods	Supply of Lire	Price of Lire
Decreases	Increases	Falls
Increases	Falls	Rises

What makes the supply of lire increase? What makes the price of lire rise?

How Payments Are Made in International Trade

A department store in the United States orders sweaters from a French manufacturer at a price of 30,000 francs. The exchange rate for francs at the time was $1 = 6$ francs. The U.S. store manager writes a check for $5,000, which she deposits with a local bank. The local bank purchases 30,000 francs (5,000 × 6) in the foreign exchange market and provides its customer with a check for that amount. The importer sends the check to the French company, which deposits the check in its bank account and ships the sweaters. The French bank now has a check from a U.S. bank promising to pay 30,000 francs to the French bank.

Meanwhile, a French music store orders $5,000 worth of CDs (compact discs) from an exporter in the United States. In similar fashion, the manager of the French music store writes a check for 30,000 francs and deposits the check at the store's bank. A local bank uses the funds to purchase $5,000 (30,000 ÷ 6) in the foreign exchange market, and provides the French business firm with a check for that amount. The music store sends the check to the U.S. exporter in return for the CDs. The U.S. exporter deposits the check in its local bank. Figure 22.2 summarizes these transactions.

From viewing Figure 22.2, we can see that:

● the dollars used to purchase francs exactly equal the francs used to purchase dollars. Consequently,
● supply of, demand for, and the exchange rate of the two countries remain the same, and
● exports enable nations to acquire foreign exchange.

THE GOLD STANDARD

From 1870 to 1971, foreign exchange rates hardly moved at all. Fixed exchange rates were the order of the day because the world's currencies were tied directly or indirectly to gold. This "tie" to gold gave the international monetary system its name: the "gold standard." Nations on the gold standard agreed to exchange their currencies for a fixed amount of gold.

One of the advantages of the gold standard was that it made for stable and easily calculated exchange rates. During the 1930s, for example, the U.S. government converted its currency at the rate of 23.22 grains of gold to the dollar. At the same time, a British pound (£) was convertible into 113 grains of gold, or 4.87 times as much as the U.S. dollar (113 grains of gold ÷ 23.22 grains = 4.87). For that reason, the exchange rate between the pound and the dollar was £1 = $4.87.

Figure 22.2 The Process of Foreign Exchange

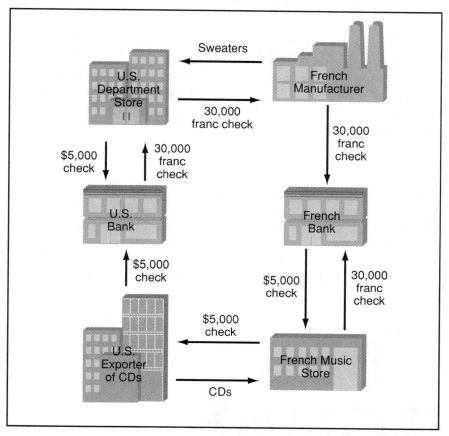

In theory, the gold standard also served to keep international trade in balance. That is, no country could export more than it imported for very long because importers made payment in either gold or a currency convertible into gold. Exports increased the supply of gold of the exporting country. Since the money supply was tied to gold, an excess of exports served to increase the money supply as its supply of gold increased. As we discussed in Chapter 14, prices will increase (all other things being equal) as the money supply increases. Under the gold standard, therefore, an excess of exports brought about an increase in prices in the exporting country.

The larger the quantity of gold in the United States the greater was the quantity of dollars placed in circulation. We can see how that worked from the following example. Assume that the United States government converted dollars into gold at the ratio of 23.22 grains to the dollar and that the U.S. Treasury held only 23.22 grains of gold. Under these conditions, the Treasury could have printed only one $1 bill or coin. Now assume that the Treasury had one thousand times that quantity of gold (23,220 grains instead of 23.22). Then $1,000 in bills and coins could have been issued.

Under the gold standard, an excess of exports over imports resulted in an inflow of gold. The inflow of gold, in turn, increased the export nation's money supply. But an increase in the supply of money resulted in price increases in the exporting country. Higher prices in the exporting country tended to discourage exports and brought the favorable trade balance to an end. (Remember that in Chapter 3 we discussed how demand varies inversely with price.)

Suppose that U.S. firms had ordered 10,000 cashmere sweaters from British firms at a cost of £10 per sweater. Under the gold standard, Great Britain would have received 11,300,000 grains of gold. (113 grains of gold per £ × £10 = 1,130 grains of gold per sweater. 10,000 sweaters × 1,130 = 11,300,000 grains of gold.) The additional gold in the British treasury would have increased the money supply in Great Britain. All other things being equal, an increase in the money supply in Great Britain would result in a rise in British prices. Assume that prices of cashmere sweaters increased from £10 to £11 each. At the higher price, U.S. firms would have ordered fewer cashmere sweaters from the British. The net result would have been that British exports would decline. As exports declined, so would the inflow of gold to Great Britain.

Nations store their gold reserves as gold bars formed by melting gold and pouring it into molds.

Countries whose imports exceeded their exports lost gold because their imports had to be paid for in gold. In our example, the money supply in the United States declined because gold was leaving the United States and going to Great Britain to pay for U.S. imports of sweaters. Prices in the United States declined, as we can see from the formula $P = \frac{M}{Q}$ (P = price; M = money supply; and Q = GDP.) If we assume that M in the United States fell from $100 billion to $50 billion and Q remained the same at $100 billion, P would have fallen from $1 (100 ÷ 100) to $.50 (50 ÷ 100). Lower U.S. prices would have attracted foreign buyers to purchase goods from the United States. As U.S. exports increased (assuming imports remained unchanged), a more favorable trade balance would have resulted.

Let us summarize what we have just discussed.

● A nation with a favorable trade balance experienced an inflow of gold.
● An inflow of gold increased the nation's money supply.
● Increases in the supply of money caused price increases.
● Higher prices resulted in a reduction in that nation's exports.
● The nation with an unfavorable trade balance experienced a gold outflow.
● A reduction in a nation's supply of gold reduced the nation's money supply.
● A decrease in the supply of money resulted in price declines.
● Lower prices brought about an increase in exports.
● Increased exports resulted in an inflow of gold.

Weaknesses within the gold standard led to its downfall. Most serious of these was the inability of nations to manage their money supply. In Chapter 18, we discussed how countries rely upon monetary policy (i.e., changes in the money supply) to regulate their economies. This was not possible in countries where the money supply was directly tied to gold. Under the gold standard, the money supply depended upon how much gold a nation possessed. In many instances, the output of privately owned gold mines had a greater impact on a nation's economy than government actions did. An increase in gold output from a private mine would bring about an increase in the money supply and a rise in prices at a time when the government might have wished to reduce inflationary pressures.

Suppose a nation wished to increase its money supply in order to encourage price increases. Under the gold standard, the nation could increase its money supply only if it increased its supply of gold. The need to manage the economies of many nations and the difficulty in doing so while tied to the gold standard became apparent during the Great Depression of the 1930s.

The 1930s was a period of worldwide depression and hardship. In efforts to fight the effects of the depression, nations printed currency in quantities greater than their gold supplies could support. Unable to acquire enough of the precious metal to redeem their currencies, the nations simply abandoned the gold standard. In the absence of gold to compare the value of one currency with another, international trade slowed drastically.

World trade almost disappeared for an additional reason—the disruption caused by World War II (1939–1945). In 1944, the powers that were winning the war called a conference for the purpose of restoring order to international trade. The rules that they drew up took their name from the town where they met—Bretton Woods, New Hampshire.

The Bretton Woods System (1945–1973)

Toward the end of World War II, representatives of 44 nations met at Bretton Woods to plan the restoration of world trade. As a first step, the conference delegates hoped to re-establish a system of fixed exchange rates. We have seen that this was a simple matter in the days when nations relied upon gold to back their currencies. But during the war (as Allied countries bought arms to win the conflict), most of the world's gold supplies went in payment to the United States.

It was left, therefore, to the delegates at Bretton Woods to find something other than gold upon which to base exchange rates. They found it in the U.S. dollar. With most of the world's mined gold supply in its vaults, the United States guaranteed to continue to exchange dollars presented by foreign countries for gold at the rate of $35 per ounce. Meanwhile, nations without a gold supply agreed to swap their currencies for dollars at a fixed rate of exchange. By relying upon the gold-supported dollar, nations continued to base the value of their currencies on gold without actually owning any of the metal.

One of the essentials to the success of the old Bretton Woods system had been the ability of nations to offer dollars in exchange for their currencies. Since foreign countries could not print dollars, the only ways they could acquire dollars was by: (1) exporting goods or services, (2) borrowing the funds, or (3) receiving dollars as gifts. Under the Bretton Woods system, it was possible for a nation to run short of dollars. In fact, many nations did become seriously short of dollars. This situation, in turn, made it difficult for these nations to import the capital (machinery, fertilizers, etc.) they needed to produce goods for export. With little to export, countries found it all but impossible to maintain stable exchange rates based on the dollar. For that reason,

Delegates from many countries met at the Bretton Woods Conference in 1944. Here U.S. Secretary of the Treasury Henry Morgenthau, Jr., addressed the opening meeting.

the Bretton Woods conferees also created the **International Monetary Fund (IMF)**.

The International Monetary Fund is a specialized agency of the United Nations. Its principal goal is to enable nations to obtain the foreign exchange necessary to conduct international trade. For that reason, the IMF will lend dollars and other currencies to countries as needed. The countries that borrow are expected to repay the loan within a stipulated time.

For as long as the United States was able to exchange gold for dollars, the Bretton Woods system of fixed exchange rates worked well. In the 1960s, however, the U.S. gold supply began to diminish. U.S. trade deficits with Japan and Western European countries led to a flow of dollars into these countries. Then, as these countries redeemed their dollars for gold, U.S. supplies of the metal diminished.

The End of the Bretton Woods System

In August 1971, President Richard Nixon announced that the United States would no longer exchange dollars for gold. This action was an attempt to devalue the dollar. (*Devaluation* is the reduction in value of a nation's currency in terms of foreign currencies.) U.S. leaders hoped that a cheaper dollar would stimulate U.S. exports,

Figure 22.3 The Gold Standard in Action

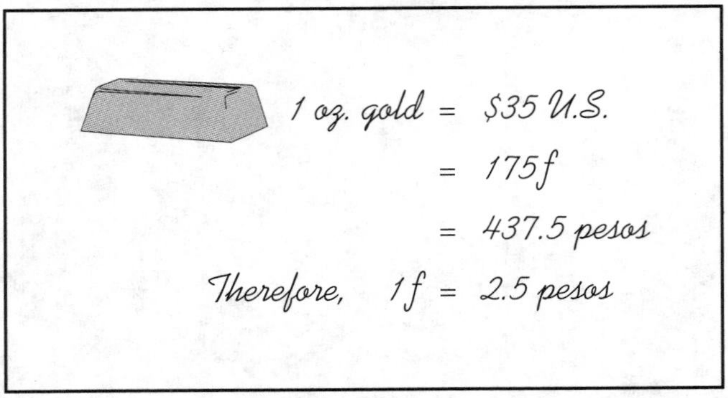

$$1 \text{ oz. gold} = \$35 \text{ U.S.}$$
$$= 175f$$
$$= 437.5 \text{ pesos}$$
$$\text{Therefore, } 1f = 2.5 \text{ pesos}$$

In the 1960s, the Mexican peso was pegged (i.e., fixed) at 12.5 to the dollar, while the French franc was pegged at 5 to the dollar. Since the dollar was convertible to gold at 35:1, 175 francs was equal in value to an ounce of gold (because 5 × 35 = 175). Similarly, it took 12.5 × 35, or 437.5 pesos to equal an ounce of gold. Can you explain why one franc equaled 2.5 pesos?

discourage imports (because a cheaper dollar would make imports more expensive to U.S. buyers), and thereby slow the outflow of dollars. The Bretton Woods agreement, however, prohibited devaluating a nation's currency. Thus, President Nixon had unilaterally canceled the Bretton Woods system.

For a time, the United States and other industrial nations tried to maintain the dollar at a fixed rate of exchange with other currencies. By 1973, this effort, too, had proven futile. Since they were no longer able to maintain fixed exchange values of currencies, the United States and the world's other industrialized nations announced their intention to allow their currencies to *float* (find their own values in relation to one another in the marketplace). The era of fixed exchange rates was over; the era of floating rates had begun.

Floating Exchange Rates

Floating exchange rates are determined in accordance with the laws of supply and demand in foreign exchange markets. The mechanics are much the same as that in which securities are priced in stock exchanges. Demand for a nation's currency comes from the desire of foreigners to obtain a country's goods and services or invest in a country's securities. Supply is derived from the desire of that nation's citizens to import the goods and services and invest in the securities of others. As the demand for Japanese goods and services increases, so too will the demand for the Japanese currency to pay for them. If, at the same time, there is no change in the pattern of Japanese imports, the price of the yen is likely to rise.

In the mid 1990s, both Germany and Japan were experiencing large favorable trade balances. Consequently, the price of German marks and Japanese yen increased relative to other currencies. By contrast, the value of U.S. imports from Germany and Japan exceeded the value of U.S. exports. The supply of dollars in foreign hands increased, and the value of the dollar (relative to the mark and the yen) declined. Although the U.S. dollar was falling against the mark and the yen, it was increasing in value relative to the Mexican peso and the Canadian dollar. This increase occurred because the United States was exporting more to Mexico and Canada than it was importing from those countries during this period.

Although foreign exchange markets function without government direction or supervision, nations monitor them so as to prevent their own currencies from fluctuating so widely as to create problems at home. They do this by buying or selling their own currencies as the circumstances dictate.

Special Drawing Rights

The flow of U.S. spending abroad increased dramatically during the years of U.S. participation in the Vietnam War (1965–1973). This mostly military spending was taking place at a time when U.S. imports were increasing. Consequently, foreign nationals had many dollars— more than they were willing to keep. The international currency markets went from a dollar shortage to a dollar glut. In 1968, in an effort to relieve the pressure on the dollar, the IMF created *Special Drawing Rights (SDRs)*. The SDRs represented an attempt to provide another reserve currency for international trade that could substitute for gold and dollars. SDRs were created out of a pool of foreign exchange deposited by 16 major nations that belonged to the IMF. SDR balances were credited to the member nation, which could then use them in place of dollars or gold to settle accounts with other countries.

The International Monetary Fund no longer buys and sells gold in exchange for foreign currencies. In its stead, SDRs have become the primary asset that countries will accept in payment for their goods and services.

Recent Trends in the Value of the Dollar

How well people live depends in part on what they can buy with their money. What they can buy with their money (the value of the dollar) fluctuates as prices for the goods and services they want to buy either increase or decrease. We have discussed that the value of the dollar (relative to foreign currencies) also fluctuates. When the dollar is high relative to the kroner, Norwegian-made goods become cheaper to Americans and U.S.-made goods become more costly to Norwegians.

Table 22.3   EXCHANGE RATES—INDEXES OF VALUE OF FOREIGN CURRENCY RELATIVE TO U.S. DOLLAR, 1980–1994

Year	United States	Canada	France	Germany	Hong Kong	Japan	Mexico
1980	100.0	105.6	155.9	133.8	122.0	110.4	245.5
1985	100.0	90.3	73.3	82.5	77.9	104.4	22.0
1990	100.0	105.7	120.8	150.2	77.9	171.8	2.0
1994	100.0	90.3	118.6	149.7	78.5	243.7	1.7

Therefore, fluctuations in exchange rates are important. On a cautionary note, however, nearly 90 percent of what Americans buy is produced in the United States. Therefore, a rise or fall in the value of the dollar in comparison with foreign currencies by 10 percent, for example, does not mean a 10 percent increase or decrease in average prices for the goods and services U.S. consumers purchase. The increase or decrease in average prices would be much less than 10 percent because many other factors also influence prices.

Note in Table 22.3 that the U.S. dollar is shown as 100 for each year. This means that the dollar is the base figure and the other currencies are compared with it. Thus, the French franc was worth 155.9 cents in U.S. currency in 1980 and 118.6 cents in 1994. In this instance, the value of the dollar relative to the French franc was greater in 1994 than it was in 1980. Now compare the value of the U.S. dollar to the Japanese yen in the years from 1980 to 1994. You can see that the yen rapidly increased in value relative to the dollar particularly in the period from 1985 to 1994. The Mexican peso shows the most serious decline (relative to the U.S. dollar) of the nations listed in the table.

RECORDING INTERNATIONAL TRADE: BALANCE OF PAYMENTS

International trade involves the buying and selling of goods and services by nations. With few exceptions, payments are made in U.S. dollars or other currencies. Nations collect and summarize their international transactions in a financial statement known as the *balance of payments*. In the United States, the responsibility for preparing its balance of payments falls to the Department of Commerce.

Imports of goods and services flowing into the country are recorded on one side of the scale, exports on the other. As for payments, you might recall from Chapter 21 that sellers in international trade expect to be paid in their local currencies. That is, U.S. merchants expect to receive U.S. dollars for their wares; Japanese sellers

Devaluation—The Cure for Economic Ills?

Some people suggest that floating exchange rates provide a remedy for certain economic problems. They want the U.S. government to devalue its currency as a way to increase exports and reduce imports. Devaluation would make the dollar less expensive in terms of foreign currencies. By reducing the value of the dollar, U.S. goods and services would become less expensive to foreigners. This situation, it is claimed, would increase exports and reduce the deficit in our balance of trade.

All economists would agree that, other things being equal, a cheaper dollar would stimulate exports of both goods and services. Most economists, however, would agree that this stimulation of exports would work only in the short run. In the long run, a devaluation of the dollar would have little or no effect on foreign trade.

● With the dollar worth less in terms of foreign currencies, people in the United States would have to pay more for imported goods and services.

● Since many imported goods and services go into the manufacture of U.S. products, sooner or later domestic prices would also rise.

● Rising prices would, in turn, lead to demands for wage increases, still further price increases, and the return of exports to approximately the same level as they were before the devaluation.

In the long run, say most economists, exchange rates are merely a reflection of a nation's competitive strength and productivity. The key to increasing exports is to produce goods and services that other nations will want, at prices they can afford.

expect to receive yen; French vendors, francs; and so on. For that reason, payments for U.S. exports are shown as U.S. dollars, while payments for imports are shown as foreign exchange.

Since U.S. imports and U.S. exports of goods and services are rarely, if ever, equal within a given year, additional funds need to be moved to bring the payments into balance. For the first 25 or so years following the Second World War, the United States exported far more than it imported. Payment differences were settled with *capital movements* in the form of loans, investments, or gifts from the United States to foreign lands. In recent years, the opposite has occurred: U.S. imports of goods and services have outstripped exports. Differences have been made up in the form of capital movements into the United States

from abroad. Examples of these capital movements are foreign investments in U.S. corporations, in real estate, and in U.S. government
bonds and notes.

Published quarterly by the U.S. Department of Commerce, the *U.S.
Balance Of Payments* summarizes such financial transactions between
the United States and the rest of the world. Table 22.4 illustrates a recent balance of payments statement. Let us study its major components and see how the transactions are brought into balance.

Table 22.4   U.S. BALANCE OF PAYMENTS, 1995 (BILLIONS OF DOLLARS)

	Inflows	*Outflows*	*Net*
Current Account			
GOODS, SERVICES, AND INCOME			
Goods			
Merchandise exports	$574.9		
Merchandise imports		$749.3.6	
			−174.4
Services			
Military	12.7	9.9	
Travel	68.3	45.5	
Passenger fares	18.2	13.4	
Other transportation	28.6	29.6	
Royalties and fees	25.9	6.5	
Other services	62.5	38.1	
Total Services	208.8	146.8	63.9
Income			
Income on foreign investments	92.2		
Foreign income on U.S. investments		131.5	
Other receipts from abroad	85.5		
Government income on assets abroad	4.6		
Government payments on foreign assets			
in the United States		61.3	
Total Income	182.3	192.8	−10.5
UNILATERAL TRANSFERS			
Government grants and pensions		14.1	
Private remittances		16.0	
			−30.1
Capital Account			
U.S. ASSETS ABROAD			
U.S. Government assets		10.0	
Private assets		270.0	
			−280.0
FOREIGN ASSETS IN THE UNITED STATES			
Foreign government assets	110.5		
Other assets	317.8		
			428.3
STATISTICAL DISCREPANCY	4.7		
Totals	$1,399.0	$1,399.0	

The Current Account

Most, but not all, international trade involves the import and export of goods and services. The *current account* summarizes those activities in the sections headed: (1) goods, services, and income; and (2) unilateral transfers.

Goods, Services, and Income. We will discuss each of these topics separately.

1. Goods. When people think of foreign trade, most picture the exporting and importing of goods (also called "merchandise"). And well they might, for trade in goods constitutes over half of all global trade.

Imports of merchandise are paid for with foreign exchange and are recorded as an *outflow of funds*. Thus, when Tom Terrific's Toyota Agency imported $200,000 worth of automobiles, the company paid for the shipment with Japanese yen, which they purchased from their bank. The $200,000 payment was included in the $749.3 billion outflow in the merchandise imports account for the year.

Merchandise exports generate an *inflow of funds*. When, for example, a Venezuelan manufacturer purchased a $75,000 knitting machine from a U.S. firm, the sum was included in the $574.9 billion recorded in the U.S. Balance of Payments statement.

As long ago as the 16th century and continuing on and off almost to the present day, economists focused on the relationship between merchandise imports and exports. They described this relationship as the *balance of trade*. In their view, a favorable balance of trade was a situation in which merchandise exports were greater than imports. An unfavorable balance of trade was one in which merchandise imports were greater than exports. (See pages 512–513 for a discussion of these ideas.)

Most economists today do not attach a great deal of importance to this balance of trade in goods. They prefer, instead, to study the entire balance of payments as a way of getting a more complete picture of a nation's strengths and/or weaknesses in the global economy.

2. Services. Since goods can be seen and felt, they are often referred to as "visible." But there are other items of value in international trade that can be neither seen nor touched. These "invisible" imports and exports are generally described as "services." Roughly 25 percent of U.S. trade with the rest of the world is in the form of services. Table 22.4 summarizes the principal service transactions. An explanation of these transactions follows:

MILITARY. Payments by foreign governments to the U.S. government to train their armed forces are treated as exports of services. Similarly, payments by the U.S. government to foreign governments for allowing it to establish bases in their countries are included in this category as imports of services.

Although, strictly speaking, the purchase and sale of military hardware represents the exchange of goods (not a service), the U.S. Department of Commerce includes these transactions in this category.

TRAVEL. Foreign tourists visiting the United States spend money for food, hotel accommodations, sightseeing excursions, and a host of other items. The money spent by these tourists has much the same effect on our balance of payments as do U.S. exports. Both represent inflows of foreign funds to the United States.

Similarly, the money spent by Americans traveling in foreign lands are recorded as outflows of funds in the Travel section of the U.S. balance of payments.

PASSENGER FARES. By reading Table 22.4, we can see that in 1995 Americans spent some $13 billion in fares to travel on foreign airlines, ships, and the like. That same year, foreigners spent about $18 billion in fares on U.S. carriers. Like other imports, Americans' spending as passengers on foreign carriers was recorded as an outflow of funds. Meanwhile, foreign passengers using U.S. carriers represented an export of services. These transactions were recorded as an inflow of funds in the balance of payments.

OTHER TRANSPORTATION. The cost of shipping merchandise imports and exports is reflected in this category. Foreign use of U.S. ships results in an inflow of funds. Meanwhile, the cost of shipping U.S. exports on foreign ships, planes, railroads, and trucks results in an outflow.

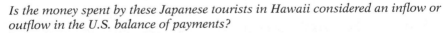

Is the money spent by these Japanese tourists in Hawaii considered an inflow or outflow in the U.S. balance of payments?

ROYALTIES AND FEES. *Royalties* are payments for the use of creative works. Royalties paid to U.S. musicians, publishers, film companies, and the like by foreign users of their materials represent exports of services and are recorded as inflows of funds. Royalties and other fees paid by Americans to foreign sources are treated as imports.

3. Income. U.S. investments in foreign corporations, real estate, or other assets generate income. Depending on the type of investments, the income will be in the form of interest, dividends, and rents. The income is summarized as an inflow of funds in the balance of payments statement. Similarly, foreign investment in U.S. assets generate an outflow of funds from the United States to foreign lands.

As indicated by Table 22.4, both private investors and governments are included in the income category.

Unilateral Transfers. In most instances, funds are transferred in payment for a good or service. This is not true of *unilateral transfers*, one-way transactions in which funds are simply given as gifts or foreign aid. The information contained in the balance of payments shows *net differences* between U.S. government transfers to foreign lands and foreign government transfers to the United States and private transfers of a similar nature. As we can see in Table 22.4, unilateral transfers in 1995 amounted to:

- an outflow of $14.1 billion resulting from transfers by governments, and
- an outflow of $16.0 billion from transfers by private individuals and institutions.

The Capital Account

So far, we have been discussing the current account in the balance of payment statement. Now we will turn to the capital account. Since imports and exports of goods and services are never equal, additional funds need to be moved to bring the payments into balance. This occurs with the movement of capital.

The *capital account* describes how the inflows and outflows of payments were brought into balance. You will find these descriptions in the accounts headed *U.S. ASSETS ABROAD* and *FOREIGN ASSETS IN THE UNITED STATES*.

Loans or investments made abroad by individuals, corporations, and governments are recorded as either outflows or inflows in the capital account of the balance of payments. Saudi Arabian investment in Iowa farmland creates an inflow of funds, just as the purchase by a U.S. corporation of an oil refinery in West Africa would create an outflow of funds. Over the years, the income, if any, generated by these

Figure 22.4 International Trade and the Balance of Payments

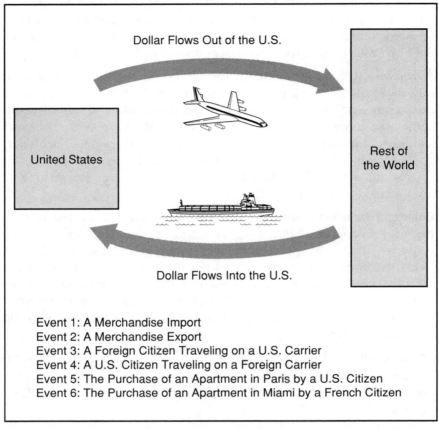

Dollar Flows Out of the U.S.

United States

Rest of
the World

Dollar Flows Into the U.S.

Event 1: A Merchandise Import
Event 2: A Merchandise Export
Event 3: A Foreign Citizen Traveling on a U.S. Carrier
Event 4: A U.S. Citizen Traveling on a Foreign Carrier
Event 5: The Purchase of an Apartment in Paris by a U.S. Citizen
Event 6: The Purchase of an Apartment in Miami by a French Citizen

What effect would each of the events in the illustration have on the balance of payments?

investments will be noted under investment income in the current account.

In the course of a year, some Americans sell off their overseas assets while others purchase new ones. Similarly, some foreigners will sell their holdings while others will add to theirs. The net result of these transactions in 1995 is summarized in Table 22.4.

U.S. Assets Abroad. The value of the dollar in terms of foreign currencies is determined in the foreign exchange markets. One of the more important things that the U.S. government does to promote foreign trade is to enter the foreign exchange market as a buyer or seller. It does so to maintain the value of the dollar.

Since foreign exchange is used to purchase foreign goods and services, a decrease in the U.S. government's supply of foreign exchange is recorded as an outflow of funds in the balance of payments. Similarly, an increase in the government's supplies of foreign exchange is shown as an inflow.

In 1995, the purchase by private individuals and institutions of foreign assets (securities, corporations, etc.) is an outflow in the Capital Account of $270 billion.

Foreign Assets in the United States. Investment by foreign governments and private individuals and institutions in U.S. securities, real estate, business firms, and other assets appear as an inflow of funds on the balance of payments statement. Foreign assets in the United States in 1995 totaled over $428 billion.

Statistical Discrepancy. Because it accounts for literally millions of transactions in international trade, the balance of payments is bound to have a number of errors. These are summarized under the heading *STATISTICAL DISCREPANCY*. The statistical discrepancy is whatever it takes to bring the balance of payments into balance. In 1995, this amounted to $4.7 billion.

Summary

The rate of exchange is the price of one country's currency in terms of another's. The value of a nation's currency depends upon the supply and demand for that currency in the international market, which in turn depends on the demand for the goods and services of that nation.

Foreign exchange rates were fixed when most industrialized nations adhered to the gold standard. In 1944, many countries adopted a standard of fixed exchange rates based on the U.S. dollar. In 1971, the United States devalued the U.S. dollar and would no longer exchange U.S. dollars at a fixed rate. Thus, exchange rates began to "float" in value in accord with the supply and demand for the currency on the international market.

The U.S. Balance of Payments is a financial statement that summarizes the country's international transactions. Exports of goods and services cause funds to flow into the country. Imports of goods and services result in an outflow of payments. When imports exceed exports, a nation has an unfavorable balance of trade. When exports exceed imports, a nation has a favorable balance of trade. When the balance of trade is not exactly equal, a balance is achieved either by an inflow or outflow of funds.

REVIEWING THE CHAPTER

Building Vocabulary

Match each item in Column A with its definition in Column B.

COLUMN A	COLUMN B
1. Special Drawing Rights	*a.* a summary of financial transactions between one country and the rest of the world
2. fixed exchange rate	*b.* the value of a currency that is determined by the laws of supply and demand on the open market
3. Bretton Woods system	
4. gold standard	*c.* the reduction in the value of a nation's currency in terms of foreign currencies
5. floating exchange rate	
6. statistical discrepancy	*d.* the relationship between a country's imports and its exports
7. International Monetary Fund	*e.* credits to the account of member nations in the IMF that can be used to purchase foreign currencies
8. devaluation	*f.* a system whereby currencies of most countries were exchangeable for a fixed amount of gold
9. balance of payments	
10. balance of trade	*g.* the value of a currency that is set by a government
	h. a summary of errors in recording transactions
	i. a system whereby foreign currencies were exchanged for dollars at a fixed rate of $35 per ounce of gold
	j. a specialized agency of the United Nations that promotes international monetary cooperation

Understanding What You Have Read

1. Which is the best explanation as to why the Mexican peso has value outside Mexico? (*a*) Anyone can walk into a bank and exchange the peso for gold. (*b*) Merchants throughout the world will accept the peso in exchange for their goods. (*c*) The peso can be used to buy Mexican goods and services. (*d*) There is an ample supply of pesos.

2. Assume that the exchange rate for the Chilean peso is $1 = 135 pesos. How much would a U.S. importer pay in dollars for wool worth 202,500 pesos? (*a*) $15,000 (*b*) $1,500 (*c*) $150 (*d*) $15.

3. Suppose that a few days before the U.S. importer made payment on the wool purchased in Question 2, the Chilean peso was devalued. What effect would this have on the importer? (*a*) It would have no effect. (*b*) It would make the wool more expensive. (*c*) It would make the wool less expensive. (*d*) It would make it impossible for the importer to make payment.

4. Assume that exchange rates are allowed to float and that the demand for German marks has been increasing. Under these circumstances, which of the following is most likely to occur? (*a*) It will take fewer dollars to buy German marks. (*b*) The price of German goods in terms of dollars will fall. (*c*) Germans will find that imported goods are getting more expensive. (*d*) Americans will have to pay more for goods made in Germany.

5. If a nation's reserves of dollars or other foreign currencies were running low, it might look to the International Monetary Fund for (*a*) a loan of foreign exchange (*b*) the printing of any foreign currency it needed (*c*) an investment loan to build up-to-date production facilities (*d*) a market for its surplus production so as to restore a "favorable balance of trade."

6. Special Drawing Rights (SDRs) were created to provide all of the following, *except* (*a*) an international monetary reserve currency (*b*) an alternative to gold (*c*) currency that can be used by tourists as they travel from one country to another (*d*) a substitute for U.S. dollars as a "reserve currency."

7. Which was a serious weakness of the gold standard? (*a*) Having the gold standard made it difficult to determine rates of exchange. (*b*) People did not want to accept gold in exchange for a currency. (*c*) As the supply of gold in a country on the gold standard increased, imports became more costly. (*d*) Having the gold standard made it difficult for a nation to increase or decrease its money supply.

8. What would likely happen to the Italian lira if Italy suddenly became the world's leading exporter of automobiles and electronic equipment? (*a*) The lira would increase in value, thereby making imports less expensive in Italy. (*b*) The lira would decrease in value, thereby making imports more expensive in Italy. (*c*) The change would not affect the value of the lira. (*d*) The change would compel the Italian government to devalue the lira.

9. A nation's balance of trade describes (*a*) the total flow of money into and out of the country (*b*) its exports and imports of merchandise (*c*) its overall economic health (*d*) how well it is doing in international trade.

10. A nation's balance of payments summarizes the nation's business transactions   (*a*) with multinational corporations based in that country   (*b*) with the European Union   (*c*) with the International Monetary Fund   (*d*) with the rest of the world.

Thinking Critically

1. Sweater Trends, Inc., distributes sweaters manufactured to its specifications to department stores and boutiques around the country. In seeking a manufacturer for its latest design, Sweater Trends narrowed down its choices to three firms. One, a U.S. company, has offered to deliver the sweaters for $10 each. A Taiwanese firm can do the same, including delivery to the United States for 48 NT$ each. The third, an Ecuadorian manufacturer, offered to deliver the sweaters for 14,400 sucres each.

    Exchange rates at the time stood at:

    $$\$1 = 7.5 \text{ NT\$}$$
    $$\$1 = 2,400 \text{ sucres}$$

    Since the initial order was to be for 10,000 sweaters, Sweater Trends selected the manufacturer that made the lowest bid. (*a*) Which manufacturer did the distributor select?   (*b*) Suppose that by the time Sweater Trends was ready to place its order, exchange rates had shifted so that $1 was now equal to 4 NT$ and 1,300 sucres. (*1*) Which manufacturer would Sweater Trends have then engaged? (*2*) What happened to the value of the U.S. dollar as a result of the shift in exchange rates? (*3*) How did the shift in exchange rates affect standards of living in the United States? (*4*) What might have caused such a shift in exchange rates?

2. "A nation's exports pay for its imports." Explain this statement.

3. Even today, some economists argue that the world's trading nations ought to return to the gold standard.   (*a*) What was the gold standard?   (*b*) Identify and explain one advantage that the gold standard offered in international trade.   (*c*) Identify and explain a principal weakness of the gold standard.

4. In the early 1990s, the dollar depreciated in value when compared with the currencies of Germany, Switzerland, France, and Japan. More funds were flowing out of the United States economy than were flowing in.

    a. Explain why the dollar depreciates with respect to the currencies of Germany, Switzerland, France, and Japan when more funds flow out of the U.S. economy than flow in.

    b. How does a decrease in the supply of foreign funds affect the U.S. balance of payments?

c. Discuss how a fall in the value of the dollar affects *(1)* U.S. demand for German, Swiss, French, and Japanese products, and *(2)* the demand for U.S. products by those countries whose currencies have appreciated in value relative to the dollar.

d. Why are U.S. workers involved in the import trade concerned when they hear that the value of the dollar is falling? How are U.S. workers involved in the export trade affected by a falling dollar?

SKILLS: Using a Foreign Exchange Rate Table

Imagine that you are on a long trip through Latin America, Europe, and Asia. To pay for purchases in each country you visit, you will exchange U.S. currency for the currency of the country you are in. Complete the following chart. Use the information in Table 22.1 (on page 538) to determine the cost in U.S. dollars and in a foreign currency for each of your purchases.

Country	Purchase	Cost in Local Currency	Cost in U.S. Dollars
Argentina	dinner for two	22 pesos	$?
France	perfume	150 francs	$?
China	ceramic vase	? yuan	$100
Mexico	shawl	100 pesos	$?
Ecuador	hotel room	84,001.75 sucres	$?
Peru	rug	20 new sol	$?
Russia	1 oz. caviar	? rubles	$150
Switz.	1 lb. cheese	6 francs	$?
Taiwan	TV set	5,272 NT$	$?

Note: To convert from a foreign currency to U.S. currency, divide the foreign currency by *How Much $1 U.S. Equals in Foreign Currency*, or multiply the foreign currency by *How Much One Unit of Foreign Currency Equals in U.S. Dollars*.

To convert from U.S. currency to foreign currency, multiply the amount in U.S. currency by *How Much $1 U.S. Equals in Foreign Currency*, or divide the amount in U.S. currency by *How Much One Unit of Foreign Currency Equals in U.S. Dollars*.

If you were to use two methods to compute a conversion, you may find a slight discrepancy. This happens because the figures quoted in Table 22.1 are rounded off.

Chapter 23

OTHER ECONOMIC SYSTEMS

Overview

A specter is haunting Europe—the specter of Communism. All the powers of old Europe have entered into a holy alliance to exorcise this specter. . . .

The Communists disdain to conceal their aims. . . . They openly declare that their ends can be attained only by the forcible overthrow of all existing social relations. Let the ruling classes tremble at a Communist revolution. The proletarians have nothing to lose but their chains. They have a world to win.
                              —Marx and Engels, **Communist Manifesto**, 1848

Does it surprise you that this quote is from a pamphlet written in 1848? **Karl Marx** and fellow socialist **Friedrich Engels** wrote it at a time of social unrest in Germany and elsewhere in Western Europe. The *Communist Manifesto* is not only a call for revolution, but a severe critique of capitalism. Many people in the 19th century blamed the capitalist economic system for the terrible working and living conditions in Europe. Western Europeans were going through the Industrial Revolution then. Unlike today, in the mid-19th century there were few labor unions to organize workers and help them demand better wages and working conditions. Governments were not yet involved in protecting workers from their employers. Socialism was in its infancy, and communism had not yet been born in 1848. Not until the 20th century would socialism and communism become strong competitors with capitalism as ways to organize economic society.

In this chapter, we will compare different economic systems. After briefly reviewing the market economy, we will discuss the theories of Karl Marx and the Communist economy of the Soviet Union. Then we will look at democratic socialism as practiced in Sweden and elsewhere. Finally, we will discuss Japan's economic system, which can be labeled "managed capitalism."

COMPARING ECONOMIC SYSTEMS

The message of economics is as clear as it is universal: you can't have everything, we can't have everything, and they can't have everything. . . .
                                                          —Anonymous

As we discussed in Chapter 1, scarcity forces all societies to make choices and decide WHAT will be produced, HOW they will be produced, and WHO will receive them? You may recall from your reading of Chapter 1 that the way a group or nation organizes itself for production in order to answer these fundamental questions is known as its "economic system."

Thus far we have mainly described one economic system—capitalism. While capitalism is the economic system of choice in the United States and in many other countries, other systems exist also. Indeed, prior to the 1990s more of the world's population lived in socialist or Communist economies than in market economies. Since the collapse of the Soviet Union in 1991, however, most of the Communist and socialist countries have been converting their economic systems to some form of capitalism.

The economic systems of nations today are mixtures of command, tradition, and free market. In a traditional economic system, people grow crops, raise herds, or fish, using the same tools and techniques that have been used for many generations past. The family is the main organizational unit of traditional economic life. WHAT is produced and HOW it is produced is not the result of conscious planning but rather a matter of custom and tradition.

In a command economy, the fundamental questions of WHAT, HOW, and WHO are pretty much decided by a central authority, usually the government. The degree of power exercised by the central authority may vary from one country to another, but the principle means of production remain in government hands. Since government owns most of the industry in command economies, government central-planning agencies determine WHAT to produce and HOW it would be produced.

We give the economic systems labels in an attempt to describe their main characteristics—labels such as "capitalism," "socialism," "communism," or "managed capitalism." As you read this chapter, though, remember that whatever we call the economy of a particular country, it is only a label. We have to search deeper in order to understand how the economy of that nation really works.

Economic systems are most frequently compared in terms of the ownership of the means of production and how these means of production are coordinated.

Ownership

Ownership as a trait of an economic system refers to the extent to which the means of production are either privately or publicly owned. In the United States, private individuals and corporations own most

What does the cartoonist show the Russian bear doing?

farms, factories, offices, shops, and other businesses. In some other countries, the government owns (and operates) a large share of the means of production.

Coordination

Coordination is a term economists use to describe the way in which the economic system answers the fundamental WHAT, HOW, and WHO questions. Nations organize their economic systems in one of three ways: (1) around the market, as in a capitalist system; (2) through government planning, as in a socialist system; or (3) a combination of the first two ways, in what is described as a "mixed economic system." Tradition may still play a role in economic activities, but the role that tradition plays diminishes as an economy industrializes. We begin our comparison of economic systems with a review of our own system of capitalism.

CAPITALISM

In Chapter 2, we described the U.S. economic system—capitalism. Let us review here the main points. In a capitalist or market economy, the means of production are, for the most part, privately owned. Prices, as determined by the forces of supply and demand, drive the system. Consumers cast their votes for **WHAT** is produced in the form of the prices they are willing to pay for particular goods and services. Producers strive to satisfy those demands as best they can. When not enough of a product is offered for sale, prices move upward until supply and demand are equal. When too much is produced, prices fall. As a result, output is reduced until supply and demand are once again equal.

Prices also determine **HOW** goods will be produced. In their efforts to maximize profits, producers strive to combine productive factors in such a way as to achieve the highest level of output for the least amount of input. For example, manufacturers of loose-leaf paper could be expected to use their machines, labor, and raw materials in such a way as to produce the greatest amount of paper (of a given type and quality) at the lowest possible cost. For their part, suppliers of raw materials used by paper producers will also do their best to offer their products and services at the prices that allow them to beat out their competition but still earn a profit.

It is important to note that the system of capitalism we have just described is an ideal. It does not exist as such in the real world. In the United States, for example, government ownership of productive facilities exists at the federal, state, and local levels. Then, too, the Federal Reserve System manages the supply of money and credit in the economy. Monopolistic and oligopolistic firms (both discussed in Chapter 7) may interfere with the free forces of the market. Moreover, many government laws protect U.S. consumers. At the same time, some other laws help individual firms or industries. In short, the United States is really a mixed economy rather than a completely *laissez-faire* capitalist economy.

KARL MARX'S ECONOMIC THOUGHT

In the mid-19th century, Karl Marx wrote several powerful critiques of capitalism as it was developing during the Industrial Revolution. Marx's ideas became the basis for both modern socialism and communism. In studying his ideas, we can learn about both of these economic systems. Some of the major theories advanced by Marx were:

The History of Society Is a History of Class Struggle

Marx argued that throughout history one class has dominated the others. He claimed that during the Middle Ages in Western Europe, the landed classes (church officials and nobility) were triumphant. At a later time, these classes were replaced as the dominant ones by the *bourgeoisie* (people of the middle class, including capitalists). Marx claimed that capitalists grew fat through the exploitation of the *proletariat*—Marx's term for people who work for wages. Marx predicted that the proletariat would eventually overthrow the capitalists and create a classless society.

Workers Are Paid Less Than the Value of the Goods They Produce

Marx called the difference between the value of workers' wages and the value of the goods that workers produce *surplus value*. Many Marxists equate surplus value with profits and suggest that this surplus value rightfully belongs to the workers.

Capitalism Will Inevitably Lead to an Endless Round of Economic Depressions

Marx argued that because of competition among firms, capitalists are under constant pressure to reduce their costs. Capitalists reduce costs by investing in labor-saving machinery, reducing wages, or both. Since labor-saving machinery requires fewer workers to produce a given output, unemployment increases. Meanwhile, those firms unable to compete successfully are forced out of business, and their workers are added to the rolls of the unemployed. As unemployment mounts and wages decline, depression is the inevitable result.

The trend is reversed as wealthier businesses buy up those that have failed. As time goes by and surplus stocks are consumed, the remaining businesses hire increasing numbers of workers, and prosperity returns. Eventually, however, the cycle is repeated, more economic power is concentrated in fewer hands, and the proletariat endures greater suffering.

Marx predicted that under capitalism the rich would get richer, the poor poorer, and (with business firms' increasing reliance upon machinery) the army of unemployed would grow and grow.

Revolution Is Inevitable

Marx believed that the mounting discontent among workers would unite them. Furthermore, Marx said that the proletariat would rise up, overthrow the capitalists, and establish a socialist state.

Communism Is the Ultimate Goal

Marx wrote that the ultimate goal for workers is communism. But to achieve this goal, he said, a society would have to advance through the stage of the dictatorship of the proletariat.

Karl Marx

To the world's Communists, the book *Das Kapital* (1867) is a kind of bible and Karl Marx is its prophet. Even socialists who are not Communists revere Karl Marx. Who was this dark-eyed, bewhiskered man, whose portrait peered down from walls in homes and offices wherever communism was the official state doctrine?

Karl Marx was born in the German city of Trier in 1818. Educated at the universities of Bonn and Berlin, he became a journalist. Forced to leave Germany because of his radical views, he settled in Paris, France. There Marx met Friedrich Engels (1820–1895), the son of a wealthy Prussian textile manufacturer. The two men became lifelong friends, a fact that is significant for several reasons. First, Marx and Engels collaborated on writing the *Communist Manifesto* (1848), which set forth a declaration of principles for a newly created Communist group known first as the "League of the Just" and later as the "Communist League." Second, had it not been for Engels' financial aid, it is unlikely that Marx would have finished writing his greatest work, *Das Kapital.*

Because of Marx's support for the 1848 revolution in Austria, he was banished from continental Europe. In 1849, Marx moved his family to London. There he spent nearly every day doing research and writing in the Reading Room of the British Museum.

Marx and his family lived in wrenching poverty for many years. Much of his meager income came from articles he wrote for a U.S. newspaper, the *New York Tribune*, and from money that Engels gave him.

In 1864, Marx helped to organize The International Workingmen's Association. The **First International**, as the association was commonly known, was a forerunner of modern Communist parties. Later, in 1867, the first volume of his *Das Kapital* was published. After Marx's death in 1883, two more volumes of the work were edited by Engels and published, in 1885 and 1894.

Dictatorship of the Proletariat. If the proletariat are victorious, Marx argued, the country that they control would be immediately surrounded by hostile capitalist states. It would be necessary, therefore (claimed Marx), to establish a dictatorship in order to organize the state along socialist lines and to fight its capitalist neighbors. This dictatorship of the proletariat would permit the victorious revolutionaries to develop a socialist economy, one in which the workers or the government would own all the means of production.

Communism. Ultimately, Marx said, the socialist economic system would advance far enough technologically so that communism would be possible. Under communism the economy would supply sufficient quantities of goods and services to satisfy everyone. All workers would work to the best of their abilities and would be paid in accordance with the principle "to each according to one's needs." There would be no classes under communism. Thus, the absence of want and of any struggle between classes would make government unnecessary. The state, declared Marx, would "wither away."

Theory and Reality

Although most Americans reject the theories and conclusions of Karl Marx, his ideas can hardly be ignored since they influenced the economic thinking of such a large portion of the world. Some things that Marx predicted about capitalism proved to be true. He was right when he predicted that there would be recurring depressions and that giant firms would come to dominate the industrial scene. Nevertheless, Marx's most important conclusion—that capitalism would inevitably collapse—has not been borne out. To the contrary, in the last decade capitalism has replaced communism in many countries.

Why was Marx wrong? Why has capitalism survived? One answer is that governments with capitalist economies have protected consumers and workers. Marx had pictured capitalism as a system that was completely dominated by the greed of the capitalists. As Marx saw it, a society so dominated would be incapable of reforming its economic system to give workers a greater share of the goods and services they produce. As a result, this exploited group would rise up and overthrow its masters. Beginning in the late 19th century, however, the governments of many capitalist countries did many things to help workers. In the United States, for example, Congress passed laws that protect consumers and workers (as well as business firms) and promote the more equitable distribution of income. Moreover, contrary to Marx's predictions of class struggle, labor and management have learned to work together within the framework of the capitalist system.

Some of the most powerful countries in the world have regarded Marxism as the theoretical basis of their economies. In the pages that follow, we will take a closer look at how the Soviet Union applied Marxist philosophy. To some extent, the Soviet system became a model for Communist systems in China, North Korea, Vietnam, Cuba, Hungary, Czechoslovakia, Yugoslavia, Bulgaria, Poland, Albania, Laos, Ethiopia, and elsewhere.

THE SOVIET EXPERIENCE, 1917–1991

Prior to 1917, communism had not been tried out by any country. In 1917, however, two revolutions took place in Russia. In the second one, the Russian Communist party under **V.I. Lenin** seized control. Thus began the first Communist state—Soviet Russia—whose name was changed to the Soviet Union in 1922. Although many observers predicted the imminent downfall of the Soviet experiment, its economy developed to a great extent. The Soviet government spent a large part of its resources building up heavy industry and a strong military. Within three decades of the revolution, the Soviet Union had become one of the two most powerful nations in the world (the other being the United States). Although Soviet leaders called their government and

May Day (May 1st) was a major holiday in the Soviet Union. This parade on May 1, 1960, in Moscow emphasized the country's military strength. The banner pictures Marx and Lenin and reads, "Forward, Toward the Victory of Communism!"

society "Communist," they did not claim that their economic system had achieved communism. Instead, communism was always a goal toward which the Communist party and its supporters were working.

Special Role of the Government in the Soviet Economy

As described earlier, the economic system of the Soviet Union was a command economy. Because the Soviet state owned almost all the means of production and distribution (including factories, mines, farms, and stores), it determined how the basic questions of WHAT, HOW, and WHO would be answered. Moreover, because the Communist party was the only legal political party, it exercised ultimate power over the government. Thus, the Communists decided what the general economic goals for the coming years would be. These goals were written down in formal plans for the coming years.

Five-Year Plans. When **Joseph Stalin** rose to power in the USSR in the mid-1920s, he found himself at the head of an industrially backward nation. In an attempt to modernize the Soviet economy as rapidly as possible, Stalin instituted a series of *five-year plans*. Each plan was a detailed statement of the nation's production goals for the next five years. The plans applied to all aspects of the economy, including industry, agriculture, trades, and the professions. For example, the government expected lawyers to handle their quota of cases, taxi drivers to log so many miles, and barbers to perform a minimum number of haircuts.

The five-year plans not only set forth production goals but also tried to *allocate* (assign) the resources necessary to achieve them. If, for example, Soviet leaders determined that steel production should be increased, the plan provided for the construction of additional steel production facilities and allocated the raw materials and labor needed to meet that goal. With the exception of the war years 1939–1945, five-year plans or their equivalent (there was one seven-year plan) were in force from 1928 to the end of the Soviet era in 1991.

Deciding WHAT to Produce. The Soviet agency responsible for preparing and administering the central economic plan was the State Planning Committee, or **Gosplan.** After consulting with the various economic ministries and industries, Gosplan prepared production quotas, or targets, for each of the 350,000 business enterprises within the Soviet economy and sent them on to the individual managers.

The managers then estimated the quantities of raw materials and the amount of labor they would need to meet their quotas. The managers' estimates were sent back to Gosplan. Since the managers' requests for inputs rarely matched the available resources, Gosplan had to modify many of its quotas and reassign tasks among the enterprises until a final plan was achieved. The plan, which was binding on all Soviet enterprises, set forth target quotas for sales, costs, profits, and productivity increases for the coming year.

Deciding HOW Goods Were to Be Produced. The responsibility for carrying out the annual plan rested with the managers of the local factories, farms, stores, and offices. They hired and fired workers, purchased machinery and equipment, and made the everyday decisions necessary to running a business. But, unlike capitalist entrepreneurs (whose primary motivation is to earn profits), the Soviet managers' goal was to conduct their "businesses" in ways that would meet their quotas.

Deciding WHO Was to Receive the Goods and Services. Since the government controlled nearly all of the nation's output, it could reward some people by allowing them to purchase goods and services that were unavailable to most others. For example, while the government controlled rents so that almost everyone could afford housing, there simply were not enough apartments to go around. Nevertheless, good housing was made available for certain categories of workers who were deemed essential by the government, such as Olympic athletes, scientists, and high party officials. Similarly, high party officials and other privileged people were able to obtain scarce items in stores set aside for their exclusive use.

The Failure of the Soviet Economy

The Communist party governed the Soviet Union until December 1991. Then, with the economic system in chaos, Soviet leaders dissolved the Soviet Union. The collapse of both the Soviet economy and the Soviet empire came as a shock to most Americans. As recently as 1987, the U.S. Central Intelligence Agency had listed Soviet production as greater than that of Japan and second only to that of the United States. As events were to prove, the Soviet Union was in reality an impoverished nation whose collapse was largely the result of its failed economic system.

Why Did the Soviet Economy Fail? Although opinions differ, most experts would agree that the system's inability to allocate scarce resources was a major reason for the failure of the Soviet economy. By allowing planners (rather than supply and demand) to determine what goods and services were to be produced, the Soviet economy was overwhelmed with products for which there were no buyers. At the same time, the Soviet economy was burdened with enormous shortages of products that were in demand.

Another major reason for the failure of the Soviet economy was the government's overemphasis on military expenditures. During the years 1945–1991, the Soviet Union devoted approximately 14 percent of its budget each year to defense. At the same time, the United States allocated about 6 percent and Japan only 1 percent of the yearly national budget for military expenditures. As a result of Soviet planners' decisions to emphasize military production, not enough resources were available for the production of consumer goods and services.

In the absence of a capitalist-type price system in the Soviet Union, resources were often undervalued by the central planners. This undervaluation, in turn, encouraged inefficient and wasteful manufacturing processes. Many plant managers, for example, looked upon Soviet petroleum, natural gas, and other raw material as cheap and limitless. They had no need to conserve these resources and had no incentive to change production methods to save money.

Under the Soviet system of low, fixed prices for consumer goods, people could afford to buy the food and appliances they wanted. The problem was that there often was not enough of these items to go around. So although the price of a commodity like eggs was low enough, at times there were not enough eggs produced to meet consumer demand. The same type of shortage existed for automobiles, appliances, and other goods. In a free enterprise economy, you will recall, when demand outruns supply, the market is brought back into balance with price increases. But the Soviet Union had made a political decision to maintain fixed prices at levels that everyone could afford. Therefore, ways other than the price system had to be developed in order to allocate consumer goods and other resources. One way was waiting in long lines for scarce goods. Another was political favoritism. And a third was the black market.

Queues. When members of the general public wanted to buy food or clothing, they had to wait their turn in long *queues* (lines) outside shops that had something to sell. When one store ran out of merchandise, shoppers might then go to other stores and wait on line there. Some people would even sneak away from their workplace to get a good place in a line. This practice interfered with the efficiency of workplaces. Queues in the Soviet Union served the same purpose as prices do in the United States. Both are ways of allocating resources.

Political Favoritism. A second means of distributing scarce resources in the Soviet Union was political favoritism. Important government and party officials and other influential citizens could avoid the indignities of waiting on line by shopping at stores run exclusively for their benefit. There the shelves were always well stocked with goods unavailable to ordinary folk. Similarly, factory managers with the right connec-

A woman stands before empty shelves in a Soviet bakery. What does the photograph tell us about the Soviet economy?

tions could always obtain the materials needed to keep their operations running smoothly. Those without connections could buy their raw materials only when they became available from government sources.

Black Market. The black market provided a third means of distributing scarce resources. Soviet citizens commonly bought fruits, vegetables, meats, shoes, petrol—in fact, almost anything they wanted—at illegal stands and stores. Products unavailable in the official government stores were often available, for a price, on the unofficial black market. The prices for goods in the black market were higher than the official prices for goods sold at government stores. But remember that the government stores often had shelves empty of certain desired items. So, if a Soviet citizen wanted a certain product that was in demand, that person sometimes had to get it on the black market and pay the going price or go without.

The Gorbachev Years. For many years, the Soviet Union was able to make up for the scarcity of consumer goods by paying for imports with exports of its natural resources. But by the 1980s, it was no longer possible to export enough raw materials to offset the shortages. In 1985, leadership of the Soviet Union and its Communist party passed to

Mikhail Gorbachev. With the Soviet economy in a shambles, Gorbachev made economic reform his top priority. Toward that end, he introduced the policies of *glasnost* and *perestroika*.

Glasnost (the Russian word for "openness") encouraged discussion and some criticism of government programs by the press and the public.

Perestroika, or "restructuring," referred to the fundamental changes that Gorbachev began making to the structure of the economy and the political system. Economic changes included: the introduction of limited private enterprise; the reform of the price system so that the costs of raw materials supplied to factories would be negotiated by buyers and sellers; and self-sufficiency for government enterprises, which were told to earn a profit or be put out of business.

By 1991, *perestroika* still had not rescued the Soviet economy. Budget deficits had reached the highest levels since the end of World War II. The economic growth rate was declining, and food had to be imported in record quantities from the United States and elsewhere. Worse still, Soviet living standards, as measured by per capita gross domestic product, were far behind those in the West.

POST-SOVIET RUSSIA

Mortally weakened by its failed economy, the Soviet Union collapsed in December 1991. It was replaced by the **Commonwealth of Independent States (CIS),** a loose association of 12 independent republics that had once been part of the Soviet Union. In Russia, the largest of the republics, the Communists gave up power to non-Communists. One former Communist, **Boris Yeltsin**, became the head of Russia.

Economic Reform in Russia

After his election as president in 1991, Boris Yeltsin continued Gorbachev's economic reforms and added some more radical ones. His goal was to revitalize the Russian economy and raise the standard of living. Some of the changes that Yeltsin and his advisers proposed were so drastic that they were characterized as "shock therapy." He called for:

- lifting of price controls
- ending central planning
- privatizing state enterprises
- balancing the national budget
- permitting the free movement of goods and capital in and out of the country.

Proponents of shock therapy said that free pricing and privatization would give profit-seeking enterprises the incentives they needed to produce the goods that consumers want. Meanwhile, opening the country to international trade and investment would provide much needed foreign technology and financing.

Yeltsin's economic reforms went into effect in January 1992. With abolition of price controls, store shelves began to fill and waiting lines outside shops disappeared. But the Russian economy was still in deep trouble. At the heart of the problem was the inability of business and industry to increase output. Indeed, GDP in 1992 dropped by about 20 percent from that in 1991. With goods and services continuing in short supply, and prices no longer fixed (as they had been in the days of communism), inflation spiraled at a rate of 20 to 30 percent per month. Meanwhile, as the now privately owned firms struggled to earn profits, many workers were laid off.

Not all Russians suffered as a result of privatization. Those able to acquire the capital necessary to purchase government assets and start a business often succeeded. Unfortunately, a sizable proportion of those early entrepreneurs became members of organized crime. According to one report published by the Russian government, organized crime controlled between 70 and 80 percent of all banking activities. Another survey found that over 25 percent of Russia's entrepreneurs said that they had been pressured to make extortion payments.

Another consequence of the early failures of Russia's conversion to a market economy was that it added to the unequal distribution of income. According to a 1995 study, the richest 20 percent of the population earned 50 percent of the country's revenue, while the poorest 20 percent received only 3.5 percent. Worse yet, one-third of all Russians lived below the poverty line.

COMMUNISM TODAY

Few countries today call themselves Communist. Examples include China, North Korea, Vietnam, and Cuba. While North Korea and Cuba have resisted introducing many elements of capitalism into their economies, China, and more recently Vietnam, are creating real mixed economies. Let us look at the example of China to see how well the label "Communist" can be applied today.

Red China

Mao Zedong and the Chinese Communist party came to power in China in 1949. They established a Soviet-style economic system in China that included a planned economy and government ownership of most of the means of production. In 1978, Mao died. Leadership of the Communist party fell to Deng Xiaoping, who turned China toward a semicapitalist dictatorship. One Chinese official jokingly commented on the changes, "Under the leadership of the Communist Party, we're advancing from socialism to capitalism."

The Rural Scene. First to break with Communist tradition were the farms. From the 1950s to 1979, farming in China was done on *communes* of 2,000 to 4,000 people. Residents of the communes were organized military style in shared living quarters and mess halls. Everyone worked at assigned tasks and received wages. Private farms had been abolished.

In 1979, the agricultural system was reformed to allow individual households and groups of households to lease land from the state for a specified number of years. During that time, the renters would have to pay taxes and fulfill planned production quotas. The goods produced to meet these quotas had to be sold to the state at set prices. After meeting these obligations, though, rural households would be free to produce what they could and sell surplus products on the free market at whatever price they could get. The rural reforms were very successful. Chinese farm output and the peasants' standard of living increased dramatically.

Industries and Other Businesses. Under Mao, the Chinese government controlled all factories, stores, and means of transportation. Copying the Soviet example, the government instituted five-year plans for all economic units. Then under Deng, the government encouraged private ownership of light and medium industries (such as the manufacturing of toys, textiles, garments, shoes, and consumer electronics). Many state factories have been privatized and have sold stock to the public. China still has five-year plans that govern the state-run industries. But since Deng's economic restructuring began, the role of the state sector in the economy has been greatly reduced. It accounts for only about half of the country's industrial production. Private businesses produce another 12 percent.

In addition to the private and the state-run factories, today many factories are owned collectively by local governments or by the people who work in the factories. Collectives account for one-third of industrial output.

China has given priority to increasing overseas trade and attracting foreign investments in Chinese factories and other businesses. As a result, over 51,000 foreign business ventures were set up between 1991 and 1994. Meanwhile, international trade as a percentage of China's GDP increased from 15 percent in 1983 to 35 percent in 1994.

Workers in a Chinese factory assemble bicycles. The market for bicycles in China is large (about 400 million riders), but this government-owned factory has to compete with a number of privately owned ones.

China's combination of political dictatorship and limited capitalism has had considerable economic success. Although its average household annual income of $685 is still relatively low (when compared with income of households in the United States or Japan), between 1979 and 1995 China's economy grew more rapidly than that of any other developing country. In fact, China's average annual rate of growth exceeded that of the United States and Japan as well. China's GDP, which amounted to $298 billion in 1980, increased to $508 billion in 1994. As a result, consumption levels more than doubled.

Problems Remain

The government has less control than before over business activity and local authorities. In Shenzhen, businesspeople in 1990 set up a stock exchange—the very symbol of capitalism—without first getting permission from the central government. Corruption is widespread in China, especially among government officials. To conduct business, Chinese entrepreneurs must often bribe Chinese officials.

Economic growth in China has been achieved at a price. While many in the new middle class live well, inflation has been running at around 20 percent through much of the 1990s. Inflation has been particularly hard on those living on pensions and other fixed incomes.

Nowhere has the income gap widened more rapidly than between the urban and rural areas. Although rural regions were among the first to benefit from privatization, many of the less efficient farmers found themselves unable to earn a good living. In 1994, annual urban income was the equivalent of $373 per capita, while rural income was only $142. Some 100 million Chinese people are estimated to have moved from the countryside to the cities in search of work. These people form a vast, sometimes-migrating labor pool that entrepreneurs tap to run their new businesses. Unemployment and overcrowding in the cities have pushed up urban crime rates. Homelessness and begging are now common in Chinese cities.

Although China is moving in the direction of free-market capitalism, it is not becoming democratic. It still has a one-party government. Communist party leaders are willing to free prices, but they are not willing to free the press. Nor will the party tolerate dissenters. In June 1989, for example, the government cracked down on pro-democracy demonstrators in Beijing's Tiananmen Square. Hundreds of students and workers died in an army-led assault on the night of June 3 and the morning of June 4. Deng justified the government's use of force by accusing the protesters of trying to overthrow the Communist party and demolish the socialist system. The Chinese Communist party shows no signs of giving up its rigid control over political life in China.

SOCIALISM

Socialism is not easy to describe because so many different nations have called themselves socialist. The Communist countries that we just described are (or, in some cases, were) socialist. In contrast to these examples is *democratic socialism*—the type of socialism that has been practiced in certain Western European countries and in India, New Zealand, Australia, and elsewhere.

Certain features help distinguish democratic socialism from communism. Although socialism is a form of command economy, the degree of power exercised by the central government varies from one socialist country to another. For example, the governments of Great Britain and Sweden when socialists were in power had much less power than the Communist governments of China and Cuba. Government ownership of productive resources and government planning are limited in democratic socialist countries but are quite extensive in Communist countries. Although socialist and Communist economic systems are both forms of a command economy, communism is the more extreme model.

Democratic Socialism

In addition to having command economies, democratic socialist countries have other traits in common. They have democratically elected governments with freedom for their population and press. They have all *nationalized* (taken control of by the government) their major industries, such as coal, railroads, airlines, and banks. After World War II, democratic socialist countries (with their high taxes on wealth) established "cradle-to-grave" welfare services, including free medical care and generous pension benefits.

Democratic socialism still exists in some countries (but only periodically) after socialists are elected to power. After winning an election, the socialist leaders introduce elaborate welfare programs and nationalize major industries. Typically, though, socialist programs are cut back in these countries after the socialists lose elections. Let us take a look at Sweden as one example of democratic socialism.

Sweden: the Middle Way

Some economists refer to the Swedish economy as the "middle way," meaning that the nation has adopted many socialist programs while maintaining the kind of private ownership normally associated with capitalism. One social program pays for all maternity expenses as well as paid leaves of absence for new parents. Regardless of need, every family in Sweden receives a child-care allowance for each child. The government subsidizes child-care centers to keep costs low for working families. Another government program pays the entire cost of medical and dental care and guarantees close to a full income for people who become sick or unemployed. All Swedish children are entitled to a free education from kindergarten through college. Students' meals, books, and school supplies are provided without charge until they are 16. Thereafter, they receive from the government a monthly allowance for as long as they remain in school.

Upon entering the world of work, Swedish young adults are eligible for different kinds of government-sponsored benefits. Unemployment insurance will reimburse them if they lose their jobs, and government programs will train them for new ones. Free transportation is available if a new job involves commuting to another town. Years later upon retirement, Swedish workers will receive pensions and other forms of government assistance, such as housing and health care.

The Swedish social welfare system was highly successful from the 1930s until the 1990s, when Sweden (like much of Western Europe) went through a recession. Unemployment rates went from almost nothing in 1991 to 13 percent in 1994. Unemployment compensation and other government benefits surged, and so did the nation's deficit. Worse still, between 1991 and 1993 the country's economy shrank by 5 percent.

In an effort to pull itself out of its recession, Sweden cut many of its welfare programs. For example, unemployment benefits were reduced from 90 percent of one's former salary to 75 percent. The austerity campaign seemed to work. In 1994, Sweden's GDP grew for the first time in three years. In the aftermath of the recession, many Swedes now call for an overhaul of the welfare system so that it will be more in line with what Swedish taxpayers can afford.

MANAGED CAPITALISM

For hundreds of years, the strongest economies were the industrialized countries of Western Europe and North America. More recently, however, new names have begun to appear on lists of very successful economies—Japan, Malaysia, South Korea, Singapore, and Thailand (see Figure 23.1). These nations share at least three things in common: (1) All are located in East or Southeast Asia, (2) they all embrace capitalism, and (3) their kind of capitalism differs from the type practiced in the United States.

What benefits does the Swedish government provide its people?

Figure 23.1   The Global Superstars of Economic Growth, 1960–1993

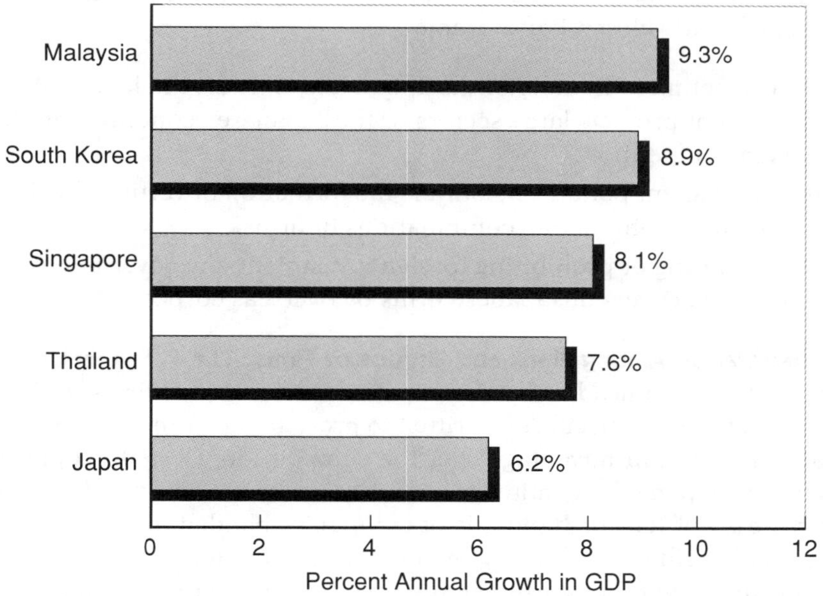

Percent Annual Growth in GDP

Malaysia — 9.3%
South Korea — 8.9%
Singapore — 8.1%
Thailand — 7.6%
Japan — 6.2%

Economists sometimes ask why some Asian nations are doing so well. Perhaps one key to their successes lies in *managed capitalism*, which includes strong government intervention in an economy and co-operation among corporations.

Japan's Managed Capitalism

One way of comparing the U.S. model and the Japanese version of capitalism is in terms of competition vs. collaboration. In the United States, competition among producers is the key to increased output, reduced costs, and improved living standards. Indeed, the principal goal of U.S. antitrust legislation is to encourage competition. In order to promote competition, the government prohibits efforts by firms in the same industry to collaborate in the production or distribution of their products. (This topic is discussed in Chapter 7, pages 160–161.)

In contrast to the emphasis the United States gives to competition among producers, the stress in the Japanese economy is placed on *collaboration* (active cooperation). This includes (1) collaboration between industry and government, (2) collaboration among groups of firms within and across industries, and (3) collaboration between limited numbers of shareholders and management.

Collaboration Between Industry and Government. As we have discussed in other chapters, government has an important role to play in the U.S. economy. In Japan, the relationship between government and industry is significantly closer. For example:

- By erecting tariff and non-tariff barriers to trade, the Japanese government protects large sectors of the Japanese economy from foreign competition.
- Government policies encourage the formation of vertical, horizontal, and conglomerate combinations of firms.
- By limiting or prohibiting foreign investment, the government prevents takeovers of Japanese firms by overseas corporations.

Collaboration Among Firms and Groups of Firms. The U.S. market system is based on head-to-head competition among rival firms. U.S. antitrust laws were specifically written to prevent one or more firms from gaining an unfair advantage over the competition. Quite the opposite is true in Japan where industry is dominated by the *keiretsu*. A *keiretsu* is a family of tens or hundreds of companies banded together for the mutual benefit of the "family" members. *Keiretsu* members are free to invest in one another's firms, share directors, and maintain close social links. Listed on page 584 are the principal firms associated with the Sumitomo Group, one of Japan's largest *keiretsu*.

Collaboration Between Shareholders and Management. Unlike in the United States (where corporations are primarily owned by private individuals), controlling shares of large Japanese firms are primarily owned by other corporations. This is especially true among the *keiretsu*, where as much as 60 to 80 percent of a corporation's stock may be owned by other member corporations. Since these shares are rarely (if ever) traded, member companies do not have to worry about falling stock prices, takeover attempts, and shareholder demands for dividend payments.

One of the benefits of collaboration between shareholders and management is that Japanese managers (unlike their U.S. counterparts) can focus on long-term rather than short-term results. For example, if forced to choose between skipping a dividend payment or laying off experienced workers, U.S. managers will often keep their stockholders happy by paying the dividend and laying off experienced workers. The decision to lay off experienced workers is a short-term decision often connected with concern for end-of-year profits. Since an experienced staff is a valuable resource, laying people off can be damaging to a business in the long term.

Should U.S. Corporations Be Allowed to Behave More Like Japanese Firms?

U.S. antitrust laws prohibit U.S. corporations from cooperating with one another by setting prices, assigning markets, and refusing to trade with outsiders. But much of Japanese companies' successes are, it is argued, partly the result of these practices. According to a number of U.S. economists and business managers, cooperation among Japanese firms has placed U.S. industry at a disadvantage in international trade. In order to "equal the playing field," they suggest that the United States revise its antitrust laws and consider alternatives to free trade. Those who hold this view hope to imitate the Japanese by (1) allowing competing U.S. firms to coordinate their planning, production, and marketing, and (2) asking the U.S. government to restrict foreign competition.

Those opposed to the above suggestions argue against a weakening of U.S. antitrust laws and against protectionist laws. They claim that both types of action would be harmful to U.S. workers, consumers, and businesses. Workers and consumers would be harmed because, in the absence of competition, firms would be tempted to raise prices, reduce wages, and produce inferior goods and services. (Arguments against protectionism are discussed in Chapter 21.)

Competition at Home. Instead of cooperation, many economists say that competition inside Japan is the main reason for Japanese successes abroad. Although collaboration between industry and government does restrict competition from foreign companies, competition is extensive within Japan. Japan has about 580 companies in the electronics business, 7,000 textile manufacturers, and 114 firms manufacturing machine tools. Price cutting within Japan is as ruthless as one might find anywhere.

Competition, as we discussed in Chapter 3, results in more efficient production, improved quality, and lower prices. Much of Japan's success is due to competition among its producers. U.S. consumers (and consumers worldwide) have recognized that Japanese products are often of superior quality and design and competitive in price compared to products made in the United States. It must be emphasized, though, that competition in the Japanese economy exists together with cooperation and collaboration in the Japanese economy.

Imitating Japanese Practices. There are a number of Japanese production techniques that are being copied by U.S. firms.

1. Quality Circles. One such technique, *quality circles*, organizes employees into teams that work together to solve any production problems that might arise. When a new Japanese employee enters a company, the company becomes the worker's family. Success is very important to the Japanese worker. But success is measured in terms of group success, not individual success. In the Japanese factory or office, a team of workers forms a quality circle. New ideas and production techniques are evaluated openly by the quality circle, and a decision is reached by the whole team. All members of the quality circle receive credit, or take blame, for the team's results. A number of U.S. corporations have adopted the team approach to production.

2. Inventory on Demand. A second Japanese practice that is gaining favor among U.S. firms is *inventory on demand* (also known as "just-in-time manufacturing"). Traditionally, most U.S. firms have maintained large stocks of inventory at the factory. This practice, however, is expensive. With inventory on demand, supplies are kept by a wholesaler and delivered immediately when requested. When a production unit needs left-front fenders, for example, an order is placed for left-front fenders and the supplies are delivered from a warehouse that holds thousands of fender parts. Thus, Japanese firms do not need to carry large inventories at their production facilities. By keeping supplies

At this Nissan auto plant in Tennessee, Japanese production techniques have increased production and workers' loyalties.

to a minimum, Japanese firms save the costs of storage.

U.S. Productivity Exceeds That of Japan. A yardstick of international competitiveness is productivity. Recent studies indicate that the United States leads European countries and Japan in productivity per worker. Japanese factory workers, for example, produce 80 percent as much as U.S. workers on an hourly basis. Some U.S. economists argue that the United States does relatively well in productivity because our government is reluctant to protect U.S. firms from the rigors of competition—domestic or foreign.

Whereas U.S. firms freely lay off unnecessary workers and close down outmoded plants, Japanese firms are reluctant to do so. Therefore, while the jobs of some Japanese workers are protected, their production costs are higher than they need be. If lifetime employment did not exist in Japan, production costs would be lower, leading to lower prices to consumers. With lower prices, consumers would be able to purchase more goods and services, resulting in a higher standard of living. Lifetime employment, then, survives in Japan at the expense of higher living standards.

Some economists in Japan and the United States disagree that lifetime employment leads to higher production costs and, consequently, lowers living standards for the nation. These economists argue that U.S. firms, by emphasizing the making of profits rather than producing goods

and services, are taking a short-sighted view. Leaders of Japanese corporations, in contrast, believe that the company should become the world's most efficient producer of the product or service it offers, and that when this happens, profits will follow. Thus, when a U.S. firm suffers an economic shock, it will "downsize" and lay off highly skilled workers and managers. Japanese firms, faced with similar conditions, absorb economic shocks not by laying off employees but by reducing dividends and salaries. Surplus scientists, managers, engineers, and workers are retrained and prepared to produce new products more efficiently once the market recovers. Lifetime employment, then, insures stability to the Japanese firms, while U.S. firms suffer from high turnover rates of their management and technical staff.

Recent Changes in Japanese Practices. Facing a continued recession in the mid-1990s, some Japanese business leaders instituted reforms in the ways their firms operate. Some Japanese firms have introduced practices to increase productivity and lower costs. For example, at management levels in many large Japanese firms, *merit pay* (pay in which those who perform better are paid more) is replacing seniority in determining salary. The Japanese institution of "life-time employment" is also under attack as workers are being asked to retire early. These reforms are bringing practices to Japan that are similar to those common in the United States.

Some Japanese business leaders think that Japan should open up its economy more to foreign competition. They also think that there should be less collaboration between the Japanese government and Japanese firms. These measures, they claim, will make Japanese businesses more efficient and better able to compete on the world market.

Perhaps the question, "Should U.S. firms be allowed to behave more like the Japanese businesses?" should be, "What can we learn from each other?" What do you think?

Table 23.1   PRINCIPAL COMPONENTS OF THE SUMITOMO GROUP

Type of Industry	Name of Company
Financial Services	Sumitomo Bank
	Sumitomo Bank and Trust Co.
	Sumitomo Life Insurance Co.
	Sumitomo Marine and Fire Insurance
Electronics	NEC
Autos	Mazda Motors
Retailing	Sumitomo
Construction	Sumitomo Construction
Metals	Sumitomo Metal Industries
	Sumitomo Metal Mining
	Sumitomo Electric Industries
Real Estate	Sumitomo Realty and Development
Glass	Nippon Sheet Glass
Chemicals	Sumitomo Chemicals
	Sumitomo Bakelite
Mining and Forestry	Sumitomo Forestry
	Sumitomo Coal Mining
Industrial Equipment	Sumitomo Heavy Industries
Cement	Sumitomo Cement
Transportation	Sumitomo Warehouse Company

With how many of these companies are you familiar? The Mazda Corporation is a member of the Sumitomo keiretsu. *In the early 1970s when Mazda was close to bankruptcy, other members of the* keiretsu *saved the troubled automaker by offering financial and other assistance. The Sumitomo Bank extended loans to Mazda; other* keiretsu *firms agreed to employ Mazda employees temporarily until the company was out of trouble; and all employees of member companies of the* keiretsu *were directed to purchase only Mazda cars.*

Summary

In capitalist countries, private ownership predominates, and co-ordination is through the marketplace. In socialist and the Communist countries, the means of production are principally owned by the state and coordination of economic activities is largely carried out through government planning. By contrast, the Japanese model of managed capitalism emphasizes cooperation and collaboration among firms and between the government and businesses.

In comparing the economic systems of two or more nations, labels can be confusing. All countries that call themselves capitalist (including the United States) have some degree of government ownership and planning. China, a Communist country, allows some private ownership of the means of production and has stock exchanges. Some democratic countries, such as Sweden, Australia, New Zealand, Britain, and France, have at times been labeled "socialist" even though in each country most of the means of production have been in private hands.

REVIEWING THE CHAPTER

Understanding What You Have Read

1. The first major nation to become Communist was (a) Russia (b) Germany (c) France (d) China.

2. In which type of economic system would the forces of supply and demand play the most important role? (a) capitalism (b) socialism (c) a command system (d) a traditional system.

3. In which respect did the economy of the Soviet Union differ from that of the United States? (a) the emphasis on technological progress (b) the use of money as a medium of exchange (c) the emphasis given to the problem of continued economic growth (d) the manner of deciding what goods and services would be produced.

4. Which statement about socialism is false? (a) The concept of socialism has changed since the time of Karl Marx. (b) All socialist systems are the same. (c) Some socialist states nationalize privately owned businesses. (d) Socialism can exist in a democratic society.

5. Which of the following was the most important factor in determining what goods and services would be produced by the Soviet Union's Communist economy? (*a*) supply and demand (*b*) government planning (*c*) labor unions (*d*) consumers.

6. All of the following reforms were introduced into the Soviet Union under the policy of *perestroika*, except (*a*) self-sufficiency of government enterprise (*b*) price reform (*c*) the profit motive (*d*) five-year plans.

7. Sweden is said to follow a "middle way" because it (*a*) maintains elements of both socialism and capitalism (*b*) combines a blend of totalitarian dictatorship with democracy (*c*) follows an economic path somewhere between communism and socialism (*d*) it is geographically located between Eastern and Western Europe.

8. Which statement is false? (*a*) All Communists are Marxists. (*b*) All Marxists are Communists. (*c*) The Soviet Union was a Communist nation. (*d*) North Korea is a Communist nation.

9. The Japanese version of capitalism differs from the U.S. model in that the Japanese government (*a*) encourages collaboration rather than competition among industries (*b*) discourages the formation of business combinations (*c*) allows foreign countries easy entry into the Japanese market (*d*) prohibits large corporations from owning controlling shares of other firms.

10. Lifetime employment, quality circles, and inventory on demand are characteristics of the economy of (*a*) the United States (*b*) Poland (*c*) China (*d*) Japan.

Thinking Critically

1. Economists usually look at the *ownership of means of production* and the *coordination of economic activity* when they compare economic systems. With reference to the italicized phrases, compare the economic system of a past or present socialist or Communist country with the economic system of the United States today.

2. Communism had its origins in the writings of Karl Marx. With respect to *two* of Marx's theories (*a*) describe each theory, and (*b*) explain the extent to which you would agree or disagree with it.

3. What were the inefficiencies in the Soviet economic system that may have contributed to the system's collapse?

4. Explain the role played by Mikhail Gorbachev in changing the Soviet economy.

5. Japan today is one of the leading industrial nations of the world. Its currency is usually strong. Japanese workers enjoy high wages and a high standard of living. Some economists and business leaders attribute the success of Japanese industries to the country's reliance on managed capitalism and Japanese production and employment techniques.

   a. Compare practices in the United States with those in Japan in terms of managed capitalism, production techniques, and employment techniques.

   b. Present arguments why the United States should or should not adopt the Japanese economic model.

Building Vocabulary

Match each term in Column A with its definition in Column B.

Column A	Column B
1. bourgeoisie	a. people who work for wages
2. socialism	b. the way in which an economic system answers the WHAT, HOW, and WHO questions
3. *perestroika*	
4. managed capitalism	c. the difference between workers' wages and the value of the goods and service they produce
5. commune	
6. coordination	d. a market economy with strong government intervention and cooperation among firms
7. proletariat	e. members of the middle class
8. surplus value	f. an economic system characterized by government ownership and management and planned production
9. five-year plan	
10. *glasnost*	g. a community of farmers who work collectively
	h. a policy that encourages public discussion and criticism
	i. a detailed statement of a country's production goals
	j. the restructuring of an economy

SKILLS: Analyzing an Editorial Cartoon

Study the cartoon below and answer the questions that follow:

1. Who does the figure labeled "China" represent?
2. Identify the symbols at the ends of the balancing rod and explain what China is doing in this cartoon.
3. Why is the figure drawn standing on a razor blade?
4. What can you say about the cartoonist's point of view toward China?
5. What title would you give this cartoon? Why?
6. How does the cartoon relate to the discussion of economic systems in this chapter?

Chapter 24

ECONOMICS OF DEVELOPMENT

Overview

More than half the people of the world are living in conditions approaching misery. . . . Their poverty is a handicap, and a threat, both to them and to more prosperous areas.

—Harry S. Truman

Little has changed since President Harry S. Truman spoke these words in 1949. The planet is still divided between the wealthy countries and the poorer ones. Of course, poverty exists in all nations, including our own. In some countries, however, poverty is much worse.

Why should we, living in one of the most economically advanced countries, be concerned about the poorer countries? The answer is not simply that we should be selfless and concerned with the plight of humanity everywhere. We might also be motivated by the fact that it is in our self-interest to promote the well-being of nations everywhere. Why? Because of increasing international economic interdependence, economic conditions and policies in one nation affect economic conditions in many other nations, including our own.

In this chapter, we will discuss how we measure and compare economic development in different nations, the factors that hinder development, and programs to promote economic growth in developing nations.

HOW CAN WE MEASURE DEVELOPMENT?

In measuring economic development, economists distinguish between developed and developing countries. The *developed countries* are industrialized nations with relatively high GDP and income per capita. *Developing countries*, by contrast, have basically agricultural economies, with relatively low income and GDP per capita. The United Nations uses slightly different terminology in discussing development. It differentiates between *more developed countries (MDCs)* and *less developed countries (LDCs)*. According to the UN, there are approximately 45 MDCs, mostly in Europe and North America. The UN lists over 120 LDCs.

How do the less developed countries compare to the more developed ones? One basis of comparison is *quality of life*, that is, how well

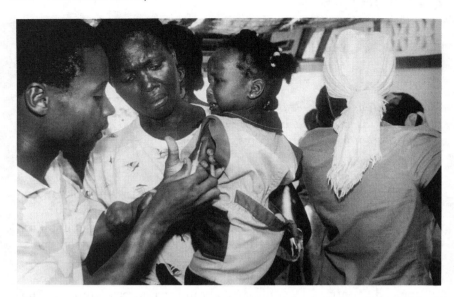

A Haitian child receives a vaccination provided by the United Nations Children's Fund (UNICEF). The medical services a country has is one of the indicators of its economic development.

the average person in each country under consideration lives. The quality of life is relatively high in the United States and in the other developed countries. People eat better, live longer, and are better educated and cared for. They have more material things. People living in the developed countries are the major beneficiaries of humankind's scientific, technological, and cultural achievements. A child born in a developed country is likely to grow to adulthood enjoying a higher quality of life than one born in a developing country. A few statistics, summarized in Table 24.1, will serve to illustrate these differences. The following discussion is based on the contents of the table.

1. Per Capita GDP

Poverty is the common denominator shared by the developing countries, while the developed countries are considered wealthier. One of the most frequently cited measures of a nation's wealth is per capita gross domestic product (first discussed in Chapter 17). This statistic is determined by dividing a nation's total GDP by its population. Economists measure living standards by the amount of goods and services available to an individual or society. GDP per capita enables them to compare the living standard of one nation to that of another. Among the more developed countries in a recent year, per capita GDP averaged $23,090. This figure is to be compared with $380 for the less developed countries.

Table 24.1 MORE DEVELOPED AND LESS DEVELOPED COUNTRIES: MEASURING THE DIFFERENCES

Regions or Country	Per Capita GDP (U.S. Dollars)	Infant Mortality (per 1,000)	Life Expectancy (years)	Literacy Rate (percent)	Energy Consumption Per Capita (kilowatt-hrs.)	1995 Population (millions)	Annual Population Growth Rate (percent)	Projected Population 2025 (millions)	Percent of GDP Devoted to Agriculture
More Developed Countries	23,090	7	77	n.a.	n.a.	812.0	0.5	908.0	4
Less Developed Countries	380	108	62	41	n.a.	3,092.0	2.9	4,987.0	28
Bangladesh	220	106	56	35	79	128.1	2.3	248.0	30
Brazil	2,930	57	67	81	1,570	160.7	1.2	230.0	11
China	490	30	69	73	647	1,203.1	1.0	1,471.0	19
Egypt	620	64	64	48	849	62.4	2.0	86.0	18
Ethiopia	100	117	48	n.a.	25	56.0	2.9	127.0	60
Germany	23,560	6	76	99	6,693	81.3	.4	82.0	1
India	300	80	61	51	373	936.5	1.8	1,392.0	31
Indonesia	740	56	63	77	233	203.6	1.6	280.0	19
Japan	31,490	4	80	99	7,211	125.5	0.2	127.0	2
Kenya	270	61	58	69	130	28.8	2.9	46.0	29
Malaysia	3,140	13	71	78	1,612	19.7	2.2	32.0	24
Mexico	3,610	35	71	87	1,381	94.0	1.9	137.0	8
South Korea	7,660	11	71	99	2,996	45.6	1.0	54.0	7
Russia	2,340	21	65	98	6,820	148.9	0.2	146.0	9
Switzerland	35,760	6	80	99	8,471	7.1	0.7	8.0	1
United States	24,740	9	76	99	12,900	263.8	0.7	331.0	2

Source: **World Development Report, 1995**

2. Medical Services

The next two columns tell us something about the state of medical and public health services in various countries. *Infant mortality rate* is the number of babies (out of every 1,000 live births) who die before their first birthday. *Life expectancy* is the number of years the average newly born infant within the designated nation may expect to live. Once again, there is a difference between the developed and the developing countries. Infant mortality is only 7 per 1,000 in the MDCs as compared to 108 per 1,000 in the LDCs. Life expectancy averages 77 years in the MDCs as compared to 62 years in the LDCs.

3. Literacy Rate

The ability to read and write is one of the essential ingredients in economic development. The percentage of an adult population who can read and write is expressed in its *literacy rate*. In the more developed countries (where compulsory education is a fact of life), most people are literate. In the less developed countries, low literacy rates are common. For that reason, governments all over the globe have declared universal literacy to be a principal goal.

The opportunity costs of universal education can be high, especially in the short run. In the desperately poor countries of Africa and Asia, parents often look to their children to help them scratch out a living. Thus, they are reluctant to have them spend time in school. Similarly, governments intent on retaining or expanding political power are likely to give spending on their armed forces a higher priority than education. Education, however, is an essential ingredient in economic growth and development. According to a study of developing nations:

> ... economies—such as Japan and the Republic of Korea—which committed themselves to education and training made great strides in human development and economic growth ... and that ... a one-year increase in schooling augmented wages by more than 10 percent; raised farm output by anywhere from 2 to 5 percent; and resulted in an increase in earnings in family-owned business.
>
> International Bank for Development,
> ***The Challenge of Development***

4. Energy Consumption Per Capita

Energy is needed for heat, light, power, and transportation. Energy is created most commonly with the help of a variety of fuels, including petroleum, natural gas, coal, and nuclear varieties. We measure a country's progress in making these vital fuels available by the statistic *energy consumption per capita*—a nation's total energy consumption divided by its population. The statistics in this column are stated in terms of kilowatt-hours.

5. Population Data

The next three columns compare the populations of the selected nations and show how they are changing. The first of these columns lists the country's total population in a recent year. The second shows its present rate of population growth per year, and the third estimates the population, based on the given rate of growth, for the year 2025.

6. Percent of GDP Devoted to Agriculture

The relative importance of agriculture in the LDCs and MDCs is illustrated in the last column. Nations obtain the food they need to feed their populations by either producing it themselves or importing it from abroad. The more industrialized a nation becomes, the fewer resources it needs to devote to growing its own food. This is true because: (1) industrialized nations can use the proceeds from the export of manufactured goods to purchase food, and (2) agricultural productivity in industrialized nations is generally higher than that in the less developed countries. In contrast to the situation in industrialized countries, agriculture generally plays a much larger role in the economies of less developed countries.

In Bangladesh, many farmers rely on animals to power plows. What percent of Bangladesh's GDP is devoted to agriculture?

THE STAGES OF DEVELOPMENT

Why are some countries more developed than others? One of the most accepted explanations of economic growth was made by economist **W.W. Rostow** of M.I.T. In his *The Stages of Economic Growth: A Non-Communist Manifesto*, Rostow argued that, at one time or another, all industrialized nations could have been classified as "less developed." At some later time, however, each began a process of development that transformed its economy. The process, as described by Rostow, involved five stages of economic growth:

- Traditional society
- Preconditions for takeoff
- Takeoff
- Drive to maturity
- Age of high mass consumption.

Rostow's work provides us with a simple framework for understanding how nations increase real per capita income through the process of economic development. Let us take a closer look at each of the stages of economic growth.

Stage 1: Traditional Society

At the traditional stage, society has not yet come to use technology to increase its production of goods and services. Because its methods of production are primitive, virtually all of society's productive energies must be directed toward feeding its people. The class structure of such a society is often rigid, and whatever surplus people produce inevitably finds its way into the hands of a small wealthy class. Since this surplus is not used to increase the level of production, economic life continues more or less the same from one year to the next.

Stage 2: Preconditions for Takeoff

Before a society can undertake a dramatic move toward development, it has to prepare itself by making certain breaks with the past. These preconditions, according to Rostow, are:

Breakdown of Old Traditions. The attitudes and traditions that dominated society in the past must be broken down so that new social, political, and economic methods may be introduced.

Emergence of Nationalism. It is easier to develop an economy along modern lines if a population accepts the rule of a central government. This was not the case in Europe during the Middle Ages. Under feudalism, a person's main allegiance was to the local lord rather than to a monarch. Similarly, in some of today's less developed countries, individual loyalties lie with a tribe rather than a national government. This tendency serves as an obstacle to modernization because a central government is needed, among other reasons, to make laws governing commerce that apply to the whole nation.

Development of a Middle Class. Economic development requires a group willing to form businesses and take risks in pursuit of profit. Such a group is described as the middle class, or bourgeoisie.

Accumulation of Savings. Before increasing output, a portion of the profits from current output needs to be saved for later purchases of capital goods. Closely allied with the accumulation of savings is the development of financial institutions and markets that can pool funds and make them available to businesses in need of capital.

Stage 3: Takeoff

Rostow defines *takeoff* as a dramatic movement toward development that includes increased productivity. Just as a plane becomes airborne at one point along the runway, so too will a developing economy "take off" with a sharp increase in output. As this occurs, production will increase at a faster rate than its population. Then, as the surplus is invested in capital goods, output will increase still further. The Industrial Revolution in the textile industry in 18th-century England is a classic example of what Professor Rostow meant by the "takeoff."

Stage 4: The Drive to Maturity

With production increasing faster than the population, living standards will increase. Simultaneously, the manufacturing and service sectors of the economy will increase in importance, while the agricultural sector will become less important.

Stage 5: Age of High Mass Consumption

Roughly 60 years after the breakdown of traditional society, said Rostow, the nation will mature to the point where it can produce or acquire anything that consumers want. With high mass consumption, consumers will have achieved a high standard of living. Meanwhile, society will be able to devote an increasing share of its resources to social welfare programs. According to the World Bank, the economies of the following high-income nations would fall into this category: New Zealand, Ireland, Spain, Israel, Australia, Hong Kong, United Kingdom, Finland, Kuwait, Italy, Singapore, Canada, Netherlands, United Arab Emirates, Belgium, France, Austria, Germany, Sweden, the United States, Norway, Denmark, Japan, and Switzerland.

WHAT FACTORS HELP OR HINDER DEVELOPMENT?

Since the developing countries are not all alike, any summary of the reasons for their poverty must be generalized. Each differs from the others in many ways. Each has its own strength and weaknesses.

Some developing countries (such as China, South Korea, Mexico, and several South American countries) are well on their way toward development. They seem to fall outside most of the generalizations that follow. Then, too, there are those developing nations whose holdings of a natural resource are extensive. It is reasonable to assume that they will more easily be able to raise capital for development than the less fortunately endowed nations. One such group includes the nations of the Organization of Petroleum Exporting Countries (OPEC). Their wealth from the sale of oil gives them an enormous advantage over other developing nations and helps explain why two OPEC members—Kuwait and the United Arab Emirates—have already reached the fifth stage of economic growth. (Other members of OPEC include Algeria, Gabon, Indonesia, Iran, Iraq, Libya, Nigeria, Qatar, Saudi Arabia, and Venezuela.) As we will read, money flowing into a country is not the only factor needed for growth. Many of the OPEC nations share some of the same obstacles to growth that the less fortunate developing countries experience.

In their fight against poverty, the developing countries tend to suffer from some or all of the following handicaps.

1. Traditions That Are Obstacles to Economic Growth

Traditional societies need to overcome any number of obstacles in their efforts to meet the preconditions for takeoff. Deeply ingrained religious and social customs and traditions may limit their ability to increase production. In some Muslim countries, for example, women are excluded from the labor force because of custom. For a long time in India, the caste system locked many people in the social class into which they were born. Those in the lowest castes were not free to work where they chose.

People in traditional economic societies are often reluctant to adopt new methods of production. Farmers who barely grow enough to feed their families, for example, may be reluctant to try a new plowing technique because they fear failure, which could result in starvation.

2. Unfavorable Social and Political Conditions

History has shown that government can be a major factor in a society's economic growth and development. In many of the less developed countries, political instability and repression have added to the na-

Women in Saudi Arabia are excluded from many jobs and are prohibited from driving motor vehicles.

tions' woes. Many of Ethiopia's problems had their origin in the harsh policies of the Marxist government that ruled from 1974 to 1991. It forced 1.5 million farmers off their land, triggered a nationwide famine, and plunged the country into a civil war.

Some governments spend more on human development (health, education, and social services) than others, with predictable results. For example, in 1989, both Sri Lanka and Guinea had about the same per capita income. But the Sri Lankan government then committed more of the nation's resources to human development than the government of Guinea. By 1993, Sri Lanka's per capita income exceeded that of Guinea by 20 percent. Moreover, life expectancy in Sri Lanka grew and is now two-thirds longer than in Guinea.

Military spending, particularly in less developed countries, is another ingredient likely to affect economic growth and development. For a number of years, Angola, Cuba, Chad, North Korea, and Uganda —all poor countries—each spent more on their armed forces than they could afford. This money could have been better used to help obtain industries or infrastructure. Some of these countries now even have difficulty feeding their own population.

Corruption is still another factor that can impede a developing nation's efforts to grow its economy. Corrupt individuals steal much money from governments—money that could be used for development. Moreover, businesspeople often have to pay bribes to get matters approved by government officials. Corruption was a major justification for the military overthrow of the government of Nigeria in 1993. Yet corruption continued in Nigeria. In 1996, for example, newspapers revealed that someone had stolen $100 million that had been in a Nigerian fund to set up a state-run airline company.

3. Rapid Population Growth

As we can see in Table 24.1, the population in developing countries is growing at a much faster rate than it is in the developed world (2.9 percent vs. 0.5 percent). At these rates, the average population in the developing nations will double in 25 years, while it will take over 140 years to double in the developed nations. Imagine the kinds of problems this population explosion might create. To maintain living standards at present levels, production in developing countries would have to double in the next 25 years. But this increase in production is unlikely to happen. Developing countries rarely achieve economic growth rates that exceed their population growth.

Remember, too, that life expectancy in developing countries is 15 years less than that in the developed societies. Combined with high birthrates, lower life expectancy means that the developing countries have a predominantly young population. As a result, an estimated half of the population of many of the developing nations are too young to work. After adding the number of those needed to rear children and those too old to work, we see that a substantial portion of the population is simply unavailable to join the labor force.

4. Shortage of Capital

Because developed nations possess the kinds of factories, equipment, and tools necessary to the tasks of modern production, they can turn out more goods and services than they themselves need. Excess production can then be exchanged for the goods and services necessary to maintain and improve the nation's living standards. The less developed countries, by contrast, are woefully short of capital and, thus, have much fewer surplus goods and services. But in order to acquire capital goods, LDCs need to set enough savings aside to finance necessary investments. In the more developed countries, individual savings in banks and other financial institutions provide a pool of funds that can be borrowed and invested in capital projects. However, in places where most of the population lives at the subsistence level, little is available for savings and investment.

In these circumstances, governments may choose to impose savings on the nation. In centrally planned economies like those of North Korea and Cuba, government can use its powers to regulate all aspects of the economy to force high savings rates. Central planners can, for example, limit the production of consumer goods. With few goods to buy, consumers are compelled to save currency.

5. Poorly Educated Labor Force

Most economists would agree that education is essential for raising individual productivity. General education gives children skills that in later years they can transfer from one job to another. All too often, however, the labor force in less developed nations suffers from inadequate education and training. The relationship between education and productivity was demonstrated in a recent study by the World Bank (*World Development Report, 1995*). Among other things, the study found that farmers in China's Hunan Province, where education is a priority, out-produced less educated farmers in other Chinese provinces. Similarly, areas of India in which few farmers had primary schooling experienced less economic growth than other areas of India in which farmers were better educated.

A PROGRAM FOR THE DEVELOPING COUNTRIES

Economists have suggested that developing countries follow a number of measures in their efforts to achieve economic growth and, in so doing, reduce poverty.

1. Increase Farm Productivity

More than half the total labor force in the developing countries works in agriculture. In the poorest nations, the average is closer to 70 percent. Contrast these percentages with the 6 percent figure for the industrialized world's agricultural labor force.

Agricultural productivity accounts for the difference. Modern technology enables farmers in the developed countries to produce (with fewer workers) far more than their counterparts in the developing countries. Whereas farms in the developed nations typically produce a surplus, much of the agriculture in the developing countries consists of *subsistence farming*. Farms operating at subsistence levels produce just enough to feed the farmers and their families.

If poor nations would modernize their farming methods, fewer farm workers would be needed. Thus, additional workers would be available for service in other forms of production, thereby increasing total output. The increase in total output could lead to an overall improvement in living standards.

In addition to improved technology, some experts suggest *land reform* as a means to improve agricultural productivity in the less developed world. Land reform refers to the breakup by government of large estates into smaller plots that can be owned and farmed individually. The process of land reform gives those who work as tenant farmers an opportunity to own the land on which they labor. Those who

A successful agricultural economy is one of the basic steps toward development. This Hmong woman works a field in Thailand.

favor land reform argue that farmers who own their land are likely to be more productive than those who work for others.

In Latin America, most farmland is still in the hands of giant landowners. Peasants who work the land do so for a minimal wage and/or a share of an estate's resources. One of the earliest efforts at land reform in Latin America occurred in Mexico in the 1930s. During that decade, some 45 million acres of land acquired in the aftermath of that country's revolution was distributed to 800,000 peasant families. More recently, Guatemala, Bolivia, Venezuela, Cuba, Ecuador, Nicaragua, Chile, and Peru have broken up some estates and redistributed the farmland.

Land reform is not unique to Latin America. In Thailand, where 60 percent of the population still makes its living from the land, land ownership and reform is that nation's most sensitive political issue. Indeed, in one two-year period (1993–1995), the Thai government distributed 4.5 acre parcels to some 600,000 families. The government of Indonesia also regards land reform as an essential part of that country's development plans. Similarly, land reform is at the top of the political agenda of the governments of South Africa and Zimbabwe.

Not all economists agree, however, that land reform leads to greater agricultural productivity. Some claim that dividing large estates into tiny, privately owned plots can be inefficient. A farmer with a small plot might not earn enough from the land to invest in agricultural machinery and make other improvements. Defenders of land reform counter with the argument that the new landowners who benefit from land reform could form cooperatives to purchase tractors and other expensive machinery. Members of the cooperatives would share the costs and the uses of such technology.

2. Reduce Population Growth

If a nation's per capita gross domestic product is to grow, total GDP must increase faster than the increase in population. With this in mind, a number of developing nations introduced family-planning programs. *Family planning* refers to efforts to limit the size of families. Family-planning programs may vary from privately sponsored organizations that give out brochures and contraceptives to clinics that perform abortions to government-imposed limits on family size. China, for example, limits families to one child and imposes penalties on parents who have more than their limit.

While most people would agree that population growth affects living standards, some efforts to limit family size are highly controversial. In some poor, agricultural countries, for example, family planning flies in the face of tradition. In those societies, people often look to their children as a kind of social security. By the time they are 10 or 11 years old, they are expected to help the family work the land. In later years, when the parents are too old to care for themselves, the children will be expected to attend to their parents' needs. Without children to care for them, many elderly people might die of hunger or neglect.

Family-planning programs often conflict with people's religious beliefs and practices. In India, where the population has been increasing by more than 10 million a year, opposition by followers of traditional Hinduism has been an obstacle to the success of that country's birth control programs. Similarly, the Roman Catholic Church has been a leader in opposing most birth control methods in countries around the world.

3. Accumulate Capital Goods

Modern production requires the application of machinery and tools and up-to-date manufacturing plants. Since the developing countries are unable to manufacture most of their own equipment, they have to purchase it abroad. They often need foreign assistance to set up modern manufacturing plants. Developing countries accumulate capital goods in the following ways:

Buy Equipment With Own Funds. About 80 percent of the capital needed for development in the developing countries comes from internal sources (that is, from within the countries).

Amartya Sen

Professor Amartya Sen of Harvard University specializes in the areas of welfare economics and economic growth and development. A citizen of India, Professor Sen was educated at Calcutta University in India and Cambridge University in Britain. Before coming to Harvard in 1980, he taught at the University of Delhi, the London School of Economics, and Oxford University.

In his landmark study *Poverty and Famine*, published in 1981, Amartya Sen argued that more lives could be saved by giving money instead of food to victims of famine. (*Famine* is defined as large-scale starvation.) In arriving at this conclusion, Professor Sen used the following arguments:

One of the most desperate problems faced by certain underdeveloped nations has been that of famine. In their efforts to fight the malnutrition,

hunger, and death that often follows in famine's wake, governments and international agencies strive to deliver and distribute food to those in need. In doing so, they undoubtedly save millions of lives. But as the death tolls show, food aid usually arrives too late to save everyone. Then, when help finally arrives, it often harms farmers who have crops or livestock to sell because people will not pay for food that they can obtain for free. As local farmers abandon the soil, the impoverished country finds itself even more dependent on outside aid when drought and famine return.

By way of illustration, Sen cited the famine in Ethiopia in 1973. While the country as a whole in 1973 produced roughly as much food as in previous years, there was a famine in the province of Wollo, where food production suffered a big decline. Most of the famine victims were subsistence farmers whose crops had failed. They lacked enough money to buy food from elsewhere in Ethiopia, which had enough food. Trade was possible because the roads into Wollo were open. Indeed, some of Wollo's farmers had surplus food and sold it outside the province.

This scenario led Professor Sen to suggest that cash, rather than food, would save more famine victims. Unlike food aid, cash can be dispatched quickly to the famine areas and is less disruptive to the local economy. With money in hand, those facing starvation could buy food from those who have enough. Moreover, cash aid will push up food prices, thereby encouraging food imports, and, even more importantly, greater production of food at home.

Of course, cash aid will work only if there is already enough food in a famine-stricken country to feed everyone, and only if food can be bought and sold relatively freely. But, as Professor Sen's research has shown, these conditions exist more often than is usually supposed.

Encourage Foreign Investments. Developing countries often encourage foreign companies to establish businesses on their soil. These investments (along with domestic investments) serve to stimulate economic growth. In keeping with this philosophy, Vietnam launched in 1986 its *doi moi* (economic renovation) policy, which, among other things, encourages foreign investment. As of 1995, *doi moi* had resulted in pledges by some 800 foreign firms of more than $17 billion of investment in 1,400 different projects.

In 1995, 35 percent of cross-border private investments were made to developing countries. Of that $161 billion, about one-third was invested in China and another third in the Asian countries of South Korea, Malaysia, Indonesia, and Thailand. Except for Mexico, Argentina, and Brazil, the rest of the developing world did not receive much private foreign investments.

Join International Financial Agencies. International organizations provide grants, loans, and technical advice to developing nations. A major source of this aid is the United Nations and its affiliated organizations. The most important of these are the International Monetary Fund (IMF) and the International Bank for Reconstruction and Development (or as it is more commonly called, the **World Bank**). The IMF and the World Bank complement one another. They do this by specializing in different aspects of the financial problems most frequently faced by developing nations.

International Monetary Fund. The IMF's job is to help insure that in periods of economic downturn the value of a nation's currency will remain stable. This task is important because a fluctuating currency can interfere with a nation's foreign trade. For example, in 1994 Venezuela considered devaluing its currency. To have done so would have created all kinds of inflationary problems for the nation's economy and its citizens. With the help of $3 billion in credits from the IMF, Venezuela brought the economy under control. As 1995 drew to a close, consumer prices in Venezuela began to drift downward.

World Bank. The fundamental role of the World Bank is to make loans to the governments of developing nations that want to build expensive infrastructure projects, such as dams, power plants, and highways. Private investors are often unwilling or unable to carry out such projects. Yet an infrastructure is necessary to attract private investment in other sectors of the economy, such as manufacturing and natural resource exploitation. In 1995, for example, guarantees by the World Bank enabled Pakistan to raise additional funding from private sources toward the building of its Hub hydroelectric plant. That same year, the Bank provided loans for road-building projects in Poland and India, and a railroad-improvement program in Bulgaria.

Regional Organizations. In addition to international agencies like the World Bank and the IMF, regional agencies (such as the Asian Development Bank, the Inter-American Development Bank, and the African Development Bank) also make loans, but only to countries within their particular regions. For example, in one recent year, the African Development Bank disbursed about $14 billion in loans for projects in Egypt, Nigeria, Morocco, Zaire, Tunisia, Algeria, and Côte d'Ivoire.

Accept Grants and Loans From Private Banks and Corporations. Private banks and corporations, if they feel that they have a reasonable chance to earn a profit, also invest in the less developed countries. Since making a profit is a primary focus of private funds, however, private sources generally prefer to do business in the stronger economies.

Accept Grants and Loans From Foreign Governments. Since the end of the Second World War, economic and technical assistance from foreign governments has been an essential ingredient in the industrialization of underdeveloped nations. However, the amount of assistance available for distribution to the underdeveloped countries has been decreasing. While in the late 1940s the U.S. government spent 2 percent of the country's GDP on foreign aid programs, by the mid-1990s this spending had declined to less than .4 percent of GDP.

The industrialized nations of Europe have also been losing their enthusiasm for helping underdeveloped nations. In 1975, the member nations of the Common Market agreed to lend economic and technical assistance to the 70 countries that had been their colonies in Africa, the Caribbean, and the Pacific. Support for this agreement, known as the **Lomé Convention,** has begun to decline. Some representatives of EU countries have argued that there has been too little to show for the

$39 billion that they had spent in economic assistance during the first 20 years. Moreover, say the critics, other nations (including some in Eastern Europe) also need EU assistance. Although the European Union has agreed to continue supporting the former colonies until 2000, the Lomé Convention may come to an end that year.

Other Help. Finally, U.S. government agencies such as the **Peace Corps** and a variety of church and other nonprofit groups also contribute to the development process. By teaching, assisting in health projects, working on construction sites, and consulting with local leaders, they bring the benefits of technology to the developing nations.

4. Introduce or Improve the Market System

To promote efficiency in their domestic economies, developing nations need to strengthen the institutions that make a market system work. A traditional economy, which many of the developing nations still have, does not promote economic growth. Command economies, such as existed in the former Soviet Union, have been found ineffective. As a result, many developing countries have been turning to the market economy as the most desirable economic model.

Strengthening Institutions. To promote efficiency in their domestic economies, developing nations need to strengthen the institutions that make a market system work. In most instances, this means that government will need to create and protect financial institutions, such as banks, securities markets, and currency exchanges. The World Bank, for example, has a program to help developing nations set up their own stock exchanges.

In recent years, Ghana has taken steps to promote private enterprise by making it easier for entrepreneurs to borrow and obtain foreign currencies.

Irene Dufu owns Cactus Enterprises, Ltd., a fishing company headquartered in Tema, Ghana. She started with only a single wooden vessel and a crew of 12. Mrs. Dufu credits her success to a government program that made it possible for her (and other small business owners) to obtain low-cost bank loans and foreign exchange. The loans and foreign currencies enabled Mrs. Dufu to purchase and maintain three modern boats. She now employs 65 people on these boats.

Improving Infrastructure. Sanitation systems, transportation facilities, communications networks, and public utilities are examples of infrastructure. Many of these vital ingredients are lacking in the developing countries. This situation discourages foreign investors and makes it difficult to develop poor countries or parts of countries.

In Nigeria, for example, there was only one telephone line for every 500 inhabitants in 1993. Business firms had to depend upon radios and messengers for basic communication. To expand and improve the nation's telecommunications networks, Nigerian leaders are privatizing them. In this way, it is hoped, the new telephone companies will have more money to invest in expanding telephone service. Other national priorities of Nigeria include programs to improve roads, water supply systems, solid waste disposal systems, and sanitation services.

Re-Establishing Credit. Borrowing from abroad is a major means that developing nations use to finance capital investment. But many of the world's poorest countries can no longer borrow. They are so heavily in debt that they can no longer meet interest payments on the loans that they have already made.

The World Bank classifies any country with an annual income of less than $695 per person as a "low-income country." Of the 54 countries in that group, 32 have severe debt problems. One of those 32 is the African country of Guinea-Bissau. It is so heavily in debt that it would have to pay out two and a half times more than it earns in exports just to meet its import payments. In an effort to save Guinea-Bissau and other nations with similar problems from bankruptcy, the International Monetary Fund and the World Bank have provided them with additional loans.

5. Invest in People

Few policies promote development as effectively as investments in human resources. These investments include expanding primary, secondary, and post-secondary education and improving health care.

With two-thirds of its population illiterate, Bangladesh has undertaken to expand its primary schools. In order to accomplish its goals, the nation will look abroad for financial assistance.

Problems of Development in Latin America

Most economists agree that developing nations can benefit from open markets, fewer government regulations (deregulation), privatization of government enterprises, and fiscal discipline. But this path toward economic growth has its problems, as we can see from examples in Latin America.

Latin America stretches south from the U.S.-Mexican border to the southernmost tip of Argentina and also includes the Caribbean Islands. Throughout the region, nations have developed and modernized their industries. At the same time, they have opened up their markets to foreign investment, pulled down many of their protective barriers to trade, controlled inflation, stabilized their currencies, and created new jobs. As a result, the region has enjoyed economic growth at a rate equal to that of the United States.

Nevertheless, all is not well in Latin America. In 1994, peasants in the state of Chiapas in Mexico rose up in rebellion. That same year, Bolivian workers staged national strikes and workers in Argentina marched on their national capital. The discontent in these countries and elsewhere in Latin America was caused by the fact that economic growth has proven very uneven. The rich are getting richer, while the poor are getting poorer. The few new jobs that have been created for the illiterate poor are largely low-paying and short-term.

Some 38 percent of Latin America's population lack basic minimums of income, food, shelter, health, and educational services. United Nations economists estimate that 46 million people in Latin America are homeless; 85 million live in homes that deserve to be demolished; and some 100 million people lack water and electricity in their homes. Thus, a high portion of the area's population live in poverty despite the economic growth brought about by the introduction of the market economy.

It is clear that more spending on social programs to develop the area's human resources is essential. But where will the money for these programs come from—private sources or government? Will wealthy Latin Americans accept paying a much larger share of taxes—something that they have not so far been accustomed to doing? Will high taxes discourage private investments?

Few economists will argue that introducing the market economy to Latin America has been a mistake or a failure. Opening the doors to more investment and to privatization is working. But in Latin America, old ways are not easily changed. Bureaucracies need to be streamlined, corruption and crime reduced, and more land reforms implemented. It may take some time before the benefits of these reforms trickle down to the mass of poverty-stricken people in Latin America.

According to Argentine economist **Miguel Angel Broda**, Latin American countries may either turn to the economic model of the Western European social-welfare state (where six out of ten new jobs since the 1970s have been created in the public sector) or follow the direction of the more market-oriented U.S. economic model (where five of six new jobs in the same period were created in the private sector). Mr. Broda argues that the U.S. model is the more desirable in the long run. But the "long run" is little comfort to people who must buy food, pay rent, and support their families in the present. These hardships, coupled with the widening gap between rich and poor in Latin America contribute to social unrest and political instability. Under such conditions, Latin Americans who have not benefited from market economy might very well look to other economic models.

If you were an economist living in Latin America today, which path to economic development would you choose—the U.S. economic model or the Western European social welfare state?

Shacks coexist with high-rise apartments in Rio de Janeiro, Brazil.

Summary

The developed nations are industrialized countries with relatively high GDP and income per capita. Developing countries, by contrast, have basically agricultural economies, with relatively low income and GDP per capita. The common factors hindering economic growth in the developing countries include: economic systems based on tradition that do not adapt easily to change; unstable political and social conditions with a small, wealthy elite and a very large number of poor citizens; population growth at a rate greater than economic growth; a shortage of capital needed for development; and a need for education and training of a population that is largely illiterate.

Programs to help the developing nations attempt to deal with the factors hindering economic growth. These programs include introducing modern technology to improve farm productivity; land reform; slowing down population growth; encouraging foreign investment; improving the market system; introducing basic improvements in the infrastructure; and improving the educational system.

The developing nations might choose a market system or a more socialized, welfare-state path to economic development. Actions that strengthen the market system in the developing nations have brought about economic growth, but the benefits of this growth have not been distributed equally among the populations of the developing countries.

REVIEWING THE CHAPTER

Building Vocabulary

Match each item in Column A with its definition in Column B.

COLUMN A	COLUMN B
1. developed country	*a.* an agricultural system in which a family produces just enough to feed itself
2. developing country	*b.* the number of years a newly born infant is expected to live
3. family planning	
4. life expectancy	*c.* an institution that grants loans to solve temporary economic problems
5. infant mortality rate	*d.* an agricultural nation with low income and per capita GDP
6. subsistence farming	*e.* efforts to limit the number of children that couples have
7. land reform	
8. takeoff	*f.* the percentage of the adult population who can read and write
9. International Monetary Fund	*g.* a stage in the economic growth of a country
	h. an industrialized nation with high per capita GDP and income
10. literacy rate	*i.* government efforts to break up large landholdings
	j. the number of infants per 1,000 born who die before their first birthday

Understanding What You Have Read

1. Which of the following describes an aspect of life that is more characteristic of developed than developing countries? (*a*) a high birthrate (*b*) a shortage of capital goods (*c*) widespread poverty (*d*) a large, industrial labor force.

2. Roads, water supply, and communications networks are part of a nation's (*a*) infrastructure (*b*) subsistence farming (*c*) foreign aid (*d*) social order.

3. Land reform is frequently suggested as a key to solving some of the economic problems of developing countries. Land reform is (*a*) the application of scientific farming methods (*b*) the use by farmers of only their most fertile land (*c*) programs to enable farmers to own land (*d*) a soil conservation program.

4. As compared to the more developed countries, developing countries usually have (*a*) greater political stability (*b*) a greater willingness to accept change (*c*) a higher percentage of their GDP devoted to agriculture (*d*) larger accumulations of capital.

5. Which of the following is an international organization known best for lending capital to needy nations for development projects? (*a*) World Bank (*b*) United Arab Emirates (*c*) European Union (*d*) OPEC.

6. Which of the following is *not* one of the five stages of economic growth? (*a*) traditional society (*b*) increased tribal loyalties (*c*) takeoff (*d*) high mass consumption.

7. A major problem facing developing nations is (*a*) slow population growth (*b*) rapid industrialization (*c*) high living standards (*d*) low output per farmer.

8. The reason developing nations are poor is that they (*a*) are located in Africa, Asia, and Latin America (*b*) are not yet industrialized (*c*) have a relatively small percentage of their population working on farms (*d*) have high rates of savings.

9. Developing countries are (*a*) all exactly alike (*b*) likely to enjoy high life expectancy, high literary rates, and low birth rates (*c*) greater in number than developed countries (*d*) incapable of change.

10. Japan is one of the world's leading industrial nations. This fact proves that (*a*) development is not limited to Europe and North America (*b*) only nations in Western Europe and North America are developed (*c*) it is relatively easy for a nation to industrialize (*d*) the Japanese people are naturally smarter than most other people.

Thinking Critically

1. Developing nations need to accumulate capital goods in order to increase their productive output. Capital formation may be financed through *personal savings, taxation, borrowing,* or *aid from sources outside their own country.*

   a. With reference to *three* of the italicized items above, explain how each serves to finance capital formation.

   b. For each item you have selected, explain the problems that a developing nation might face in applying that method to finance capital formation.

2. Imagine that you are an economic advisor to the president of the United States. The leader of a developing country in Asia visits you and asks your government for a loan of $40 billion to improve her nation's infrastructure, including hospitals, roads, schools, and communication networks. Your analysis shows that in the past much of the foreign grants and loans this nation received had been wasted or had gone into the hands of corrupt officials. Without U.S. help, however, the economy might collapse and a revolution or political coup might take place.

   a. Describe the economic, political, and strategic issues involved in this request.

   b. Based on your analysis, what would you advise the president to do?

3. A major problem facing the developing nations has been that of poverty. Economists have advised achieving economic development by opening up a country's markets, deregulating industries, privatizing state-owned industries, and promoting fiscal responsibility. Where such measures have been applied, however, economic growth has not reduced poverty. In fact, the gap between the rich and poor has widened. Because of this widening gap, some Latin American nations might imitate the economic policies of socialist countries rather than those of the United States.

   a. What are the advantages and disadvantages of industrialization to a developing nation?

   b. Would you recommend that any areas of the economy be in government hands? Explain your answer.

   c. Is it in the interest of the United States government and people to be concerned with the problems of people in developing countries? Explain your answer.

SKILLS: Constructing and Analyzing a Map of Economic Development

Use Table 24.1, "Measuring the Differences," on page 591 to help you construct a map of economic development in the world today. Do your work on an outline map of the world.

1. To get a better picture of where the developed and developing nations of the world are located, color yellow the nations that fit the description of less developed. Color green those nations that seem to be on the road to development, and color blue the developed nations.

   Use the following as guidelines as to what stage of development a country has reached.

Stage of Development	Per Capita GDP	Energy Consumption Per Capita (kilowatt-hrs.)	Percent of GDP Devoted to Agriculture
Developed	$10,000+	5,000+	less than 6%
On Road to Development	$1,000–9,999	1,000–4,999	6–20%
Less Developed	under $1,000	below 1,000	more than 20%

2. Using the same map, label all of the following regions: North America, Central America, South America, Western Europe, Eastern Europe and Russia, Middle East, Africa, South Asia, Southeast Asia, and East Asia. Although you are working with a limited number of the nations of the world, what generalizations can you suggest concerning where most of the developed nations are located? Where those that are on the road to development are located? Where most of the less developed nations are located?

3. Mark with diagonal lines going like this (\\\) those nations from the table whose literacy rate is 91 percent or greater; and with diagonal lines going like this (///) those nations whose literacy rate is 50–90 percent. What generalizations can you make with regard to the relationship between a nation's literacy rate and its level of economic development?

4. For extra credit, improve your map by gathering information about other nations of the world and adding the correct coloring and shadings of these nations to your map. You can find comparative international statistics in the *Statistical Abstract of the United States*, *The World Almanac*, and *Information Please Almanac*.

Glossary

ability-to-pay principle the idea that people who are best able to afford to pay taxes should pay more than others

absolute advantage a situation whereby one nation can produce a good or service at a lower cost than another nation

acceleration principle (or accelerator) the idea that small changes in consumption lead to proportionately greater changes in investment

administrative red tape bureaucrats' efforts to slow down the government's approval process

ad valorem tariff a tax on imports calculated as a percentage of their value

affirmative action the active hiring and promotion of members of certain groups because of past patterns of discrimination

after-tax income the income that remains after paying taxes

agency shop a workplace where nonunion workers are required to pay dues to the union that represents them

aggregate demand the total of all spending by all sectors of the nation's economy: consumers, business, and government

allocate to assign parts of a whole

annual percentage rate (APR) the percentage cost of credit on a purchase, figured on a yearly basis

annual report a report by a company on its financial operations over the past year

annuity a fund purchased for a fixed sum in order to provide periodic income at a later time

antitrust law legislation that limits monopolistic practices

arbitration the process of settling a labor-management dispute by which an impartial third party renders a binding decision

arbitrator the third party in arbitration

assessment the official evaluation of a property

asset anything of value that is owned by an individual or a business

automated teller machine (ATM) a bank device that allows a customer to make deposits and withdrawals

automatic stabilizer a feature built into an economic system that automatically compensates for changes in the business cycle

automation the substitution of modern machinery for human labor in the production process

balanced budget one in which planned income and expenses are equal

balanced fund a mutual fund that invests in both stocks and bonds

balance of payments a financial statement that summarizes a nation's economic transactions with the rest of the world

balance sheet a financial report that summarizes the assets, liabilities, and net worth of an individual or organization

balance of trade the difference between the cost of a nation's merchandise imports and the value of its merchandise exports

bank reserves the funds a bank sets aside to meet withdrawal demands

bankruptcy a legal declaration that a firm is unable to pay its debts

barter the exchange of a good or service for another good or service

bear an investor who acts in expectation that the price of a stock will decline

benefits-received principle the idea that taxes should be paid by those who will benefit from the money collected

bilateral having to do with two nations or two parties

bimetallic monetary standard a money system based on the ability to exchange currency for two metals, usually gold and silver

black market an unofficial, illegal market

blank endorsement a check endorsement that transfers title to anyone holding the check

block grant federal aid to state or local government to achieve broad policy goals

blue-collar worker one employed in craft, operative, or manual labor

board of directors the elected representatives of the stockholders of a corporation

bond a certificate issued by a unit of government or a corporation in exchange for a long-term loan

bond fund a mutual fund that invests only in bonds

bourgeoisie people of the middle class

boycott an organized refusal to buy goods or services from a company or nation

broker one who carries out customers' orders to buy and sell securities

budget a plan for dealing with future income and expenses

bull an investor who believes that the price of a stock will rise

bull market a general rise in prices of stocks

business cycle the fluctuations in a nation's economic activity

buying long purchasing securities in the expectation of selling them later at a higher price

by-product a secondary good produced along with a major item of production

capacity maximum output in the short run

capital machines, tools, buildings, and other things used to produce goods and services; money

capital account the summary of capital movements in a balance of payment statement

capital consumption the sums that all businesses set aside in a year to replace worn-out plant and equipment; also called *depreciation*

capital formation the production of capital goods

capital gain the profit realized from the sale of an asset

capital goods see *capital*

capital growth the increase in value of a stock over time

capitalism an economic system in which most of the resources of production are privately owned, and most economic decisions are made by individuals and business firms

capital movement an investment, loan, or gift from one country to another to settle differences between a country's imports and its exports

capital resource see *capital*

cartel a group of sellers who formally agree among themselves to restrict output and/or control prices of their products

cash in vault money that a bank has on hand to use

caveat emptor "let the buyer beware"

ceiling price a maximum, government-set price for something

central bank a national institution that supervises other banks in a country; sometimes called a *national bank*

certificate of deposit (CD) a savings instrument whose owner agrees not to withdraw his or her deposit for a set period of time

certify to approve something officially

charge account an arrangement that allows a consumer to purchase goods on credit

charter a government license for people to form a corporation

checkoff a clause in some union contracts that requires the employer to withhold union dues from workers' paychecks

circular flow the movement of money, goods, and services through the economy

clearing a check the process whereby a bank deducts the amount of a check from the account of the person who wrote it

closed shop a business in which only workers belonging to a specified union may be hired

coincident indicator a set of data whose up-and-down movements over time parallel the business cycle

collaboration active cooperation

collateral any item of value that a lender may seize should a borrower default on a loan

collective bargaining a series of discussions between representatives of a union and representatives of management to arrive at a contract that will spell out the terms of employment

collusion an agreement or agreements among competing firms to limit competition

command economy one in which decisions to allocate resources are made by the government

commercial bank a privately owned institution that provides a wide array of financial services, especially to business customers

commodity inflation general price increases caused by run-ups in the prices of key commodities

common stock a stock that entitles its owners to vote for candidates to the board of directors

commune a community of farmers who work collectively

comparative advantage the principle that a nation should specialize in the production of those goods and services in which it is most efficient, and trade its surplus goods and services for the things it needs

competition the rivalry among buyers and among sellers for goods and services

compound interest the interest earned on the principal and on the interest already earned

concentration ratio the percentage of an industry's output that is produced by its four largest firms

conglomerate merger one that combines firms that produce unrelated products

constant dollar a value of the dollar that has been adjusted to eliminate the effects of inflation or deflation

consumer one who buys goods and services for personal use

consumer cooperative a retail business owned by some or all of its customers

Consumer Price Index (CPI) the series of index numbers measuring changes in the level of prices over a period of time

consumer sovereignty the freedom consumers have to choose which goods and services to buy

consumption the act of buying final goods or services

contraction the phase of a business cycle during which economic activity is in decline

cooperative an association of individuals who wish to buy, market, or produce products as a group

coordination the way in which an economic system answers the WHAT, HOW, and WHO questions

copayment the amount of a medical bill that a patient with health insurance must pay

copyright a government grant of legal control over records, literary, musical, and artistic works

corporate income tax a tax on net profits of incorporated businesses

corporate raider an outsider who tries to take control of a corporation by buying stock

corporation a business chartered under state or federal law and owned by its stockholders

cost-benefit analysis a weighing of the costs and benefits of something to reach a numerical answer

cost-push inflation a rise in the level of prices caused by an increase in the costs of doing business

countercyclical fiscal policy one calculated to check excessive developments in a business cycle

counterfeit to produce money illegally

craft a skilled occupation

craft union an organization of members of the same skilled trade

credit card a piece of plastic that allows holders to purchase goods and services on credit at participating businesses

credit history a record of how one has paid bills and repaid loans

credit union a depository institution whose members are its depositors and borrowers

current account the summary of all imports and exports of goods, services, income, and unilateral transfers in a balance of payments

cyclical unemployment the status of workers who have lost their job because of insufficient demand for goods and services during the downswing of a business cycle

debtor one who owes money

deductible the yearly amount of total medical bills that a patient with health insurance must pay

deficit the status of a budget in which revenue is less than expenditures

deflation a general decline in prices

degree of inequality the distance between equal income distribution and actual distribution

demand the quantity of a product or service that would be purchased at a particular price

demand curve a line on a graph that shows the amount of a product or service that will be purchased at each price

demand deposit an account in a bank that promises to pay on demand a specified amount of money; a checking account

demand-pull inflation a rise in the level of prices caused by an increase in demand

democratic socialism an economic system with a command economy, elected government, and freedoms for the population and the press

deposit multiplier the number of times deposits could be ncreased by the banking system for every dollar in reserves

depository institution a business that holds people's deposits

depreciation a decline in the value of capital assets caused by use, the passage of time, or both

depression a serious, long-lasting decline in a nation's business activity

deregulate to remove regulations

derived demand the demand for something that is caused by the demand for something else

devaluation a reduction in the price of one currency in terms of the currencies of other nations

developed country an industrialized country with relatively high GDP and income per capita

developing country one with a largely agricultural economy and relatively low income and GDP per capita

diminishing returns the point at which the extra output, resulting from the addition of more units of a productive factor, will begin to decline

direct tax a tax paid to the government by the person or business that is taxed; a tax that cannot be shifted

discount rate the interest on loans that the Federal Reserve charges its member banks

discretionary fiscal policy a fiscal policy that the government may or may not use to regulate the economy

discrimination the favoring or slighting of someone because of the racial, religious, ethnic, or gender group to which that person belongs

diseconomy of scale an increase in the cost of doing business that results when a business has grown too large

disposable income the income a person or family has left after paying personal taxes

dividends profits that are distributed by corporations to share-holders

drawee the bank upon which a check is drawn

drawer the person writing a check

durable good a product that is expected to last several years or more

easy-money policy a Fed policy to expand the money supply

econometrics a branch of economics that uses mathematics and statistics in solving economic problems

economic growth the increase in output of goods and services over time; an increase over time in either real GDP or real GDP per capita

economic indicator a set of statistics about the performance of a sector of the nation's economy

economics the study of how people and societies use limited resources to satisfy unlimited wants

economic stability a period of modest changes in the level of prices, employment, and business activity

economic system the way in which a society answers the WHAT, HOW, and WHO questions

economy of scale a reduction in the cost of doing business that results from increases in the size of operations

educational attainment the number of years of school completed or degrees obtained

elastic currency one that expands and contracts with the needs of businesses

elasticity of demand the extent to which total spending for an item will fluctuate with changes in prices

elasticity of supply the extent to which total spending for an item will fluctuate with changes in supply

embargo a ban on importing goods

eminent domain the right of government to acquire private property for public use by paying a reasonable price to the owner

endorsement the act of passing title to a check to another party

energy consumption per capita a nation's total energy consumption divided by its population

energy tax a tax on the consumption of energy

Engel's Law the rule that as a family's income increases, the percentage spent on food decreases while the percentage spent on luxuries, medical care, personal care, and savings increases

entrepreneur a person who gathers together the factors of production to create and operate a business enterprise in the hope of earning profits

entrepreneurship the process of bringing together the factors of production

equation of exchange $MV = PQ$, where M equals the money supply, V equals velocity, P equals the average price paid, and Q equals the quantity of goods and services produced

equilibrium price the price at which the quantity of a good or service supplied equals the amount demanded

equity financing a corporation's method of obtaining capital by selling its stock

equity fund a mutual fund that invests only in corporate stocks

escalator clause a section of a union contract that ties wage increases to a cost-of-living index

estate tax a federal tax levied on a person's personal property at the time of death

exchange rate the amount of one currency that can be purchased for a certain amount of another currency

excise tax a tax on the manufacture, sale, or use of a good or service

expansion the phase of a business cycle during which the economy advances out of a trough

expenditures approach a way of calculating GDP by measuring purchases by consumers, businesses, and government, and by international buyers of U.S. goods and services

exports a nation's goods and services that are sold abroad

external cost a business expense paid for by society as a whole

external debt money that the federal government owes to foreign institutions and individuals

externality a cost or benefit of an economic activity that is paid for or enjoyed by those who had neither produced nor consumed it

factor of production a resource (such as labor, land, or capital) that is used to produce a good or service

favorable balance of trade an excess in the value of merchandise exports over imports

Federal Reserve note paper currency issued by the Federal Reserve System

fiat currency standard a paper money system not based on metals

final goods products sold at retail

finance charge the total amount one pays to use credit in a purchase

financial assistance cash payments by a government to individuals in need

fiscal policy the use by the government of its powers to tax and spend in order to regulate the economy

fiscal year an accounting period of 12 months

five-year plan a detailed statement of a nation's production goals for a five-year period

fixed costs those that remain unchanged regardless of the number of units a business produces

flat tax a tax with a single rate that is applied to all income above a certain level

floating exchange rate the value of a nation's currency that moves up and down to reflect roughly the laws of supply and demand

fluctuate to move up and down in value

food stamp a federal government coupon that eligible recipients can use to purchase food at many stores

401(k) plan a fund run by an employer into which a worker (and sometimes the employer) contributes to provide income upon retirement

fractional currency U.S. coins that are worth less than $1
free enterprise see *capitalism*
frictional unemployment the status of workers who have left one job and are likely soon to find another
fringe benefit the compensation received by employees in addition to wages
full employment the condition in which all of an economy's resources are being utilized
full endorsement a check endorsement that transfers title of the check to a specific party

GDP per capita total value of all goods and services produced by a national economy in a year divided by the population
gift tax a federal tax on gifts in excess of specified limits
glasnost a Soviet policy introduced by Mikhail Gorbachev that encouraged public discussion and criticism
global economy the combined economies of all nations
global warming the idea that the earth's surface temperatures are increasing over time
goldsmith a person who makes and sells articles of gold for a living
gold standard the tying of the value of a nation's currency to a fixed amount of gold
goods tangible items of value
grant-in-aid a payment by one level of government to a lower one, usually designated to be spent for a specific purpose
Great Depression the severe economic downturn in the United States and elsewhere, 1929-1939
greenhouse effect the trapping of the sun's heat by atmospheric gases
greenmail the practice of buying enough of a company's stock to threaten a hostile takeover and then reselling the stock to that company at a price above market value
Gresham's Law the idea that cheap money drives out expensive money
grievance a formal complaint by a union member against his or her employer
grievance machinery established methods of resolving disputes between employers and workers who belong to a union
gross domestic product (GDP) the total value of all goods and services produced by a national economy in a year
gross private domestic investment the sum of business spending for new equipment, construction, and changes in business inventories
gross receipts tax one levied on a business firm's retail and wholesale sales

health maintenance organization (HMO) a group of health-care providers who offer prepaid, coordinated health care
hidden tax one included in the selling price of a good or service without the buyer knowing about it

holding company a corporation that has a controlling interest in the shares of one or more other corporations

home equity loan a consumer loan in which one's home is used as collateral

horizontal merger a merger of two or more firms that produce competing products

human resources the people whose efforts and skills go into the production of goods and services

imports goods and services that are purchased from abroad

income approach a way of calculating GDP by measuring the total income of all employees and businesses

income distribution the percentage of total income received by various groups in society

income-maintenance program government efforts to reduce poverty by transferring income to the poor

income security government welfare

income statement a summary of the financial activities of a firm over a period of time

indirect tax a tax that can be shifted from the person or business taxed to someone else, who is frequently unaware of that fact

individual retirement account (IRA) a fund into which an individual may pay a limited amount each year to provide income upon retirement

inelastic demand a market situation in which a decrease or increase in price results in a less than proportionate increase or decrease in the quantity demanded

infant industry an industry which, because it is newly developed, is unable to compete with the same industry in other nations

infant mortality rate the number of babies (out of every 1,000 live births) who die before their first birthday

inflation a general rise in prices

inflationary gap the excess of aggregate demand over total output at full employment

infrastructure the physical capital that supports a society's activities; includes roads, power lines, water facilities, and schools

injunction a court order to cease a certain activity

in-kind payment a government's provision of a good or service to needy individuals

innovation a new way of doing something

insider trading the buying or selling of stock by someone who uses information not available to the general public

installment plan a method of purchasing something on credit with payments scheduled over time

interlocking directorate a situation in which the same people sit on the boards of directors of competing firms

internal cost a business expense paid for by the firm incurring it

internal debt money that the federal government owes to U.S. institutions and individuals

inventory the goods that a business has on hand to sell and the materials used in their manufacture

inventory on demand a method of obtaining supplies needed for manufacturing only just before they are needed

inverse the reverse of

investing the use of savings to buy property that is expected to increase in value

investment the property that people or institutions purchase while investing

investment bank an institution that underwrites corporations' issues of stocks and bonds

investment-grade bond a bond ranked Baa or BBB and above

investor one who buys something of value for income and/or long-term growth

job outlook the chances of finding work in a particular occupation, region, season, etc.

junk bond a highly risky bond ranked below investment grade

jurisdictional strike one caused by a dispute between two unions over which one can represent certain workers

keiretsu a closely knit network of business firms in Japan

L the measure of the nation's money supply that consists of M3 plus savings bonds and certain private and government securities

labor contract a written agreement between an employer and a union

labor force the number of people 16 years of age, or older, who are working or looking for work

labor productivity output per worker per time period

lagging indicator a set of data that experiences the ups and downs of business activity some time after it occurs in the business cycle

laissez-faire a government's policy of not interfering with its nation's economy

land reform the breakup by a government of large estates into smaller, farmer-owned plots

Law of Demand the principle that the demand for a good or service varies inversely with its price

Law of Diminishing Returns the principle that in adding factors of production, a firm eventually reaches a point where productivity begins to decline

Law of Supply the principle that the quantity of a good or service supplied varies directly with its price

leading indicator a set of data that experiences the ups and downs of business activity some time before it occurs in the business cycle

legal tender a currency that by law must be accepted in payment of debt

less developed country (LDC) see *developing country*

leverage the use of borrowed funds to finance business operations

liability an obligation or debt

life expectancy the number of years the average newly born infant is expected to live

limited liability the legal exemption of stockholders from the debts of the corporation in which they own stock

limited life a business's legal status that it will not continue to exist after the death of its owner

line of credit a bank's arrangement with a firm that allows the firm to borrow, up to a limit, whenever it needs money

liquidate to sell off the assets of a firm and go out of business

liquidity the ease with which a savings vehicle can be turned into cash

literacy rate the percentage of the adult population who can read and write

lockout the shutting down of a plant by management in hopes of getting its union workers to agree to certain contract proposals

long run a period of time during which any or all of the factors of production could vary

long-term financing loans that need to be repaid in a year or more

long-term unemployed those who have been jobless for 6 months or more

Lorenz Curve a graph that compares income distribution as it actually is with what income distribution would be if everyone received an equal share

luxury a nonessential good or service that adds comfort and pleasure to life

M1 the nation's money supply as measured by the total currency, checkbook money, and traveler's checks in circulation on any given day

M2 the nation's money supply as measured by M1 plus individual savings accounts, money market funds, and certain foreign assets

M3 the nation's money supply as measured by M2 plus business and other large savings accounts

macroeconomics the study of the forces affecting the economy as a whole

managed capitalism a market economy with strong government intervention and cooperation among corporations

managed competition the provision of health care by a local or regional network of providers

margin a down payment required when purchasing securities on credit

marginal cost the addition to costs resulting from the production of one extra unit

marginalism the evaluation of the usefulness of adding one more of an item to the production of a good or service

marginal productivity the value of the output of the last worker hired by a company

marginal propensity to consume (MPC) the rate at which the public spends as national income goes up

marginal propensity to save (MPS) the rate at which the public saves as national income goes up

marginal revenue the income from the production of one more unit

marginal utility the additional usefulness received from each added unit of a product or service

market a place where goods and services are bought and sold

market economy one in which the allocation of resources is determined by the free operation of the forces of supply and demand and market prices

market power the ability of buyers and sellers to influence prices

market price see *equilibrium price*

mass production the making of a product in quantity, usually with machinery

maturity the date at which a bond is set to be redeemed at face value

maximum employment a goal whereby everyone who wants to work has a job

maximum production the level at which entrepreneurs believe it no longer profitable to add more workers, land, or capital to the production process

maximum purchasing power consumers' ability to buy the greatest amount possible with limited numbers of dollars

mediation a nonbinding process in which an impartial party, or mediator, tries to bring both sides in a labor dispute into agreement

mercantilism a set of economic practices of the 16th to 18th centuries based on the premise that a nation's wealth could be measured by its stock of gold and silver

merger the absorption of one or more firms by another

merit pay a system of compensation based on the idea that those who perform better are paid more

microeconomics the study of the effects of economic forces on individual parts of the economy

mint to manufacture coins; a place where coins are made

monetary policy an action taken by the Federal Reserve System to regulate the nation's supply of money and credit

monetary standard the commodity or benchmark that a society chooses to use for its money

money market fund a mutual fund that invests in short-term credit instruments such as Treasury bills

monopolistic competition a market situation in which there are many firms selling similar items on the basis of product differentiation

monopoly a market situation in which there is only one seller of a particular good or service

monopoly power the ability of a group of firms to act as if it were a monopoly

monopsony a market that has only one buyer

more developed country (MDC) see *developed country*

mortgage a pledge of property as security for a loan

most-favored-nation clause a treaty provision requiring a signatory to extend the same preferential trade terms to other signatories that it extends to a nonsignatory

multilateral having to do with many nations or parties

multinational corporation a firm that has operations in two or more countries

multiplier (or multiplier effect) a numerical factor by which an increase in investment or spending is multiplied to find the effect on national income

mutual fund a corporation that uses the proceeds from the sale of its stocks to purchase the securities of other corporations

mutual savings bank a bank that is owned by its depositors

national debt the total of all money owed by the federal government

national health insurance a system whereby a central government pays for the nation's health-care system

national income the total of incomes earned by individuals and business firms in the production of the GDP

national union a labor group organized on a national level

natural resource a factor of production obtained from the land, sea, or air

necessity a product or service needed to sustain daily life

net exports the difference between a country's imports and exports of goods and services in a year

net interest the difference between the total interest received and that paid out by all businesses in a year

net worth the value of a business as measured by its assets minus its liabilities

nondurable good a product that is quickly consumed or worn out

nonrenewable resource one incapable of being replaced or renewed by nature

not-for-profit business a firm that does not distribute profits, but reinvests its earnings

NOW (negotiable order of withdrawal) account a checking account that pays interest on deposited money

oligopoly a market dominated by only a few sellers

on-the-job training a program whereby workers earn money while they are learning a skill

open market operation the buying or selling of government bonds by the Federal Open Market Committee

open shop a business or factory in which the employer is free to hire either union or nonunion workers

opportunity cost the amount of goods and services that must be done without in order to obtain another good and service

outlay an expenditure

outpatient a medical patient who is treated at a hospital or clinic but who does not stay overnight

over-the-counter market places where stocks are bought and sold other than the stock exchanges

paradox of thrift the assertion that if individuals increase the level of their savings, society as a whole will have less to save

parity a price that gives farmers the same purchasing power from the sale of their goods that they enjoyed during certain base years

partnership an unincorporated business owned by two or more people

patent a government grant giving ownership rights to an invention

payee the person to whom a check is payable

peak the upper turning point of a business cycle

perestroika attempts at restructuring the Soviet economy under Mikhail Gorbachev to allow elements of free enterprise

personal consumption expenditures spending by consumers

personal income the total income received by individuals before they pay income taxes

personal property tax a tax on one's personal property

Phillips Curve a graph illustrating the trade-off between inflation and unemployment

picketing the marching of workers with signs outside a place of business, usually to proclaim a strike

"play-or-pay" program a proposed law requiring employers to buy health insurance for their employees or pay a payroll tax

pork (or pork-barrel legislation) laws passed mainly to benefit people and businesses in an electoral district so that voters will re-elect the legislators who supported the laws

portfolio a group of investments owned by an investor

poverty level (or poverty threshold) the income level below which people are considered poor

poverty rate the percentage of a population or group whose income is below the poverty level

preferred stock the shares of stock that are entitled to a fixed dividend before profits are distributed to holders of common stock

price floor the minimum, government-set price for a commodity

price leadership a characteristic of an oligopoly by which firms match each other's price increases and decreases

price supports a government program that sets a floor on the selling price of some farm products by offering to buy the products at that floor

principal the face value of a loan

privatization the transformation of a publicly owned business into a privately owned one

producer cooperative an organization of producers who cooperate in buying equipment and supplies and in marketing

product differentiation the creation by sellers of the appearance that their products are different from those of their competitors, while, in fact, they are similar

production possibilities curve a graph showing the various combinations of goods and services that an economy might produce if all its resources were fully and effectively employed

productive capacity the amount of goods and services that the economy is able to produce at a given time

productivity a measure of the efficiency of a factor of production, as measured by *output per unit of input*

profit the income that remains after the costs of doing business have been deducted from the receipts of the sale of goods and services

profit maximization efforts to earn the greatest profits

profit motive the desire of business owners to earn the greatest profits

progressive tax one that increases in the percentage paid as the tax-payer's income increases

proletariat people of the working class

promissory note a written promise to repay a loan, plus interest, by a specific date

propensity to consume the tendency to consume a portion of one's income

propensity to save the tendency to save a portion of one's income

proportional tax one that applies the same rate to all persons regardless of their income

proprietors' income the profits earned by the owners of the nation's unincorporated businesses

prospectus a document for investors that describes the operations of a company that is issuing new securities

protective tariff a tax whose primary purpose is to protect domestic production from foreign competition

proxy a certificate signed by a stockholder authorizing someone else to cast ballots at a stockholders' meeting

public corporation one whose stock can be bought and sold by the general public

public franchise a government license to a business for an exclusive market

public good or service one that can benefit everyone in the society; a good or service that is provided mainly by government

public utility an industry that produces a good or service in the public interest

pure competition a market in which there are many buyers and sellers, none of whom can alone affect prices

quality circle a team of employees who work together to solve production problems

quality of life how well the average person lives

quota a limit on the import of a good

rate of population growth the percentage that a population increases over time

real estate (or real property) land and anything more-or-less permanently attached to it, such as buildings

real GDP (or real gross domestic product) the measurement of gross domestic product in dollars of a base year

real property tax a tax on the value of land or anything permanently attached to it

rebate to return part of a fee already paid, such as a tax

recession a contraction in economic activity that lasts for six months or more

recessionary gap the amount by which aggregate demand falls short of the total needed to sustain full employment

reciprocal the reverse of something

recovery the expansion phase of a business cycle

regional trade bloc a group of countries of the same region that have made a trade agreement

regressive tax one that takes a larger proportion of the earnings of people with low incomes than of those with higher incomes

renewable resource one capable of being replaced or renewed

rent subsidy a partial payment of a person's rent by a government

reserve ratio (or reserve requirement) the percentage of its total deposits that a bank is required to keep in its Federal Reserve district bank or as cash in its vaults

restrictive endorsement a check endorsement that restricts how funds are to be used

retained earnings profits of a business that are not distributed to its owners

revenue income from sales of goods and services

revenue tariff a tax on imports whose primary purpose is to generate income

right to private property a principle that allows individuals to own property and use it in any lawful manner that they choose

right-to-work law a state regulation that makes it illegal to require workers to join labor unions

royalties payments to creative individuals (such as inventors, songwriters, and authors) by those who use their works

run on a bank large withdrawals from a bank by many depositors at the same time

sales tax one on the value of certain retail sales of goods and services

savings any income that is not spent

savings and loan association (S&L) a financial institution whose funds are used primarily to finance home mortgages

S corporation a type of small corporation that has the tax benefits of a partnership

securities stocks and bonds

selling short selling stock that you do not own (that you borrow from a broker) in the hope of buying it back later at a lower price

seniority the status of a worker in being employed for more years than others in a workplace

service an intangible item of value, such as medical care

service worker one employed in the service industries, such as transportation, trade, finance, and government

shareholder (or stockholder) one who owns stock of a corporation

shifting the process of transferring the burden of a tax to another party

short run the operation of a plant using existing equipment

short-term financing loans that need to be repaid in less than a year

silver certificate former U.S. paper currency that could be exchanged for silver

simple interest the interest earned on the principal alone

slowdown a deliberate reduction of output by workers

socialism an economic system in which the means of production are owned by the state and resources are allocated through central planning

sole proprietorship an unincorporated business owned by one person

Special Drawing Rights (SDRs) credits to the accounts of member nations in the International Monetary Fund that can be used to purchase foreign currencies

specialization a situation in which a worker or company specializes in one activity

specific tariff a tax on imports calculated by a set amount per unit

speculator one who buys things of value to turn a quick profit

stagflation a period of both a recession and inflation

standard of living the quantity and quality of goods and services available to an individual or society

statement of cash flows a summary of a firm's sources and uses of cash over time

statistical discrepancy a line in a financial statement that summarizes errors in recording transactions

stock a certificate that represents ownership in a corporation

stock exchange a place where shares of stock in major corporations are bought and sold

stock market a collective term for places where shares of stock are bought and sold

strike a work stoppage by a firm's employees

strikebreaker (or scab) one hired to replace a striking union member

structural unemployment the status of workers who have lost their job because of changes in technology, consumer preferences, or the movement of job opportunities from one region to another

subsistence farming the operation of a farm that does not produce more than enough to feed the farm family

supply the quantity of a product or service offered for sale at a particular price

supply-side economics an economic theory that calls for a shift in the focus of government from the demand (consumption) side of the economy to the supply (production) side

surplus the status of a budget in which revenue is greater than expenditures

surplus value the difference between workers' wages and the value of the goods and services they produce

sustainable economic growth the idea that economic growth is desirable as long as every generation passes on a stock of net resources to future generations

take-off a dramatic movement toward economic development that includes increased productivity

target pricing the guarantee of a minimum price to a farmer by the government

tariff a tax on imports

tax credit the amount one can reduce one's tax liability because of one's poverty status or participation in certain activities

tax deduction an amount that individuals and families can deduct from their taxable income

tax exemption a set amount of one's income that can be exempted by law from income tax for each member of a family

tax incidence the person on whom the burden of a tax ultimately falls

technological revolution rapid changes in the ways of producing goods and services

technology a culture's methods and tools for making things

thrift institution a term used for mutual savings banks, S&Ls, and credit unions

tight money a Fed policy that attempts to slow down the growth of the money supply

time deposit a bank account for which the bank might require of the depositor an advance notice of a withdrawal

token money coins whose metallic value is less than their face value

trade credit the practice of suppliers' giving businesses time to pay for orders

trade-off the giving up of one thing to obtain something else

traditional economy one in which resources are allocated according to tradition and custom

transfer payment a government money payment to an individual for which nothing is received in return

traveler's check a check that one can purchase at most banks and easily cash at most places of business

trough the lowest point in a business cycle

trust a large business monopoly of the 19th century whose shareholders placed control of the firm in the hands of trustees

underconsumption a time when consumer expenditures lag behind output

underground economy the part of the economy whose activities are not included in official government statistics

unemployment compensation state-provided cash benefits to eligible unemployed workers for a limited period

unfavorable balance of trade an excess in the value of merchandise imports over exports

unfunded mandate a requirement imposed by one level of government on a subordinate level to enact some program for which no financing is provided

unilateral transfer a gift from individuals or institutions of one country to those of another

unincorporated income tax a tax on net income of businesses that are not incorporated

union shop a firm that has a union contract that states nonunion members may be hired on condition that they join the union

unit production cost the average cost of producing an item

unlimited liability a situation in a sole proprietorship or partner-ship whereby the personal property of any owner may be taken to pay the debts of the business

United States notes paper currency issued by the U.S. Treasury Department

value-added tax (VAT) a tax paid on the value added to a good at each stage of production

variable cost one that increases or decreases with the level of production

vault a protected storage area of a bank

vertical merger a consolidation of two or more businesses that are each other's suppliers or customers

wage-price spiral an inflation marked by rising wages causing prices to rise *and* rising prices causing wages to rise

white-collar worker one employed in a clerical, professional, or managerial occupation

worker mobility the willingness of workers to move to where jobs are

yield the rate of return on an investment based on the purchase price

zero economic growth the idea that the GDP should increase only enough to accommodate population growth

Index

Acknowledgments

Cover   Ted Bernstein
Text Design   Kay Wanous
Drawn Art   Burmar Technical Corporation

Photographs and Prints

Unit I   1, Telegraph/FPG International Corp.; 5, Rafael Macia/Photo Researchers; 6, UN/DPI Photo (#90398); 11, UPI/Corbis-Bettmann; 13, Corbis-Bettmann; 27, UPI/Corbis-Bettmann; 53, Joe Tabacca/AP/Wide World Photos; 63, Richard Hutchings/Photo Researchers.

Unit II   75, Mark Lennihan/AP/Wide World Photos; 79, Renee Lynn/Photo Researchers; 82, AP/Wide World Photos; 88, The New York Times/NYT Pictures; 99, New York Stock Exchange Archives; 103, UPI/Corbis-Bettmann; 106, Spencer Grant/Photo Researchers; 112 and 124, Corbis-Bettmann; 132, UPI/Corbis-Bettmann; 146, Arthur Grace, NYT Pictures; 147, Library of Congress; 150, Michael Hayman/Stock Boston.

Unit III   171, Barbara Rios/Photo Researchers; 181(l), Dion Ogust/The Image Works; 181(r), Michael Powers/Stock Boston; 186(l), Laimute E. Druskis/Stock Boston; 186(c), Kathy Sloane/Photo Researchers; 186(r), Bettye Lane/Photo Researchers; 199, both Corbis-Bettmann; 207, Steve and Mary Skjold/The Image Works; 210, Reuters/Corbis-Bettmann; 213 and 215, UPI/Corbis-Bettmann; 224, Barbara Rios/Photo Researchers; 226, Michael Siluk/The Image Works; 231, Perry Morse; 234, Paul Levesque.

Unit IV   247, Library of Congress; 250, Nina Berman/SIPA Press; 251, Bedrich Grunzweig/Photo Researchers; 265, UPI/Corbis-Bettmann; 280, Dorothy Littell Greco/The Image Works; 285, Jim Mahoney/The Image Works; 299, Perry Morse; 312, Itsuo Inouye/AP/Wide World Photos; 314, Rhoda Sidney/Stock Boston; 316, George Bellerose/Stock Boston; 318, Corbis-Bettmann.

Unit V   329, Weisburg; 331, Corbis-Bettmann; 340, Bureau of Engraving and Printing, U.S. Treasury Department; 345, UPI/Corbis-Bettmann; 358, Corbis-Bettmann; 361, Spencer Grant/Photo Researchers; 366, UPI/Corbis-Bettmann; 375, Corbis-Bettmann; 381, Federal Reserve System; 385, Joe Marquette/AP/Wide World Photos.

Unit VI   391, Michael Simpson/FPG International Corp.; 396, Corbis-Bettmann; 397, UPI/Corbis-Bettmann; 403 and 404, Corbis-Bettmann; 421, AP/Wide World Photos; 423, Bryce Flynn/Stock Boston; 445, Owen Franken/Stock Boston; 448, UPI/Corbis-Bettmann; 471, Michael Dwyer/Stock Boston; 473, UPI/Corbis-Bettmann; 475, Elizabeth Crews/Stock Boston; 486, Cathy Cheney/Stock Boston; 488, Spencer Grant/Stock Boston.

Unit VII   499, Telegraph/FPG International Corp.; 502 and 504, UN/DPI Photos (#140420 and 141224); 509, Culver Pictures; 510, Reuters/Corbis-Bettmann; 514, Corbis-Bettmann; 517, David Scull/NYT Pictures; 521, Reuters/Corbis-Bettmann; 523, Spencer Grant/Photo Researchers; 527, Asea Brown Boveri; 539, Reuters/Corbis-Bettmann; 542, Corbis-Bettmann; 545, UPI/Corbis-Bettmann; 552, Eric Reisberg/AP/Wide World Photos; 565, Corbis-Bettmann; 567, Library of Congress; 571 and 575, Reuters/Corbis-Bettmann; 578, Judy Gelles/Stock Boston; 582, UPI/Corbis-Bettmann; 590, Steve Winter/UN/DPI Photo; 593, K. Bubriski/UN/DPI Photo; 597, David Longstreath/AP/Wide World Photos; 600, UN/DPI Photo (#158657); 602, Harvard University News Office; 608, UN/DPI Photo (#5096).